PERSPECTIVES:
READINGS
FOR WRITERS

Perspectives:
Readings for Writers

Robert DiYanni
Pace University, Pleasantville

McGRAW-HILL, INC.
New York · St. Louis · San Francisco · Auckland · Bogotá · Caracas · Lisbon · London
Madrid · Mexico City · Milan · Montreal · New Delhi · San Juan · Singapore · Sydney
Tokyo · Toronto

Perspectives: Readings for Writers

Permissions Acknowledgments appear on pages 541–545, and on this page by reference.

This book is printed on acid-free paper.

1 2 3 4 5 6 7 8 9 0 DOC DOC 9 0 9 8 7 6 5

ISBN 0-07-016967-5

This book was set in Lucida Bright by ComCom, Inc.
The editors were Tim Julet and James R. Belser;
the design was done by Top Desk Publishers' Group;
the production supervisor was Richard A. Ausburn.
The photo editor was Kathy Bendo;
the photo researcher was Mia Galison.
R. R. Donnelley & Sons Company was printer and binder.

Library of Congress Cataloging-in-Publication Data

DiYanni, Robert.
    Perspectives: readings for writers / Robert DiYanni.
        p.   cm.
    Includes index.
    ISBN 0-07-016967-5
    1. College readers.   2. English language—Rhetoric.   I. Title.
PE1417.D58   1996
808'.0427—dc20   95-8885

About the Author

Robert DiYanni is Professor of English at Pace University, Pleasantville, New York, where he teaches courses in literature, writing, and humanities. He has also taught at Queens College of the City University of New York, at New York University in the Graduate Rhetoric Program, and most recently in the Expository Writing Program at Harvard University. He received his B.A. from Rutgers University (1968) and his Ph.D. from the City University of New York (1976).

Professor DiYanni has written articles and reviews on various aspects of literature, composition, and pedagogy. His books include *The McGraw-Hill Book of Poetry; Women's Voices; Reading Poetry; Like Season'd Timber: New Essays on George Herbert;* and *Modern American Poets: Their Voices and Visions* (a text to accompany the Public Broadcasting Television series that aired in 1988). He has also published *The Scribner Handbook for Writers* and is currently at work on *An Introduction to the Humanities.*

For Mary

Contents in Brief

RHETORICAL CONTENTS   xxi
TO THE STUDENT   xxv
TO THE INSTRUCTOR   xxvii
ACKNOWLEDGMENTS   xxix

Introduction: Reading toward Writing   1

Communities

Scott Russell Sanders	*Wayland*	32
Mary Gordon	*More Than Just a Shrine: Paying Homage to the Ghosts of Ellis Island*	43
Marianna De Marco Torgovnick	*On Being White, Female, and Born in Bensonhurst*	48
Amy Tan	*Mother Tongue*	58
Tom Wolfe	*The Right Stuff*	64
Maxine Hong Kingston	*Silence*	75
Alice Walker	*In Search of Our Mothers' Gardens*	80
Eric Kim	*Family Portrait (student essay)*	89
William Faulkner	*A Rose for Emily (story)*	94
Maya Angelou	*On the Pulse of Morning (poem)*	102

Culture and Society

Tom Wolfe	*Only One Life*	111
Joan Didion	*Marrying Absurd*	116
Larry L. King	*Playing Cowboy*	120
Gloria Anzaldúa	*How to Tame a Wild Tongue*	130
Diane Ravitch	*Multiculturalism*	140
George Orwell	*Marrakech*	156
Henry Louis Gates, Jr.	*2 Live Crew, Decoded*	162
Marie Ribisi	*The Health Craze (student essay)*	165
Leslie Marmon Silko	*The Man to Send Rain Clouds (story)*	170
Louis Simpson	*Walt Whitman at Bear Mountain (poem)*	175

Gender

Susan Brownmiller	*Femininity*	181
Pat C. Hoy II	*Mosaics of Southern Masculinity*	186
Maxine Hong Kingston	*No Name Woman*	201
Annie Dillard	*The Deer at Providencia*	211
Scott Russell Sanders	*The Men We Carry in Our Minds*	216
Deborah Tannen	*Different Words, Different Worlds*	222
Paul Theroux	*Being a Man*	235

Maile Meloy   *The Voice of the Looking-Glass*
                       (student essay)   240
John Updike   *A & P (story)*   246
Emily Dickinson   *"I'm wife—I've finished that" (poem)*   252

Race
James Baldwin   *Notes of a Native Son*   257
Roger Wilkins   *In Ivory Towers*   273
June Jordan   *Where Is the Love?*   277
Cornel West   *Race Matters*   282
N. Scott Momaday   *from The Way to Rainy Mountain*   288
Richard Rodriguez   *Complexion*   293
Shelby Steele   *The New Sovereignty*   298
Suyin So   *Grotesques (student essay)*   309
Ralph Ellison   *Battle Royal (story)*   313
Langston Hughes   *Theme for English B (poem)*   325

Language
Michiko Kakutani   *The Word Police*   331
Robin Lakoff   *Talking Like a Lady*   336
Barbara Lawrence   *Four-Letter Words Can Hurt You*   345
Nancy Mairs   *On Being a Cripple*   349
Neil Postman   *"Now . . . This"*   359
James Baldwin   *If Black English Isn't a Language,*
                       Then Tell Me, What Is?   369
George Orwell   *Politics and the English Language*   373
Lisa Bogdonoff   *Police! Police! (student essay)*   384
Gish Jen   *What Means Switch? (story)*   387
Pablo Neruda   *The Word (poem)*   401

The Arts
Joan Didion   *Georgia O'Keeffe*   407
Ralph Ellison   *Living with Music*   411
Mary Gordon   *Mary Cassatt*   419
Mark Strand   *Crossing the Tracks to Hopper's*
                       World   423
William Zinsser   *Shanghai*   427
James Agee   *The Comic Acting of Buster Keaton*   438
John Berger   *Looking at a Photograph*   443
Elizabeth MacDonald   *Odalisque (student essay)*   446
James Baldwin   *Sonny's Blues (story)*   451
Langston Hughes   *Trumpet Player (poem)*   475

Nature

Sharman Apt Russell · *The Mimbres* · 481

Edward Hoagland · *The Courage of Turtles* · 490

Lewis Thomas · *The World's Biggest Membrane* · 496

Annie Dillard · *Living Like Weasels* · 500

George Orwell · *Some Thoughts on the Common Toad* · 505

Leslie Marmon Silko · *Landscape, History, and the Pueblo Imagination* · 509

Loren Eiseley · *The Flow of the River* · 516

Maile Meloy · *Horse-Love (student essay)* · 523

Tess Gallagher · *The Lover of Horses (story)* · 527

Elizabeth Bishop · *The Fish (poem)* · 537

PERMISSIONS ACKNOWLEDGMENTS · 541

INDEX · 547

Contents

RHETORICAL CONTENTS   xxi

TO THE STUDENT   xxv

TO THE INSTRUCTOR   xxvii

ACKNOWLEDGMENTS   xxix

Introduction: Reading toward Writing   1
  Why Read, and Why Write?   1
  An Approach to Reading   3
    Experience   3
  Zora Neale Hurston—How It Feels to Be Colored Me   3
    Interpretation   5
    Evaluation   8
    Moving toward Writing—Preliminary Strategies   10
    Annotating   10
  Gretel Ehrlich—About Men   10
    Questioning   12
    Freewriting   13
    Using a Double-Column Notebook   15
    Beyond Preliminary Writing Strategies   16
    Notes on Essay Form   18
  A Student Essay and How It Originated   20

Communities

Scott Russell Sanders   *Wayland*   32

    "Since we give labels to all that puzzles us, as we name every blank space on the map, I could say that what I stumbled into in Wayland were the mysteries of death, life, beasts, food, mind, sex, and God."

Mary Gordon   *More Than Just a Shrine: Paying Homage to the Ghosts of Ellis Island*   43

    "I suppose it is part of being an American to be engaged in a somewhat tiresome but always self-absorbing process of national definition. And in this process, I have found in traveling to Ellis Island an important piece of evidence that could remind me I was right to feel my differentness."

Marianna De Marco Torgovnick *Growing up White, Female, and Born in Bensonhurst*   48

    "Now, as I write about the neighborhood, I recognize that although I've come far in physical and material distance, the emotional distance is harder to gauge. Bensonhurst has everything to do with who I am and even with what I write. Occasionally I get reminded of my roots, of their simultaneously choking and nutritive power."

Amy Tan   *Mother Tongue*   58

    "Lately, I've been giving more thought to the kind of English my mother speaks. Like others, I have described it to people as 'broken' or 'fractured' English. But I wince when I say that. It has always bothered me that I can think of no way to describe it other than 'broken,' as if it were damaged and needed to be fixed . . ."

Tom Wolfe   *The Right Stuff*   64
"In this fraternity, even though it was military, men were not rated by their outward rank. . . . No, herein the world was divided into those who had it and those who did not. This quality, this *it,* was never named, however, nor was it talked about in any way."

Maxine Hong Kingston   *Silence*   75
"Normal Chinese women's voices are strong and bossy. We American-Chinese girls had to whisper to make ourselves American-feminine. Apparently we whispered even more softly than the Americans. . . . Most of us eventually found some voice, however faltering. We invented an American-feminine speaking personality."

Alice Walker   *In Search of Our Mothers' Gardens*   80
"How they did it—those millions of black women . . . —brings me to the title of this essay, 'In Search of Our Mothers' Gardens,' which is a personal account that is yet shared, in its theme and its meaning, by all of us."

Eric Kim (student)   *Family Portrait*   89
"A few weeks ago I received a small package from home. It was a set of pictures our family took during Christmas break. My mother and father are sitting together in the front. . . . We still don't look comfortable, but then again, we aren't leaning away from each other this time. It is beginning to look like a family portrait."

William Faulkner   *A Rose for Emily (story)*   94
"When Miss Emily Grierson died, our whole town went to her funeral: the men through a sort of respectful affection for a fallen monument, the women mostly out of curiosity to see the inside of her house, which no one save an old manservant—a combined gardener and cook—had seen in at least ten years."

Maya Angelou   *On the Pulse of Morning (poem)*   102
"Here on the pulse of this new day / You may have the grace to look up and out / And into your sister's eyes, / And into your brother's face . . .'"

Culture and Society

Tom Wolfe   *Only One Life*   111
"Much of what is now known as the 'sexual revolution' has consisted of both women and men filling in the blank this way: 'If I've only one life, let me live it as . . .' "

Joan Didion   *Marrying Absurd*   116
"What people who get married in Las Vegas actually do expect—what, in the largest sense, their 'expectations' are—strikes one as a curious and self-contradictory business."

Larry L. King   *Playing Cowboy*   120
"Texas is my mind's country, that place I most want to understand and record and preserve. Four generations of my people sleep in its soil; I have children there, and a grandson; the dead past and the living future tie me to it. Not that I always approve of it or love it."

Gloria Anzaldúa   *How to Tame a Wild Tongue*   130
"For a people who are neither Spanish nor live in a country in which Spanish is the first language; for a people who live in a country in which English is the reigning tongue but who are not Anglo; for a people who cannot entirely identify with either standard . . . Spanish nor standard English, what recourse is left to them but to create their own language?"

Diane Ravitch   *Multiculturalism*   140
"Given the diversity of American society, it has been impossible to insulate the schools from pressures that result from differences and tensions among groups. When people differ about basic values, sooner or later those disagreements turn up in battles about how schools are organized or what the schools should teach."

George Orwell   *Marrakech*   156
"When you walk through a town like this—two hundred thousand inhabitants, of whom at least twenty thousand own literally nothing except the rags they stand up in—when you see how the people live, and still more how easily they die, it is always difficult to believe that you are walking among human beings."

Henry Louis Gates, Jr.   *2 Live Crew, Decoded*   162
"Is 2 Live Crew more 'obscene' than, say, the comic Andrew 'Dice' Clay? Clearly, this rap group is seen as more threatening than others that are just as sexually explicit. Can this be completely unrelated to the specter of the young black male as a figure of sexual and social disruption, the very stereotypes 2 Live Crew seems determined to undermine?"

Marie Ribisi (student)   *The Health Craze*   165
"Much of what is presently recognized as the "fitness craze" has consisted of both men and women completing the statement this way: 'Why not keep your age your secret . . . and take up jogging or wear designer jeans'?"

Leslie Marmon Silko   *The Man to Send Rain Clouds (story)*   170
"Across the brown wrinkled forehead he drew a streak of white and along the high cheekbones he drew a strip of blue paint. He paused and watched Ken throw pinches of corn meal and pollen into the wind that fluttered the small gray feather . . . 'Send us rain clouds, Grandfather'."

Louis Simpson   *Walt Whitman at Bear Mountain (poem)*   175
"What are you, Walt? / The Open Road goes to the used-car lot. / Where is the nation you promised?"

Gender

Susan Brownmiller   *Femininity*   181
"As I passed through a stormy adolescence to a stormy maturity, femininity increasingly became an exasperation. . . . 'Don't lose your femininity' and 'Isn't it remarkable how she manages to retain her femininity?' had terrifying implications."

Pat C. Hoy II   *Mosaics of Southern Masculinity*   186
"My father, I used to think, simply was not there. I have discovered over time, that he was, still is. He's there, like the place; he's in my bones. I know it by the fives I make. I know it by the cars I drive and the way I drive them, know it too by the smiling way I ask for recognition and confirmation."

Maxine Hong Kingston   *No Name Woman*   201
" 'You must not tell anyone'," my mother said, 'what I am about to tell you. In China your father had a sister who killed herself. She jumped into the family well. We say that your father has all brothers because it is as if she had never been born'."

Annie Dillard   *The Deer at Providencia*   211
"They had looked to see how I, the only woman, and the youngest, was taking the sight of the deer's struggles. I looked detached, apparently, or hard, or calm, or focused, still. I don't know. I remember feeling very old and energetic."

Scott Russell Sanders   *The Men We Carry in Our Minds*   216
" 'This must be a hard time for women'," I say to my friend Anneke. 'They have so many paths to choose from, and so many voices calling them.' 'I think it's a lot harder for men,' she replies."

Deborah Tannen   *Different Words, Different Worlds*   222
"If women speak and hear a language of connection and intimacy, while men speak and hear a language of status and independence, then communication between men and women can be like cross-cultural communication, prey to a clash of conversational styles."

Paul Theroux   *Being a Man*   235
"I have always disliked being a man. The whole idea of manhood in America is pitiful, in my opinion. . . . Even the expression 'Be a man!' strikes me as insulting and abusive."

Maile Meloy (student)   *The Voice of the Looking-Glass*   240
"Little girls (and little boys) learn early that the way women are treated is determined by the way they appear. . . . It is a woman's ever-present task to monitor her image, not to survey a situation to determine the appropriate action, as a man does, but to survey herself and define by her presentation the way she wishes others to act toward her."

John Updike   *A & P (story)*   246
"In walks these three girls in nothing but bathing suits. I'm in the third check-out slot, with my back to the door, so I don't see them until they're over by the bread. The one that caught my eye first was the one in the plaid green two-piece."

Emily Dickinson   *I'm "wife"—I've finished that" (poem)*   252
I'm "wife"—I've finished that—
That other state—
I'm Czar—I'm "Woman" now—
It's safer so—

Race

James Baldwin   *Notes of a Native Son*   257
"It was necessary to hold on to the things that mattered. The dead man mattered, the new life mattered; blackness and whiteness did not matter; to believe that they did was to acquiesce in one's own destruction. Hatred, which could destroy so much, never failed to destroy the man who hated and this was an immutable law."

Roger Wilkins   *In Ivory Towers*   273
" 'You're upset because you think *affirmative action* makes white folks look at you funny. Hell, white folks were looking at black folks funny long before affirmative action was invented."

June Jordan   *Where Is the Love?*   277
"It is here in this extreme, inviolable coincidence of my status as a Black feminist, my status as someone twice stigmatized, my status as a Black woman who is twice kin to the despised majority of all the human life that there is, it is here, in that extremity. . . . that I ask, of myself, and of any one who would call me sister, *Where is the love?*"

Cornel West   *Race Matters*   282
"To engage in a serious discussion of race in America, we must begin not with the problems of black people but with the flaws of American society— flaws rooted in historic inequalities and longstanding cultural stereotypes.

How we set up the terms for discussing racial issues shapes our perception and response to these issues."

N. Scott Momaday   *from The Way to Rainy Mountain*   288
"My grandmother had a reverence for the sun, a holy regard that now is all but gone out of mankind. There was a wariness in her, and an ancient awe. She was a Christian in her later years, but she had come a long way about, and she never forgot her birthright."

Richard Rodriguez   *Complexion*   293
"Throughout adolescence, I felt myself mysteriously marked. Nothing else about my appearance would concern me so much as the fact my complexion was dark."

Shelby Steele   *The New Sovereignty*   298
"In a liberal democracy, collective entitlements based upon race, gender, ethnicity, or some other group grievance are always undemocratic expedients. . . . I think it is time for those who seek identity and power through grievance groups to fashion identities apart from grievance . . ."

Suyin So (student)   *Grotesques*   309
"Once I asked my father whether he thought, if we weren't what we were we would be black or white. He looked at me in profound astonishment and with a hint of irritation. 'Suyin,' he told me, 'we are Asian. . . . We cannot change what we are'."

Ralph Ellison   *Battle Royal (story)*   313
"He was an odd old guy, my grandfather, and I am told I take after him. . . . On his deathbed he called my father to him and said, 'Son, after I'm gone I want you to keep up the fight. I never told you, but our life is a war and I have been a traitor all my born days, a spy in the enemy's country. . . . I want you to overcome 'em with yeses, undermine 'em with grins, agree 'em to death and destruction, let 'em swoller you till they vomit or bust wide open."

Langston Hughes   *Theme for English B (poem)*   325
"As I learn from you, / I guess you learn from me— / although you're older— and white— / and somewhat more free."

Language

Michiko Kakutani   *The Word Police*   331
"In the case of the politically correct, the prohibition of certain words, phrases and ideas is advanced in the cause of building a brave new world free of racism and hate, but this vision of harmony clashes with the very ideals of diversity and inclusion that the multicultural movement holds dear, and it's purchased at the cost of freedom of expression and freedom of speech."

Robin Lakoff   *Talking Like a Lady*   336
"Little girls are indeed taught to talk like little ladies, in that their speech is in many ways more polite than that of boys or men, and the reason for this is that politeness involves an absence of a strong statement, and women's speech is devised to prevent the expression of strong statements."

Barbara Lawrence   *Four-Letter Words Can Hurt You*   345
"No one that I know, least of all my students, would fail to question the values of a society whose literature and entertainment rested heavily on racial or ethnic pejoratives. Are the values of a society whose literature and entertainment rest as heavily as ours on sexual pejoratives any less questionable?"

Nancy Mairs   *On Being a Cripple*   349
"I am a cripple. I choose this word to name me. I choose from among several possibilities, the most common of which are 'handicapped' and 'disabled.' . . . 'Cripple' seems to me a clean word, straightforward and precise."

Neil Postman   *"Now . . . This"*   359
"There is no murder so brutal, no earthquake so devastating, no political
blunder so costly—for that matter, no ball score so tantalizing or weather
report so threatening—that it cannot be erased from our minds by a newscaster saying, 'Now . . . this'."

James Baldwin   *If Black English Isn't a Language,*
                                 Then Tell Me, What Is?   369
"It goes without saying, then, that language is also a political instrument,
means and proof of power. It is the most vivid and crucial key to identity: It
reveals the private identity, and connects one with, or divorces one from,
the larger, public, or communal identity."

George Orwell   *Politics and the English Language* 373
"Thus political language has to consist largely of euphemism, question-
begging and sheer cloudy vagueness. Defenceless villages are bombarded
from the air, the inhabitants driven out into the countryside, the cattle
machine-gunned, the huts set on fire with incendiary bullets: this is called
pacification."

Lisa Bogdonoff (student)   *Police! Police!*   384
"Very often we refer to the conservators of public peace as 'police,' 'cops,'
'fuzz,' even 'pigs.' Although each of these words refers to members of the
peacekeeping force, the implications connoted by each are quite different."

Gish Jen   *What Means Switch? (story)*   387
"There we are, nice Chinese family—father, mother, two born-here girls.
Where should we live next? My parents slide the question back and forth like
a cup of ginseng neither one wants to drink. Until finally it comes to them,
what they really want is a milkshake (chocolate) and to go with it a house in
Scarsdale."

Pablo Neruda   *The Word (poem)*   401
"The word / was born in the blood, / grew in the dark body, beating, / and
took flight through the lips and the mouth."

The Arts

Joan Didion   *Georgia O'Keeffe*   407
"She told adults that she wanted to be an artist and was embarrassed when
they asked what kind of artist she wanted to be: she had no idea 'what kind.'
She had no idea what artists did."

Ralph Ellison   *Living with Music*   411
"In those days it was either live with music or die with noise, and we chose
rather desperately to live. In the process our apartment—what with its
booby-trappings of audio equipment, wires, discs and tapes—came to resemble the Collier mansion, but that was later. First there was the neighborhood,
assorted drunks and a singer."

Mary Gordon   *Mary Cassatt*   419
"Cassatt's reputation has suffered because of the prejudice against her subject matter. Mothers and children: what could be of lower prestige, more vulnerable to the charge of sentimentality? Yet if one looks at the work of Mary
Cassatt, one sees how triumphantly she avoids the pitfalls of sentimentality because of the astringent rigor of her eye and craft."

Mark Strand   *Crossing the Tracks to Hopper's World*   423

"The remarkable number of roads, highways, and railroad tracks in his paintings speak for Hopper's fascination with passage. Often, while looking at his work, we are made to feel like transients, momentary visitors to a scene that will endure without us and that suffers our presence with aggressive reticence."

William Zinsser   *Shanghai*   427

"There was no translating 'hambone' into Mandarin, but Ruff quickly had an intricate rhythm going to demonstrate, slapping himself with the palms of his hands and smacking his open mouth to create a series of resonating pops. Applause greeted this proof that the body could be its own drum."

James Agee   *The Comic Acting of Buster Keaton*   438

"Keaton's face ranked almost with Lincoln's as an early American archetype; it was haunting, handsome, almost beautiful, yet it was irreducibly funny; he improved matters by topping it off with a deadly horizontal hat, as flat and thin as a phonograph record."

John Berger   *Looking at a Photograph*   443

"A mother with her child is staring intently at a soldier. Perhaps they are speaking. We cannot hear their words. Perhaps they are saying nothing and everything is being said by the way they are looking at each other."

Elizabeth MacDonald (student)   *Odalisque*   446

"I do not remember the first time that I made myself throw up. It may have been in eleventh grade, but the circumstances have faded under the shame and horror."

James Baldwin   *Sonny's Blues (story)*   451

"I had never before thought of how awful the relationship must be between the musician and his instrument. He has to fill it, this instrument, with the breath of life, his own. He has to make it do what he wants it to do."

Langston Hughes   *Trumpet Player (poem)*   475

"The music / From the trumpet at his lips / Is honey / Mixed with liquid fire. / The rhythm / From the trumpet at his lips / Is ecstasy / Distilled from old desire—"

Nature

Sharman Apt Russell   *The Mimbres*   481

"On the morning of the second 'hundred-year flood,' we woke to a triumphant roar and strangely clear view. Below our house, what had last night been a field of winter rye was a mass of brown water lapping at the goat's pen. Something important seemed to be missing. . . ."

Edward Hoagland   *The Courage of Turtles*   490

"Turtles cough, burp, whistle, grunt and hiss, and produce social judgments. They put their heads together amicably enough, but then one drives the other back with the suddenness of two dogs who have been conversing in tones too low for an onlooker to hear."

Lewis Thomas   *The World's Biggest Membrane*   496

"It is hard to feel affection for something as totally impersonal as the atmosphere, and yet there it is, as much a part and product of life as wine or bread. . . . It breathes for us, and it does another thing for our pleasure. . . ."

Annie Dillard   *Living Like Weasels*   500
"I don't think I can learn from a wild animal how to live in particular—shall
I suck warm blood, hold my tail high, walk with my footprints precisely over
the prints of my hands?—but I might learn something of mindlessness,
something of the purity of living in the physical senses and the dignity of
living without bias or motive."

George Orwell   *Some Thoughts on the Common Toad*   505
"How many a time have I stood watching the toads mating, or a pair of hares
having a boxing match in the young corn, and thought of all the important
persons who would stop me enjoying this if they could. But luckily they
can't."

Leslie Marmon Silko   *Landscape, History, and the Pueblo*
                               Imagination   509
"The land, the sky, and all that is within them—the landscape—includes
human beings. Interrelationships in the Pueblo landscape are complex and
fragile. . . . Survival depended upon harmony and cooperation not only
among human beings, but among all things—the animate and the less animate, since rocks and mountains were known to move, to travel occasionally."

Loren Eiseley   *The Flow of the River*   516
"Once in a lifetime, perhaps, one escapes the actual confines of the flesh.
Once in a lifetime, if one is lucky, one so merges with sunlight and air and
running water that whole eons, the eons that mountains and deserts know,
might pass in a single afternoon without discomfort."

Maile Meloy (student)   *Horse-Love*   523
"Nothing is more unapologetically physical and natural than the birth of a
horse. . . . Around this strange nativity are gathered the worried midwives:
unshaven and rumpled horsemen in plaid flannel, women in rubber boots
caked with manure, a vet with rolled up sleeves. Each stands by, blinking
from lost sleep and patient vigilance, but alert."

Tess Gallagher   *The Lover of Horses (story)*   527
"They say my great-grandfather was a gypsy, but the most popular explanation for his behavior was that he was a drunk. How else could the women
have kept up the scourge of his memory all these years, had they not had the
usual malady of our family to blame? Probably he was both a gypsy and a
drunk."

Elizabeth Bishop   *The Fish (poem)*   537
"I caught a tremendous fish / and held him beside the boat / half out of
water, with my hook / fast in a corner of his mouth."

PERMISSIONS ACKNOWLEDGMENTS   541
INDEX   547

Rhetorical Contents

Description

	2
How It Feels to Be Colored Me	3
More Than Just a Shrine	43
The Right Stuff	64
In Search of Our Mothers' Gardens	80
A Rose for Emily	94
On the Pulse of Morning	102
Only One Life	111
Marrying Absurd	116
Playing Cowboy	120
Marrakech	156
The Health Craze	165
Walt Whitman at Bear Mountain	170
The Deer at Providencia	211
The Voice of the Looking-Glass	240
"I'm wife—I've finished that"	252
from The Way to Rainy Mountain	288
Complexion	293
The Word	401
Mary Cassatt	411
The Comic Acting of Buster Keaton	438
Looking at a Photograph	443
Odalisque	446
Trumpet Player	475
The Fish	537

Narration

Wayland	32
On Being White, Female, and Born in Bensonhurst	48
Family Portrait	89
A Rose for Emily	94
The Man to Send Rain Clouds	170
Mosaics of Southern Masculinity	186
No Name Woman	201
A & P	246
Notes of a Native Son	257
Grotesques	309
Battle Royal	313
What Means Switch?	387
Living with Music	411
Shanghai	427
Sonny's Blues	451
The Mimbres	481
Living Like Weasels	500
The Flow of the River	516
The Lover of Horses	527

Exposition

About Men (Illustration)	10
Wayland (Examples)	32

Mother Tongue (Illustration)   58
The Right Stuff (Definition)   64
Marrying Absurd (Illustration and Cause/Effect)   111
Playing Cowboy (Comparison/Contrast)   120
Multiculturalism (Comparison/Contrast)   140
Femininity (Illustration)   181
Mosaics of Southern Masculinity (Reasons/Examples)   186
No Name Woman (Cause/Effect)   201
The Men We Carry in Our Minds (Comparison/Contrast)   216
Different Words, Different Worlds (Comparison/Contrast)   222
Notes of a Native Son (Cause/Effect)   257
Complexion (Illustration)   293
Theme for English B (Comparison/Contrast)   325
Talking Like a Lady (Illustration)   331
Four Letter Words Can Hurt You (Illustration)   345
"Now . . . This" (Reasons/Examples)   359
Politics and the English Language (Illustration)   373
Police! Police! (Illustration)   384
Georgia O'Keeffe (Illustration)   407
Mary Cassatt (Comparison/Contrast)   411
Crossing the Tracks to Hopper's World (Illustration)   423
Odalisque (Cause/Effect)   446
The Courage of Turtles (Illustration)   490
The World's Biggest Membrane (Analogy)   496
Horse-Love (Illustration)   523

Persuasion
How It Feels to Be Colored Me   3
About Men   10
More Than Just a Shrine   43
On Being White, Female, and Born in Bensonhurst   48
Mother Tongue   58
The Right Stuff   64
In Search of Our Mothers' Gardens   80
How to Tame a Wild Tongue   130
Multiculturalism   140
Marrakech   156
2 Live Crew, Decoded   162
Femininity   181
Being a Man   235
The Voice of the Looking-Glass   240
In Ivory Towers   257
Where Is the Love?   277
Race Matters   282
The New Sovereignty   298
The Word Police   331
On Being a Cripple   349
"Now . . . This"   359
If Black English Isn't a Language, Then Tell Me, What Is?   369
Politics and the English Language   373

Looking at a Photograph 443
The World's Biggest Membrane 496
Living Like Weasels 500
Some Thoughts on the Common Toad 505
Landscape, History, and the Pueblo Imagination 509

To the Student

The way to read better is to read more and to reflect more thoughtfully on what you read. The way to write better is to practice. If you have not had a lot of experience reading widely, or if you lack sufficient practice in writing, that is no cause for concern. You can learn to read with confidence and to write with competence; you can achieve greater understanding of what you read and a surer sense of how to say what you think in writing.

This book presents an approach to reading that embodies a method you can employ for reading many kinds of materials—essays, poems, stories, editorials, Op-Ed pieces, critical analyses, textbooks, advertisements, graffiti, and many other types of texts. The approach invites you to do three things:

1. consider your experience—both your experience in living and your experience of reading
2. analyze the elements or aspects of texts you read according to a four-step method: observing textual details, relating and connecting them, drawing inferences from those connections, and formulating an interpretation from your inferences
3. evaluate the texts you read by reflecting on the social, cultural, and other values they reflect, and by considering the validity and persuasiveness of the arguments they make or the perspectives on experience they offer.

The book's approach to writing is intricately linked with its approach to reading. This approach involves learning to respond to texts you read by annotating them, by freewriting and asking questions about them, and by keeping a special double-column notebook about your reading.

The introduction provides you with a discussion of the approach to reading with examples of each part: responding, interpreting, and evaluating.

Additional guidance for this approach to reading is provided in the questions and writing suggestions that follow each selection. After every reading, however brief, you will find three sets of questions. The first questions (experience) ask you to consider aspects of experience—either your experience in reading the selection or your personal experience as it relates to the selection. The second questions (interpretation) ask you to consider the meaning(s) of the selection. And the third questions (evaluation) ask you either to consider the values the selection reflects or to evaluate the selection's effectiveness.

Complementing these guiding questions for reading and understanding, you will find three writing suggestions after each selection. The first of these writing suggestions (exploring) invites you to rely on personal experience to explore your thoughts and feelings about a situation similar or related to that described in the selection. The second writing suggestion (interpreting) invites you to analyze the selection, sometimes by focusing on its structure; sometimes on its language and style; sometimes on its details, examples, and other forms of evidence. The third writing suggestion *(evaluating)* invites you to make a judgment about the selection, and sometimes to consider your own values as you respond to the values reflected in the selection.

In responding to any of the questions or writing suggestions, you are encouraged to think for yourself and develop your powers of mind. The questions and writing suggestions are designed to guide you toward critical and creative thinking—toward the kind of thoughtful and imaginative response that reflects who you are, what you believe, how you think, and why you think the way you do.

Robert DiYanni

To the Instructor

This book has been designed to give students the kind of practice in reading that will enable them to become better readers and writers. To that end a broad selection of readings has been collected under seven headings: communities, culture and society, language, gender, the arts, nature, and race. Each topic constitutes a chapter that includes seven professional prose pieces, one student essay, one short story, and one poem (in that order). The topics and the selections within the chapters are wide-ranging in scope and provocative in perspective and point of view. The selections, by writers of different cultures who espouse different values and ideas, are evenly divided between women and men, and they include a high representation of minority voices. The readings are meant to be engaging, readable, and interesting.

Half of the book's 72 selections are by women. Minority writers account for more than a third of the pieces, and they include Latino/Latina authors, Native Americans, Asian Americans, and African American writers representing a wide range of styles and voices. Of the 51 professional essays, about one-third are arguments, or involve extensive argumentation. These argument-centered texts, moreover, reflect differing styles and voices as well as varying levels of accessibility and complexity.

The book's topics (chapter headings) have been chosen with care to reflect both traditional categories familiar to teachers and students ("language," "nature," "the arts") and categories currently attracting pedagogical and academic attention ("communities," "race," "gender," "culture and society").

The pedagogy on which the book is based offers less a system than a method. That is, instead of being an inflexible set of rules to follow, it provides an approach to reading. The method allows for and encourages the kinds of reading and writing associated with reader-response approaches. It also includes the kinds of analysis and interpretation affiliated with various types of close reading. In addition, it invites the making of judgments and the consideration of values that reflect various concerns of cultural studies.

The book's approach to reading, which divides into three parts—experience, interpretation, and evaluation—provides a useful way to introduce students to the scope and complexity of reading. Its attention to their experience of reading and living invites students to see these readings as relevant both to how they live and to how they read. Its attention to analysis and interpretation encourages students to read closely and attend to detail, to relate one aspect or one part of a text to other aspects and other parts so as to arrive at a coherent interpretation. And, finally, the book's attention to evaluation involves respect for the values students bring to the text along with a concern that they understand values reflected in the text that may differ, perhaps in significant ways, from their own.

The questions that follow each selection, moreover, have been devised and arranged as lines of inquiry focused on the three aspects of reading: experience, interpretation, and evaluation. The questions attempt to stimulate thoughtful responses based on previous knowledge and experience, rather than on a quick scan of the text for a simple and single correct answer.

The approach to writing in the book reinforces and grows out of its approach to reading. Students are encouraged to write informally while they read and more discursively afterwards. Two extended examples walk students through the steps of turning careful reading into thoughtful writing. For the second example students are invited to participate in contributing annotations, freewriting, questions, and double-column notebook entries. Writing assignments, which follow every selection, invite different kinds of essays: personal (exploratory), analytical, and argumentative.

The book's selections and pedagogy aim, overall, to make students' reading and writing interesting, relevant, and enjoyable.

Robert DiYanni

Acknowledgments

I would like to thank, first of all, those at McGraw-Hill who encouraged me and supported my work on this book: Alison Zetterquist, who lobbied for its signing; Phil Butcher, who nurtured its development; and Tim Julet, who suggested improvements and oversaw its completion. Thanks also to Jim Belser, Senior Editing Supervisor, for his professionalism and attention to detail; to Joe Piliero who created the book's elegant design; and to Rich Ausburn for overseeing the many phases of production.

A number of insightful reviewers offered wise counsel, from which I happily benefitted. Thanks go to Tuziline Jita Allan, Baruch College; Steve Beck, Southeastern Community College; Michael Berberich, Galveston College; Kathleen Shine Caine, Merrimack College; Robin Calitri, Merced College; Walter Cannon, Central College; Michael Cochran, Santa Fe Community College; Kirk Combe, Denison University; John Davis, University of Texas at San Antonio; Dale Flynn, University of California, Davis; Marjorie Ford, Stanford University; Susan Forrest, Santa Rosa Junior College; Paula Gibson, Cardinal Stritch College; Larry Griffin, Midland College; Ruth Haber, Worcester State College; David Hoffman, Averett College; Kathleen Krager, Walsh University; Hedda Marcus, Nassau Community College; Joseph Martin, Cornell University; Elizabeth Nolan, Westchester University; Jerry Olsen, Middlesex County College; Alan Powers, Bristol Community College; Gerald Richman, Suffolk University; Donnalee Rubin, Salem State College; Ken Wolfskill, Chowan College; and Edith Wollin, North Seattle Community College.

Robert DiYanni

PERSPECTIVES:
READINGS
FOR WRITERS

INTRODUCTION

Reading Toward Writing

WHY READ, AND WHY WRITE?

We read for information about topics that interest us, about people and places, about activities we enjoy. And we read newspapers and magazines for pleasure. We may read to escape, to amuse ourselves, to deepen our understanding of an issue, to solve a problem, to satisfy our curiosity. We do that kind of reading for ourselves.

We also read to learn about subjects and fields that, for one reason or another, we need to study—at least for a time. Some of this reading we may do for a job, some for academic courses of study toward fulfilling requirements for a college degree.

Whatever its purpose, reading can make us more aware of our world and more aware of ourselves. It can stretch our imagination and deepen and enliven our experience. It can provoke us to think by challenging our assumptions. And it can help us make sense of our lives and our world by providing us with explanations that relate what we see, hear, think, and learn. Reading, in short, can enrich our understanding of issues that affect our world and our lives.

As educated people living in a complex and rapidly changing world, we must think about our culture and society, our communities large and small—especially where and how we fit into them. We need to be aware of debates occurring over issues of race and gender, since everyone is a member of both and since race and gender are burning issues for our time. We also need to be alert to how language reflects and affects racial attitudes, gender roles, and cultural dispositions. Moreover, the more we know about how language works, the better we will be able to understand it, enjoy it, and use it ourselves.

These and other subjects serve as chapter topics in this book because they are about life in all its variety, complexity, and richness. Some of the topics may relate more immediately and dramatically to our concerns. Others may seem more remote from our immediate experience. If, for example, you live in a city, concern about nature may not be so important to you. And conversely, if you live far from an urban or suburban cultural center, the arts may seem remote.

But consider that nature and art form part of the environment in which we all live. Our relations with the natural world are becoming increasingly complex, with the earth's resources diminishing. As inhabitants of a planet of which we are not the sole occupants, we need to better understand and appreciate the rest of creation if we are to exist comfortably in the future. And we need to understand works of art, because those works embody human experience in all its joy and pain and express the deepest and most resonant ideas and emotions. No society has ever existed that didn't express its values through one or another of the arts, and ours is no different.

Reading is one way toward acquiring such understanding and appreciation. And like reading, writing remains necessary even in a world of phones and faxes, of instant communication. Writing, like reading, fosters thinking, for in order to write, you have to think about what you want to say and how best to say it. In the process of doing that, you may find yourself thinking of things to say that you did not know you were going to say when you started. That is simply because the act of writing stimulates thought.

Writing, like reading, is also active. It requires intellectual energy. It requires attention to meaning and attentiveness to evidence in support of that meaning. For the evidence you need to support the ideas and opinions you write about, you rely on your experience of life, on your observation of the world, and on your reading.

One of the most important kinds of writing you will do in many types of college courses is writing about reading. In history courses you will write about historical events, perhaps on the basis of original documents or sources (called "primary sources"), perhaps using secondary sources (sources about sources) as your texts to write about. In literature courses you will write about novels and stories, poems and plays and essays, which are also primary sources. In writing about literature you may need to use secondary sources, perhaps to write a research essay about different interpretations of a particular literary work, such as *Hamlet.* The same goes for the rest of the curriculum—psychology, economics, philosophy and religion, the arts, even, to some extent, the sciences. In all these disciplines you can expect to receive assignments requiring you to write based on your reading of primary sources, observations, or experimental data and on your reading of secondary sources that explain the primary sources or data.

We can write about texts in these and other disciplines for three reasons at least. First, writing about a text leads us to read it attentively, to see things about it we might overlook on a more casual reading. Second, writing stimulates thinking. Putting words on paper gets our minds into gear. Third, we may want to react to what a text says, perhaps to endorse its views, perhaps to disagree with or qualify them. Finally, writing and reading are mutually supporting. Because these two intellectual acts stimulate and reinforce one another, we should make our reading as active as our writing. And we should use both reading and writing as ways to develop our thinking.

AN APPROACH TO READING

When we read a text of any kind, we do essentially three things: We respond, we interpret, and we evaluate. We react emotionally and intellectually to what we read (our immediate response). We try to understand what the writer is saying, what the text means (our interpretation). And we make judgments about its persuasiveness and effectiveness (our evaluation). We can use these three categories to describe how we read various kinds of texts—essays and other prose works as well as literary works such as short stories and poems. In the process we will illustrate ways of experiencing, interpreting, and evaluating texts that can lead to deeper understanding of what we read.

Experience

One of the first things that occurs when we read a text is that we bring to it our particular background and experience. This includes both our experience of living in the world and our experience of reading. We bring to our reading of any text both who we are and what we know. As we read, we form initial impressions that begin to coalesce as we read further. Consider what happens, for example, as you read the opening section of Zora Neale Hurston's essay "How It Feels to Be Colored Me."

1   I am colored but I offer nothing in the way of extenuating circumstances except the fact that I am the only Negro in the United States whose grandfather on the mother's side was *not* an Indian chief.

2   I remember the very day that I became colored. Up to my thirteenth year I lived in the little Negro town of Eatonville, Florida. It is exclusively a colored town. The only white people I knew passed through the town going to or coming from Orlando. The native whites rode dusty horses, the Northern tourists chugged down the sandy village road in automobiles. The town knew the Southerners and never stopped cane chewing when they passed. But the Northerners were something else again. They were peered at cautiously from behind curtains by the timid. The more venturesome would come out on the porch to watch them go past and got just as much pleasure out of the tourists as the tourists got out of the village.

3   The front porch might seem a daring place for the rest of the town, but it was a gallery seat for me. My favorite place was atop the gate-post. Proscenium box for a born first-nighter. Not only did I enjoy the show, but I didn't mind the actors knowing that I liked it. I usually spoke to them in passing. I'd wave at them and when they returned my salute, I would say something like this: "Howdy-do-well-I-thank-you-where-you-goin'?" Usually the automobile or the horse paused at this, and after a

queer exchange of compliments, I would probably "go a piece of the way" with them, as we say in farthest Florida. If one of my family happened to come to the front in time to see me, of course negotiations would be rudely broken off. But even so, it is clear that I was the first "welcome-to-our-state" Floridian, and I hope the Miami Chamber of Commerce will please take notice.

During this period, white people differed from colored to me only in that they rode through town and never lived there. They liked to hear me "speak pieces" and sing and wanted to see me dance the parse-me-la, and gave me generously of their small silver for doing these things, which seemed strange to me for I wanted to do them so much that I needed bribing to stop. Only they didn't know it. The colored people gave no dimes. They deplored any joyful tendencies in me, but I was their Zora nevertheless. I belonged to them, to the nearby hotels, to the county—everybody's Zora.

But changes came in the family when I was thirteen, and I was sent to school in Jacksonville. I left Eatonville, the town of the oleanders, as Zora. When I disembarked from the river-boat at Jacksonville, she was no more. It seemed that I had suffered a sea change. I was not Zora of Orange County any more. I was now a little colored girl. I found it out in certain ways. In my heart as well as in the mirror. I became a fast brown—warranted not to rub nor run.

Whatever you understand from this passage, your response to what Hurston describes will be affected by what you know about being "colored," by what you know about racial and regional differences, by what you know about changes people undergo from innocence to experience. Your experience in reading this passage, will also be affected by moments when you learned something about your race, your ethnicity, your social class, or some other aspect of your identity. Moreover, as you read this opening passage you begin to gain a sense of Zora Neale Hurston the writer as well as Zora the "little colored girl," as she describes herself. You begin to sense something of the writer's wit as well as the little girl's potential vulnerability.

Your experience of reading is affected, that is, by your own past experience in living, by your knowledge gained through observation and reading, and by the way the writer organizes and arranges her text. When Hurston notes that her young self, for example, found out that she was colored "in certain ways," you expect that Hurston will describe those ways later in her essay. You also expect, perhaps, that they will be somewhat painful experiences for her when Hurston writes that young Zora found out this fact of life in her "heart as well as in the mirror."

In reading this opening section of Hurston's essay, you have been invited into her world. And you have been invited to respond to what she describes there not only intellectually, but emotionally, as well. You do not have to have seen or directly experienced the kind of situation Hurston describes to respond to what she depicts. Imagining will be enough. Your capacity to imagine, in fact, is an important way to bring your experience to bear on your reading of essays. For experience does not mean only what you yourself have actually lived through; it also includes what you have learned or are capable of imagining.

And finally, concerning your experience of reading, you will have certain subjective impressions of the text, including, perhaps, emotional reactions. These elements of response are inevitable. And while they are preliminary and may change as you read further into the essay, they are important to acknowledge, for your emotional apprehension of a work is every bit as important as your intellectual comprehension.

Intellectual comprehension, however, is the provenance of interpretation, which is the next aspect of reading to consider, and one that is critical for academic work.

Interpretation

When you interpret a text, you explain it to yourself and make sense of it. In interpreting, you do not entirely disregard your subjective impressions of what you read, but you try to be objective, to think less of your own immediate reactions than of what the writer is saying or suggesting. Your interpretation of a text such as an essay, poem, or story is one way of understanding it, one way of making sense of it. Other ways of understanding the text, other interpretations, will exist; they, too, will make sense. Your interpretation should rely on your intellectual comprehension and not on your emotional response to or your subjective impressions of the text. Your goal is to understand what the writer is saying or suggesting.

In reading a text such as an essay, poem, or story, you attempt to discover the writer's idea. Your effort to comprehend the idea of the text is the goal of interpretation. Consider, from the standpoint of interpretation, the second section of Hurston's essay, "How It Feels to Be Colored Me."

6   But I am not tragically colored. There is no great sorrow dammed up in my soul, nor lurking behind my eyes. I do not mind at all. I do not belong to the sobbing school of Negrohood who hold that nature somehow has given them a lowdown dirty deal and whose feelings are all hurt about it. Even in the helter-skelter skirmish that is my life, I have seen that the world is to the strong regardless of a little pigmentation more or less. No, I do not weep at the world—I am too busy sharpening my oyster knife.

7   Someone is always at my elbow reminding me that I am the granddaughter of slaves. It fails to register depression with me. Slavery is sixty years in the past. The operation was successful and the patient is doing well, thank you. The terrible struggle that made me an American out of a potential slave said "On the line!" The Reconstruction said "Get set!": and the generation before said "Go!" I am off to a flying start and I must not halt in the stretch to look behind and weep. Slavery is the price I paid for civilization, and the choice was not with me. It is a bully

adventure and worth all that I have paid through any ancestors for it. No one on earth ever had a greater chance for glory. The world to be won and nothing to be lost. It is thrilling to think—to know that for any act of mine, I shall get twice as much praise or twice as much blame. It is quite exciting to hold the center of the national stage, with the spectators not knowing whether to laugh or to weep.

8   The position of my white neighbors is much more difficult. No brown specter pulls up a chair beside me when I am down to eat. No dark ghost thrusts its leg against mine in bed. The game of keeping what one has is never so exciting as the game of getting.

Hurston suggests that she does not regret being born black. In fact, she is delighted with her race, since, as she says, "no one on earth ever had a greater chance for glory." She sees being "colored" as an opportunity rather than a drawback, and she announces her satisfaction by distinguishing herself from those who see themselves as "tragically colored."

In addition, Hurston argues that unlike her white neighbors, she does not have to live with a heritage of guilt for legal and moral crimes committed against black people. "No brown specter" and "no dark ghost" haunt her, she says.

It is not merely the idea Hurston expresses here, however, that is important; it is the attitude she takes toward it and the tone in which she expresses it. She appears to relish her chance to shine; she is thrilled to think about what opportunities she has in "the game of getting" (which is how she sees life).

Although Hurston does not deny that the institution of slavery exacted a price—a price she believes has been paid by her ancestors— she is not one to weep over the past. Rather, she is "off to a flying start" toward success and enjoyment in life. As she puts it, she is "busy sharpening [her] oyster knife."

But let us consider a bit further the process of interpretation. Interpretation involves four interrelated acts:

1. observing details
2. relating those details
3. developing inferences on the basis of related details
4. formulating a conclusion in light of our inferences.

To understand a fictional work, for example, you observe its details of language, scene, and action. You listen to what the characters say and to how they say it. You note how the characters interact. You observe how the writer describes them and perhaps comments on their thoughts or behavior. You then relate your observations, connecting them into meaningful units. On the bases of these connections you form inferences or interpretive hypotheses about their significance. Ultimately, you arrive at a conclusion about the story's meaning.

The process is similar for a poem or essay. The four intellectual acts

are the same: observing, connecting, inferring, and concluding. The differences result from different features of each genre. With poetry you
pay even greater attention to details of language—to images and
metaphors, for example—than you do when you read stories and essays.
You consider the sounds of words and their connotations, and you
observe the poem's structural patterns for clues to its meaning. With
essays you attend to the writer's tone, to his or her attitude toward the
subject. You think about the idea of the essay, and you consider the evidence the writer uses to illustrate, advance, and support that idea.

Before we consider our last element of reading—evaluation—we
need to provide the last two sections of Hurston's essay.

9   Sometimes it is the other way around. A white person is set down in
our midst, but the contrast is just as sharp for me. For instance, when I
sit in the drafty basement that is The New World Cabaret with a white
person, my color comes. We enter chatting about any little nothing that
we have in common and are seated by the jazz waiters. In the abrupt
way that jazz orchestras have, this one plunges into a number. It loses
no time in circumlocutions, but gets right down to business. It constricts
the thorax and splits the heart with its tempo and narcotic harmonies.
This orchestra grows rambunctious, rears on its hind legs and attacks
the tonal veil with primitive fury, rending it, clawing it until it breaks
through to the jungle beyond. I follow those heathen—follow them
exultingly. I dance wildly inside myself; I yell within, I whoop; I shake
my assegai above my head. I hurl it true to the mark *yeeeeooww!* I am in
the jungle and living in the jungle way. My face is painted red and yellow
and my body is painted blue. My pulse is throbbing like a war drum. I
want to slaughter something—give pain, give death to what, I do not
know. But the piece ends. The men of the orchestra wipe their lips and
rest their fingers. I creep back slowly to the veneer we call civilization
with the last tone and find the white friend sitting motionless in his
seat, smoking calmly.

10   "Good music they have here," he remarks, drumming the table with
his fingertips.

11   Music. The great blobs of purple and red emotions have not touched
him. He has only heard what I felt. He is far away and I see him but
dimly across the ocean and the continent that have fallen between us.
He is so pale with his whiteness then and I am *so* colored.

12   I do not always feel colored. Even now I often achieve the unconscious Zora of Eatonville before the Hegira. I feel most colored when I
am thrown against a sharp white background.

13   For instance at Barnard. "Beside the waters of the Hudson" I feel my
race. Among the thousand white persons, I am a dark rock surged upon,
and overswept, but through it all, I remain myself. When covered by the
waters, I am; and the ebb but reveals me again.

14   At certain times I have no race, I am *me*. When I set my hat at a certain angle and saunter down Seventh Avenue, Harlem City, feeling as
snooty as the lions in front of the Forty-Second Street Library, for

instance. So far as my feelings are concerned, Peggy Hopkins Joyce on the Boule Mich with her gorgeous raiment, stately carriage, knees knocking together in a most aristocratic manner, has nothing on me. The cosmic Zora emerges. I belong to no race nor time. I am the eternal feminine with its string of beads.

15   I have no separate feeling about being an American citizen and colored. I am merely a fragment of the Great Soul that surges within the boundaries. My country, right or wrong.

16   Sometimes, I feel discriminated against, but it does not make me angry. It merely astonishes me. How *can* any deny themselves the pleasure of my company? It's beyond me.

17   But in the main, I feel like a brown bag of miscellany propped against a wall. Against a wall in company with other bags, white, red and yellow. Pour out the contents, and there is discovered a jumble of small things priceless and worthless. A first-water diamond, an empty spool, bits of broken glass, lengths of string, a key to a door long since crumbled away, a rusty knife-blade, old shoes saved for a road that never was and never will be, a nail bent under the weight of things too heavy for any nail, a dried flower or two still a little fragrant. In your hand is the brown bag. On the ground before you is the jumble it held—so much like the jumble in the bags, could they be emptied, that all might be dumped in a single heap and the bags refilled without altering the content of any greatly. A bit of colored glass more or less would not matter. Perhaps that is how the Great Stuffer of Bags filled them in the first place—who knows?

Evaluation

When you evaluate an essay, you consider its value for yourself as a reader. Evaluation consists essentially of two different kinds of assessment: (1) a judgment about the work's achievement, including the power and validity of its ideas, and (2) a consideration of the cultural values the work reflects or endorses.

When you evaluate an idea, you consider its accuracy as a description, its validity as a statement, its persuasiveness as a proposal, or its credibility as an imaginative construction. In order to evaluate any text you first have to identify the writer's idea, whether explicitly stated or implied. Then you need to restate the idea as a generalization. Evaluation depends on interpretation. Your understanding of a work's idea will influence your evaluation of it.

To make this kind of evaluation, of course, you must analyze the work, considering how well the writer employs words to create meaning, how well he or she dramatizes ideas in memorable ways, and how well the work persuades you intellectually or moves you emotionally.

Let us consider briefly some questions we might raise in an evaluation of Hurston's "How It Feels to Be Colored Me." You might consider, for example, how engaging you find Hurston's essay, or how broadly it reflects the feelings of other African Americans. Does Hurston's description accurately reflect your own knowledge or experience? Do you think most African Americans would agree with Hurston? Do you think her essay makes white American readers comfortable with their relationship with African Americans? Why or why not?

Another aspect of your evaluation of "How It Feels to Be Colored Me" concerns the values Hurston's essay endorses. Do you agree that being colored provides people with greater opportunities than are available to those in positions of power or control in a society, whatever their race or color? What do you think of Hurston's celebration of her race, of her self-confidence, and of her stance toward life?

In assessing the personal values of the writer and the cultural values displayed in her essay, you will, of course, bring your own values into play. It is precisely for this reason that it is important to consider the values Hurston's essay reflects. It is not so much that she is right or wrong about those values, but that considering her values by measuring them against your own will lead you to both a greater appreciation of her values and a better understanding of your own.

Other important kinds of values that surface in reading texts are the various social attitudes, moral beliefs, and cultural dispositions that animate them. How you respond to any text is determined in part by your understanding of such values and by your sense of how they mesh or clash with your own values. The essays, stories, and poems in this book reflect strongly held convictions based on particular social, moral, and cultural values. Annie Dillard's "The Deer at Providencia," for example, raises the subject of cruelty to animals, especially with respect to cultural expectations about how women respond to an animal's suffering. Maxine Hong Kingston's "No Name Woman" focuses on the clash between Chinese and American cultural norms, especially with regard to behavior considered reprehensible. James Baldwin's "Notes of a Native Son" deals with race relations and family dynamics within the context of bitter social antagonism. In these essays and others, arguments are presented, positions taken, and meanings made, all with social, moral, and cultural values paramount.

Evaluation in this sense involves our appraisal of the social, cultural, and moral ideals a work seems to support. Our social values reflect our attitudes toward the beliefs and ways of living of communities of which we are a part. Our cultural values, which derive from our ethnic and familial heritage, are affected by our race, our gender, and our language. Our moral values reflect our ethical norms—what we consider to be good and evil, right and wrong. These values are influenced by our religious beliefs and may reflect our political convictions.

With education and experience, our values may change. Through contact with other languages and cultures, we may come to understand the limiting perspective of our own. When we live or work or learn with people different from ourselves, we may be persuaded to different ways of seeing things we had previously taken for granted. Some of our beliefs, assumptions, and attitudes about marriage and family, sex and love, work and money, along with other aspects of life, are likely to change over time.

MOVING TOWARD WRITING—PRELIMINARY STRATEGIES

Our earlier discussion of Zora Neale Hurston's "How It Feels to Be Colored Me" demonstrates the process of careful reading necessary for thoughtful writing about a text. This section will take you farther along the road from reading an essay toward writing about it. In this section you will explore and practice some preliminary writing strategies. These should prove useful ways to begin thinking about what you read by doing relatively brief bursts of writing.

To help you move in that direction—from reading toward writing— we have printed the following essay by Gretel Ehrlich in sections. Each section consists of from one to three paragraphs. For each section you will find a different preliminary writing technique and thinking strategy illustrated. The illustrations of jotting annotations, asking questions, freewriting, and using a double-column notebook, however, are there only to help you get started. They begin the process and show you what to do. But you need to participate by adding your own writing—your own annotations, freewriting, questions, and double-column notebook comments to those provided as a start.

Each of these preliminary writing strategies is "writer based." That is, each technique invites your personal reflection on the text in writing that you produce for yourself rather than for other readers. These preliminary writing exercises help you find out what you think, which you can develop later in a more formal piece of writing—an essay or research paper, for example—for a public audience beyond yourself.

What shape that more formal writing takes, how it is organized and developed, will vary greatly depending on your instructor's requirements and the kind of essay, paper, or report you will be writing. Some general guidelines about essays follow discussion of the preliminary writing strategies.

Annotating

Annotating is one way to increase your involvement in reading a text by writing about it while you read. When you annotate or make notes about a text, you respond actively to it. Usually you make annotations in the margins around a text, but you can also make them within it by underlining or highlighting words, circling phrases, or bracketing sentences or paragraphs. You can also draw arrows, add question and exclamation marks, and employ any abbreviations you find useful.

Annotating a text offers a convenient and relatively painless way to begin writing about it. Your annotations can get you started zeroing in on what you think is important or interesting. You can use them to highlight points of contention and disagreement. And you can use them to signal textual details that may puzzle or disconcert you.

Annotations generally take one of the following forms:

· Labels or shorthand abbreviations of your reactions. You might write, for example, "good" or "nonsense" or "perhaps." You might also use labels to highlight important textual features with annotations such as "main point" or "evidence" or "irony."

· Summaries of important ideas or attitudes you discover in the text. These marginal notes, though brief, are more extensive than labels. They are often statements or exclamations. "This is nonsense," for example, or "An essential point—the world of *Hamlet* is full of riddles, puzzles, and mysteries."

· Questions such as "Why this?" or "Significant?" Or perhaps more extensively, "How does this section relate to the previous section?" "Where is the evidence for this assertion?"

In annotating a text, you begin to clarify your understanding of it. The act of writing such notes, however brief, encourages you to focus and to think. A further advantage of annotation is that if you write nothing more for a while, you have at least marked up the text for rereading, for subsequent study, and for class discussion. Annotating your required course readings is an effective way to prepare for class participation. And if and when you write more formally and extensively about the text, your annotations provide you with a place to pick up your thinking.

Here is the opening paragraph of Ehrlich's essay, with a few annotations to get you started. Read the paragraph, and add your own annotations. You can focus your annotations on the kinds of details Ehrlich includes (and what purpose they serve) or on particular words, phrases, or images that strike you as interesting.

When I'm in New York but feeling lonely for Wyoming I look for the Marlboro ads in the subway. What I'm aching to see is horseflesh, the glint of a spur, a line of distant mountains, brimming creeks, and a reminder of the ranchers and cowboys I've ridden with for the last eight years. But the men I see in those posters with their stern, humorless looks remind me of no one I know here. In our hellbent earnestness to romanticize the cowboy we've ironically disesteemed his true character. If he's "strong and silent" it's because there's probably no one to talk to. If he "rides away into the sunset" it's because he's been on horseback since four in the morning moving cattle and he's trying, fifteen hours later, to get home to his family. If he's "a rugged individualist" he's also part of a team: ranch work is teamwork and even the glorified open-range cowboys of the 1880s rode up and down the Chisholm Trail in the company of twenty or thirty other riders. Instead of the macho, trigger-happy man our culture

Is this her concern?

She cites familiar images— clichés

Where's this?

has perversely wanted him to be, the cowboy is more apt to be *toughness* convivial, quirky, and softhearted. To be "tough" on a ranch has *vs* nothing to do with conquests and displays of power. More often *toughing it out* than not, circumstances—like the colt he's riding or an unexpect- ed blizzard—are overpowering him. It's not toughness but "toughing it out" that counts. In other words, this macho, cultur- *cowboy or* al artifact the cowboy has become is simply a man who possess- *part of* es resilience, patience, and an instinct for survival. "Cowboys are *Am. culture* just like a pile of rocks—everything happens to them. They get climbed on, kicked, rained and snowed on, scuffed up by wind. Their job is 'just to take it,' " one old-timer told me.

Questioning

Now that you have read the opening paragraph and made some annota- tions, you can ask some questions you have about the piece. You can raise questions about Ehrlich's ideas, about her evidence, perhaps about her uses of language (like the term "rugged individualist" in the first paragraph or "iconic myth" in the second).

Asking questions about the text is one way to become engaged with its argument and its evidence. You might choose to focus some of your questions on Ehrlich's claims (her thesis or idea) and on the kinds of evi- dence she uses to support them. Or you may choose to ask questions that push the essay's argument beyond its bounds to consider whether Ehrlich's ideas apply to American men generally and not just to cow- boys. You might prefer to write your questions in a letter to the author. In the course of your letter, you could explain what you think she is say- ing and use your questions as a way of confirming your interpretation, satisfying your curiosity, or deepening your understanding.

One interesting possibility is to imagine that you were interviewing Gretel Ehrlich. What would you ask her, based on your reading of the first two paragraphs?

Here is Ehrlich's second paragraph, accompanied by a few questions to get you started. After considering them, add a few of your own.

2   A cowboy is someone who loves his work. Since the hours are long—ten to fifteen hours a day—and the pay is $30 he has to. What's required of him is an odd mixture of physical vigor and maternalism. His part of the beef-raising industry is to birth and nurture calves and take care of their mothers. For the most part his work is done on horse- back and in a lifetime he sees and comes to know more animals than people. The iconic myth surrounding him is built on American notions of heroism: the index of a man's value as measured in physical courage. Such ideas have perverted manliness into a self-absorbed race for cheap thrills. In a rancher's world, courage has less to do with facing danger than with acting spontaneously—usually on behalf of an animal or

another rider. If a cow is stuck in a boghole he throws a loop around her neck, takes his dally (a half hitch around the saddle horn), and pulls her out with horsepower. If a calf is born sick, he may take her home, warm her in front of the kitchen fire, and massage her legs until dawn. One friend, whose favorite horse was trying to swim a lake with hobbles on, dove under water and cut her legs loose with a knife, then swam her to shore, his arm around her neck lifeguard-style, and saved her from drowning. Because these incidents are usually linked to someone or something outside himself, the westerner's courage is selfless, a form of compassion.

General Questions

Does Ehrlich really mean to suggest that cowboys need to be maternal— that they need to develop the kind of caring instincts of mothers for their children?

Have things changed very much since Ehrlich published this essay in 1985?

Interview Questions

Do you think that the compassion you describe as essential for cowboy life is something westerners possess more than, say, easterners or southerners?

How often does the kind of heroic action performed by your friend who saved his horse from drowning actually occur? What other examples of this kind of selfless and compassionate behavior can you offer?

Your Questions

General questions:

Interview questions:

Freewriting

Your initial impressions of a text, which you can record with annotations, will often lead you to further thoughts about it. You can develop this additional thinking with *freewriting.* In freewriting you record your thoughts about a text without arranging them in any special order, putting them down as they occur to you. You simply write down what you think without worrying about organization or spelling or grammar. The point is to get your thinking recorded, to let your mind spin with thoughts and not to censor those thoughts prematurely.

Freewriting offers you a way to pursue an idea—to develop your thinking to see where it may lead. Like annotating, it provides a fairly easy way to begin writing that can be developed in more elaborate or organized ways later.

You can try your hand at freewriting about the following paragraphs of Ehrlich's essay. Just add your own freewriting to that provided as an example.

3   The physical punishment that goes with cowboying is greatly under-played. Once fear is dispensed with, the threshold of pain rises to meet the demands of the job. When Jane Fonda asked Robert Redford (in the film *Electric Horseman*) if he was sick as he struggled to his feet one morning, he replied, "No, just bent." For once the movies had it right. The cowboys I was sitting with laughed in agreement. Cowboys are rarely complainers: they show their stoicism by laughing at themselves.

4   If a rancher or cowboy has been thought of as a "man's man"—laconic, hard-drinking, inscrutable—there's almost no place in which the balancing act between male and female, manliness and femininity, can be more natural. If he's gruff, handsome, and physically fit on the out-side, he's androgynous at the core. Ranchers are midwives, hunters, nur-turers, providers, and conservationists all at once. What we've inter-preted as toughness—weathered skin, calloused hands, a squint in the eye and a growl in the voice—only masks the tenderness inside. "Now don't go telling me these lambs are cute," one rancher warned me the first day I walked into the football-field-sized lambing sheds. The next thing I knew he was holding a black lamb. "Ain't this little rat good-lookin'?"

5   So many of the men who came to the West were southerners—men looking for work and a new life after the Civil War—that chivalrousness and strict codes of honor were soon thought of as western traits. There were very few women in Wyoming during territorial days, so when they did arrive (some as mail-order brides from places like Philadelphia) there was a stand-offishness between the sexes and a formality that per-sists now. Ranchers still tip their hats and say, "Howdy, ma'am" instead of shaking hands with me.

Example of Freewriting

Androgynous? Cowboys as half men and half women? Does Ehrlich mean that cowboys are (or need to be) something of both—maternal and paternal, womanly or motherly as well as manly macho? She plays with typical macho characteristics of toughness—weathered skin, callouses, a squint—and balances them against those of tenderness—comments about cute lambs and critters and actions such as their midwifery.

Does Ehrlich like being addressed with "Howdy, ma'am," or would she prefer a handshake? Does the androgyny apply to her—a cowgirl—as well?

Your Freewriting

Using a Double-Column Notebook

One strategy for developing your thinking in response to an essay is to use a double-column notebook. In this notebook you divide your page in half, reserving one half for notes and the other half for comments. On the "notes" side you summarize the writer's idea(s) by recording as carefully as you can what the writer is saying. Here, you interpret the essay. In addition, on this "notes" side you can make observations about the text, recording things you see going on in it. On the "comments" side you go beyond interpreting the essay to evaluating it. There, you consider the writer's ideas and respond to them. In addition, you can use the comments side to relate the essay you are reading to other texts you have come across.

Here is the remainder of Ehrlich's essay, her last three paragraphs, followed by an example of how to write double-column notebook entries.

6   Even young cowboys are often evasive with women. It's not that they're Jekyll and Hyde creatures—gentle with animals and rough on women—but rather, that they don't know how to bring their tenderness into the house and lack the vocabulary to express the complexity of what they feel. Dancing wildly all night becomes a metaphor for the explosive emotions pent up inside, and when these are, on occasion, released, they're so battery-charged and potent that one caress of the face or one "I love you" will peal for a long while.

7   The geographical vastness and the social isolation here make emotional evolution seem impossible. Those contradictions of the heart between respectability, logic, and convention on the one hand, and impulse, passion, and intuition on the other, played out wordlessly against the paradisical beauty of the West, give cowboys a wide-eyed but drawn look. Their lips pucker up, not with kisses but with immutability. They may want to break out, staying up all night with a lover just to

talk, but they don't know how and can't imagine what the consequences will be. Those rare occasions when they do bare themselves result in confusion. "I feel as if I'd sprained my heart," one friend told me a month after such a meeting.

8   My friend Ted Hoagland wrote, "No one is as fragile as a woman but no one is as fragile as a man." For all the women here who use "fragile-ness" to avoid work or as a sexual ploy, there are men who try to hide theirs, all the while clinging to an adolescent dependency on women to cook their meals, wash their clothes, and keep the ranch house warm in winter. But there is true vulnerability in evidence here. Because these men work with animals, not machines or numbers, because they live outside in landscapes of torrential beauty, because they are confined to a place and a routine embellished with awesome variables, because calves die in the arms that pulled others into life, because they go to the mountains as if on a pilgrimage to find out what makes a herd of elk tick, their strength is also a softness, their toughness, a rare delicacy.

This is how your double-column notebook will look. You have been given three "notes" and three "comments" entries. On a separate sheet of paper you can add your own notes and comments—at least three for each side. (You can focus on the essay's last three paragraphs, or you can go back to earlier ones and to your annotations, questions, and freewriting to further develop your thinking.)

Notes (Toward Interpretation)	**Comments (Toward Evaluation)**
Ehrlich debunks the stereotypical image of the cowboy without denying that cowboys are tough, strong, silent individualists.	Is Ehrlich's own image of the cowboy overly romanticized? In making cowboys maternal, does she make too much of their gentleness? Maybe not.
She uses direct quotes from cowboys as one kind of evidence. She refers to images from popular culture—the Marlboro ad and a film, *The Electric Horseman*— as examples of cowboy manliness.	Ehrlich's historical explanation may be an oversimplification, though its broad outline makes sense.
Your Notes	**Your Comments**
(Toward Interpretation)	(Toward Evaluation)

BEYOND PRELIMINARY WRITING STRATEGIES

Once you have read Ehrlich's essay through, annotating it and making notes and comments, you should be ready to develop a more formal piece of writing for other readers. The following questions encourage you further toward developing an essay of your own. The first group of questions, "experience," invites you to think about your own life in relation to Ehrlich's essay. These questions could lead you to write a personal or exploratory essay. The second group, "interpretation," guides you toward analyzing Ehrlich's essay. These questions lead you toward writing an essay of analysis and interpretation. The third set of questions, "evaluation," encourages you to consider the values displayed there. These questions lead toward a persuasive essay in which you develop an argument about an issue.

The three sets of guiding questions are accompanied by three suggestions for writing, each leading to a different kind of essay—a personal essay based on experience, an analytical essay that provides an interpretation, and an argumentative essay that weighs ideas and values. Each of the essays in this book is followed by three sets of questions and three types of suggestions for writing arranged in just this way. You can use those questions and writing suggestions in conjunction with the advice given here about annotating, questioning, freewriting, and using a double-column notebook to fulfill your instructor's writing assignments and to do other writing for yourself. By working carefully and thoroughly with these questions and techniques, you will read and write more thoughtfully and effectively. And at your best you should produce work you can be proud of.

Your instructor may require one or another of these types of essays as a class assignment based on Ehrlich's "About Men" (or other selections in the book). You may also be free to choose among the different writing suggestions to satisfy a particular writing assignment. But whatever writing assignment you are given, you should use those preliminary "Moving Toward Writing" techniques that best enable you to engage the writer's work actively and thoughtfully. While you should not feel obliged to perform all of the "Moving Toward Writing" techniques every time you write in response to what you read, you should certainly use those most helpful to you.

QUESTIONS

Experience

- As you read Ehrlich's piece, what sorts of things were running through your mind? Did you find yourself "seeing" the Marlboro cowboy? Did you recall television commercials or magazine ads that play off this image?
- Later in the essay Ehrlich describes the "vastness" of the West. To what extent did you find yourself imagining what she was describing? Why? To what extent can you relate her experience of the West's grandeur and beauty to your experience of a place—whether or not it is a western place like Ehrlich's Wyoming?

Interpretation

- Is this essay primarily about cowboys? About men generally? To what extent does Ehrlich limit what she says to western males? To what extent does what she says about cowboys apply to men in general—or perhaps at least to American men?

· Explain how Ehrlich uses the image—the stereotype, really—of the cowboy to develop and advance her argument. What does she do with this stereotype?

Evaluation

· Do you find Ehrlich's thinking persuasive? Do you accept her evidence—her personal testimony? Does she achieve her aims in this essay?

· What cultural values are at the center of Ehrlich's argument? To what extent do your own values—your own sense of what a "man" might be—mesh with those espoused by Ehrlich?

WRITING

Exploring

· Write your own essay entitled "About Men." You can begin, if you like, with a familiar image, perhaps with an image from a popular film or song. Use this image to suggest particular qualities or characteristics you think essential to being a man—or at least to being considered a real man, a successful man, or something similar. Use your own experience as one form of evidence.

Interpreting

· Write an interpretation of "About Men." Explain what Ehrlich's purpose seems to be and how she goes about achieving it. Analyze her use of dialogue and her references to popular media and to history. Explain what they contribute to her essay.

Evaluating

· Write a response to Ehrlich in which you debate her celebration of the androgynous man. That is, evaluate her argument, and explain how and why it should be modified to account for what you think about Ehrlich's idea. Be sure you are careful to represent her idea and argument accurately and fairly.

Notes on Essay Form

While instructors vary, sometimes widely, in their expectations about what constitutes a good student essay, a number of general essay features are frequently expected. You can be expected to provide a clear statement of your idea, sometimes called a *thesis.* This statement of thesis or idea should appear early in your essay, though on occasion your idea or thesis may be implied or stated toward the end of your essay.

A thesis is not a topic but is, instead, an idea about the topic. You can think of your thesis or idea as a perspective or point of view expressed toward your topic. For example, in writing an essay about cowboys you would need to do more than simply provide information about them. You would need to express an idea, as Gretel Ehrlich does in her essay "About Men," in which she suggests the idea that cowboys are androgynous—that is, that they possess qualities typically thought of as female as well as those more traditionally thought of as "manly" ones. In writing your own essay about cowboys, you might express a different idea about cowboys. For example, you might wish to explore how or why men (or women) born and raised in the West differ from those born and raised in the East. Or, you might write an essay about Ehrlich's essay, perhaps grafting onto her idea one of your own, or perhaps by arguing against her idea about the cowboy's androgynous nature.

There are many possibilities for finding ideas when you write an essay. The essential thing, however, is that your essay must be grounded in something you wish to say about the subject—the something that is, essentially, your thesis or idea.

In the same way as there are multiple possibilities for finding ideas in essays, so, too, there are many ways to organize and develop them. One of the most common ways is to introduce your idea in your opening paragraph; provide a few arguments, details, or examples to support or illustrate it (in three or more following paragraphs, one supporting point per paragraph); and supply a conclusion that wraps up your discussion, perhaps giving your readers something further to think about, perhaps simply reinforcing the point of your introductory paragraph.

This traditional essay model, though efficient, has limitations. While it provides a clearly organized structure for explaining an idea or supporting an argument, it is also predictable. Some instructors value this essay model highly; others prefer alternative essay forms that are less tightly structured, yet that still follow the basic framework of introduction, body, and conclusion. This basic three-part framework requires that you introduce your subject before you get down to details of information and evidence that you will provide in the body of your essay. It also requires that you devise a conclusion that follows logically from the information and evidence you provide in the body of your essay.

In looking at Gretel Ehrlich's essay "About Men," for example, you might see that Ehrlich's opening paragraph serves as her introduction, paragraphs 2 through 7 as the body of her essay, and paragraph 8 as her conclusion. Look at how she introduces her essay by identifying the central concerns of her topic—her focus. Look at how she concludes her essay by leaving her readers with a perspective on the cowboy's dual nature. And look, also, at how she organizes the body of her essay by devoting individual paragraphs to different examples and elements that support and illustrate her view of cowboys.

Or consider how Zora Neale Hurston organizes her very different personal essay, in which she explains why she has always been happy to be a black woman. Hurston's essay differs from Ehrlich's in being less of an explanation and illustration of a general idea (that cowboys are androgynous) than of a revelation about her self and an expression of how she feels about who she is. Ehrlich's essay is expository (or explanatory), while Hurston's is personal (or familiar). While Ehrlich uses personal experience from time to time as part of her evidence, she also uses other kinds of evidence in support of her claim about cowboys. Hurston, on the other hand, sticks with her experience all the way, since her purpose is less to persuade her readers of an idea than to share with them her perspective about her own identity. One could argue, on the other hand, that Hurston's essay also contains an implied argument that racist attitudes do not really harm minority individuals but only make them stronger and more confident.

Even though Hurston and Ehrlich are writing different kinds of essays, both of them have something to say—Ehrlich about cowboys and Hurston about herself. Each writer introduces her topic and provides a perspective on it (Ehrlich in her first paragraph, Hurston in paragraphs 1 through 4) before developing her thought in the body of the essay (Ehrlich in paragraphs 2 through 7, Hurston in paragraphs 5 through 13). Each then provides a conclusion to her essay (Ehrlich in paragraph 8 and Hurston in paragraphs 14 through 17).

In writing your own essays, you will need to organize them so readers can determine what constitutes your introduction, body, and conclusion. You will need to decide on an arrangement of your body paragraphs that seems both natural and logical both to you and to your readers. There is no single best way to do this. But you should check with your instructor about his or her guidelines for organizing the middle or body of an essay as well as about acceptable kinds of introduction and conclusion. In addition, you should consult your college handbook or other books containing advice about writing for ways to make your writing reader based, that is, written so that it is easy for a reader to follow. One way to do this, for example, is to provide transitional words and phrases that help readers see how one sentence or point is related to another. Look back two sentences, for example, to see how the phrase "in addition" works to let you know that another point is being introduced. Or look back one sentence to see how the phrase "for example" works to indicate that an illustration is to come.

These expectations and others concerning accurate grammar, careful spelling, and logical thinking hold for many types of essays. Your handbook or book of writing instruction will suggest guidelines for writing along with appropriate organizational patterns you might use in constructing different types of essays in which you explain, analyze, interpret, evaluate, argue, describe, and/or narrate. Check with your instructor or your handbook for appropriate ways to proceed in organizing and developing the types of essays you are required to write.

A STUDENT ESSAY AND HOW IT ORIGINATED

Since analysis and interpretation are central concerns in most college courses, the following sample student essay exemplifies one way to analyze and interpret a text—in this case Hurston's "How It Feels to Be Colored Me." Be aware that what the student writer, Jennifer Song, has done in exploring Hurston's essay can also be done when writing about literary works such as poems or novels as well as about films, works of music or art, or works of philosophy, history, or religion.

The assignment to which Jennifer Song's essay is a response involved a series of brief exercises preliminary to writing a full draft of an essay for a freshman college composition course. For her first exercise Jennifer was asked to read carefully, annotate, and highlight an essay she would eventually write about. Along with the rest of her class, Jennifer was advised of the importance of this form of active reading for comprehension—gaining a solid understanding of what she read. As a second part of this first exercise, Jennifer was asked to select two key passages from an essay and explain why they were particularly important. She was also asked to show a relationship between the two passages she selected, either by asking a series of questions about them or by identifying specific connections between their details. Like her classmates, Jennifer had the option of using freewriting or the double-column notebook to explore her questions, thoughts, and observations. This first exercise had a limit of 500 words.

The second exercise required students to identify and analyze three or more images or metaphors in the essay and to see if there was a pattern that linked the images and/or metaphors. The writing exercise of no more than 500 words required explaining how the images and metaphors revealed the writer's idea or attitude about his or her subject.

The exercises were written for successive class meetings. At each class meeting for which the exercises were due, Jennifer discussed her work with other classmates who were also working on Hurston. Students made both oral and written observations, asked questions, and otherwise shared ideas about each other's responses to the exercise assignments. The instructor added written comments, mostly about how the exercises might be further developed into a more extensive piece of writing—an analytical essay about the text each student had chosen.

The essay assignment, which was designed to have students develop their thinking beyond what they had discovered in doing the two preliminary 500-word exercises, was as follows:

> You are asked to do a "close" reading of a single essay by one of the writers from *Modern American Prose.* Your task is to analyze the essay's images, metaphors, and symbols, along with its organization and selection of detail, so you can describe its overall effect and explain its overarching idea. The evidence for your interpretation must be found in the essay itself—in its words and phrases, its language and structure, rather than in comments others may have made about it. Be sure to provide evidence for your interpretation with specific references to the text you analyze. Five typed pages double spaced.

Jennifer wrote a draft in response to this essay assignment, which was then brought to class for group discussion, and which also received written comments from her instructor. At this point Jennifer had a conference with the instructor to discuss possible ways to strengthen her essay through revision. The revised and graded version of Jennifer's essay follows some of the notes she made while doing the two preliminary exercises.

Some of Jennifer's Notes

Jennifer divided her notes into observations, questions, inferences, and an overview of the essay's structure. Here are a few of each that she made.

Observations

Hurston writes as an adult looking back on her childhood.

She includes scenes of white and black people together.

She uses many comparisons

—as an actress on the stage of the world

—the town gate-post as a seat to view the world

—slavery as a wound already operated on.

She describes her feelings—being astonished, not angry, happy.

She uses images—the stone statue of a lion, the brown bag of miscellany, the primal warrior, the dark rock.

Questions

Why does she feel different about Eatonville and Jacksonville?

What is her focus in each of the essay's four parts?

When does she feel most colored, and why?

Is her experience typical of others, or is she different in how she feels about being black?

How much is Hurston suggesting about a person's identity?

Inferences

Hurston seems proud to be black and a woman.

She sees herself making a strong impression on others.

She doesn't seem to care if others don't respond to her favorably.

She seems unbothered by the prejudice of whites—it's their loss.

She thinks it's better to be black than white.

Structure

4 parts: (1) being "colored," (2) being optimistic, (3) being different, (4) being an individual.

Or perhaps: (1) a girl, (2) a woman, (3) a black American, (4) her self, Zora!

Although Jennifer did not use all these notes in her essay, she did use many of them. She also thought of other details of the essay she wished to comment on as she wrote her exercises and her drafts. Her writing process thus involved many things: reading carefully and making annotations, asking questions, making notes, writing exercises for class, sharing ideas with others in class, writing a draft based on her preliminary writing and her exercises, conferring with her instructor, and revising her draft as an essay to be submitted and graded.

Even though Jennifer's essay was considered "finished" or "final," it could, of course, be further revised and improved. Most writing, however good, can be made even better. What you should strive for in producing your own essays is the best work you can create in the time available. At the very least you should give yourself time for preliminary writing strategies to help you get started thinking and writing. Regardless of the types of essays you will be writing, you should remember to begin with small-scale approaches such as annotating or freewriting and with shorter exercises and preliminary drafts. Try also to get feedback from other readers between your exercises and drafts—feedback you can use to revise your writing successfully.

> Jennifer Song
> The Essay, S-17
> R. DiYanni
> 8/1/94

~~Analytical Essay I—Interpretation/Explanation~~

~~On~~ "How It Feels to Be Colored Me" ~~By Zora Neale Hurston~~ *An Analysis and Interpretation*

Better title needed

Zora Neale Hurston's charm lies in her powerful sense of self. *Fully aware,* ~~She writes (aware.)~~ Her essay, "How It Feels to Be Colored Me," is a statement and assertion. It is a journey of self and a testimony of identity. In discovering the facets and faces of Zora Neale Hurston, we can see our own.

The power of this essay stems from the unique attitude ~~of~~ Hurston's. She sees things in a new and daring light, challenging even our own sturdy notions. She dispels the norm more often than not and throws mass expected behavior to the wind. As Hurston grows into her identity, she realizes that who and what she is is natural. She discovers her inherent black qualities and at the same time discovers herself—physically, emotionally, spiritually.

Throughout this essay, readers are aware that Zora Neale Hurston is far from ordinary. She is unique. After all, like she says in the piece's first paragraph: "I am the only Negro in the United States whose grandfather on the mother's side was *not* an Indian chief." This statement paves the way for similar comments illustrating that Hurston is not afraid to break stereotypes.

Neither is Hurston afraid to rebel, to rise above and beyond what she calls the "tragically colored." As a black woman, Hurston may be expected to be depressed and dejected, consumed by the "great sorrow," haunted by the memory that she is the "granddaughter of slaves." She isn't. The wound of slavery has been "past operated on." It is time to heal, time to dry the tears of America's "sobbing school of Negrohood."

Hurston even goes as far as to explain to us the advantages of the day in a metaphor of stage and show. The world is like a "national stage" and hers is the chance to hold "center"; "the world to be won and nothing to be lost." There was "no one on earth [who] ever had a greater chance for glory." "Getting twice as much praise or twice as much blame," Hurston found herself, as a black woman, in the very heart of an exciting controversy, a controversy either hailing or denouncing black achievement. The world, she felt, was "thrilling."

In describing her childhood, Hurston uses the same metaphor of the stage to show the relationship between black and white as she saw it during her youth. The local town gate-post is her personal first-rate spectator seat to the world; but the world, a big show, serves also as a stage and platform for her to sing and dance upon. Performing for white travelers passing through town makes Zora, the first "welcome-to-our-state" Floridian, happy. Yet to some, perhaps, the relationship Zora is so content with is actually detrimental to her.

To some, perhaps, she is a white man's puppet, at his beck and call for a cheap and passing amusement, the symbol of black American servitude towards the white race. They might see it as a servile relationship: a trick—a song, a dance, a parse-me-la—for a mear and meager pittance of silver. Remember, however, that Zora Neale Hurston was a performer with a love to perform—silver or not, white audience or black audience.

The idea that Hurston's mind is not confined to the proper, expected attitudes of thought is emphasized by her flippant language and creative use of diction. In describing slavery, she uses the word "bully adventure" and relates its history to an exhilarating race with the words: "On the line! . . . Get set! . . . Go!" However, the tone is more excited and optimistic than irreverent.

Hurston sees the brighter side to life, refusing to let any preconceived notion squelch her own vibrant spirit. She insists upon moving on, upon looking forward and not back. Being genuinely straightforward in a way few would dare to be, the author sees, along with the pain and hurt and tragedy she understands and accepts, an opportunity.

Structurally, the piece is formed in a careful manner. This essay flows through the episodes of Hurston's growing identity—as a girl, a woman, a black American, and Zora. For each identity, Hurston dedicates a section. To string these parts together in a coherent and effective manner, Hurston uses a common thread—an image of water. It is a journey by river-boat that makes Zora the "little colored girl"; and "covered by waters," it is the "ebb" that reveals her "race"; and then again it is "dimly across the ocean and continent" that Hurston separates herself from her white friend. The image of water is not just a convenient metaphor, but an important symbol within the context of the essay. The water signifies life, birth, and baptism; and so it can also signify a new realization of self and of selves.

Hurston takes us through each of these self-realizations one by one. We start with Zora as a girl, the "unconscious Zora of Eatonville," and move on to a someone more aware of race differences. From there, Hurston takes us to a Zora who is struck by the power of her color and the vitality of her roots, and then on to a woman concerned with herself as "*me,*" the cosmic Zora. The word "I" is used often, many times at the beginning of the sentence as a marked point of emphasis. This technique makes Hurston seem all the more sure of herself and her identity. The testimony she relates follows a path from the unconscious to the conscious, from the naïve unknowing to the deepest realization of self and nothing more.

Hurston uses a series of images throughout the essay that metaphorically serve to represent herself, the individual. In the beginning, we have Zora as a performer, naïvely dancing for the world, readily eager for its applause. After that, she moves to the image of herself as a rock—a "dark rock surged upon, and over swept, but through it all, I remain myself." A rock is strong and permanent, eroded only gradually by the trials of time. And because "the world is to the strong regardless of a little pigmentation more or less," Hurston, too, is strong like the rock.

Another key image in this essay is that of the primal warrior, nestled deep in the heart of Hurston's emotions. In the drafty basement of the New York cabaret, the primitive emotions of the author rip loose. The*y* come wildly and vibrantly, pulsating much like the blues rhythms that call forth this grand spirit. This image is Hurston's culture come alive.

As Hurston undergoes this metamorphosis from college girl to primitive being, the structure and pattern of her sentence*s* echo her thoughts. The sentences she use*s here* are short, tumultuous, and have an almost beat-like quality. They rise i*n* *a* crescendo, like the emotions Hurston experiences, and fall in calm, cool suddenness as the composed image of the friend drums his finger tips on the table.

The scene of this image is a crucial turning point. It begins a section of the essay that introduces a new image within herself. It is here that Hurston starts to realize the true, instinctive qualities of her personality—not what she should be or what she is and shouldn't be, but what Zora Neale Hurston actually is. It is here that she realizes the difference between herself and her friend so "pale with his whiteness"; and it is here that she recognizes the unique richness of her race.

In the last episode of the essay, Hurston is yet another object: a bag of objects—"a brown bag of miscellany propped against a wall." For us, the image is delectable in it*s* creativ*e*~~ity and~~ simplicity. For Hurston, the image holds a deeper truth, explaining the equality of people. We, she *implies* ~~infers~~, are all the same: red, yellow, white, and brown; our stuffing is all the same—give or take a "a bit of colored glass," of course.

Hurston ends this scene and essay with the question—"who knows?" The answer is no one. To us, Hurston *is* all those things: a dancer, a rock, a warrior, a bag of miscellany. She *is* all those things and more. Perhaps, in searching for our own identities, Hurston leaves us that one bit of advice. Perhaps she wants us to realize that we must find our own identity, discover our own destiny. We realize then that we are so many things—our past and our future, our beliefs and our culture, our strengths and our weaknesses. We realize then that our "stuffing" is not made by others, but by and through ourselves.

ONE

Communities

SCOTT RUSSELL SANDERS
  Wayland

MARY GORDON
  More Than Just a Shrine: Paying Homage to the Ghosts of Ellis Island

MARIANNA DE MARCO TORGOVNICK
  On Being White, Female, and Born in Bensonhurst

AMY TAN
  Mother Tongue

TOM WOLFE
  The Right Stuff

MAXINE HONG KINGSTON
  Silence

ALICE WALKER
  In Search of Our Mothers' Gardens

ERIC KIM
  Family Portrait

WILLIAM FAULKNER
  A Rose for Emily

MAYA ANGELOU
  On the Pulse of Morning

Each of us is a member of many communities. Whether we are born and raised in city or country, suburbia or exurbia, we grow up in a particular world with distinct physical and social elements. Our neighborhood may be a block of detached homes large or small, close or near; it may be an apartment house raised high or spread low over a couple of storeys. This early physical community is complemented by others: the communities of family and friends, the community of school, and later, the community of work.

We exist in relationship to others. To the manifold communities we belong to, we take our multiple identities. For these same communities we assume multiple roles—as husband or wife or child, as student or teacher, as brother, sister, acquaintance, friend. Community involves places as well as people, beliefs and attitudes and ways of thinking as well as simply living or working together. Each of the communities to which we belong binds us to others who share common ideals, attitudes, perspectives, beliefs, customs, and so on. The communities to which we belong, moreover, stretch back in time to embrace our ancestors and reach forward into the future to touch those who will come after us.

The selections in this chapter invite you to think about the different communities of which you are a member. They explore these and other aspects of community in ways that illustrate the richness of community without hiding its tensions, dangers, and problems. Notions of community represented in these selections go beyond our ordinary notions of geographical, social, or religious community. They include, in addition, gender, racial, and ethnic communities. One piece, Tom Wolfe's "The Right Stuff," describes a subcommunity within the military—fighter pilots training to become United States astronauts. Another, Amy Tan's "Mother Tongue," illustrates different linguistic communities to which the writer belongs and how she uses varied ways of speaking to establish her differing communal relationships.

Mary Gordon writes about the community of heritage through imagining her ancestors emigrating from Ireland after she herself visits Ellis Island, the port of entry for many immigrants coming to America. In "Wayland" Scott Sanders describes another kind of visit, one to a town he lived in many years before, taking us into a small midwestern community. Like Sanders, Marianna De Marco Torgovnick returns home to her roots in Bensonhurst, Brooklyn, New York, from her North Carolina home, where she lives and works as a professor of literature at Duke. Torgovnick contrasts the values and life-styles of her two communities, not only providing a sense of Italian American family life in Bensonhurst, but also raising questions about racial tensions and ethnic identity.

In "Family Portrait" Eric Kim describes the lack of community in his family and the struggle he and his parents undergo to begin to find some semblance of it. Ethnic and religious communal values also figure prominently in Kim's essay, generating considerable tension. Tension is also a keynote in William Faulkner's short story "A Rose for Emily," which describes a woman's inability to adopt to the changes in a small Southern town. Faulkner's story raises questions about tradition and its influence on behavior. His macabre work is complemented by the optimism and joy of Maya Angelou's celebration of diversity and community in her poem "On the Pulse of Morning," which she read at the presidential inauguration of Bill Clinton.

SCOTT RUSSELL SANDERS
(b. 1945)

Wayland

Scott Russell Sanders is a professor of English at Indiana University. He has published fiction and literary criticism in addition to three volumes of essays, The Paradise of Bombs *(1987),* Secrets of the Universe *(1992), and* Staying Put *(1993). In the following selection from his latest book, Sanders describes the pleasures of being rooted in a community where you know others and they know you. His essay, the last chapter of* Staying Put, *is organized around a visit to the town where he grew up and seven key elements he found there: death, life, beasts, food, mind, sex, and God.*

Sanders organizes his essay around those seven mysteries, taking them up in order by telling a story of how and where he encountered each. He also uses the image of the crossroads to suggest a place of learning, growing, moving beyond. And his sentences are rife with images and metaphors, as this example suggests: "What had brought me back to Wayland was a need to dig through the fluff and debris of ordinary life, down to some bedrock of feeling and belief."

1   Two blacktop roads, broken by frost and mended with tar, running from nowhere to nowhere, cross at right angles in the rumpled farm country of northeastern Ohio. The neighborhood where they intersect is called Wayland— not a village, not even a hamlet, only a cluster of barns and silos and frame houses and a white steepled Methodist church. Just north of Wayland, the Army fenced in fifty square miles of ground for a bomb factory, and just to the south the Corps of Engineers built a dam and flooded even more square miles for a reservoir. I grew up behind those government fences in the shadows of bunkers, and on farms that have since vanished beneath those government waters. Family visits to church began carrying me to Wayland when I was five, romance was carrying me there still at seventeen, and in the years between I was drawn there often by duty or desire. Thus it happened that within shouting distance of the Wayland crossroads I met seven of the great mysteries.

2   Even as a boy, oblivious much of the time to all save my own sensations, I knew by the tingle in my spine when I had bumped into something utterly new. I groped for words to describe what I had felt, as I grope still. Since we give labels to all that puzzles us, as we name every blank space on the map, I could say that what I stumbled into in Wayland were the mysteries of death, life, beasts, food, mind, sex, and God. But these seven words are only tokens, worn coins that I drop onto the page, hoping to bribe you, coins I finger as reminders of those awful encounters.

3   The roads that cross at Wayland are too humble to show on the Ohio map, too small even to wear numbers. And yet, without maps or mistakes, without quite meaning to, I recently found my way back there from half a thousand miles away, after an absence of twenty-five years, led along the grooves of memory.

4   The grooves are deep, and they set me vibrating well before I reached the place, as the spiral cuts in phonograph records will shake music from a needle. I was heading toward Cleveland when I took a notion to veer off the interstate and see what had become of Akron, which led me to see what had become of Kent, which led me to Ravenna, the seat of Portage County. Nothing aside from stoplights made me pause. Not sure what I was looking for, I drove east from the county seat along a highway hurtling with trucks. Soon the rusted chain link fence of the Ravenna Arsenal came whipping by on my left and the raised bed of the Baltimore & Ohio tracks surged by on the right. Then I realized where I was going. My knuckles whitened on the steering wheel as I turned from the highway, put my back toward the trucks and bombs, and passed under the railroad through a concrete arch. Beyond the arch, the woods and fields and houses of Wayland shimmered in the October sunlight, appearing to my jealous eye scarcely changed after a quarter of a century.

5   I knew the place had changed, of course, if only because in the years since I had come here last—drawn in those days like a moth to the flame of a girl—the population of the earth had nearly doubled. Every crossroads, every woods, every field on the planet is warping under the pressure of our terrible hunger. So I knew that Wayland had changed, for all its pastoral shimmer in the autumn light. Yet I was grateful that on the surface it so much resembled my childhood memories, for in my effort to live adequately in the present, I had come here to conduct some business with the past. What had brought me back to Wayland was a need to dig through the fluff and debris of ordinary life, down to some bedrock of feeling and belief.

6   I left my car in the graveled parking lot of the church and set out walking. Without planning my steps, I meandered where memory led, and where it led was from station to station of my childhood astonishment. Not yet ready for the church, I went next door to the parsonage, where I had first caught a whiff of death. The white clapboard house, a two-story box with a porch across the front and a green hipped roof, could have belonged to any of the neighboring farms. That was appropriate, for the ministers who succeeded one another in the house often preached as though they were farmers, weeding out sins, harvesting souls.

7   The minister whom I knew first was the Reverend Mr. Knipe, a bulky man sunken with age, his hair as white as the clapboards on the parsonage, his voice like the cooing of pigeons in the barn. Much in life amused him. Whenever he told you something that struck him as funny, he would cover his mouth with a hand to hide his smile. Despite the raised hand, often his laugh burst free and rolled over you. I began listening to him preach and pray and lead hymns when I was five, and for the next two years I heard Reverend Knipe every Sunday, until his voice became for me that of the Bible itself, even the voice of God. Then one Sunday when I was seven, I shook his great hand after the service as usual, suffering him to bend down and pat my head, and I went home to my dinner and he went home to his. While his wife set the table in the parsonage, Reverend Knipe rested on the front porch in his caned rocking chair, drifted off to sleep, and never woke up.

8   When Mother told me of this, the skin prickled on my neck. To sleep and never wake! To be a white-haired man with a voice like a barnful of pigeons, and

the next minute to be nothing at all! Since my parents considered me too young to attend the funeral, I could only imagine what had become of his body, and I imagined not decay but evaporation—the flesh dispersing into thin air like morning mist from a pond.

9   The following Sunday, while a visitor preached, I stole from church and crept over to the parsonage. I drew to the edge of the porch, wrapped my fingers around the spindles of the railing, and stared at the empty rocker. Reverend Knipe will never sit in that chair again, I told myself. Never, never, never. I tried to imagine how long forever would last. I tried to imagine how it would feel to be nothing. No thing. Suddenly chair and house and daylight vanished, and I was gazing into a dark hole, I was falling, I was gone. I caught a whiff of death, the damp earthy smell seeping from beneath the porch. It was also the smell of mud, of leaping grass, of spring. Clinging to that sensation, I pulled myself up out of the hole. There was the house again, the chair. I let go of the railing, swung away, and ran back to the church, chanting to myself: *He was old and I am young. He was old and I am young.*

10   Nights, often, and sometimes in the broad light of day, I still have to scrabble up out of that hole. We all do. Sometime in childhood, each of us bangs head-on into the blank fact we call death. Once that collision takes place, the shock of it never wears off. We may find ourselves returning to the spot where it occurred as to the scene of an accident, the way I found myself drawn, half a lifetime later, to the front steps of this parsonage. I was a stranger to the family who lived there now. Not wishing to intrude on them, I paused by the steps and surveyed the porch. Vinyl siding had covered the clapboard. An aluminum folding chair had replaced the rocker. I squatted by the railing, lowering my face to the height of a seven-year-old, closed my eyes against the shadows, and sniffed. From below the sill of the porch came the earth's dank perennial breath, fetid and fertile. Yes, I thought, filling myself with the smell: this abides, this is real; no matter the name we give it, life or death, it is a fact as rough and solid as a stone squeezed in the palm of the hand.

11   A dog yapped inside the parsonage. I stood up hurriedly and backed away, before anyone could appear at the door to ask me what in tarnation I was looking for under that porch.

12   Still following the grooves of memory, I crossed the road to stand in the driveway of another white frame house. It was not so much the house that drew me as it was the side yard, where, about this time each fall, we brought our apples for pressing. The old press with its wooden vat and iron gears used to balance on concrete blocks in the shade of a willow. We would pick apples in the military reservation, from orchards that had been allowed to go wild after the government bulldozed the farmsteads. Unsprayed, blotched and wormy, these apples were also wonderfully sweet. We kept them in bushel baskets and cardboard boxes in the cellar, their fragrance filling the house, until we had accumulated enough to load our station wagon. Then we drove here, parked beside the willow, and fed our fruit into the press.

13   On this mild October day, the willow looked as I remembered it, thick in the trunk and gold in the leaves. There was no sign of a press, but that did not keep me from remembering what it was like to squeeze apples. First we pulped them in

a mill, then we wrapped them in cheesecloth and tamped them down, layer by layer, into the slotted wooden vat. To mash them, we spun a cast iron wheel. It was easy to begin with, so easy that my brother and sister and I could make the spokes whirl. Later, the cranking would become too hard for us, and our mother would take her turn, then our father, then both of them together. The moment that set me trembling, however, came early on, while my hand was still on the iron wheel, the moment when cider began to ooze through the cheesecloth, between the slats, and down the spout into a waiting bucket. Out of the dirt, out of the gnarled trunks and wide-flung branches, out of the ripe red fruit had come this tawny juice. When my arms grew tired, I held a Mason jar under the spout, caught a glassful, and drank it down. It was as though we had squeezed the planet and out had poured sweetness.

14   What came back to me, musing there by the willow all these years later, was the sound of cider trickling into the bucket, the honeyed taste of it, and my bewilderment that rain and wood and dirt and sun had yielded this juice. Amazing, that we can drink the earth! Amazing, that it quenches our thirst, answers our hunger! Who would have predicted such an outlandish thing? Who, having sipped, can forget that it is the earth we swallow?

15   Well, I had forgotten; or at least I had buried under the habits of casual eating that primal awareness of the meaning of food. And so here was another fundamental perception, renewed for me by my sojourn in Wayland. This image of cider gushing from a spout was my cornucopia, proof of the dazzling abundance that sustains us.

16   From the cider house I walked downhill to the crossroads. One corner was still a pasture, browsed by three horses, another was a scrubby field grown up in brush and weeds, and the other two corners were expansive lawns. Through the brushy field meandered a creek where I used to hunt frogs with a flashlight and bucket. As in all the Octobers I could remember, the maples in the yards were scarlet, the pasture oaks were butterscotch, and the sycamores along the creek were stripped down to their voluptuous white limbs. Yellow mums and bright red pokers of salvia were still thriving in flowerbeds. A portly older man on a riding mower was cutting one of the lawns, while from a stump beside the driveway an older woman observed his progress, a hand shading her eyes. I knew them from childhood, but their names would not come. I waved, and they waved back. That was conversation enough. I had no desire to speak with them or with anyone in Wayland, since I would have been hard put to explain who I was or why I had come back. Maybe I also wanted to keep the past pure, unmixed with the present.

17   Because the crossroads are laid out on the grid of survey lines, the blacktop runs due north and south, east and west. The roads were so little traveled that I could stand in the intersection, the tar gummy beneath my boots, and gaze along the pavement in each of the cardinal directions. I had just come from the south, where the church gleamed on its hill. My view to the north was cut off by the railroad, except for the arched opening of the underpass, through which I could see the rusted fence of the Arsenal. Memories of a girl I had courted were beckoning from the west; but less feverish memories beckoned from the opposite direction, and that is where I chose to go next.

18   A quarter mile east of the crossroads I came to a farm where the Richards

family used to breed and board and train horses. Although the name on the mailbox had changed, ten or twelve horses were grazing, as before, in a paddock beside the barn. I leaned against the fence and admired them.

19   In boyhood I had raised and ridden horses of my own, a stocky mixture of Shetland pony and the high-stepping carriage breed known as hackney. They all came out of a single ornery mare called Belle, and they all had her color, a sorrel coat that grew sleek in summer and shaggy in winter. We used to bring Belle here to the Richards place for mating with a hackney stallion. Years before the voltage of sex began to make my own limbs jerk, I had been amazed by the stallion's urgency and the mare's skittishness. He nipped and nuzzled and pursued her; she danced and wheeled. Their energy seemed too great for the paddock to hold. Surely the fence would give way, the barn itself would fall! Then at length Belle shivered to a standstill and allowed the stallion to lift his forelegs onto her rump, his back legs jigging, hoofs scrambling for purchase, her legs opening to his dark pizzle, the two of them momentarily one great plunging beast. And then, if luck held, twelve months later Belle would open her legs once more and drop a foal. Within minutes of entering the world, the foal would be tottering about on its wobbly stilts, drunk on air, and it would be ramming its muzzle into Belle's belly in search of milk. What a world, that the shivering union of mare and stallion in the barnyard should lead to this new urgency!

20   Musing there by the paddock on this October afternoon, I felt toward the grazing horses a huge affection. Each filled its hide so gloriously. I gave a low whistle. Several massive heads bobbed up and swung toward me, jaws working on grass, ears pricked forward. Their black eyes regarded me soberly, then all but one of the heads returned to grazing. The exception was a palomino gelding, who tossed his white mane, switched his white tail, and started ambling in my direction. As he drew near, I stretched my right arm toward him, palm open. Had I known I would be coming here, I would have brought apples or sugar cubes. My father would have pulled a cigarette from his pocket and offered that. But all I had to offer was the salt on my skin. The palomino lowered his muzzle to my palm, sniffed cautiously, then curled out his rasping red tongue and licked.

21   I knew that sandpapery stroke on my hand as I knew few other sensations. Just so, my own horses had nibbled oats and sugar and sweat from my palm. The pressure of their tongues made my whole body sway. There by the fence, past and present merged, and I was boy and man, swaying. I reveled in the muscular touch, animal to animal. Contact! It assured me that I was not alone in the world. I was a creature among creatures.

22   When the palomino lost interest in my right hand, I offered my left. He sniffed idly, and, finding it empty, turned back to the greater temptation of grass. But the rasp of his tongue on my palm stayed with me, another clean, hard fact, another piece of bedrock on which to build a life.

23 The field across the road from the Richards place was grown up into a young woods, mostly staghorn sumac and cedar and oak. When I had seen it last, twenty-five years earlier, this had been a meadow luxuriant with grasses and wildflowers. Back where the far edge of the field ran up against the sinuous line of willows bordering the creek, there had been a cottage, low and brown, moss grow-

ing on the roof, weeds lapping at the windows, a place that looked from a distance more like a forgotten woodpile than a house. Today, no cottage showed above the vigorous trees. But near my feet I could see the twin ruts of the dirt track that used to lead back to the place. I followed them, my boots knocking seeds from thistle and wild rye.

24   I knew the meadow and the cottage because the woman who used to live here was my science teacher in high school. Fay Givens must have been in her early sixties when I met her in my freshman year. Many students mocked her for being so unthinkably old, for looking like a schoolmarm, for loving science, for trembling when she spoke about nature. She would gaze fervently into a beaker as though an entire galaxy spun before her. She grew so excited while recounting the habits of molecules that she would skip about the lab and clap her spotted hands. She would weep for joy over what swam before her in a microscope. Mrs. Givens wept easily, more often than not because of a wisecrack or prank from one of the students. Our cruelty was a defense against the claim she made on us. For she was inviting us to share her passionate curiosity. She called us to hunger and thirst after knowledge of the universe.

25   I would not join the others in mocking her. I supposed it was pity that held me back, or an ingrained respect for my elders. Only in the fall of my freshman year, on a day when Mrs. Givens brought us here to this field for a botany class, did I realize that I could not mock her because I loved her. She led us through her meadow, naming every plant, twirling the bright fallen leaves, telling which birds ate which berries, opening milkweed pods, disclosing the burrows of groundhogs, parting the weeds to reveal caterpillars and crickets, showing where mice had severed blades of grass. Much of the meadow she had planted, with seeds carried in her pockets from the neighboring countryside. Every few years she burned it, as the Indians had burned the prairies, to keep the woods from reclaiming it.

26   While Mrs. Givens told us these things in her quavery voice, students kept sidling away to smoke or joke or dabble their hands in the creek, until there were only three of us following her. I stayed with her not from a sense of obedience but from wonder. To know this patch of land, I dimly realized, would be the work of a lifetime. But in knowing it deeply, right down to the foundations, you would comprehend a great deal more, perhaps everything. As she touched the feathery plants of her meadow, as she murmured the names and histories of the creatures who shared the place with her, I came to feel that this was holy ground. And if the meadow was holy, why not the entire earth?

27   At one point, Mrs. Givens knelt amid the bristly spikes of a tall russet grass. "You see why it's called foxtail, don't you?" she said. "Livestock won't eat it, but you can twist the stalks together and make a fair rope. Farmers used to bind up corn fodder with hanks of foxtail." She grasped one of the spikes, and, with a rake of her thumb, brushed seeds into her palm. She poured a few seeds into my hand and a few into the hands of the other two students who had remained with her. "Now what do you have there?" she asked us.

28   We stared at the barbed grains in our palms. "Seeds," one of us replied.

29   "That's the universe unfolding," she told us, "right there in your hands. The same as in every cell of our bodies. Now *why?* That's the question I can't ever get behind. Why should the universe be alive? Why does it obey laws? And why

these particular laws? For that matter, why is there a universe at all?" She gave a rollicking laugh. "And isn't it curious that there should be creatures like us who can walk in this beautiful field and puzzle over things?"

30   She asked her questions gaily, and I have carried them with me all these years in the same spirit. They rose in me again on this October afternoon as I followed the dirt track to the spot where her cottage used to be. Stones marked the cellar hole and the front stoop. Brush grew up through the space left by her death. The woods had reclaimed her meadow. Yet the ground still felt holy. Her marveling gaze had disclosed for me the force and shapeliness of things, and that power survived her passing. She taught me that genius is not in our looking but in what we see. If only we could be adequate to the given world, we need not dream of paradise.

31   Reversing my steps, I walked back to the crossroads and kept going west for a hundred yards or so, until I fetched up before the house where, as a simmering teenager, I had wooed a girl. Let me call her Veronica. She and her family moved from Wayland soon after the Army Corps of Engineers built that needless dam, and so on this October day her house was for me another shell filled only with memory. The present kept abrading the past, however, because during the few minutes while I stood there a grown man in a go-cart kept zooming around the yard, following a deeply gouged path. Every time he roared past, he peered at me from beneath his crash helmet. I nodded, assuming the look of one who is infatuated with loud machines, and that appeared to satisfy him.

32   Veronica had the face of a queen on the deck of cards with which I learned to play poker, a face I considered perfect. Words tumbled from her lush lips, impulsively, like rabbits fleeing a burrow. Black wavy hair tumbled down her back, twitching nearly to her slender hips. Having learned in marriage what it means to love a woman, I cannot say that what I felt for Veronica was quite love. Nor was it simply lust, although for much of my seventeenth year the mere thought of her set me aching. At that age, I would have been reluctant to see myself as the urgent stallion and Veronica as the skittish mare. Later, I would realize that horseflesh and humanflesh dance to the same ardent music, even though our human dance is constrained by rules that horses never know. During the season of our affection, Veronica was a chased girl but also a chaste one, and I was a polite boy, both of us keenly aware of boundaries.

33   In her backyard there was a sycamore tree that loomed high over the house, its fat trunk a patchwork of peeling bark and its crooked upper branches as creamy as whole milk. Wooden crossbars nailed to the trunk formed a ladder up to a treehouse. Veronica and I often sat beneath the sycamore on a stone bench, talking and falling silent, aware of parental eyes watching us from the kitchen. With our backs to the house, our sides pressed together, I could risk brushing a hand over her knee, she could run a fingernail under my chin. But even a kiss, our mouths so visibly meeting, would have prompted a visit from the kitchen.

34   One October day, a day very like this one of my return to Wayland, Veronica and I were sitting on the bench, hunting for words to shape our confusion, when suddenly she leapt to her feet and said, "Let's go up to the treehouse."

35   "We'll get filthy," I said. I glanced with misgiving at my white knit shirt and

chino pants, so carefully pressed. Her lemony blouse was protected by a green corduroy jumper.

36   "It'll wash out," she said, tugging me by the hand.

37   I stood. Without waiting for me, she kicked off her shoes and clambered up the wooden rungs, but instead of halting at the rickety platform of the treehouse, she kept on, swaying from limb to limb. I watched until the flashing of her bare legs made me look away. When she had gone as high as she dared, high enough to escape the view from the kitchen, she balanced on a branch and called to me, "Come on up! Are you afraid?"

38   I was afraid—but not of the tree. I stepped onto a crossbrace and started climbing, and as I climbed there was nowhere else to look but up, and there was nothing else to see above me except those white legs parted within the green hoop of her skirt. Her creamy forked limbs and the creamy forked limbs of the sycamore merged in my sight, as they merge now in memory, and I was drawn upward into the pale shadows between her thighs. My knowledge of what I was climbing toward would remain abstract for a number of years. I understood only that where her legs joined there was an opening, a gateway for life coming and going. When I reached Veronica I put my hand, briefly, where my gaze had gone, just far enough to feel the surprising warmth of that secret, satiny place. Then I withdrew my hand and she smoothed her skirt, neither of us risking a word, and we teetered there for a hundred heartbeats on those swaying branches, shaken by inner as well as outer winds. Then the kitchen door creaked open and her mother's voice inquired as to our sanity, and we climbed down. I went first, as though to catch Veronica should she fall, my eyes toward the ground.

39   The buzzing of the go-cart eventually wore through the husk of memory, and my lungs filled with the present. I became again what I was, a man long married, a man with a daughter the age Veronica had been on that day of our climb into the tree. The sycamore still rose behind the house, twenty-five years taller, crisp brown leaves rattling in the wind, the pale upper limbs as pale and silky as ever.

40   I had a choice of returning to the church by the road or across the stubble of a cornfield. I chose the field. All the way, I could see the white steepled box gleaming on its rise. The only car in the parking lot was mine. Beyond a treeline to the southwest, beyond the annihilating waters of the reservoir that I could not bear to look at, the sun wallowed down toward dusk. The church might already be locked, I thought, so late on a weekday afternoon. Still I did not hurry. My boots scuffed the ridges where corn had stood. Raccoons and crows would find little to feast on in this stubble, for the harvester had plucked it clean. I recalled the biblical injunction to farmers, that they leave the margins of their fields unpicked, for the poor and the beasts. I thought of the margins in a life, in my life, the untended zones beyond the borders of clarity, the encircling wilderness out of which new powers and visions come.

41   A cornfield is a good approach to a church, for you arrive with dirt on your boots, the smell of greenery in your nostrils, dust on your tongue. The door would be locked, I figured, and the main door was, the broad entrance through which the Methodist women carried their piety and their pies, through which men carried mortgages and mortality, through which children like myself carried headfuls of

questions. But the rear door was unlocked. I left my boots on the stoop and went inside.

42   The back room I entered had the familiarity of a place one returns to in dream: the squeaky pine boards of the floor, the dwarf tables where children would sit on Sundays to color pictures of Jesus, the brass hooks where the choir would hang their robes and the minister his hat, the folding chairs collapsed into a corner, the asthmatic furnace, and on a counter the stack of lathe-turned walnut plates for the offering.

43   Every few paces I halted, listening. The joints of the church cricked as the sun let go. Birds fussed beyond the windows. But no one else was about; this relieved me, for here least of all was I prepared to explain myself. I had moved too long in circles where to confess an interest in religious things marked one as a charlatan, a sentimentalist, or a fool. No doubt I have all three qualities in my character. But I also have another quality, and that is an unshakable hunger to know who I am, where I am, and into what sort of cosmos I have been so briefly and astonishingly sprung. Whatever combination of shady motives might have led me here, the impulse that shook me right then was a craving to glimpse the very source and circumference of things.

44   I made my way out through the choir door into the sanctuary. Cushionless pews in somber ranks, uncarpeted floor, exposed beams in the vault overhead and whitewashed plaster on the walls: it was a room fashioned by men and women who knew barns, for preachers who lived out of saddlebags, in honor of a God who cares nothing for ornament. No tapestries, no shrines, no racks of candles, no gold on the altar, no bragging memorials to vanished patrons. The window glass, unstained, let in the plain light of day.

45   I sat in a pew midway along the central aisle and looked out through those clear windows. My reasons for coming here were entwined with that sky full of light. As a boy I had looked out, Sunday after Sunday, to see corn grow and clouds blow, to watch crows bustle among the tops of trees, to follow hawks, unmindful of the Sabbath, on their spiraling hunts, and to sense in all this radiant surge the same rush I felt under my fingers when I pressed a hand to my throat. There was no gulf between outside and inside. We gathered in this room not to withdraw, but more fully to enter the world.

46   On this day of my return, I kept watching the sky as the light thinned and the darkness thickened. I became afraid. Afraid of dying, yes, but even more of not having lived, afraid of passing my days in a stupor, afraid of squandering my moment in the light. I gripped the pew in front of me to still my trembling. I wanted to dive down to the center of being, touch bedrock, open my eyes and truly, finally, unmistakably see. I shifted my gaze from the darkening window to the altar, to the wooden cross, to the black lip of the Bible showing from the pulpit. But those were only props for a play that was forever in rehearsal, the actors clumsy, the script obscure. I was myself one of the actors, sustained in my own clumsy efforts by the hope that one day the performance would be perfect, and everything would at last come clear.

47   One cannot summon grace with a whistle. The pew beneath me, the air around me, the darkening windows did not turn to fire. The clouds of unknowing

did not part. I sat there for a long while, and then I rose and made my way down the aisle, past the organ, through the choir door and back room, out into the freshening night. On the stoop I drew on my boots and laced them up. The chrome latch of my car was already cool. I drove back through the crossroads with headlights glaring, alert for animals that might dash before me in the confusion of dusk.

48 There is more to be seen at any crossroads than one can see in a lifetime of looking. My return visit to Wayland was less than two hours long. Once again half a thousand miles distant from that place, making this model from slippery words, I cannot be sure where the pressure of mind has warped the surface of things. If you were to go there, you would not find every detail exactly as I have described it. How could you, bearing as you do a past quite different from mine? No doubt my memory, welling up through these lines, has played tricks with time and space.

49 What memory is made of I cannot say; my body, at least, is made of atoms on loan from the earth. How implausible, that these atoms should have gathered to form this *I,* this envelope of skin that walks about and strokes horses and tastes apples and trembles with desire in the branches of a sycamore and gazes through the windows of a church at the ordinary sky. Certain moments in one's life cast their influence forward over all the moments that follow. My encounters in Wayland shaped me first as I lived through them, then again as I recalled them during my visit, and now as I write them down. That is of course why I write them down. The self is a fiction. I make up the story of myself with scraps of memory, sensation, reading, and hearsay. It is a tale I whisper against the dark. Only in rare moments of luck or courage do I hush, forget myself entirely, and listen to the silence that precedes and surrounds and follows all speech.

50 If you have been keeping count, you may have toted up seven mysteries, or maybe seven times seven, or maybe seven to the seventh power. My hunch is that, however we count, there is only one mystery. In our nearsightedness, we merely glimpse the light scintillating off the numberless scales of Leviathan, and we take each spark for a separate wonder.

51 Could we bear to see all the light at once? Could we bear the roar of infinite silence? I sympathize with science, where, in order to answer a question, you limit the variables. You draw a circle within which everything can be measured, and you shut out the rest of the universe. But every enclosure is a makeshift, every boundary an illusion. With great ingenuity, we decipher some of the rules that govern this vast shining dance, but all our efforts could not change the least of them.

52 Nothing less than the undivided universe can be our true home. Yet how can one speak or even think about the whole of things? Language is of only modest help. Every sentence is a wispy net, capturing a few flecks of meaning. The sun shines without vocabulary. The salmon has no name for the desire that drives it upstream. The newborn groping for the nipple knows hunger long before it knows a single word. Even with an entire dictionary in one's head, one eventually comes to the end of words. Then what? Then drink deep like the baby, swim like the salmon, burn like any brief star.

QUESTIONS

Experience

· Think about a time when you revisited a place you once lived—a former house or apartment, the street on which you once lived or the town or city, perhaps a school you attended. What were your feelings and thoughts upon returning?

· Early in the essay (in paragraph 2) Sanders says that he has attempted to bribe his readers with seven words that suggest what he will be writing about: "death, life, beasts, food, mind, sex, and God." To what extent did you accept his "bribe"? Why?

Interpretation

· What does Sanders learn in returning to Wayland? Do you agree with Sanders when he writes, "There is more to be seen at any crossroads than one can see in a lifetime of looking"? Why, or why not? And what do you think he means by saying that "the self is a fiction"?

Evaluation

· What are the values that drive Sanders on his return visit? What is he looking for? What does he find that helps him understand himself? How do you understand the advice he offers in his final sentence: "Then drink deep like the baby, swim like the salmon, burn like any brief star"?

WRITING

Exploring

· Write an essay about a return visit you once made to a place that was once important in your life. You may wish to organize your essay by describing what you expected to find and what you actually found. Or perhaps you may wish to focus on a single aspect of the place, perhaps even a single eventful moment of the visit.

Interpreting

· Using Sanders's seven "bribes," explain the point he conveys about each. What does he say about death, life, beasts, food, mind, sex, and God? Try to relate his point about each to one or more details of what he says about the others.

Evaluating

· Compare this essay with another that Sanders has written (see pp. 216–220). What elements do the essays share? How do they differ? Which essay do you like better? Why?

MARY GORDON
(b. 1949)

More Than Just a Shrine: Paying Homage to the Ghosts of Ellis Island

Mary Gordon was born in Far Rockaway, New York. She graduated with a B.A. from Barnard College, where she now teaches, and has also earned an M.A. from Syracuse University. Her books include the fictional works Final Payments *(1978),* The Company of Women *(1981),* Men and Angels *(1986),* Temporary Shelter *(1988), and* The Other Side *(1990). The following selection is taken from her collection of essays,* Good Boys and Dead Girls and Other Essays *(1991).*

In "More Than Just a Shrine," Gordon describes a visit she made to Ellis Island, the way station for immigrants coming to the United States. Neither Gordon's visit nor her essay pays patriotic tribute to the place. Instead, Ellis Island for her is a shrine to the people who passed through it—those countless immigrants, the majority poor and uneducated, coming to a vast country of which they knew little beyond that it symbolized hope and an opportunity to improve their lives. Gordon does not sentimentalize either the place or the people who embarked there, nor does she ignore the indignities visited upon them. Blending personal and social history, Gordon communes with the "ghosts" who haunt her imagination and her essay in inspiring ways.

1   I once sat in a hotel in Bloomsbury trying to have breakfast alone. A Russian with a habit of compulsively licking his lips asked if he could join me. I was afraid to say no; I thought it might be bad for détente. He explained to me that he was a linguist and that he always liked to talk to Americans to see if he could make any connection between their speech and their ethnic background. When I told him about my mixed ancestry—my mother is Irish and Italian, my father was a Lithuanian Jew—he began jumping up and down in his seat, rubbing his hands together and licking his lips even more frantically.

2   "Ah," he said, "so you are really somebody who comes from what is called the boiling pot of America." Yes, I told him; yes, I was; but I quickly rose to leave. I thought it would be too hard to explain to him the relation of the boiling potters to the main course, and I wanted to get to the British Museum. I told him that the only thing I could think of that united people whose backgrounds, histories, and points of view were utterly diverse was that their people had landed at a place called Ellis Island.

3   I didn't tell him that Ellis Island was the only American landmark I'd ever visited. How could I describe to him the estrangement I'd always felt from the kind of traveler who visits shrines to America's past greatness, those rebuilt forts with

muskets behind glass and sabers mounted on the walls and gift shops selling maple sugar candy in the shape of Indian headdresses, those reconstructed villages with tables set for fifty and the Paul Revere silver gleaming? All that Americana—Plymouth Rock, Gettysburg, Mount Vernon, Valley Forge—it all inhabits for me a zone of blurred abstraction with far les hold on my imagination than the Bastille or Hampton Court. I suppose I've always known that my uninterest in it contains a large component of the willed: I am American, and those places purport to be my history. But they are not mine.

4   Ellis Island is, though; it's the one place I can be sure my people are connected to. And so I made a journey there to find my history, like any Rotarian traveling in his Winnebago to Antietam to find his. I had become part of that humbling democracy of people looking in some site for a past that has grown unreal. The monument I traveled to was not, however, a tribute to some old glory. The minute I set foot upon the island I could feel all that it stood for: insecurity, obedience, anxiety, dehumanization, the terrified and careful deference of the displaced. I hadn't traveled to the Battery and boarded a ferry across from the Statue of Liberty to raise flags or breathe a richer, more triumphant air. I wanted to do homage to the ghosts.

5   I felt them everywhere, from the moment I disembarked and saw the building with its high-minded brick, its hopeful little lawn, its ornamental cornices. The place was derelict when I arrived; it had not functioned for more than thirty years—almost as long as the time it had operated at full capacity as a major immigration center. I was surprised to learn what a small part of history Ellis Island had occupied. The main building was constructed in 1892, then rebuilt between 1898 and 1900 after a fire. Most of the immigrants who arrived during the latter half of the nineteenth century, mainly northern and western Europeans, landed not at Ellis Island but on the western tip of the Battery, at Castle Garden, which had opened as a receiving center for immigrants in 1855.

6   By the 1880s, the facilities at Castle Garden had grown scandalously inadequate. Officials looked for an island on which to build a new immigration center, because they thought that on an island immigrants could be more easily protected from swindlers and quickly transported to railroad terminals in New Jersey. Bedloe's Island was considered, but New Yorkers were aghast at the idea of a "Babel" ruining their beautiful new treasure, "Liberty Enlightening the World." The statue's sculptor, Frédéric-Auguste Bartholdi, reacted to the prospect of immigrants landing near his masterpiece in horror; he called it a "monstrous plan." So much for Emma Lazarus.

7   Ellis Island was finally chosen because the citizens of New Jersey petitioned the federal government to remove from the island an old naval powder magazine that they thought dangerously close to the Jersey shore. The explosives were removed; no one wanted the island for anything. It was the perfect place to build an immigration center.

8   I thought about the island's history as I walked into the building and made my way to the room that was the center in my imagination of the Ellis Island experience: the Great Hall. It had been made real for me in the stark, accusing photographs of Louis Hine and others, who took those pictures to make a point. It was in the Great Hall that everyone had waited—waiting, always, the great voca-

tion of the dispossessed. The room was empty, except for me and a handful of other visitors and the park ranger who showed us around. I felt myself grow insignificant in that room, with its huge semicircular windows, its air, even in dereliction, of solid and official probity.

9   I walked in the deathlike expansiveness of the room's disuse and tried to think of what it might have been like, filled and swarming. More than sixteen million immigrants came through that room; approximately 250,000 were rejected. Not really a large proportion, but the implications for the rejected were dreadful. For some, there was nothing to go back to, or there was certain death; for others, who left as adventurers, to return would be to adopt in local memory the fool's role, and the failure's. No wonder that the island's history includes reports of three thousand suicides.

10   Sometimes immigrants could pass through Ellis Island in mere hours, though for some the process took days. The particulars of the experience in the Great Hall were often influenced by the political events and attitudes on the mainland. In the 1890s and the first years of the new century, when cheap labor was needed, the newly built receiving center took in its immigrants with comparatively little question. But as the century progressed, the economy worsened, eugenics became both scientifically respectable and popular, and World War I made American xenophobia seem rooted in fact.

11   Immigration acts were passed; newcomers had to prove, besides moral correctness and financial solvency, their ability to read. Quota laws came into effect, limiting the number of immigrants from southern and eastern Europe to less than 14 percent of the total quota. Intelligence tests were biased against all non-English-speaking persons, and medical examinations became increasingly strict, until the machinery of immigration nearly collapsed under its own weight. The Second Quota Law of 1924 provided that all immigrants be inspected and issued visas at American consular offices in Europe, rendering the center almost obsolete.

12   On the day of my visit, my mind fastened upon the medical inspections, which had always seemed to me most emblematic of the ignominy and terror the immigrants endured. The medical inspectors, sometimes dressed in uniforms like soldiers, were particularly obsessed with a disease of the eyes called trachoma, which they checked for by flipping back the immigrants' top eyelids with a hook used for buttoning gloves—a method that sometimes resulted in the transmission of the disease to healthy people. Mothers feared that if their children cried too much, their red eyes would be mistaken for a symptom of the disease and the whole family would be sent home. Those immigrants suspected of some physical disability had initials chalked on their coats. I remembered the photographs I'd seen of people standing, dumbstruck and innocent as cattle, with their manifest numbers hung around their necks and initials marked in chalk upon their coats: "E" for eye trouble, "K" for hernia, "L" for lameness, "X" for mental defects, "H" for heart disease.

13   I thought of my grandparents as I stood in the room: my seventeen-year-old grandmother, coming alone from Ireland in 1896, vouched for by a stranger who had found her a place as a domestic servant to some Irish who had done well. I tried to imagine the assault it all must have been for her; I've been to her hometown, a collection of farms with a main street—smaller than the athletic field of my

local public school. She must have watched the New York skyline as the first- and second-class passengers were whisked off the gangplank with the most cursory of inspections while she was made to board a ferry to the new immigration center.

14   What could she have made of it—this buff-painted wooden structure with its towers and its blue slate roof, a place *Harper's Weekly* described as "a latter-day watering place hotel"? It would have been the first time she had heard people speaking something other than English. She would have mingled with people carrying baskets on their heads and eating foods unlike any she had ever seen—dark-eyed people, like the Sicilian she would marry ten years later, who came over with his family at thirteen, the man of the family, responsible even then for his mother and sister. I don't know what they thought, my grandparents, for they were not expansive people, nor romantic; they didn't like to think of what they called "the hard times," and their trip across the ocean was the single adventurous act of lives devoted after landing to security, respectability, and fitting in.

15   What is the potency of Ellis Island for someone like me—an American, obviously, but one who has always felt that the country really belonged to the early settlers, that, as J. F. Powers wrote in *Morte D'Urban,* it had been "handed down to them by the Pilgrims, George Washington and others, and that they were taking a risk in letting you live in it." I have never been the victim of overt discrimination; nothing I have wanted has been denied me because of the accidents of blood. But I suppose it is part of being an American to be engaged in a somewhat tiresome but always self-absorbing process of national definition. And in this process, I have found in traveling to Ellis Island an important piece of evidence that could remind me I was right to feel my differentness. Something had happened to my people on that island, a result of the eternal wrongheadedness of American protectionism and the predictabilities of simple greed. I came to the island, too, so I could tell the ghosts that I was one of them, and that I honored them—their stoicism, and their innocence, the fear that turned them inward, and their pride. I wanted to tell them that I liked them better than I did the Americans who made them pass through the Great Hall and stole their names and chalked their weaknesses in public on their clothing. And to tell the ghosts what I have always thought: that American history was a very classy party that was not much fun until they arrived, brought the good food, turned up the music, and taught everyone to dance.

QUESTIONS

Experience

· Have you ever visited any of what Gordon calls "shrines to America's past greatness," places such as Plymouth Rock, Gettysburg, Mount Vernon, Valley Forge, Lexington? How about the Statue of Liberty or the Liberty Bell? If you have been to one of these places or to another historical landmark, what was your experience like? If you have not visited such a place, explain why you would or would not like to.

Interpretation

· What is there about Ellis Island that makes Gordon feel "American"? Besides the factual information she provides about Ellis Island, what idea does she convey about the place? Where do you find her explanation of the significance and meaning of Ellis Island strongest and clearest?

Evaluation

· How well does Gordon convey the spirit of Ellis Island? To what extent can you understand what she feels about the place? To what extent do you agree with the kinds of values she ascribes to Ellis Island? Why?

· Explain what Gordon is saying in her final paragraph.

WRITING

Exploring

· Write an essay about a visit you once made to a historic place, perhaps to one of those identified in the essay or to another, such as the Alamo or the Vietnam Veterans Memorial in Washington, D.C. Explain the significance of the visit for you. Focus on a key aspect rather than describing everything that happened on the trip.

Interpreting

· Write an analysis and interpretation of a significant historical landmark or place, whether or not you have ever visited it. Some possibilities are the ones mentioned in the essay or in the previous writing assignment. Others are the following: the Lincoln or Jefferson memorials, the St. Gaudens's sculpture on the Boston Common, a Civil War or Revolutionary War battlefield, or a western "ghost" town.

Evaluating

· Write a piece in which you explain the values—personal, social, cultural, or religious—that impelled your ancestors to come to America (or that influenced others to bring them here by force). Consider not only why they came but also how they lived once they arrived, and perhaps what kind of legacy they have left you.

· Or write an essay that supports, qualifies, or disputes Gordon's contention that "it is part of being an American to be engaged in a somewhat tiresome but always self-absorbing process of national definition."

MARIANNA DE MARCO TORGOVNICK
(b. 1949)

On Being White, Female, and Born in Bensonhurst

Marianna De Marco Torgovnick is the author of three books on literature, society, and the arts. She has written for general-interest periodicals such as South Atlantic Quarterly, Partisan Review, *and* Art Forum, *publishing articles on a wide range of interdisciplinary topics. Her most recent book, a collection of personal essays entitled* Crossing Ocean Parkway, *takes its name from a Brooklyn, New York, thoroughfare that divides neighborhoods of different religions and ethnicities—specifically Italian Catholics and East European Jews.*

In her essay, Torgovnick links her personal experience with social issues such as integration, class differences, and racial tension. She writes about the larger social concerns partly from the inside, so to speak, through explaining values of her clan. She brings Bensonhurst to life by describing specific scenes, and she brings the scenes to life through the use of dialogue and sharply etched detail.

1   The Mafia protects the neighborhood, our fathers say, with that peculiar satisfied pride with which law-abiding Italian Americans refer to the Mafia: the Mafia protects the neighborhood from "the coloreds." In the fifties and sixties, I heard that information repeated, in whispers, in neighborhood parks and in the yard at school in Bensonhurst. The same information probably passes today in the parks (the word now "blacks," not "coloreds") but perhaps no longer in the schoolyards. From buses each morning, from neighborhoods outside Bensonhurst, spill children of all colors and backgrounds—American black, West Indian black, Hispanic, and Asian. But the blacks are the only ones especially marked for notice. Bensonhurst is no longer entirely protected from "the coloreds." But in a deeper sense, at least for Italian Americans, Bensonhurst never changes.

2   Italian-American life continues pretty much as I remember it. Families with young children live side by side with older couples whose children are long gone to the suburbs. Many of those families live "down the block" from the last generation or, sometimes still, live together with parents or grandparents. When a young family leaves, as sometimes happens, for Long Island or New Jersey or (very common now) for Staten Island, another arrives, without any special effort being required, from Italy or a poorer neighborhood in New York. They fill the neat but anonymous houses that make up the mostly tree-lined streets: two-, three-, or four-family houses for the most part (this is a working, lower to middle-middle class area, and people need rents to pay mortgages), with a few single family or small apartment houses tossed in at random. Tomato plants, fig trees, and plaster madonnas often decorate small but well-tended yards which face out

onto the street; the grassy front lawn, like the grassy back yard, is relatively uncommon.

3   Crisscrossing the neighborhood and marking out ethnic zones—Italian, Irish, and Jewish, for the most part, though there are some Asian Americans and some people (usually Protestants) called simply Americans—are the great shopping streets: Eighty-sixth Street, Kings Highway, Bay Parkway, Eighteenth Avenue, each with its own distinctive character. On Eighty-sixth Street, crowds bustle along sidewalks lined with ample, packed fruit stands. Women wheeling shopping carts or baby strollers check the fruit carefully, piece by piece, and often bargain with the dealer, cajoling for a better price or letting him know that the vegetables, this time, aren't up to snuff. A few blocks down, the fruit stands are gone and the streets are lined with clothing and record shops, mobbed by teenagers. Occasionally, the el rumbles overhead, a few stops out of Coney Island on its way to the city, a trip of around one hour.

4   On summer nights, neighbors congregate on stoops which during the day serve as play yards for children. Air conditioning exists everywhere in Bensonhurst, but people still sit outside in the summer—to supervise children, to gossip, to stare at strangers. *"Buona sera,"* I say, or *"Buona notte,"* as I am ritually presented to Sal and Lily and Louie, the neighbors sitting on the stoop. *"Grazie,"* I say when they praise my children or my appearance. It's the only time I use Italian, which I learned at high school, although my parents (both second-generation Italian Americans, my father Sicilian, my mother Calabrian) speak it at home to each other but never to me or my brother. My accent is the Tuscan accent taught at school, not the southern Italian accents of my parents and the neighbors.

5   It's important to greet and please the neighbors; any break in this decorum would seriously offend and aggrieve my parents. For the neighbors are the stern arbiters of conduct in Bensonhurst. Does Mary keep a clean house? Did Gina wear black long enough after her mother's death? Was the food good at Tony's wedding? The neighbors know and pass judgment. Any news of family scandal (my brother's divorce, for example) provokes from my mother the agonized words: "But what will I *tell* people?" I sometimes collaborate in devising a plausible script.

6   A large sign on the church I attended as a child sums up for me the ethos of Bensonhurst. The sign urges contributions to the church building fund with the message, in huge letters: "EACH YEAR ST. SIMON AND JUDE SAVES THIS NEIGHBORHOOD ONE MILLION DOLLARS IN TAXES." Passing the church on the way from largely Jewish and middle-class Sheepshead Bay (where my in-laws live) to Bensonhurst, year after year, my husband and I look for the sign and laugh at the crass level of its pitch, its utter lack of attention to things spiritual. But we also understand exactly the values it represents.

7   In the summer of 1989, my parents were visiting me at my house in Durham, North Carolina, from the apartment in Bensonhurst where they have lived since 1942: three small rooms, rent-controlled, floor clean enough to eat off, every corner and crevice known and organized. My parents' longevity in a single apartment is unusual even for Bensonhurst, but not that unusual; many people live for decades in the same place or move within a ten-block radius. When I lived in this apartment, there were four rooms; one has since been ceded to a demanding

landlord, one of the various landlords who have haunted my parents' life and must always be appeased lest the ultimate threat—removal from the rent-controlled apartment—be brought into play. That summer, during their visit, on August 23 (my younger daughter's birthday) a shocking, disturbing, news report issued from the neighborhood: it had become another Howard Beach.

8   Three black men, walking casually through the streets at night, were attacked by a group of whites. One was shot dead, mistaken, as it turned out, for another black youth who was dating a white, although part-Hispanic, girl in the neighborhood. It all made sense: the crudely protective men, expecting to see a black arriving at the girl's house and overreacting; the rebellious girl dating the outsider boy; the black dead as a sacrifice to the feelings of the neighborhood.

9   I might have felt outrage, I might have felt guilt or shame, I might have despised the people among whom I grew up. In a way I felt all four emotions when I heard the news. I expect that there were many people in Bensonhurst who felt the same rush of emotions. But mostly I felt that, given the set-up, this was the only way things could have happened. I detested the racial killing, but I also understood it. Those streets, which should be public property available to all, belong to the neighborhood. All the people sitting on the stoops on August 23 knew that as well as they knew their own names. The black men walking through probably knew it too—though their casual walk sought to deny the fact that, for the neighbors, even the simple act of blacks walking through the neighborhood would be seen as invasion.

10   Italian Americans in Bensonhurst are notable for their cohesiveness and provinciality; the slightest pressure turns those qualities into prejudice and racism. Their cohesiveness is based on the stable economic and ethical level that links generation to generation, keeping Italian Americans in Bensonhurst and the Italian-American community alive as the Jewish-American community of my youth is no longer alive. (Its young people routinely moved to the suburbs or beyond and were never replaced, so that Jews in Bensonhurst today are almost all very old people.) Their provinciality results from the Italian Americans' devotion to jealous distinctions and discriminations. Jews are suspect, but (the old Italian women admit) "they make good husbands." The Irish are okay, fellow Catholics, but not really "like us"; they make bad husbands because they drink and gamble. Even Italians come in varieties, by region (Sicilian, Calabrian, Neapolitan, very rarely any region further north) and by history in this country (the newly arrived and ridiculed "gaffoon" versus the second or third generation).

11   Bensonhurst is a neighborhood dedicated to believing that its values are the only values; it tends toward certain forms of inertia. When my parents visit me in Durham, they routinely take chairs from the kitchen and sit out on the lawn in front of the house, not on the chairs on the back deck; then they complain that the streets are too quiet. When they walk around my neighborhood (these De Marcos who have friends named Travaglianti and Occhipinti), they look at the mailboxes and report that my neighbors have strange names. Prices at my local supermarket are compared, in unbelievable detail, with prices on Eighty-sixth Street. Any rearrangement of my kitchen since their last visit is registered and criticized. Difference is not only unwelcome, it is unacceptable. One of the most characteristic things my mother ever said was in response to my plans for renovating my house

in Durham. When she heard my plans, she looked around, crossed her arms, and said, "If it was me, I wouldn't change nothing." My father once asked me to level with him about a Jewish boyfriend who lived in a different part of the neighborhood, reacting to his Jewishness, but even more to the fact that he often wore Bermuda shorts: "Tell me something, Marianna. Is he a Communist?" Such are the standards of normality and political thinking in Bensonhurst.

12   I often think that one important difference between Italian Americans in New York neighborhoods like Bensonhurst and Italian Americans elsewhere is that the others moved on—to upstate New York, to Pennsylvania, to the Midwest. Though they frequently settled in communities of fellow Italians, they did move on. Bensonhurst Italian Americans seem to have felt that one large move, over the ocean, was enough. Future moves could be only local: from the Lower East Side, for example, to Brooklyn, or from one part of Brooklyn to another. Bensonhurst was for many of these people the summa of expectations. If their America were to be drawn as a *New Yorker* cover, Manhattan itself would be tiny in proportion to Bensonhurst and to its satellites, Staten Island, New Jersey, and Long Island.

13   "Oh, no," my father says when he hears the news about the shooting. Though he still refers to blacks as "coloreds," he's not really a racist and is upset that this innocent youth was shot in his neighborhood. He has no trouble acknowledging the wrongness of the death. But then, like all the news accounts, he turns to the fact, repeated over and over, that the blacks had been on their way to look at a used car when they encountered the hostile mob of whites. The explanation is right before him but, "Yeah," he says, still shaking his head, "yeah, but what were they *doing* there? They didn't belong."

14   Over the next few days, the television news is even more disturbing. Rows of screaming Italians lining the streets, most of them looking like my relatives. I focus especially on one woman who resembles almost completely my mother: stocky but not fat, mid-seventies but well preserved, full face showing only minimal wrinkles, ample steel-gray hair neatly if rigidly coiffed in a modified beehive hairdo left over from the sixties. She shakes her fist at the camera, protesting the arrest of the Italian-American youths in the neighborhood and the incursion of more blacks into the neighborhood, protesting the shooting. I look a little nervously at my mother (the parent I resemble), but she has not even noticed the woman and stares impassively at the television.

15   What has Bensonhurst to do with what I teach today and write? Why did I need to write about this killing in Bensonhurst, but not in the manner of a news account or a statistical sociological analysis? Within days of hearing the news, I began to plan this essay, to tell the world what I knew, even though I was aware that I could publish the piece only someplace my parents or their neighbors would never see or hear about it. I sometimes think that I looked around from my baby carriage and decided that someday, the sooner the better, I would get out of Bensonhurst. Now, much to my surprise, Bensonhurst—the antipodes of the intellectual life I sought, the least interesting of places—had become a respectable intellectual topic. People would be willing to hear about Bensonhurst—and all by the dubious virtue of a racial killing in the streets.

16   The story as I would have to tell it would be to some extent a class narrative: about the difference between working class and upper middle class, dependence

and a profession, Bensonhurst and a posh suburb. But I need to make it clear that I do not imagine myself as writing from a position of enormous self-satisfaction, or even enormous distance. You can take the girl out of Bensonhurst (that much is clear), but you may not be able to take Bensonhurst out of the girl. And upward mobility is not the essence of the story, though it is an important marker and symbol.

17   In Durham today, I live in a twelve-room house surrounded by an acre of trees. When I sit on my back deck on summer evenings, no houses are visible through the trees. I have a guaranteed income, teaching English at an excellent university, removed by my years of education from the fundamental economic and social conditions of Bensonhurst. The one time my mother ever expressed pleasure at my work was when I got tenure, what my father still calls, with no irony intended, "ten years." "What does that mean?" my mother asked when she heard the news. Then she reached back into her experience as a garment worker, subject to periodic layoffs. "Does it mean they can't fire you just for nothing and can't lay you off?" When I said that was exactly what it means, she said, "Very good. Congratulations. That's *wonderful.*" I was free from the *padrones,* from the network of petty anxieties that had formed, in large part, her very existence. Of course, I wasn't really free of petty anxieties: would my salary increase keep pace with my colleagues', how would my office compare, would this essay be accepted for publication, am I happy? The line between these worries and my mother's is the line between the working class and the upper middle class.

18   But getting out of Bensonhurst never meant to me a big house, or nice clothes, or a large income. And it never meant feeling good about looking down on what I left behind or hiding my background. Getting out of Bensonhurst meant freedom—to experiment, to grow, to change. It also meant knowledge in some grand, abstract way. All the material possessions I have acquired, I acquired simply along the way—and for the first twelve years after I left Bensonhurst, I chose to acquire almost nothing at all. Now, as I write about the neighborhood, I recognize that although I've come far in physical and material distance, the emotional distance is harder to gauge. Bensonhurst has everything to do with who I am and even with what I write. Occasionally I get reminded of my roots, of their simultaneously choking and nutritive power.

19   Scene one: It's after a lecture at Duke, given by a visiting professor from Princeton. The lecture was long and a little dull and—bad luck—I had agreed to be one of the people having dinner with the lecturer afterward. We settle into our table at the restaurant: this man, me, the head of the comparative literature program (also a professor of German), and a couple I like who teach French, the husband at my university, the wife at one nearby. The conversation is sluggish, as it often is when a stranger, like the visiting professor, has to be assimilated into a group, so I ask the visitor from Princeton a question to personalize things a bit. "How did you get interested in what you do? What made you become a professor of German?" The man gets going and begins talking about how it was really unlikely that he, a nice Jewish boy from Bensonhurst, would have chosen, in the mid-fifties, to study German. Unlikely indeed.

20   I remember seeing *Judgment at Nuremberg* in a local movie theater and having a woman in the row in back of me get hysterical when some clips of a con-

centration camp were shown. "My God," she screamed in a European accent, "look at what they did. Murderers, MURDERERS!"—and she had to be supported out by her family. I couldn't see, in the dark, whether her arm bore the neatly tattooed numbers that the arms of some of my classmates' parents did—and that always affected me with a thrill of horror. Ten years older than me, this man had lived more directly through those feelings, lived with and *among* those feelings. The first chance he got, he raced to study in Germany. I myself have twice chosen not to visit Germany, but I understand his impulse to identify with the Other as a way of getting out of the neighborhood.

21   At the dinner, the memory about the movie pops into my mind but I pick up instead on the Bensonhurst—I'm also from there, but Italian American. Like a flash, he asks something I haven't been asked in years: Where did I go to high school and (a more common question) what was my maiden name? I went to Lafayette High School, I say, and my name was De Marco. Everything changes: his facial expression, his posture, his accent, his voice. "Soo, Dee Maw-ko," he says, "dun anything wrong at school today—got enny pink slips? Wanna meet me later at the parrk or maybe bye the Baye?" When I laugh, recognizing the stereotype that Italians get pink slips for misconduct at school and the notorious chemistry between Italian women and Jewish men, he says, back in his Princetonian voice: "My God, for a minute I felt like I was turning into a werewolf."

22   It's odd that although I can remember almost nothing else about this man— his face, his body type, even his name—I remember this lapse into his "real self" with enormous vividness. I am especially struck by how easily he was able to slip into the old, generic Brooklyn accent. I myself have no memory of ever speaking in that accent, though I also have no memory of trying not to speak it, except for teaching myself, carefully, to say "oil" rather than "earl."

23   But the surprises aren't over. The female French professor, whom I have known for at least five years, reveals for the first time that she is also from the neighborhood, though she lived across the other side of Kings Highway, went to a different, more elite high school, and was Irish American. Three of six professors, sitting at an eclectic vegetarian restaurant in Durham, all from Bensonhurst— a neighborhood where (I swear) you couldn't get the *New York Times* at any of the local stores.

24   Scene two: I still live in Bensonhurst. I'm waiting for my parents to return from a conference at my school, where they've been summoned to discuss my transition from elementary to junior high school. I am already a full year younger than any of my classmates, having skipped a grade, a not uncommon occurrence for "gifted" youngsters. Now the school is worried about putting me in an accelerated track through junior high, since that would make me two years younger. A compromise was reached: I would be put in a special program for gifted children, but one that took three, not two, years. It sounds okay.

25   Three years later, another wait. My parents have gone to school this time to make another decision. Lafayette High School has three tracks: academic, for potentially college-bound kids; secretarial, mostly for Italian-American girls or girls with low aptitude-test scores (the high school is de facto segregated, so none of the tracks is as yet racially coded, though they are coded by ethnic group and gender); and vocational, mostly for boys with the same attributes, ethnic or intel-

lectual. Although my scores are superb, the guidance counselor has recommended the secretarial track; when I protested, the conference with my parents was arranged. My mother's preference is clear: the secretarial track—college is for boys; I will need to make a "good living" until I marry and have children. My father also prefers the secretarial track, but he wavers, half proud of my aberrantly high scores, half worried. I press the attack, saying that if I were Jewish I would have been placed, without question, in the academic track. I tell him I have sneaked a peek at my files and know that my IQ is at genius level. I am allowed to insist on the change into the academic track.

26   What I did, and I was ashamed of it even then, was to play upon my father's competitive feelings with Jews: his daughter could and should be as good as theirs. In the bank where he was a messenger, and at the insurance company where he worked in the mailroom, my father worked with Jews, who were almost always his immediate supervisors. Several times, my father was offered the supervisory job but turned it down after long conversations with my mother about the dangers of making a change, the difficulty of giving orders to friends. After her work in a local garment shop, after cooking dinner and washing the floor each night, my mother often did piecework making bows; sometimes I would help her for fun, but it *wasn't* fun, and I was free to stop while she continued for long, tedious hours to increase the family income. Once a week, her part-time boss, Dave, would come by to pick up the boxes of bows. Short, round, with his shirt-tails sloppily tucked into his pants and a cigar almost always dangling from his lips, Dave was a stereotyped Jew but also, my parents always said, a nice guy, a decent man.

27   Years later, similar choices come up, and I show the same assertiveness I showed with my father, the same ability to deal for survival, but tinged with Bensonhurst caution. Where will I go to college? Not to Brooklyn College, the flagship of the city system—I know that, but don't press the invitations I have received to apply to prestigious schools outside of New York. The choice comes down to two: Barnard, which gives me a full scholarship, minus five hundred dollars a year that all scholarship students are expected to contribute from summer earnings, or New York University, which offers me one thousand dollars above tuition as a bribe. I waver. My parents stand firm: they are already losing money by letting me go to college; I owe it to the family to contribute the extra thousand dollars plus my summer earnings. Besides, my mother adds, harping on a favorite theme, there are no boys at Barnard; at NYU I'm more likely to meet someone to marry. I go to NYU and do marry in my senior year, but he is someone I didn't meet at college. I was secretly relieved, I now think (though at the time I thought I was just placating my parents' conventionality), to be out of the marriage sweepstakes.

28   The first boy who ever asked me for a date was Robert Lubitz, in eighth grade: tall and skinny to my average height and teenage chubbiness. I turned him down, thinking we would make a ridiculous couple. Day after day, I cast my eyes at stylish Juliano, the class cutup; day after day, I captivated Robert Lubitz. Occasionally, one of my brother's Italian-American friends would ask me out, and I would go, often to ROTC dances. My specialty was making political remarks so shocking that the guys rarely asked me again. After a while I recognized destiny: the Jewish

man was a passport out of Bensonhurst. I of course did marry a Jewish man, who gave me my freedom and, very important, helped remove me from the expectations of Bensonhurst. Though raised in a largely Jewish section of Brooklyn, he had gone to college in Ohio and knew how important it was, as he put it, "to get past the Brooklyn Bridge." We met on neutral ground, in Central Park, at a performance of Shakespeare. The Jewish-Italian marriage is a common enough catastrophe in Bensonhurst for my parents to have accepted, even welcomed, mine—though my parents continued to treat my husband like an outsider for the first twenty years ("Now Marianna. Here's what's going on with you brother. But don't tell-a you husband").

29   Along the way I make other choices, more fully marked by Bensonhurst cautiousness. I am attracted to journalism or the arts as careers, but the prospects for income seem iffy. I choose instead to imagine myself as a teacher. Only the availability of NDEA fellowships when I graduate, with their generous terms, propels me from high school teaching (a thought I never much relished) to college teaching (which seems like a brave new world). Within the college teaching profession, I choose offbeat specializations: the novel, interdisciplinary approaches (not something clear and clubby like Milton or the eighteenth century). Eventually I write the book I like best about primitive others as they figure within Western obsessions: my identification with "the Other," my sense of being "Other," surfaces at last. I avoid all mentoring structures for a long time but accept aid when it comes to me on the basis of what I perceive to be merit. I'm still, deep down, Italian-American Bensonhurst, though by this time I'm a lot of other things as well.

30   Scene three: In the summer of 1988, a little more than a year before the shooting in Bensonhurst, my father woke up trembling and in what appeared to be a fit. Hospitalization revealed that he had a pocket of blood on his brain, a frequent consequence of falls for older people. About a year earlier, I had stayed home, using my children as an excuse, when my aunt, my father's much loved sister, died, missing her funeral; only now does my mother tell me how much my father resented my taking his suggestion that I stay home. Now, confronted with what is described as brain surgery but turns out to be less dramatic than it sounds, I fly home immediately.

31   My brother drives three hours back and forth from New Jersey every day to chauffeur me and my mother to the hospital: he is being a fine Italian-American son. For the first time in years, we have a long conversation alone. He is two years older than I am, a chemical engineer who has also left the neighborhood but has remained closer to its values, with a suburban, Republican inflection. He talks a lot about New York, saying that (except for neighborhoods like Bensonhurst) it's a "third-world city now." It's the summer of the Tawana Brawley incident, when Brawley accused white men of abducting her and smearing racial slurs on her body with her own excrement. My brother is filled with dislike for Al Sharpton and Brawley's other vocal supporters in the black community—not because they're black, he says, but because they're troublemakers, stirring things up. The city is drenched in racial hatred that makes itself felt in the halls of the hospital: Italians and Jews in the beds and as doctors; blacks as nurses and orderlies.

32   This is the first time since I left New York in 1975 that I have visited Brooklyn

without once getting into Manhattan. It's the first time I have spent several days alone with my mother, living in her apartment in Bensonhurst. My every move is scrutinized and commented on. I feel like I am going to go crazy.

33   Finally, it's clear that my father is going to be fine, and I can go home. She insists on accompanying me to the travel agent to get my ticket for home, even though I really want to be alone. The agency (a Mafia front?) has no one who knows how to ticket me for the exotic destination of North Carolina and no computer for doing so. The one person who can perform this feat by hand is out. I have to kill time for an hour and suggest to my mother that she go home, to be there for my brother when he arrives from Jersey. We stop in a Pork Store, where I buy a stash of cheeses, sausages, and other delicacies unavailable in Durham. My mother walks home with the shopping bags, and I'm on my own.

34   More than anything I want a kind of *sorbetto* or ice I remember from my childhood, a *cremolata,* almond-vanilla-flavored with large chunks of nuts. I pop into the local bakery (at the unlikely hour of 11 A.M.) and ask for a *cremolata,* usually eaten after dinner. The woman—a younger version of my mother—refuses: they haven't made a fresh ice yet, and what's left from the day before is too icy, no good. I explain that I'm about to get on a plane for North Carolina and want that ice, good or not. But she has her standards and holds her ground, even though North Carolina has about the same status in her mind as Timbuktoo and she knows I will be banished, perhaps forever, from the land of *cremolata.*

35   Then, while I'm taking a walk, enjoying my solitude, I have another idea. On the block behind my parents' house, there's a club for men, for men from a particular town or region in Italy: six or seven tables, some on the sidewalk beneath a garish red, green, and white sign; no women allowed or welcome unless they're with men, and no women at all during the day when the real business of the club—a game of cards for old men—is in progress. Still, I know that inside the club would be coffee and a *cremolata* ice. I'm thirty-eight, well dressed, very respectable looking; I know what I want. I also know I'm not supposed to enter that club. I enter anyway, asking the teenage boy behind the counter firmly, in my most professional tones, for a *cremolata* ice. Dazzled, he complies immediately. The old men at the card table have been staring at this scene, unable to place me exactly, though my facial type is familiar. Finally, a few old men's hisses pierce the air. *"Strega,"* I hear as I leave, *"mala strega"*—"witch," or "brazen whore." I have been in Bensonhurst less than a week, but I have managed to reproduce, on my final day there for this visit, the conditions of my youth. Knowing the rules, I have broken them. I shake hands with my discreetly rebellious past, still an outsider walking through the neighborhood, marked and insulted—though unlikely to be shot.

QUESTIONS

Experience

· To what extent do you share Torgovnick's experience of growing up in an ethnically diverse neighborhood? To what extent does the neighborhood in which you grew up differ from the kind of neighborhood in which Torgovnick grew up? Of what importance is this similarity or difference?

Interpretation

· Why do you think Torgovnick distinguishes between the Tuscan Italian accent she learned in high school and the southern Italian accents of her parents' speech?

· Why does she say that blacks walking in her Bensonhurst neighborhood would be interpreted by residents there as invaders?

· Why does Torgovnick feel compelled to write this essay? Is it therapeutic? An attempt to apologize? To clarify and explain? Something else?

Evaluation

· How well do you think Torgovnick conveys her sense of Bensonhurst? Do you acquire a sense of its values and concerns?

· What values are represented by the sign on the church of St. Simon and St. Jude? Why do you think Torgovnick mentions it? What values are suggested by Torgovnick's house in North Carolina? How do those values compare with the values of her Bensonhurst neighborhood?

WRITING

Exploring

· Write an essay about your own neighborhood—one you have lived in most of your life or another that made a strong impression on you. Characterize the values of the people who live there. Try to provide an overall impression of who its residents are, why they live there, and what their lives are like.

Interpreting

· Explain what you think is the central idea of Torgovnick's essay. You might choose to focus on an aspect of race, class, or ethnicity, since all three figure prominently in her essay.

Evaluating

· Write an essay in which you discuss how the values of your past—as inscribed in your neighborhood—have influenced the values you hold today. Consider the extent to which the values reflected by your former neighborhood continue to influence you.

AMY TAN
(b. 1952)

Mother Tongue

Amy Tan was born in Stockton, California, and raised there until after her father's death, when she moved with her mother to Switzerland, where she attended high school. She attended college in Oregon before taking a job with IBM as a writer of computer manuals. A few years later, having been inspired by Louise Erdrich's interlocked stories about Native American (Chippewa) life in her book Love Medicine, *Tan began writing the interlocking stories that soon became her best-selling novel,* The Joy Luck Club *(1989).*

Like the stories in The Joy Luck Club *and those in her later novel,* The Kitchen God's Wife, *the essay that follows concerns Tan's exploration of cultural difference and cultural connectedness through language. One of its most interesting features is Tan's consideration of what she calls "the different Englishes" she uses with her mother (and her mother uses with her), with her husband, in public, and in her writing. Tan exhibits these Englishes skillfully in the essay, letting us hear them, for the most part, in action—a compositional strategy that brings Tan's writing to life, making it, as her mother said of her novel* The Joy Luck Club, *"so easy to read."*

1   I am not a scholar of English or literature. I cannot give you much more than personal opinions on the English language and its variations in this country or others.

2   I am a writer. And by that definition, I am someone who has always loved language. I am fascinated by language in daily life. I spend a great deal of my time thinking about the power of language—the way it can evoke an emotion, a visual image, a complex idea, or a simple truth. Language is the tool of my trade. And I use them all—all the Englishes I grew up with.

3   Recently, I was made keenly aware of the different Englishes I do use. I was giving a talk to a large group of people, the same talk I had already given to half a dozen other groups. The nature of the talk was about my writing, my life, and my book, *The Joy Luck Club.* The talk was going along well enough, until I remembered one major difference that made the whole talk sound wrong. My mother was in the room. And it was perhaps the first time she had heard me give a lengthy speech, using the kind of English I have never used with her. I was saying things like, "The intersection of memory upon imagination" and "There is an aspect of my fiction that relates to thus-and-thus"—a speech filled with carefully wrought grammatical phrases, burdened, it suddenly seemed to me, with nominalized forms, past perfect tenses, conditional phrases, all the forms of standard English that I had learned in school and through books, the forms of English I did not use at home with my mother.

4   Just last week, I was walking down the street with my mother, and I again

found myself conscious of the English I was using, the English I do use with her. We were talking about the price of new and used furniture and I heard myself saying this: "Not waste money that way." My husband was with us as well, and he didn't notice any switch in my English. And then I realized why. It's because over the twenty years we've been together I've often used that same kind of English with him, and sometimes he even uses it with me. It has become our language of intimacy, a different sort of English that relates to family talk, the language I grew up with.

5   So you'll have some idea of what this family talk I heard sounds like, I'll quote what my mother said during a recent conversation which I videotaped and then transcribed. During this conversation, my mother was talking about a political gangster in Shanghai who had the same last name as her family's, Du, and how the gangster in his early years wanted to be adopted by her family, which was rich by comparison. Later, the gangster became more powerful, far richer than my mother's family, and one day showed up at my mother's wedding to pay his respects. Here's what she said in part:

6   "Du Yusong having business like fruit stand. Like off the street kind. He is Du like Du Zong—but not Tsung-ming Island people. The local people call putong, the river east side, he belong to that side local people. That man want to ask Du Zong father take him in like become own family. Du Zong father wasn't look down on him, but didn't take seriously, until that man big like become a mafia. Now important person, very hard to inviting him. Chinese way, came only to show respect, don't stay for dinner. Respect for making big celebration, he shows up. Mean gives lots of respect. Chinese custom. Chinese social life that way. If too important won't have to stay too long. He come to my wedding. I didn't see, I heard it. I gone to boy's side, they have YMCA dinner. Chinese age I was nineteen."

7   You should know that my mother's expressive command of English belies how much she actually understands. She reads the *Forbes* report, listens to *Wall Street Week,* converses daily with her stockbroker, reads all of Shirley MacLaine's books with ease—all kinds of things I can't begin to understand. Yet some of my friends tell me they understand 50 percent of what my mother says. Some say they understand 80 to 90 percent. Some say they understand none of it, as if she were speaking pure Chinese. But to me, my mother's English is perfectly clear, perfectly natural. It's my mother tongue. Her language, as I hear it, is vivid, direct, full of observation and imagery. That was the language that helped shape the way I saw things, expressed things, made sense of the world.

8   Lately, I've been giving more thought to the kind of English my mother speaks. Like others, I have described it to people as "broken" or "fractured" English. But I wince when I say that. It has always bothered me that I can think of no way to describe it other than "broken," as if it were damaged and needed to be fixed, as if it lacked a certain wholeness and soundness. I've heard other terms used, "limited English," for example. But they seem just as bad, as if everything is limited, including people's perceptions of the limited English speaker.

9   I know this for a fact, because when I was growing up, my mother's "limited" English limited *my* perception of her. I was ashamed of her English. I believed that her English reflected the quality of what she had to say. That is, because she

expressed them imperfectly her thoughts were imperfect. And I had plenty of empirical evidence to support me: the fact that people in department stores, at banks, and at restaurants did not take her seriously, did not give her good service, pretended not to understand her, or even acted as if they did not hear her.

10   My mother has long realized the limitations of her English as well. When I was fifteen, she used to have me call people on the phone to pretend I was she. In this guise, I was forced to ask for information or even to complain and yell at people who had been rude to her. One time it was a call to her stockbroker in New York. She had cashed out her small portfolio and it just so happened we were going to go to New York the next week, our very first trip outside California. I had to get on the phone and say in an adolescent voice that was not very convincing, "This is Mrs. Tan."

11   And my mother was standing in the back whispering loudly, "Why he don't send me check, already two weeks late. So mad he lie to me, losing me money."

12   And then I said in perfect English, "Yes, I'm getting rather concerned. You had agreed to send the check two weeks ago, but it hasn't arrived."

13   Then she began to talk more loudly. "What he want, I come to New York tell him front of his boss, you cheating me?" And I was trying to calm her down, make her be quiet, while telling the stockbroker, "I can't tolerate any more excuses. If I don't receive the check immediately, I am going to have to speak to your manager when I'm in New York next week." And sure enough, the following week there we were in front of this astonished stockbroker, and I was sitting there red-faced and quiet, and my mother, the real Mrs. Tan, was shouting at his boss in her impeccable broken English.

14   We used a similar routine just five days ago, for a situation that was far less humorous. My mother had gone to the hospital for an appointment, to find out about a benign brain tumor a CAT scan had revealed a month ago. She said she had spoken very good English, her best English, no mistakes. Still, she said, the hospital did not apologize when they said they had lost the CAT scan and she had come for nothing. She said they did not seem to have any sympathy when she told them she was anxious to know the exact diagnosis, since her husband and son had both died of brain tumors. She said they would not give her any more information until the next time and she would have to make another appointment for that. So she said she would not leave until the doctor called her daughter. She wouldn't budge. And when the doctor finally called her daughter, me, who spoke in perfect English—lo and behold—we had assurances the CAT scan would be found, promise that a conference call on Monday would be held, and apologies for any suffering my mother had gone through for a most regrettable mistake.

15   I think my mother's English almost had an effect on limiting my possibilities in life as well. Sociologists and linguists probably will tell you that a person's developing language skills are more influenced by peers. But I do think that the language spoken in the family, especially in immigrant families which are more insular, plays a large role in shaping the language of the child. And I believe that it affected my results on achievement tests, IQ tests, and the SAT. While my English skills were never judged as poor, compared to math, English could not be considered my strong suit. In grade school I did moderately well, getting perhaps B's, sometimes B-pluses, in English and scoring perhaps in the sixtieth or seven-

tieth percentile on achievement tests. But those scores were not good enough to override the opinion that my true abilities lay in math and science, because in those areas I achieved A's and scored in the ninetieth percentile or higher.

16   This was understandable. Math is precise; there is only one correct answer. Whereas, for me at least, the answers on English tests were always a judgment call, a matter of opinion and personal experience. Those tests were constructed around items like fill-in-the-blank sentence completion, such as, "Even though Tom was ————, Mary thought he was ————." And the correct answer always seemed to be the most bland combinations of thoughts, for example, "Even though Tom was shy, Mary thought he was charming," with the grammatical structure "even though" limiting the correct answer to some sort of semantic opposites, so you wouldn't get answers like, "Even though Tom was foolish, Mary thought he was ridiculous." Well, according to my mother, there were very few limitations as to what Tom could have been and what Mary might have thought of him. So I never did well on tests like that.

17   The same was true with word analogies, pairs of words in which you were supposed to find some sort of logical, semantic relationship—for example, "*Sunset* is to *nightfall* as ———— is to ————." And here you would be presented with a list of four possible pairs, one of which showed the same kind of relationship: *red* is to *stoplight, bus* is to *arrival, chills* is to *fever, yawn* is to *boring*. Well, I could never think that way. I knew what the tests were asking, but I could not block out of my mind the images already created by the first pair, "*sunset* is to *nightfall*"— and I would see a burst of color against a darkening sky, the moon rising, the lowering of a curtain of stars. And all the other pairs of words—red, bus, stoplight, boring—just threw up a mass of confusing images, making it impossible for me to sort out something as logical as saying: "A sunset precedes nightfall" is the same as "a chill precedes a fever." The only way I would have gotten that answer right would have been to imagine an associative situation, for example, by being disobedient and staying out past sunset, catching a chill at night which turns into feverish pneumonia as punishment, which indeed did happen to me.

18   I have been thinking about all this lately, about my mother's English, about achievement tests. Because lately I've asked, as a writer, why there are not more Asian Americans represented in American literature. Why are there few Asian Americans enrolled in creative writing programs? Why do so many Chinese students go into engineering? Well, these are broad sociological questions I can't begin to answer. But I have noticed in surveys—in fact, just last week—that Asian students, as a whole, always do significantly better on math achievement tests than in English. And this makes me think that there are other Asian-American students whose English spoken in the home might also be described as "broken" or "limited." And perhaps they also have teachers who are steering them away from writing and into math and science, which is what happened to me.

19   Fortunately, I happen to be rebellious in nature and enjoy the challenge of disproving assumptions made about me. I became an English major my first year in college, after being enrolled as pre-med. I started writing nonfiction as a freelancer the week after I was told by my former boss that writing was my worst skill and I should hone my talents toward account management.

20   But it wasn't until 1985 that I finally began to write fiction. And at first I wrote using what I thought to be wittily crafted sentences, sentences that would finally prove I had mastery over the English language. Here's an example from the first draft of a story that later made its way into *The Joy Luck Club,* but without this line: "That was my mental quandary in its nascent state." A terrible line, which I can hardly pronounce.

21   Fortunately, for reasons I won't get into today, I later decided I should envision a reader for the stories I would write. And the reader I decided upon was my mother, because these were stories about mothers. So with this reader in mind— and in fact she did read my early drafts—I began to write stories using all the Englishes I grew up with: the English I spoke to my mother, which for lack of a better term might be described as "simple"; the English she used with me, which for lack of a better term might be described as "broken"; my translation of her Chinese, which could certainly be described as "watered down"; and what I imagine to be her translation of her Chinese if she could speak in perfect English, her internal language, and for that I sought to preserve the essence, but neither an English nor a Chinese structure. I wanted to capture what language ability tests can never reveal: her intent, her passion, her imagery, the rhythms of her speech and the nature of her thoughts.

22   Apart from what any critic had to say about my writing, I knew I had succeeded where it counted when my mother finished reading my book and gave me her verdict: "So easy to read."

QUESTIONS

Experience

- Tan describes how the English she uses with her mother and her husband differs from the language she uses with others in public. To what extent do you use language differently with different groups, on different occasions, in different circumstances? What special forms of language do you use with friends, family, and others you may be intimate with?
- Tan mentions that she had once been ashamed of her mother's English. Have you ever been ashamed of your own use of English or of another's? Why?

Interpretation

- What impression might one get from hearing Tan's mother speak? Does Tan convince you that her mother's "expressive command of English belies how much she actually understands"? Why, or why not?
- Why does Tan reject terms such as "limited," "broken," or "fractured" English to describe her mother's spoken English? Do you agree with her point? Why, or why not?
- What does Tan mean by suggesting that her mother's English nearly limited her own possibilities in life? Do you find Amy Tan's explanation convincing? Why, or why not?

Evaluation

· Why is her mother's English so important to Amy Tan herself—as her mother's daughter and as a writer? What does Tan find especially valuable about her mother's English? Why?

· Do you find Amy Tan's writing in this essay "easy to read"? Why, or why not?

WRITING

Exploring

· Write about your own experience with language. Perhaps you speak or write more than one type or dialect of English. Perhaps you speak or write a language other than English. Write about one or more occasions when your use of language had a significant effect on something that happened to you or on your own or another's feelings.

Interpreting

· Select one aspect of Tan's essay for analysis and interpretation. Identify what you think is one of her most important ideas, and explain how Tan develops and presents it. You may wish to consider, for example, Tan's point about why many Asian American students go into engineering and the sciences. Or her idea that "language spoken in the family, especially in immigrant families . . . plays a large role in shaping the language of the child."

Evaluating

· Write an evaluation of Tan's essay. Assess how well you think she succeeds in conveying her ideas about language. You may wish to consider as well the techniques of writing she uses (her use of example, incident, direct quotation, and the like).

TOM WOLFE
(b. 1931)

The Right Stuff

Tom Wolfe began his career as an academic, earning a doctorate in American Studies at Yale. But his inclination was more journalistic than academic, and he began working as a reporter for the Washington Post *and later as a magazine writer for the now defunct* New York Herald-Tribune. *Wolfe has written articles and essays on trends in popular culture—many of them later collected in books such as* The Kandy-Kolored Tangerine-Flake Streamline Baby *(1965),* The Pump House Gang *(1968), and* Mauve Gloves and Madmen, Clutter and Vine *(1976). His book about the space program,* The Right Stuff *(1979), was made into a movie, as was his only novel,* Bonfire of the Vanities *(1988). In the following chapter from* The Right Stuff, *Wolfe describes the qualities men require to become successful test pilots and astronauts. He describes the community of men who strive to join an even more special fraternity—those with "the right stuff" for success.*

Among the noteworthy stylistic features of The Right Stuff *are its blend of colloquial language with technical terms; its inclusion of some very long sentences; its use of dialogue, italicized words, and repetition; and its emphatic conclusions of paragraphs. Overall, the essay is a stylistic tour de force, a pyrotechnical verbal display akin to the feats and stunts performed by the test pilots, whose world and ways Wolfe so gloriously captures.*

1   A young man might go into military flight training believing that he was entering some sort of technical school in which he was simply going to acquire a certain set of skills. Instead, he found himself all at once enclosed in a fraternity. And in this fraternity, even though it was military, men were not rated by their outward rank as ensigns, lieutenants, commanders, or whatever. No, herein the world was divided into those who had it and those who did not. This quality, this *it,* was never named, however, nor was it talked about in any way.

2   As to just what this ineffable quality was . . . well, it obviously involved bravery. But it was not bravery in the simple sense of being willing to risk your life. The idea seemed to be that any fool could do that, if that was all that was required, just as any fool could throw away his life in the process. No, the idea here (in the all-enclosing fraternity) seemed to be that a man should have the ability to go up in a hurtling piece of machinery and put his hide on the line and then have the moxie, the reflexes, the experience, the coolness, to pull it back in the last yawning moment—and then to go up again *the next day,* and the next day, and every next day, even if the series should prove infinite—and, ultimately, in its best expression, do so in a cause that means something to thousands, to a people, a nation, to humanity, to God. Nor was there *a test* to show whether or not a pilot had this righteous quality. There was, instead, a seemingly infinite series of tests. A career in flying was like climbing one of those ancient Babylonian pyramids

made up of a dizzy progression of steps and ledges, a ziggurat, a pyramid extra-ordinarily high and steep; and the idea was to prove at every foot of the way up that pyramid that you were one of the elected and anointed ones who had *the right stuff* and could move higher and higher and even—ultimately, God willing, one day—that you might be able to join that special few at the very top, that elite who had the capacity to bring tears to men's eyes, the very Brotherhood of the Right Stuff itself.

3   None of this was to be mentioned, and yet it was acted out in a way that a young man could not fail to understand. When a new flight (i.e., a class) of trainees arrived at Pensacola, they were brought into an auditorium for a little lec-ture. An officer would tell them: "Take a look at the man on either side of you." Quite a few actually swiveled their heads this way and that, in the interest of appearing diligent. Then the officer would say: "One of the three of you is not going to make it!"—meaning, not get his wings. That was the opening theme, the *motif* of primary training. We already know that one-third of you do not have the right stuff—it only remains to find out who.

4   Furthermore, that was the way it turned out. At every level in one's progress up that staggeringly high pyramid, the world was once more divided into those men who had the right stuff to continue the climb and those who had to be *left behind* in the most obvious way. Some were eliminated in the course of the open-ing classroom work, as either not smart enough or not hardworking enough, and were left behind. Then came the basic flight instruction, in single-engine, propeller-driven trainers, and a few more—even though the military tried to make this stage easy—were washed out and left behind. Then came more demanding levels, one after the other, formation flying, instrument flying, jet train-ing, all-weather flying, gunnery, and at each level more were washed out and left behind. By this point easily a third of the original candidates had been, indeed, eliminated . . . from the ranks of those who might prove to have the right stuff.

5   In the Navy, in addition to the stages that Air Force trainees went through, the neophyte always had waiting for him, out in the ocean, a certain grim gray slab; namely, the deck of an aircraft carrier; and with it perhaps the most difficult routine in military flying, carrier landings. He was shown films about it, he heard lectures about it, and he knew that carrier landings were hazardous. He first prac-ticed touching down on the shape of a flight deck painted on an airfield. He was instructed to touch down and gun right off. This was safe enough—the shape did-n't move, at least—but it could do terrible things to, let us say, the gyroscope of the soul. *That shape!—it's so damned small!* And more candidates were washed out and left behind. Then came the day, without warning, when those who remained were sent out over the ocean for the first of many days of reckoning with the slab. The first day was always a clear day with little wind and a calm sea. The carrier was so steady that it seemed, from up there in the air, to be resting on pilings, and the candidate usually made his first carrier landing successfully, with relief and even *élan.* Many young candidates looked like terrific aviators up to that very point—and it was not until they were actually standing on the carrier deck that they first began to wonder if they had the proper stuff, after all. In the training film the flight deck was a grand piece of gray geometry, perilous, to be sure, but an amazing abstract shape as one looks down upon it on the screen. And yet once

the newcomer's two feet were on it . . . *Geometry*—my God, man, this is a . . . skillet! It *heaved,* it moved up and down underneath his feet, it pitched up, it pitched down, it rolled to port (this great beast *rolled!*) and it rolled to starboard, as the ship moved into the wind and, therefore, into the waves, and the wind kept sweeping across, sixty feet up in the air out in the open sea, and there were no railings whatsoever. This was a *skillet!*—a frying pan!—a short-order grill!—not gray but black, smeared with skid marks from one end to the other and glistening with pools of hydraulic fluid and the occasional jet-fuel slick, all of it still hot, sticky, greasy, runny, virulent from God knows what traumas—still ablaze!—consumed in detonations, explosions, flames, combustion, roars, shrieks, whines, blasts, horrible shudders, fracturing impacts, as little men in screaming red and yellow and purple and green shirts with black Mickey Mouse helmets over their ears skittered about on the surface as if for their very lives (you've said it now!), hooking fighter planes onto the catapult shuttles so that they can explode their afterburners and be slung off the deck in a red-mad fury with a *kaboom!* that pounds through the entire deck—a procedure that seems absolutely controlled, orderly, sublime, however, compared to what he is about to watch as aircraft return to the ship for what is known in the engineering stoicisms of the military as "recovery and arrest." To say that an F-4 was coming back onto this heaving barbecue from out of the sky at a speed of 135 knots . . . that might have been the truth in the training lecture, but it did not begin to get across the idea of what the newcomer saw from the deck itself, because it created the notion that perhaps the plane was gliding in. On the deck one knew differently! As the aircraft came closer and the carrier heaved on into the waves and the plane's speed did not diminish and the deck did not grow steady—indeed, it pitched up and down five or ten feet per greasy heave—one experienced a neural alarm that no lecture could have prepared him for: This is not an *airplane* coming toward me, it is a brick with some poor sonofabitch riding it *(someone much like myself!),* and it is not *gliding,* it is *falling,* a fifty-thousand-pound brick, headed not for a stripe on the deck but for *me*—and with a horrible *smash!* it hits the skillet, and with a blur of momentum as big as a freight train's it hurtles toward the far end of the deck—another blinding storm!—another roar as the pilot pushes the throttle up to full military power and another smear of rubber screams out over the skillet—and this is nominal!—quite okay!—for a wire stretched across the deck has grabbed the hook on the end of the plane as it hit the deck tail down, and the smash was the rest of the fifteen-ton brute slamming onto the deck, as it tripped up, so that it is now straining against the wire at full throttle, in case it hadn't held and the plane had "boltered" off the end of the deck and had to struggle up into the air again. And already the Mickey Mouse helmets are running toward the fiery monster . . .

6   And the candidate, looking on, begins to *feel* that great heaving sun-blazing deathboard of a deck wallowing in his own vestibular system—and suddenly he finds himself backed up against his own limits. He ends up going to the flight surgeon with so-called conversion symptoms. Overnight he develops blurred vision or numbness in his hands and feet or sinusitis so severe that he cannot tolerate changes in altitude. On one level the symptom is real. He really cannot see too well or use his fingers or stand the pain. But somewhere in his subconscious he knows it is a plea and a beg-off; he shows not the slightest concern (the flight sur-

geon notes) that the condition might be permanent and affect him in whatever life awaits him outside the arena of the right stuff.

7   Those who remained, those who qualified for carrier duty—and even more so those who later on qualified for *night* carrier duty—began to feel a bit like Gideon's warriors. *So many have been left behind!* The young warriors were now treated to a deathly sweet and quite unmentionable sight. They could gaze at length upon the crushed and wilted pariahs who had washed out. They could inspect those who did not have the righteous stuff.

8   The military did not have very merciful instincts. Rather than packing up these poor souls and sending them home, the Navy, like the Air Force and the Marines, would try to make use of them in some other role, such as flight controller. So the washout has to keep taking classes with the rest of his group, even though he can no longer touch an airplane. He sits there in the classes staring at sheets of paper with cataracts of sheer human mortification over his eyes while the rest steal looks at him . . . this man reduced to an ant, this untouchable, this poor son-ofabitch. And in what test had he been found wanting? Why, it seemed to be nothing less than *manhood* itself. Naturally, this was never mentioned, either. Yet there it was. *Manliness, manhood, manly courage* . . . there was something ancient, primordial, irresistible about the challenge of this stuff, no matter what a sophisticated and rational age one might think he lived in.

9   Perhaps because it could not be talked about, the subject began to take on superstitious and even mystical outlines. A man either had it or he didn't! There was no such thing as having *most* of it. Moreover, it could blow at any seam. One day a man would be ascending the pyramid at a terrific clip, and the next—bingo!—he would reach his own limits in the most unexpected way. Conrad and Schirra met an Air Force pilot who had had a great pal at Tyndall Air Force Base in Florida. This man had been the budding ace of the training class; he had flown the hottest fighter-style trainer, the T-38, like a dream; and then he began the routine step of being checked out in the T-33. The T-33 was not nearly as hot an aircraft as the T-38; it was essentially the old P-80 jet fighter. It had an exceedingly small cockpit. The pilot could barely move his shoulders. It was the sort of airplane of which everybody said, "You don't get into it, you *wear* it." Once inside a T-33 cockpit this man, this budding ace, developed claustrophobia of the most para-lyzing sort. He tried everything to overcome it. He even went to a psychiatrist, which was a serious mistake for a military officer if his superiors learned of it. But nothing worked. He was shifted over to flying jet transports, such as the C-135. Very demanding and necessary aircraft they were, too, and he was still spoken of as an excellent pilot. But as everyone knew—and, again, it was never explained in so many words—only those who were assigned to fighter squadrons, the "fighter jocks," as they called each other with a self-satisfied irony, remained in the true fraternity. Those assigned to transports were not humiliated like washouts—*some-body* had to fly those planes—nevertheless, they, too, had been *left behind* for lack of the right stuff.

10   Or a man could go for a routine physical one fine day, feeling like a million dollars, and be grounded for *fallen arches*. It happened!—just like that! (And try raising them.) Or for breaking his wrist and losing only *part* of its mobility. Or for a minor deterioration of eyesight, or for any of hundreds of reasons that would make

no difference to a man in an ordinary occupation. As a result all fighter jocks began looking upon doctors as their natural enemies. Going to see a flight surgeon was a no-gain proposition; a pilot could only hold his own or lose in the doctor's office. To be grounded for a medical reason was no humiliation, looked at objectively. But it was a humiliation, nonetheless!—for it meant you no longer had that indefinable, unutterable, integral stuff. (It could blow at *any* seam.)

11   All the hot young fighter jocks began trying to test the limits themselves in a superstitious way. They were like believing Presbyterians of a century before who used to probe their own experience to see if they were truly among *the elect.* When a fighter pilot was in training, whether in the Navy or the Air Force, his superiors were continually spelling out strict rules for him, about the use of the aircraft and conduct in the sky. They repeatedly forbade so-called hot-dog stunts, such as outside loops, buzzing, flathatting, hedgehopping and flying under bridges. But somehow one got the message that the man who truly *had* it could ignore those rules—not that he should make a point of it, but that he *could*—and that after all there was only one way to find out—and that in some strange unofficial way, peeking through his fingers, his instructor halfway expected him to challenge all the limits. They would give a lecture about how a pilot should never fly without a good solid breakfast—eggs, bacon, toast, and so forth— because if he tried to fly with his blood-sugar level too low, it could impair his alertness. Naturally, the next day every hot dog in the unit would get up and have a breakfast consisting of one cup of black coffee and take off and go up into a vertical climb until the weight of the ship exactly canceled out the upward pull of the engine and his air speed was zero, and he would hang there for one thick adrenal instant—and then fall like a rock, until one of three things happened: he keeled over nose first and regained his aerodynamics and all was well, he went into a spin and fought his way out of it, or he went into a spin and had to eject or crunch it, which was always supremely possible.

12   Likewise, "hassling"—mock dogfighting—was strictly forbidden, and so naturally young fighter jocks could hardly wait to go up in, say, a pair of F-100s and start the duel by making a pass at each other at 800 miles an hour, the winner being the pilot who could slip in behind the other one and get locked in on his tail ("wax his tail"), and it was not uncommon for some eager jock to try too tight an outside turn and have his engine flame out, whereupon, unable to restart it, he has to eject . . . and he shakes his fist at the victor as he floats down by parachute and his half-a-million-dollar aircraft goes *kaboom!* on the palmetto grass or the desert floor, and he starts thinking about how he can get together with the other guy back at the base in time for the two of them to get their stories straight before the investigation: "I don't know what happened, sir. I was pulling up after a target run, and it just flamed out on me." Hassling was forbidden, and hassling that led to the destruction of an aircraft was a serious court-martial offense, and the man's superiors knew that the engine hadn't *just flamed out,* but every unofficial impulse on the base seemed to be saying: "Hell, we wouldn't give you a nickel for a pilot who hasn't done some crazy rat-racing like that. It's all part of the right stuff."

13   The other side of this impulse showed up in the reluctance of the young jocks to admit it when they had maneuvered themselves into a bad corner they couldn't get out of. There were two reasons why a fighter pilot hated to declare an

emergency. First, it triggered a complex and very public chain of events at the field: all other incoming flights were held up, including many of one's comrades who were probably low on fuel; the fire trucks came trundling out to the runway like yellow toys (as seen from way up there), the better to illustrate one's hapless state; and the bureaucracy began to crank up the paper monster for the investigation that always followed. And second, to declare an emergency, one first had to reach that conclusion in his own mind, which to the young pilot was the same as saying: "A minute ago I still *had* it—now I need your help!" To have a bunch of young fighter pilots up in the air thinking this way used to drive flight controllers crazy. They would see a ship beginning to drift off the radar, and they couldn't rouse the pilot on the microphone for anything other than a few meaningless mumbles, and they would know he was probably out there with engine failure at a low altitude, trying to reignite by lowering his auxiliary generator rig, which had a little propeller that was supposed to spin in the slipstream like a child's pinwheel.

14   "Whiskey Kilo Two Eight, do you want to declare an emergency?"

15   *This* would rouse him!—to say: "Negative, negative, Whiskey Kilo Two Eight is not declaring an emergency."

16   Kaboom. Believers in the right stuff would rather crash and burn.

17   One fine day, after he had joined a fighter squadron, it would dawn on the young pilot exactly how the losers in the great fraternal competition were now being left behind. Which is to say, not by instructors or other superiors or by failures at prescribed levels of competence, but by death. At this point the essence of the enterprise would begin to dawn on him. Slowly, step by step, the ante had been raised until he was now involved in what was surely the grimmest and grandest gamble of manhood. Being a fighter pilot—for that matter, simply taking off in a single-engine jet fighter of the Century series, such as an F-102, or any of the military's other marvelous bricks with fins on them—presented a man, on a perfectly sunny day, with more ways to get himself killed than his wife and children could imagine in their wildest fears. If he was barreling down the runway at two hundred miles an hour, completing the takeoff run, and the board started lighting up red, should he (a) abort the takeoff (and try to wrestle with the monster, which was gorged with jet fuel, out in the sand beyond the end of the runway) or (b) eject (and hope that the goddamned human cannonball trick works at zero altitude and he doesn't shatter an elbow or a kneecap on the way out) or (c) continue the takeoff and deal with the problem aloft (knowing full well that the ship may be on fire and therefore seconds away from exploding)? He would have one second to sort out the options and act, and this kind of little workaday decision came up all the time. Occasionally a man would look coldly at the binary problem he was now confronting every day—Right Stuff/Death—and decide it wasn't worth it and voluntarily shift over to transports or reconnaissance or whatever. And his comrades would wonder, for a day or so, what evil virus had invaded his soul . . . as they left him behind. More often, however, the reverse would happen. Some college graduate would enter Navy aviation through the Reserves, simply as an alternative to the Army draft, fully intending to return to civilian life, to some waiting profession or family business; would become involved in the obsessive business of ascending the ziggurat pyramid of flying;

and, at the end of his enlistment, would astound everyone back home and very likely himself as well by signing up for another one. What on earth got into him? He couldn't explain it. After all, the very words for it had been amputated. A Navy study showed that two-thirds of the fighter pilots who were rated in the top rungs of their groups—i.e., the hottest young pilots—reenlisted when the time came, and practically all were college graduates. By this point, a young fighter jock was like the preacher in *Moby Dick* who climbs up into the pulpit on a rope ladder and then pulls the ladder up behind him; except the pilot could not use the words necessary to express the vital lessons. Civilian life, and even home and hearth, now seemed not only far away but far *below,* back down many levels of the pyramid of the right stuff.

18   A fighter pilot soon found he wanted to associate only with other fighter pilots. Who else could understand the nature of the little proposition (right stuff/death) they were all dealing with? And what other subject could compare with it? It was riveting! To talk about it in so many words was forbidden, of course. The very words *death, danger, bravery, fear* were not to be uttered except in the occasional specific instance or for ironic effect. Nevertheless, the subject could be adumbrated in *code* or *by example.* Hence the endless evenings of pilots huddled together talking about flying. On these long and drunken evenings (the bane of their family life) certain theorems would be propounded and demonstrated— and all by *code* and *example.* One theorem was: There are no *accidents* and no fatal flaws in the machines; there are only pilots with the wrong stuff. (I.e., blind Fate can't kill me.) When Bud Jennings crashed and burned in the swamps at Jacksonville, the other pilots in Peter Conrad's squadron said: *How could he have been so stupid?* It turned out that Jennings had gone up in the SNJ with his cockpit canopy opened in a way that was expressly forbidden in the manual, and carbon monoxide had been sucked in from the exhaust, and he passed out and crashed. All agreed that Bud Jennings was a good guy and a good pilot, but his epitaph on the ziggurat was: *How could he have been so stupid?* This seemed shocking at first, but by the time Conrad had reached the end of that bad string at Pax River, he was capable of his own corollary to the theorem: viz., no single factor ever killed a pilot; there was always a chain of mistakes. But what about Ted Whelan, who fell like a rock from 8,100 feet when his parachute failed? Well, the parachute was merely part of the chain: first, someone should have caught the structural defect that resulted in the hydraulic leak that triggered the emergency; second, Whelan did not check out his seat-parachute rig, and the drogue failed to separate the main parachute from the seat; but even after those two mistakes, Whelan had fifteen or twenty seconds, as he fell, to disengage himself from the seat and open the parachute manually. Why just stare at the scenery coming up to smack you in the face! And everyone nodded. (He failed—but I wouldn't have!) Once the theorem and the corollary were understood, the Navy's statistics about one in every four Navy aviators dying meant nothing. The figures were averages, and averages applied to those with average stuff.

19   A riveting subject, especially if it were one's own hide that was on the line. Every evening at bases all over America, there were military pilots huddled in officers clubs eagerly cutting the right stuff up in coded slices so they could talk about it. What more compelling topic of conversation was there in the world? In the Air

Force there were even pilots who would ask the tower for priority landing clear-
ance so that they could make the beer call on time, at 4 P.M. sharp, at the Officers
Club. They would come right out and state the reason. The drunken rambles began
at four and sometimes went on for ten or twelve hours. Such conversations! They
diced that righteous stuff up into little bits, bowed ironically to it, stumbled blindfolded around it, groped, lurched, belched, staggered, bawled, sang, roared, and
feinted at it with self-deprecating humor. Nevertheless!—they never mentioned it
by name. No, they used the approved codes, such as: "Like a jerk I got myself
into a hell of a corner today." They told of how they "lucked out of it." To get
across the extreme peril of his exploit, one would use certain oblique cues. He
would say, "I looked over at Robinson"—who would be known to the listeners as
a non-com who sometimes rode backseat to read radar—"and he wasn't talking
any more, he was just staring at the radar, like this, giving it that *zombie* look.
Then I *knew* I was in trouble." Beautiful! Just right! For it would also be known to
the listeners that the non-coms advised one another: "*Never* fly with a lieutenant.
Avoid captains and majors. Hell, man, do yourself a favor: don't fly with anybody
below colonel." Which in turn said: "Those young bucks shoot dice with death!"
And yet once in the air the non-com had his own standards. He was determined
to remain as outwardly cool as the pilot, so that when the pilot did something
that truly petrified him, he would say nothing; instead, he would turn silent, cata-
tonic, like a zombie. Perfect! *Zombie.* There you had it, compressed into a single
word all of the foregoing. I'm a hell of a pilot! I shoot dice with death! And now all
you fellows know it! And I haven't spoken of that unspoken stuff even once!

20   The talking and drinking began at the beer call, and then the boys would
break for dinner and come back afterward and get more wasted and more garru-
lous or else more quietly fried, drinking good cheap PX booze until 2 A.M. The
night was young! Why not get the cars and go out for a little proficiency run? It
seemed that every fighter jock thought himself an ace driver, and he would do
anything to obtain a hot car, especially a sports car, and the drunker he was, the
more convinced he would be about his driving skills, as if the right stuff, being
indivisible, carried over into any enterprise whatsoever, under any conditions. A
little proficiency run, boys! (There's only one way to find out!) And they would
roar off in close formation from, say, Nellis Air Force Base, down Route 15, into Las
Vegas, barreling down the highway, rat-racing, sometimes four abreast, jockeying
for position, piling into the most listless curve in the desert flats as if they were trying to root each other out of the groove at the Rebel 500—and then bursting into
downtown Las Vegas with a rude fraternal roar like the Hell's Angels—and the
natives chalked it up to youth and drink and the bad element that the Air Force
attracted. They knew nothing about the right stuff, of course.

21   More fighter pilots died in automobiles than in airplanes. Fortunately, there
was always some kindly soul up the chain to certify the papers "line of duty," so
that the widow could get a better break on the insurance. That was okay and only
proper because somehow the system itself had long ago said *Skol!* and *Quite
right!* to the military cycle of Flying & Drinking and Drinking & Driving, as if there
were no other way. Every young fighter jock knew the feeling of getting two or
three hours' sleep and then waking up at 5:30 A.M. and having a few cups of coffee, a few cigarettes, and then carting his poor quivering liver out to the field for

another day of flying. There were those who arrived not merely hungover but still drunk, slapping oxygen tank cones over their faces and trying to burn the alcohol out of their systems, and then going up, remarking later: "I don't *advise* it, you understand, but it *can* be done." (Provided you have the right stuff, you miserable pudknocker.)

22   Air Force and Navy airfields were usually on barren or marginal stretches of land and would have looked especially bleak and Low Rent to an ordinary individual in the chilly light of dawn. But to a young pilot there was an inexplicable bliss to coming out to the flight line while the sun was just beginning to cook up behind the rim of the horizon, so that the whole field was still in shadow and the ridges in the distance were in silhouette and the flight line was a monochrome of Exhaust Fume Blue, and every little red light on top of the water towers or power stanchions looked dull, shriveled, congealed, and the runway lights, which were still on, looked faded, and even the landing lights on a fighter that had just landed and was taxiing in were no longer dazzling, as they would be at night, and looked instead like shriveled gobs of candlepower out there—and yet it was beautiful, exhilarating!—for he was revved up with adrenalin, anxious to take off before the day broke, to burst up into the sunlight over the ridges before all those thousands of comatose souls down there, still dead to the world, snug in home and hearth, even came to their senses. To take off in an F-100F at dawn and cut on the afterburner and hurtle twenty-five thousand feet up into the sky in thirty seconds, so suddenly that you felt not like a bird but like a trajectory, yet with full control, full control of *four tons* of thrust, all of which flowed from your will and through your fingertips, with the huge engine right beneath you, so close that it was as if you were riding it bareback, until all at once you were supersonic, an event registered on earth by a tremendous cracking boom that shook windows, but up here only by the fact that you now felt utterly free of the earth—to describe it, even to wife, child, near ones and dear ones, seemed impossible. So the pilot kept it to himself, along with an even more indescribable . . . an even more sinfully inconfessable . . . feeling of superiority, appropriate to him and to his kind, lone bearers of the right stuff.

23   From *up here* at dawn the pilot looked down upon poor hopeless Las Vegas (or Yuma, Corpus Christi, Meridian, San Bernardino, or Dayton) and began to wonder. How can all of them down there, those poor souls who will soon be waking up and trudging out of their minute rectangles and inching along their little noodle highways toward whatever slots and grooves make up their everyday lives—how could they live like that, with such earnestness, if they had the faintest idea of what it was like up here in this righteous zone?

24   But of course! Not only the washed-out, grounded, and dead pilots had been left behind—but also all of those millions of sleepwalking souls who never even attempted the great gamble. The entire world below . . . *left behind.* Only at this point can one begin to understand just how big, how titanic, the ego of the military pilot could be. The world was used to enormous egos in artists, actors, entertainers of all sorts, in politicians, sports figures, and even journalists, because they had such familiar and convenient ways to show them off. But that slim young man over there in uniform, with the enormous watch on his wrist and the withdrawn look on his face, that young officer who is so shy that he can't even open his

mouth unless the subject is flying—that young pilot—well, my friends, his ego is even *bigger!*—so big, it's *breathtaking!* Even in the 1950's it was difficult for civilians to comprehend such a thing, but *all* military officers and many enlisted men tended to feel superior to civilians. It was really quite ironic, given the fact that for a good thirty years the rising business classes in the cities had been steering their sons away from the military, as if from a bad smell, and the officer corps had never been held in lower esteem. Well, career officers returned the contempt in trumps. They looked upon themselves as men who lived by higher standards of behavior than civilians, as men who were the bearers and protectors of the most important values of American life, who maintained a sense of discipline while civilians abandoned themselves to hedonism, who maintained a sense of honor while civilians lived by opportunism and greed. Opportunism and greed: there you had your much-vaunted corporate business world. Khrushchev was right about one thing: when it came time to hang the capitalist West, an American businessman would sell him the rope. When the showdown came—and the showdowns always came—not all the wealth in the world or all the sophisticated nuclear weapons and radar and missile systems it could buy would take the place of those who had the uncritical willingness to face danger, those who, in short, had the right stuff.

25   In fact, the feeling was so righteous, so exalted, it could become religious. Civilians seldom understood this, either. There was no one to teach them. It was no longer the fashion for serious writers to describe the glories of war. Instead, they dwelt upon its horrors, often with cynicism or disgust. It was left to the occasional pilot with a literary flair to provide a glimpse of the pilot's self-conception in its heavenly or spiritual aspect. When a pilot named Robert Scott flew his P-43 over Mount Everest, quite a feat at the time, he brought his hand up and snapped a salute to his fallen adversary. He thought he had *defeated* the mountain, surmounting all the forces of nature that had made it formidable. And why not? "God is my co-pilot," he said—that became the title of his book—and he meant it. So did the most gifted of all the pilot authors, the Frenchman Antoine de Saint-Exupéry. As he gazed down upon the world . . . from up there . . . during transcontinental flights, the good Saint-Ex saw civilization as a series of tiny fragile patches clinging to the otherwise barren rock of Earth. He felt like a lonely sentinel, a protector of those vulnerable little oases, ready to lay down his life in their behalf, if necessary; a saint, in short, true to his name, flying up here at the right hand of God. The good Saint-Ex! And he was not the only one. He was merely the one who put it into words most beautifully and anointed himself before the altar of the right stuff.

QUESTIONS

Experience

· Describe your experience of reading Wolfe's essay, especially what it is like to read sentences with numerous italicized words, ellipses (. . .), exclamation points (!), quotation marks, and dashes.
· Relate Wolfe's description of how the test pilots formed a tight-knit group to

your own experience of belonging to some kind of special group (a sports team, perhaps, or a special club or organization).

Interpretation

· Explain just what "the right stuff" is that Wolfe shows test pilots need to succeed.

· Explain what Wolfe means by saying that the men were in "an enclosing fraternity." How does that fact affect their view of themselves? How does it affect their behavior?

· What is Wolfe's attitude toward the test pilots? Is he praising them? Celebrating them? Criticizing them? Satirizing them? Something else? How do you know?

Evaluation

· What do you think of Wolfe's verbal high jinks, his extravagant style of writing? Are you impressed with how Wolfe handles language, are you confused by it, or are you simply uninterested? Why?

· What social and cultural values do the pilots espouse? (What is most important to them?) Does Wolfe share these values? Why, or why not?

WRITING

Exploring

· Write your own essay about a group you have observed or about one you belong to. Try to give your readers a sense of what it is like to be a member of this group.

Interpreting

· Analyze Wolfe's essay to show how he achieves the effects he does. Identify what you see as the primary effects Wolfe does achieve. Then identify and illustrate the techniques he uses to achieve them. (Consider such things as the kinds of words he uses, the types and lengths of his sentences, his use of punctuation, his comparisons, and so on.)

Evaluating

· Write an essay responding to the values Wolfe associates with the pilots. Agree or disagree with what he says about them. Support, qualify, or argue against the image of the pilots he creates.

MAXINE HONG KINGSTON
(b. 1940)

Silence

Maxine Hong Kingston was raised in the Chinese American community of Stockton, California, and graduated from the University of California. Her first two books, The Woman Warrior *(1976) and* China Men *(1980), brought her literary recognition and a measure of fame. She has also published a novel,* The Tripmaster Monkey *(1992). The first two works blend fact and fiction in strikingly original ways. In the selection that follows, taken from* The Woman Warrior, *Kingston describes her first experiences speaking English and her strategies for keeping silent.*

Kingston uses the contrast between silence and noise as one of her organizing principles. She contrasts the ability of the native speakers to break silence with her own keeping of it. And she contrasts her silence in American kindergarten with her comfortable speech at Chinese school, one example of the cultural contrasts Kingston describes. Kingston renders this contrast of cultures with precisely drawn examples such as the differences between the letter "I" in English and Chinese.

1   When I went to kindergarten and had to speak English for the first time, I became silent. A dumbness—a shame—still cracks my voice in two, even when I want to say "hello" casually, or ask an easy question in front of the checkout counter, or ask directions of a bus driver. I stand frozen, or I hold up the line with the complete, grammatical sentence that comes squeaking out at impossible length. "What did you say?" says the cab driver, or "Speak up," so I have to perform again, only weaker the second time. A telephone call makes my throat bleed and takes up that day's courage. It spoils my day with self-disgust when I hear my broken voice come skittering out into the open. It makes people wince to hear it. I'm getting better, though. Recently I asked the postman for special-issue stamps; I've waited since childhood for postmen to give me some of their own accord. I am making progress, a little every day.

2   My silence was thickest—total—during the three years that I covered my school paintings with black paint. I painted layers of black over houses and flowers and suns, and when I drew on the blackboard, I put a layer of chalk on top. I was making a stage curtain, and it was the moment before the curtain parted or rose. The teachers called my parents to school, and I saw they had been saving my pictures, curling and cracking, all alike and black. The teachers pointed to the pictures and looked serious, talked seriously too, but my parents did not understand English. ("The parents and teachers of criminals were executed," said my father.) My parents took the pictures home. I spread them out (so black and full of possibilities) and pretended the curtains were swinging open, flying up, one after another, sunlight underneath, mighty operas.

3   During the first silent year I spoke to no one at school, did not ask before

going to the lavatory, and flunked kindergarten. My sister also said nothing for three years, silent in the playground and silent at lunch. There were other quiet Chinese girls not of our family, but most of them got over it sooner than we did. I enjoyed the silence. At first it did not occur to me I was supposed to talk or to pass kindergarten. I talked at home and to one or two of the Chinese kids in class. I made motions and even made some jokes. I drank out of a toy saucer when the water spilled out of the cup, and everybody laughed, pointing at me, so I did it some more. I didn't know that Americans don't drink out of saucers.

4   I liked the Negro students (Black Ghosts) best because they laughed the loudest and talked to me as if I were a daring talker too. One of the Negro girls had her mother coil braids over her ears Shanghai-style like mine; we were Shanghai twins except that she was covered with black like my paintings. Two Negro kids enrolled in Chinese school, and the teachers gave them Chinese names. Some Negro kids walked me to school and home, protecting me from the Japanese kids, who hit me and chased me and stuck gum in my ears. The Japanese kids were noisy and tough. They appeared one day in kindergarten, released from concentration camp, which was a tic-tac-toe mark, like barbed wire, on the map.

5   It was when I found out I had to talk that school become a misery, that the silence became a misery. I did not speak and felt bad each time that I did not speak. I read aloud in first grade, though, and heard the barest whisper with little squeaks come out of my throat. "Louder," said the teacher, who scared the voice away again. The other Chinese girls did not talk either, so I knew the silence had to do with being a Chinese girl.

6   Reading out loud was easier than speaking because we did not have to make up what to say, but I stopped often, and the teacher would think I'd gone quiet again. I could not understand "I." The Chinese "I" has seven strokes, intricacies. How could the American "I," assuredly wearing a hat like the Chinese, have only three strokes, the middle so straight? Was it out of politeness that this writer left off the strokes the way a Chinese has to write her own name small and crooked? No, it was not politeness; "I" is a capital and "you" is lower-case. I stared at that middle line and waited so long for its black center to resolve into tight strokes and dots that I forgot to pronounce it. The other troublesome word was "here," no strong consonant to hang on to, and so flat, when "here" is two mountainous ideographs. The teacher, who had already told me every day how to read "I" and "here," put me in the low corner under the stairs again, where the noisy boys usually sat.

7   When my second grade class did a play, the whole class went to the auditorium except the Chinese girls. The teacher, lovely and Hawaiian, should have understood about us, but instead left us behind in the classroom. Our voices were too soft or nonexistent, and our parents never signed the permission slips anyway. They never signed anything unnecessary. We opened the door a crack and peeked out, but closed it again quickly. One of us (not me) won every spelling bee, though.

8   I remember telling the Hawaiian teacher, "We Chinese can't sing 'land where our fathers died.' " She argued with me about politics, while I meant because of curses. But how can I have that memory when I couldn't talk? My mother says that we, like the ghosts, have no memories.

9   After American school, we picked up our cigar boxes, in which we had arranged books, brushes, and an inkbox neatly, and went to Chinese school, from 5:00 to 7:30 P.M. There we changed together, voices rising and falling, loud and soft, some boys shouting, everybody reading together, reciting together and not alone with one voice. When we had a memorization test, the teacher let each of us come to his desk and say the lesson to him privately, while the rest of the class practiced copying or tracing. Most of the teachers were men. The boys who were so well behaved in the American school played tricks on them and talked back to them. The girls were not mute. They screamed and yelled during recess, when there were no rules; they had fistfights. Nobody was afraid of children hurting themselves or of children hurting school property. The glass doors to the red and green balconies with the gold joy symbols were left wide open so that we could run out and climb the fire escapes. We played capture-the-flag in the auditorium, where Sun Yat-sen and Chiang Kai-shek's pictures hung at the back of the stage, the Chinese flag on their left and the American flag on their right. We climbed the teak ceremonial chairs and made flying leaps off the stage. One flag headquarters was behind the glass door and the other on stage right. Our feet drummed on the hollow stage. During recess the teachers locked themselves up in their office with the shelves of books, copybooks, inks from China. They drank tea and warmed their hands at a stove. There was no play supervision. At recess we had the school to ourselves, and also we could roam as far as we could go—downtown, Chinatown stores, home—as long as we returned before the bell rang.

10   At exactly 7:30 the teacher again picked up the brass bell that sat on his desk and swung it over our heads, while we charged down the stairs, our cheering magnified in the stairwell. Nobody had to line up.

11   Not all of the children who were silent at American school found voice at Chinese school. One new teacher said each of us had to get up and recite in front of the class, who was to listen. My sister and I had memorized the lesson perfectly. We said it to each other at home, one chanting, one listening. The teacher called on my sister to recite first. It was the first time a teacher had called on the second-born to go first. My sister was scared. She glanced at me and looked away; I looked down at my desk. I hoped that she could do it because if she could, then I would have to. She opened her mouth and a voice came out that wasn't a whisper, but it wasn't a proper voice either. I hoped that she would not cry, fear breaking up her voice like twigs underfoot. She sounded as if she were trying to sing through weeping and strangling. She did not pause or stop to end the embarrassment. She kept going until she said the last word, and then she sat down. When it was my turn, the same voice came out, a crippled animal running on broken legs. You could hear splinters in my voice, bones rubbing jagged against one another. I was loud, though. I was glad I didn't whisper.

12   How strange that the emigrant villagers are shouters, hollering face to face. My father asks, "Why is it I can hear Chinese from blocks away? Is it that I understand the language? Or is it they talk loud?" They turn the radio up full blast to hear the operas, which do not seem to hurt their ears. And they yell over the singers that wail over the drums, everybody talking at once, big arm gestures, spit flying. You can see the disgust on American faces looking at women like that. It isn't just the loudness. It is the way Chinese sounds, ching-chong ugly, to Amer-

ican ears, not beautiful like Japanese sayonara words with the consonants and vowels as regular as Italian. We make guttural peasant noise and have Ton Duc Thang names you can't remember. And the Chinese can't hear Americans at all; the language is too soft and western music unhearable. I've watched a Chinese audience laugh, visit, talk-story, and holler during a piano recital, as if the musician could not hear them. A Chinese-American, somebody's son, was playing Chopin, which has no punctuation, no cymbals, no gongs. Chinese piano music is five black keys. Normal Chinese women's voices are strong and bossy. We American-Chinese girls had to whisper to make ourselves American-feminine. Apparently we whispered even more softly than the Americans. Once a year the teachers referred my sister and me to speech therapy, but our voices would straighten out, unpredictably normal, for the therapists. Some of us gave up, shook our heads, and said nothing, not one word. Some of us could not even shake our heads. At times shaking my head no is more self-assertion than I can manage. Most of us eventually found some voice, however faltering. We invented an American-feminine speaking personality.

QUESTIONS

Experience

· Think back to times in your own life when you preferred silence over speech. Why might you have wanted to avoid speaking? Was that possible? Necessary? Why, or why not? Consider in particular your use of language and silence in school, in unfamiliar situations, among strangers, and so on.

Interpretation

· Kingston suggests that her silence was not peculiar to her—that instead, "the silence had to do with being a Chinese girl." Do you think her gender or her race and ethnicity were more important? Why?
· What point does Kingston make with her reference to the letter "I"? Why does it pose a problem for her and other Chinese American girls as well?
· One of the structural principles of this selection is the contrast Kingston sets up between silence and noise. Identify and explain the significant features of the noise-silence contrast.

Evaluation

· At one point Kingston says that she and her friends "invented an American-feminine speaking personality." Do you think this was a good thing to do? Why, or why not?
· Kingston compares the sounds of Chinese with the sounds of Japanese when she writes that "it is the way Chinese sounds, ching-chong ugly, to American ears, not beautiful like Japanese sayonara words with the consonants and vowels as regular as Italian." Consider what aspects of language you value; or consider what aspects of language the cultural group you belong to values.

WRITING

Exploring

· Discuss a time when you were more comfortable with silence than with speech. Identify the circumstances; describe your feelings; and explain how and why you moved from silence to speech—or how and why you did not.

Interpreting

· Analyze the way Kingston develops her ideas about silence. You may wish to consider her use of contrast, her use of examples, or her references to different racial and ethnic groups.

· Identify and explain the major differences Kingston singles out between Chinese and American ways of speaking.

Evaluating

· Discuss how attitudes toward language and ways of using it differ among different groups of people. You may wish to elaborate on differences between Chinese and Americans in this respect, or you may wish to focus on smaller groups—family versus friends, for example, or school versus home.

ALICE WALKER
(b. 1944)

*In Search of
Our Mothers' Gardens*

Alice Walker was born in Georgia, the youngest of eight children of black sharecroppers. She attended Spelman College and Sarah Lawrence College, from which she graduated with a B.A. During her college years she became deeply involved in the Civil Rights Movement, and she participated in a variety of social programs—working for voter registration, welfare rights, and Head Start. She has taught at Jackson State College, Wellesley College, Brandeis University, and the University of California at Berkeley. Throughout her life Walker has exhibited a confidence, learned from her mother, that will not be shaken by discouragement or doubt. Through her work as a poet, novelist, essayist, editor, speaker, and teacher, Walker has consistently revealed an ability to see things fresh and to see them whole.

"In Search of Our Mothers' Gardens," though originally presented as a talk, is a carefully wrought essay. One of its most striking features is its rich range of reference. Walker includes references to the African American writers Jean Toomer, Phillis Wheatley, and Zora Neale Hurston; the African poet Okot p'Bitek; and the English novelist and essayist Virginia Woolf. Walker also includes references to one of her own novels. She includes a short poem she wrote and a description of an anonymously made quilt that hangs in the Smithsonian Institution in Washington, D.C. This quilt serves as an image of Walker's essay, itself quilted out of the many patches of reference and quotation Walker introduces into it, not the least of which is her mother's stunning garden, which Walker celebrates in the essay's title and in the most lyrical prose passage in the essay.

> I described her own nature and temperament. Told how they needed a larger life for their expression. . . . I pointed out that in lieu of proper channels, her emotions had overflowed into paths that dissipated them. I talked, beautifully I thought, about an art that would be born, an art that would open the way for women the likes of her. I asked her to hope, and build up an inner life against the coming of that day. . . . I sang, with a strange quiver in my voice, a promise song.
>
> —"AVEY," JEAN TOOMER, *Cane*
> *The poet speaking to a prostitute who falls
> asleep while he's talking*

1 When the poet Jean Toomer walked through the South in the early twenties, he discovered a curious thing: black women whose spirituality was so intense, so deep, so *unconscious*, they were themselves unaware of the richness they held. They stumbled blindly through their lives: creatures so abused and mutilated in body, so dimmed and confused by pain, that they considered them-

selves unworthy even of hope. In the selfless abstractions their bodies became to the men who used them, they became more than "sexual objects," more even than mere women; they became "Saints." Instead of being perceived as whole persons, their bodies became shrines: what was thought to be their minds became temples suitable for worship. These crazy Saints stared out at the world, wildly, like lunatics—or quietly, like suicides; and the "God" that was in their gaze was as mute as a great stone.

2   Who were these Saints? These crazy, loony, pitiful women?

3   Some of them, without a doubt, were our mothers and grandmothers.

4   In the still heat of the post-Reconstruction South, this is how they seemed to Jean Toomer: exquisite butterflies trapped in an evil honey, toiling away their lives in an era, a century, that did not acknowledge them, except as "the *mule* of the world." They dreamed dreams that no one knew—not even themselves, in any coherent fashion—and saw visions no one could understand. They wandered or sat about the countryside crooning lullabies to ghosts, and drawing the mother of Christ in charcoal on courthouse walls.

5   They forced their minds to desert their bodies and their striving spirits sought to rise, like frail whirlwinds from the hard red clay. And when those frail whirlwinds fell, in scattered particles, upon the ground, no one mourned. Instead, men lit candles to celebrate the emptiness that remained, as people do who enter a beautiful but vacant space to resurrect a God.

6   Our mothers and grandmothers, some of them: moving to music not yet written. And they waited.

7   They waited for a day when the unknown thing that was in them would be made known; but guessed, somehow in their darkness, that on the day of their revelation they would be long dead. Therefore to Toomer they walked, and even ran, in slow motion. For they were going nowhere immediate, and the future was not yet within their grasp. And men took our mothers and grandmothers, "but got no pleasure from it." So complex was their passion and their calm.

8   To Toomer, they lay vacant and fallow as autumn fields, with harvest time never in sight: and he saw them enter loveless marriages, without joy; and become prostitutes, without resistance; and become mothers of children, without fulfillment.

9   For these grandmothers and mothers of ours were not Saints, but Artists; driven to a numb and bleeding madness by the springs of creativity in them for which there was no release. They were Creators, who lived lives of spiritual waste, because they were so rich in spirituality—which is the basis of Art—that the strain of enduring their unused and unwanted talent drove them insane. Throwing away this spirituality was their pathetic attempt to lighten the soul to a weight their work-worn, sexually abused bodies could bear.

10   What did it mean for a black woman to be an artist in our grandmothers' time? In our great-grandmothers' day? It is a question with an answer cruel enough to stop the blood.

11   Did you have a genius of a great-great-grandmother who died under some ignorant and depraved white overseer's lash? Or was she required to bake biscuits for a lazy backwater tramp, when she cried out in her soul to paint watercolors of sunsets, or the rain falling on the green and peaceful pasturelands? Or was

her body broken and forced to bear children (who were more often than not sold away from her)—eight, ten, fifteen, twenty children—when her one joy was the thought of modeling heroic figures of rebellion, in stone or clay?

12   How was the creativity of the black woman kept alive, year after year and century after century, when for most of the years black people have been in America, it was a punishable crime for a black person to read or write? And the freedom to paint, to sculpt, to expand the mind with action did not exist. Consider, if you can bear to imagine it, what might have been the result if singing, too, had been forbidden by law. Listen to the voices of Bessie Smith, Billie Holiday, Nina Simone, Roberta Flack, and Aretha Franklin, among others, and imagine those voices muzzled for life. Then you may begin to comprehend the lives of our "crazy," "Sainted" mothers and grandmothers. The agony of the lives of women who might have been Poets, Novelists, Essayists, and Short-Story Writers (over a period of centuries), who died with their real gifts stifled within them.

13   And, if this were the end of the story, we would have cause to cry out in my paraphrase of Okot p'Bitek's great poem:

> O, my clanswomen
> Let us all cry together!
> Come,
> Let us mourn the death of our mother,
> The death of a Queen
> The ash that was produced
> By a great fire!
> O, this homestead is utterly dead
> Close the gates
> With *lacari* thorns,
> For our mother
> The creator of the Stool is lost!
> And all the young men
> Have perished in the wilderness!

14   But this is not the end of the story, for all the young women—our mothers and grandmothers, *ourselves*—have not perished in the wilderness. And if we ask ourselves why, and search for and find the answer, we will know beyond all efforts to erase it from our minds, just exactly who, and of what, we black American women are.

15   One example, perhaps the most pathetic, most misunderstood one, can provide a backdrop for our mothers' work: Phillis Wheatley, a slave in the 1700s.

16   Virginia Woolf, in her book *A Room of One's Own,* wrote that in order for a woman to write fiction she must have two things, certainly: a room of her own (with key and lock) and enough money to support herself.

17   What then are we to make of Phillis Wheatley, a slave, who owned not even herself? This sickly, frail black girl who required a servant of her own at times—her health was so precarious—and who, had she been white, would have been easily considered the intellectual superior of all the women and most of the men in the society of her day.

18   Virginia Woolf wrote further, speaking of course not of our Phillis, that "any woman born with a great gift in the sixteenth century [insert "eighteenth century,"

insert "black woman," insert "born or made a slave"] would certainly have gone crazed, shot herself, or ended her days in some lonely cottage outside the village, half witch, half wizard [insert "Saint"], feared and mocked at. For it needs little skill and psychology to be sure that a highly gifted girl who had tried to use her gift of poetry would have been so thwarted and hindered by contrary instincts [add "chains, guns, the lash, the ownership of one's body by someone else, submission to an alien religion"], that she must have lost her health and sanity to a certainty."

19   The key words, as they relate to Phillis, are "contrary instincts." For when we read the poetry of Phillis Wheatley—as when we read the novels of Nella Larsen or the oddly false-sounding autobiography of that freest of all black women writers, Zora Hurston—evidence of "contrary instincts" is everywhere. Her loyalties were completely divided, as was, without question, her mind.

20   But how could this be otherwise? Captured at seven, a slave of wealthy, doting whites who instilled in her the "savagery" of the Africa they "rescued" her from . . . one wonders if she was even able to remember her homeland as she had known it, or as it really was.

21   Yet, because she did try to use her gift for poetry in a world that made her a slave, she was "so thwarted and hindered by . . . contrary instincts, that she . . . lost her health. . . ." In the last years of her brief life, burdened not only with the need to express her gift but also with a penniless, friendless "freedom" and several small children for whom she was forced to do strenuous work to feed, she lost her health, certainly. Suffering from malnutrition and neglect and who knows what mental agonies, Phillis Wheatley died.

22   So torn by "contrary instincts" was black, kidnapped, enslaved Phillis that her description of "the Goddess"—as she poetically called the Liberty she did not have—is ironically, cruelly humorous. And, in fact, has held Phillis up to ridicule for more than a century. It is usually read prior to hanging Phillis's memory as that of a fool. She wrote:

> The Goddess comes, she moves divinely fair,
> Olive and laurel binds her *golden* hair.
> Wherever shines this native of the skies,
> Unnumber'd charms and recent graces rise. [My italics]

23   It is obvious that Phillis, the slave, combed the "Goddess's" hair every morning; prior, perhaps, to bringing in the milk, or fixing her mistress's lunch. She took her imagery from the one thing she saw elevated above all others.

24   With the benefit of hindsight we ask, "How could she?"

25   But at last, Phillis, we understand. No more snickering when your stiff, struggling, ambivalent lines are forced on us. We know now that you were not an idiot or a traitor; only a sickly little black girl, snatched from your home and country and made a slave; a woman who still struggled to sing the song that was your gift, although in a land of barbarians who praised you for your bewildered tongue. It is not so much what you sang, as that you kept alive, in so many of our ancestors, *the notion of song.*

26   Black women are called, in the folklore that so aptly identified one's status in society, "the *mule* of the world," because we have been handed the burdens that

everyone else—*everyone* else—refused to carry. We have also been called "Matri-archs," "Superwomen," and "Mean and Evil Bitches." Not to mention "Castraters" and "Sapphire's Mama." When we have pleaded for understanding, our character has been distorted; when we have asked for simple caring, we have been handed empty inspirational appellations, then stuck in the farthest corner. When we have asked for love, we have been given children. In short, even our plainer gifts, our labors of fidelity and love, have been knocked down our throats. To be an artist and a black woman, even today, lowers our status in many respects, rather than raises it: and yet, artists we will be.

27   Therefore we must fearlessly pull out of ourselves and look at and identify with our lives the living creativity some of our great-grandmothers were not allowed to know. I stress *some* of them because it is well known that the majority of our great-grandmothers knew, even without "knowing" it, the reality of their spirituality, even if they didn't recognize it beyond what happened in the singing at church—and they never had any intention of giving it up.

28   How they did it—those millions of black women who were not Phillis Wheat-ley, or Lucy Terry or Frances Harper or Zora Hurston or Nella Larsen or Bessie Smith; or Elizabeth Catlett, or Katherine Dunham, either—brings me to the title of this essay, "In Search of Our Mothers' Gardens," which is a personal account that is yet shared, in its theme and its meaning, by all of us. I found, while thinking about the far-reaching world of the creative black woman, that often the truest answer to a question that really matters can be found very close.

29 In the late 1920s my mother ran away from home to marry my father. Marriage, if not running away, was expected of seventeen-year-old girls. By the time she was twenty, she had two children and was pregnant with a third. Five children later, I was born. And this is how I came to know my mother: she seemed a large, soft, loving-eyed woman who was rarely impatient in our home. Her quick, violent temper was on view only a few times a year, when she battled with the white landlord who had the misfortune to suggest to her that her children did not need to go to school.

30   She made all the clothes we wore, even my brothers' overalls. She made all the towels and sheets we used. She spent the summers canning vegetables and fruits. She spent the winter evenings making quilts enough to cover all our beds.

31   During the "working" day, she labored beside—not behind—my father in the fields. Her day began before sunup, and did not end until late at night. There was never a moment for her to sit down, undisturbed, to unravel her own private thoughts; never a time free from interruption—by work or the noisy inquiries of her many children. And yet, it is to my mother—and all our mothers who were not famous—that I went in search of the secret of what has fed that muzzled and often mutilated, but vibrant, creative spirit that the black woman has inherited, and that pops out in wild and unlikely places to this day.

32   But when, you will ask, did my overworked mother have time to know or care about feeding the creative spirit?

33   The answer is so simple that many of us have spent years discovering it. We have constantly looked high, when we should have looked high—and low.

34   For example: in the Smithsonian Institution in Washington, D.C., there hangs

a quilt unlike any other in the world. In fanciful, inspired, and yet simple and identifiable figures, it portrays the story of the Crucifixion. It is considered rare, beyond
price. Though it follows no known pattern of quilt-making, and though it is made
of bits and pieces of worthless rags, it is obviously the work of a person of powerful imagination and deep spiritual feeling. Below this quilt I saw a note that says
it was made by "an anonymous black woman in Alabama, a hundred years ago."

35   If we could locate this "anonymous" black woman from Alabama, she would
turn out to be one of our grandmothers—an artist who left her mark in the only
materials she could afford, and in the only medium her position in society allowed
her to use.

36   As Virginia Woolf wrote further, in *A Room of One's Own:*

> Yet genius of a sort must have existed among women as it must have existed
> among the working class. [Change this to "slaves" and "the wives and daughters
> of sharecroppers."] Now and again an Emily Brontë or a Robert Burns [change this
> to "a Zora Hurston or a Richard Wright"] blazes out and proves its presence. But
> certainly it never got itself on to paper. When, however, one reads of a witch
> being ducked, or a woman possessed by devils [or "Sainthood"], of a wise
> woman selling herbs [our root workers], or even a very remarkable man who had
> a mother, then I think we are on the track of a lost novelist, a suppressed poet, or
> some mute and inglorious Jane Austen. . . . Indeed, I would venture to guess that
> Anon, who wrote so many poems without singing them, was often a woman. . . .

37   And so our mothers and grandmothers have, more often than not anonymously, handed on the creative spark, the seed of the flower they themselves
never hoped to see: or like a sealed letter they could not plainly read.

38   And so it is, certainly, with my own mother. Unlike "Ma" Rainey's songs,
which retained their creator's name even while blasting forth from Bessie Smith's
mouth, no song or poem will bear my mother's name. Yet so many of the stories
that I write, that we all write, are my mother's stories. Only recently did I fully
realize this: that through years of listening to my mother's stories of her life, I have
absorbed not only the stories themselves, but something of the manner in which
she spoke, something of the urgency that involves the knowledge that her stories—like her life—must be recorded. It is probably for this reason that so much of
what I have written is about characters whose counterparts in real life are so much
older than I am.

39   But the telling of these stories, which came from my mother's lips as naturally as breathing, was not the only way my mother showed herself as an artist. For
stories, too, were subject to being distracted, to dying without conclusion. Dinners
must be started, and cotton must be gathered before the big rains. The artist that
was and is my mother showed itself to me only after many years. This is what I
finally noticed:

40   Like Mem, a character in *The Third Life of Grange Copeland,* my mother
adorned with flowers whatever shabby house we were forced to live in. And not
just your typical straggly country stand of zinnias, either. She planted ambitious
gardens—and still does—with over fifty different varieties of plants that bloom
profusely from early March until late November. Before she left home for the
fields, she watered her flowers, chopped up the grass, and laid out new beds.

When she returned from the fields she might divide clumps of bulbs, dig a cold pit, uproot and replant roses, or prune branches from her taller bushes or trees—until night came and it was too dark to see.

41   Whatever she planted grew as if by magic, and her fame as a grower of flowers spread over three counties. Because of her creativity with her flowers, even my memories of poverty are seen through a screen of blooms—sunflowers, petunias, roses, dahlias, forsythia, spirea, delphiniums, verbena . . . and on and on.

42   And I remember people coming to my mother's yard to be given cuttings from her flowers; I hear again the praise showered on her because whatever rocky soil she landed on, she turned into a garden. A garden so brilliant with colors, so original in its design, so magnificent with life and creativity, that to this day people drive by our house in Georgia—perfect strangers and imperfect strangers—and ask to stand or walk among my mother's art.

43   I notice that it is only when my mother is working in her flowers that she is radiant, almost to the point of being invisible—except as Creator: hand and eye. She is involved in work her soul must have. Ordering the universe in the image of her personal conception of Beauty.

44   Her face, as she prepares the Art that is her gift, is a legacy of respect she leaves to me, for all that illuminates and cherishes life. She has handed down respect for the possibilities—and the will to grasp them.

45   For her, so hindered and intruded upon in so many ways, being an artist has still been a daily part of her life. This ability to hold on, even in very simple ways, is work black women have done for a very long time.

46   This poem is not enough, but it is something, for the woman who literally covered the holes in our walls with sunflowers:

> They were women then
> My mama's generation
> Husky of voice—Stout of
> Step
> With fists as well as
> Hands
> How they battered down
> Doors
> And ironed
> Starched white
> Shirts
> How they led
> Armies
> Headragged Generals
> Across mined
> Fields
> Booby-trapped
> Kitchens
> To discover books
> Desks

> A place for us
> How they knew what we
> *Must* know
> Without knowing a page
> Of it
> Themselves

47   Guided by my heritage of a love of beauty and a respect for strength—in search of my mother's garden, I found my own.

48   And perhaps in Africa over two hundred years ago, there was just such a mother; perhaps she painted vivid and daring decorations in oranges and yellows and greens on the walls of her hut; perhaps she sang—in a voice like Roberta Flack's—*sweetly* over the compounds of her village; perhaps she wove the most stunning mats or told the most ingenious stories of all the village storytellers. Perhaps she was herself a poet—though only her daughter's name is signed to the poems that we know.

49   Perhaps Phillis Wheatley's mother was also an artist.

50   Perhaps in more than Phillis Wheatley's biological life is her mother's signature made clear.

QUESTIONS

Experience

· Describe your experience in reading "In Search of Our Mothers' Gardens." Consider both your emotional response to Walker's writing and the way you made sense of it as you read through it.

· Relate at least one aspect of Walker's essay to your own experience or to the experience of someone you know or someone you have read or heard about.

Interpretation

· Single out a sentence or a paragraph you believe contains Walker's central idea. Interpret the sentence, or comment on the paragraph, explaining her idea in your own words.

· Explain the importance of the garden and flower images Walker includes toward the end of the essay. How is this imagery related to the quilt Walker describes earlier?

· What does Walker mean when she writes: "in search of my mother's garden, I found my own"?

Evaluation

· This essay can be read as a tribute to Walker's mother and a celebration of other African American women of her generation and earlier. What does Walker especially value about these women? What does she value about her mother? Why?

WRITING

Exploring

· Write an essay in which you pay tribute to an individual, a group of people, or both. You can include in your essay stories about the person or group; factual information; references to books, music, photographs, paintings, or other works of art and craft; and anything else you consider relevant.

Interpreting

· Analyze the different pieces of Walker's essay—the different elements she includes in it. Identify the pieces of Walker's quiltlike essay, and explain how the pieces fit together to clarify and enforce Walker's idea about African American women.

Evaluating

· Evaluate Walker's essay by considering how well the writer conveys her ideas. Consider her use of language, her use of imagery, her references to other writers and historical figures such as Jean Toomer and Phillis Wheatley, and her use of epigraphs. Decide, too, what the poem included at the end contributes to her essay.

ERIC KIM
(b. 1972)

Family Portrait

Eric Kim was educated at Harvard University, where he majored in visual and environmental studies in preparation for a career as an architect. "Family Portrait" was written as an assignment for a freshman course in expository writing. To get to his finished essay, Eric initially wrote a short exercise in which he described a picture of his family. Then, in response to a second exercise, he wrote a short account of an argument with his father. Out of those two brief pieces Eric developed his essay.

The piece is noteworthy for its striking use of dialogue, its honest presentation of family tension, and its vivid description. Kim is careful to balance the scene of conflict with his father with another conflict between him and his mother. One of the essay's nicest touches is the way Eric Kim introduces a second photograph at the end of his essay—a photograph that contains a positive note for improved family relations.

1   In my house hangs a large portrait of my family taken just before my junior year. It does not look like a family portrait at all. None of us look like we want to be there together. My mother is sitting on a wrought-iron bench, with my younger sister Laura on her right and me on her left. We are all leaning away from each other. Behind us, my older sister Joan is leaning unnaturally on my father. The strain of unnatural posing shows on all of our faces. We are all tense. It is an uncomfortable picture.

2   For years our family has been troubled and tense. We have never been the closest of families, and events in the past several years have pulled us farther apart. Our move to Los Angeles five years ago was a pivotal event. It is impossible to say exactly why our family fell apart after that move. Certainly my older sister Joan and I sped the process as we poured out our teenage angst into the easiest channel: our family. Southern Californian freedom and individuality played a role as well. The long hours my father had to spend in downtown Los Angeles, an hour from our suburban home, certainly helped alienate us from him. The single most divisive element in our lives, however, was unquestionably the church.

3   The church was the reason why our family had moved to Los Angeles three years earlier. My father had been a minister for two years when in my eighth grade year the oldest Korean church in Los Angeles asked him to be its assistant pastor. My father finally agreed when the senior founding pastor told him that he was stepping down within a year and would give my father his position. That year, however, various circumstances kept the senior pastor, Don Kim, away from the church. While he was away, my father won friends and admiration as he reorganized the chaotic church offices and programs.

4   None of this pleased Don Kim when he returned a year later. He saw the

church as his own creation, his daughter, and my father as a guest turned inter-loper. Angered and threatened by my father's new influence, Don Kim began a yearlong battle to make him leave. Denying that he had ever offered the original agreement, he forbade my father from preaching and denounced him from the pulpit. He wrote letters to church members and to the Korean newspapers slan-dering my father. He even dissolved existing Bible study groups and resumed a program that the church federation had banned because it engenders cults of per-sonality around its leaders. In short, he did everything he could to humiliate my father and to reassert his own authority.

5   My father responded with silence. In his typical fashion, he took the punish-ment by himself. He continued his administrative duties, which often took so much of his time that he would spend several nights a week at the church. My sophomore year I saw very little of my father. What I did see of him was frighten-ing. His jovial humor and endless patience faded into grim bitterness, silent intro-spection, and a flaring temper.

6   The troubles at church inevitably wrecked the relationships in our family. My parents suffered the most. They argued every night when he was home and most nights when he wasn't. They disagreed so much because their personalities are so similar. They are both stubborn, self-assured, and closed-minded. In spite of that, they might get along if they could ever agree on anything. Unfortunately, they seldom do. Every night my father was home they fought. My mother would tell my father how he should be handling his life, and he would thunder at her to be silent and mind her place. Their fights always ended with her wailing and screaming and him thundering out of the house. Every night! You would think several years of it would have made them stop. It only made them angrier. One night I heard my mother screaming through her tears at my father. "You never loved me! I know it! You never loved me! You should just kill me now!" The door flew open and my father stormed out, muttering violently in Korean. He slammed the front door on his way out, and drove away. He didn't come back till late that night.

7   The slam of the front door woke me several months later. It was the morning of Christmas Eve. It was obvious enough what had driven my father away. My mother was seething, and spent the morning screaming at us to get ready for the day's special church service. There was no reason for me to be any angrier than usual that particular day; nevertheless, my mother and I were bickering all morn-ing. Things were worse in the car. I was driving, my mother was in the front, and my sisters were sitting in the back. My mother, still ranting at what rotten chil-dren we were, started clipping her nails, letting the clippings lay where they fell. I had spent two hours cleaning the car the day before, and got unreasonably mad. I sped up to 70, then to 80 miles an hour. Sheer fright usually shuts her up at around 75, but that day she chose instead to yell even more, saying I was insane and would kill us all. I don't know why I lost control. My rage consumed me and I did the stupidest thing possible. I threw the car to the right, then to the left. At 80 miles an hour the small tires on our Honda gave up, and the car spun. The world flashed by in a maniacal blur for what seemed an eternity. When we stopped in a cloud of acrid smoke, we were parked on an exit ramp on the left-hand side of the freeway, parallel to the wall. We had made a perfect 360° spin.

8   When I thought about the incident later, I realized that we could all have died. Traffic had been heavy with Yuletide travelers that morning, but we, somehow, had been in an open patch of road. I have never seen another left-hand off-ramp from Interstate 5 in Los Angeles, but we ended up parked on one. Had we been thirty yards down the highway in either direction, we would certainly have hit other cars on the way to slamming into the concrete retaining wall. My mother was silent the rest of the way to church. She never realized quite how closely death missed us, and I never told her. As it was, she avoided me for days, giving me strange looks. I am convinced she thought I was truly crazy. At least she stopped nagging me for a while.

9   At that moment in the car, I truly hated my mother. Usually, however, that boiling fury cooled to mere annoyance in a few days. I could never take her seriously enough to sustain hatred toward her. But I could, and did, hate my father. I didn't realize it until a Saturday afternoon my senior year. We were parked in the deserted lot of a local elementary school, where we had driven to "have a discussion about a few things." What the "discussion" had turned out to be was yet another customs sermon for me and a long personal revelation about him. I had heard most of it before, but only now could I really understand how my father had rationalized the problems in the church and in our home and how completely blameless he believed himself to be. In a flash I was struck by how very calculating and condescending, how very *Korean* my father was. I saw a man embittered and withdrawn, in whom a life of study and a previous career in engineering had instilled both a worship of logic and a superior conviction of his own rightness. I was revolted and angered. It was as though I had discovered he was a leper.

10   I could no longer make myself listen to his voice. Instead I studied my fingers, the faint texture of the brown plastic dashboard, the design on the fabric door inserts, the reflections of bright sunlight off a Honda parked down the street. Finally he stopped and watched me for a moment. *"Yaima!"* he shouted. "Why aren't you listening to me?"

11   Without turning, I told him that if he had dragged me along to be his punching bag I had better things to do. Now his tirades came crashing down on me. I was an insolent son, I never tried to understand him, and I was a shame to our family. I opened the door and stepped out. I bent down to face him and started to bawl at him. I told him how I had felt fatherless for the past two years, how he never tried to listen to or understand anyone, and that *he* was a shame to *me*. In the end the violence of my own sobbing choked off my shouts, and tears ran burning down my face. I slammed the door shut and started to walk home.

12   He drove up beside me and told me to get in the car. He said I was being a fool and that everyone could see me. I didn't answer him, and he drove on. His car was parked outside when I reached our house. I stepped straight into our other car and drove away. I came back after midnight, and my father was gone.

13   Things didn't get much better in my family until I left for college. My father eventually left the church to start his own, but that solved few problems. The new church is even farther away than the old one, and the stress of starting any new venture is immense. My mother, of course, kept chiming in every night with how my father should be running his life and the church, and my father kept storming

out of the house. For a long time he kept spare clothes and a bedroll in the trunk of his car. As for myself, I stayed out of the house and the church as much as possible. I was disillusioned by the dirty politics I had found in the church, and embittered by the sordid battle I found at home each day. I turned away from church and home, relying instead on my friends for the support and camaraderie I could not find elsewhere in my life.

14   Many of my friends, even my own sister, have told me that relationships with their parents have improved vastly since they left for college. Such stories once amazed me. It still seems paradoxical in a way that when maintaining a relationship is hardest, the relationships can turn around, get closer and stronger. Perhaps there is something in old clichés about distance and the heart. When I went home for Christmas, we had our inevitable clashes, but something seemed different. Our fights ended a little sooner, and we made up a little earlier. My parents seemed anxious to keep our home peaceful. They even tried to sit down and talk with me seriously. It was unnerving in a way. I didn't know how to respond or what to say. After eighteen years, we barely knew each other.

15 A few weeks ago I received a small package from home. It was a set of pictures our family took during Christmas break. My mother and father are sitting together in the front, and Laura is now leaning on my father. Joan and I are standing behind them, smiling. We still don't look comfortable, but then again, we aren't leaning away from each other this time. It is beginning to look like a family portrait.

QUESTIONS

Experience

· As you read Eric Kim's essay, what was your reaction? Why?
· To what extent, if at all, does Kim's experience relate to your own? Have you felt hostility and hatred toward your parents, for example? If so, why? If not, why not?
· How does Kim's depiction of his parents' relationship strike you? Is it convincing? Why, or why not?

Interpretation

· In part, "Family Portrait" is about Eric Kim's family. What comes through strongest about his family? What does the picture he describes at the beginning and end of his essay contribute?
· What is Kim's attitude toward religion (or toward the ethnic Korean church)?

Evaluation

· What are the most important values of Eric Kim's father? Of his mother and sister? What matters most to him?
· How do you assess Kim's chances for reconciling with his family? For his parents to get along better? Why?

WRITING

Exploring

· Write your own "family portrait." Focus on your relationship with one or more family members. Use anecdote, descriptive detail, direct quotation. You may wish to refer to one or more photographs of family members as well.

Interpreting

· Analyze Kim's essay. Identify its major parts, and explain the logic of their ordering. Consider Kim's use of the two family photographs.

Evaluating

· Select what for you is one of the most important values that surfaces in Kim's essay (a cultural, religious, educational, or social value). Discuss your own ideas about the subject, perhaps using Kim's essay as a starting point.

WILLIAM FAULKNER
[1897–1962]

A Rose for Emily

Chronicler of the American South, William Faulkner has long been considered one of America's most gifted writers. Writing about historical change in the South, Faulkner created, in a series of novels and stories, the mythological Yoknapatawpha county, the setting for novels such as The Sound and The Fury, Light in August, *and* Absalom, Absalom! *Born and raised in Mississippi, Faulkner attended the University of Missippi for two years without taking a degree, before serving for a short time in the Royal Canadian Air Force, and working as a reporter in New Orleans. He returned to Mississippi in the 1920s to devote himself to writing.*

Among his numerous fine short stories, "A Rose for Emily" remains one of his best known and most highly valued. Faulkner once described it as a ghost story, though that is only one of its dimensions. At its heart is the character of Miss Emily, an embodiment of the values and ideals of the old South, which were being eroded by the encroachment of the modern world. One of the story's many provocative considerations is how the community— represented as a plural narrative "we"—responds to Miss Emily.

I

1   When Miss Emily Grierson died, our whole town went to her funeral: the men through a sort of respectful affection for a fallen monument, the women mostly out of curiosity to see the inside of her house, which no one save an old manservant—a combined gardener and cook—had seen in at least ten years.

2   It was a big, squarish frame house that had once been white, decorated with cupolas and spires and scrolled balconies in the heavily lightsome style of the seventies, set on what had once been our most select street. But garages and cotton gins had encroached and obliterated even the august names of that neighborhood; only Miss Emily's house was left, lifting its stubborn and coquettish decay above the cotton wagons and the gasoline pumps—an eyesore among eyesores. And now Miss Emily had gone to join the representatives of those august names where they lay in the cedar-bemused cemetery among the ranked and anonymous graves of Union and Confederate soldiers who fell at the battle of Jefferson.

3   Alive, Miss Emily had been a tradition, a duty, and a care; a sort of hereditary obligation upon the town, dating from that day in 1894 when Colonel Sartoris, the mayor—he who fathered the edict that no Negro woman should appear on the streets without an apron—remitted her taxes, the dispensation dating from the death of her father on into perpetuity. Not that Miss Emily would have accepted charity. Colonel Sartoris invented an involved tale to the effect that Miss

Emily's father had loaned money to the town, which the town, as a matter of business, preferred this way of repaying. Only a man of Colonel Sartoris' generation and thought could have invented it, and only a woman could have believed it.

4   When the next generation, with its more modern ideas, became mayors and aldermen, this arrangement created some little dissatisfaction. On the first of the year they mailed her a tax notice. February came, and there was no reply. They wrote her a formal letter, asking her to call at the sheriff's office at her convenience. A week later the mayor wrote her himself, offering to call or to send his car for her, and received in reply a note on paper of an archaic shape, in a thin, flowing calligraphy in faded ink, to the effect that she no longer went out at all. The tax notice was also enclosed, without comment.

5   They called a special meeting of the Board of Aldermen. A deputation waited upon her, knocked at the door through which no visitor had passed since she ceased giving china-painting lessons eight or ten years earlier. They were admitted by the old Negro into a dim hall from which a stairway mounted into still more shadow. It smelled of dust and disuse—a close, dank smell. The Negro led them into the parlor. It was furnished in heavy, leather-covered furniture. When the Negro opened the blinds of one window, they could see that the leather was cracked; and when they sat down, a faint dust rose sluggishly about their thighs, spinning with slow motes in the single sun-ray. On a tarnished gilt easel before the fireplace stood a crayon portrait of Miss Emily's father.

6   They rose when she entered—a small, fat woman in black, with a thin gold chain descending to her waist and vanishing into her belt, leaning on an ebony cane with a tarnished gold head. Her skeleton was small and spare; perhaps that was why what would have been merely plumpness in another was obesity in her. She looked bloated, like a body long submerged in motionless water, and of that pallid hue. Her eyes, lost in the fatty ridges of her face, looked like two small pieces of coal pressed into a lump of dough as they moved from one face to another while the visitors stated their errand.

7   She did not ask them to sit. She just stood in the door and listened quietly until the spokesman came to a stumbling halt. Then they could hear the invisible watch ticking at the end of the gold chain.

8   Her voice was dry and cold. "I have no taxes in Jefferson. Colonel Sartoris explained it to me. Perhaps one of you can gain access to the city records and satisfy yourselves."

9   "But we have. We are the city authorities, Miss Emily. Didn't you get a notice from the sheriff, signed by him?"

10   "I received a paper, yes," Miss Emily said. "Perhaps he considers himself the sheriff. . . . I have no taxes in Jefferson."

11   "But there is nothing on the books to show that, you see. We must go by the—"

12   "See Colonel Sartoris. I have no taxes in Jefferson."

13   "But, Miss Emily—"

14   "See Colonel Sartoris." (Colonel Sartoris had been dead almost ten years.) "I have no taxes in Jefferson. Tobe!" The Negro appeared. "Show these gentlemen out."

2

15 So she vanquished them, horse and foot, just as she had vanquished their fathers thirty years before about the smell. That was two years after her father's death and a short time after her sweetheart—the one we believed would marry her—had deserted her. After her father's death she went out very little; after her sweetheart went away, people hardly saw her at all. A few of the ladies had the temerity to call, but were not received, and the only sign of life about the place was the Negro man—a young man then—going in and out with a market basket.

16 "Just as if a man—any man—could keep a kitchen properly," the ladies said; so they were not surprised when the smell developed. It was another link between the gross, teeming world and the high and mighty Griersons.

17 A neighbor, a woman, complained to the mayor, Judge Stevens, eighty years old.

18 "But what will you have me do about it, madam?" he said.

19 "Why, send her word to stop it," the woman said. "Isn't there a law?"

20 "I'm sure that won't be necessary," Judge Stevens said. "It's probably just a snake or a rat that nigger of hers killed in the yard. I'll speak to him about it."

21 The next day he received two more complaints, one from a man who came in diffident deprecation. "We really must do something about it, Judge. I'd be the last one in the world to bother Miss Emily, but we've got to do something." That night the Board of Aldermen met—three graybeards and one younger man, a member of the rising generation.

22 "It's simple enough," he said. "Send her word to have her place cleaned up. Give her a certain time to do it in, and if she don't. . . ."

23 "Dammit, sir," Judge Stevens said, "will you accuse a lady to her face of smelling bad?"

24 So the next night, after midnight, four men crossed Miss Emily's lawn and slunk about the house like burglars, sniffing along the base of the brickwork and at the cellar openings while one of them performed a regular sowing motion with his hand out of a sack slung from his shoulder. They broke open the cellar door and sprinkled lime there, and in all the outbuildings. As they recrossed the lawn, a window that had been dark was lighted and Miss Emily sat in it, the light behind her, and her upright torso motionless as that of an idol. They crept quietly across the lawn and into the shadow of the locusts that lined the street. After a week or two the smell went away.

25 That was when people had begun to feel really sorry for her. People in our town, remembering how old lady Wyatt, her great-aunt, had gone completely crazy at last, believed that the Griersons held themselves a little too high for what they really were. None of the young men were quite good enough for Miss Emily and such. We had long thought of them as a tableau, Miss Emily a slender figure in white in the background, her father a spraddled silhouette in the foreground, his back to her and clutching a horsewhip, the two of them framed by the backflung front door. So when she got to be thirty and was still single, we were not pleased exactly, but vindicated; even with insanity in the family she wouldn't have turned down all of her chances if they had really materialized.

26 When her father died, it got about that the house was all that was left to her;

and in a way, people were glad. At last they could pity Miss Emily. Being left alone, and a pauper, she had become humanized. Now she too would know the old thrill and the old despair of a penny more or less.

27   The day after his death all the ladies prepared to call at the house and offer condolence and aid, as is our custom. Miss Emily met them at the door, dressed as usual and with no trace of grief on her face. She told them that her father was not dead. She did that for three days, with the ministers calling on her, and the doctors, trying to persuade her to let them dispose of the body. Just as they were about to resort to law and force, she broke down, and they buried her father quickly.

28   We did not say she was crazy then. We believed she had to do that. We remembered all the young men her father had driven away, and we knew that with nothing left, she would have to cling to that which had robbed her, as people will.

3

29 She was sick for a long time. When we saw her again, her hair was cut short, making her look like a girl, with a vague resemblance to those angels in colored church windows—sort of tragic and serene.

30   The town had just let the contracts for paving the sidewalks, and in the summer after her father's death they began the work. The construction company came with niggers and mules and machinery, and a foreman named Homer Barron, a Yankee—a big, dark, ready man, with a big voice and eyes lighter than his face. The little boys would follow in groups to hear him cuss the niggers, and the niggers singing in time to the rise and fall of picks. Pretty soon he knew everybody in ttown. Whenever you heard a lot of laughing anywhere about the square, Homer Barron would be in the center of the group. Presently, we began to see him and Miss Emily on Sunday afternoons driving in the yellow-wheeled buggy and the matched team of bays from the livery stable.

31   At first we were glad that Miss Emily would have an interest, because the ladies all said, "Of course a Grierson would not think seriously of a Northerner, a day laborer." But there were still others, older people, who said that even grief could not cause a real lady to forget *noblesse oblige*—without calling it *noblesse oblige*. They just said, "Poor Emily. Her kinsfolk should come to her." She had some kin in Alabama; but years ago her father had fallen out with them over the estate of old lady Wyatt, the crazy woman, and there was no communication between the two families. They had not even been represented at the funeral.

32   And as soon as the old people said, "Poor Emily," the whispering began. "Do you suppose it's really so?" they said to one another. "Of course it is. What else could. . . ." This behind their hands; rustling of craned silk and satin behind jalousies closed upon the sun of Sunday afternoon as the thin, swift clop-clop-clop of the matched team passed: "Poor Emily."

33   She carried her head high enough—even when we believed that she was fallen. It was as if she demanded more than ever the recognition of her dignity as the last Grierson; as if it had wanted that touch of earthiness to reaffirm her imper-

viousness. Like when she bought the rat poison, the arsenic. That was over a year after they had begun to say "Poor Emily," and while the two female cousins were visiting her.

34   "I want some poison," she said to the druggist. She was over thirty then, still a slight woman, though thinner than usual, with cold, haughty black eyes in a face the flesh of which was strained across the temples and about the eyesockets as you imagine a lighthouse-keeper's face ought to look. "I want some poison," she said.

35   "Yes, Miss Emily. What kind? For rats and such? I'd recom——"

36   "I want the best you have. I don't care what kind."

37   The druggist named several. "They'll kill anything up to an elephant. But what you want is——"

38   "Arsenic," Miss Emily said. "Is that a good one?"

39   "Is . . . arsenic? Yes, ma'am. But what you want——"

40   "I want arsenic."

41   The druggist looked down at her. She looked back at him, erect, her face like a strained flag. "Why, of course," the druggist said. "If that's what you want. But the law requires you to tell what you are going to use it for."

42   Miss Emily just stared at him, her head tilted back in order to look him eye for eye, until he looked away and went and got the arsenic and wrapped it up. The Negro delivery boy brought her the package; the druggist didn't come back. When she opened the package at home there was written on the box, under the skull and bones: "For rats."

4

43 So the next day we all said, "She will kill herself'; and we said it would be the best thing. When she had first begun to be seen with Homer Barron, we had said, "She will marry him." Then we said, "She will persuade him yet," because Homer himself had remarked—he liked men, and it was known that he drank with the younger men in the Elks' Club—that he was not a marrying man. Later we said, "Poor Emily" behind the jalousies as they passed on Sunday afternoon in the glittering buggy, Miss Emily with her head high and Homer Barron with his hat cocked and a cigar in his teeth, reins and whip in a yellow glove.

44   Then some of the ladies began to say that it was a disgrace to the town and a bad example to the young people. The men did not want to interfere, but at last the ladies forced the Baptist minister—Miss Emily's people were Episcopal—to call upon her. He would never divulge what happened during that interview, but he refused to go back again. The next Sunday they again drove about the streets, and the following day the minister's wife wrote to Miss Emily's relations in Alabama.

45   So she had blood-kin under her roof again and we sat back to watch developments. At first nothing happened. Then we were sure that they were to be married. We learned that Miss Emily had been to the jeweler's and ordered a man's toilet set in silver, with the letters H.B. on each piece. Two days later we

learned that she had bought a complete outfit of men's clothing, including a night-shirt, and we said, "They are married." We were really glad. We were glad because the two female cousins were even more Grierson than Miss Emily had ever been.

46   So we were not surprised when Homer Barron—the streets had been finished some time since—was gone. We were a little disappointed that there was not a public blowing-off, but we believed that he had gone on to prepare for Miss Emily's coming, or to give her a chance to get rid of the cousins. (By that time it was a cabal, and we were all Miss Emily's allies to help circumvent the cousins.) Sure enough, after another week they departed. And, as we had expected all along, within three days Homer Barron was back in town. A neighbor saw the Negro man admit him at the kitchen door at dusk one evening.

47   And that was the last we saw of Homer Barron. And of Miss Emily for some time. The Negro man went in and out with the market basket, but the front door remained closed. Now and then we would see her at the window for a moment, as the men did that night when they sprinkled the lime, but for almost six months she did not appear on the streets. Then we knew that this was to be expected too; as if that quality of her father which had thwarted her woman's life so many times had been too virulent and too furious to die.

48   When we next saw Miss Emily, she had grown fat and her hair was turning gray. During the next few years it grew grayer and grayer until it attained an even pepper-and-salt iron-gray, when it ceased turning. Up to the day of her death at seventy-four it was still that vigorous iron-gray, like the hair of an active man.

49   From that time on her front door remained closed, save during a period of six or seven years, when she was about forty, during which she gave lessons in china-painting. She fitted up a studio in one of the downstairs rooms, where the daughters and granddaughters of Colonel Sartoris' contemporaries were sent to her with the same regularity and in the same spirit that they were sent to church on Sundays with a twenty-five-cent piece for the collection plate. Meanwhile her taxes had been remitted.

50   Then the newer generation became the backbone and the spirit of the town, and the painting pupils grew up and fell away and did not send their children to her with boxes of color and tedious brushes and pictures cut from the ladies' magazines. The front door closed upon the last one and remained closed for good. When the town got free postal delivery, Miss Emily alone refused to let them fasten the metal numbers above her door and attach a mailbox to it. She would not listen to them.

51   Daily, monthly, yearly we watched the Negro grow grayer and more stooped, going in and out with the market basket. Each December we sent her a tax notice, which would be returned by the post office a week later, unclaimed. Now and then we would see her in one of the downstairs windows—she had evidently shut up the top floor of the house—like the carven torso of an idol in a niche, looking or not looking at us, we could never tell which. Thus she passed from generation to generation—dear, inescapable, impervious, tranquil, and perverse.

52   And so she died. Fell ill in the house filled with dust and shadows, with only a doddering Negro man to wait on her. We did not even know she was sick; we

had long since given up trying to get any information from the Negro. He talked to no one, probably not even to her, for his voice had grown harsh and rusty, as if from disuse.

53　　She died in one of the downstairs rooms, in a heavy walnut bed with a curtain, her gray head propped on a pillow yellow and moldy with age and lack of sunlight.

5

54　The Negro met the first of the ladies at the front door and let them in, with their hushed, sibilant voices and their quick, curious glances, and then he disappeared. He walked right through the house and out the back and was not seen again.

55　　The two female cousins came at once. They held the funeral on the second day, with the town coming to look at Miss Emily beneath a mass of bought flowers, with the crayon face of her father musing profoundly above the bier and the ladies sibilant and macabre; and the very old men—some in their brushed Confederate uniforms—on the porch and the lawn, talking of Miss Emily as if she had been a contemporary of theirs, believing that they had danced with her and courted her perhaps, confusing time with its mathematical progression, as the old do, to whom all the past is not a diminishing road but, instead, a huge meadow which no winter ever quite touches, divided from them now by the narrow bottleneck of the most recent decade of years.

56　　Already we knew that there was one room in that region above stairs which no one had seen in forty years, and which would have to be forced. They waited until Miss Emily was decently in the ground before they opened it.

57　　The violence of breaking down the door seemed to fill this room with pervading dust. A thin, acrid pall as of the tomb seemed to lie everywhere upon this room decked and furnished as for a bridal: upon the valance curtains of faded rose color, upon the rose-shaded lights, upon the dressing table, upon the delicate array of crystal and the man's toilet things backed with tarnished silver, silver so tarnished that the monogram was obscured. Among them lay a collar and tie, as if they had just been removed, which, lifted, left upon the surface a pale crescent in the dust. Upon a chair hung the suit, carefully folded; beneath it the two mute shoes and the discarded socks.

58　　The man himself lay in the bed.

59　　For a long while we just stood there, looking down at the profound and fleshless grin. The body had apparently once lain in the attitude of an embrace, but now the long sleep that outlasts love, that conquers even the grimace of love, had cuckolded him. What was left of him, rotted beneath what was left of the nightshirt, had become inextricable from the bed in which he lay; and upon him and upon the pillow beside him lay that even coating of the patient and biding dust.

60　　Then we noticed that in the second pillow was the indentation of a head. One of us lifted something from it, and leaning forward, that faint and invisible dust dry and acrid in the nostrils, we saw a long strand of iron-gray hair.

QUESTIONS

Experience

· What was it like to read "A Rose for Emily"? Which parts of the story engaged you most and which parts least? Why?

· To what extent are you familiar with someone like Miss Emily?

Interpretation

· What do you think Faulkner's story shows about people? About history? About society?

· To what extent do you think this is a "ghost story" and to what extent a story about life in a particular time and place?

Evaluation

· What social and cultural values does the story embody? How important are the attitudes and perspectives expressed by the "we" that narrates the story?

WRITING

Exploring

· Write an essay in which you discuss someone you know who reminds you of Miss Emily.

· Or write about your own experience of being confronted by changes you or someone you know were unwilling or unable to accept or adapt to.

Interpreting

· Write an essay in which you explain the significance of the opening paragraphs or of the concluding paragraphs for the meaning of the story as a whole.

Evaluating

· Write an essay in which you relate the social and cultural values embodied in the story to your life in a particular place in the United States today.

MAYA ANGELOU
(b. 1928)

On the Pulse of Morning

Maya Angelou, poet and memoirist, was born and raised in Stamps, Arkansas. As a young woman, Angelou worked as a singer, dancer, and actress. She has been a civil rights activist and a performer of her own prose and verse. She has also been featured on Bill Moyers's public television series of broadcasts about creative Americans. Angelou's life is richly recorded in three volumes of autobiography, I Know Why the Caged Bird Sings *(1970),* Gather Together in My Name *(1974), and* Singin' and Swingin' and Gettin' Merry Like Christmas *(1976).*

Her poem "On the Pulse of Morning," read at Bill Clinton's presidential inauguration, celebrates the diversity of America, including a catalogue of immigrants among its stanzas. The poet uses a tree, a rock, and a river as symbols, and she includes other elements of nature, especially images of light and morning, to suggest hope for a new beginning. Angelou also uses simple and direct language, and she makes the poem an invitation to human solidarity.

1
A Rock, A River, A Tree
Hosts to species long since departed,
Marked the mastodon,
The dinosaur, who left dried tokens
5
Of their sojourn here
On our planet floor,
Any broad alarm of their hastening doom
Is lost in the gloom of dust and ages.

But today, the Rock cries out to us, clearly, forcefully,
10
Come, you may stand upon my
Back and face your distant destiny,
But seek no haven in my shadow,
I will give you no hiding place down here.

You, created only a little lower than
15
The angels, have crouched too long in
The bruising darkness
Have lain too long
Facedown in ignorance,
Your mouths spilling words

20
Armed for slaughter.
The Rock cries out to us today,
You may stand upon me;
But do not hide your face.

Across the wall of the world,
25   A River sings a beautiful song. It says,
Come, rest here by my side.

Each of you, a bordered country,
Delicate and strangely made proud,
Yet thrusting perpetually under siege.
30   Your armed struggles for profit
Have left collars of waste upon
My shore, currents of debris upon my breast.
Yet today I call you to my riverside,
If you will study war no more.

35   Come, clad in peace,
And I will sing the songs
The Creator gave to me when I and the
Tree and the Rock were one.
Before cynicism was a bloody sear across your brow
40   And when you yet knew you still knew nothing.
The River sang and sings on.

There is a true yearning to respond to
The singing River and the wise Rock.
So say the Asian, The Hispanic, The Jew
45   The African, the Native American, the Sioux,
The Catholic, the Muslim, the French, the Greek,
The Irish, the Rabbi, the Priest, the Sheik,
The Gay, the Straight, the Preacher,
The privileged, the homeless, the Teacher.
50   They hear. They all hear
The speaking of the Tree.

They hear the first and last of every Tree
Speak to humankind today.
Come to me,
55   Here beside the River.
Plant yourself beside the River.

Each of you, descendant of some passed-
On traveler, has been paid for.
You, who gave me my first name, you,
60   Pawnee, Apache, Seneca, you
Cherokee Nation, who rested with me, then
Forced on bloody feet,
Left me to the employment of
Other seekers—desperate for gain,
65   Starving for gold.

You, the Turk, the Arab, the Swede,
The German, the Eskimo, the Scot,
The Italian, the Hungarian, the Pole,
You the Ashanti, the Yoruba, the Kru, bought
70 Sold, stolen, arriving on a nightmare
Praying for a dream.

Here, root yourselves beside me.
I am that Tree planted by the River,
Which will not be moved.
75 I, the Rock, I, the River, I, the Tree
I am yours—your passages have been paid.
Lift up your faces, you have a piercing need
For this bright morning dawning for you.
History, despite its wrenching pain,
80 Cannot be unlived, but if faced
With courage, need not be lived again.

Lift up you eyes
Upon this day breaking for you.
Give birth again
85 To the dream.

Women, children, men,
Take it into the palms of your hands,
Mold it into the shape of your most
Private need. Sculpt it into
90 The image of your most public self.
Lift up you hearts
Each new hour holds new chances
For a new beginning.
Do not be wedded forever
95 To fear, yoked eternally
To brutishness.

The horizon leans forward,
Offering you space
To place new steps of change
100 Here, on the pulse of this fine day
You may have the courage
To look up and out and upon me,
The Rock, the River, the Tree, your country.
No less to Midas than the mendicant.
105 No less to you now than the mastodon then.

Here on the pulse of this new day
You may have the grace to look up and out
And into your sister's eyes,

And into your brother's face,
Your country,
And say simply
Very simply
With hope—
Good morning.

QUESTIONS

Experience

· What was your reaction to your initial reading (or hearing) of this poem? How do you respond when the speaker talks to a rock and a tree? Do you find this sort of conversation between humans and nature sensible, silly, or what? Why?

Interpretation

· What image of America does Angelou present in her poem? Do you think this is an appropriate poem to read at a presidential inauguration? Why, or why not?

· What image of community is presented in the poem? How does Angelou convey her sense of community? What lines are most important in establishing her perspective?

Evaluation

· What cultural and social values does the poem celebrate? Is the poet successful in communicating her vision of these values? Why, or why not?

· Do you think this is an effective poem? Why, or why not?

WRITING

Exploring

· Write an essay or poem in which you present your own vision of the American or university community either as it presently exists or as you wish it to exist in the future.

Interpreting

· Analyze Angelou's poem by identifying its major sections or parts and explaining the significance or point of each part. Be sure to explain the significance of elements of nature she cites as well as the catalogue of peoples she includes.

Evaluating

· Consider Angelou's poem in light of Michiko Kakutani's essay "The Word Police" on p. 331. Kakutani refers to "On the Pulse of Morning" in her essay as an example of politically correct language. Evaluate the poem as an example of political correctness.

COMMUNITIES—CONSIDERATIONS FOR THINKING AND WRITING

1. Compare the depiction of female communities in the selections by Maxine Hong Kingston and Alice Walker. Consider how Kingston and Walker present their communities of women, what values animate those womanly communities, and the roles men play in relation to women. You may wish to expand your discussion by including Robin Lakoff's "Talking Like a Lady" (in "Language") or Deborah Tannen's "Different Words, Different Worlds" (in "Gender").

2. Compare the depiction of male communities in the selections by Tom Wolfe in this section with the ways men relate to one another as described by Pat Hoy, Paul Theroux, or Scott Russell Sanders—all in the "Gender" section. You may also wish to consider how one or another of these writers portrays how women relate to men.

3. Discuss the clash of cultures reflected in the selections by Amy Tan, Marianna De Marco Torgovnick, and Maxine Hong Kingston. Consider both the common elements of cultural conflict these writers describe and different conflicting elements, especially what accounts for those differences. You may wish to expand your selection by introducing observations about Robin Lakoff's "Talking Like a Lady" (in "Language") or Gloria Anzaldúa's "How to Tame a Wild Tongue" (in "Culture and Society").

4. Discuss the portraits of family life in the selections by Eric Kim, Amy Tan, and Marianna De Marco Torgovnick. Explain how each writer characterizes his or her family and how each relates to specific family members. You may also introduce additional observations about family relations based on your reading of Pat Hoy's "Mosaics of Southern Masculinity" ("Gender") and Gish Jen's "What Means Switch?" ("Language").

5. Compare the ideal image of community as depicted in Maya Angelou's "On the Pulse of Morning" with that of Mary Gordon's "More Than Just a Shrine." You may wish to include destructive images of community as they appear in Diane Ravitch's "Multiculturalism" (in "Culture and Society"). Explain which images of community you find more compelling or persuasive, and why.

6. Describe the kinds of communities found in your college or university. Consider not only the sense of community (or lack thereof) of the school overall, but the smaller communities within it in which you find yourself included or excluded. You may wish to focus on one or more of these smaller communities. Try to identify the community's values and to account for its defining characteristics.

7. Do a piece of creative writing in which you explore an aspect of community. You may wish to write a poem, song, short story, or a scene for a play or a

film. You may wish to focus on a particular small community within a larger one, such as the community of varsity basketball players, Asian Americans, accounting majors, and so on.

8. Write a research essay that investigates a question about community raised by one of the writers in this chapter. Your community issue may involve race, ethnicity, class, language, gender, or another category you devise. Your topic should be narrow enough to explore from a fresh perspective.

T W O

Culture and Society

TOM WOLFE
Only One Life

JOAN DIDION
Marrying Absurd

LARRY L. KING
Playing Cowboy

GLORIA ANZALDÚA
How to Tame a Wild Tongue

DIANE RAVITCH
Multiculturalism

GEORGE ORWELL
Marrakech

HENRY LOUIS GATES, JR.
2 Live Crew, Decoded

MARIE RIBISI
The Health Craze

LESLIE MARMON SILKO
The Man to Send Rain Clouds

LOUIS SIMPSON
Walt Whitman at Bear Mountain

The word "culture" refers to common patterns of behavior and to customary ways of living. It encompasses the language we speak and the various communities we belong to. Culture includes our country (our national culture); our social standing as a member of the lower, middle, or upper class, the leisured or working class; our sexual orientation (gay or straight culture); our heritage, race, and ethnicity (as a Japanese American, a Latino or a Chicana, a Haitian, or a Canadian, for example).

Culture includes what we have been handed down through tradition, what we have learned, and what we share with others. Like language, culture surrounds us, immersing us in ways of thinking about how we live our lives. Culture, in short, defines who we are and reflects what we value. The writers in this chapter reveal social and cultural values, sometimes to celebrate them, sometimes to call them into question.

Tom Wolfe and Joan Didion, for example, satirize elements of American culture they consider vulgar and self-indulgent. Wolfe pokes fun at tendencies Americans displayed in the 1960s to take themselves very seriously, a period Wolfe dubs "The Me Decade." Didion turns her satiric sights on Las Vegas, particularly on its wedding industry, which she anatomizes with trenchant irony. Larry L. King, on the other hand, pokes fun at himself as he explores the ways he switches cultural roles between acting like a Texan in New York and acting like an easterner in his home state of Texas. Gloria Anzaldúa explores other facets of cultural switching in her "How to Tame a Wild Tongue," in which she employs several languages and dialects. Diane Ravitch's approach to the issue of multiculturalism is one that celebrates pluralism while castigating what she calls "particularism," an emphasis on the contributions of one cultural element to the neglect and detriment of others.

In "Marrakech," George Orwell portrays a society of the poor and the powerless, and he argues implicitly that the two go hand in hand. Henry Louis Gates, Jr., makes a different kind of argument in his "2 Live Crew, Decoded," in which he defends the sexist and racist lyrics of the notorious rappers, 2 Live Crew, by setting their music in both cultural and artistic contexts.

Marie Ribisi's "The Health Craze" uses the style and tone of Tom Wolfe's "Only One Life" to satirize the increasing emphasis Americans have been putting on diet and fitness. And both Leslie Marmon Silko's short story "The Man to Send Rain Clouds" and Louis Simpson's poem "Walt Whitman at Bear Mountain" invite readers to consider ways that conventionally accepted social values may be challenged as inadequate.

TOM WOLFE
(b. 1931)

Only One Life

Tom Wolfe began his career as an academic, earning a doctorate in American Studies at Yale. But his inclination was more journalistic than academic, and he began working as a reporter for the Washington Post *and later as a magazine writer for the now defunct* New York Herald-Tribune. *Wolfe has written articles and essays on trends in popular culture, many of them later collected in books such as* The Kandy-Kolored Tangerine-Flake Streamline Baby *(1965),* The Pump House Gang *(1968), and* Mauve Gloves & Madmen, Clutter & Vine *(1976). His book about the space program,* The Right Stuff *(1979), was made into a movie, as was his only novel,* Bonfire of the Vanities *(1988).*

In the following excerpt from Mauve Gloves & Madmen, Clutter & Vine, *Wolfe takes satirical aim at characteristics of what he calls "the Me Decade" by keying in on a popular advertising slogan and referring to events of the 1960s. Among the interesting features of Wolfe's essay are his use of advertising slogans and signal phrases that capture the spirit of the times: "If I've only one life, let me live it as a ———!" And: "Let's talk about Me." In these and other instances, Wolfe uses, for emphasis, quotation marks, italics, and capital letters for normally uncapitalized words. He also uses ellipses (. . .), long sentences, dialogue, and numerous contemporary references to create a swinging, colloquial style that suits his subject.*

1   In 1961 a copy writer named Shirley Polykoff was working for the Foote, Cone & Belding advertising agency on the Clairol hair-dye account when she came up with the line: "If I've only one life, let me live it as a blonde!" In a single slogan she had summed up what might be described as the secular side of the Me Decade. "If I've only one life, let me live it as a ———!" (You have only to fill in the blank.)

2   This formula accounts for much of the popularity of the women's liberation or feminist movement. "What does a woman want?" said Freud. Perhaps there are women who want to humble men or reduce their power or achieve equality or even superiority for themselves and their sisters. But for every one such woman, there are nine who simply want to *fill in the blank* as they see fit. "If I've only one life, let me live it as . . . a free spirit!" (Instead of . . . a house slave: a cleaning woman, a cook, a nursemaid, a stationwagon hacker, and an occasional household sex aid.) But even that may be overstating it, because often the unconscious desire is nothing more than: *"Let's talk about Me."* The great unexpected dividend of the feminist movement has been to elevate an ordinary status—woman, housewife—to the level of drama. One's very existence as *a woman* . . . as *Me* . . . becomes something all the world analyzes, agonizes over, draws cosmic conclusions from, or, in any event, takes seriously. Every woman becomes Emma Bovary, Cousin Bette, or Nora . . . or Erica Jong or Consuelo Saah Baehr.

3   Among men the formula becomes "If I've only one life, let me live it as a . . .

Casanova or a Henry VIII" (instead of a humdrum workadaddy, eternally faithful, except perhaps for a mean little skulking episode here and there, to a woman who now looks old enough to be your aunt and needs a shave or else has electrolysis lines above her upper lip, as well as atrophied calves, and is an embarrassment to be seen with when you take her on trips). The right to shuck overripe wives and take on fresh ones was once seen as the prerogative of kings only, and even then it was scandalous. In the 1950's and 1960's it began to be seen as the prerogative of the rich, the powerful, and the celebrated (Nelson Rockefeller, Henry Ford, and Show Business figures), although it retained the odor of scandal. Wife-shucking damaged Adlai Stevenson's chances of becoming President in 1952 and 1956 and Rockefeller's chances of becoming the Republican nominee in 1964 and 1968. Until the 1970's wife-shucking made it impossible for an astronaut to be chosen to go into space. Today, in the Me Decade, it becomes *normal behavior,* one of the factors that has pushed the divorce rate above 50 percent.

4   When Eugene McCarthy filled in the blank in 1972 and shucked his wife, it was hardly noticed. Likewise in the case of several astronauts. When Wayne Hays filled in the blank in 1976 and shucked his wife of thirty-eight years, it did not hurt his career in the slightest. Copulating with the girl in the office, however, was still regarded as scandalous. (Elizabeth Ray filled in the blank in another popular fashion: If I've only one life, let me live it as a . . . Celebrity!" As did Arthur Bremer, who kept a diary during his stalking of Nixon and, later, George Wallace . . . with an eye toward a book contract. Which he got.) Some wiseacre has remarked, supposedly with levity, that the federal government may in time have to create reservations for women over thirty-five, to take care of the swarms of shucked wives and widows. In fact, women in precisely those categories have begun setting up communes or "extended families" to provide one another support and companionship in a world without workadaddies. ("If I've only one life, why live it as an anachronism?")

5   Much of what is now known as the "sexual revolution" has consisted of both women and men filling in the blank this way: "If I've only one life, let me live it as . . . a Swinger!" (Instead of a frustrated, bored monogamist.) In "swinging," a husband and wife give each other license to copulate with other people. There are no statistics on the subject that mean anything, but I do know that it pops up in conversation today in the most unexpected corners of the country. It is an odd experience to be in De Kalb, Illinois, in the very corncrib of America, and have some conventional-looking housewife (not *housewife,* damn it!) come up to you and ask: "Is there much tripling going on in New York?"

6   *"Tripling?"*

7   Tripling turns out to be a practice, in De Kalb, anyway, in which a husband and wife invite a third party—male or female, but more often female—over for an evening of whatever, including polymorphous perversity, even the practices written of in the one-hand magazines, such as *Hustler,* all the things involving tubes and hoses and tourniquets and cups and double-jointed sailors.

8   One of the satisfactions of this sort of life, quite in addition to the groin spasms, is talk: *Let's talk about Me.* Sexual adventurers are given to the most relentless and deadly serious talk . . . about Me. They quickly succeed in placing themselves onstage in the sexual drama whose outlines were sketched by Freud

and then elaborated by Wilhelm Reich. Men and women of all sorts, not merely swingers, are given just now to the most earnest sort of talk about the Sexual Me. A key drama of our own day is Ingmar Bergman's movie *Scenes from a Marriage.* In it we see a husband and wife who have good jobs and a well-furnished home but who are unable to "communicate"—to cite one of the signature words of the Me Decade. Then they begin to communicate, and thereupon their marriage breaks up and they start divorce proceedings. For the rest of the picture they communicate endlessly, with great candor, but the "relationship"—another signature word—remains doomed. Ironically, the lesson that people seem to draw from this movie has to do with . . . "the need to communicate."

9   *Scenes from a Marriage* is one of those rare works of art, like *The Sun Also Rises,* that not only succeed in capturing a certain mental atmosphere in fictional form . . . but also turn around and help radiate it throughout real life. I personally know of two instances in which couples, after years of marriage, went to see *Scenes from a Marriage* and came home convinced of the "need to communicate." The discussions began with one of the two saying, Let's try to be completely candid for once. You tell me exactly what you don't like about me, and I'll do the same for you. At this, the starting point, the whole notion is exciting. We're going to talk about *Me!* (And I can take it.) I'm going to find out what he (or she) really thinks about me! (Of course, I have my faults, but they're minor . . . or else exciting.)

10   She says, "Go ahead. What don't you like about me?"

11   They're both under the Bergman spell. Nevertheless, a certain sixth sense tells him that they're on dangerous ground. So he decides to pick something that doesn't seem too terrible.

12   "Well," he says, "one thing that bothers me is that when we meet people for the first time, you never know what to say. Or else you get nervous and start chattering away, and it's all so banal, it makes me look bad."

13   Consciously she's still telling herself, "I can take it." But what he has just said begins to seep through her brain like scalding water. What's he talking about?—makes *him* look bad? *He's saying I'm unsophisticated, a social liability and an embarrassment. All those times we've gone out, he's been ashamed of me!* (And what makes it worse—it's the sort of disease for which there's no cure!) She always knew she was awkward. His crime is: he *noticed!* He's known it, too, all along. He's had *contempt* for me.

14   Out loud she says, "Well, I'm afraid there's nothing I can do about that."

15   He detects the petulant note. "Look," he says, "you're the one who said to be candid."

16   She says, "I know. I *want* you to be."

17   He says, "Well, it's your turn."

18   "Well," she says, "I'll tell *you* something about when we meet people and when we go places. You never clean yourself properly—you don't know how to wipe yourself. Sometimes we're standing there talking to people, and there's . . . a smell. And I'll tell you something else: People can tell it's you."

19   And he's still telling *him*self, "I can take it"—but what inna namea Christ is *this?*

20   He says, "But you've never said anything—about anything like that."

21   She says, "But I *tried* to. How many times have I told you about your dirty drawers when you were taking them off at night?"

22   Somehow this really makes him angry . . . All those times . . . and his mind immediately fastens on Harley Thatcher and his wife, whom he has always wanted to impress . . . From underneath my $350 suits I smelled of *shit!* What infuriates him is that this is a humiliation from which there's no recovery. *How often have they sniggered about it later?—or not invited me places? Is it something people say every time my name comes up?* And all at once he is intensely annoyed with his wife, not because she never told him all these years, but simply because she *knows* about his disgrace—and she was the one who *brought him the bad news!*

23   From that moment on they're ready to get the skewers in. It's only a few minutes before they've begun trying to sting each other with confessions about their little affairs, their little slipping around, their little coitus on the sly—"Remember that time I told you my flight from Buffalo was canceled?"—and at that juncture the ranks of those *who can take it* become very thin indeed. So they communicate with great candor! and break up! and keep on communicating! and they find the relationship hopelessly doomed.

24   One couple went into group therapy. The other went to a marriage counselor. Both types of therapy are very popular forms, currently, of *Let's talk about Me.* This phase of the breakup always provides a rush of exhilaration—for what more exhilarating topic is there than . . . *Me?* Through group therapy, marriage counseling, and other forms of "psychological consultation" they can enjoy that same *Me* euphoria that the very rich have enjoyed for years in psychoanalysis. The cost of the new Me sessions is only $10 to $30 an hour, whereas psychoanalysis runs from $50 to $125. The woman's exhilaration, however, is soon complicated by the fact that she is (in the typical case) near or beyond the cutoff age of thirty-five and will have to retire to the reservation.

25   Well, my dear Mature Moderns . . . Ingmar never promised you a rose garden!

QUESTIONS

Experience

- Written nearly twenty years ago, Wolfe's essay refers to people in the news at the time (such as Arthur Bremer and Erica Jong) as well as to historical figures such as Henry Ford and King Henry VIII of England. To what extent do either the historical references or those current with the time of the essay's writing help or hinder your understanding of Wolfe's point?

Interpretation

- What is Wolfe's subject here? Is it the early feminist movement toward women's liberation? Talk therapy? Selfishness? Something else? What is Wolfe's attitude toward his subject? How do you know?
- "Only One Life" falls into two major parts: paragraphs 1 through 8 and paragraphs 9 through 23, followed by a brief conclusion in paragraphs 24 and 25.

Identify the subject and point of the two long parts, and explain how Wolfe moves in paragraphs 8 and 9 from the subject of the first part to that of the second.

Evaluation

· What is Wolfe's attitude toward feminism as conveyed by the following quotations:

1. "The great unexpected dividend of the feminist movement has been to elevate an ordinary status—woman, housewife—to the level of drama."

2. "One's very existence as *a woman* . . . as *Me* . . . becomes something all the world analyzes, agonizes over, draws cosmic conclusions from, or, in any event, takes seriously." What is your response to his attitude?

WRITING

Exploring

· Write an essay describing the decade of the 1990s. You can treat the subject seriously or humorously. But be sure to characterize the decade and to illustrate whatever traits you consider to define it.

Interpreting

· Compare Wolfe's analysis of test plane fighter pilots in "The Right Stuff" with his approach to the Me Decade in "Only One Life." Include his use of examples and comparisons as well as any other aspects of style you consider important.

Evaluating

· Take a popular slogan from print advertising or a TV commercial about a contemporary issue. Write an essay examining its implications and ramifications. Explain how the slogan sums up and epitomizes important attitudes, ideals, and values of whoever uses it, believes in it, or lives by it. You may wish to imitate Wolfe by using variations on the slogan throughout your essay.

JOAN DIDION
(b. 1934)

Marrying Absurd

*Joan Didion, essayist and novelist, was born in Sacramento, California. Did-
ion earned her B.A. from the University of California at Berkeley and won
Vogue magazine's Prix de Paris the year she graduated. She has been an
associate editor at Vogue, has taught creative writing, and has contributed
stories, articles, and reviews to numerous periodicals. Her books include
River Run, Play It as It Lays, A Book of Common Prayer, and Democracy (all
novels); Slouching Toward Bethlehem, The White Album, Salvador, and After
Henry (essays and journal articles). The following selection reveals Didion's
skill at trenchant social criticism.*

   *In "Marrying Absurd" Didion savagely satirizes the Las Vegas wedding
industry. She does so through creating a series of brief scenes in which the
dialogue spoken by the characters reflects views at odds with those of the
writer (and presumably Didion's readers as well). Irony, thus, is Didion's
instrument for her satire. This irony takes many forms, including ironic dialogue, the ironic signs posted everywhere in Las Vegas, and Didion's artful
juxtaposing of scenes that comment indirectly on the vulgar and shallow
values she sees as endemic not only in Las Vegas but, by implication,
throughout America.*

ₗ   To be married in Las Vegas, Clark County, Nevada, a bride must swear that she
is eighteen or has parental permission and a bridegroom that he is twenty-one
or has parental permission. Someone must put up five dollars for the license. (On
Sundays and holidays, fifteen dollars. The Clark County Courthouse issues marriage licenses at any time of the day or night except between noon and one in
the afternoon, between eight and nine in the evening, and between four and five
in the morning.) Nothing else is required. The State of Nevada, alone among these
United States, demands neither a premarital blood test nor a waiting period before
or after the issuance of a marriage license. Driving in across the Mojave from Los
Angeles, one sees the signs way out on the desert, looming up from that moon-
scape of rattlesnakes and mesquite, even before the Las Vegas lights appear like a
mirage on the horizon: "GETTING MARRIED? Free License Information First Strip Exit."
Perhaps the Las Vegas wedding industry achieved its peak operational efficiency
between 9:00 p.m. and midnight of August 26, 1965, an otherwise unremarkable
Thursday which happened to be, by Presidential order, the last day on which anyone could improve his draft status merely by getting married. One hundred and
seventy-one couples were pronounced man and wife in the name of Clark County
and the State of Nevada that night, sixty-seven of them by a single justice of the
peace, Mr. James A. Brennan. Mr. Brennan did one wedding at the Dunes and
the other sixty-six in his office, and charged each couple eight dollars. One bride

lent her veil to six others. "I got it down from five to three minutes," Mr. Brennan said later of his feat. "I could've married them *en masse,* but they're people, not cattle. People expect more when they get married."

2   What people who get married in Las Vegas actually do expect—what, in the largest sense, their "expectations" are—strikes one as a curious and self-contra-dictory business. Las Vegas is the most extreme and allegorical of American set-tlements, bizarre and beautiful in its venality and in its devotion to immediate gratification, a place the tone of which is set by mobsters and call girls and ladies' room attendants with amyl nitrite poppers in their uniform pockets. Almost every-one notes that there is no "time" in Las Vegas, no night and no day and no past and no future (no Las Vegas casino, however, has taken the obliteration of the ordinary time sense quite so far as Harold's Club in Reno, which for a while issued, at odd intervals in the day and night, mimeographed "bulletins" carrying news from the world outside); neither is there any logical sense of where one is. One is standing on a highway in the middle of a vast hostile desert looking at an eighty-foot sign which blinks "Stardust" or "Caesar's Palace." Yes, but what does that explain? This geographical implausibility reinforces the sense that what happens there has no connection with "real" life; Nevada cities like Reno and Carson are ranch towns, Western towns, places behind which there is some historical imper-ative. But Las Vegas seems to exist only in the eye of the beholder. All of which makes it an extraordinarily stimulating and interesting place, but an odd one in which to want to wear a candlelight satin Priscilla of Boston wedding dress with Chantilly lace insets, tapered sleeves and a detachable modified train.

3   And yet the Las Vegas wedding business seems to appeal to precisely that impulse. "Sincere and Dignified Since 1954," one wedding chapel advertises. There are nineteen such wedding chapels in Las Vegas, intensely competitive, each offering better, faster, and, by implication, more sincere services than the next: Our Photos Best Anywhere, Your Wedding on A Phonograph Record, Can-dlelight with Your Ceremony, Honeymoon Accommodations, Free Transportation from Your Motel to Courthouse to Chapel and Return to Motel, Religious or Civil Ceremonies, Dressing Rooms, Flowers, Rings, Announcements, Witnesses Avail-able, and Ample Parking. All of these services, like most others in Las Vegas (sauna baths, payroll-check cashing, chinchilla coats for sale or rent), are offered twenty-four hours a day, seven days a week, presumably on the premise that mar-riage, like craps, is a game to be played when the table seems hot.

4   But what strikes one most about the Strip chapels, with their wishing wells and stained-glass paper windows and their artificial bouvardia, is that so much of their business is by no means a matter of simple convenience, of late-night liaisons between show girls and baby Crosbys. Of course there is some of that. (One night about eleven o'clock in Las Vegas I watched a bride in an orange minidress and masses of flame-colored hair stumble from a Strip chapel on the arm of her bride-groom, who looked the part of the expendable nephew in movies like *Miami Syn-dicate.* "I gotta get the kids," the bride whimpered. "I gotta pick up the sitter, I gotta get to the midnight show." "What you gotta get," the bridegroom said, opening the door of a Cadillac Coupe de Ville and watching her crumple on the seat, "is sober.") But Las Vegas seems to offer something other than "conve-

nience"; it is merchandising "niceness," the facsimile of proper ritual, to children who do not know how else to find it, how to make the arrangements, how to do it "right." All day and evening long on the Strip, one sees actual wedding parties, waiting under the harsh lights at a crosswalk, standing uneasily in the parking lot of the Frontier while the photographer hired by The Little Church of the West ("Wedding Place of the Stars") certifies the occasion, takes the picture: the bride in a veil and white satin pumps, the bridegroom usually in a white dinner jacket, and even an attendant or two, a sister or a best friend in hot-pink *peau de soie*, a flirtation veil, a carnation nosegay. "When I Fall in Love It Will Be Forever," the organist plays, and then a few bars of Lohengrin. The mother cries; the stepfather, awkward in his role, invites the chapel hostess to join them for a drink at the Sands. The hostess declines with a professional smile; she has already transferred her interest to the group waiting outside. One bride out, another in, and again the sign goes up on the chapel door: "One moment please—Wedding."

5   I sat next to one such wedding party in a Strip restaurant the last time I was in Las Vegas. The marriage had just taken place; the bride still wore her dress, the mother her corsage. A bored waiter poured out a few swallows of pink champagne ("on the house") for everyone but the bride, who was too young to be served. "You'll need something with more kick than that," the bride's father said with heavy jocularity to his new son-in-law; the ritual jokes about the wedding night had a certain Panglossian character, since the bride was clearly several months pregnant. Another round of pink champagne, this time not on the house, and the bride began to cry. "It was just as nice," she sobbed, "as I hoped and dreamed it would be."

QUESTIONS

Experience

· How does Didion's description of a Las Vegas wedding compare with your experience of weddings? Identify any similarities and differences between weddings you have attended and the one Didion describes.

· Do you agree with Didion's view of Las Vegas marriages? Why, or why not? What is your own view of the wedding described in "Marrying Absurd"?

Interpretation

· Besides describing and satirizing the Las Vegas wedding industry, what larger issues does Didion identify in her essay?

· Comment on each of the scenes Didion includes in the essay. Explain the function of each scene and what the scenes together have in common.

Evaluation

· Identify the values of the marrying couple and their guests. Identify as well the values of the justice of the peace and the hostess. To what extent are they involved in the wedding and celebration? Why?

WRITING

Exploring

· Write an essay about weddings or other important social or religious rituals, such as bar mitzvahs, funerals, or graduations. You can treat the subject seriously or humorously, and you can bring into your discussion references to the ritual you write about from popular music, television and movies, and your own experience.

Interpreting

· Analyze the techniques Didion uses to satirize Las Vegas weddings. Some possibilities: irony, comparisons, the title. Explain the effects Didion achieves through using these techniques.

Evaluating

· Discuss one of the following quotations:

   1. "Las Vegas is the most extreme and allegorical of American settlements, bizarre and beautiful in its venality and in its devotion to immediate gratification."

   2. "[Las Vegas] is merchandising 'niceness,' the facsimile of proper ritual, to children who do not know how else to find it, how to make the arrangements, how to do it 'right.'"

· You need not restrict your discussion to or even focus it on Las Vegas. You may prefer to discuss the cultural values identified in each quotation in a broader context.

LARRY L. KING
(b. 1929)

Playing Cowboy

Larry L. King was born and raised in Texas. He has worked as a farmhand, oil field worker, journalist, and politician. Although skeptical of academics, King has accepted academic distinctions and appointments, including a Neiman Fellowship at Harvard, a fellowship in communications at Duke, and a visiting professorship in journalism and political science at Princeton.

Mostly, however, Larry L. King has been a writer, and most persistently a political journalist. He has served as writer-in-residence for the Washington Star, *and he has been a contributing editor for* Harper's, The Texas Monthly, The Texas Observer, *and* New Times. *In addition to writing for many periodicals, he has published a novel,* The One-Eyed Man *(1966), and five books of nonfiction:* Wheeling and Dealing *(1978), . . .* And Other Dirty Stories *(1968),* The Old Man and Other Lesser Mortals *(1974),* Confessions of a White Racist *(1971), and* Of Outlaws, Con Men, Whores, Politicians, and Other Artists *(1980). He has also coauthored two plays, one of which,* The Best Little Whorehouse in Texas *(1978), was a Broadway hit. His* None But a Blockhead *(1985) reviews his life as a writer.*

In "Playing Cowboy" King amusingly recounts his experience of living in two different cultural worlds. His essay centers on his dual behavior: in New York he "plays cowboy," wearing boots and hat and using a southern drawl when he speaks; in Texas he acts the sophisticated easterner, eschewing western ways. King's writing in the essay is often lively and occasionally brash. His diction moves from the vulgar to the formal, sometimes within the confines of a single sentence. And his humor makes "Playing Cowboy" fun to read.

1   When I was young, I didn't know that when you leave a place, it may not be forever. The past, I thought, had served its full uses and could bury its own dead; bridges were for burning; "good-bye" meant exactly what it said. One never looked back except to judge how far one had come.

2   Texas was the place I left behind. And not reluctantly. The leave-taking was so random I trusted the United States Army to relocate me satisfactorily. It did, in 1946, choosing to establish in Queens (then but a five-cent subway ride from the clamorous glamour of Manhattan) a seventeen-year-old former farm boy and small-town sapling green enough to challenge chlorophyll. The assignment would shape my life far more than I then suspected; over the years it would teach me to "play cowboy"—to become, strangely, more "Texas" than I had been.

3   New York offered everything to make an ambitious kid dizzy; I moved through its canyons in a hot walking dream. Looking back, I see myself starring in a bad movie I then accepted as high drama: the Kid, a.k.a. the Bumptious Innocent, discovering the theater, books, a bewildering variety of nightclubs and bars;

subways and skyscrapers and respectable wines. There were glancing encounters with Famous Faces: Walter Winchell, the actor Paul Kelly, the ex-heavyweight champion Max Baer, bandleader Stan Kenton. It was easy; spotting them, I simply rushed up, stuck out my hand, sang out my name, and began asking personal questions.

4   Among my discoveries was that I dreaded returning to Texas; where were its excitements, celebrities, promises? As corny as it sounds, one remembers the final scene of that bad movie. Crossing the George Washington Bridge in a Greyhound bus in July 1949—Army discharge papers in my duffel bag—I looked back at Manhattan's spires and actually thought, *I'll be back, New York.* I did not know that scene had been played thousands of times by young men or young women from the provinces, nor did I know that New York cared not a whit whether we might honor the pledge. In time, I got back. On my recent forty-sixth birthday, it dawned that I had spent more than half my life—or twenty-four years—on the eastern seaboard. I guess there's no getting around the fact that this makes me an expatriate Texan.

5   "Expatriate" remains an exotic word. I think of it as linked to Paris or other European stations in the 1920s: of Sylvia Beach and her famous bookstore; of Hemingway, Fitzgerald, Dos Passos, Ezra Pound, and Gertrude Stein Stein Stein. There is wine in the Paris air, wine and cheese and sunshine, except on rainy days when starving young men in their attics write or paint in contempt of their gut rumbles. Spain. The brave bulls. Dublin's damp fog. Movable feasts. *That's* what "expatriate" means, so how can it apply to one middle-aged grandfather dodging Manhattan's muggers and dogshit pyramids while grunting a son through boarding school and knocking on the doors of magazine editors? True expatriates, I am certain, do not wait in dental offices, the Port Authority Bus Terminal, or limbo. Neither do they haunt their original root sources three or four times each year, while dreaming of accumulating enough money to return home in style as a gentlemanly rustic combining the best parts of J. Frank Dobie, Lyndon Johnson, Stanley Walker, and the Old Man of the Mountain. Yet that is my story, and that is my plan.

6   I miss the damned place. Texas is my mind's country, that place I most want to understand and record and preserve. Four generations of my people sleep in its soil; I have children there, and a grandson; the dead past and the living future tie me to it. Not that I always approve it or love it. It vexes and outrages and disappoints me—especially when I am there. It is now the third most urbanized state, behind New York and California, with all the tangles, stench, random violence, architectural rape, historical pillage, neon blight, pollution, and ecological imbalance the term implies. Money and mindless growth remain high on the list of official priorities, breeding a crass boosterism not entirely papered over by an infectious energy. The state legislature—though improving as slowly as an old man's mending bones—still harbors excessive, coon-ass, rural Tory Democrats who fail to understand that 79.7 percent of Texans have flocked to urban areas and may need fewer farm-to-market roads, hide-and-tick inspectors, or outraged orations almost comically declaiming against welfare loafers, creeping socialism, the meddling ol' feds, and sin in the aggregate.

7   Too much, now, the Texas landscape sings no native notes. The impersonal,

standardized superhighways—bending around or by most small towns, and then blatting straightaway toward the urban sprawls—offer homogenized service stations, fast-food-chain outlets, and cluttered shopping centers one might find duplicated in Ohio, Maryland, Illinois, or Anywhere, U.S.A. Yes, there is much to make me protest, as did Mr. Faulkner's Quentin Compson, of the South—"I *don't* hate it. I don't hate it, I *don't. . . .*" For all its shrinkages of those country pleasures I once eschewed, and now covet and vainly wish might return, Texas remains in my mind's eye that place to which I shall eventually return to rake the dust for my formative tracks; that place where one hopes to grow introspective and wise as well as old. It is a romantic foolishness, of course; the opiate dream of a nostalgia junkie. When I go back to stay—and I fancy that I will—there doubtless will be opportunities to wonder at my plan's imperfections.

8   For already I have created in my mind, you see, an improbable corner of paradise: the rustic, rambling ranch house with the clear-singing creek nearby, the clumps of shade trees (under which, possibly, the Sons of the Pioneers will play perpetual string-band concerts), the big cozy library where I will work and read and cogitate between issuing to the Dallas *Times-Herald* or the Houston *Post* those public pronouncements befitting an Elder Statesman of Life and Letters. I will become a late-blooming naturalist and outdoorsman: hiking and camping, and piddling in cattle; never mind that to date I have preferred the sidewalks of New York, and my beef not on the hoof but tricked up with mushroom sauces.

9   All this will occur about one easy hour out of Austin—my favorite Texas city— and exactly six miles from a tiny, unnamed town looking remarkably like what Walt Disney would have built for a cheery, heart-tugging Texas-based story happening about 1940. The nearest neighbor will live 3.7 miles away, have absolutely no children or dogs, but will have one beautiful young wife, who adores me; it is she who will permit me, by her periodic attentions, otherwise to live the hermit's uncluttered life. Politicians will come to my door hats in hand, and fledgling Poets and young Philosophers. Basically, they will want to know exactly what is Life's Purpose. Looking out across the gently blowing grasslands, past the grazing blooded cattle, toward a perfect sunset, with even the wind in my favor, and being the physical reincarnation of Hemingway with a dash of Twain in my mood, I shall—of course—be happy to tell them.

10 Well, we all know that vast gap between fantasy and reality when True Life begins playing the scenario. Likely I will pay twice to thrice the value for a run-down old "farmhouse" where the plumbing hasn't worked since Coolidge, and shall die of a heart attack while digging a cesspool. The nearest neighbor will live directly across the road; he will own seven rambunctious children, five mad dogs, and an ugly harridan with sharp elbows, a shrill voice, and a perverse hatred for dirty old writing men. The nearest town—less than a half mile away and growing by leaps, separated from my digs only by a subdivision of mock Bavarian castles and the new smeltering plant—will be made of plastics, paved parking lots, and puppy-dog tails. The trip to Austin will require three hours if one avoids rush hour crushes; when I arrive—to preen in Scholz Garten or The Raw Deal or other watering holes where artists congregate—people will say, "Who's that old fart?" Unfortunately I may try to tell them. My books will long have been out of print, probably my

secret yearning will be to write a column for the local weekly newspaper. Surrounded by strangers, memories, and galloping growth, I shall sit on my porch—rocking and cackling and talking gibberish to the wind—while watching them build yet another Kwik Stop Kwality Barbecue Pit on the west edge of my crowded acreage. Occasionally I will walk the two dozen yards to the interstate highway to throw stones at passing trucks; my ammunition will peter out long before traffic does. But when I die digging that cesspool, by God, I'll have died at home. That knowledge makes me realize where my heart is.

11   But the truth, dammit, is that I feel much more the Texan when in the East. New Yorkers, especially, encourage and expect one to perform a social drill I think of as "playing cowboy." Even as a young soldier I discovered a presumption among a high percentage of New Yorkers that my family owned shares in the King Ranch and that my natural equestrian talents were unlimited; all one needed to affirm such groundless suspicions were a drawl and a grin. To this day you may spot me in Manhattan wearing boots and denim jeans with a matching vest and western-cut hat—topped by a furry cattleman's coat straight out of Marlboro Country; if you've seen Dennis Weaver play McCloud, then you've seen me, without my beard.

12   Never mind that I *like* such garb, grew up wearing it, or that I find it natural, practical, and inexpensive; no, to a shameful degree, I dress for my role. When I learned that Princeton University would pay good money to a working writer for teaching his craft—putting insulated students in touch with the workaday salts and sours of the literary world—do you think I went down there wrapped in an ascot and puffing a briar pipe from Dunhill's? No, good neighbors, I donned my Cowboy Outfit to greet the selection committee and aw-shucksed and consarned 'em half to death; easterners just can't resist a John Wayne quoting Shakespeare; I've got to admit there's satisfaction in it for every good ol' boy who country-slicks the city dudes.

13   New Yorkers tend to think of Mississippians or Georgians or Virginians under the catchall category of "southerners," of Californians as foreigners, and of Texans as the legendary Texan. We are the only outlanders, I think, that they define within a specific state border and assign the burden of an obligatory—i.e., "cowboy"—culture. Perhaps we court such treatment; let it be admitted that Texans are a clannish people. We tend to think of ourselves as Texans no matter how long ago we strayed or how tenuous our home connections. When I enter a New York store and some clerk—alerted by my nasal twang—asks where I am from, I do not answer "East Thirty-second Street," but "Texas," yet my last permanent address there was surrendered when Eisenhower was freshly President and old George Blanda was little more than a rookie quarterback.

14   More than half my close friends—and maybe 20 percent of my overall eastern seaboard acquaintances—are expatriate Texans: writers, musicians, composers, editors, lawyers, athletes, showfolk, a few businessmen, and such would-be politicians or former politicians as Bill Moyers and Ramsey Clark. Don Meredith, Liz Smith, Judy Buie, Dan Jenkins, you name 'em, and to one degree or another we play cowboy together. Many of us gather for chili suppers, tell stories with origins in Fort Worth or Odessa or Abilene; sometimes we even play dominoes or listen to country-western records.

15   There is, God help us, an organization called The New York Texans, and about 2,000 of us actually belong to it. We meet each March 2—Texas Independence Day—to drink beer, hoo-haw at each other in the accents of home, and honor some myth that we can, at best, only ill define. We even have our own newspaper, published quarterly by a lady formerly of Spur, Texas, which largely specializes in stories bragging on how well we've done in the world of the Big Apple. Since people back home are too busy to remind us of our good luck and talents, we remind ourselves.

16   No matter where you go, other Texans discover you. Sometimes they are themselves expatriates, sometimes tourists, sometimes business-bent travelers. In any case, we whoop a mutual recognition, even though we're strangers or would be unlikely to attract each other if meeting within our native borders. Indeed, one of the puzzling curiosities is why the Dallas banker, or the George Wallace fanatic who owns the little drygoods store in Beeville, and I may drop all prior plans in order to spend an evening together in Monterrey or Oshkosh when—back home—we would consider each other social lepers. Many times I have found myself buddy-buddying with people not all that likable or interesting, sharing Aggie jokes or straight tequila shots or other peculiarities of home.

17   If you think that sounds pretty dreadful, it often is. Though I am outraged when called a "professional Texan," or when I meet one, certainly I am not always purely innocent. Much of it is a big put-on, of course. We enjoy sharing put-ons against those who expect all Texans to eat with the wrong fork, offer coarse rebel yells, and get all vomity-drunk at the nearest football game. There is this regional defensiveness—LBJ would have known what I mean—leading us to order "a glass of clabber and a mess of chitlins" when faced by the haughty ministrations of the finest French restaurants. (My group does, anyway, though I don't know about the stripe of Texan epitomized, say, by Rex Reed; that bunch has got so smooth you can't see behind the sheen). I hear my Texas friends, expatriates and otherwise, as their accents thicken and their drawls slow down on approaching representatives of other cultures. I observe them as they attempt to come on more lordly and sophisticated than Dean Acheson or more country than Ma and Pa Kettle, depending on what they feel a need to prove.

18   That they (or I) need to prove anything is weird in itself. It tells you what they—yes, the omnipotent They—put in our young Texas heads. The state's history is required teaching in the public schools, and no student by law may escape the course. They teach Texas history very much fumigated—the Alamo's martyrs, the Indian-killing frontiersmen, the heroic Early Day Pioneers, the Rugged Plainsmen, the Builders and Doers; these had hearts pure where others were soiled—and they teach it and teach it and teach it. I came out of the public schools of Texas knowing naught of Disraeli, Darwin, or Darrow—though well versed in the lore of Sam Houston, Stephen F. Austin, Jim Bowie, the King Ranch, the Goodnight-Loving Trail over which thundered the last of the big herds. No school day was complete but that we sang "The Eyes of Texas," "Texas Our Texas," "Beautiful Texas." I mean, try substituting "Rhode Island" or "North Dakota," and it sounds about half-silly even to a Texan. We were taught again and again that Texas was the biggest state, one of the richest, possibly the toughest, surely the most envied. Most Americans, I guess, grow up convinced that their little corners

of the universe are special; Texas, however, takes care to institutionalize the preachment.

19   To discover a wider world, then, where others fail to hold those views—to learn that Texans are thought ignorant or rich or quite often both, though to the last in number capable of sitting a mean steed—is to begin at once a new education and feel sneaky compulsions toward promoting useless old legends. Long after I knew that the Texas of my youth dealt more with myth than reality, and long past that time when I knew that the vast majority of Texans lived in cities, I continued to play cowboy. This was a social and perhaps a professional advantage in the East; it marked one as unique, permitted one to pose as a son of yesterday, furnished a handy identity among the faceless millions. In time one has a way of becoming in one's head something of the role one has assumed. Often I have actually felt myself the reincarnation or the extension of the old range lords or bedroll cowpokes or buffalo hunters. Such playacting is harmless so long as one confines it to wearing costumes or to speech patterns—"I'm a-hankerin' for a beefsteak, y'all, and thank I'll mosey on over to P. J. Clarke's"—but becomes counterproductive unless regulated. Nobody has been able to coax me atop a horse since that day a dozen years ago when I proved to be the most comic equestrian ever to visit a given riding stable on Staten Island. Misled by my range garb, accent, and sunlamp tan, the stable manager assigned what surely must have been his most spirited steed. Unhorsed after much graceless grabbing and grappling, I heard my ride described by a laughing fellow with Brooklyn in his voice: "Cheez, at foist we thought youse was a trick rider. But just before youse fell, we seen youse wasn't nothing but a shoemaker."

20   Though I wear my Texas garb in Texas, I am more the New Yorker there; not so much in my own mind, perhaps, as in the minds of others. People hold me to account for criticisms I've written of Texas or accuse me of having gone "New York" in my thinking or attitudes. "Nobody's more parochial than a goddamn New Yorker," some of my friends snort—and often they are right. I, too, feel outraged at Manhattan cocktail parties when some clinch-jawed easterner makes it clear he thinks that everything on the wrong side of the George Washington Bridge is quaint, hasn't sense enough to come in from the rain, and maybe lacks toilet training. Yet my Texas friends have their own misconceptions of my adopted home and cause me to defend it. They warn of its violent crime, even though Houston annually vies with Detroit for the title of "Murder Capital of the World." They deride New York's slums and corruptions, even though in South El Paso (and many another Texas city) may be found shameful dirt poverty and felonious social neglect, and Texas erupts in its own political Watergates—banking, insurance, real estate scandals—at least once each decade. So I find myself in the peculiar defense of New York, waving my arms, and my voice growing hotter, saying things like "You goddamn Texans gotta learn that you're not so damned special. . . ." *You* goddamn Texas, now.

21   My friends charge that despite my frequent visits home and my summering on Texas beaches, my view of the place is hopelessly outdated. Fletcher Boone, an Austin artist and entrepreneur—now owner of The Raw Deal—was the latest to straighten out my thinking. "All you goddamn expatriates act like time froze

somewhere in the nineteen-fifties or earlier," he said. "You'd think we hadn't discovered television down here, or skin flicks, or dope. Hell, we grew us a *President* down here. We've got tall buildings and long hairs and some of us know
how to ski!" Mr. Boone had recently visited New York and now held me to
account for its sins: "It's mental masturbation. You go to a party up there, and
instead of people making real conversation, they stop the proceedings so somebody can sing opera or play the piano or do a tap dance. It's show biz, man—
buncha egomaniacal people using a captive audience to stroke themselves.
Whatta they talk about? 'I, I, I. Me, me, me. Mine, mine, mine.' " Well, no, I rebut;
they also talk about books, politics, and even *ideas;* only the middle of these, I
say, is likely to be remarked in Texas. Boone is offended; he counterattacks that
easterners do not live life so much as they attempt to dissect it or, worse, dictate
how others should live it by the manipulations of fashion, art, the media. We shout
gross generalities, overstatements, "facts" without support. I become the Visiting
Smart-ass New Yorker, losing a bit of my drawl.

22   Well, bless him, there may be something to Fletcher Boone's charge, I found
recently when I returned as a quasi sociologist. It was my plan to discover some
young, green blue-collar or white-collar, recently removed to the wicked city from
upright rural upbringings, and record that unfortunate hick's slippages or shocks.
Then I would return to the hick's small place of origin, comparing what he or she
had traded for a mess of modern city pottage; family graybeards left behind would
be probed for their surrogate shocks and would reveal their fears for their urbanized young. It would be a whiz of a story, having generational gaps and cultural
shocks and more disappointments or depletions than the Nixon White House. It
would be at once nostalgic, pitiful, and brave; one last angry shout against moder-
nity before Houston sinks beneath the waves, Lubbock dries up and blows away
for lack of drinking water, and Dallas-Fort Worth grows together as firmly as
Siamese twins. Yes, it would have everything but three tits and, perhaps, origi-
nality.

23   Telephone calls to old friends produced no such convenient study. Those recommended turned out to have traveled abroad, attended college in distant
places, or otherwise been educated by an urban, mobile society. A young airline
hostess in Houston talked mainly of San Francisco or Hawaii; a bank clerk in Dallas
sniggered that even in high school days he had spent most of his weekends away
from his native village—in city revelry—and thought my idea of "cultural shock"
quaint; a petrochemical plant worker failed to qualify when he said, "Shit, life's
not all that much different. I live here in Pasadena"—an industrial morass with all
the charms and odors of Gary, Indiana—"and I go to my job, watch TV, get drunk
with my buddies. Hail, it's not no different from what it was back there in Mona-
hans. Just more traffic and more people and a little less sand." I drove around the
state for days, depressed by the urbanization of my former old outback even as I
marveled at its energy, before returning to New York, where I might feel, once
more, like a Texan: where I might play cowboy; dream again the ancient dreams.

24   It is somehow easier to conjure up the Texas I once knew from Manhattan.
What an expatriate most remembers are not the hardscrabble times of the 1930s,
or the narrow attitudes of a people not then a part of the American mainstream,
but a way of life that was passing without one's then realizing it. Quite without

knowing it, I witnessed the last of the region's horse culture. Schoolboys tied their mounts to mesquite trees west of the Putnam school and at noon fed them bundled roughage; the pickup truck and the tractor had not yet clearly won out over the horse, though within the decade they would. While the last of the great cattle herds had long ago disappeared up the Chisholm or the Goodnight-Loving Trail, I would see small herds rounded up on my Uncle Raymond's Bar-T-Bar Ranch and loaded from railside corrals for shipment to the stockyards of Fort Worth—or "Cowtown," as it was then called without provoking smiles. (The rough-planked saloons of the brawling North Side of "Cowtown," near the old stockyards, are gone now save for a small stretch lacquered and refurbished in a way so as to make tourists feel they've been where they ain't.) In Abilene, only thirty-two miles to the west, I would hear the chants of cattle auctioneers while smelling feedlot dung, tobacco, saddle leather, and the sweat of men living the outdoor life. Under the watchful eye of my father, I sometimes rode a gentle horse through the shinnery and scrub oaks of the old family farm, helping him bring in the five dehorned milk cows while pretending to be a bad-assed gunslinger herding longhorns on a rank and dangerous trail drive.

25   But it was all maya, illusion. Even a dreaming little tad knew the buffalo hunters were gone, along with the old frontier forts, the Butterfield stage, the first sodbusters whose barbed wire fenced in the open range and touched off wars continuing to serve Clint Eastwood or James Arness. This was painful knowledge for one succored on myths and legends, on real-life tales of his father's boyhood peregrinations in a covered wagon. Nothing of my original time and place, I felt, would be worth living through or writing about. What I did not then realize (and continue having trouble remembering) is that the past never was as good as it looks from a distance.

26   The expatriate, returning, thus places an unfair burden upon his native habitat: He demands it to have impossibly marked time, to have marched in place, during the decades he has absented himself. He expects it to have preserved itself as his mind recalls it; to furnish evidence that he did not memorize in vain its legends, folk and folklore, mountains and streams and villages. Never mind that he may have removed himself to other places because they offered rapid growth, new excitements, and cultural revolutions not then available at home.

27   We expatriate sons may sometimes be unfair: too critical; fail to give due credit; employ the double standard. Especially do those of us who write flay Texas in the name of our disappointments and melted snows. Perhaps it's good that we do this, the native press being so boosterish and critically timid; but there are times, I suspect, when our critical duty becomes something close to a perverse pleasure. Easterners I have known, visiting my homeplace, come away impressed by its dynamic qualities; they see a New Frontier growing in my native bogs, a continuing spirit of adventure, a bit of trombone and swashbuckle, something fresh and good. Ah, but they did not know Texas when she was young.

28   There is a poignant tale told by the writer John Graves of the last, tamed remnants of a formerly free and proud Indian tribe in Texas: how a small band of them approached an old rancher, begged a scrawny buffalo bull from him, and— spurring their thin ponies—clattered and whooped after it, running it ahead of them, and killed it in the old way—with lances and arrows. They were foolish, I

guess, in trying to hold history still for one more hour; probably I'm foolish in the same sentimental way when I sneak off the freeways to snake across the Texas back roads in search of my own past. But there are a couple of familiar stretches making the ride worth it; I most remember one out in the lonely windblown ranch country, between San Angelo and Water Valley, with small rock-dotted hills ahead at the end of a long, flat stretch of road bordered by grasslands, random clumps of trees, wild flowers, grazing cattle, a single distant ranch house whence—one fancies—issues the perfume of baking bread, simmering beans, beef over the flames. There are no billboards, no traffic cloverleafs, no neon, no telephone poles, no Jiffy Tacos or Stuckey's stands, no oil wells, no Big Rich Bastards, no ship channels threatening to ignite because of chemical pollutions, no Howard Johnson flavors. Though old Charley Goodnight lives, Lee Harvey Oswald and Charles Whitman remain unborn.

29   Never have I rounded the turn leading into that peaceful valley, with the spiny ridge of hills beyond it, that I failed to feel new surges and exhilarations and hope. For a precious few moments I exist in a time warp: I'm back in Old Texas, under a high sky, where all things are again possible and the wind blows free. Invariably, I put the heavy spurs to my trusty Hertz or Avis steed: go flying lickety-split down that lonesome road, whooping a crazy yell and taking deep joyous breaths, sloshing Lone Star beer on my neglected dangling safety belt, and scattering roadside gravel like bursts of buckshot. Ride 'im, cowboy! *Ride* 'im. . . .

QUESTIONS

Experience

· Describe what it is like to read King's essay. To what extent did you find yourself amused by his writing? To what extent did you find yourself gaining a better understanding of King and of Texans?

Interpretation

· In what sense is the title, "Playing Cowboy," a clue to King's idea and attitude in the piece? What does King mean by "playing cowboy"?

· What is King's attitude toward Texas? What does it mean to him? How has it influenced who and what he is?

· What does King mean when he says that though he wears his Texas garb when in Texas, he feels more like a New Yorker there?

Evaluation

· What cultural values does King associate with Texas? With New York? To what extent are the images he offers of Texans and New Yorkers accurate and convincing?

· What is King's attitude toward "New York Texans"?

WRITING

Exploring

· Discuss your experience in returning to a place after having moved away, perhaps attempting to escape it. Discuss its hold on you, particularly how you may have tried to neutralize its influence, and whether or not you succeeded, and why.

· Or, if you have always lived in the same place, write about your desire to move or to stay put.

· Or discuss the place(s) in which you have lived in terms of comfort and convenience, opportunities and advantages, setting and style.

Interpreting

· Write an essay explaining one of the following quotations from King's "Playing Cowboy." Consider the context of the quotation you choose.

1. "One has a way of becoming in one's head something of the role one has assumed."

2. "The past never [is] as good as it looks from a distance."

Evaluating

· Assess the persuasiveness of King's characterizations of New Yorkers or Texans, or both. Support, modify, or refute his views of them through evidence from your experience, your reading, or both.

· Or, discuss the values associated with a place in which you currently live or a place in which you once lived. Consider the extent to which the place has left its cultural impression on you. Consider the extent to which the community's values have helped form who you are.

GLORIA ANZALDÚA
(b. 1942)

How to Tame a Wild Tongue

Gloria Anzaldúa was raised in southwest Texas. She describes herself as "a border woman," living between the Mexican and Anglo cultures. Her books include two edited volumes, This Bridge Called My Back: Writing by Radical Women of Color *(1983) and* Haciendo Caras: Making Face/Making Soul *(1990).*

"How to Tame a Wild Tongue," from Borderlands/La Frontera *(1987), is a bold and innovative piece of writing. Its most striking feature involves the way Anzaldúa crosses language borders by mixing Spanish and English while combining different essay genres such as autobiography, critical theory, and argument. It is a rich brew, concocted not only of different languages and dialects, but of different voices, some of them the voices of other writers that Anzaldúa absorbs into her text. It is a challenging and exciting essay to read.*

> "We're going to have to control your tongue," the dentist says, pulling out all the metal from my mouth. Silver bits plop and tinkle into the basin. My mouth is a motherlode.
> The dentist is cleaning out my roots. I get a whiff of the stench when I gasp. "I can't cap that tooth yet, you're still draining," he says.
> "We're going to have to do something about your tongue," I hear the anger rising in his voice. My tongue keeps pushing out the wads of cotton, pushing back the drills, the long thin needles. "I've never seen anything as strong or as stubborn," he says. And I think, how do you tame a wild tongue, train it to be quiet, how do you bridle and saddle it? How do you make it lie down?
>
> Who is to say that robbing a people of its language is less violent than war?
>
> —RAY GWYN SMITH[1]

1   I remember being caught speaking Spanish at recess—that was good for three licks on the knuckles with a sharp ruler. I remember being sent to the corner of the classroom for "talking back" to the Anglo teacher when all I was trying to do was tell her how to pronounce my name. "If you want to be American, speak 'American.' If you don't like it, go back to Mexico where you belong."

2   "I want you to speak English. *Pa' hallar buen trabajo tienes que saber hablar el inglés bien. Qué vale toda tu educación si todavía hablas inglés con un* 'accent,' " my mother would say, mortified that I spoke English like a Mexican. At Pan American University, I and all Chicano students were required to take two speech classes, their purpose: to get rid of our accents.

3   Attacks on one's form of expression with the intent to censor are a violation of the First Amendment. *El Anglo con cara de inocente nos arrancó la lengua.* Wild tongues can't be tamed, they can only be cut out.

OVERCOMING THE TRADITION OF SILENCE

Ahogadas, escupimos el oscuro.
Peleando con nuestra propia sombra
el silencio nos sepulta.

4   *En boca cerrada no entran moscas.* "Flies don't enter a closed mouth" is a saying I kept hearing when I was a child. *Ser habladora* was to be a gossip and a liar, to talk too much. *Muchachitas bien criadas,* well-bred girls don't answer back. *Es una falta de respeto* to talk back to one's mother or father. I remember one of the sins I'd recite to the priest in the confession box the few times I went to confession: talking back to my mother, *hablar pa' 'tras, repelar. Hocicona, repelona, chismosa,* having a big mouth, questioning, carrying tales are all signs of being *mal criada.* In my culture they are all words that are derogatory if applied to women— I've never heard them applied to men.

5 The first time I heard two women, a Puerto Rican and a Cuban, say the word *"nosotras,"* I was shocked. I had not known the word existed. Chicanas use *nosotros* whether we're male or female. We are robbed of our female being by the masculine plural. Language is a male discourse.

And our tongues have become
dry   the wilderness has
dried out our tongues   and
we have forgotten speech.
                                                —IRENA KLEPFISZ[2]

6   Even our own people, other Spanish speakers *nos quieren poner candados en la boca.* They would hold us back with their bag of *reglas de academia.*

OYÉ COMO LADRA:
EL LENGUAJE DE LA FRONTERA

Quien tiene boca se equivoca.
                        —Mexican saying

7   *"Pocho,* cultural traitor, you're speaking the oppressor's language by speaking English, you're ruining the Spanish language," I have been accused by various Latinos and Latinas. Chicano Spanish is considered by the purist and by most Latinos deficient, a mutilation of Spanish.

8   But Chicano Spanish is a border tongue which developed naturally. Change, *evolución, enriquecimiento de palabras nuevas por invención o adopción* have created variants of Chicano Spanish, *un nuevo lenguaje. Un lenguaje que corresponde a un modo de vivir.* Chicano Spanish is not incorrect, it is a living language.

9   For a people who are neither Spanish nor live in a country in which Spanish is the first language; for a people who live in a country in which English is the reigning tongue but who are not Anglo; for a people who cannot entirely identify with

either standard (formal, Castilian) Spanish nor standard English, what recourse is left to them but to create their own language? A language which they can connect their identity to, one capable of communicating the realities and values true to themselves—a language with terms that are neither *español ni inglés,* but both. We speak a patois, a forked tongue, a variation of two languages.

10   Chicano Spanish sprang out of the Chicanos' need to identify ourselves as a distinct people. We needed a language with which we could communicate with ourselves, a secret language. For some of us, language is a homeland closer than the Southwest—for many Chicanos today live in the Midwest and the East. And because we are a complex, heterogeneous people, we speak many languages. Some of the languages we speak are

1. Standard English
2. Working class and slang English
3. Standard Spanish
4. Standard Mexican Spanish
5. North Mexican Spanish dialect
6. Chicano Spanish (Texas, New Mexico, Arizona, and California have regional variations)
7. Tex-Mex
8. *Pachuco* (called *caló*)

11   My "home" tongues are the languages I speak with my sister and brothers, with my friends. They are the last five listed, with 6 and 7 being closest to my heart. From school, the media, and job situations, I've picked up standard and working class English. From Mamagrande Locha and from reading Spanish and Mexican literature, I've picked up Standard Spanish and Standard Mexican Spanish. From *los recién llegados,* Mexican immigrants, and *braceros,* I learned the North Mexican dialect. With Mexicans I'll try to speak either Standard Mexican Spanish or the North Mexican dialect. From my parents and Chicanos living in the Valley, I picked up Chicano Texas Spanish, and I speak it with my mom, younger brother (who married a Mexican and who rarely mixes Spanish with English), aunts, and older relatives.

12   With Chicanas from *Nuevo México* or *Arizona* I will speak Chicano Spanish a little, but often they don't understand what I'm saying. With most California Chicanas I speak entirely in English (unless I forget). When I first moved to San Francisco, I'd rattle off something in Spanish, unintentionally embarrassing them. Often it is only with another Chicana *tejano* that I can talk freely.

13 Words distorted by English are known as anglicisms or *pochismos*. The *pocho* is an anglicized Mexican or American of Mexican origin who speaks Spanish with an accent characteristic of North Americans and who distorts and reconstructs the language according to the influence of English.[3] Tex-Mex, or Spanglish, comes most naturally to me. I may switch back and forth from English to Spanish in the same sentence or in the same word. With my sister and my brother Nune and with Chicano *tejano* contemporaries I speak in Tex-Mex.

14   From kids and people my own age I picked up *Pachuco. Pachuco* (the language of the zoot suiters) is a language of rebellion, both against Standard Spanish and Standard English. It is a secret language. Adults of the culture and outsiders cannot understand it. It is made up of slang words from both English and Spanish. *Ruca* means girl or woman, *vato* means guy or dude, *chale* means no, *simón* means yes, *churro* is sure, talk is *periquiar, pigionear* means petting, *que gacho* means how nerdy, *ponte águila* means watch out, death is called *la pelona.* Through lack of practice and not having others who can speak it, I've lost most of the *Pachuco* tongue.

CHICANO SPANISH

15   Chicanos, after 250 years of Spanish/Anglo colonization, have developed significant differences in the Spanish we speak. We collapse two adjacent vowels into a single syllable and sometimes shift the stress in certain words such as *maíz/maiz, cohete/cuete.* We leave out certain consonants when they appear between vowels: *lado/lao, mojado/mojao.* Chicanos from South Texas pronounce *f* as *j* as in *jue (fue).* Chicanos use "archaisms," words that are no longer in the Spanish language, words that have been evolved out. We say *semos, truje, haiga, ansina,* and *naiden.* We retain the "archaic" *j,* as in *jalar,* that derives from an earlier *h* (the French *halar* or the Germanic *halon* which was lost to standard Spanish in the sixteenth century), but which is still found in several regional dialects such as the one spoken in South Texas. (Due to geography, Chicanos from the Valley of South Texas were cut off linguistically from other Spanish speakers. We tend to use words that the Spaniards brought over from Medieval Spain. The majority of the Spanish colonizers in Mexico and the Southwest came from Extremadura—Hernán Cortés was one of them—and Andalucía. Andalucians pronounce *ll* like a *y,* and their *d*'s tend to be absorbed by adjacent vowels: *tirado* becomes *tirao.* They brought *el lenguaje popular, dialectos y regionalismos.*)[4]

16   Chicanos and other Spanish speakers also shift *ll* to *y* and *z* to *s.*[5] We leave out initial syllables, saying *tar* for *estar, toy* for *estoy, hora* for *ahora* (*cubanos* and *puertorriqueños* also leave out initial letters of some words). We also leave out the final syllable such as *pa* for *para.* The intervocalic *y,* the *ll* as in *tortilla, ella, botella,* gets replaced by *tortia* or *tortiya, ea, botea.* We add an additional syllable at the beginning of certain words: *atocar* for *tocar, agastar* for *gastar.* Sometimes we'll say *lavaste las vacijas,* other times *lavates* (substituting the *ates* verb endings for the *aste*).

17   We used anglicisms, words borrowed from English: *bola* from ball, *carpeta* from carpet, *máchina de lavar* (instead of *lavadora*) from washing machine. Tex-Mex argot, created by adding a Spanish sound at the beginning or end of an English word such as *cookiar* for cook, *watchar* for watch, *parkiar* for park, and *rapiar* for rape, is the result of the pressures on Spanish speakers to adapt to English.

18   We don't use the word *vosotros/as* or its accompanying verb form. We don't say *claro* (to mean yes), *imagínate,* or *me emociona,* unless we picked up Spanish from Latinas, out of a book, or in a classroom. Other Spanish-speaking groups are going through the same, or similar, development in their Spanish.

LINGUISTIC TERRORISM

> Deslenguadas. Somos los del español deficiente. *We are your linguistic nightmare, your linguistic aberration, your linguistic* mestisaje, *the subject of your* burla. *Because we speak with tongues of fire we are culturally crucified. Racially, culturally, and linguistically* somos huérfanos—*we speak an orphan tongue.*

19　Chicanas who grew up speaking Chicano Spanish have internalized the belief that we speak poor Spanish. It is illegitimate, a bastard language. And because we internalize how our language has been used against us by the dominant culture, we use our language differences against each other.

20　Chicana feminists often skirt around each other with suspicion and hesitation. For the longest time I couldn't figure it out. Then it dawned on me. To be close to another Chicana is like looking into the mirror. We are afraid of what we'll see there. *Pena.* Shame. Low estimation of self. In childhood we are told that our language is wrong. Repeated attacks on our native tongue diminish our sense of self. The attacks continue throughout our lives.

21　Chicanas feel uncomfortable talking in Spanish to Latinas, afraid of their censure. Their language was not outlawed in their countries. They had a whole lifetime of being immersed in their native tongue; generations, centuries in which Spanish was a first language, taught in school, heard on radio and TV, and read in the newspaper.

22　If a person, Chicana or Latina, has a low estimation of my native tongue, she also has a low estimation of me. Often with *mexicanas y latinas* we'll speak English as a neutral language. Even among Chicanas we tend to speak English at parties or conferences. Yet, at the same time, we're afraid the other will think we're *agringadas* because we don't speak Chicano Spanish. We oppress each other trying to out-Chicano each other, vying to be the "real" Chicanas, to speak like Chicanos. There is no one Chicano language just as there is no one Chicano experience. A monolingual Chicana whose first language is English or Spanish is just as much a Chicana as one who speaks several variants of Spanish. A Chicana from Michigan or Chicago or Detroit is just as much a Chicana as one from the Southwest. Chicano Spanish is as diverse linguistically as it is regionally.

23　By the end of this century, Spanish speakers will comprise the biggest minority group in the United States, a country where students in high schools and colleges are encouraged to take French classes because French is considered more "cultured." But for a language to remain alive it must be used.[6] By the end of this century English, and not Spanish, will be the mother tongue of most Chicanos and Latinos.

24　So, if you want to really hurt me, talk badly about my language. Ethnic identity is twin skin to linguistic identity—I am my language. Until I can take pride in my language, I cannot take pride in myself. Until I can accept as legitimate Chicano Texas Spanish, Tex-Mex, and all the other languages I speak, I cannot accept the legitimacy of myself. Until I am free to write bilingually and to switch codes without having always to translate, while I still have to speak English or Spanish when I would rather speak Spanglish, and as long as I have to accommodate the English

speakers rather than having them accommodate me, my tongue will be illegitimate.

25   I will no longer be made to feel ashamed of existing. I will have my voice:
Indian, Spanish, white. I will have my serpent's tongue—my woman's voice, my
sexual voice, my poet's voice. I will overcome the tradition of silence.

> *My fingers*
> *move sly against your palm*
> *Like women everywhere, we speak in code. . . .*
>
> —MELANIE KAYE/KANTROWITZ[7]

"VISTAS," CORRIDOS, Y COMIDA: MY NATIVE TONGUE

26   In the 1960s, I read my first Chicano novel. It was *City of Night* by John Rechy, a
gay Texan, son of a Scottish father and a Mexican mother. For days I walked
around in stunned amazement that a Chicano could write and could get published.
When I read *I Am Joaquín*[8] I was surprised to see a bilingual book by a Chicano in
print. When I saw poetry written in Tex-Mex for the first time, a feeling of pure
joy flashed through me. I felt like we really existed as a people. In 1971, when I
started teaching High School English to Chicano students, I tried to supplement
the required texts with works by Chicanos, only to be reprimanded and forbidden
to do so by the principal. He claimed that I was supposed to teach "American"
and English literature. At the risk of being fired, I swore my students to secrecy
and slipped in Chicano short stories, poems, a play. In graduate school, while
working toward a Ph.D., I had to "argue" with one adviser after the other, semester after semester, before I was allowed to make Chicano literature an area of focus.

27   Even before I read books by Chicanos or Mexicans, it was the Mexican movies
I saw at the drive-in—the Thursday night special of $1.00 a carload—that gave
me a sense of belonging. *"Vámonos a las vistas,"* my mother would call out and
we'd all—grandmother, brothers, sister, and cousins—squeeze into the car. We'd
wolf down cheese and bologna white bread sandwiches while watching Pedro
Infante in melodramatic tearjerkers like *Nosotros los pobres,* the first "real" Mexican movie (that was not an imitation of European movies). I remember seeing
Cuando los hijos se van and surmising that all Mexican movies played up the love
a mother has for her children and what ungrateful sons and daughters suffer when
they are not devoted to their mothers. I remember the singing-type "westerns" of
Jorge Negrete and Miguel Aceves Mejía. When watching Mexican movies, I felt a
sense of homecoming as well as alienation. People who were to amount to something didn't go to Mexican movies, or *bailes,* or tune their radios to *bolero,*
rancherita, and *corrido* music.

28   The whole time I was growing up, there was *norteño* music sometimes called
North Mexican border music, or Tex-Mex music, or Chicano music, or *cantina* (bar)
music. I grew up listening to *conjuntos,* three- or four-piece bands made up of
folk musicians playing guitar, *bajo sexto,* drums, and button accordion, which Chi-

canos had borrowed from the German immigrants who had come to Central Texas and Mexico to farm and build breweries. In the Rio Grande Valley, Steve Jordan and Little Joe Hernández were popular, and Flaco Jiménez was the accordion king. The rhythms of Tex-Mex music are those of the polka, also adapted from the Germans, who in turn had borrowed the polka from the Czechs and Bohemians.

29   I remember the hot, sultry evenings when *corridos*—songs of love and death on the Texas-Mexican borderlands—reverberated out of cheap amplifiers from the local *cantinas* and wafted in through my bedroom window.

30   *Corridos* first became widely used along the South Texas/Mexican border during the early conflict between Chicanos and Anglos. The *corridos* are usually about Mexican heroes who do valiant deeds against the Anglo oppressors. Pancho Villa's song, *"La cucaracha,"* is the most famous one. *Corridos* of John F. Kennedy and his death are still very popular in the Valley. Older Chicanos remember Lydia Mendoza, one of the great border *corrido* singers who was called *la Gloria de Tejas.* Her *"El tango negro,"* sung during the Great Depression, made her a singer of the people. The ever-present *corridos* narrated one hundred years of border history, bringing news of events as well as entertaining. These folk musicians and folk songs are our chief cultural mythmakers, and they made our hard lives seem bearable.

31   I grew up feeling ambivalent about our music. Country-western and rock-and-roll had more status. In the fifties and sixties, for the slightly educated and *agringado* Chicanos, there existed a sense of shame at being caught listening to our music. Yet I couldn't stop my feet from thumping to the music, could not stop humming the words, nor hide from myself the exhilaration I felt when I heard it.

32 There are more subtle ways that we internalize identification, especially in the forms of images and emotions. For me food and certain smells are tied to my identity, to my homeland. Woodsmoke curling up to an immense blue sky; woodsmoke perfuming my grandmother's clothes, her skin. The stench of cow manure and the yellow patches on the ground; the crack of a .22 rifle and the reek of cordite. Homemade white cheese sizzling in a pan, melting inside a folded *tortilla.* My sister Hilda's hot, spicy *menudo, chile colorado* making it deep red, pieces of *panza* and hominy floating on top. My brother Carito barbequing *fajitas* in the backyard. Even now and 3,000 miles away, I can see my mother spicing the ground beef, pork, and venison with *chile.* My mouth salivates at the thought of the hot steaming *tamales* I would be eating if I were home.

SI LE PREGUNTAS A MI MAMÁ, "¿QUÉ ERES?"

*Identity is the essential core of who
we are as individuals, the conscious
experience of the self inside.*

—GERSHEN KAUFMAN[9]

33   *Nosotros los* Chicanos straddle the borderlands. On one side of us, we are constantly exposed to the Spanish of the Mexicans, on the other side we hear the Anglos' incessant clamoring so that we forget our language. Among ourselves we don't say *nosotros los americanos, o nosotros los españoles, o nosotros los*

hispanos. We say *nosotros los mexicanos* (by *mexicanos* we do not mean citizens of Mexico; we do not mean a national identity, but a racial one). We distinguish between *mexicanos del otro lado* and *mexicanos de este lado.* Deep in our hearts we believe that being Mexican has nothing to do with which country one lives in. Being Mexican is a state of soul—not one of mind, not one of citizenship. Neither eagle nor serpent, but both. And like the ocean, neither animal respects borders.

> Dime con quien andas y te diré quien eres.
> *(Tell me who your friends are and I'll tell you who you are.)*
> —Mexican saying

34   *Si le preguntas a mi mamá, "¿Qué eres?" te dirá, "Soy mexicana."* My brothers and sister say the same. I sometimes will answer *"soy mexicana"* and at others will say *"soy Chicana" o "soy tejana."* But I identified as *"Raza"* before I ever identified as *"mexicana"* or "Chicana."

35   As a culture, we call ourselves Spanish when referring to ourselves as a linguistic group and when copping out. It is then that we forget our predominant Indian genes. We are 70–80 percent Indian.[10] We call ourselves Hispanic[11] or Spanish-American or Latin American or Latin when linking ourselves to other Spanish-speaking peoples of the Western hemisphere and when copping out. We call ourselves Mexican-American[12] to signify we are neither Mexican nor American, but more the noun "American" than the adjective "Mexican" (and when copping out).

36   Chicanos and other people of color suffer economically for not acculturating. This voluntary (yet forced) alienation makes for psychological conflict, a kind of dual identity—we don't identify with the Anglo-American cultural values and we don't totally identify with the Mexican cultural values. We are a synergy of two cultures with various degrees of Mexicanness or Angloness. I have so internalized the borderland conflict that sometimes I feel like one cancels out the other and we are zero, nothing, no one. *A veces no soy nada ni nadie. Pero hasta cuando no lo soy, lo soy.*

37   When not copping out, when we know we are more than nothing, we call ourselves Mexican, referring to race and ancestry; *mestizo* when affirming both our Indian and Spanish (but we hardly ever own our Black) ancestry; Chicano when referring to a politically aware people born and/or raised in the United States; *Raza* when referring to Chicanos; *tejanos* when we are Chicanos from Texas.

38   Chicanos did not know we were a people until 1965 when Cesar Chavez and the farmworkers united and *I Am Joaquín* was published and *la Raza Unida* party was formed in Texas. With that recognition, we became a distinct people. Something momentous happened to the Chicano soul—we became aware of our reality and acquired a name and a language (Chicano Spanish) that reflected that reality. Now that we had a name, some of the fragmented pieces began to fall together—who we were, what we were, how we had evolved. We began to get glimpses of what we might eventually become.

39   Yet the struggle of identities continues, the struggle of borders is our reality still. One day the inner struggle will cease and a true integration take place. In the meantime, *tenémos que hacer la lucha. ¿Quién está protegiendo los ranchos de mi*

gente? ¿Quién está tratando de cerrar la fisura entre la india y el blanco en nuestra sangre? El Chicano, si, el Chicano que anda como un ladrón en su propia casa.

40 *Los Chicanos,* how patient we seem, how very patient. There is the quiet of the Indian about us.[13] We know how to survive. When other races have given up their tongue we've kept ours. We know what it is to live under the hammer blow of the dominant *norteamericano* culture. But more than we count the blows, we count the days the weeks the years the centuries the aeons until the white laws and commerce and customs will rot in the deserts they've created, lie bleached. *Humildes* yet proud, *quietos* yet wild, *nosotros los mexicanos-Chicanos* will walk by the crumbling ashes as we go about our business. Stubborn, persevering, impenetrable as stone, yet possessing a malleability that renders us unbreakable, we, the *mestizas* and *mestizos,* will remain.

NOTES

[1] Ray Gwyn Smith, *Moorland Is Cold Country,* unpublished book.

[2] Irena Klepfisz, *"Di rayze aheym*/The Journey Home," in *The Tribe of Dina: A Jewish Women's Anthology,* Melanie Kaye/Kantrowitz and Irena Klepfisz, eds. (Montpelier, VT: Sinister Wisdom Books, 1986), 49.

[3] R. C. Ortega, *Dialectología Del Barrio,* trans. Hortencia S. Alwan (Los Angeles, CA: R. C. Ortega Publisher & Bookseller, 1977), 132.

[4] Eduardo Hernandéz-Chávez, Andrew D. Cohen, and Anthony F. Beltramo, *El Lenguaje de los Chicanos: Regional and Social Characteristics of Language Used by Mexican Americans* (Arlington, VA: Center for Applied Linguistics, 1975), 39.

[5] Hernandéz-Chávez, xvii.

[6] Irena Klepfisz, "Secular Jewish Identity: Yidishkayt in America," in *The Tribe of Dina,* Kaye/Kantrowitz and Klepfisz, eds., 43.

[7] Melanie Kaye/Kantrowitz, "Sign," in *We Speak in Code: Poems and Other Writings* (Pittsburgh, PA: Motheroot Publications, Inc., 1980), 85.

[8] Rodolfo Gonzales, *I Am Joaquín/Yo Soy Joaquín* (New York, NY: Bantam Books, 1972). It was first published in 1967.

[9] Gershen Kaufman, *Shame: The Power of Caring* (Cambridge, MA: Schenkman Books, Inc., 1980), 68.

[10] John R. Chávez, *The Lost Land: The Chicano Images of the Southwest* (Albuquerque, NM: University of New Mexico Press, 1984), 88–90.

[11] "Hispanic" is derived from *Hispanis* (*España,* a name given to the Iberian Peninsula in ancient times when it was a part of the Roman Empire) and is a term designated by the U.S. government to make it easier to handle us on paper.

[12] The Treaty of Guadalupe Hidalgo created the Mexican-American in 1848.

[13] Anglos, in order to alleviate their guilt for dispossessing the Chicano, stressed the Spanish part of us and perpetrated the myth of the Spanish Southwest. We have accepted the fiction that we are Hispanic, that is Spanish, in order to accommodate ourselves to the dominant culture and its abhorrence of Indians. Chávez, 88–91.

QUESTIONS

Experience

· Describe your experience of reading "How to Tame a Wild Tongue." To what extent did you find Anzaldúa's use of Spanish confusing, helpful, enriching?

How did you respond to her use of quotations from other writers? Why? Where were you on home ground? Where were you lost, confused, excluded? Why?

· What was your response to Anzaldúa's description of the nine languages she speaks? Do you agree that these are all languages? Why, or why not? How do you define a "language"?

Interpretation

· What argument does Anzaldúa make for the need for a Chicano Spanish? And why does she characterize it as "a forked tongue"? Why does she say that "often it is only with another Chicana *tejano* that I can talk freely"?

· What is the point of her section on Chicano Spanish? Of her section on linguistic terrorism? And what does she mean by "linguistic terrorism"? What accounts for the varieties of Chicano Spanish she describes?

Evaluation

· Why does Anzaldúa speak so many different dialects and languages? Why doesn't she simply use standard English and standard Spanish?

· What cultural values are associated with the different languages and dialects Anzaldúa describes? Which are most important to her, and why? Which are most important to you? Why?

WRITING

Exploring

· Write a paper describing the different languages, dialects, or other forms of language you use. Describe where you use them, with whom, and why. Provide plenty of specific examples.

Interpreting

· Write a paper analyzing and interpreting "How to Tame a Wild Tongue." Include in your analysis a description or inventory of the different kinds of materials Anzaldúa includes in her piece and the effects they have. Consider the various meanings of her title.

Evaluating

· Explain the importance of music for Anzaldúa as she was growing up. Consider the values associated with the different types of music she describes and the feelings she has about each.

· Or explain her own valuation of her dual identity described in the last section of her essay. Consider the language, tone, and idea of her final paragraph.

DIANE RAVITCH
(b. 1938)

Multiculturalism

Diane Ravitch is an historian of education who has served as a government consultant and who has worked as a college professor at Teachers College, Columbia University. Her books include The Troubled Crusade: American Education, 1945–1980 *(1981),* What Do Our Seventeen-Year-Olds Know? *(1987), and* The American Reader *(1990).*

The following essay, originally published in the American Scholar *(1990), has become a standard item in the debate about multiculturalism in American education. Diane Ravitch's strategy is to summarize the views she wishes to oppose and then present a schema—particularist versus pluralist forms of multiculturalism—to develop her position and point out weaknesses in the opposition perspective.*

1   Questions of race, ethnicity, and religion have been a perennial source of conflict in American education. The schools have often attracted the zealous attention of those who wish to influence the future, as well as those who wish to change the way we view the past. In our history, the schools have been not only an institution in which to teach young people skills and knowledge, but an arena where interest groups fight to preserve their values, or to revise the judgments of history, or to bring about fundamental social change. In the nineteenth century, Protestants and Catholics battled over which version of the Bible should be used in school, or whether the Bible should be used at all. In recent decades, bitter racial disputes—provoked by policies of racial segregation and discrimination—have generated turmoil in the streets and in the schools. The secularization of the schools during the past century has prompted attacks on the curricula and textbooks and library books by fundamentalist Christians, who object to whatever challenges their faith-based views of history, literature, and science.

2   Given the diversity of American society, it has been impossible to insulate the schools from pressures that result from differences and tensions among groups. When people differ about basic values, sooner or later those disagreements turn up in battles about how schools are organized or what the schools should teach. Sometimes these battles remove a terrible injustice, like racial segregation. Sometimes, however, interest groups politicize the curriculum and attempt to impose their views on teachers, school officials, and textbook publishers. Across the country, even now, interest groups are pressuring local school boards to remove myths and fables and other imaginative literature from children's readers and to inject the teaching of creationism in biology. When groups cross the line into extremism, advancing their own agenda without regard to reason or to others, they threaten public education itself, making it difficult to teach any issues honestly and making the entire curriculum vulnerable to political campaigns.

3   For many years, the public schools attempted to neutralize controversies over

race, religion, and ethnicity by ignoring them. Educators believed, or hoped, that the schools could remain outside politics; this was, of course, a vain hope since the schools were pursuing policies based on race, religion, and ethnicity. Nonetheless, such divisive questions were usually excluded from the curriculum. The textbooks minimized problems among groups and taught a sanitized version of history. Race, religion, and ethnicity were presented as minor elements in the American saga; slavery was treated as an episode, immigration as a sidebar, and women were largely absent. The textbooks concentrated on presidents, wars, national politics, and issues of state. An occasional "great black" or "great woman" received mention, but the main narrative paid little attention to minority groups and women.

4   With the ethnic revival of the 1960s, this approach to the teaching of history came under fire, because the history of national leaders—virtually all of whom were white, Anglo-Saxon, and male—ignored the place in American history of those who were none of the above. The traditional history of elites had been complemented by an assimilationist view of American society, which presumed that everyone in the American melting pot would eventually lose or abandon those ethnic characteristics that distinguished them from mainstream Americans. The ethnic revival demonstrated that many groups did not want to be assimilated or melted. Ethnic studies programs popped up on campuses to teach not only that "black is beautiful," but also that every other variety of ethnicity is "beautiful" as well; everyone who had "roots" began to look for them so that they too could recover that ancestral part of themselves that had not been homogenized.

5   As ethnicity became an accepted subject for study in the late 1960s, textbooks were assailed for their failure to portray blacks accurately; within a few years, the textbooks in wide use were carefully screened to eliminate bias against minority groups and women. At the same time, new scholarship about the history of women, blacks, and various ethnic minorities found its way into the textbooks. At first, the multicultural content was awkwardly incorporated as little boxes on the side of the main narrative. Then some of the new social historians (like Stephan Thernstrom, Mary Beth Norton, Gary Nash, Winthrop Jordan, and Leon Litwack) themselves wrote textbooks, and the main narrative itself began to reflect a broadened historical understanding of race, ethnicity, and class in the American past. Consequently, today's history textbooks routinely incorporate the experiences of women, blacks, American Indians, and various immigrant groups.

6   Although most high school textbooks are deeply unsatisfactory (they still largely neglect religion, they are too long, too encyclopedic, too superficial, and lacking in narrative flow), they are far more sensitive to pluralism than their predecessors. For example, the latest edition of Todd and Curti's *Triumph of the American Nation,* the most popular high school history text, has significantly increased its coverage of blacks in America, including profiles of Phillis Wheatley, the poet; James Armistead, a revolutionary war spy for Lafayette; Benjamin Banneker, a self-taught scientist and mathematician; Hiram Revels, the first black to serve in the Congress; and Ida B. Wells-Barnett, a tireless crusader against lynching and racism. Even better as a textbook treatment is Jordan and Litwack's *The United States,* which skillfully synthesizes the historical experiences of blacks, Indians, immigrants, women, and other groups into the mainstream of American

social and political history. The latest generation of textbooks bluntly acknowledges the racism of the past, describing the struggle for equality by racial minorities while identifying individuals who achieved success as political leaders, doctors, lawyers, scholars, entrepreneurs, teachers, and scientists.

7   As a result of the political and social changes of recent decades, cultural pluralism is now generally recognized as an organizing principle of this society. In contrast to the idea of the melting pot, which promised to erase ethnic and group differences, children now learn that variety is the spice of life. They learn that America has provided a haven for many different groups and has allowed them to maintain their cultural heritage or to assimilate, or—as is often the case—to do both; the choice is theirs, not the state's. They learn that cultural pluralism is one of the norms of a free society; that differences among groups are a national resource rather than a problem to be solved. Indeed, the unique feature of the United States is that its common culture has been formed by the interaction of its subsidiary cultures. It is a culture that has been influenced over time by immigrants, American Indians, Africans (slave and free) and by their descendants. American music, art, literature, language, food, clothing, sports, holidays, and customs all show the effects of the commingling of diverse cultures in one nation. Paradoxical though it may seem, the United States has a common culture that is multicultural.

8   Our schools and our institutions of higher learning have in recent years begun to embrace what Catherine R. Stimpson of Rutgers University has called "cultural democracy," a recognition that we must listen to a "diversity of voices" in order to understand our culture, past and present. This understanding of the pluralistic nature of American culture has taken a long time to forge. It is based on sound scholarship and has led to major revisions in what children are taught and what they read in school. The new history is—indeed, must be—a warts-and-all history; it demands an unflinching examination of racism and discrimination in our history. Making these changes is difficult, raises tempers, and ignites controversies, but gives a more interesting and accurate account of American history. Accomplishing these changes is valuable, because there is also a useful lesson for the rest of the world in America's relatively successful experience as a pluralistic society. Throughout human history, the clash of different cultures, races, ethnic groups, and religions has often been the cause of bitter hatred, civil conflict, and international war. The ethnic tensions that now are tearing apart Lebanon, Sri Lanka, Kashmir, and various republics of the Soviet Union remind us of the costs of unfettered group rivalry. Thus, it is a matter of more than domestic importance that we closely examine and try to understand that part of our national history in which different groups competed, fought, suffered, but ultimately learned to live together in relative peace and even achieved a sense of common nationhood.

9   Alas, these painstaking efforts to expand the understanding of American culture into a richer and more varied tapestry have taken a new turn, and not for the better. Almost any idea, carried to its extreme, can be made pernicious, and this is what is happening now to multiculturalism. Today, pluralistic multiculturalism must contend with a new, particularistic multiculturalism. The pluralists seek a richer common culture; the particularists insist that no common culture is possible or desirable. The new particularism is entering the curriculum in a number of school systems across the country. Advocates of particularism propose an ethno-

centric curriculum to raise the self-esteem and academic achievement of children from racial and ethnic minority backgrounds. Without any evidence, they claim that children from minority backgrounds will do well in school *only* if they are immersed in a positive, prideful version of their ancestral culture. If children are of, for example, Fredonian ancestry, they must hear that Fredonians were important in mathematics, science, history, and literature. If they learn about great Fredonians and if their studies use Fredonian examples and Fredonian concepts, they will do well in school. If they do not, they will have low self-esteem and will do badly.

10   At first glance, this appears akin to the celebratory activities associated with Black History Month or Women's History Month, when schoolchildren learn about the achievements of blacks and women. But the point of those celebrations is to demonstrate that neither race nor gender is an obstacle to high achievement. They teach all children that everyone, regardless of their race, religion, gender, ethnicity, or family origin, can achieve self-fulfillment, honor, and dignity in society if they aim high and work hard.

11   By contrast, the particularistic version of multiculturalism is unabashedly filiopietistic and deterministic. It teaches children that their identity is determined by their "cultural genes." That something in their blood or their race memory or their cultural DNA defines who they are and what they may achieve. That the culture in which they live is not their own culture, even though they were born here. That American culture is "Eurocentric,"[1] and therefore hostile to anyone whose ancestors are not European. Perhaps the most invidious implication of particularism is that racial and ethnic minorities are not and should not try to be part of American culture; it implies that American culture belongs only to those who are white and European; it implies that those who are neither white nor European are alienated from American culture by virtue of their race or ethnicity; it implies that the only culture they do belong to or can ever belong to is the culture of their ancestors, even if their families have lived in this country for generations.

12   The war on so-called Eurocentrism is intended to foster self-esteem among those who are not of European descent. But how, in fact, is self-esteem developed? How is the sense of one's own possibilities, one's potential choices, developed? Certainly, the school curriculum plays a relatively small role as compared to the influence of family, community, mass media, and society. But to the extent that curriculum influences what children think of themselves, it should encourage children of all racial and ethnic groups to believe that they are part of this society and that they should develop their talents and minds to the fullest. It is enormously inspiring, for example, to learn about men and women from diverse backgrounds who overcame poverty, discrimination, physical handicaps, and other obstacles to achieve success in a variety of fields. Behind every such biography of accomplishment is a story of heroism, perseverance, and self-discipline. Learning these stories will encourage a healthy spirit of pluralism, of mutual respect, and of self-respect among children of different backgrounds. The children of American society today will live their lives in a racially and culturally diverse nation, and their education should prepare them to do so.

---

[1] Centered or focused on Europe.

13   The pluralist approach to multiculturalism promotes a broader interpretation of the common American culture and seeks due recognition for the ways that the nation's many racial, ethnic, and cultural groups have transformed the national culture. The pluralists say, in effect, "American culture belongs to us, all of us; the U.S. is us, and we remake it in every generation." But particularists have no interest in extending or revising American culture; indeed, they deny that a common culture exists. Particularists reject any accommodation among groups, any interactions that blur the distinct lines between them. The brand of history that they espouse is one in which everyone is either a descendant of victims or oppressors. By doing so, ancient hatreds are fanned and re-created in each new generation. Particularism has its intellectual roots in the ideology of ethnic separatism and in the black nationalist movement. In the particularist analysis, the nation has five cultures: African American, Asian American, European American, Latino/Hispanic, and Native American. The huge cultural, historical, religious, and linguistic differences within these categories are ignored, as is the considerable intermarriage among these groups, as are the linkages (like gender, class, sexual orientation, and religion) that cut across these five groups. No serious scholar would claim that all Europeans and white Americans are part of the same culture, or that all Asians are part of the same culture, or that all people of Latin-American descent are of the same culture, or that all people of African descent are of the same culture. Any categorization this broad is essentially meaningless and useless.

14   Several districts—including Detroit, Atlanta, and Washington, D.C.—are developing an Afrocentric curriculum. *Afrocentricity* has been described in a book of the same name by Molefi Kete Asante of Temple University. The Afrocentric curriculum puts Africa at the center of the student's universe. African Americans must "move away from an [*sic*] Eurocentric framework" because "it is difficult to create freely when you use someone else's motifs, styles, images, and perspectives." Because they are not Africans, "white teachers cannot inspire in our children the visions necessary for them to overcome limitations." Asante recommends that African Americans choose an African name (as he did), reject European dress, embrace African religion (not Islam or Christianity) and love "their own" culture. He scorns the idea of universality as a form of Eurocentric arrogance. The Eurocentrist, he says, thinks of Beethoven or Bach as classical, but the Afrocentrist thinks of Ellington or Coltrane as classical; the Eurocentrist lauds Shakespeare or Twain, while the Afrocentrist prefers Baraka, Shange, or Abiola. Asante is critical of black artists like Arthur Mitchell and Alvin Ailey who ignore Afrocentricity. Likewise, he speaks contemptuously of a group of black university students who spurned the Afrocentrism of the local Black Student Union and formed an organization called Inter-race: "Such madness is the direct consequence of self-hatred, obligatory attitudes, false assumptions about society, and stupidity."

15   The conflict between pluralism and particularism turns on the issue of universalism. Professor Asante warns his readers against the lure of universalism: "Do not be captured by a sense of universality given to you by the Eurocentric viewpoint; such a viewpoint is contradictory to your own ultimate reality." He insists that there is no alternative to Eurocentrism, Afrocentrism, and other ethnocentrisms. In contrast, the pluralist says, with the Roman playwright Terence, "I am a man: nothing human is alien to me." A contemporary Terence would say "I am a person" or might be a woman, but the point remains the same: You don't have to

be black to love Zora Neale Hurston's fiction or Langston Hughes's poetry or Duke Ellington's music. In a pluralist curriculum, we expect children to learn a broad and humane culture, to learn about the ideas and art and animating spirit of many cultures. We expect that children, whatever their color, will be inspired by the courage of people like Helen Keller, Vaclav Havel, Harriet Tubman, and Feng Lizhe. We expect that their response to literature will be determined by the ideas and images it evokes, not by the skin color of the writer. But particularists insist that children can learn only from the experiences of people from the same race.

16   Particularism is a bad idea whose time has come. It is also a fashion spreading like wildfire through the education system, actively promoted by organizations and individuals with a political and professional interest in strengthening ethnic power bases in the university, in the education profession, and in society itself. One can scarcely pick up an educational journal without learning about a school district that is converting to an ethnocentric curriculum in an attempt to give "self-esteem" to children from racial minorities. A state-funded project in a Sacramento high school is teaching young black males to think like Africans and to develop the "African Mind Model Technique," in order to free themselves of the racism of American culture. A popular black rap singer, KRS-One, complained in an op-ed article in the *New York Times* that the schools should be teaching blacks about their cultural heritage, instead of trying to make everyone Americans. "It's like trying to teach a dog to be a cat," he wrote. KRS-One railed about having to learn about Thomas Jefferson and the Civil War, which had nothing to do (he said) with black history.

17   Pluralism can easily be transformed into particularism, as may be seen in the potential uses in the classroom of the Mayan contribution to mathematics. The Mayan example was popularized in a movie called *Stand and Deliver,* about a charismatic Bolivian-born mathematics teacher in Los Angeles who inspired his students (who are Hispanic) to learn calculus. He told them that their ancestors invented the concept of zero; but that wasn't all he did. He used imagination to put across mathematical concepts. He required them to do homework and to go to school on Saturdays and during the Christmas holidays, so that they might pass the Advanced Placement mathematics examination for college entry. The teacher's reference to the Mayans' mathematical genius was a valid instructional device: It was an attention-getter and would have interested even students who were not Hispanic. But the Mayan example would have had little effect without the teacher's insistence that the class study hard for a difficult examination.

18   Ethnic educators have seized upon the Mayan contribution to mathematics as the key to simultaneously boosting the ethnic pride of Hispanic children and attacking Eurocentrism. One proposal claims that Mexican-American children will be attracted to science and mathematics if they study Mayan mathematics, the Mayan calendar, and Mayan astronomy. Children in primary grades are to be taught that the Mayans were first to discover the zero and that Europeans learned it long afterwards from the Arabs, who had learned it in India. This will help them see that Europeans were latecomers in the discovery of great ideas. Botany is to be learned by study of the agricultural techniques of the Aztecs, a subject of some-what limited relevance to children in urban areas. Furthermore, "ethnobotanical" classifications of plants are to be substituted for the Eurocentric Linnaean system. At first glance, it may seem curious that Hispanic children are deemed to have no

cultural affinity with Spain; but to acknowledge the cultural tie would confuse the ideological assault on Eurocentrism.

19   This proposal suggests some questions: Is there any evidence that the teaching of "culturally relevant" science and mathematics will draw Mexican-American children to the study of these subjects? Will Mexican-American children lose interest or self-esteem if they discover that their ancestors were Aztecs or Spaniards, rather than Mayans? Are children who learn in this way prepared to study the science and mathematics that are taught in American colleges and universities and that are needed for advanced study in these fields? Are they even prepared to study the science and mathematics taught in *Mexican* universities? If the class is half Mexican-American and half something else, will only the Mexican-American children study in a Mayan and Aztec mode or will all the children? But shouldn't all children study what is culturally relevant for them? How will we train teachers who have command of so many different systems of mathematics and science?

20   The efficacy of particularist proposals seems to be less important to their sponsors than their value as ideological weapons with which to criticize existing disciplines for their alleged Eurocentric bias. In a recent article titled "The Ethnocentric Basis of Social Science Knowledge Production" in the *Review of Research in Education,* John Stanfield of Yale University argues that neither social science nor science are objective studies, that both instead are "Euro-American" knowledge systems which reproduce "hegemonic racial domination." The claim that science and reason are somehow superior to magic and witchcraft, he writes, is the product of Euro-American ethnocentrism. According to Stanfield, current fears about the misuse of science (for instance, "the nuclear arms race, global pollution") and "the powerplays of Third World nations (the Arab oil boycott and the American-Iranian hostage crisis) have made Western people more aware of nonscientific cognitive styles. These last events are beginning to demonstrate politically that which has begun to be understood in intellectual circles: namely, that modes of social knowledge such as theology, science, and magic are different, not inferior or superior. They represent different ways of perceiving, defining, and organizing knowledge of life experiences." One wonders: if Professor Stanfield broke his leg, would he go to a theologian, a doctor, or a magician?

21   Every field of study, it seems, has been tainted by Eurocentrism, which was defined by a professor at Manchester University, George Ghevarughese Joseph, in *Race and Class* in 1987, as "intellectual racism." Professor Joseph argues that the history of science and technology—and in particular, of mathematics—in non-European societies was distorted by racist Europeans who wanted to establish the dominance of European forms of knowledge. The racists, he writes, traditionally traced mathematics to the Greeks, then claimed that it reached its full development in Europe. These are simply Eurocentric myths to sustain an "imperialist/racist ideology," says Professor Joseph, since mathematics was found in Egypt, Babylonia, Mesopotamia, and India long before the Greeks were supposed to have developed it. Professor Joseph points out too that Arab scientists should be credited with major discoveries traditionally attributed to William Harvey, Isaac Newton, Charles Darwin, and Sir Francis Bacon. But he is not concerned only to argue historical issues; his purpose is to bring all of these different mathematical traditions into the school classroom so that children might study, for

example, "traditional African designs, Indian *rangoli* patterns and Islamic art" and "the language and counting systems found across the world."

22   This interesting proposal to teach ethnomathematics comes at a time when American mathematics educators are trying to overhaul present practices, because of the poor performance of American children on national and international assessments. Mathematics educators are attempting to change the teaching of their subject so that children can see its uses in everyday life. There would seem to be an incipient conflict between those who want to introduce real-life applications of mathematics and those who want to teach the mathematical systems used by ancient cultures. I suspect that most mathematics teachers would enjoy doing a bit of both, if there were time or student interest. But any widespread movement to replace modern mathematics with ancient ethnic mathematics runs the risk of disaster in a field that is struggling to update existing curricula. If, as seems likely, ancient mathematics is taught mainly to minority children, the gap between them and middle-class white children is apt to grow. It is worth noting that children in Korea, who score highest in mathematics on international assessments, do not study ancient Korean mathematics.

23   Particularism is akin to cultural Lysenkoism,[2] for it takes as its premise the spurious notion that cultural traits are inherited. It implies a dubious, dangerous form of cultural predestination. Children are taught that if their ancestors could do it, so could they. But what happens if a child is from a cultural group that made no significant contribution to science or mathematics? Does this mean that children from that background must find a culturally appropriate field in which to strive? How does a teacher find the right cultural buttons for children of mixed heritage? And how in the world will teachers use this technique when the children in their classes are drawn from many different cultures, as is usually the case? By the time that every culture gets its due, there may be no time left to teach the subject itself. This explosion of filiopietism (which, we should remember, comes from adults, not from students) is reminiscent of the period some years ago when the Russians claimed that they had invented everything first; as we now know, this nationalistic braggadocio did little for their self-esteem and nothing for their economic development. We might reflect, too, on how little social prestige has been accorded in this country to immigrants from Greece and Italy, even though the achievements of their ancestors were at the heart of the classical curriculum.

24   Filiopietism and ethnic boosterism lead to all sorts of odd practices. In New York State, for example, the curriculum guide for eleventh grade American history lists three "foundations" for the United States Constitution, as follows:

A. Foundations.
    1. 17th and 18th century Enlightenment thought
    2. Haudenosaunee political system
        a. Influence upon colonial leadership and European intellectuals (Locke, Montesquieu, Voltaire, Rousseau)
        b. Impact on Albany Plan of Union, Articles of Confederation, and U.S. Constitution
    3. Colonial experience

---

[2] A genetic doctrine asserting that acquired characteristics are inheritable.

25   Those who are unfamiliar with the Haudenosaunee political system might wonder what it is, particularly since educational authorities in New York State rank it as equal in importance to the European Enlightenment and suggest that it strongly influenced not only colonial leaders but the leading intellectuals of Europe. The Haudenosaunee political system was the Iroquois confederation of five (later six) Indian tribes in upper New York State, which conducted war and civil affairs through a council of chiefs, each with one vote. In 1754, Benjamin Franklin proposed a colonial union at a conference in Albany; his plan, said to be inspired by the Iroquois Confederation, was rejected by the other colonies. Today, Indian activists believe that the Iroquois Confederation was the model for the American Constitution, and the New York State Department of Education has decided that they are right. That no other state sees fit to give the American Indians equal billing with the European Enlightenment may be owing to the fact that the Indians in New York State (numbering less than forty thousand) have been more politically effective than elsewhere or that other states have not yet learned about this method of reducing "Eurocentrism" in their American history classes.

26   Particularism can easily be carried to extremes. Students of Fredonian descent must hear that their ancestors were seminal in the development of all human civilization and that without the Fredonian contribution, we would all be living in caves or trees, bereft of art, technology, and culture. To explain why Fredonians today are in modest circumstances, given their historic eminence, children are taught that somewhere, long ago, another culture stole the Fredonians' achievements, palmed them off as their own, and then oppressed the Fredonians.

27   I first encountered this argument almost twenty years ago, when I was a graduate student. I shared a small office with a young professor, and I listened as she patiently explained to a student why she had given him a D on a term paper. In his paper, he argued that the Arabs had stolen mathematics from the Nubians in the desert long ago (I forget in which century this theft allegedly occurred). She tried to explain to him about the necessity of historical evidence. He was unconvinced, since he believed that he had uncovered a great truth that was beyond proof. The part I couldn't understand was how anyone could lose knowledge by sharing it. After all, cultures are constantly influencing one another, exchanging ideas and art and technology, and the exchange usually is enriching, not depleting.

28   Today, there are a number of books and articles advancing controversial theories about the origins of civilization. An important work, *The African Origin of Civilization: Myth or Reality,* by Senegalese scholar Cheikh Anta Diop, argues that ancient Egypt was a black civilization, that all races are descended from the black race, and that the achievements of "western" civilization originated in Egypt. The views of Diop and other Africanists have been condensed into an everyman's paperback titled *What They Never Told You in History Class* by Indus Khamit Kush. This latter book claims that Moses, Jesus, Buddha, Mohammed, and Vishnu were Africans; that the first Indians, Chinese, Hebrews, Greeks, Romans, Britains, and Americans were Africans; and that the first mathematicians, scientists, astronomers, and physicians were Africans. A debate currently raging among some classicists is whether the Greeks "stole" the philosophy, art, and religion of the ancient Egyptians and whether the ancient Egyptians were black Africans. George G. M. James's *Stolen Legacy* insists that the Greeks "stole the Legacy of

the African Continent and called it their own." James argues that the civilization of Greece, the vaunted foundation of European culture, owed everything it knew and did to its African predecessors. Thus, the roots of western civilization lie not in Greece and Rome, but in Egypt and, ultimately, in black Africa.

29   Similar speculation was fueled by the publication in 1987 of Martin Bernal's *Black Athena: The Afroasiatic Roots of Classical Civilization,* Volume 1, *The Fabrication of Ancient Greece, 1785–1985,* although the controversy predates Bernal's book. In a fascinating foray into the politics of knowledge, Bernal attributes the preference of Western European scholars for Greece over Egypt as the fount of knowledge to nearly two centuries of racism and "Europocentrism," but he is uncertain about the color of the ancient Egyptians. However, a review of Bernal's book last year in the *Village Voice* began, "What color were the ancient Egyptians? Blacker than Mubarak,[3] baby." The same article claimed that white racist archeologists chiseled the noses off ancient Egyptian statues so that future generations would not see the typically African facial characteristics. The debate reached the pages of the *Biblical Archeology Review* last year in an article titled "Were the Ancient Egyptians Black or White?" The author, classicist Frank J. Yurco, argues that some Egyptian rulers were black, others were not, and that "the ancient Egyptians did not think in these terms." The issue, wrote Yurco, "is a chimera, cultural baggage from our own society that can only be imposed artificially on ancient Egyptian society."

30   Most educationists are not even aware of the debate about whether the ancient Egyptians were black or white, but they are very sensitive to charges that the schools' curricula are Eurocentric, and they are eager to rid the schools of the taint of Eurocentrism. It is hardly surprising that America's schools would recognize strong cultural ties with Europe since our nation's political, religious, educational, and economic institutions were created chiefly by people of European descent, our government was shaped by European ideas, and nearly 80 percent of the people who live here are of European descent. The particularists treat all of this history as a racist bias toward Europe, rather than as the matter-of-fact consequences of European immigration. Even so, American education is not centered on Europe. American education, if it is centered on anything, is centered on itself. It is "Americentric." Most American students today have never studied any world history; they know very little about Europe, and even less about the rest of the world. Their minds are rooted solidly in the here and now. When the Berlin Wall was opened in the fall of 1989, journalists discovered that most American teenagers had no idea what it was, nor why its opening was such a big deal. Nonetheless, Eurocentrism provides a better target than Americentrism.

31   In school districts where most children are black and Hispanic, there has been a growing tendency to embrace particularism rather than pluralism. Many of the children in these districts perform poorly in academic classes and leave school without graduating. They would fare better in school if they had well-educated and well-paid teachers, small classes, good materials, encouragement at home and school, summer academic programs, protection from the drugs and crime that ravage their neighborhoods, and higher expectations of satisfying careers

---

[3] Hosni Mubarak (b. 1928), Egyptian political leader.

upon graduation. These are expensive and time-consuming remedies that must also engage the larger society beyond the school. The lure of particularism is that it offers a less complicated anodyne, one in which the children's academic deficiencies may be addressed—or set aside—by inflating their racial pride. The danger of this remedy is that it will detract attention from the real needs of schools and the real interests of children, while simultaneously arousing distorted race pride in children of all races, increasing racial antagonism, and producing fresh recruits for white and black racist groups.

32   The particularist critique gained a major forum in New York in 1989, with the release of a report called "A Curriculum of Inclusion," produced by a task force created by the State Commissioner of Education, Thomas Sobol. In 1987, soon after his appointment, Sobol appointed a Task Force on Minorities to review the state's curriculum for instances of bias. He did this not because there had been complaints about bias in the curriculum, but because—as a newly appointed state commissioner whose previous job had been to superintend the public schools of a wealthy suburb, Scarsdale—he wanted to demonstrate his sensitivity to minority concerns. The Sobol task force was composed of representatives of African American, Hispanic, Asian American, and American Indian groups.

33   The task force engaged four consultants, one from each of the aforementioned racial or ethnic minorities, to review nearly one hundred teachers' guides prepared by the state. These guides define the state's curriculum, usually as a list of facts and concepts to be taught, along with model activities. The primary focus of the consultants, not surprisingly, was the history and social studies curriculum. As it happened, the history curriculum had been extensively revised in 1987 to make it multicultural, in both American and world history. In the 1987 revision the time given to Western Europe was reduced to one-quarter of one year, as part of a two-year global studies sequence in which equal time was allotted to seven major world regions, including Africa and Latin America.

34   As a result of the 1987 revisions in American and world history, New York State had one of the most advanced multicultural history–social studies curricula in the country. Dozens of social studies teachers and consultants had participated, and the final draft was reviewed by such historians as Eric Foner of Columbia University, the late Hazel Hertzberg of Teachers College, Columbia University, and Christopher Lash of the University of Rochester. The curriculum was overloaded with facts, almost to the point of numbing students with details and trivia, but it was not insensitive to ethnicity in American history or unduly devoted to European history.

35   But the Sobol task force decided that this curriculum was biased and Eurocentric. The first sentence of the task force report summarizes its major thesis: "African Americans, Asian Americans, Puerto Ricans/Latinos, and Native Americans have all been the victims of an intellectual and educational oppression that has characterized the culture and institutions of the United States and the European American world for centuries."

36   The task force report was remarkable in that it vigorously denounced bias without identifying a single instance of bias in the curricular guides under review. Instead, the consultants employed harsh, sometimes inflammatory, rhetoric to treat every difference of opinion or interpretation as an example of racial bias. The

African American consultant, for example, excoriates the curriculum for its "White Anglo-Saxon (WASP) value system and norms," its "deep-seated pathologies of racial hatred" and its "white nationalism"; he decries as bias the fact that children study Egypt as part of the Middle East instead of as part of Africa. Perhaps Egypt should be studied as part of the African unit (geographically, it is located on the African continent); but placing it in one region rather than the other is not what most people think of as racism or bias. The "Latino" consultant criticizes the use of the term "Spanish-American War" instead of "Spanish-Cuban-American War." The Native American consultant complains that tribal languages are classified as "foreign languages."

37   The report is consistently Europhobic. It repeatedly expresses negative judgments on "European Americans" and on everything Western and European. All people with a white skin are referred to as "Anglo-Saxons" and "WASPs." Europe, says the report, is uniquely responsible for producing aggressive individuals who "were ready to 'discover, invade and conquer' foreign land because of greed, racism and national egoism." All white people are held collectively guilty for the historical crimes of slavery and racism. There is no mention of the "Anglo-Saxons" who opposed slavery and racism. Nor does the report acknowledge that some whites have been victims of discrimination and oppression. The African American consultant writes of the Constitution, "There is something vulgar and revolting in glorifying a process that heaped undeserved rewards on a segment of the population while oppressing the majority."

38   The New York task force proposal is not merely about the reconstruction of what is taught. It goes a step further to suggest that the history curriculum may be used to ensure that "children from Native American, Puerto Rican/Latino, Asian American, and African American cultures will have higher self-esteem and self-respect, while children from European cultures will have a less arrogant perspective of being part of the group that has 'done it all.' "

39   In February 1990, Commissioner Sobol asked the New York Board of Regents to endorse a sweeping revision of the history curriculum to make it more multicultural. His recommendations were couched in measured tones, not in the angry rhetoric of his task force. The board supported his request unanimously. It remains to be seen whether New York pursues the particularist path marked out by the Commissioner's advisory group or finds its way to the concept of pluralism within a democratic tradition.

40 The rising tide of particularism encourages the politicization of all curricula in the schools. If education bureaucrats bend to the political and ideological winds, as is their wont, we can anticipate a generation of struggle over the content of the curriculum in mathematics, science, literature, and history. Demands for "culturally relevant" studies, for ethnostudies of all kinds, will open the classroom to unending battles over whose version is taught, who gets credit for what, and which ethno-interpretation is appropriate. Only recently have districts begun to resist the demands of fundamentalist groups to censor textbooks and library books (and some have not yet begun to do so).

41   The spread of particularism throws into question the very idea of American public education. Public schools exist to teach children the general skills and

knowledge that they need to succeed in American society, and the specific skills and knowledge that they need in order to function as American citizens. They receive public support because they have a public function. Historically, the public schools were known as "common schools" because they were schools for all, even if the children of all the people did not attend them. Over the years, the courts have found that it was unconstitutional to teach religion in the common schools, or to separate children on the basis of their race in the common schools. In their curriculum, their hiring practices, and their general philosophy, the public schools must not discriminate against or give preference to any racial or ethnic group. Yet they are permitted to accommodate cultural diversity by, for example, serving food that is culturally appropriate or providing library collections that emphasize the interests of the local community. However, they should not be expected to teach children to view the world through an ethnocentric perspective that rejects or ignores the common culture. For generations, those groups that wanted to inculcate their religion or their ethnic heritage have instituted private schools—after school, on weekends, or on a full-time basis. There, children learn with others of the same group—Greeks, Poles, Germans, Japanese, Chinese, Jews, Lutherans, Catholics, and so on—and are taught by people from the same group. Valuable as this exclusive experience has been for those who choose it, this has not been the role of public education. One of the primary purposes of public education has been to create a national community, a definition of citizenship and culture that is both expansive and *inclusive.*

42   The curriculum in public schools must be based on whatever knowledge and practices have been determined to be best by professionals—experienced teachers and scholars—who are competent to make these judgments. Professional societies must be prepared to defend the integrity of their disciplines. When called upon, they should establish review committees to examine disputes over curriculum and to render judgment, in order to help school officials fend off improper political pressure. Where genuine controversies exist, they should be taught and debated in the classroom. Was Egypt a black civilization? Why not raise the question, read the arguments of the different sides in the debate, show slides of Egyptian pharaohs and queens, read books about life in ancient Egypt, invite guest scholars from the local university, and visit museums with Egyptian collections? If scholars disagree, students should know it. One great advantage of this approach is that students will see that history is a lively study, that textbooks are fallible, that historians disagree, that the writing of history is influenced by the historian's politics and ideology, that history is written by people who make choices among alternative facts and interpretations, and that history changes as new facts are uncovered and new interpretations win adherents. They will also learn that cultures and civilizations constantly interact, exchange ideas, and influence one another, and that the idea of racial or ethnic purity is a myth. Another advantage is that students might once again study ancient history, which has all but disappeared from the curricula of American schools. (California recently introduced a required sixth grade course in ancient civilizations, but ancient history is otherwise *terra incognita*[4] in American education.)

43   The multicultural controversy may do wonders for the study of history, which

has been neglected for years in American schools. At this time, only half of our high school graduates ever study any world history. Any serious attempt to broaden students' knowledge of Africa, Europe, Asia, and Latin America will require at least two, and possibly three years of world history (a requirement thus far only in California). American history, too, will need more time than the one-year high-school survey course. Those of us who have insisted for years on the importance of history in the curriculum may not be ready to assent to its redemptive power, but hope that our new allies will ultimately join a constructive dialogue that strengthens the place of history in the schools.

44   As cultural controversies arise, educators must adhere to the principle of "E Pluribus Unum." That is, they must maintain a balance between the demands of the one—the nation of which we are common citizens—and the many—the varied histories of the American people. It is not necessary to denigrate either the one or the many. Pluralism is a positive value, but it is also important that we preserve a sense of an American community—a society and a culture to which we all belong. If there is no overall community with an agreed-upon vision of liberty and justice, if all we have is a collection of racial and ethnic cultures, lacking any common bonds, then we have no means to mobilize public opinion on behalf of people who are not members of our particular group. We have, for example, no reason to support public education. If there is no larger community, then each group will want to teach its own children in its own way, and public education ceases to exist.

45   History should not be confused with filiopietism. History gives no grounds for race pride. No race has a monopoly on virtue. If anything, a study of history should inspire humility, rather than pride. People of every racial group have committed terrible crimes, often against others of the same group. Whether one looks at the history of Europe or Africa or Latin America or Asia, every continent offers examples of inhumanity. Slavery has existed in civilizations around the world for centuries. Examples of genocide can be found around the world, throughout history, from ancient times right through to our own day. Governments and cultures, sometimes by edict, sometimes simply following tradition, have practiced not only slavery, but human sacrifice, infanticide, cliterodectomy,[5] and mass murder. If we teach children this, they might recognize how absurd both racial hatred and racial chauvinism are.

46   What must be preserved in the study of history is the spirit of inquiry, the readiness to open new questions and to pursue new understandings. History, at its best, is a search for truth. The best way to portray this search is through debate and controversy, rather than through imposition of fixed beliefs and immutable facts. Perhaps the most dangerous aspect of school history is its tendency to become Official History, a sanctified version of the Truth taught by the state to captive audiences and embedded in beautiful mass-market textbooks as holy writ. When Official History is written by committees responding to political pressures, rather than by scholars synthesizing the best available research, then the errors of the past are replaced by the politically fashionable errors of the present. It may be difficult to teach children that history is both important and uncertain, and that even the best historians never have all the pieces of the jigsaw puzzle, but it is necessary to do so. If state education departments permit the revision of their history courses

and textbooks to become an exercise in power politics, then the entire process of state-level curriculum-making becomes suspect, as does public education itself.

47   The question of self-esteem is extraordinarily complex, and it goes well beyond the content of the curriculum. Most of what we call self-esteem is formed in the home and in a variety of life experiences, not only in school. Nonetheless, it has been important for blacks—and for other racial groups—to learn about the history of slavery and of the civil rights movement; it has been important for blacks to know that their ancestors actively resisted enslavement and actively pursued equality; and it has been important for blacks and others to learn about black men and women who fought courageously against racism and who provide models of courage, persistence, and intellect. These are instances where the content of the curriculum reflects sound scholarship, and at the same time probably lessens racial prejudice and provides inspiration for those who are descendants of slaves. But knowing about the travails and triumphs of one's forebears does not necessarily translate into either self-esteem or personal accomplishment. For most children, self-esteem—the self-confidence that grows out of having reached a goal—comes not from hearing about the monuments of their ancestors but as a consequence of what they are able to do and accomplish through their own efforts.

48   As I reflected on these issues, I recalled reading an interview a few years ago with a talented black runner. She said that her model is Mikhail Baryshnikov. She admires him because he is a magnificent athlete. He is not black; he is not female; he is not American-born; he is not even a runner. But he inspires her because of the way he trained and used his body. When I read this, I thought how narrow-minded it is to believe that people can be inspired *only* by those who are exactly like them in race and ethnicity.

QUESTIONS

Experience

· Comment on your experience in school and community life with racial and ethnic difference. To what extent have you come in contact with people of different racial, ethnic, and religious backgrounds than yours? What principles govern your relationships with people who differ from you in these ways?

Interpretation

· According to Diane Ravitch, what distinguishes pluralistic multiculturalism from particularistic multiculturalism? Which does she favor, and why?

· What does Ravitch mean when she writes that "the conflict between pluralism and particularism turns on the issue of universalism"?

Evaluation

· Evaluate Ravitch's argument about particularistic multiculturalism. Consider the examples she cites in paragraphs 15 through 20. Whose arguments do you find more convincing—those of Ravitch or those of the particularists? Why?

· What do you think of the example Ravitch uses to conclude her essay? Why?

WRITING

Exploring

· Make a list of people you admire along with the characteristics for which you admire them. Include both living and historical figures. Ask some of your classmates, friends, and teachers whom they admire and why. Then take stock to see whether those mentioned on your list or those admired by your classmates, friends, and teachers are exactly like you or them in race and ethnicity.

Interpreting

· Write an essay in which you analyze your own education from a multicultural standpoint. Explain in what ways your education has been or has not been multicultural (and whether it has been pluralistic or particularistic). Consider whether it could have been made more or less multicultural and whether this would have been a good thing.

Evaluating

· Write an essay that identifies and examines the cultural values that underlie the two approaches to multiculturalism Ravitch discusses: pluralistic multiculturalism and particularistic multiculturalism. Explain which version of multiculturalism you prefer and why.

GEORGE ORWELL
(1903–1950)

Marrakech

George Orwell is the pen name of Eric Blair, born in 1903 to English parents in Bengal, India. Orwell was educated in England, at Crossgates School and at Eton as King's Scholar. After university, he went to Burma, where he served as subdivisional officer in the Indian Imperial Police.

Best known for his fictional allegories, Animal Farm *and* 1984, *Orwell has also written remarkable nonfiction, including both books and essays.* Homage to Catalonia *(1938) provides an eyewitness account of the Spanish Civil War, Orwell having served as a soldier on the Republican side. The* Road to Wigan Pier *(1937) provides an angry account of mining conditions in northern England.*

Orwell's essay "Marrakech" is constructed of a series of interlocking vignettes that depict the Moroccan city, especially the poverty of its inhabitants. Orwell's rhetorical strategy in the essay is to work by implication and suggestion rather than to state his idea explicitly. Each of the five little scenes reveals an aspect of the place and its people. Through brief but telling snatches of dialogue and through carefully selected descriptive detail, Orwell provides a memorable expression of his viewpoint.

I

1 As the corpse went past the flies left the restaurant table in a cloud and rushed after it, but they came back a few minutes later.

2 The little crowd of mourners—all men and boys, no women—threaded their way across the market-place between the piles of pomegranates and the taxis and the camels, wailing a short chant over and over again. What really appeals to the flies is that the corpses here are never put into coffins, they are merely wrapped in a piece of rag and carried on a rough wooden bier on the shoulders of four friends. When the friends get to the burying-ground they hack an oblong hole a foot or two deep, dump the body in it and fling over it a little of the dried-up, lumpy earth, which is like broken brick. No gravestone, no name, no identifying mark of any kind. The burying-ground is merely a huge waste of hummocky earth, like a derelict building-lot. After a month or two no one can even be certain where his own relatives are buried.

II

3 When you walk through a town like this—two hundred thousand inhabitants, of whom at least twenty thousand own literally nothing except the rags they stand up in—when you see how the people live, and still more how easily they die, it is

always difficult to believe that you are walking among human beings. All colonial empires are in reality founded upon that fact. The people have brown faces— besides, there are so many of them! Are they really the same flesh as yourself? Do they even have names? Or are they merely a kind of undifferentiated brown stuff, about as individual as bees or coral insects? They rise out of the earth, they sweat and starve for a few years, and then they sink back into the nameless mounds of the graveyard and nobody notices that they are gone. And even the graves themselves soon fade back into the soil. Sometimes, out for a walk, as you break your way through the prickly pear, you notice that it is rather bumpy under- foot, and only a certain regularity in the bumps tells you that you are walking over skeletons.

4   I was feeding one of the gazelles in the public gardens.

5   Gazelles are almost the only animals that look good to eat when they are still alive, in fact, one can hardly look at their hindquarters without thinking of mint sauce. The gazelle I was feeding seemed to know that this thought was in my mind, for though it took the piece of bread I was holding out it obviously did not like me. It nibbled rapidly at the bread, then lowered its head and tried to butt me, then took another nibble and then butted again. Probably its idea was that if it could drive me away the bread would somehow remain hanging in mid-air.

6   An Arab navvy working on the path nearby lowered his heavy hoe and sidled slowly towards us. He looked from the gazelle to the bread and from the bread to the gazelle, with a sort of quiet amazement, as though he had never seen any- thing quite like this before. Finally he said shyly in French:

7   "*I* could eat some of that bread."

8   I tore off a piece and he stowed it gratefully in some secret place under his rags. This man is an employee of the Municipality.

III

9 When you go through the Jewish quarters you gather some idea of what the medieval ghettoes were probably like. Under their Moorish rulers the Jews were only allowed to own land in certain restricted areas, and after centuries of this kind of treatment they have ceased to bother about overcrowding. Many of the streets are a good deal less than six feet wide, the houses are completely windowless, and sore-eyed children cluster everywhere in unbelievable numbers, like clouds of flies. Down the centre of the street there is generally running a little river of urine.

10   In the bazaar huge families of Jews, all dressed in the long black robe and lit- tle black skull-cap, are working in dark fly-infested booths that look like caves. A carpenter sits cross-legged at a prehistoric lathe, turning chair-legs at lightning speed. He works the lathe with a bow in his right hand and guides the chisel with his left foot, and thanks to a lifetime of sitting in this position his left leg is warped out of shape. At his side his grandson, aged six, is already starting on the simpler parts of the job.

11   I was just passing the coppersmiths' booths when somebody noticed that I was lighting a cigarette. Instantly, from the dark holes all round, there was a fren- zied rush of Jews, many of them old grandfathers with flowing grey beards, all

clamoring for a cigarette. Even a blind man somewhere at the back of one of the booths heard a rumour of cigarettes and came crawling out, groping in the air with his hand. In about a minute I had used up the whole packet. None of these people, I suppose, works less than twelve hours a day, and every one of them looks on a cigarette as a more or less impossible luxury.

12   As the Jews live in self-contained communities they follow the same trades as the Arabs, except for agriculture. Fruit-sellers, potters, silversmiths, blacksmiths, butchers, leather-workers, tailors, water-carriers, beggars, porters—whichever way you look you see nothing but Jews. As a matter of fact there are thirteen thousand of them, all living in the space of a few acres. A good job Hitler wasn't here. Perhaps he was on his way, however. You hear the usual dark rumours about the Jews, not only from the Arabs but from the poorer Europeans.

13   "Yes, mon vieux, they took my job away from me and gave it to a Jew. The Jews! They're the real rulers of this country, you know. They've got all the money. They control the banks, finance—everything."

14   "But," I said, "isn't it a fact that the average Jew is a labourer working for about a penny an hour?"

15   "Ah, that's only for show! They're all moneylenders really. They're cunning, the Jews."

16   In just the same way, a couple of hundred years ago, poor old women used to be burned for witchcraft when they could not even work enough magic to get themselves a square meal.

IV

17 All people who work with their hands are partly invisible, and the more important the work they do, the less visible they are. Still, a white skin is always fairly conspicuous. In northern Europe, when you see a labourer ploughing a field, you probably give him a second glance. In a hot country, anywhere south of Gibraltar or east of Suez, the chances are that you don't even see him. I have noticed this again and again. In a tropical landscape one's eye takes in everything except the human beings. It takes in the dried-up soil, the prickly pear, the palm tree and the distant mountain, but it always misses the peasant hoeing at his patch. He is the same colour as the earth, and a great deal less interesting to look at.

18   It is only because of this that the starved countries of Asia and Africa are accepted as tourist resorts. No one would think of running cheap trips to the Distressed Areas. But where the human beings have brown skins their poverty is simply not noticed. What does Morocco mean to a Frenchman? An orange-grove or a job in Government service. Or to an Englishman? Camels, castles, palm trees, Foreign Legionnaires, brass trays, and bandits. One could probably live there for years without noticing that for nine-tenths of the people the reality of life is an endless, back-breaking struggle to wring a little food out of an eroded soil.

19   Most of Morocco is so desolate that no wild animal bigger than a hare can live on it. Huge areas which were once covered with forest have turned into a treeless waste where the soil is exactly like broken-up brick. Nevertheless a good deal of it is cultivated, with frightful labour. Everything is done by hand. Long lines

of women, bent double like inverted capital L's, work their way slowly across the fields, tearing up the prickly weeds with their hands, and the peasant gathering lucerne for fodder pulls it up stalk by stalk instead of reaping it, thus saving an inch or two on each stalk. The plough is a wretched wooden thing, so frail that one can easily carry it on one's shoulder, and fitted underneath with a rough iron spike which stirs the soil to a depth of about four inches. This is as much as the strength of the animals is equal to. It is usual to plough with a cow and a donkey yoked together. Two donkeys would not be quite strong enough, but on the other hand two cows would cost a little more to feed. The peasants possess no harrows, they merely plough the soil several times over in different directions, finally leaving it in rough furrows, after which the whole field has to be shaped with hoes into small oblong patches to conserve water. Except for a day or two after the rare rainstorms there is never enough water. Along the edges of the fields channels are hacked out to a depth of thirty or forty feet to get at the tiny trickles which run through the subsoil.

20   Every afternoon a file of very old women passes down the road outside my house, each carrying a load of firewood. All of them are mummified with age and the sun, and all of them are tiny. It seems to be generally the case in primitive communities that the women, when they get beyond a certain age, shrink to the size of children. One day a poor old creature who could not have been more than four feet tall crept past me under a vast load of wood. I stopped her and put a five-sou piece (a little more than a farthing) into her hand. She answered with a shrill wail, almost a scream, which was partly gratitude but mainly surprise. I suppose that from her point of view, by taking any notice of her, I seemed almost to be violating a law of nature. She accepted her status as an old woman, that is to say as a beast of burden. When a family is travelling it is quite usual to see a father and a grown-up son riding ahead on donkeys, and an old woman following on foot, carrying the baggage.

21   But what is strange about these people is their invisibility. For several weeks, always at about the same time of day, the file of old women had hobbled past the house with their firewood, and though they had registered themselves on my eyeballs I cannot truly say that I had seen them. Firewood was passing—that was how I saw it. It was only that one day I happened to be walking behind them, and the curious up-and-down motion of a load of wood drew my attention to the human being beneath it. Then for the first time I noticed the poor old earth-coloured bodies, bodies reduced to bones and leathery skin, bent double under the crushing weight. Yet I suppose I had not been five minutes on Moroccan soil before I noticed the overloading of the donkeys and was infuriated by it. There is no question that the donkeys are damnably treated. The Moroccan donkey is hardly bigger than a St. Bernard dog, it carries a load which in the British Army would be considered too much for a fifteen-hands mule, and very often its pack-saddle is not taken off its back for weeks together. But what is peculiarly pitiful is that it is the most willing creature on earth, it follows its master like a dog and does not need either bridle or halter. After a dozen years of devoted work it suddenly drops dead, whereupon its master tips it into the ditch and the village dogs have torn its guts out before it is cold.

22   This kind of thing makes one's blood boil, whereas—on the whole—the plight

of the human beings does not. I am not commenting, merely pointing to a fact. People with brown skins are next door to invisible. Anyone can be sorry for the donkey with its galled back, but it is generally owing to some kind of accident if one even notices the old woman under her load of sticks.

V

23 As the storks flew northward the Negroes were marching southward—a long, dusty column, infantry, screw-gun batteries, and then more infantry, four or five thousand men in all, winding up the road with a clumping of boots and a clatter of iron wheels.

24 They were Senegalese, the blackest Negroes in Africa, so black that sometimes it is difficult to see whereabouts on their necks the hair begins. Their splendid bodies were hidden in reach-me-down khaki uniforms, their feet squashed into boots that looked like blocks of wood, and every tin hat seemed to be a couple of sizes too small. It was very hot and the men had marched a long way. They slumped under the weight of their packs and the curiously sensitive black faces were glistening with sweat.

25 As they went past a tall, very young Negro turned and caught my eye. But the look he gave me was not in the least the kind of look you might expect. Not hostile, not contemptuous, not sullen, not even inquisitive. It was the shy, wide-eyed Negro look, which actually is a look of profound respect. I saw how it was. This wretched boy, who is a French citizen and has therefore been dragged from the forest to scrub floors and catch syphilis in garrison towns, actually has feelings of reverence before a white skin. He has been taught that the white race are his masters, and he still believes it.

26 But there is one thought which every white man, and in this connection it doesn't matter twopence if he calls himself a socialist, thinks when he sees a black army marching past. "How much longer can we go on kidding these people? How long before they turn their guns in the other direction?"

27 It was curious, really. Every white man there had this thought stowed somewhere or other in his mind. I had it, so had the other onlookers, so had the officers on their sweating chargers and the white N.C.O.'s marching in the ranks. It was a kind of secret which we all knew and were too clever to tell; only the Negroes didn't know it. And really it was like watching a flock of cattle to see the long column, a mile or two miles of armed men, flowing peacefully up the road, while the great white birds drifted over them in the opposite direction, glittering like scraps of paper.

QUESTIONS

Experience

· As you read the opening vignette of "Marrakech," what did make of the behavior of the flies? How did you react to the description of the burial?

· As you read the second and subsequent vignettes, to what extent did you try to relate them to the opening section? To what extent did you see them as self-contained units, yet related on the basis of a general idea?

Interpretation

· What do the five sections of "Marrakech" have in common? What general theme links them?

· Look back at section III, which itself contains a series of smaller subsections. Identify the scenes within section III, and explain how they are related.

Evaluation

· Orwell avoids stating outright his attitude about what he sees in Marrakech. Yet we understand that he is not simply describing the place neutrally. Instead, he is making a judgment, offering a perspective on the poverty and powerlessness he sees there. What is Orwell's attitude, and where do you sense it most powerfully?

WRITING

Exploring

· Write an essay about a place by creating a series of descriptive vignettes or scenes, as Orwell does in "Marrakech." You may wish to write about an area of your city or hometown, your neighborhood, or your campus, for which you might focus on such areas as the library, student center, gymnasium, classrooms, cafeteria, and so on. You may wish to convey your sense of the campus (or other place) indirectly, through the kinds of details you select and the way you organize them.

Interpreting

· Write an analysis of "Marrakech," focusing on one part at a time. Identify the central issue in each scene, and explain how Orwell conveys his attitude through his selection of detail and his use of dialogue. Write one or two paragraphs of analysis for each section of Orwell's essay. You may wish to conclude by writing an additional paragraph in which you explain Orwell's overall point and attitude.

Evaluating

· Argue for or against the indirect strategy Orwell adopts in "Marrakech." Consider whether his essay is more or less effective for not presenting a thesis directly but instead letting his idea and attitude emerge indirectly.

HENRY LOUIS GATES, JR.
(b. 1950)

2 Live Crew, Decoded

Henry Louis Gates is a professor and a critic. He has taught at Duke and Princeton and is currently a professor at Harvard University, where he heads the program in Afro-American studies. Gates has published a number of books, including Black Literature and Literary Theory *(1984) and* The Signifying Monkey, *which won a 1989 National Book Award. He is also the general editor of the Schomberg Library of American Writers and the author of a recent memoir,* Colored People *(1994). His article in response to the publicity generated by 2 Live Crew was published in the* New York Times, *June 19, 1990.*

Gates's brief essay turns on his explanation of the urban black street tradition of "signifying" or "playing the dozens." Rather than argue whether 2 Live Crew's lyrics are obscene or artful, he places the group's music in a cultural context in which parody and sexual carnival have prominent places. In defense of lyrics like those of 2 Live Crew, Gates also introduces notions of censorship and racism, most evident in his final sentence.

1   The rap group 2 Live Crew and their controversial hit recording "As Nasty as They Wanna Be" may well earn a signal place in the history of First Amendment rights. But just as important is how these lyrics will be interpreted and by whom.

2   For centuries, African-Americans have been forced to develop coded ways of communicating to protect them from danger. Allegories and double meanings, words redefined to mean their opposites ("bad" meaning "good," for instance), even neologisms ("bodacious") have enabled blacks to share messages only the initiated understood.

3   Many blacks were amused by the transcripts of Marion Barry's sting operation, which reveals that he used the traditional black expression about one's "nose being opened." This referred to a love affair and not, as Mr. Barry's prosecutors have suggested, to the inhalation of drugs. Understanding this phrase could very well spell the difference (for the mayor) between prison and freedom.

4   2 Live Crew is engaged in heavy-handed parody, turning the stereotypes of black and white American culture on their heads. These young artists are acting out, to lively dance music, a parodic exaggeration of the age-old stereotypes of the oversexed black female and male. Their exuberant use of hyperbole (phantasmagoric sexual organs, for example) undermines—for anyone fluent in black cultural codes—a too literal-minded hearing of the lyrics.

5   This is the street tradition called "signifying" or "playing the dozens," which has generally been risqué, and where the best signifier or "rapper" is the one who invents the most extravagant images, the biggest "lies," as the culture says. (H. "Rap" Brown earned his nickname in just this way.) In the face of racist stereo-

types about black sexuality, you can do one of two things: you can disavow them or explode them with exaggeration.

6   2 Live Crew, like many "hip-hop" groups, is engaged in sexual carnivalesque. Parody reigns supreme, from a take-off of standard blues to a spoof of the black power movement; their off-color nursery rhymes are part of a venerable Western tradition. The group even satirizes the culture of commerce when it appropriates popular advertising slogans ("Tastes great!" "Less filling!") and puts them in a bawdy context.

7   2 Live Crew must be interpreted within the context of black culture generally and of signifying specifically. Their novelty, and that of other adventuresome rap groups, is that their defiant rejection of euphemism now voices for the mainstream what before existed largely in the "race record" market—where the records of Redd Foxx and Rudy Ray Moore once were forced to reside.

8   Rock songs have always been about sex but have used elaborate subterfuges to convey that fact. 2 Live Crew uses Anglo-Saxon words and is self-conscious about it: a parody of a white voice in one song refers to "private personal parts," as a coy counterpart to the group's bluntness.

9   Much more troubling than its so-called obscenity is the group's overt sexism. Their sexism is so flagrant, however, that it almost cancels itself out in a hyperbolic war between the sexes. In this, it recalls the inter-sexual jousting in Zora Neale Hurston's novels. Still, many of us look toward the emergence of more female rappers to redress sexual stereotypes. And we must not allow ourselves to sentimentalize street culture: the appreciation of verbal virtuosity does not lessen one's obligation to critique bigotry in all of its pernicious forms.

10   Is 2 Live Crew more "obscene" than, say, the comic Andrew "Dice" Clay? Clearly, this rap group is seen as more threatening than others that are just as sexually explicit. Can this be completely unrelated to the specter of the young black male as a figure of sexual and social disruption, the very stereotypes 2 Live Crew seems determined to undermine?

11   This question—and the very large question of obscenity and the First Amendment—cannot even be addressed until those who would answer them become literate in the vernacular traditions of African-Americans. To do less is to censor through the equivalent of intellectual prior restraint—and censorship is to art what lynching is to justice.

QUESTIONS

Experience

· What has been your experience with rap music generally and with that of 2 Live Crew in particular? Is this music you care for? Why, or why not?

Interpretation

· Why, according to Gates, has 2 Live Crew used exaggeration and hyperbole in expressing themselves? To what extent can their use of exaggeration be attributed to what Gates terms "signifying" or "playing the dozens"? How convincing is his explanation that 2 Live Crew's style of sexual suggestion is an attempt to explode sexual stereotypes with exaggeration?

Evaluation

· To what extent has 2 Live Crew's music been misunderstood by mainstream audiences? Do you agree with Gates that in order to understand the significance of this rap group's performances, you must place it within the contexts of western "carnivalesque" and, even more important, "black culture generally and of signifying specifically"? Why, or why not?

WRITING

Exploring

· Describe your own response to the performances of 2 Live Crew.
· Or explain why you have not paid much attention to the group.
· Or compare the music of 2 Live Crew with that of another, less notorious rap or hip-hop group.

Interpreting

· Summarize Gates's argument in defense of 2 Live Crew. What does Gates say about their alleged sexism? Their obscenity? Their use of racial and sexual stereotypes? Explain the significance of Gates's references to traditional western (white) culture, and comment on his use of comparisons such as that made in the article's final sentence.

Evaluating

· Discuss the phenomenon of rap music in general or the events surrounding the performances of 2 Live Crew in particular as manifestations of a clash of cultural attitudes and values. Try to place the group or rap music in a larger cultural context by relating it to other social and cultural forces.

MARIE RIBISI
(b. 1962)

The Health Craze

Marie Ribisi wrote "The Health Craze" for a college composition course she took as a sophomore at Queens College, City University of New York. She had been reading essays by contemporary American writers, when she was assigned to write an essay about a social or cultural issue, imitating the style of one of the writers studied in the course. Marie chose Tom Wolfe as her author and his "Only One Life" (pp. 111–114) as her model essay. Her own essay, while reflecting her thinking about an aspect of health in American society in the early 1980s, hews closely to the sentence structures and tone of Wolfe's essay.

1   In 1982 a middle-class woman's magazine entitled COSMOPOLITAN was circulating various advertisements for the Noxell Raintree moisturizing beauty lotion, which attempts to sell the product with the line: "Why not keep your age your secret!" In a single catchword it had captured what may be delineated as the laic side of the Youth Era. "Why not keep your age your secret . . ." (And anything else you want to conceal that may cause you to feel old.)

2   This prescription accounts for most of the notoriety of the nation's fitness or health craze. "How young can I look?" most women ask their hairdressers. Without a doubt there are women who want to look younger or conceal their age or be noticed by their male peers or just keep their heads above water. But for every such woman, there are twenty young fifteen-year-olds who simply want to "steal the limelight" and be noticed by the same male group. "Why not keep your age your secret . . . and your wrinkles too!" (Not to mention . . . a few sags here and there, dark circles, age spots, crow's feet, and graying, mousy-brown hair.) But even that is not really covering the half of it, because usually the subconscious implication is nothing less than: "If you're old, you're out." The critical coup de main extra of the youth movement has been to cultivate a female population—middle-aged women—to the state of eternal beauty. One's very being as a female . . . as a person . . . becomes something all of society ignores, overlooks constantly, places little importance on, or, in any event, takes lightly. Every woman becomes paranoid, insecure, or worrisome . . . or feels rejected or excluded.

3   Among the men, the prescription becomes: "Why not keep your age a secret . . . as long as you keep fit or have money (instead of going to pot, harboring a beer belly, except perhaps allowing a few distinguished wrinkles to appear here and there, to a man who preserves himself well enough to look 45 all his life and knows that aging or the appearance of a receding hairline will not be noticed but only looked upon as addenda to the process of comely male maturity.) The possibility of being an unaffected individual and ignoring the preoccupation with looking young is possible for men only, and even for them it is difficult at times. In the 1960's and 1970's it began to be seen as the solicitude of the young, the elite,

and the female population (Twiggy, Cheryl Tiegs, and famous fashion models), although it also touched the matrons of the middle class. Losing weight enabled opportunists such as Jack LaLanne to open up his own health spas in the late 1960's and Weight Watchers to become internationally acclaimed as an authoritative organization in aiding the obese in pound depletion. Until 1978 the fitness fad made it impossible for any young women over 105 pounds to fit into snug, sear-sucking, french-cut jeans. Today, in the "I am thin, now what should I do to stay this way?" Era, being slim is matter-of-fact—as long as one counts the Cadburys, chugalugs eight glasses of water each day, and takes the Special K pinch every morning.

4   When Elizabeth Taylor found herself in the overweight category in 1980 and was ridiculed by journalists, it was noticed. Likewise in the situations of countless females. When beautiful women gained weight in particular areas and got out of shape, it tainted their respectability and stature to a great degree. Working off the excess baggage in a health spa, in fact, was the only hope for undergoing the coveted emaciation. (Louise Lasser completed the declaration in a contrary unpopular manner: "Why not keep your age your secret . . . and gain as many pounds as you like regardlessly." As did Shelley Winters, who kept her weight at a steady 190 pound reading, and, later, Jane Russell . . . with an eye toward a Playtex full-figured girdle commercial. Which she got.) Some wiseasses remark, supposedly with an angle of wit, that the federal government may eventually have to develop more land to make room for overweight women, to accommodate the masses of corpulent maidens and matrons. However, voicing such opinions has simply demonstrated to women or the female population that to succeed and be accepted, one must remain trim in a world of chauvinists. ("Why not keep your age a secret . . . and stop living as an anomaly.")

5   Much of what is presently recognized as the "fitness craze" has consisted of both women and men completing the statement this way: "Why not keep your age your secret . . . and take up jogging or wear designer jeans." (Instead of remaining sedentary and living in polyester specials.) In "jogging" a guy and a girl can exercise with one another to lose pounds without feeling alone. There are no statistics on the exercise that prove anything, but I do know that it surfaces in conversation today in the most unexpected corners of the United States. It is a peculiar event to be in Montpelier, Vermont, in the heart of the eastern ski country, and have some hotdog daredevil (and I mean blonde-haired, blue-eyed!) come up to you and ask: "Is there much jogging going on in New York?"

6   "JOGGING?"

7   Jogging turns out to be a ritual, in Montpelier, in any case, in which acrobatic skiers engage in the summer months—men and women, often in teams—running for promoting fitness, building up leg muscles, strengthening knee power crucial to good skiers, such as slalom racers, all the downhillers, and ballet skiers, and free-style jumpers.

8   One of the satisfactions of this kind of activity, quite in addition to the trolly horses, is belonging: I want to belong like everyone else. Young and old alike are given to the most relentless and serious endeavor . . . being like everyone else. People quickly succeed in placing themselves on the same level in the health drama whose effects are immediate loss of weight and emotional security. Men

and women of all walks of life, not merely skiers, are given just now to the achievement of being accepted in peer circles while still maintaining their individuality. A key drama of our own day is Peter Yates' movie BREAKING AWAY. In it we see a group of young adults who have graduated high school and live in the vicinity of a famous university but who are unable to develop a true sense of "belonging"—to cite one of the signature feelings of the Fitness Decade. Then each character begins to belong, and thereupon their individuality flourishes and they begin to spread out. For the remainder of the picture they grow limitlessly, with some fear, but the "self-assertion"—another signature word—begins to emerge. Obviously, the lesson that the audience draws from this picture is related to the "need to belong." The dialogues begin with the main character saying something like, "We'll always be buddies no matter what happens. We're cutters and that makes us a team. There isn't a chance in the world I could ever desert you." At this, the starting line, the entire scene seems familiar. We yearn to belong to something (or someone in one way or another). I'm going to do something that will make me like him (or her) and then I'll undoubtedly belong! (Of course, I have my individuality, but that will develop . . . in time.)

9   He says, "We'll always be cutters. It's a special bond that will always keep us together. Won't it?"

10   He was struggling dearly to hold his ground. Nevertheless, a certain sixth sense indicates that he's on a quaking earth. So he repeats the process of rationalizing in his mind in hopes of convincing himself.

11   "Well," his friend says as he looks across the lake, "those college shmucks aren't wasting any time in claiming their corner of the quarry. It seems that being a cutter just isn't what it used to be."

12   Consciously our hero is telling himself, "I wonder if that's true?" But what his friend has just said begins to pound in his brain like an irritating tune you try to forget. What's he trying to say?—Good-bye? He's saying we don't belong with each other anymore, we're outcasts in this present state, the growing has stopped. All of the times through which we struggled together are over! (And what makes matters worse is—I have to find something that will make me feel part of a greater whole again!) He always knew, deep in his heart, that this day would come. His mistake was: he believed he belonged. His friends knew it, too, all along. They felt unsure of themselves.

13   Out loud our hero says, "Well, I'm afraid there's nothing we can do about those asshole co-eds."

14   The group detects the pessimistic note. "Look," he says, "We may as well face up to the facts for our own good."

15   His friend says, "You're right. We're no longer in high school."

16   He says, "Well, what about the rest of you."

17   "Well," says one of them, "I'll tell you something about how we'll have to decide what to do with ourselves and how we want to go through life. You never really think about it seriously—you just don't know how to go about it—you know? Sometimes we're bummin' round havin' a good time, and suddenly there's a click . . . somethin's missin'. You just know there's an emptiness."

18   And the hero's still telling himself, "I can make it—but what the hell do I do?"

19   He says, "We never said anything—about anything like this."

20   One of the group says, "It's not the same. How many times have I told you that dese days it just ain't the same no more?"

21   Somehow this really makes our hero upset . . . all those times . . . and his mind instantaneously fastens on his mom and dad whom he always wanted to make proud . . . After feeling so secure I suddenly don't BELONG! What infuriates him is that this is a trauma which cannot be easily put aside. HOW MUCH LONGER WILL I HAVE TO WAIT UNTIL I WILL KNOW WHAT TO DO—OR FEEL THAT SENSE OF BELONGING? WHAT CAN I DO TO BECOME PART OF IT ALL AGAIN? And all at once he is suddenly disillusioned with life in general, not because things never worked out for themselves, but simply because nothing's ever permanent—and he would have to be the one to decide what to do with himself this time to FEEL THAT SENSE OF BELONGING once again—IT WOULD HAVE TO COME FROM HIM.

22   From that moment on, our heroes are ready to develop their individuality. It's only a few minutes before they each begin attempting to "break away" from each other with courage of the highest caliber, with true heart—"Don't look back at yesterday—it's gone"—and at that juncture when things get tough they all get going, but on their own. So they make attempts with great hopes! and break away! and keep on searching! and they find themselves suddenly belonging.

23   One young man gets married. The other, our hero, decides to enter college. Both decisions are vehicles, in essence, of acquiring acceptance via whatever undertaking the characters involve themselves in, similar to those who choose to become "fit" or look "young" or "jog". This phase of the game finally reveals that universal truth—that one must do what one has to, to belong—including keeping one's age a secret or going to college. Through marriage, sharing one's life with another person, and engaging oneself in mutual projects, two people can enjoy an intimate sense of "belonging" that many people have enjoyed for centuries. The cost of this is only one's insecurity, whereas college will probably run from $30,000–$100,000. The entire belonging process, however, is well worth whatever it takes to feel wanted in today's society or keep a secret.

24   Well, my dear Security Seekers . . . the rest is up to you.

QUESTIONS

Experience

· How would you characterize the experience of reading Marie Ribisi's essay? Why? Where did you find yourself most and least engaged? Why?

· To what extent can you relate to the references and allusions she makes—her references to *Cosmopolitan* and Noxell Raintree moisturing lotion, for example, and to Elizabeth Taylor and Cheryl Tiegs?

Interpretation

· What is the central subject of this essay, and what is the writer's attitude toward it?

· How effective are the techniques Marie Ribisi uses to convey her attitude toward the subject? What are the effects, for example, of her use of ellipses (. . .), of words in all capital letters, of exclamation points and parentheses?

Evaluation

· What cultural values are described or otherwise suggested in "keep your age your secret"?

· What is your own view of the behaviors and attitudes Ribisi refers to, such as dieting, jogging, and keeping one's age a secret?

WRITING

Exploring

· Select a contemporary fad or fashion which is associated with a catchy phrase or advertising slogan. Use that phrase or slogan to describe the fad or fashion. Reveal your attitude toward it by treating the subject either seriously or playfully. You may wish to use some of Ribisi's writing techniques.

Interpreting

· Analyze Ribisi's essay and provide an interpretation of it. Identify her main point, and describe how she goes about conveying it.

· Or analyze a print or video advertisement. Identify its major parts or segments. Explain how its language and images convey its message, and comment on the ad's selling strategies.

Evaluating

· Evaluate the success of Ribisi's essay as an imitation of Tom Wolfe's "Only One Life" (p. 111).

· Or evaluate the persuasiveness of "keep your age your secret."

· Or select one of the cultural concerns Ribisi refers to and write your own essay about it.

LESLIE MARMON SILKO
(b. 1948)

The Man to Send Rain Clouds

Leslie Marmon Silko, poet, essayist, and storyteller, was born in New Mexico of Laguna parentage. She spent her childhood on the Laguna Pueblo Indian reservation. She has published a volume of poetry, Laguna Woman *(1974); a collection of short stories,* Storyteller *(1981); and two novels,* Ceremony *(1977) and* Almanac of the Dead *(1991). She has been the recipient of a MacArthur fellowship as well as other awards.*

"The Man to Send Rain Clouds" reveals a direct clash of cultural perspectives. The story turns on a conflict between Catholic and Native American burial rituals. Especially noteworthy is Silko's use of symbolism in her description of water at the story's conclusion.

1　They found him under a big cottonwood tree. His Levi jacket and pants were faded light blue so that he had been easy to find. The big cottonwood tree stood apart from a small grove of winterbare cottonwoods which grew in the wide, sandy arroyo. He had been dead for a day or more, and the sheep had wandered and scattered up and down the arroyo. Leon and his brother-in-law, Ken, gathered the sheep and left them in the pen at the sheep camp before they returned to the cottonwood tree. Leon waited under the tree while Ken drove the truck through the deep sand to the edge of the arroyo. He squinted up at the sun and unzipped his jacket—it sure was hot for this time of year. But high and northwest the blue mountains were still in snow. Ken came sliding down the low, crumbling bank about fifty yards down, and he was bringing the red blanket.

2　Before they wrapped the old man, Leon took a piece of string out of his pocket and tied a small gray feather in the old man's long white hair. Ken gave him the paint. Across the brown wrinkled forehead he drew a streak of white and along the high cheekbones he drew a strip of blue paint. He paused and watched Ken throw pinches of corn meal and pollen into the wind that fluttered the small gray feather. Then Leon painted with yellow under the old man's broad nose, and finally, when he had painted green across the chin, he smiled.

3　"Send us rain clouds, Grandfather." They laid the bundle in the back of the pickup and covered it with a heavy tarp before they started back to the pueblo.

4　They turned off the highway onto the sandy pueblo road. Not long after they passed the store and post office they saw Father Paul's car coming toward them. When he recognized their faces he slowed his car and waved for them to stop. The young priest rolled down the car window.

5　"Did you find old Teofilo?" he asked loudly.

6　Leon stopped the truck. "Good morning, Father. We were just out to the sheep camp. Everything is OK now."

7   "Thank God for that. Teofilo is a very old man. You really shouldn't allow him to stay at the sheep camp alone."

8   "No, he won't do that anymore now."

9   "Well, I'm glad you understand. I hope I'll be seeing you at Mass this week— we missed you last Sunday. See if you can get old Teofilo to come with you." The priest smiled and waved at them as they drove away.

10   Louise and Teresa were waiting. The table was set for lunch, and the coffee was boiling on the black iron stove. Leon looked at Louise and then at Teresa.

11   "We found him under a cottonwood tree in the big arroyo near sheep camp. I guess he sat down to rest in the shade and never got up again." Leon walked toward the old man's bed. The red plaid shawl had been shaken and spread carefully over the bed, and a new brown flannel shirt and pair of stiff new Levi's were arranged neatly beside the pillow. Louise held the screen door open while Leon and Ken carried in the red blanket. He looked small and shriveled, and after they dressed him in the new shirt and pants he seemed more shrunken.

12   It was noontime now because the church bells rang the Angelus. They ate the beans with hot bread, and nobody said anything until after Teresa poured the coffee.

13   Ken stood up and put on his jacket. "I'll see about the gravediggers. Only the top layer of soil is frozen. I think it can be ready before dark."

14   Leon nodded his head and finished his coffee. After Ken had been gone for a while, the neighbors and clanspeople came quietly to embrace Teofilo's family and to leave food on the table because the gravediggers would come to eat when they were finished.

15 The sky in the west was full of pale yellow light. Louise stood outside with her hands in the pockets of Leon's green Army jacket that was too big for her. The funeral was over, and the old men had taken their candles and medicine bags and were gone. She waited until the body was laid into the pickup before she said anything to Leon. She touched his arm, and he noticed that her hands were still dusty from the corn meal that she had sprinkled around the old man. When she spoke, Leon could not hear her.

16   "What did you say? I didn't hear you."

17   "I said that I had been thinking about something."

18   "About what?"

19   "About the priest sprinkling holy water for Grandpa. So he won't be thirsty."

20   Leon stared at the new moccasins that Teofilo had made for the ceremonial dances in the summer. They were nearly hidden by the red blanket. It was getting colder, and the wind pushed gray dust down the narrow pueblo road. The sun was approaching the long mesa where it disappeared during the winter. Louise stood there shivering and watching his face. Then he zipped up his jacket and opened the truck door. "I'll see if he's there."

21 Ken stopped the pickup at the church, and Leon got out; and then Ken drove down the hill to the graveyard where people were waiting. Leon knocked at the

old carved door with its symbols of the Lamb. While he waited he looked up at the twin bells from the king of Spain with the last sunlight pouring around them in their tower.

22   The priest opened the door and smiled when he saw who it was. "Come in! What brings you here this evening?"

23   The priest walked toward the kitchen, and Leon stood with his cap in his hand, playing with the earflaps and examining the living room—the brown sofa, the green armchair, and the brass lamp that hung down from the ceiling by links of chain. The priest dragged a chair out of the kitchen and offered it to Leon.

24   "No thank you, Father. I only came to ask you if you would bring your holy water to the graveyard."

25   The priest turned away from Leon and looked out the window at the patio full of shadows and the dining-room windows of the nuns' cloister across the patio. The curtains were heavy, and the light from within faintly penetrated; it was impossible to see the nuns inside eating supper. "Why didn't you tell me he was dead? I could have brought the Last Rites anyway."

26   Leon smiled. "It wasn't necessary, Father."

27   The priest stared down at his scuffed brown loafers and the worn hem of his cassock. "For a Christian burial it was necessary."

28   His voice was distant, and Leon thought that his blue eyes looked tired.

29   "It's OK, Father, we just want him to have plenty of water."

30   The priest sank down into the green chair and picked up a glossy missionary magazine. He turned the colored pages full of lepers and pagans without looking at them.

31   "You know I can't do that, Leon. There should have been the Last Rites and a funeral Mass at the very least."

32   Leon put on his green cap and pulled the flaps down over his ears. "It's getting late, Father. I've got to go."

33   When Leon opened the door Father Paul stood up and said, "Wait." He left the room and came back wearing a long brown overcoat. He followed Leon out the door and across the dim churchyard to the adobe steps in front of the church. They both stooped to fit through the low adobe entrance. And when they started down the hill to the graveyard only half of the sun was visible above the mesa.

34   The priest approached the grave slowly, wondering how they had managed to dig into the frozen ground; and then he remembered that this was New Mexico, and saw the pile of cold loose sand beside the hole. The people stood close to each other with little clouds of steam puffing from their faces. The priest looked at them and saw a pile of jackets, gloves, and scarves in the yellow, dry tumbleweeds that grew in the graveyard. He looked at the red blanket, not sure that Teofilo was so small, wondering if it wasn't some perverse Indian trick—something they did in March to ensure a good harvest—wondering if maybe old Teofilo was actually at sheep camp corraling the sheep for the night. But there he was, facing into a cold dry wind and squinting at the last sunlight, ready to bury a red wool blanket while the faces of his parishioners were in shadow with the last warmth of the sun on their backs.

35   His fingers were stiff, and it took him a long time to twist the lid off the holy

water. Drops of water fell on the red blanket and soaked into dark icy spots. He sprinkled the grave and the water disappeared almost before it touched the dim, cold sand; it reminded him of something—he tried to remember what it was, because he thought if he could remember he might understand this. He sprinkled more water; he shook the container until it was empty, and the water fell through the light from sundown like August rain that fell while the sun was still shining, almost evaporating before it touched the wilted squash flowers.

36   The wind pulled at the priest's brown Franciscan robe and swirled away the corn meal and pollen that had been sprinkled on the blanket. They lowered the bundle into the ground, and they didn't bother to untie the stiff pieces of new rope that were tied around the ends of the blanket. The sun was gone, and over on the highway the eastbound lane was full of headlights. The priest walked away slowly. Leon watched him climb the hill, and when he had disappeared within the tall, thick walls, Leon turned to look up at the high blue mountains in the deep snow that reflected a faint red light from the west. He felt good because it was finished, and he was happy about the sprinkling of the holy water; now the old man could send them big thunderclouds for sure.

QUESTIONS

Experience

· Whether or not you are familiar with Native American burial rituals, how well were you able to follow and make sense of the story's developing action?

· How do the burial and the rituals that accompany it compare with others you may have witnessed?

Interpretation

· What is the significance for the priest of the water sprinkled over the dead man and his grave? Why was the priest reluctant, initially, to come and perform that ritual? Why does Leon want the priest to sprinkle the holy water? What does the ritual mean for him?

Evaluation

· Whose values are being endorsed and whose values questioned in this story? How do you know? What bits of action and dialogue most strongly convey the story's values?

WRITING

Exploring

· Describe one or more ritualistic actions performed at a funeral or other service for the dead you have attended or have seen in a film.

Interpreting

· Analyze and explain the series of rituals performed in a service for the dead from a religious, military, or other tradition you are familiar with.

Evaluating

· Compare the treatment of death in this story with that in Shirley Jackson's "The Lottery," or compare the attitude toward the dead man in this story with that toward the land in Leslie Marmon Silko's essay "Landscape, History and the Pueblo Imagination" (pp. 509–514).

LOUIS SIMPSON
(b. 1923)

Walt Whitman at Bear Mountain

Louis Simpson was born in Jamaica, West Indies. He was educated there at Munro College and in New York at Columbia University, where he received his master's and doctoral degrees. He has taught at Columbia and at the University of California at Berkeley and is currently professor of English at the State University of New York at Stony Brook. His numerous awards include a Guggenheim fellowship and a Pulitzer Prize.

His poem on Walt Whitman begins with a description of a sculpture of the poet at Bear Mountain in New York State. It addresses the poet in a series of questions about the American nation and its people. Among its notable features are the conversation Simpson includes between Whitman and his poem's speaker and the vision of America, present and future, that the poem implies.

> *. . . life which does not give the preference to any other life, of any previous period, which therefore prefers its own existence . . .*
>
> ORTEGA Y GASSET

1 Neither on horseback nor seated,
But like himself, squarely on two feet,
The poet of death and lilacs
Loafs by the footpath. Even the bronze looks alive
5 Where it is folded like cloth. And he seems friendly.

"Where is the Mississippi panorama
And the girl who played the piano?
What are you, Walt?
The Open Road goes to the used-car lot.

10 "Where is the nation you promised?
These houses built of wood sustain
Colossal snows,
And the light above the street is sick to death.

"As for the people—see how they neglect you!
15 Only a poet pauses to read the inscription."

"I am here," he answered.
"It seems you have found me out.
Yet, did I not warn you that it was Myself
I advertised? Were my words not sufficiently plain?

20   "I gave no prescriptions,
        And those who have taken my moods for prophecies
        Mistake the matter."
        Then, vastly amused—"Why do you reproach me?
        I freely confess I am wholly disreputable.
25   Yet I am happy, because you have found me out."

        A crocodile in wrinkled metal loafing . . .

        Then all the realtors,
        Pickpockets, salesmen, and the actors performing
        Official scenarios,
30   Turned a deaf ear, for they had contracted
        American dreams.

        But the man who keeps a store on a lonely road,
        And the housewife who knows she's dumb,
        And the earth, are relieved.

35   All that grave weight of America
        Cancelled! Like Greece and Rome.
        The future in ruins!
        The castles, the prisons, the cathedrals
        Unbuilding, and roses
40   Blossoming from the stones that are not there . . .

        The clouds are lifting from the high Sierras.
        The Bay mists clearing;
        And the angel in the gate, the flowering plum,
        Dances like Italy, imagining red.

QUESTIONS

Experience

· As you were reading the poem, where did you find it easiest to follow and where hardest? Why?

· How do you respond to the idea of the poem's speaker (or the poet himself) speaking with a poet who died more than a century ago? Why?

Interpretation

· What kinds of questions is the speaker asking Walt Whitman? What kinds of answers does Whitman provide? How would you characterize the question-and-answer part of the poem?

· What sense do you make of the references to Greece, Rome, and Italy?

Evaluation

· What do you think Simpson means by writing that the "realtors / Pickpockets, salesmen," and others "Turned a deaf ear, for they had contracted / American dreams"? What kinds of American dreams are implied?

· What values does the poem seem to question? Does it endorse any particular kind of values? How do the values expressed in the poem correspond to your own?

WRITING

Exploring

· Do a little exploring in one or another poem of Whitman's. The ones alluded to in Simpson's poem include "Song of the Open Road," "When Lilacs Last in the Dooryard Bloom'd," "Crossing Brooklyn Ferry," and the final three sections (50–52) of "Song of Myself." Write a few paragraphs presenting your sense of Whitman from reading one or more of those poems.

Interpreting

· Provide a stanza-by-stanza analysis of Simpson's poem. Write a brief comment for each, even if you find some stanzas puzzling or confusing.

· Where would you divide the poem into its major parts? Why?

· How is the epigraph related to the rest of the poem?

Evaluating

· Identify and discuss the values that seem central to the poem. What is it about America that Simpson is concerned with, and what is his attitude toward those things?

· Or discuss the values you find in one or more of the Whitman poems mentioned in the "Exploring" writing assignment.

CULTURE AND SOCIETY—CONSIDERATIONS FOR THINKING AND WRITING

1. Location, or place, is important in some of the selections in this section. Compare what two of the following writers say about place and the cultural values associated with the places they describe: Joan Didion (Las Vegas), Larry L. King (Texas and New York), George Orwell (Marrakech), Gloria Anzaldúa (the Southwest).

2. A few of the selections deal with rituals or cultural behavior. Select one essay from the following and explain the writer's attitude toward the rituals he or she describes. Didion's "Marrying Absurd" (weddings), Gates's "2 Live Crew, Decoded" (rap music), Ribisi's "The Health Craze" (jogging and exercise), Orwell's "Marrakech" and Silko's "The Man to Send Rain Clouds" (burials).

3. In a few selections, issues of multiculturalism are especially important. Explain what two of the following essays reveal about the importance of understanding forms of cultural expression that differ from our own: Ravitch's "Multiculturalism," Anzaldúa's "How to Tame a Wild Tongue," Gates's "2 Live Crew, Decoded," Silko's "The Man to Send Rain Clouds."

4. Compare two of the following selections for what they say about language: Anzaldúa's "How to Tame a Wild Tongue" and Gates's "2 Live Crew, Decoded" (from this chapter) and Baldwin's "If Black English Isn't a Language," Lawrence's "Four-Letter Words Can Hurt You," and Kakutani's "The Word Police" (all in "Language").

5. Compare the way irony and satire are used in two of the following: Wolfe's "Only One Life," Didion's "Marrying Absurd," and Ribisi's "The Health Craze."
    Or compare the humor of King's "Playing Cowboy" with that of Theroux's "Being a Man" or Updike's "A & P" (both in "Gender").

6. Try to write an extended definition of "culture" by identifying the characteristic features of cultural groups in general. All cultural groups, for example, subscribe to a set of attitudes and encourage a set of behaviors toward those in authority. Use the essays in this section along with information from your reading and personal experience to illustrate each cultural characteristic you identify.

7. Create a dialogue (or a trialogue) on cultural difference by having two or three of the writers from this chapter engage in an imaginary conversation.
    Or make up a set of interview questions that you would ask two of the writers if you could speak with them personally.

8. Write an essay based on research into an aspect of culture that interests you. You may wish to investigate a cultural issue, attitude, behavior, or idea raised by one of the writers in this chapter, such as Didion's look into the culture of the Las Vegas wedding.

THREE

Gender

SUSAN BROWNMILLER
   Femininity

PAT C. HOY II
   Mosaics of Southern Masculinity

MAXINE HONG KINGSTON
   No Name Woman

ANNIE DILLARD
   The Deer at Providencia

SCOTT RUSSELL SANDERS
   The Men We Carry in Our Minds

DEBORAH TANNEN
   Different Words, Different Worlds

PAUL THEROUX
   Being a Man

MAILE MELOY
   The Voice of the Looking-Glass

JOHN UPDIKE
   A & P

EMILY DICKINSON
   "I'm 'wife'—I've finished that"

It is no accident that the first question people have after the birth of a child concerns its sex. "Is it a boy or a girl?" they typically ask. From the color of blanket the child sleeps under and the color of clothing he or she initially wears, the child's sex is marked for difference. People's attitudes about the child's future activities, goals, ambitions, and dreams are linked inextricably with gender. Sexual differentiation, for better or worse, is a human reality. What we do with this reality and how we come to terms with differences between the sexes form the subject of many of the essays in this section.

Not every writer here sees gender differences the same way. Nor do all the writers agree on conceptions of masculinity and femininity. While the images of femininity presented by Susan Brownmiller and Maile Meloy, for example, may coincide, those images clash, to some extent, with the image of the feminine found in Annie Dillard's "The Deer at Providencia" and in Emily Dickinson's "I'm 'wife'—I've finished that—." In the same way, the images of masculinity found in Paul Theroux's "Being a Man" are not entirely consistent with images of masculinity found in Scott Russell Sander's "The Men We Carry in Our Minds" and Pat C. Hoy's "Mosaics of Southern Masculinity." Hoy's essay adds a twist to the topic by introducing the notion of region or place, and Maxine Hong Kingston adds still another by considering the clash in the cultural perspectives on gender between the United States and China.

Deborah Tannen and John Updike show men and women (in Updike's story, adolescent boys and girls) interacting in part according to conventional cultural stereotypes. Tannen argues that men and women communicate differently both in what they say and in how they say it, while Updike portrays a boy acting in concord with romanticized notions of masculine behavior.

All the writers have something interesting to say about being male or female, and in the process they invite us to think about this distinctive aspect of our common humanity.

SUSAN BROWNMILLER
(b. 1935)

Femininity

Susan Brownmiller has been an actress, editor, researcher, and writer for a variety of publications. Her books include Against Our Will *(1975), a study of rape in America, and* Waverly Place *(1989), a novel that centers on a murder case involving wife battering and child abuse. Her book* Femininity *(1984), from which the following excerpt is taken, looks at the limitations that society's concept of the feminine has imposed upon women. Throughout the book (and the excerpt) Brownmiller introduces personal experience as part of the evidence she amasses from her reading.*

In describing femininity, Brownmiller implicitly defines it. Her main purpose, however, in this introduction to her book of the same title, is to explain its uses and to account for its usefulness. To some extent her argument on behalf of femininity comes in response to those who oppose femininity as a cultural condition that enslaves and diminishes women. Brownmiller's examples and her approach reveal her counterargumentative intent.

1   We had a game in our house called "setting the table" and I was Mother's helper. Forks to the left of the plate, knives and spoons to the right. Placing the cutlery neatly, as I recall, was one of my first duties, and the event was alive with meaning. When a knife or a fork dropped on the floor, that meant a man was unexpectedly coming to dinner. A falling spoon announced the surprise arrival of a female guest. No matter that these visitors never arrived on cue, I had learned a rule of gender identification. Men were straight-edged, sharply pronged and formidable, women were softly curved and held the food in a rounded well. It made perfect sense, like the division of pink and blue that I saw in babies, an orderly way of viewing the world. Daddy, who was gone all day at work and who loved to putter at home with his pipe tobacco and tool chest, was knife and fork. Mommy and Grandma, with their ample proportions and pots and pans, were grownup soup spoons, large and capacious. And I was a teaspoon, small and slender, easy to hold and just right for pudding, my favorite dessert.

2   Being good at what was expected of me was one of my earliest projects, for not only was I rewarded, as most children are, for doing things right, but excellence gave pride and stability to my childhood existence. Girls were different from boys, and the expression of that difference seemed mine to make clear. Did my loving, anxious mother, who dressed me in white organdy pinafores and Mary Janes and who cried hot tears when I got them dirty, give me my first instruction? Of course. Did my doting aunts and uncles with their gifts of pretty dolls and miniature tea sets add to my education? Of course. But even without the appropriate toys and clothes, lessons in the art of being feminine lay all around me and I absorbed them all: the fairy tales that were read to me at night, the brightly colored advertisements I pored over in magazines before I learned to decipher the

words, the movies I saw, the comic books I hoarded, the radio soap operas I happily followed whenever I had to stay in bed with a cold. I loved being a little girl, or rather I loved being a fairy princess, for that was who I thought I was.

3   As I passed through a stormy adolescence to a stormy maturity, femininity increasingly became an exasperation, a brilliant, subtle esthetic that was bafflingly inconsistent at the same time that it was minutely, demandingly concrete, a rigid code of appearance and behavior defined by do's and don't-do's that went against my rebellious grain. Femininity was a challenge thrown down to the female sex, a challenge no proud, self-respecting young woman could afford to ignore, particularly one with enormous ambition that she nursed in secret, alternately feeding or starving its inchoate life in tremendous confusion.

4   "Don't lose your femininity" and "Isn't it remarkable how she manages to retain her femininity?" had terrifying implications. They spoke of a bottom-line failure so irreversible that nothing else mattered. The pinball machine has registered "tilt," the game had been called. Disqualification was marked on the forehead of a woman whose femininity was lost. No records would be entered in her name, for she had destroyed her birthright in her wretched, ungainly effort to imitate a man. She walked in limbo, this hapless creature, and it occurred to me that one day I might see her when I looked in the mirror. If the danger was so palpable that warning notices were freely posted, wasn't it possible that the small bundle of resentments I carried around in secret might spill out and place the mark on my own forehead? Whatever quarrels with femininity I had I kept to myself; whatever handicaps femininity imposed, they were mine to deal with alone, for there was no women's movement to ask the tough questions, or to brazenly disregard the rules.

5   Femininity, in essence, is a romantic sentiment, a nostalgic tradition of imposed limitations. Even as it hurries forward in the 1980s, putting on lipstick and high heels to appear well dressed, it trips on the ruffled petticoats and hoop-skirts of an era gone by. Invariably and necessarily, femininity is something that women had more of in the past, not only in the historic past of prior generations, but in each woman's personal past as well—in the virginal innocence that is replaced by knowledge, in the dewy cheek that is coarsened by age, in the "inherent nature" that a woman seems to misplace so forgetfully whenever she steps out of bounds. Why should this be so? The XX chromosomal message has not been scrambled, the estrogen-dominated hormonal balance is generally as biology intended, the reproductive organs, whatever use one has made of them, are usually in place, the breasts of whatever size are most often where they should be. But clearly, biological femaleness is not enough.

6   Femininity always demands more. It must constantly reassure its audience by a willing demonstration of difference, even when one does not exist in nature, or it must seize and embrace a natural variation and compose a rhapsodic symphony upon the notes. Suppose one doesn't care to, has other things on her mind, is clumsy or tone-deaf despite the best instruction and training? To fail at the feminine difference is to appear not to care about men, and to risk the loss of their attention and approval. To be insufficiently feminine is viewed as a failure in core sexual identity, or as a failure to care sufficiently about oneself, for a woman found

wanting will be appraised (and will appraise herself) as mannish or neutered or simply unattractive, as men have defined these terms.

7   We are talking, admittedly, about an exquisite esthetic. Enormous pleasure can be extracted from feminine pursuits as a creative outlet or purely as relaxation; indeed, indulgence for the sake of fun, or art, or attention, is among femininity's great joys. But the chief attraction (and the central paradox, as well) is the competitive edge that femininity seems to promise in the unending struggle to survive, and perhaps to triumph. The world smiles favorably on the feminine woman: it extends little courtesies and minor privilege. Yet the nature of this competitive edge is ironic, at best, for one works at femininity by accepting restrictions, by limiting one's sights, by choosing an indirect route, by scattering concentration and not giving one's all as a man would to his own, certifiably masculine, interests. It does not require a great leap of imagination for a woman to understand the feminine principle as a grand collection of compromises, large and small, that she simply must make in order to render herself a successful woman. If she has difficulty in satisfying femininity's demands, if its illusions go against her grain, or if she is criticized for her shortcomings and imperfections, the more she will see femininity as a desperate strategy of appeasement, a strategy she may not have the wish or the courage to abandon, for failure looms in either direction.

8   It is fashionable in some quarters to describe the feminine and masculine principles as polar ends of the human continuum and to sagely profess that both polarities exist in all people. Sun and moon, yin and yang, soft and hard, active and passive, etcetera, may indeed be opposites, but a linear continuum does not illuminate the problem. (Femininity, in all its contrivances, is a very active endeavor.) What, then, is the basic distinction? The masculine principle is better understood as a driving ethos of superiority designed to inspire straightforward, confident success, while the feminine principle is composed of vulnerability, the need for protection, the formalities of compliance and the avoidance of conflict— in short, an appeal of dependence and good will that gives the masculine principle its romantic validity and its admiring applause.

9   Femininity pleases men because it makes them appear more masculine by contrast; and, in truth, conferring an extra portion of unearned gender distinction on men, an unchallenged space in which to breathe freely and feel stronger, wiser, more competent, is femininity's special gift. One could say that masculinity is often an effort to please women, but masculinity is known to please by displays of mastery and competence while femininity pleases by suggesting that these concerns, except in small matters, are beyond its intent. Whimsy, unpredictability and patterns of thinking and behavior that are dominated by emotion, such as tearful expressions of sentiment and fear, are thought to be feminine precisely because they lie outside the established route to success.

10   If in the beginnings of history the feminine woman was defined by her physical dependency, her inability for reasons of reproductive biology to triumph over the forces of nature that were the tests of masculine strength and power, today she reflects both an economic and emotional dependency that is still considered "natural," romantic and attractive. After an unsettling fifteen years in

which many basic assumptions about the sexes were challenged, the economic disparity did not disappear. Large numbers of women—those with small children, those left high and dry after a mid-life divorce—need financial support. But even those who earn their own living share a universal need for connectedness (call it love, if you wish). As unprecedented numbers of men abandon their sexual interest in women, others, sensing opportunity, choose to demonstrate their interest through variety and a change in partners. A sociological fact of the 1980s is that female competition for two scarce resources—men and jobs—is especially fierce.

11　　So it is not surprising that we are currently witnessing a renewed interest in femininity and an unabashed indulgence in feminine pursuits. Femininity serves to reassure men that women need them and care about them enormously. By incorporating the decorative and the frivolous into its definition of style, femininity functions as an effective antidote to the unrelieved seriousness, the pressure of making one's way in a harsh, difficult world. In its mandate to avoid direct confrontation and to smooth over the fissures of conflict, femininity operates as a value system of niceness, a code of thoughtfulness and sensitivity that in modern society is sadly in short supply.

12　　There is no reason to deny that indulgence in the art of feminine illusion can be reassuring to a woman, if she happens to be good at it. As sexuality undergoes some dizzying revisions, evidence that one is a woman "at heart" (the inquisitor's question) is not without worth. Since an answer of sorts may be furnished by piling on additional documentation, affirmation can arise from such identifiable but trivial feminine activities as buying a new eyeliner, experimenting with the latest shade of nail color, or bursting into tears at the outcome of a popular romance novel. Is there anything destructive in this? Time and cost factors, a deflection of energy and an absorption in fakery spring quickly to mind, and they need to be balanced, as in a ledger book, against the affirming advantage.

QUESTIONS

Experience

· To what extent (if you are female) has your experience with what Brownmiller calls "gender identification" matched hers? Have you, for example, been advised to preserve your femininity or to avoid appearing overly "masculine" (perhaps by appearing to need help to solve a problem or repair something that needed it)?

· Did you, on the other hand, as Brownmiller did, "love being a little girl"? If so, why, and if not, why not?

· If you are male, to what extent has your experience reflected the gender markers that Brownmiller provides for men? Consider, for example, her comment that the masculine principle is best understood "as a driving ethos of superiority designed to inspire straightforward, confident success."

Interpretation

· Brownmiller presents femininity as both a threat and a challenge. In what sense does it threaten women? How does it limit them? And how is it a challenge?

· How is the Women's Movement relevant to Brownmiller's discussion of femininity? What is Brownmiller's view of the movement, and how does she see herself in relation to it?

· Cull from the essay those characteristics Brownmiller identifies as "feminine." What is her point about these feminine qualities?

Evaluation

· Do you agree with Brownmiller's idea of a feminine approach to living? Why, or why not? What value does Brownmiller see in this idea, particularly in how women relate to men? (See especially her last two paragraphs.)

· Do you think Brownmiller adequately expresses here the way gender roles have changed in the last decade? If not, does that vitiate or perhaps limit the value of her viewpoint? Why, or why not?

WRITING

Exploring

· Write an essay in which you describe how you were made aware of gender roles. You may wish to explore how gender roles play out in your family.

Interpreting

· Brownmiller's essay is essentially an argument about the value of femininity. In the course of making the case for femininity, she defines her conception of the term. She also introduces personal experience as evidence. Analyze the structure of Brownmiller's piece. Consider where and how she uses her experience, where she defines the term, and where and why she makes her point.

Evaluating

· Argue for or against the ideas Brownmiller advances about femininity. You can modify her definition if you like. And you can agree or disagree with what she says about masculinity, as well.

PAT C. HOY II
(b. 1938)

Mosaics of Southern Masculinity

Pat Hoy has taught English literature and expository writing at the United States Military Academy and at Harvard University as well as at Bergen County Community College. He is currently director of the Expository Writing Program at New York University and a professor of English. He has published articles, reviews, and familiar (or personal) essays on a wide range of subjects for periodicals such as Sewanee Review, Virginia Quarterly Review, Agni, *and* Twentieth-Century Literature. *His first book of familiar essays,* Instinct for Survival, *was published by the University of Georgia Press in 1992. In the piece that follows, taken from that collection, Hoy explores images of masculinity as they impinge upon his understanding of himself and his relation to his father.*

One of the most interesting features of Hoy's essay is its use of stories, especially how his stories are structured as a series of interrelated fragments of memory, differently colored and sized, juxtaposed to form a mosaic of his experience. Hoy includes, for example, stories about his father and stories about himself, stories about how as a young boy he made the number 5, stories about reading and dancing, about women and music and war. Hoy connects these stories and suggests their interrelatedness, in the process both explaining and exploring an idea about gender. His essay provides a prime example of how to use stories—of living, of reading, of remembering—as evidence for ideas rather than simply as interesting anecdotes bereft of meaning.

> *Nobody under forty can believe how nearly* everything's *inherited.*
>
> REYNOLDS PRICE

1   He simply wasn't there. My sister and two of her friends were comforting my mom as we sat out front of our bus station in the 1943 sedan. As I scampered over the front seat into the back, I was stunned by her grief. It caught me in midair, and as I toppled into the space between Ellisene and Dot, I stopped my squirming and snuggled down deep. He was gone, and he wouldn't be back. They were trying to help her through the ordeal, trying to stop the heaving and the suffering. And even though their words made no sense to me, I could feel her loss in my five-year-old bones. He was gone.

2   I saw him occasionally for brief periods over the next twenty-four years, but when he died at fifty-six of cirrhosis of the liver, I had not known him. I had no cause to miss him until I was thirty-five and it seemed my own marriage wouldn't survive. I missed him again at forty-three when Patrick left for college, and I began

to wonder if I had done enough for him and his younger brother Tim, began to rummage around in my memories recalling signs of my father's influence, began, for the first time, to try to assemble a mosaic of my own masculinity.

3   I must have been seven or eight, sitting at my desk on the sleeping porch, working under the glare of a hanging light bulb, when my half-brother, home on furlough, walked through the room and stopped to watch me do my arithmetic. I was absorbed in the figuring and could hear only the thud and soft glide of the iron as Mom touched up her dress for work. After a few minutes Willard interrupted me.

4   "Make a five again."

5   "Huh?"

6   "Make a five."

7   I made one. Starting at the bottom of the half-circle, I moved the pencil around counter-clockwise to the top of the curve, made a short vertical line straight up and moved the lead point to the right completing the horizontal bar, all without ever lifting my pencil from the paper. One smooth, natural motion. Easy. A five from the bottom up.

8   "Look at this, Mother," he exclaimed, obviously beside himself. "Have you ever seen Butch make a five? Pat Hoy! No one but Pat Hoy makes a five like that!"

9   I didn't understand his excitement, but I remembered the moment—my first conscious memory of my dad's influence, all the more interesting to me now because I know he didn't teach me to make fives. Neither did Miss Culbertson, nor Miss Barnes, nor any of my other teachers. It was a genetic remnant that came along with his smile lines, his love of fast cars, and his damning fascination with women. I knew none of this at seven.

10   The last time I drove Mom from Hamburg to Little Rock, she was eighty-five. I was forty-two. We had just left Monticello heading north for Star City, and I was stuck behind a log truck and a couple of straggling cars. When an opening came, I made my move, whizzed past the three vehicles, and eased back into my lane as a southbound eighteen-wheeler breezed by. I turned to Mom with a smile breaking on my face.

11   "Pat Hoy!" she said.

12   "What?"

13   "I've seen him do it a thousand times."

14   "Do what?"

15   "Turn to me with that look and a grin from ear to ear, wait'n for approval."

16   Three years later, in the fall of the year, I was at Fort Leonard Wood, Missouri, with two younger Army officers. After two hard days of trying to teach high-ranking civil servants and senior officers to write more effectively, we needed sustenance. Leonard Wood had only a steak-and-fries restaurant on the strip and a small night club. We opted first for the mediocre food and then on a whim drove across the highway to the honky-tonk. We had spent six summer weeks with our traveling word show, laughing our way through airports, making students laugh while they learned in the classroom. We had a fairly good sense of each other's daytime habits. At nights we had gone our separate ways, visiting friends at each

of the posts, Army life being very much a small-town experience. The communities were separate, spread all over the world, but nonetheless of a piece. I was never a stranger in any one of them.

17   Our favorite pastime during the previous summer had been a Jungian game. We tried to second-guess each other's taste in women, tried to guess the nature of the woman in the other man's head. It was a game of images. We tried to predict "grid overlap," guessing when the woman in the classroom or the airport or on the plane would match the imagined woman in one of our buddy's heads. We joked about "anima seizures": spellbinding image overlap. The game was an older man's contribution to the summer fun.

18   The club across the street from the restaurant was small and close, but it felt friendly when we walked in in our khakis, polo shirts, and docksiders. The Missouri cowboys paid no attention, but the waitress seemed amused when she brought the beers. A Willie Nelson number drew couples out into the hazy space of the dance floor where refracting lights played softly around cowboy hats and occasionally found a patch of sequined hair. A strapping, lithe woman and her little man caught my eye. They were feeling their way around the floor, lost in the rhythms of those "lonely, lonely times."

19   Before I knew it, one of my buddies was on the floor, cutting in. The little man went back to his table, sat down, and tilted his hat forward just a bit. He sat with his back to us, but I could see him hook the heels of his boots over the bottom rung of the chair, slightly defiant.

20   The woman seemed unaware that she had changed partners. When she went back to the table, her man continued to stare at the door.

21   The vocalist didn't sound much like Anne Murray, but when she launched into "Son of a Rotten Gambler," I knew I couldn't sit there drinking beer any longer. I walked over to the strapping woman and asked her if she'd like to dance.

22   Reaching for my hand, she said, "I'd really like to, but I can't."

23   I asked her why not.

24   "He doesn't want me to dance with anyone else."

25   I looked over at him, sitting there immobilized, still staring at the front door. He might not have moved for three songs. They hadn't danced again. So I moved between them.

26   "Would you mind if I danced with your friend?" I asked, feeling my way into the protocol.

27   He didn't move his eyes.

28   "Look," I said pulling up a stool from the table behind us, "I'm not after your woman. I just want to dance this song with her."

29   He cleared his throat but kept up his business with the door.

30   She reached up and put her hand on my arm, pulling me down in her direction as she said, "I'm sorry. I really would like to dance, but I can't do it tonight."

31   I made it back to our table as the singer slid into the last stanza: "He'd be the son of his father / His father the teacher." But the teacher wasn't there to ask. I wondered what he would have done, wondered what the honky-tonk rules called for?

32   I remember his stopping by our house late one afternoon when I was about

thirteen; he was on the way out of town, on the move as usual. I could smell vodka over Dentyne. Mom asked him where he was headed.

33   "Juking."

34   "Where to?"

35   "Chula."

36   I didn't know where Chula was, but I guessed it was the Howdy Club in El Dorado, miles away over the dump, a long stretch of suspended roadway surrounded on both sides by the Ouachita river. I expected him to die there. But in those days, his life seemed charmed. Chula, I now suspect, was Xanadu. It was there he built his "dome of pleasure," there he "drunk the milk of Paradise." And perhaps, like me, as he listened to the "woman wailing," he "heard from far/Ancestral voices." I felt close to him that night in Missouri, very close, felt him in my bones again. And I felt too a painful advantage. He didn't have the wherewithal to distinguish the woman in his head from the one outside. Seizures carried him through life, and when his charms wore out, his liver couldn't carry the load.

37   The next morning at the post exchange, I saw the strapping woman. The image had dissipated; it couldn't hold up under the light of day. But she held up quite well. She apologized again, said her man had had a hard day, said he wasn't usually like that, said he was a good man. She thanked me for letting them be the night before. I liked her, liked my dad. I think he would have left the cowboy alone too. He was good at that, leaving people alone. Until that morning, it had never seemed a virtue.

38   When my father began to reappear in my imagination, I turned to Erich Neumann for clarification. He claims that all of us have two fathers (as well as two mothers), one actual, the other archetypal, spiritual—a collective Father. Sons, in the decidedly patriarchal psychology of Neumann's *Origins and History of Consciousness,* must overcome both of the World Parents and both of the actual parents in order to gain independence and reach maturity. The son-hero initially fears the threat to "the spiritual, masculine principle," fears "being swallowed by the maternal unconscious," and needs help at the outset from the fathers. Because I had shut my real father out of my life and out of my imagination for so long, he was no help to me as a youngster. What independence I gained from the Mothers, I gained at the hands of the town Fathers who saw to my upbringing in a small southern hamlet that bears even today the indelible stamp of masculinity.

39   Neumann tells us " 'The fathers' are the representatives of law and order, from the earliest taboos to the most modern judicial systems; they hand down the highest values of civilization, whereas the mothers control the highest, i.e., deepest, values of life and nature." Those gender differences ring true of my experience. The collective voice, the voice of the fathers there in that little hamlet called Hamburg, said this: you will be in the Boy Scouts; you will play football; you will go on the hunt; you will expose yourself to trials so that you can test your strength and independence; you will be a man and uphold the institutional values (never mind our own waywardness; what we represent, not what we do, that's what's important). The deepest voices said something different: you will be a gentle man; you will go to church; you will love and honor your mother and father (even if he has deserted you); you will avoid conflict and danger; you will remain always loyal to us, the deepest voices; you will never abandon us.

40   But there were ironic inconsistencies. The town fathers held up only part of their bargain. They understood too little of the myth they were unconsciously enacting. They pushed me into tests but did not draw me into community. My time on the hunt was limited to a day at a time, no weekends, no continuity, no time for fellowship. They forced Mom to let me play football, not because they were concerned about my development but because I was fairly tough and wiry; they wanted a winning team. The scouting activities were more satisfying; the men looked after our development. They drew all of us together, gave us their time and their guidance, took us in the woods, took us west to a national jamboree in California, taught us teamwork and responsibility. But always, at the end of those activities, the scoutmasters went home with their own sons. I could never confirm the experience, after the fact, with a man. The rituals never claimed me entirely. But, of course, no one knew anything was missing. I certainly didn't.

41   There was yet another irony at work in my life long before I was aware of it. It was my mother, not my father, who sent me off to West Point, off to war—the same woman who, sending two sons to an earlier world war, had lost one. I keep wondering, even today, whether she was seduced by the spell of the old romance, unable to see the irony of what she was doing. Did she send me away to assuage those other losses? I'll never know for sure. But I sense, even now years after her death, a touch of madness in the way she and other women send men off to war with their blessings—their own heads swimming with visions of grandeur. My mother was not at all clearheaded about West Point and the other side of soldiering.

42   Virginia Woolf was. In *Mrs. Dalloway* she mocks Peter Walsh, exposing his infantile urge to be "an adventurer," a "romantic buccaneer." To remind us of the danger of following such urges, Woolf has Walsh cross paths with Septimus Warren Smith, a young man who has been left crazed by war. Against the comic story of Peter's heroism, we hear the tragic story of how Septimus left home "a mere boy" to go up to London, leaving behind him "an absurd note . . . such as great men have written, and the world has read later when the story of their struggles has become famous."

43   But, of course, Septimus does not become a great man. Compelled and inspired by his teacher Miss Isabel Pole—who "lent him books, wrote him scraps of letters," in general fed his active male imagination with "vanity, ambition, idealism, passion, loneliness, courage, laziness, the usual seeds"—Septimus becomes "one of the first to volunteer." He goes to war "to save an England which consisted almost entirely of Shakespeare's plays and Miss Isabel Pole in a green dress walking in a square." Having gone, "he developed manliness; he was promoted." But while there, Septimus lost his mind; having lost it, he gained insight that made him no longer fit to live in the culture that had sent him out to serve.

44   Of a different generation from Septimus, I felt no deep yearning for the sound of the guns when I left my mom and that community in south Arkansas. My manliness had already been tempered by the deeper values. Lead soldiers and toy cannons, "Dixie" and rebel flags had not moved my spirit. I had built my model airplanes in youth to commemorate the loss of my brother, one of the war's turret gunners. Had I been born a decade later, I might, like my friend Sam Pickering, have decorated my model planes with flowers. But I came after the romance of

the Old South, after the other great wars too—and before the flower children. My mind's irony blossomed in a war foreign to all who had served before me.

45   When I left the South, I was certain it had not claimed me. I left under the impress of an active male imagination—young and naive, my head full of grandeur. I was looking for a way to loose the ties that bound me to family and region. I wanted independence, wanted to be cut loose, turned out on my own. Susceptible to an urge deeper than any particular war could command, I was oblivious to the consequences of where I was going. A romance far older than even the South was claiming me. I sought only the challenge and the promise. West Point offered me a way into the world of the fathers. But it was a gauntlet cast into my path by an adoring mother.

46   Years later, after Vietnam, after my own father's death, when I finally turned my mind South again, I began to understand what Allen Tate meant in "A Southern Mode of the Imagination" about the change that took place after World War I, the change that turned the southern mind inward, causing it to "shift from rhetoric to dialectic," creating what he later characterized as a "literature of introspection" rather than a "literature of romantic illusion." I was not the "old Southern *rhetor,* the speaker who was eloquent before the audience but silent in himself." Rummaging around inside my head, I was discovering my heritage, recovering lost remnants of masculinity, developing a sense of irony fit for my experiences. By that time, I had slayed the Mothers and saved my marriage, knew enough Jung to be dangerous, and had begun to make peace with the woman in my head. She was occasionally helpful as I moved into middle age, and the stories I began to tell myself in order to live seemed mythic. They began to reach beyond me into the world. I sensed for the first time in my life that I could never be alone again.

47   In "A Lost Traveller's Dream," Tate writes of memory, her feminine nature, her free will. He writes of the difficulty of arresting the "flow of inner time." Memory, he says, has "its own life and purposes; it gives what *it* wills. . . . The Latin *memoria* is properly a feminine noun, for women never forget; and likewise the soul is the *anima,* even in man, his vital principle and the custodian of memory, the image of woman that all men both pursue and flee." Tate reminds us too that the "imaginative writer is the archeologist of memory, dedicated to the minute particulars of the past, definite things—*prima sacramenti memoria.* If his 'city' is to come alive again from a handful of shards, he will try to fit them together in an elusive jigsaw puzzle, most of the pieces of which are forever lost." By the time I read Tate's words, my life had already confirmed them, but they still give me consolation. They point the way into a deeper myth.

48   When Tate illustrates what he actually means by the southern myth, he relays the old story about the curse of slavery, the invasion from outside, the destruction of a culture. Myth is historical, a story imposed on a culture from the outside, a way of accounting for what happened, rather than a story that embodies a culture's sensibility. Working from the outside, imposing a story on events, Tate buries the more powerful, stabilizing story that has always been there in the images and activities of family life. Yet he too knew that other story, the one he tells in "The Fugitive" about the "simple homogeneous background . . . a sort of unity of feeling" that he and his friends took with them to the university. He's

pointing to an inherent sensibility. The southern community itself was there before the war—masculine and feminine—the higher values of law and order underscored by the deeper values of life and nature.

49   A child of the matriarchy, I was raised on the South's deeper values. My sense of law and order, skewed by my sense of the foibles of actual men, caused me for years to undervalue the archetypal Father. I grew up in a house where dependence was more important than independence. So I grew up secure, seeing no need to hold my life together with stories of derring-do. Life was just fine until I moved out of that southern hamlet into the world of conflict—into the mania of competition, into war.

50   Yet the remnants of masculinity passed on by the town fathers served me well enough when I moved east and went, much later, to war. I carried to West Point and to Penn and to Vietnam a sense of community that had shaped my imagination without my knowing it. I had a survival kit but had no sense of its inherent ironies, complexities, contradictions, strengths. I would not begin to understand that inheritance fully until nearly thirty years later when I read Bill Berry's "Class Southerner." I was fifty. That essay gave me a sense of myself, a sense of what had made me different from almost all my northern friends. When I read literature or read the history books, I, like Bill, "wanted more than brilliance." I wanted "the fleshed body of a living past." I looked too for the story that formed around the words, the personal myth that shaped the writer's vision. I wanted meaning, wanted desperately to see how the stories I read illuminated the life I was trying to live.

51   Sitting here as I am, trying to fit the "handful of shards" together in the jigsaw puzzle that will constitute my own version of the city, I know that the masculine pieces are just now beginning to fit in place. Active all along, they have been influential in subtle ways. But my aversion to *machismo*—the boxing ring, the stench of the cadet gymnasium, the Army's insistence on masculine standards even when such standards are inappropriate—made me a maverick through my years of military service. Nevertheless, I stayed in the Army for almost three decades, stayed even when I had the chance and the inclination to leave. I think I was unwilling to turn the business of law and order over to the real men. They spend too much time building monuments to their own magnificence. They spend too much time in the gymnasium. They undervalue the deeper values.

52   It took me years to come face to face with my father. When I did, he was long dead. A number of people over the years had told me how much I looked like him, and scores of others had talked about how much they liked him, what a fine businessman he was. What they said was not meant to console me; they loved the man despite his faults, never qualifying their praise of him, never commenting about the drinking. He had won their hearts through warmth and generosity, a playful spirit, and just a touch of melancholy, I suspect. I sense it in myself, a bittersweet, desperate longing to be loved. All his friends told me how much he loved me; he never took the time.

53   Yet as I grew up I felt no need for consolation. I understood what had happened, where he had gone—his absence was one of the facts of my life. Part of my upbringing was to learn to live with that loss and to live without bitterness. I

suspect that Mom's greatest accomplishment was keeping her mouth shut over her own deep loss; she engendered stability, protected me, and preserved the memory of their life together. She had a firm hold on the deeper values and so did most of the other people I grew up around. Those folks lived earnest lives, but they had a sense of humor, and they looked out for one another. Those of us who were fatherless got on with our lives, loved by mothers and other friends. The community was our family. So I had no reason to feel put out or left out because Pat Hoy had skipped town.

54   Nevertheless, as my children grew up, I made a simple, silent commitment: I would always be there. I knew nothing else to do. My memory afforded little help. Stories about my father gave me no pattern against which to measure life with my children. Ann had her own memories, and she often tried to turn me into her father. Whatever he had done with her, I was supposed to do with Patrick and Tim. I listened and abided when her suggestions made sense, but mostly I watched and waited for the children to need me. When they did, I tried to pay attention. What I know about fathering, they taught me.

55   Looking back on our life together, I think the teaching began in Oklahoma when it seemed that I would lose them, lose the opportunity to be there with them as they grew up. Work had become my salvation. There was certainly nothing malicious in my dedication. I had been trained to be a professional soldier. My mom had taught me the value of hard work; West Point had given me a calling. I didn't see the difference until it was almost too late. Mom worked as hard as she did out of necessity. She worked on a commission, selling bus tickets. No sales, no income.

56   But my work was not for a bus company; it was for the U.S. Army. "Duty, Honor, Country," the motto said. Pay strict attention to the mission, or a million ghosts in olive drab will haunt you. That's what MacArthur had told the Corps of Cadets, just a year after I graduated from West Point. MacArthur, Eisenhower, Patton, and all those before them, "the men of the Corps long dead." To them we pledged our allegiance. To them we sang obeisance:

> The Corps, bareheaded, salute it,
>   With eyes up, thanking our God—
> That we of the Corps are treading
>   Where they of the Corps have trod—
> They are here in ghostly assemblage,
>   The men of the Corps long dead,
> And our hearts are standing attention
>   While we wait for their passing tread.

Ah yes, the men of the Corps long dead. Those men had, in a quiet, insidious way, established for me, and for thousands of others before and after me, the priorities by which we would live our lives, priorities that subordinated wife and children to the higher values. "If the Army wanted you to have a wife, they'd issue you one." Mission came first; everything else second. We never dreamed we had a choice.

57   Good soldiers, we bought the concept, every last one of us it seemed, everyone finally except the woman I married. It took her twelve years to act against

the violation. Even the two "short tours" that put me first in Korea and then in Vietnam for twelve months, even those tours we took in stride. We had been called on to make the sacrifice. It was our duty. Two for the price of one was the unwritten contract that governed our lives. Eventually, women began to say no. Ann was one of the first.

58　　　When she realized that she could no longer subordinate herself to my job, it rocked me, undercutting the very principles upon which I had begun to live out my life. Instead of fighting like a man to hold on to those principles, I sat down for the first time in my life and thought about what it meant to be a father. I thought seriously about what *I* considered the highest values and began to wonder just exactly what it would take to hold my world together. Becoming a division commander seemed far less important than being a father. I had been around in my children's lives, but hadn't been immersed in them. I had a conviction that my business in life was business. If I worked hard enough and got promoted and brought home the bacon, everything else would follow. *Being there* turned out to be more complicated than I had imagined.

59　　　At Ann's insistence, I moved to an Army apartment for bachelor officers, a BOQ. There alone, trying to figure out how to respond to Ann's *crie de cour*— her urgent plea for space, I turned to down-and-out country music. Over on the other side of Lawton, Ann was playing Carly Simon and Carole King. In the BOQ room, I was listening to Willie Nelson. In the rhythm and whine of Nelson's plaint, I found my dad . . . for the first time. What grabbed me was not the sad story of rejection so often chronicled in the songs, but the spirit of soulful resignation and the latent optimism just beneath the surface. There was actually something mythic about what I was hearing. The ballads, the stories themselves, were as old as time. Nothing that was happening to me was so bad afterall. Others had had their props knocked out and survived to sing about it. I could too. Through those songs, my own heart found its outlet, and in them I discovered solace and a father's independent spirit—a fierce and rugged individualism, a man not afraid to be fearful yet strong enough to survive. My world need not end.

60　　　Living apart from my children but near them in the same town, I got to know them better during the months of conflict and separation. When I went to them, I went with a purpose—usually to go fishing or to take them somewhere they wanted to go. I liked the fishing best because it gave us time to stand still and work together as we threaded the worms onto the hooks, bit the sinkers with our teeth, rigged the cane poles; it gave us time to wait on the banks of streams as we anticipated the thrill of the pull.

61　　　Whatever Patrick and Tim thought of those times they've never told me. For me the moments were special because they put me close to them and to my own dad. He had a reputation for being one of the best fishermen in a county full of sportsmen. The men and the women went together to the lakes and the rivers, and at the end of the long days in the sun, they got together to laugh and celebrate the day's catch. Pictures substantiate Dad's reputation—strings of fish, big ones . . . and always the smiling face, transformed by accomplishment. Standing on the creek bank together in Oklahoma, Patrick, Tim, and I gave each other lessons in fathering, and I began to sense for the first time in my life what I had actually missed. Climbing the corporate ladder had not given me such insight.

62   Many years later, after Ann and I had resolved the differences that were pushing us apart, after the children were grown, after I had found my dad in that Missouri cafe, I found him again, this time in the mountains of Wyoming. Nine of us
had gone up to a lake near the end of an eight-day excursion on horseback. I had
fishing on my mind before the trip and had asked for just one chance to catch a
trout. I had had no experience fishing in mountain lakes, had never caught a trout.
But I had heard stories, and somewhere deep in my bones I had a hankering to try
it. Before the trip, a friend loaned me his spinning gear and a cloth pouch filled
with lures and flies and other artificial whatnots.

63   Early that morning, we set out on horseback from the camp to go out of the
valley into the mountains, up to Crater Lake. It was a long, winding climb, not
nearly as steep as those on other days—no danger, nothing but the satisfaction of
going up toward the sky, higher and higher until the view out into the Wind River
Basin yanked our breath away. Near the top, we had to abandon our horses on a
plateau and work our way on foot up the rock formations for one of the views,
but our journey's end was higher yet, around the rocks and up so high we had to
go down on foot across a small glacier field, and down even farther into the crater
itself . . . to the lake. Only three of us wanted to fish.

64   I worked my way around the lake casting first one lure and then another without any luck until I found a place where I could leap out to a submerged boulder
and cast into the middle of the lake. Standing apart pleased me; I could watch
the others at the far end of the lake without being part of their noisiness. As I cast
my line far out into the lake and let the lure go deep into the water before I began
reeling, I sensed that I had found the perfect spot as well as the right technique.
Casting, reeling, relaxing occasionally to let the lure drop down deeper before I
tugged it, I had found a pleasing rhythm. The three trout I caught over the next
few hours seemed something of a gift, and I was happy up there so high, out on
the rock alone, to encounter my father's spirit.

65   He is not always easy to come across, but I've found him on other occasions
in the books I read. There aren't many traces of him in my memory—we weren't
together long enough and I know too few stories about him—so I have to depend
on others to bring him to me. When they do, he tugs at me. Often it takes no
more than an image to bring him to life. Sam Pickering, in "Son and Father," tells
of walking into his father's room one evening finding him asleep, "pajamas . . .
inside out, as mine invariably are." Sam saw on the bed an older version of himself, positions identical: "right leg pulled high toward the chest, and left thrust
back and behind with the toes pointed, seemingly pushing us up and through the
bed." During that moment of insight, "youth's false sense of superiority" fell away,
and Sam realized something about likenesses and the absurdity of repudiation.
Had my dad been standing near me on that boulder in Wyoming, watching me
land the trout, he would have known by the rhythm of my casting and my linger-
ing smile of satisfaction that we too are bound in strange ways. I no longer think of
repudiation.

66   Carthage, Tennessee, tied Sam Pickering's father to a world of particulars and
family values; it tied him to life. In turn he tied young Samuel to the same life.
Looking back on their life together, Sam claims that "Pickerings lived quiet lives,
cultivating their few acres and avoiding the larger world with its abstractions of

honor, service, and patriotism. For them country meant the counties in which they lived, not the imperial nation. . . . With the exception of the Civil War, the struggles of the nation have not touched us." He finds strength in this response to life: "we are soft and, in our desires, subconscious or conscious, to remain free, have become evasive. Few things are simple though, and this very evasiveness may be a sign of a shrewd or even tough vitality"—or perhaps a sign of some great historical myth recreating itself in human terms.

67　　Looking back on my youth, measuring it against the books I read now and the life I lived with my own sons, I yearn for only one thing my father might have given me. I grew up a child of the matriarchate, spending my life among the women. At the end of those hot, summer days, no matter what I had been doing, I returned to a house where there was no male influence. When I went away to college, I knew almost nothing about the way men and women act in the privacy of their own homes, and I knew precious little about the way grown men act in the company of other men, apart from the women. Going to West Point was a way into that world, but it was no substitute for the one I had been denied as I grew up. I sense that void in my life even today when I read about the loss in southern books, many of them written by men I have come to know and admire during these years of searching.

68　　Roy Reed gave me a glimpse into that masculine life a few years ago when I was reading *Looking for Hogeye.* At the time, I was writing an essay of my own about mother-son journeys of separation. In the early drafts, I was overvaluing the matriarchate. Roy's essays caught me up short, put me back on track, led my imagination through the mother to the father, and let me see more clearly how the higher and the deeper values can manifest themselves in the lives of men. He also renewed my interest in tough-minded perseverance at a time when I was tiring of younger Army colleagues who still persisted in subordinating their lives to a calling they had not taken time to examine.

69　　In "Spring Comes to Hogeye," it is not a woman who is close to nature but a man. Roy writes lovingly of Ira Solenberger whose life is so closely tied to the seasons that he, in concert with spring's late coming, knows intuitively to plant his crops late. Roy respects this old man's perception, cares about him. He makes us see that Ira dies in harmony with the seasons. His existence has followed a mysterious rhythm of ebb and flow. In a larger sense, Ira is important to Roy because his death signals the loss of a special breed of hill people. He relishes country folks' "plain damned meanness" and savors their sense of community; they "look after one another. . . . The trash take care of their own, not out of goodness but out of necessity. There is no one else to do it." Those hill folks know something important about community and survival, something distinctly masculine, and a touch mysterious.

70　　In "Fall" Roy takes us into the woods with a "bunch" of hunters, some old, some young. We might just be in the Mississippi woods with Faulkner tracking bear, but this ritual develops on a smaller, more accessible, scale. The hunter's primary business is squirrel hunting. Roy's is the "exhilarating mystery that puzzles every hunter: the discovery that he can detect the presence of game by some sense that is beyond hearing, seeing or even smelling." Throughout this essay, Roy intersperses another narrative that begins in 1943 against the backdrop of war. It is a story about the "expectations that every Southern boy has a right to see filled at a certain time"—a narrative of male ritual: the first hunt, the first drink, the first kill. That ritual "tied the boy not only to the uncle but, more importantly, to his father, and tied the two of them to the ancestral woods." But then, "the son lost his taste for it." Hunting became a "single ritual hunt each year," and the government flooded the land. The "bond was dissolved and the son set adrift from his own blood." "Fall" is a story of cultural disintegration embedded in a story of perpetuation, of renewal and mystery. Like Ira Solenberger, Roy's hunting neighbors live close enough to the land to live the myth of community. In that myth we find the story of our survival.

71   Compare their view of the hunt to Allen Tate's: "One September day in the valley below Sewanee, twenty-five years ago, I shot a dove that fell into the weeds, and when I found her she was lying head up with a gout of blood in each eye. I shot her again. Her life had been given to my memory; and I have never hunted from that day." Tate explains his decision: "The feminine memory says: Here is that dying dove; you must really kill it this time or you will not remember it from all the other birds you have killed; take it or leave it; I have given it to you." One writer sees only the deeper values and not the highest. The other sees beyond the killing to the continuity, sees within the image of death itself the stuff of survival. My father, I suspect, was not much of a hunter, but he had access to that community of men; he had access to the story of perpetuation; he knew about the mystery of renewal. I know it too now, as a story, but he could have given it to me as a boy, firsthand, and I could have passed it on to my sons as experience. It is a loss I can only recover secondhand.

72   William Humphrey, whom I do not know, has given me the clearest insight into what my sons, my father, and I might have missed. Humphrey discovered the stuff of survival as a kid in Texas. In his memoir, *Farther Off from Heaven,* he resurrects a tough, wiry father every bit as wild as my own dad. He frames his memoir with his father's premature death. The fatal automobile wreck on the Fourth of July, 1937, was a strange, ironic emancipation for a boy of thirteen, but he survived because of a father's gift. Hunting was for the two of them an intimate, life-sustaining experience. The father himself had taken to the woods as a sanctuary from his tyrannical parents; he was, at first, the hunted. On his own in the woods, he learned to survive. He went there to verify the stories of danger told by outsiders; he went there "to see the dragons in their den." What he learned, he passed on to his son.

73   Reinventing years later the morning on which he and his mother accompanied his father's mangled body in the ambulance ride to Paris, Texas, Humphrey thought of the magic of those woods he shared with his father. He remembered the break of day, the pristine moment of first light, remembered that the "change seemed chemical, like a photographic print in the developer in the dimness of the darkroom, the image appearing out of nothingness, then rapidly becoming distinct, recognizable, familiar." He remembered his father's transformation in the woods, that "old boyish wonder": "My oneness with him gave me some of his sense of oneness with that world." That world—their world, the world of the father and the son—was a world of trust and companionship, a world in which the two were on such intimate terms they could dispense with talk. Deep in the woods on

an alligator hunt, Humphrey claims to have found "along with the deepening strangeness . . . a familiarity, as though one had been here before, but in another life"; he expected around one of the turns that the "long-forgotten, universal mother tongue" would come back to them; he thought they might very well reenter paradise. Telling this story, Humphrey reenacts Marlow's journey up the river to visit Kurtz, but these voyagers come back bound together for life. No need for Marlow's noble lie. They do not submit. They meet the alligator-dragon, subdue it, make it their own. They return, young and renewed.

74   Death, then, was not a new experience for the thirteen-year-old boy, but the sudden, revolting loss of a father was. Premature death shocked him because it left him alone. We can judge the severity of the jolt and the power of his father's influence by Humphrey's reaction on the night before the funeral: "My last night's sleep in Clarksville, with my father's body lying in the next room, would be my last ever, I vowed. No visits home for me, no reopening of wounds. It was a vow I was to keep for thirty-two years."

75   But finally, like a salmon's, Humphrey's "homing instincts" got the best of him, and he defied his vows; he too discovered the folly of repudiation. Back in town with a guide, he comes upon two boys playing in the cemetery; they offer to help him find the grave they think he's searching for: "Looking at either of them was like looking at myself through the wrong end of binoculars. I gave them half a dollar apiece, a token repayment for all the many nickels that men of Clarksville had given me in my time . . . thanked them; said no, we were not looking for any grave, what we were looking for was just the opposite: some spot where there was not any grave, where there was still room for one. Why? Was somebody dead? No; not yet."

76   The Texas Humphrey had come back to was changed, just as Carthage, Hog-eye, and Hamburg have changed. Lytle was dead right about the onslaught of industrialism. But something remains of place that is as timeless as those river-bottoms Humphrey entered with his father, something deep. It calls us back wherever we are, calls us back into community. Whether our fathers were there or not, whether they took us literally on the hunt, whether they left us land or left us landless, there hovers about the place a presiding spirit, masculine, indomitable, inviolable.

77   There is mystery. My father, I used to think, simply was not there. I have discovered over time, that he was, still is. He's there, like the place; he's in my bones. I know it by the fives I make. I know it by the cars I drive and the way I drive them, know it too by the smiling way I ask for recognition and confirmation. I know it too by what I learned from my own sons, standing and fishing together on the banks of those streams in Oklahoma. But I know it especially by my evolving relationship with the woman in my head. Like my father, I know her power, know how easy it is to turn my life over to anima, seductress that she is, dancing there with her little cowboy in the starlight cafe. But I know too what he never seemed to learn. I know that she will not always stand up in the light of day, will not always stand up to the higher values. The real woman, outside my head, might, but the one inside is a different matter. She can lead me to destruction or she can save me. Her duality is tricky business.

78   I have discovered that anima has a partner. Anima—soul, imagination, the

woman in my head who is not a mere woman—anima and animus have been there all along in my psyche: a divine pair, a syzygy. James Hillman suggests that to "imagine in pairs and couples is to think mythologically. Mythical thinking connects pairs into tandems rather than separating them into opposites." In my own acts of imagining, I recognize animus—a shaping, criticizing spirit. It has given me what Hillman calls "distance from mood." Perhaps it has given me what Sam Pickering might call the "right distance." I see more clearly now how the syzygy manifests itself in our time, how we can have "shrewd, tough vitality" on the home front, how the farmer can live in nature, how the intimacy of the hunt can match the intimacy of a good marriage. I see again how toughness can be a virtue. What I find in my own imagination is a happy marriage of the highest and the deepest values, a mounting respect for the preservation of the community through close living, living so close to earth that we do not lose touch of it. I see there the myth of our time. And I hear from the bottom land of my imagination the deep cry of ancestral voices.

QUESTIONS

Experience

· How do you experience reading the beginning of Hoy's essay? How do you respond to the epigraph? Do you think about its idea or wonder how it will tie into the essay? And what about your reading of the opening paragraphs and the story about making 5s? Did you have the sense that you were reading an autobiography? A short story? An essay? Why?

· To what extent did you think of your own life as you were reading about Pat Hoy's? Hoy says elsewhere that writers repair memory; they make us remember what we have forgotten. Did you begin thinking, for example, about how you make 5s or about how you do something else—walk, smile, tilt your head—in the manner of one of your parents or grandparents?

Interpretation

· Early in the essay, Hoy says that his making of 5s was "a genetic remnant" that came along with some other things he believes were inherited from his father—"his love of fast cars, and his damning fascination with women." How does this notion relate to the essay's epigraph?

· This essay contains a number of stories—about making 5s, about asking a woman to dance, about being sent off to war, about reading various texts, about listening to Willie Nelson. What do Hoy's stories have in common? How are the fragments of memory held together in Hoy's "mosaic"?

Evaluation

· Various images of masculinity and femininity populate this essay. Which do you find most and which least attractive? Which most compelling? Why?

· Consider the paragraph in which Hoy explains that it was his mother and not his father who sent him off to the army—and ultimately to war. What is he suggesting here about women and war? Do you agree that mothers as well as fathers harbor idealized images of war's glory and grandeur, of their sons' courage and heroism?

· Another important arena of values that animates this essay is the one Hoy himself wrestled with as a husband and father. Consider what he says about society's ranking of a man's responsibilities to his wife and children compared with his responsibility to his work.

WRITING

Exploring

· Write an essay in which you explore an idea—about manliness or womanliness or about some other subject. Bring into your essay references to some other kinds of texts—a popular song, some lines from a poem or an advertisement, a quotation from a book. In addition, include in your essay a number of stories about yourself. These can be brief memories or longer narratives. Use the stories and the other texts to explore your idea. Try to find a suitable epigraph for your essay as well.

Interpreting

· Write a paper analyzing the style and structure of Hoy's essay. With what does it begin and end? Why? How is it developed? Explain the effects of Hoy's method of organization and his use of quotations from other writers.

Evaluating

· Write an argumentative essay supporting or disputing one or another idea Hoy advances in his essay. You can take as your starting point something Hoy himself says or something he quotes from another writer.

MAXINE HONG KINGSTON
(b. 1940)

No Name Woman

Maxine Hong Kingston was raised in the Chinese American community of Stockton, California, and graduated from the University of California. Her first two books, The Woman Warrior *(1976) and* China Men *(1980), brought her literary recognition and a measure of fame. She has also published a novel,* The Tripmaster Monkey *(1992). Both of the first two works blend fact and fiction in strikingly original ways. In the selection that follows, taken from* The Woman Warrior, *Kingston imagines some of the details of her narrative, largely because her mother, from whom she heard the remarkable story Kingston tells here, admonished her to keep silent. Silence and secrecy, in fact, are critical terms for her discourse, in which we encounter some surprising and unsettling details.*

One of the most fascinating aspects of this selection (and the book from which it is taken) is its mingling of fiction with fact. At a number of points, Kingston lets us know that she is imagining rather than reporting. For example, after reporting her mother's story about her no-name aunt, Kingston imagines what her aunt must have been like—somewhat independent and rebellious, Kingston hypothesizes—and what it must have been like for her to live amidst repression. The genre of Kingston's work, thus, is unstable—at times reading like factual discourse and at times like a short story or a novel.

1 "You must not tell anyone," my mother said, "what I am about to tell you. In China your father had a sister who killed herself. She jumped into the family well. We say that your father has all brothers because it is as if she had never been born.

2 "In 1924 just a few days after our village celebrated seventeen hurry-up weddings—to make sure that every young man who went 'out on the road' would responsibly come home—your father and his brothers and your grandfather and his brothers and your aunt's new husband sailed for America, the Gold Mountain. It was your grandfather's last trip. Those lucky enough to get contracts waved good-bye from the decks. They fed and guarded the stowaways and helped them off in Cuba, New York, Bali, Hawaii. 'We'll meet in California next year,' they said. All of them sent money home.

3 "I remember looking at your aunt one day when she and I were dressing; I had not noticed before that she had such a protruding melon of a stomach. But I did not think, 'She's pregnant,' until she began to look like other pregnant women, her shirt pulling and the white tops of her black pants showing. She could not have been pregnant, you see, because her husband had been gone for years. No one said anything. We did not discuss it. In early summer she was ready to have the child, long after the time when it could have been possible.

4   "The village had also been counting. On the night the baby was to be born the villagers raided our house. Some were crying. Like a great saw, teeth strung with lights, files of people walked zigzag across our land, tearing the rice. Their lanterns doubled in the disturbed black water, which drained away through the broken bunds. As the villagers closed in, we could see that some of them, probably men and women we knew well, wore white masks. The people with long hair hung it over their faces. Women with short hair made it stand up on end. Some had tied white bands around their foreheads, arms, and legs.

5   "At first they threw mud and rocks at the house. Then they threw eggs and began slaughtering our stock. We could hear the animals scream their deaths—the roosters, the pigs, a last great roar from the ox. Familiar wild heads flared in our night windows; the villagers encircled us. Some of the faces stopped to peer at us, their eyes rushing like searchlights. The hands flattened against the panes, framed heads, and left red prints.

6   "The villagers broke in the front and the back doors at the same time, even though we had not locked the doors against them. Their knives dripped with the blood of our animals. They smeared blood on the doors and walls. One woman swung a chicken, whose throat she had slit, splattering blood in red arcs about her. We stood together in the middle of our house, in the family hall with the pictures and tables of the ancestors around us, and looked straight ahead.

7   "At that time the house had only two wings. When the men came back, we would build two more to enclose our courtyard and a third one to begin a second courtyard. The villagers pushed through both wings, even your grandparents' rooms, to find your aunt's, which was also mine until the men returned. From this room a new wing for one of the younger families would grow. They ripped up her clothes and shoes and broke her combs, grinding them underfoot. They tore her work from the loom. They scattered the cooking fire and rolled the new weaving in it. We could hear them in the kitchen breaking our bowls and banging the pots. They overturned the great waist-high earthenware jugs; duck eggs, pickled fruits, vegetables burst out and mixed in acrid torrents. The old woman from the next field swept a broom through the air and loosed the spirits-of-the-broom over our heads. 'Pig.' 'Ghost.' 'Pig,' they sobbed and scolded while they ruined our house.

8   "When they left, they took sugar and oranges to bless themselves. They cut pieces from the dead animals. Some of them took bowls that were not broken and clothes that were not torn. Afterward we swept up the rice and sewed it back up into sacks. But the smells from the spilled preserves lasted. Your aunt gave birth in the pigsty that night. The next morning when I went for the water, I found her and the baby plugging up the family well.

9   "Don't let your father know that I told you. He denies her. Now that you have started to menstruate, what happened to her could happen to you. Don't humiliate us. You wouldn't like to be forgotten as if you had never been born. The villagers are watchful."

10   Whenever she had to warn us about life, my mother told stories that ran like this one, a story to grow up on. She tested our strength to establish realities. Those in the emigrant generations who could not reassert brute survival died young and far from home. Those of us in the first American generations have had

to figure out how the invisible world the emigrants built around our childhoods fits in solid America.

11   The emigrants confused the gods by diverting their curses, misleading them with crooked streets and false names. They must try to confuse their offspring as well, who, I suppose, threaten them in similar ways—always trying to get things straight, always trying to name the unspeakable. The Chinese I know hide their names: sojourners take new names when their lives change and guard their real names with silence.

12   Chinese-Americans, when you try to understand what things in you are Chinese, how do you separate what is peculiar to childhood, to poverty, insanities, one family, your mother who marked your growing with stories, from what is Chinese? What is Chinese tradition and what is the movies?

13   If I want to learn what clothes my aunt wore, whether flashy or ordinary, I would have to begin, "Remember Father's drowned-in-the-well sister?" I cannot ask that. My mother has told me once and for all the useful parts. She will add nothing unless powered by Necessity, a riverbank that guides her life. She plants vegetable gardens rather than lawns; she carries the odd-shaped tomatoes home from the fields and eats food left for the gods.

14   Whenever we did frivolous things, we used up energy; we flew high kites. We children came up off the ground over the melting cones our parents brought home from work and the American movie on New Year's Day—*Oh, You Beautiful Doll* with Betty Grable one year, and *She Wore a Yellow Ribbon* with John Wayne another year. After the one carnival ride each, we paid in guilt; our tired father counted his change on the dark walk home.

15   Adultery is extravagance. Could people who hatch their own chicks and eat the embryos and the heads for delicacies and boil the feet in vinegar for party food, leaving only the gravel, eating even the gizzard lining—could such people engender a prodigal aunt? To be a woman, to have a daughter in starvation time was a waste enough. My aunt could not have been the lone romantic who gave up everything for sex. Women in the old China did not choose. Some man had commanded her to lie with him and be his secret evil. I wonder whether he masked himself when he joined the raid on her family.

16   Perhaps she had encountered him in the fields or on the mountain where the daughters-in-law collected fuel. Or perhaps she first noticed her in the marketplace. He was not a stranger because the village housed no strangers. She had to have dealings with him other than sex. Perhaps he worked an adjoining field, or he sold her the cloth for the dress she sewed and wore. His demand must have surprised, then terrified her. She obeyed him; she always did as she was told.

17   When the family found a young man in the next village to be her husband, she had stood tractably beside the best rooster, his proxy, and promised before they met that she would be his forever. She was lucky that he was her age and she would be the first wife, an advantage secure now. The night she first saw him, he had sex with her. Then he left for America. She had almost forgotten what he looked like. When she tried to envision him, she only saw the black and white face in the group photograph the men had had taken before leaving.

18   The other man was not, after all, much different from her husband. They both gave orders: she followed. "If you tell your family, I'll beat you. I'll kill you. Be

here again next week." No one talked sex, ever. And she might have separated the rapes from the rest of living if only she did not have to buy her oil from him or gather wood in the same forest. I want her fear to have lasted just as long as rape lasted so that the fear could have been contained. No drawn-out fear. But women at sex hazarded birth and hence lifetimes. The fear did not stop but permeated everywhere. She told the man, "I think I'm pregnant." He organized the raid against her.

19   On nights when my mother and father talked about their life back home, sometimes they mentioned an "outcast table" whose business they still seemed to be settling, their voices tight. In a commensal tradition, where food is precious, the powerful older people made wrongdoers eat alone. Instead of letting them start separate new lives like the Japanese, who could become samurais and geishas, the Chinese family, faces averted but eyes glowering sideways, hung on to the offenders and fed them leftovers. My aunt must have lived in the same house as my parents and eaten at an outcast table. My mother spoke about the raid as if she had seen it, when she and my aunt, a daughter-in-law to a different household, should not have been living together at all. Daughters-in-law lived with their husbands' parents, not their own; a synonym for marriage in Chinese is "taking a daughter-in-law." Her husband's parents could have sold her, mortgaged her, stoned her. But they had sent her back to her own mother and father, a mysterious act hinting at disgraces not told me. Perhaps they had thrown her out to deflect the avengers.

20   She was the only daughter; her four brothers went with her father, husband, and uncles "out on the road" and for some years became western men. When the goods were divided among the family, three of the brothers took land, and the youngest, my father, chose an education. After my grandparents gave their daughter away to her husband's family, they had dispensed all the adventure and all the property. They expected her alone to keep the traditional ways, which her brothers, now among the barbarians, could fumble without detection. The heavy, deep-rooted women were to maintain the past against the flood, safe for returning. But the rare urge west had fixed upon our family, and so my aunt crossed boundaries not delineated in space.

21   The work of preservation demands that the feelings playing about in one's guts not be turned into action. Just watch their passing like cherry blossoms. But perhaps my aunt, my forerunner, caught in a slow life, let dreams grow and fade and after some months or years went toward what persisted. Fear at the enormities of the forbidden kept her desires delicate, wire and bone. She looked at a man because she liked the way the hair was tucked behind his ears, or she liked the question-mark line of a long torso curving at the shoulder and straight at the hip. For warm eyes or a soft voice or a slow walk—that's all—a few hairs, a line, a brightness, a sound, a pace, she gave up family. She offered us up for a charm that vanished with tiredness, a pigtail that didn't toss when the wind died. Why, the wrong lighting could erase the dearest thing about him.

22   It could very well have been, however, that my aunt did not take subtle enjoyment of her friend, but, a wild woman, kept rollicking company. Imagining her free with sex doesn't fit, though. I don't know any women like that, or men either. Unless I see her life branching into mine, she gives me no ancestral help.

23   To sustain her being in love, she often worked at herself in the mirror, guessing at the colors and shapes that would interest him, changing them frequently in order to hit on the right combination. She wanted him to look back.

24   On a farm near the sea, a woman who tended her appearance reaped a reputation for eccentricity. All the married women blunt-cut their hair in flaps about their ears or pulled it back in tight buns. No nonsense. Neither style blew easily into heart-catching tangles. And at their weddings they displayed themselves in their long hair for the last time. "It brushed the backs of my knees," my mother tells me. "It was braided, and even so, it brushed the backs of my knees."

25   At the mirror my aunt combined individuality into her bob. A bun could have been contrived to escape into black streamers blowing in the wind or in quiet wisps about her face, but only the older women in our picture album wear buns. She brushed her hair back from her forehead, tucking the flaps behind her ears. She looped a piece of thread, knotted into a circle between her index fingers and thumbs, and ran the double strand across her forehead. When she closed her fingers as if she were making a pair of shadow geese bite, the string twisted together catching the little hairs. Then she pulled the thread away from her skin, ripping the hairs out neatly, her eyes watering from the needles of pain. Opening her fingers, she cleaned the thread, then rolled it along her hairline and the tops of her eyebrows. My mother did the same to me and my sisters and herself. I used to believe that the expression "caught by the short hairs" meant a captive held with a depilatory string. It especially hurt at the temples, but my mother said we were lucky we didn't have to have our feet bound when we were seven. Sisters used to sit on their beds and cry together, she said, as their mothers or their slave removed the bandages for a few minutes each night and let the blood gush back into their veins. I hope that the man my aunt loved appreciated a smooth brow, that he wasn't just a tits-and-ass man.

26   Once my aunt found a freckle on her chin, at a spot that the almanac said predestined her for unhappiness. She dug it out with a hot needle and washed the wound with peroxide.

27   More attention to her looks than these pullings of hairs and pickings at spots would have caused gossip among the villagers. They owned work clothes and good clothes and they wore good clothes for feasting the new seasons. But since a woman combing her hair hexes beginnings, my aunt rarely found an occasion to look her best. Women looked like great sea snails—the corded wood, babies, and laundry they carried were the whorls on their backs. The Chinese did not admire a bent back; goddesses and warriors stood straight. Still there must have been a marvelous freeing of beauty when a worker laid down her burden and stretched and arched.

28   Such commonplace loveliness, however, was not enough for my aunt. She dreamed of a lover for the fifteen days of New Year's, the time for families to exchange visits, money, and food. She plied her secret comb. And sure enough she cursed the year, the family, the village, and herself.

29   Even as her hair lured her imminent lover, many other men looked at her. Uncles, cousins, nephews, brothers would have looked, too, had they been home between journeys. Perhaps they had already been restraining their curiosity, and they left, fearful that their glances, like a field of nesting birds, might be startled

and caught. Poverty hurt, and that was their first reason for leaving. But another, final reason for leaving the crowded house was the never-said.

30   She may have been unusually beloved, the precious only daughter, spoiled and mirror gazing because of the affection the family lavished on her. When her husband left, they welcomed the chance to take her back from the in-laws; she could live like the little daughter for just a while longer. There are stories that my grandfather was different from other people, "crazy ever since the little Jap bayoneted him in the head." He used to put his naked penis on the dinner table, laughing. And one day he brought home a baby girl, wrapped up inside his brown western-style greatcoat. He had traded one of his sons, probably my father, the youngest, for her. My grandmother made him trade back. When he finally got a daughter of his own, he doted on her. They must have all loved her, except perhaps my father, the only brother who never went back to China, having once been traded for a girl.

31   Brothers and sisters, newly men and women, had to efface their sexual color and present plain miens. Disturbing hair and eyes, a smile like no other, threatened the ideal of five generations living under one roof. To focus blurs, people shouted face to face and yelled from room to room. The immigrants I know have loud voices, unmodulated to American tones even after years away from the village where they called their friendships out across the fields. I have not been able to stop my mother's screams in public libraries or over telephones. Walking erect (knees straight, toes pointed forward, not pigeon-toed, which is Chinese-feminine) and speaking in an inaudible voice, I have tried to turn myself American-feminine. Chinese communication was loud, public. Only sick people had to whisper. But at the dinner table, where the family members came nearest one another, no one could talk, not the outcasts nor any eaters. Every word that falls from the mouth is a coin lost. Silently they gave and accepted food with both hands. A preoccupied child who took his bowl with one hand got a sideways glare. A complete moment of total attention is due everyone alike. Children and lovers have no singularity here, but my aunt used a secret voice, a separate attentiveness.

32   She kept the man's name to herself throughout her labor and dying; she did not accuse him that he be punished with her. To save her inseminator's name she gave silent birth.

33   He may have been somebody in her own household, but intercourse with a man outside the family would have been no less abhorrent. All the village were kinsmen, and the titles shouted in loud country voices never let kinship be forgotten. Any man within visiting distance would have been neutralized as a lover— "brother," "younger brother," "older brother"—one hundred and fifteen relationship titles. Parents researched birth charts probably not so much to assure good fortune as to circumvent incest in a population that has but one hundred surnames. Everybody has eight million relatives. How useless then sexual mannerisms, how dangerous.

34   As if it came from an atavism deeper than fear, I used to add "brother" silently to boys' names. It hexed the boys, who would or would not ask me to dance, and made them less scary and as familiar and deserving of benevolence as girls.

35   But, of course, I hexed myself also—no dates. I should have stood up, both arms waving, and shouted out across libraries, "Hey, you! Love me back." I had no idea, though, how to make attraction selective, how to control its direction and magnitude. If I made myself American-pretty so that the five or six Chinese boys in the class fell in love with me, everyone else—the Caucasian, Negro, and Japanese boys—would too. Sisterliness, dignified and honorable, made much more sense.

36   Attraction eludes control so stubbornly that whole societies designed to organize relationships among people cannot keep order, not even when they bind people to one another from childhood and raise them together. Among the very poor and the wealthy, brothers married their adopted sisters, like doves. Our family allowed some romance, paying adult brides' prices and providing dowries so that their sons and daughters could marry strangers. Marriage promises to turn strangers into friendly relatives—a nation of siblings.

37   In the village structure, spirits shimmered among the live creatures, balanced and held in equilibrium by time and land. But one human being flaring up into violence could open up a black hole, a maelstrom that pulled in the sky. The frightened villagers, who depended on one another to maintain the real, went to my aunt to show her a personal, physical representation of the break she had made in the "roundness." Misallying couples snapped off the future, which was to be embodied in true offspring. The villagers punished her for acting as if she could have a private life, secret and apart from them.

38   If my aunt had betrayed the family at a time of large grain yields and peace, when many boys were born, and wings were being built on many houses, perhaps she might have escaped such severe punishment. But the men—hungry, greedy, tired of planting in dry soil—had been forced to leave the village in order to send food-money home. There were ghost plagues, bandit plagues, wars with the Japanese, floods. My Chinese brother and sister had died of an unknown sickness. Adultery, perhaps only a mistake during good times, became a crime when the village needed food.

39   The round moon cakes and round doorways, the round tables of graduated size that fit one roundness inside another, round windows and rice bowls—these talismans had lost their power to warn this family of the law: a family must be whole, faithfully keeping the descent line by having sons to feed the old and the dead, who in turn look after the family. The villagers came to show my aunt and her lover-in-hiding a broken house. The villagers were speeding up the circling of events because she was too shortsighted to see that her infidelity had already harmed the village, that waves of consequences would return unpredictably, sometimes in disguise, as now, to hurt her. This roundness had to be made coin-sized so that she would see its circumference: punish her at the birth of her baby. Awaken her to the inexorable. People who refused fatalism because they could invent small resources insisted on culpability. Deny accidents and wrest fault from the stars.

40   After the villagers left, their lanterns now scattering in various directions toward home, the family broke their silence and cursed her. "Aiaa, we're going to die. Death is coming. Death is coming. Look what you've done. You've killed us.

Ghost! Dead ghost! Ghost! You've never been born." She ran out into the fields, far enough from the house so that she could no longer hear their voices, and pressed herself against the earth, her own land no more. When she felt the birth coming, she thought that she had been hurt. Her body seized together. "They've hurt me too much," she thought. "This is gall, and it will kill me." With forehead and knees against the earth, her body convulsed and then relaxed. She turned on her back, lay on the ground. The black well of sky and stars went out and out and out forever; her body and her complexity seemed to disappear. She was one of the stars, a bright dot in blackness, without home, without a companion, in eternal cold and silence. An agoraphobia rose in her, speeding higher and higher, bigger and bigger; she would not be able to contain it; there would be no end to fear.

41   Flayed, unprotected against space, she felt pain return, focusing her body. This pain chilled her—a cold, steady kind of surface pain. Inside, spasmodically, the other pain, the pain of the child, heated her. For hours she lay on the ground, alternately body and space. Sometimes a vision of normal comfort obliterated reality: she saw the family in the evening gambling at the dinner table, the young people massaging their elders' backs. She saw them congratulating one another, high joy on the mornings the rice shoots came up. When these pictures burst, the stars drew yet further apart. Black space opened.

42   She got to her feet to fight better and remembered that old-fashioned women gave birth in their pigsties to fool the jealous, pain-dealing gods, who do not snatch piglets. Before the next spasms could stop her, she ran to the pigsty, each step a rushing out into emptiness. She climbed over the fence and knelt in the dirt. It was good to have a fence enclosing her, a tribal person alone.

43   Laboring, this woman who had carried her child as a foreign growth that sickened her every day, expelled it at last. She reached down to touch the hot, wet, moving mass, surely smaller than anything human, and could feel that it was human after all—fingers, toes, nails, nose. She pulled it up on to her belly, and it lay curled there, butt in the air, feet precisely tucked one under the other. She opened her loose shirt and buttoned the child inside. After resting, it squirmed and thrashed and she pushed it up to her breast. It turned its head this way and that until it found her nipple. There, it made little snuffling noises. She clenched her teeth at its preciousness, lovely as a young calf, a piglet, a little dog.

44   She may have gone to the pigsty as a last act of responsibility: she would protect this child as she had protected its father. It would look after her soul, leaving supplies on her grave. But how would this tiny child without family find her grave when there would be no marker for her anywhere, neither in the earth nor the family hall? No one would give her a family hall name. She had taken the child with her into the wastes. At its birth the two of them had felt the same raw pain of separation, a wound that only the family pressing tight could close. A child with no descent line would not soften her life but only trail after her, ghostlike, begging her to give it purpose. At dawn the villagers on their way to the fields would stand around the fence and look.

45   Full of milk, the little ghost slept. When it awoke, she hardened her breasts against the milk that crying loosens. Toward morning she picked up the baby and walked to the well.

46   Carrying the baby to the well shows loving. Otherwise abandon it. Turn its

face into the mud. Mothers who love their children take them along. It was probably a girl; there is some hope of forgiveness for boys.

47   "Don't tell anyone you had an aunt. Your father does not want to hear her
name. She has never been born." I have believed that sex was unspeakable and
words so strong and fathers so frail that "aunt" would do my father mysterious
harm. I have thought that my family, having settled among immigrants who had
also been their neighbors in the ancestral land, needed to clean their name, and a
wrong word would incite the kinspeople even here. But there is more to this
silence: they want me to participate in her punishment. And I have.

48   In the twenty years since I heard this story I have not asked for details nor
said my aunt's name; I do not know it. People who can comfort the dead can also
chase after them to hurt them further—a reverse ancestor worship. The real punishment was not the raid swiftly inflicted by the villagers, but the family's deliberately forgetting her. Her betrayal so maddened them, they saw to it that she
would suffer forever, even after death. Always hungry, always needing, she would
have to beg food from other ghosts, snatch and steal it from those whose living
descendants give them gifts. She would have to fight the ghosts massed at crossroads for the buns a few thoughtful citizens leave to decoy her away from village
and home so that the ancestral spirits could feast unharassed. At peace, they
could act like gods, not ghosts, their descent lines providing them with paper
suits and dresses, spirit money, paper houses, paper automobiles, chicken, meat,
and rice into eternity—essences delivered up in smoke and flames, steam and
incense rising from each rice bowl. In an attempt to make the Chinese care for
people outside the family, Chairman Mao encourages us now to give our paper
replicas to the spirits of outstanding soldiers and workers, no matter whose ancestors they may be. My aunt remains forever hungry. Goods are not distributed
evenly among the dead.

49   My aunt haunts me—her ghost drawn to me because now, after fifty years of
neglect, I alone devote pages of paper to her, though not origamied into houses
and clothes. I do not think she always means me well. I am telling on her, and
she was a spite suicide, drowning herself in the drinking water. The Chinese are
always very frightened of the drowned one, whose weeping ghost, wet hair hanging and skin bloated, waits silently by the water to pull down a substitute.

QUESTIONS

Experience

· Describe your experience in reading Kingston's essay. Consider, for example,
  your reaction as you read the opening segment—the story her mother tells her
  about her aunt, the no name woman. Consider, as well, your response to the
  details Kingston invents as she imagines what her aunt must have experienced. And consider, finally, how Kingston herself experiences the story of her
  aunt's suicide.

· Think about the family stories of some of your relatives. Consider how their
  experience might be related to Kingston's, especially her experience of living in
  two cultures.

Interpretation

· Where and in what way does Kingston reveal the point of the story about her no name aunt? To what extent is Kingston's idea here limited to women and their position in society? To what extent is Kingston describing attitudes characteristic of a foreign world?

· What ideas about family life emerge from this piece? What does Kingston mean by describing the Chinese family with the image of the circle and with the word "roundness"?

· Much of Kingston's story is speculative: she imagines the "facts" about her aunt, a woman she never met from a world she only knows at second hand. Explain Kingston's interpretation of her aunt's experience.

Evaluation

· Identify the cultural values that pervade "No Name Woman." Which of these cultural norms seems most important? Why? How does Kingston dramatize its importance?

· To what extent are secrecy and silence issues for Kingston? For her family? To what extent do these issues represent a standard to which women but not men are held (a double standard)?

· Consider Kingston's distinction between being Chinese-feminine and American-feminine.

WRITING

Exploring

· Tell a family story that has been part of your family lore. It need not be as dark a story as "No Name Woman." It might even be a humorous story. In the telling try to clarify the values, social and familial, that make the story important to you or to your family. Or tell a number of brief family stories that share a common theme, whose thread you either make explicit or leave implied.

Interpreting

· Analyze the implications of Kingston's essay for sexual stereotyping. Explain what her essay suggests about the double standard that restricts women's behavior and limits their options. Or discuss the cultural conflicts evident in Kingston's essay. Consider her situation as a twentieth-century Chinese-American woman in relationship to the events she describes.

Evaluating

· Do some research in Chinese representation of women in art—especially in painting and sculpture, or look for such representations in American popular media. Use your findings to support, qualify, or challenge Kingston's ideas.

ANNIE DILLARD
(b. 1945)

The Deer at Providencia

Annie Dillard has taught creative writing at Wesleyan University in Connecticut. She lived for a time in Roanoke, Virginia, a place she used to wonderful effect in her first book, Pilgrim at Tinker Creek, *awarded a Pulitzer Prize for 1974. Since then she has lived on Puget Sound and in Connecticut. Dillard has written a number of books, including* Living by Fiction, *a critical study;* Teaching a Stone to Talk, *a collection of essays; and* An American Childhood, *a portion of her autobiography.*

Dillard's essays can be demanding both intellectually and emotionally. In "The Deer at Providencia," Dillard raises some unsettling questions about pain and suffering. She describes a series of conflicts, largely centering on aspects of gender, leaning particularly on expected responses of women to the suffering of the innocent and the helpless. Her strategy is to describe a series of brief scenes and to let them comment implicitly on each other.

1   There were four of us North Americans in the jungle, in the Ecuadorian jungle on the banks of the Napo River in the Amazon watershed. The other three North Americans were metropolitan men. We stayed in tents in one riverside village, and visited others. At the village called Providencia we saw a sight which moved us, and which shocked the men.

2   The first thing we saw when we climbed the riverbank to the village of Providencia was the deer. It was roped to a tree on the grass clearing near the thatch shelter where we would eat lunch.

3   The deer was small, about the size of a whitetail fawn, but apparently full-grown. It had a rope around its neck and three feet caught in the rope. Someone said that the dogs had caught it that morning and the villagers were going to cook and eat it that night.

4   This clearing lay at the edge of the little thatched hut village. We could see the villagers going about their business, scattering feed corn for hens about their houses, and wandering down paths to the river to bathe. The village headman was our host; he stood beside us as we watched the deer struggle. Several village boys were interested in the deer; they formed part of the circle we made around it in the clearing. So also did four businessmen from Quito who were attempting to guide us around the jungle. Few of the very different people standing in this circle had a common language. We watched the deer, and no one said much.

5   The deer lay on its side at the rope's very end, so the rope lacked slack to let it rest its head in the dust. It was "pretty," delicate of bone like all deer, and thin-skinned for the tropics. Its skin looked virtually hairless, in fact, and almost translucent, like a membrane. Its neck was no thicker than my wrist; it was rubbed open on the rope, and gashed. Trying to paw itself free of the rope, the deer had

scratched its own neck with its hooves. The raw underside of its neck showed red stripes and some bruises bleeding inside the muscles. Now three of its feet were hooked in the rope under its jaw. It could not stand, of course, on one leg, so it could not move to slacken the rope and ease the pull on its throat and enable it to rest its head.

6   Repeatedly the deer paused, motionless, its eyes veiled, with only its rib cage in motion, and its breaths the only sound. Then, after I would think, "It has given up; now it will die," it would heave. The rope twanged; the tree leaves clattered; the deer's free foot beat the ground. We stepped back and held our breaths. It thrashed, kicking, but only one leg moved; the other three legs tightened inside the rope's loop. Its hip jerked; its spine shook. Its eyes rolled; its tongue, thick with spittle, pushed in and out. Then it would rest again. We watched this for fifteen minutes.

7   Once three young native boys charged in, released its trapped legs, and jumped back to the circle of people. But instantly the deer scratched up its neck with its hooves and snared its forelegs in the rope again. It was easy to imagine a third and then a fourth leg soon stuck, like Brer Rabbit and the Tar Baby.

8   We watched the deer from the circle, and then we drifted on to lunch. Our palm-roofed shelter stood on a grassy promontory from which we could see the deer tied to the tree, pigs and hens walking under village houses, and black-and-white cattle standing in the river. There was even a breeze.

9   Lunch, which was the second and better lunch we had that day, was hot and fried. There was a big fish called *doncella,* a kind of catfish, dipped whole in corn flour and beaten egg, then deep fried. With our fingers we pulled soft fragments of it from its sides to our plates, and ate; it was delicate fish-flesh, fresh and mild. Someone found the roe, and I ate of that too—it was fat and stronger, like egg yolk, naturally enough, and warm.

10   There was also a stew of meat in shreds with rice and pale brown gravy. I had asked what kind of deer it was tied to the tree; Pepe had answered in Spanish, "*Gama.*" Now they told us this was *gama* too, stewed. I suspect the word means merely game or venison. At any rate, I heard that the village dogs had cornered another deer just yesterday, and it was this deer which we were now eating in full sight of the whole article. It was good. I was surprised at its tenderness. But it is a fact that high levels of lactic acid, which builds up in muscle tissues during exertion, tenderizes.

11   After the fish and meat we ate bananas fried in chunks and served on a tray; they were sweet and full of flavor. I felt terrific. My shirt was wet and cool from swimming; I had had a night's sleep, two decent walks, three meals, and a swim—everything tasted good. From time to time each one of us, separately, would look beyond our shaded roof to the sunny spot where the deer was still convulsing in the dust. Our meal completed, we walked around the deer and back to the boats.

12   That night I learned that while we were watching the deer, the others were watching me.

13   We four North Americans grew close in the jungle in a way that was not the usual artificial intimacy of travelers. We liked each other. We stayed up all that night talking, murmuring, as though we rocked on hammocks slung above time. The others were from big cities: New York, Washington, Boston. They all said that I had no expression on my face when I was watching the deer—or at any rate, not the expression they expected.

14   They had looked to see how I, the only woman, and the youngest, was taking the sight of the deer's struggles. I looked detached, apparently, or hard, or calm, or focused, still. I don't know. I was thinking. I remember feeling very old and energetic. I could say like Thoreau that I have traveled widely in Roanoke, Virginia. I have thought a great deal about carnivorousness; I eat meat. These things are not issues; they are mysteries.

15 Gentlemen of the city, what surprises you? That there is suffering here, or that I know it?

16   We lay in the tent and talked. "If it had been my wife," one man said with special vigor, amazed, "she wouldn't have cared *what* was going on; she would have dropped *everything* right at that moment and gone in the village from here to there to there, she would not have *stopped* until that animal was out of its suffering one way or another. She couldn't *bear* to see a creature in agony like that."

17   I nodded.

18 Now I am home. When I wake I comb my hair before the mirror above my dresser. Every morning for the past two years I have seen in that mirror, beside my sleep-softened face, the blackened face of a burnt man. It is a wire-service photograph clipped from a newspaper and taped to my mirror. The caption reads: "Alan McDonald in Miami hospital bed." All you can see in the photograph is a smudged triangle of face from his eyelids to his lower lip; the rest is bandages. You cannot see the expression in his eyes; the bandages shade them.

19   The story, headed MAN BURNED FOR SECOND TIME, begins:

> "Why does God hate me?" Alan McDonald asked from his hospital bed.
> "When the gunpowder went off, I couldn't believe it," he said. "I just couldn't believe it. I said, 'No, God couldn't do this to me again.' "

He was in a burn ward in Miami, in serious condition. I do not even know if he lived. I wrote him a letter at the time, cringing.

20   He had been burned before, thirteen years previously, by flaming gasoline. For years he had been having his body restored and his face remade in dozens of operations. He had been a boy, and then a burnt boy. He had already been stunned by what could happen, by how life could veer.

21   Once I read that people who survive bad burns tend to go crazy; they have a very high suicide rate. Medicine cannot ease their pain; drugs just leak away, soaking the sheets, because there is no skin to hold them in. The people just lie there and weep. Later they kill themselves. They had not known, before they were burned, that the world included such suffering, that life could permit them personally such pain.

22   This time a bowl of gunpowder had exploded on McDonald.

"I didn't realize what had happened at first," he recounted. "And then I heard that sound from 13 years ago. I was burning. I rolled to put the fire out and I thought, 'Oh God, not again.'

"If my friend hadn't been there, I would have jumped into a canal with a rock around my neck."

His wife concludes the piece, "Man, it just isn't fair."

23 I read the whole clipping again every morning. This is the Big Time here, every minute of it. Will someone please explain to Alan McDonald in his dignity, to the deer at Providencia in his dignity, what is going on? And mail me the carbon.

24 When we walked by the deer at Providencia for the last time, I said to Pepe, with a pitying glance at the deer, *"Pobrecito"*—"poor little thing." But I was trying out Spanish. I knew at the time it was a ridiculous thing to say.

QUESTIONS

Experience

· How do you react to reading about the struggles of the deer? What do you think you would have done had you been there? Why?
· Have you ever watched an animal suffering painfully, perhaps dying, without being able (or willing) to do anything about it? Can you relate that or some other experience to your reading of Dillard's experience?
· Did your response change, deepen, intensify when you read about Alan McDonald? How did you respond to the story of his suffering? Why?

Interpretation

· How do you connect the story of Alan McDonald with the plight of the deer?
· Of what importance is Dillard's careful description of the lunch she eats? Does it reveal something about her as a person? Does it comment obliquely on the deer? On carnivorousness? Something else?
· What interpretation does Dillard make of her experience? How do you understand what she seems to be saying? How would you interpret it?

Evaluation

· Of what importance is Dillard's mentioning that this event occurred in the Ecuadorian jungle? Is the meaning of life—of animal life especially—somehow different there? And what of the fact that Dillard was with three other North Americans? Are we to assume that the cultural values of North Americans are somehow at odds with what we are shown about life in Ecuador?
· Dillard makes explicit reference to herself as a woman. Why? What does she suggest by describing the men's reactions to her response (or apparent lack of response) to the deer's suffering? Do women respond to pain and suffering differently than men do?

· And finally, what philosophical or religious values are being raised with Dillard's references to Alan McDonald's question "Why does God hate me?" and to her request for an explanation of his and the deer's suffering?

WRITING

Exploring

· Write an essay in which you explore how men and women respond to pain and suffering. You can use your personal experience for evidence, as well as selecting examples and evidence from your reading or from recent films.

Interpreting

· Analyze the structure and style of Dillard's essay. Consider why she divides it into parts. Explain the relationship among the parts. Consider also Dillard's tone—her attitude toward the things she describes—from the deer to the burned man.

Evaluating

· Write an essay in which you confirm, qualify, or counter Dillard's thinking. If you wish, you can consider what she implies about women and their response to suffering. Or you can consider what she suggests philosophically about the problem of suffering.

SCOTT RUSSELL SANDERS
(b. 1945)

The Men We Carry in Our Minds

Scott Russell Sanders is professor of English at Indiana University. He has published fiction and literary criticism in addition to three volumes of essays, The Paradise of Bombs *(1987),* Secrets of the Universe *(1992), and* Staying Put *(1993). In the following piece from the earliest collection, Sanders suggests that the lives of most men are not nearly as glamorous and exciting as some women may think. Beginning his essay by recounting a dialogue with a woman friend, Sanders then explores questions raised in their conversation. He concludes with a question inviting us to consider whether his views can be appreciated by women, and he confesses to a conventionally unmanly envy of women, whose lives typically revolve more naturally around the things he himself loves.*

Sanders begins his essay with a conversation, which serves as a springboard to his reflections about the degree to which the lives of men are more or less difficult than the lives of women. He orders his reflections largely by grouping them into boyhood memories and college experience, the first concerning men, the second women. Although Sanders creates an apparently loose organization (you hardly notice his artful arranging as you read), he sets up his essay carefully and concludes it with a pair of questions we could imagine him raising in a conversation like the one with which he begins the essay.

1   This must be a hard time for women." I say to my friend Anneke. "They have so many paths to choose from, and so many voices calling them."

2   "I think it's a lot harder for men," she replies.

3   "How do you figure that?"

4   "The women I know feel excited, innocent, like crusaders in a just cause. The men I know are eaten up with guilt."

5   We are sitting at the kitchen table drinking sassafras tea, our hands wrapped around the mugs because this April morning is cool and drizzly. "Like a Dutch morning," Anneke told me earlier. She is Dutch herself, a writer and midwife and peacemaker, with the round face and sad eyes of a woman in a Vermeer painting who might be waiting for the rain to stop, for a door to open. She leans over to sniff a sprig of lilac, pale lavender, that rises from a vase of cobalt blue.

6   "Women feel such pressure to be everything, do everything," I say. "Career, kids, art, politics. Have their babies and get back to the office a week later. It's as if they're trying to overcome a million years' worth of evolution in one lifetime."

7   "But we help one another. We don't try to lumber on alone, like so many wounded grizzly bears, the way men do." Anneke sips her tea. I gave her the mug with owls on it, for wisdom. "And we have this deep-down sense that we're

in the *right*—we've been held back, passed over, used—while men feel they're in the wrong. Men are the ones who've been discredited, who have to search their souls."

8   I search my soul. I discover guilty feelings aplenty—toward the poor, the Vietnamese, Native Americans, the whales, an endless list of debts—a guilt in each case that is as bright and unambiguous as a neon sign. But toward women I feel something more confused, a snarl of shame, envy, wary tenderness, and amazement. This muddle troubles me. To hide my unease I say, "You're right, it's tough being a man these days."

9   "Don't laugh." Anneke frowns at me, mournful-eyed, through the sassafras steam. "I wouldn't be a man for anything. It's much easier being the victim. All the victim has to do is break free. The persecutor has to live with his past."

10   How deep is that past? I find myself wondering after Anneke has left. How much of an inheritance do I have to throw off? Is it just the beliefs I breathed in as a child? Do I have to scour memory back through father and grandfather? Through St. Paul? Beyond Stonehenge and into the twilit caves? I'm convinced the past we must contend with is deeper even than speech. When I think back on my childhood, on how I learned to see men and women, I have a sense of ancient, dizzying depths. The back roads of Tennessee and Ohio where I grew up were probably closer, in their sexual patterns, to the campsites of Stone Age hunters than to the genderless cities of the future into which we are rushing.

11   The first men, besides my father, I remember seeing were black convicts and white guards, in the cottonfield across the road from our farm on the outskirts of Memphis. I must have been three or four. The prisoners wore dingy gray and black zebra suits, heavy as canvas, sodden with sweat. Hatless, stooped, they chopped weeds in the fierce heat, row after row, breathing the acrid dust of boll-weevil poison. The overseers wore dazzling white shirts and broad shadowy hats. The oiled barrels of their shotguns flashed in the sunlight. Their faces in memory are utterly blank. Of course those men, white and black, have become for me an emblem of racial hatred. But they have also come to stand for the twin poles of my early vision of manhood—the brute toiling animal and the boss.

12   When I was a boy, the men I knew labored with their bodies. They were marginal farmers, just scraping by, or welders, steelworkers, carpenters; they swept floors, dug ditches, mined coal, or drove trucks, their forearms ropy with muscle, they trained horses, stoked furnaces, built tires, stood on assembly lines wrestling parts onto cars and refrigerators. They got up before light, worked all day long whatever the weather, and when they came home at night they looked as though somebody had been whipping them. In the evenings and on weekends they worked on their own places, tilling gardens that were lumpy with clay, fixing broken-down cars, hammering on houses that were always too drafty, too leaky, too small.

13   The bodies of the men I knew were twisted and maimed in ways visible and invisible. The nails of their hands were black and split, the hands tattooed with scars. Some had lost fingers. Heavy lifting had given many of them finicky backs and guts weak from hernias. Racing against conveyor belts had given them ulcers. Their ankles and knees ached from years of standing on concrete. Anyone who had worked for long around machines was hard of hearing. They squinted, and

the skin of their faces was creased like the leather of old work gloves. There were times, studying them, when I dreaded growing up. Most of them coughed, from dust or cigarettes, and most of them drank cheap wine or whiskey, so their eyes looked bloodshot and bruised. The fathers of my friends always seemed older than the mothers. Men wore out sooner. Only women lived into old age.

14   As a boy I also knew another sort of men, who did not sweat and break down like mules. They were soldiers, and so far as I could tell they scarcely worked at all. During my early school years we lived on a military base, an arsenal in Ohio, and every day I saw GIs in the guardshacks, on the stoops of barracks, at the wheels of olive drab Chevrolets. The chief fact of their lives was boredom. Long after I left the Arsenal I came to recognize the sour smell the soldiers gave off as that of souls in limbo. They were all waiting—for wars, for transfers, for leaves, for promotions, for the end of their hitch—like so many braves waiting for the hunt to begin. Unlike the warriors of older tribes, however, they would have no say about when the battle would start or how it would be waged. Their waiting was broken only when they practiced for war. They fired guns at targets, drove tanks across the churned-up fields of the military reservation, set off bombs in the wrecks of old fighter planes. I knew this was all play. But I also felt certain that when the hour for killing arrived, they would kill. When the real shooting started, many of them would die. This was what soldiers were *for,* just as a hammer was for driving nails.

15   Warriors and toilers: those seemed, in my boyhood vision, to be the chief destinies for men. They weren't the only destinies, as I learned from having a few male teachers, from reading books, and from watching television. But the men on television—the politicians, the astronauts, the generals, the savvy lawyers, the philosophical doctors, the bosses who gave orders to both soldiers and laborers—seemed as remote and unreal to me as the figures in tapestries. I could no more imagine growing up to become one of these cool, potent creatures than I could imagine becoming a prince.

16   A nearer and more hopeful example was that of my father, who had escaped from a red dirt farm to a tire factory, and from the assembly line to the front office. Eventually he dressed in a white shirt and tie. He carried himself as if he had been born to work with his mind. But his body, remembering the earlier years of slogging work, began to give out on him in his fifties, and it quit on him entirely before he turned sixty-five. Even such a partial escape from man's fate as he had accomplished did not seem possible for most of the boys I knew. They joined the Army, stood in line for jobs in the smoky plants, helped build highways. They were bound to work as their fathers had worked, killing themselves or preparing to kill others.

17   A scholarship enabled me not only to attend college, a rare enough feat in my circle, but even to study in a university meant for the children of the rich. Here I met for the first time young men who had assumed from birth that they would lead lives of comfort and power. And for the first time I met women who told me that men were guilty of having kept all the joys and privileges of the earth for themselves. I was baffled. What privileges? What joys? I thought about the maimed, dismal lives of most of the men back home. What had they stolen from their wives and daughters? The right to go five days a week, twelve months a year, for thirty or forty years to a steel mill or a coal mine? The right to drop bombs

and die in war? The right to feel every leak in the roof, every gap in the fence, every cough in the engine, as a wound they must mend? The right to feel, when the lay-off comes or the plant shuts down, not only afraid but ashamed?

18   I was slow to understand the deep grievances of women. This was because, as a boy, I had envied them. Before college, the only people I had ever known who were interested in art or music or literature, the only ones who read books, the only ones who ever seemed to enjoy a sense of ease and grace were the mothers and daughters. Like the menfolk, they fretted about money, they scrimped and made-do. But, when the pay stopped coming in, they were not the ones who had failed. Nor did they have to go to war, and that seemed to me a blessed fact. By comparison with the narrow, ironclad days of fathers, there was an expansiveness, I thought, in the days of mothers. They went to see neighbors, to shop in town, to run errands at school, at the library, at church. No doubt, had I looked harder at their lives, I would have envied them less. It was not my fate to become a woman, so it was easier for me to see the graces. Few of them held jobs outside the home, and those who did filled thankless roles as clerks and wait-resses. I didn't see, then, what a prison a house could be, since houses seemed to me brighter, handsomer places than any factory. I did not realize—because such things were never spoken of—how often women suffered from men's bullying. I did learn about the wretchedness of abandoned wives, single mothers, widows; but I also learned about the wretchedness of lone men. Even then I could see how exhausting it was for a mother to cater all day to the needs of young children. But if I had been asked, as a boy, to choose between tending a baby and tending a machine, I think I would have chosen the baby. (Having now tended both, I know I would choose the baby.)

19   So I was baffled when the women at college accused me and my sex of hav-ing cornered the world's pleasures. I think something like my bafflement has been felt by other boys (and by girls as well) who grew up in dirt-poor farm country, in mining country, in black ghettos, in Hispanic barrios, in the shadows of factories, in Third World nations—any place where the fate of men is as grim and bleak as the fate of women. Toilers and warriors. I realize now how ancient these identities are, how deep the tug they exert on men, the undertow of a thousand generations. The miseries I saw, as a boy, in the lives of nearly all men I continue to see in the lives of many—the body-breaking toil, the tedium, the call to be tough, the humil-iating powerlessness, the battle for a living and for territory.

20   When the women I met at college thought about the joys and privileges of men, they did not carry in their minds the sort of men I had known in my child-hood. They thought of their fathers, who were bankers, physicians, architects, stockbrokers, the big wheels of the big cities. These fathers rode the train to work or drove cars that cost more than any of my childhood houses. They were attended from morning to night by female helpers, wives and nurses and secre-taries. They were never laid off, never short of cash at month's end, never lined up for welfare. These fathers made decisions that mattered. They ran the world.

21   The daughters of such men wanted to share in this power, this glory. So did I. They yearned for a say over their future, for jobs worthy of their abilities, for the right to live at peace, unmolested, whole. Yes, I thought, yes yes. The difference between me and these daughters was that they saw me, because of my sex, as

destined from birth to become like their fathers, and therefore as an enemy to their desires. But I knew better. I wasn't an enemy, in fact or in feeling. I was an ally. If I had known, then, how to tell them so, would they have believed me? Would they now?

QUESTIONS

Experience

· Toward the end of the opening dialogue, Sanders searches his soul and discovers feelings of guilt. Do you share Sanders's guilty feelings about the kind of political and social problems he refers to? Why, or why not?

· To what extent do you share Anneke's view that women are victims and men their persecutors? How has your own experience affected your view? How would you answer Sanders's concluding questions?

Interpretation

· What images of men does Sanders describe? Where did he acquire these images? And how does the contrast between them express the idea about men Sanders develops in this essay?

· How does Sanders's portrayal of women support his idea that men's lives are more desperate and more dangerous (and thus less appealing) than the lives of women?

· Sanders suggests how stereotyping can lead to unjustified resentment and envy by indicating how pervasive is the stereotype of masculine privilege. What is Sanders's basic point about masculine privilege?

Evaluation

· How persuasive is Sanders's overall argument? How valid is the distinction he draws between different types of men? How persuasively does he portray the lives of women? And how well do you think Sanders understands women?

· Sanders refers to a number of cultural perspectives with regard to men. To what extent does Sanders's cultural background play into his argument? What characteristics of men does he draw from the cultural traditions of heartland America?

· Why and with what effect does Sanders refer to other times and places than those he has himself experienced? What cultural values are suggested by the references in paragraphs 10 and 19?

WRITING

Exploring

· Tell a story of your own that compares with something Sanders describes in his essay. Perhaps you can include as part of your essay a conversation you had with a member of the opposite sex.

Interpreting

· Analyze the way Sanders organizes his essay. Identify its basic parts; explain what he accomplishes in each part; and relate the parts to one another. Consider his use of dialogue in the beginning and his use of questions at the end as well as his use of contrast.

Evaluating

· Support or dispute Sanders's claims about men. Use evidence from your reading and experience to substantiate your assertions. Consider looking to images of men conveyed in popular songs, rap music, or films. If you do, be sure to explain their relation to Sanders's argument about men.

DEBORAH TANNEN
(b. 1945)

Different Words, Different Worlds

Deborah Tannen is professor of linguistics at Georgetown University. In addition to her scholarly publications on language, she has published a best-selling book, You Just Don't Understand, *in which she argues that men and women use language differently. Tannen contends, moreover, that even when men and women use the same words, they often mean different things. The different conversational styles of men and women reveal fundamental differences in how they perceive others and relate to others. In this excerpt from her book, Tannen writes simply and directly, using many specific examples to illustrate and support her argument.*

One of the notable features of her writing is the way she creates little scenes complete with dialogue—a compositional strategy well suited to her topic. In these miniscenes Tannen is able to show human communication in action and thus to illustrate her idea as well as explain it.

1 Many years ago I was married to a man who shouted at me, "I do not give you the right to raise your voice to me, because you are a woman and I am a man." This was frustrating, because I knew it was unfair. But I also knew just what was going on. I ascribed his unfairness to his having grown up in a country where few people thought women and men might have equal rights.

2 Now I am married to a man who is a partner and friend. We come from similar backgrounds and share values and interests. It is a continual source of pleasure to talk to him. It is wonderful to have someone I can tell everything to, someone who understands. But he doesn't always see things as I do, doesn't always react to things as I expect him to. And I often don't understand why he says what he does.

3 At the time I began working on this book, we had jobs in different cities. People frequently expressed sympathy by making comments like "That must be rough," and "How do you stand it?" I was inclined to accept their sympathy and say things like "We fly a lot." Sometimes I would reinforce their concern: "The worst part is having to pack and unpack all the time." But my husband reacted differently, often with irritation. He might respond by de-emphasizing the inconvenience: As academics, we had four-day weekends together, as well as long vacations throughout the year and four months in the summer. We even benefited from the intervening days of uninterrupted time for work. I once overheard him telling a dubious man that we were lucky, since studies have shown that married couples who live together spend less than half an hour a week talking to each other; he was implying that our situation had advantages.

4 I didn't object to the way my husband responded—everything he said was

true—but I was surprised by it. I didn't understand why he reacted as he did. He explained that he sensed condescension in some expressions of concern, as if the questioner were implying, "Yours is not a real marriage; your ill-chosen profession has resulted in an unfortunate arrangement. I pity you, and look down at you from the height of complacence, since my wife and I have avoided your misfortune." It had not occurred to me that there might be an element of one-upmanship in these expressions of concern, though I could recognize it when it was pointed out. Even after I saw the point, though, I was inclined to regard my husband's response as slightly odd, a personal quirk. He frequently seemed to see others as adversaries when I didn't.

5   Having done the research that led to this book, I now see that my husband was simply engaging the world in a way that many men do: as an individual in a hierarchical social order in which he was either one-up or one-down. In this world, conversations are negotiations in which people try to achieve and maintain the upper hand if they can, and protect themselves from others' attempts to put them down and push them around. Life, then, is a contest, a struggle to preserve independence and avoid failure.

6   I, on the other hand, was approaching the world as many women do: as an individual in a network of connections. In this world, conversations are negotiations for closeness in which people try to seek and give confirmation and support, and to reach consensus. They try to protect themselves from others' attempts to push them away. Life, then, is a community, a struggle to preserve intimacy and avoid isolation. Though there are hierarchies in this world too, they are hierarchies more of friendship than of power and accomplishment.

7   Women are also concerned with achieving status and avoiding failure, but these are not the goals they are *focused* on all the time, and they tend to pursue them in the guise of connection. And men are also concerned with achieving involvement and avoiding isolation, but they are not *focused* on these goals, and they tend to pursue them in the guise of opposition.

8   Discussing our differences from this point of view, my husband pointed out to me a distinction I had missed: He reacted the way I just described only if expressions of concern came from men in whom he sensed an awareness of hierarchy. And there were times when I too disliked people's expressing sympathy about our commuting marriage. I recall being offended by one man who seemed to have a leering look in his eye when he asked, "How do you manage this long-distance romance?" Another time I was annoyed when a woman who knew me only by reputation approached us during the intermission of a play, discovered our situation by asking my husband where he worked, and kept the conversation going by asking us all about it. In these cases, I didn't feel put down; I felt intruded upon. If my husband was offended by what he perceived as claims to superior status, I felt these sympathizers were claiming inappropriate intimacy.

INTIMACY AND INDEPENDENCE

9   *Intimacy* is key in a world of connection where individuals negotiate complex networks of friendship, minimize differences, try to reach consensus, and avoid the

appearance of superiority, which would highlight differences. In a world of status, *independence* is key, because a primary means of establishing status is to tell others what to do, and taking orders is a marker of low status. Though all humans need both intimacy and independence, women tend to focus on the first and men on the second. It is as if their lifeblood ran in different directions.

10   These differences can give women and men differing views of the same situation, as they did in the case of a couple I will call Linda and Josh. When Josh's old high-school chum called him at work and announced he'd be in town on business the following month, Josh invited him to stay for the weekend. That evening he informed Linda that they were going to have a houseguest, and that he and his chum would go out together the first night to shoot the breeze like old times. Linda was upset. She was going to be away on business the week before, and the Friday night when Josh would be out with his chum would be her first night home. But what upset her the most was that Josh had made these plans on his own and informed her of them, rather than discussing them with her before extending the invitation.

11   Linda would never make plans, for a weekend or an evening, without first checking with Josh. She can't understand why he doesn't show her the same courtesy and consideration that she shows him. But when she protests, Josh says, "I can't say to my friend, 'I have to ask my wife for permission'!"

12   To Josh, checking with his wife means seeking permission, which implies that he is not independent, not free to act on his own. It would make him feel like a child or an underling. To Linda, checking with her husband has nothing to do with permission. She assumes that spouses discuss their plans with each other because their lives are intertwined, so the actions of one have consequences for the other. Not only does Linda not mind telling someone, "I have to check with Josh"; quite the contrary—she likes it. It makes her feel good to know and show that she is involved with someone, that her life is bound up with someone else's.

13   Linda and Josh both felt more upset by this incident, and others like it, than seemed warranted, because it cut to the core of their primary concerns. Linda was hurt because she sensed a failure of closeness in their relationship: He didn't care about her as much as she cared about him. And he was hurt because he felt she was trying to control him and limit his freedom.

14   A similar conflict exists between Louise and Howie, another couple, about spending money. Louise would never buy anything costing more than a hundred dollars without discussing it with Howie, but he goes out and buys whatever he wants and feels they can afford, like a table saw or a new power mower. Louise is disturbed, not because she disapproves of the purchases, but because she feels he is acting as if she were not in the picture.

15   Many women feel it is natural to consult with their partners at every turn, while many men automatically make more decisions without consulting their partners. This may reflect a broad difference in conceptions of decision making. Women expect decisions to be discussed first and made in consensus. They appreciate the discussion itself as evidence of involvement and communication. But many men feel oppressed by lengthy discussions about what they see as minor decisions, and they feel hemmed in if they can't just act without talking

first. When women try to initiate a freewheeling discussion by asking, "What do you think?" men often think they are being asked to decide.

16   Communication is a continual balancing act, juggling the conflicting needs for intimacy and independence. To survive in the world, we have to act in concert with others, but to survive as ourselves, rather than simply as cogs in a wheel, we have to act alone. In some ways, all people are the same: We all eat and sleep and drink and laugh and cough, and often we eat, and laugh at, the same things. But in some ways, each person is different, and individuals' differing wants and preferences may conflict with each other. Offered the same menu, people make different choices. And if there is cake for dessert, there is a chance one person may get a larger piece than another—and an even greater chance that one will *think* the other's piece is larger, whether it is or not.

ASYMMETRIES

17   If intimacy says, "We're close and the same," and independence says, "We're separate and different," it is easy to see that intimacy and independence dovetail with connection and status. The essential element of connection is symmetry: People are the same, feeling equally close to each other. The essential element of status is asymmetry: People are not the same; they are differently placed in a hierarchy.

18   This duality is particularly clear in expressions of sympathy or concern, which are all potentially ambiguous. They can be interpreted either symmetrically, as evidence of fellow feeling among equals, or asymmetrically, offered by someone one-up to someone one-down. Asking if an unemployed person has found a job, if a couple have succeeded in conceiving the child they crave, or whether an untenured professor expects to get tenure can be meant—and interpreted, regardless of how it is meant—as an expression of human connection by a person who understands and cares, or as a reminder of weakness from someone who is better off and knows it, and hence as condescending. The latter view of sympathy seems self-evident to many men. For example, a handicapped mountain climber named Tom Whittaker, who leads groups of disabled people on outdoor expeditions, remarked, "You can't feel sympathetic for someone you admire"—a statement that struck me as not true at all.

19   The symmetry of connection is what creates community: If two people are struggling for closeness, they are both struggling for the same thing. And the asymmetry of status is what creates contest: Two people can't both have the upper hand, so negotiation for status is inherently adversarial. In my earlier work, I explored in detail the dynamics of intimacy (which I referred to as involvement) and independence, but I tended to ignore the force of status and its adversarial nature. Once I identified these dynamics, however, I saw them all around me. The puzzling behavior of friends and co-workers finally became comprehensible.

20   Differences in how my husband and I approached the same situation, which previously would have been mystifying, suddenly made sense. For example, in a jazz club the waitress recommended the crab cakes to me, and they turned out to be terrible. I was uncertain about whether or not to send them back. When the

waitress came by and asked how the food was, I said that I didn't really like the crab cakes. She asked, "What's wrong with them?" While staring at the table, my husband answered. "They don't taste fresh." The waitress snapped. "They're frozen! What do you expect?" I looked directly up at her and said. "We just don't like them." She said, "Well, if you don't like them, I could take them back and bring you something else."

21   After she left with the crab cakes, my husband and I laughed because we realized we had just automatically played out the scripts I had been writing about. He had heard her question "What's wrong with them?" as a challenge that he had to match. He doesn't like to fight, so he looked away, to soften what he felt was an obligatory counterchallenge: He felt instinctively that he had to come up with something wrong with the crab cakes to justify my complaint. (He was fighting for me.) I had taken the question "What's wrong with them?" as a request for information. I instinctively sought a way to be right without making her wrong. Perhaps it was because she was a woman that she responded more favorably to my approach.

22   When I have spoken to friends and to groups about these differences, they too say that now they can make sense of previously perplexing behavior. For example, a woman said she finally understood why her husband refused to talk to his boss about whether or not he stood a chance of getting promoted. He wanted to know because if the answer was no, he would start looking for another job. But instead of just asking, he stewed and fretted, lost sleep, and worried. Having no others at her disposal, this wife had fallen back on psychological explanations: Her husband must be insecure, afraid of rejection. But then, everyone is insecure, to an extent. Her husband was actually quite a confident person. And she, who believed herself to be at least as insecure as he, had not hesitated to go to her boss to ask whether he intended to make her temporary job permanent.

23   Understanding the key role played by status in men's relations made it all come clear. Asking a boss about chances for promotion highlights the hierarchy in the relationship, reminding them both that the employee's future is in the boss's hands. Taking the low-status position made this man intensely uncomfortable. Although his wife didn't especially relish taking the role of supplicant with respect to her boss, it didn't set off alarms in her head, as it did in his.

24   In a similar flash of insight, a woman who works in sales exclaimed that now she understood the puzzling transformation that the leader of her sales team had undergone when he was promoted to district manager. She had been sure he would make a perfect boss because he had a healthy disregard for authority. As team leader, he had rarely bothered to go to meetings called by management and had encouraged team members to exercise their own judgment, eagerly using his power to waive regulations on their behalf. But after he became district manager, this man was unrecognizable. He instituted more regulations than anyone had dreamed of, and insisted that exceptions could be made only on the basis of written requests to him.

25   This man behaved differently because he was now differently placed in the hierarchy. When he had been subject to the authority of management, he'd done all he could to limit it. But when the authority of management was vested in him, he did all he could to enlarge it. By avoiding meetings and flouting regulations, he

had evidenced not disregard for hierarchy but rather discomfort at being in the subordinate position within it.

26   Yet another woman said she finally understood why her fiancé, who very much believes in equality, once whispered to her that she should keep her voice down. "My friends are downstairs," he said. "I don't want them to get the impression that you order me around."

27   That women have been labeled "nags" may result from the interplay of men's and women's styles, whereby many women are inclined to do what is asked of them and many men are inclined to resist even the slightest hint that anyone, especially a woman, is telling them what to do. A woman will be inclined to repeat a request that doesn't get a response because she is convinced that her husband would do what she asks, if he only understood that she *really* wants him to do it. But a man who wants to avoid feeling that he is following orders may instinctively wait before doing what she asked, in order to imagine that he is doing it of his own free will. Nagging is the result, because each time she repeats the request, he again puts off fulfilling it.

MIXED JUDGMENTS AND MISJUDGMENTS

28   Because men and women are regarding the landscape from contrasting vantage points, the same scene can appear very different to them, and they often have opposite interpretations of the same action.

29   A colleague mentioned that he got a letter from a production editor working on his new book, instructing him to let her know if he planned to be away from his permanent address at any time in the next six months, when his book would be in production. He commented that he hadn't realized how like a parole officer a production editor could be. His response to this letter surprised me, because I have received similar letters from publishers, and my response is totally different: I like them, because it makes me feel important to know that my whereabouts matter. When I mentioned this difference to my colleague, he was puzzled and amused, as I was by his reaction. Though he could understand my point of view intellectually, emotionally he could not imagine how one could not feel framed as both controlled and inferior in rank by being told to report one's movements to someone. And though I could understand his perspective intellectually, it simply held no emotional resonance for me.

30   In a similar spirit, my colleague remarked that he had read a journal article written by a woman who thanked her husband in the acknowledgments section of her paper for helpful discussion of the topic. When my colleague first read this acknowledgment, he thought the author must be incompetent, or at least insecure: Why did she have to consult her husband about her own work? Why couldn't she stand on her own two feet? After hearing my explanation that women value evidence of connection, he reframed the acknowledgment and concluded that the author probably valued her husband's involvement in her work and made reference to it with the pride that comes of believing one has evidence of a balanced relationship.

31   If my colleague's reaction is typical, imagine how often women who think

they are displaying a positive quality—connection—are misjudged by men who perceive them as revealing a lack of independence, which the men regard as synonymous with incompetence and insecurity.

IN PURSUIT OF FREEDOM

32   A woman was telling me why a long-term relationship had ended. She recounted a recurrent and pivotal conversation. She and the man she lived with had agreed that they would both be free, but they would not do anything to hurt each other. When the man began to sleep with other women, she protested, and he was incensed at her protest. Their conversation went like this:

> SHE: How can you do this when you know it's hurting me?
> HE: How can you try to limit my freedom?
> SHE: But it makes me feel awful.
> HE: You are trying to manipulate me.

On one level, this is simply an example of a clash of wills: What he wanted conflicted with what she wanted. But in a fundamental way, it reflects the difference in focus I have been describing. In arguing for his point of view, the key issue for this man was his independence, his freedom of action. The key issue for the woman was their interdependence—how what he did made her feel. He interpreted her insistence on their interdependence as "manipulation": She was using her feelings to control his behavior.

33   The point is not that women do not value freedom or that men do not value their connection to others. It is rather that the desire for freedom and independence becomes more of an issue for many men in relationships, whereas interdependence and connection become more of an issue for many women. The difference is one of focus and degree.

34   In a study of how women and men talk about their divorces, Catherine Kohler Riessman found that both men and women mentioned increased freedom as a benefit of divorce. But the word *freedom* meant different things to them. When women told her they had gained freedom by divorce, they meant that they had gained "independence and autonomy." It was a relief for them not to have to worry about how their husbands would react to what they did, and not have to be "responsive to a disgruntled spouse." When men mentioned freedom as a benefit of divorce, they meant freedom from obligation—the relief of feeling "less confined," less "claustrophobic," and having "fewer responsibilities."

35   Riessman's findings illuminate the differing burdens that are placed on women and men by their characteristic approaches to relationships. The burden from which divorce delivered the women was perceived as internally motivated: the continual preoccupation with how their husbands would respond to them and how they should respond to their husbands. The burden from which it delivered the men was perceived as externally imposed: the obligations of the provider role and a feeling of confinement from having their behavior constrained by others. Independence was not a gift of divorce for the men Riessman interviewed, because, as one man put it, "I always felt independent and I guess it's just more so now."

36   *The Chronicle of Higher Education* conducted a small survey, asking six university professors why they had chosen the teaching profession. Among the six were four men and two women. In answering the question, the two women referred to teaching. One said, "I've always wanted to teach." The other said, "I knew as an undergraduate that I wanted to join a faculty. . . . I realized that teaching was the thing I wanted to do." The four men's answers had much in common with each other and little in common with the women's. All four men referred to independence as their main motive. Here are excerpts from each of their responses:

> I decided it was academe over industry because I would have my choice of research. There's more independence.

> I wanted to teach, and I like the freedom to set your own research goals.

> I chose an academic job because the freedoms of academia outweighed the money disadvantages—and to pursue the research interest I'd like to, as opposed to having it dictated.

> I have a problem that interests me. . . . I'd rather make $30,000 for the rest of my life and be allowed to do basic research than to make $100,000 and work in computer graphics.

Though one man also mentioned teaching, neither of the women mentioned freedom to pursue their own research interests as a main consideration. I do not believe this means that women are not interested in research, but rather that independence, freedom from being told what to do, is not as significant a preoccupation for them.

37   In describing what appealed to them about teaching, these two women focused on the ability to influence students in a positive way. Of course, influencing students reflects a kind of power over them, and teaching entails an asymmetrical relationship, with the teacher in the higher-status position. But in talking about their profession, the women focused on connection to students, whereas the men focused on their freedom from others' control.

MALE-FEMALE CONVERSATION IS CROSS-CULTURAL COMMUNICATION

38   If women speak and hear a language of connection and intimacy, while men speak and hear a language of status and independence, then communication between men and women can be like cross-cultural communication, prey to a clash of conversational styles. Instead of different dialects, it has been said they speak different genderlects.

39   The claim that men and women grow up in different worlds may at first seem patently absurd. Brothers and sisters grow up in the same families, children to parents of both genders. Where, then, do women and men learn different ways of speaking and hearing?

IT BEGINS AT THE BEGINNING

40 Even if they grow up in the same neighborhood, on the same block, or in the same house, girls and boys grow up in different worlds of words. Others talk to them differently and expect and accept different ways of talking from them. Most important, children learn how to talk, how to have conversations, not only from their parents but from their peers. After all, if their parents have a foreign or regional accent, children do not emulate it: they learn to speak with the pronunciation of the region where they grow up. Anthropologists Daniel Maltz and Ruth Borker summarize research showing that boys and girls have very different ways of talking to their friends. Although they often play together, boys and girls spend most of their time playing in same-sex groups. And, although some of the activities they play at are similar, their favorite games are different, and their ways of using language in their games are separated by a world of difference.

41   Boys tend to play outside, in large groups that are hierarchically structured. Their groups have a leader who tells others what to do and how to do it, and resists doing what other boys propose. It is by giving orders and making them stick that high status is negotiated. Another way boys achieve status is to take center stage by telling stories and jokes, and by sidetracking or challenging the stories and jokes of others. Boys' games have winners and losers and elaborate systems of rules that are frequently the subjects of arguments. Finally, boys are frequently heard to boast of their skill and argue about who is best at what.

42   Girls, on the other hand, play in small groups or in pairs; the center of a girl's social life is a best friend. Within the group, intimacy is key: Differentiation is measured by relative closeness. In their most frequent games, such as jump rope and hopscotch, everyone gets a turn. Many of their activities (such as playing house) do not have winners or losers. Though some girls are certainly more skilled than others, girls are expected not to boast about it, or show that they think they are better than the others. Girls don't give orders; they express their preferences as suggestions, and suggestions are likely to be accepted. Whereas boys say, "Gimme that!" and "Get outta here!" girls say, "Let's do this," and "How about doing that?" Anything else is put down as "bossy." They don't grab center stage—they don't want it—so they don't challenge each other directly. And much of the time, they simply sit together and talk. Girls are not accustomed to jockeying for status in an obvious way; they are more concerned that they be liked.

43   Gender differences in ways of talking have been described by researchers observing children as young as three. Amy Sheldon videotaped three- to four-year-old boys and girls playing in threesomes at a day-care center. She compared two groups of three—one of boys, one of girls—that got into fights about the same play item: a plastic pickle. Though both groups fought over the same thing, the dynamics by which they negotiated their conflicts were different. In addition to illustrating some of the patterns I have just described, Sheldon's study also demonstrates the complexity of these dynamics.

44   While playing in the kitchen area of the day-care center, a little girl named Sue wanted the pickle that Mary had, so she argued that Mary should give it up because Lisa, the third girl, wanted it. This led to a conflict about how to satisfy Lisa's (invented) need. Mary proposed a compromise, but Sue protested:

MARY: I cut it in half. One for Lisa, one for me, one for me.
SUE: But, Lisa wants a *whole* pickle!

Mary comes up with another creative compromise, which Sue also rejects:

MARY: Well, it's a whole *half* pickle.
SUE: No, it isn't.
MARY: Yes, it is, a whole *half* pickle.
SUE: *I'll* give her a whole half. I'll give her a *whole whole.* I gave her a whole one.

At this point. Lisa withdraws from the alliance with Sue, who satisfies herself by saying, "I'm pretending I gave you one."

45   On another occasion, Sheldon videotaped three boys playing in the same kitchen play area, and they too got into a fight about the plastic pickle. When Nick saw that Kevin had the pickle, he demanded it for himself:

NICK: [Screams] Kevin, but the, oh, I *have* to cut! I want to cut it! It's mine!

Like Sue, Nick involved the third child in his effort to get the pickle:

NICK: [Whining to Joe] Kevin is not letting me cut the pickle.
JOE: Oh, I know! I can pull it away from him and give it back to you. That's an idea!

The boys' conflict, which lasted two and a half times longer than the girls', then proceeded as a struggle between Nick and Joe on the one hand and Kevin on the other.

46   In comparing the boys' and girls' pickle fights, Sheldon points out that, for the most part, the girls mitigated the conflict and preserved harmony by compromise and evasion. Conflict was more prolonged among the boys, who used more insistence, appeals to rules, and threats of physical violence. However, to say that these little girls and boys used *more* of one strategy or another is not to say that they didn't use the other strategies at all. For example, the boys did attempt compromise, and the girls did attempt physical force. The girls, like the boys, were struggling for control of their play. When Sue says by mistake, *"I'll give her a whole half,"* then quickly corrects herself to say. "I'll give her a *whole whole,"* she reveals that it is not really the size of the portion that is important to her, but who gets to serve it.

47   While reading Sheldon's study, I noticed that whereas both Nick and Sue tried to get what they wanted by involving a third child, the alignments they created with the third child, and the dynamics they set in motion, were fundamentally different. Sue appealed to Mary to fulfill someone else's desire; rather than saying that *she* wanted the pickle, she claimed that Lisa wanted it. Nick asserted his own desire for the pickle, and when he couldn't get it on his own, he appealed to Joe to get it for him. Joe then tried to get the pickle by force. In both these scenarios, the children were enacting complex lines of affiliation.

48   Joe's strong-arm tactics were undertaken not on his own behalf but, chivalrously, on behalf of Nick. By making an appeal in a whining voice, Nick positioned himself as one-down in a hierarchical structure, framing himself as someone in

need of protection. When Sue appealed to Mary to relinquish her pickle, she wanted to take the one-up position of serving food. She was fighting not for the right to *have* the pickle, but for the right to *serve* it. (This reminded me of the women who said they'd become professors in order to teach.) But to accomplish her goal. Sue was depending on Mary's desire to fulfill others' needs.

49   This study suggests that boys and girls both want to get their way, but they tend to do so differently. Though social norms encourage boys to be openly competitive and girls to be openly cooperative, different situations and activities can result in different ways of behaving. Marjorie Harness Goodwin compared boys and girls engaged in two task-oriented activities: The boys were making slingshots in preparation for a fight, and the girls were making rings. She found that the boys' group was hierarchical: The leader told the others what to do and how to do it. The girls' group was egalitarian: Everyone made suggestions and tended to accept the suggestions of others. But observing the girls in a different activity—playing house—Goodwin found that they too adopted hierarchical structures: The girls who played mothers issued orders to the girls playing children, who in turn sought permission from their play-mothers. Moreover, a girl who was a play-mother was also a kind of manager of the game. This study shows that girls know how to issue orders and operate in a hierarchical structure, but they don't find that mode of behavior appropriate when they engage in task activities with their peers. They do find it appropriate in parent-child relationships, which they enjoy practicing in the form of play.

50   These worlds of play shed light on the world views of women and men in relationships. The boys' play illuminates why men would be on the lookout for signs they are being put down or told what to do. The chief commodity that is bartered in the boys' hierarchical world is status, and the way to achieve and maintain status is to give orders and get others to follow them. A boy in a low-status position finds himself being pushed around. So boys monitor their relations for subtle shifts in status by keeping track of who's giving orders and who's taking them.

51   These dynamics are not the ones that drive girls' play. The chief commodity that is bartered in the girls' community is intimacy. Girls monitor their friendships for subtle shifts in alliance, and they seek to be friends with popular girls. Popularity is a kind of status, but it is founded on connection. It also places popular girls in a bind. By doing field work in a junior high school, Donna Eder found that popular girls were paradoxically—and inevitably—disliked. Many girls want to befriend popular girls, but girls' friendships must necessarily be limited, since they entail intimacy rather than large group activities. So a popular girl must reject the overtures of most of the girls who seek her out—with the result that she is branded "stuck up."

THE KEY IS UNDERSTANDING

52 If adults learn their ways of speaking as children growing up in separate social worlds of peers, then conversation between women and men is cross-cultural communication. Although each style is valid on its own terms, misunderstandings arise because the styles are different. Taking a cross-cultural approach to

male-female conversations makes it possible to explain why dissatisfactions are justified without accusing anyone of being wrong or crazy.

53   Learning about style differences won't make them go away, but it can banish mutual mystification and blame. Being able to understand why our partners, friends, and even strangers behave the way they do is a comfort, even if we still don't see things the same way. It makes the world into more familiar territory. And having others understand why we talk and act as we do protects us from the pain of their puzzlement and criticism.

54   In discussing her novel *The Temple of My Familiar,* Alice Walker explained that a woman in the novel falls in love with a man because she sees in him "a giant ear." Walker went on to remark that although people may think they are falling in love because of sexual attraction or some other force, "really what we're looking for is someone to be able to hear us."

55   We all want, above all, to be heard—but not merely to be heard. We want to be understood—heard for what we think we are saying, for what we know we meant. With increased understanding of the ways women and men use language should come a decrease in frequency of the complaint "You just don't understand."

QUESTIONS

Experience

· To what extent can you relate Tannen's discussion to aspects of your own experience? Have you found, for example, that in talking with members of the opposite sex, you sometimes are surprised or puzzled by how your remarks are interpreted? Describe a time when someone of the opposite sex misunderstood you.

· Have you yourself sometimes misunderstood comments made by members of the opposite sex, especially or particularly if those comments were of a sexual nature? Would you deduce from this or any of your other experiences in talking with people that men and women do, indeed, use language differently?

Interpretation

· Tannen argues that women approach the world differently than men do, and that the way they use and understand language reflects this difference. Do women engage in conversation, for example, as much to establish and maintain relationships as to acquire information or to assert their authority (as she suggests that men do)? Explain your reasoning.

· Explain how Tannen uses the concepts of "asymmetries" and "mixed judgments" to develop her argument. Explain how she uses the terms "intimacy" and "independence" in distinguishing between masculine and feminine uses of language.

Evaluation

· Identify the different values that Tannen sees as motivating and sustaining the conversational needs of men and women. What do you think of Tannen's metaphor comparing conversation between women and men to "cross-cultural" communication?

· In addition to intimacy for women and independence for men, what other cultural values does Tannen mention? Do you agree with her gender associations for these values? Why, or why not?

WRITING

Exploring

· Write an essay about differences or similarities in the conversational styles of men and women. Decide which you consider more important and why. Consider one or more of the following: conversational subjects, frequency, length, intensity, loudness, degree of privacy. Use your personal experience as one form of evidence.

Interpreting

· Analyze the representations of men and women talking in television advertising or in sitcoms. What do you notice about how men and women talk in either genre? Write an essay based on your observations.
· Analyze the way television sports commentators, news broadcasters, talk-show hosts, teachers, or employers refer to men and women by name. Explain the significance of any differences you find.

Evaluating

· Argue for or against the assertions Tannen makes in her piece. Support your argument with evidence from your reading, your observation, and your experience.

PAUL THEROUX
(b. 1941)

Being a Man

Paul Theroux is a novelist and travel writer. In the following essay Theroux expresses his dissatisfaction with being expected to live up to an image of manhood that he detests. In the course of complaining about various aspects of the male mystique, Theroux raises questions about what it means to be a man in America today and what we can do to enrich our understanding of what a man ought to be. Throughout his essay, Theroux makes a number of comments about women—largely to clarify his views about masculinity, though on occasion to consider similarities between the experience of men and women.

There is more than negativism and criticism in this essay, however. Theroux is frequently humorous and often genuinely warm as well. In fact, that is one of the essay's distinctive features. Another is a striking directness, even combativeness, notable in sentences such as "I have always disliked being a man," and in "Even the expression 'Be a man!' strikes me as insulting and abusive." Theroux's combination of wit and toughness makes for good writing—and good reading.

1   There is a pathetic sentence in the chapter "Fetishism" in Dr. Norman Cameron's book *Personality Development and Psychopathology*. It goes, "Fetishists are nearly always men; and their commonest fetish is a woman's shoe." I cannot read that sentence without thinking that it is just one more awful thing about being a man—and perhaps it is an important thing to know about us.

2   I have always disliked being a man. The whole idea of manhood in America is pitiful, in my opinion. This version of masculinity is a little like having to wear an ill-fitting coat for one's entire life (by contrast, I imagine femininity to be an oppressive sense of nakedness). Even the expression "Be a man!" strikes me as insulting and abusive. It means: Be stupid, be unfeeling, obedient, soldierly, and stop thinking. Man means "manly"—how can one think about men without considering the terrible ambition of manliness? And yet it is part of every man's life. It is a hideous and crippling lie; it not only insists on difference and connives at superiority, it is also by its very nature destructive—emotionally damaging and socially harmful.

3   The youth who is subverted, as most are, into believing in the masculine ideal is effectively separated from women and he spends the rest of his life finding women a riddle and a nuisance. Of course, there is a female version of this male affliction. It begins with mothers encouraging little girls to say (to other adults) "Do you like my new dress?" In a sense, little girls are traditionally urged to please adults with a kind of coquettishness, while boys are enjoined to behave like monkeys towards each other. The nine-year-old coquette proceeds to

become womanish in a subtle power game in which she learns to be sexually indispensable, socially decorative, and always alert to a man's sense of inadequacy.

4   Femininity—being ladylike—implies needing a man as witness and seducer; but masculinity celebrates the exclusive company of men. That is why it is so grotesque; and that is also why there is no manliness without inadequacy— because it denies men the natural friendship of women.

5   It is very hard to imagine any concept of manliness that does not belittle women, and it begins very early. At an age when I wanted to meet girls—let's say the treacherous years of thirteen to sixteen—I was told to take up a sport, get more fresh air, join the Boy Scouts, and I was urged not to read so much. It was the 1950s and if you asked too many questions about sex you were sent to camp—boy's camp, of course: the nightmare. Nothing is more unnatural or prisonlike than a boy's camp, but if it were not for them we would have no Elks' Lodges, no pool rooms, no boxing matches, no Marines.

6   And perhaps no sports as we know them. Everyone is aware of how few in number are the athletes who behave like gentlemen. Just as high school basketball teaches you how to be a poor loser, the manly attitude towards sports seems to be little more than a recipe for creating bad marriages, social misfits, moral degenerates, sadists, latent rapists, and just plain louts. I regard high school sports as a drug far worse than marijuana, and it is the reason that the average tennis champion, say, is a pathetic oaf.

7   Any objective study would find the quest for manliness essentially right-wing, puritanical, cowardly, neurotic, and fueled largely by a fear of women. It is also certainly philistine. There is no book-hater like a Little League coach. But indeed all the creative arts are obnoxious to the manly ideal, because at their best the arts are pursued by uncompetitive and essentially solitary people. It makes it very hard for a creative youngster, for any boy who expresses the desire to be alone seems to be saying that there is something wrong with him.

8   It ought to be clear by now that I have something of an objection to the way we turn boys into men. It does not surprise me that when the President of the United States has his customary weekend off he dresses like a cowboy—it is both a measure of his insecurity and his willingness to please. In many ways, American culture does little more for a man than prepare him for modeling clothes in the L. L. Bean catalogue. I take this as a personal insult because for many years I found it impossible to admit to myself that I wanted to be a writer. It was my guilty secret, because being a writer was incompatible with being a man.

9   There are people who might deny this, but that is because the American writer, typically, has been so at pains to prove his manliness that we have come to see literariness and manliness as mingled qualities. But first there was a fear that writing was not a manly profession—indeed, not a profession at all. (The paradox in American letters is that it has always been easier for a woman to write and for a man to be published.) Growing up, I had thought of sports as wasteful and humiliating, and the idea of manliness was a bore. My wanting to become a writer was not a flight from that oppressive role-playing, but I quickly saw that it was at odds

with it. Everything in stereotyped manliness goes against the life of the mind. The Hemingway personality is too tedious to go into here, and in any case his exertions are well known, but certainly it was not until this aberrant behavior was examined by feminists in the 1960s that any male writer dared question the pugnacity in Hemingway's fiction. All the bullfighting and arm wrestling and elephant shooting diminished Hemingway as a writer, but it is consistent with a prevailing attitude in American writing: one cannot be a male writer without first proving that one is a man.

10   It is normal in America for a man to be dismissive or even somewhat apologetic about being a writer. Various factors make it easier. There is a heartiness about journalism that makes it acceptable—journalism is the manliest form of American writing and, therefore, the profession the most independent-minded women seek (yes, it is an illusion, but that is my point). Fiction-writing is equated with a kind of dispirited failure and is only manly when it produces wealth—money is masculinity. So is drinking. Being a drunkard is another assertion, if misplaced, of manliness. The American male writer is traditionally proud of his heavy drinking. But we are also a very literal-minded people. A man proves his manhood in America in old-fashioned ways. He kills lions, like Hemingway; or he hunts ducks, like Nathanael West, or he makes pronouncements like, "A man should carry enough knife to defend himself with," as James Jones once said to a *Life* interviewer. Or he says he can drink you under the table. But even tiny drunken William Faulkner loved to mount a horse and go fox hunting, and Jack Kerouac roistered up and down Manhattan in a lumberjack shirt (and spent every night of *The Subterraneans* with his mother in Queens). And we are familiar with the lengths to which Norman Mailer is prepared, in his endearing way, to prove that he is just as much a monster as the next man.

11   When the novelist John Irving was revealed as a wrestler, people took him to be a very serious writer, and even a bubble reputation like Eric *(Love Story)* Segal's was enhanced by the news that he ran the marathon in a respectable time. How surprised we would be if Joyce Carol Oates were revealed as a sumo wrestler or Joan Didion active in pumping iron. "Lives in New York City with her three children" is the typical woman writer's biographical note, for just as the male writer must prove he has achieved a sort of muscular manhood, the woman writer—or rather her publicists—must prove her motherhood.

12   There would be no point in saying any of this if it were not generally accepted that to be a man is somehow—even now in feminist-influenced America—a privilege. It is on the contrary an unmerciful and punishing burden. Being a man is bad enough; being manly is appalling (in this sense, women's lib has done much more for men than for women). It is the sinister silliness of men's fashions and a clubby attitude in the arts. It is the subversion of good students. It is the so-called Dress Code of the Ritz-Carlton Hotel in Boston, and it is the institutionalized cheating in college sports. It is the most primitive insecurity.

13   And this is also why men often object to feminism, but are afraid to explain why: of course women have a justified grievance, but most men believe—and with reason—that their lives are just as bad.

QUESTIONS

Experience

· In his opening paragraph Theroux says that it is an "awful thing" to be a man. Do you agree with him that it is "awful" to be a man or woman? Why, or why not?

· Theroux also says that he has "always disliked being a man." If you are a man, can you understand what he is implying—whether you yourself have always or ever disliked being a man? And if you are a woman, can you understand why a man might say this? Explain your response.

· Bring your own experience to bear on Theroux's comments on sports such as his observation that "high school basketball teaches you how to be a poor loser."

Interpretation

· What aspects of the cult of manliness does Theroux object to? Why? Why is he so hard on sports? On dressing like a cowboy? What image of femininity does he counterpoint to the masculine ideal he complains about?

· Theroux is greatly concerned with the connection between being considered "manly" and being a writer. What, specifically, does he identify as the conflict between them? And what is his point in introducing Ernest Hemingway, William Faulkner, and Norman Mailer into his argument?

Evaluation

· What evidence does Theroux use to support his claim that being a man is a "punishing burden"? Do you find his argument convincing? Why, or why not? Could you provide other evidence to support Theroux's claim?

· What cultural values are embodied in the image of manliness that Theroux criticizes? How important are these values in affecting how men think of themselves? To what extent have cultural conditions changed to alter the image of manliness Theroux condemns?

· Why might a person resent his or her gender? To what extent is it possible for people to free themselves of stereotyped ideas about gender?

· Comment on two examples of Theroux's humor. What makes them funny?

WRITING

Exploring

· Write an essay in which you explore the concept of "manliness." Identify its central features; then explain and illustrate them. You may, if you like, base your essay on personal experience, perhaps writing about someone you know who exhibits your sense of what it means to be manly. Or write an essay defining your sense of femininity. You can use Theroux's remarks about femininity as a springboard; you can include them in the midst of your essay; or you can ignore them altogether.

Interpreting

· Analyze the uses of humor in Theroux's essay. Explain what Theroux's humor contributes to his essay's tone and how humorous examples develop or support his argument.

Evaluating

· Find photographs or artworks that support Theroux's contention that being a man is a "punishing burden." Find others that contradict his claim. Develop an essay built around these photographs and/or artworks. Formulate an idea that can account for the contradictory or contrasting images of men you find.

MAILE MELOY
(b. 1972)

The Voice of the Looking-Glass

Maile Meloy is a recent graduate of Harvard University, where she majored in English. She did a part of her college study abroad, at Oxford University, where she studied Renaissance literature. She is currently completing an M.F.A. at Columbia University. Her essay considers the ways women are pressured by society to be concerned with their appearance. Weaving her reading into her experience growing up female, Meloy reflects on aspects of femininity she both relishes and disparages.

Two features of Meloy's essay can be singled out for comment. First, her epigraphs, which she uses to establish the focus of her essay. The first epigraph, from the novelist and art critic John Berger, points toward the two central concerns of her essay: how women see themselves and how they imagine that others, especially men, see them. Her second epigraph, from Casanova's memoirs, comments obliquely on the first and illustrates, to some extent, why women are concerned with how they look.

Another distinctive compositional strategy worth noting is Meloy's use of description. At two places in her text she slows down to describe a picture— the first, a picture of herself; the second, a word picture of a poor woman huddled in a doorstep. Meloy introduces these pictures as evidence for her idea and as material to think about.

> A woman must continually watch herself. She is almost continually accompanied by her own image of herself. Men look at women. Women watch themselves being looked at.
>
> John Berger
> *Ways of Seeing*

> The girl was ugly. I was bored during the whole journey.
>
> Casanova
> *History of My Life*

1   From the moment I became conscious of cause and effect I have been conscious of the importance of my own appearance. Little girls (and little boys) learn early that the way women are treated is determined by the way they appear. John Berger, in *Ways of Seeing*, has gotten it right. It is a woman's ever-present task to monitor her image, not to survey a situation to determine the appropriate action, as a man does, but to survey herself and define by her presentation the way she wishes others to act toward her.

2   I have a photograph of myself at graduation, with my hair down and fuschia and plumeria leis piled around my neck. I am laughing, with my mouth open, head tilted, and eyes cast to the side, at something the photographer has said.

The picture is not posed: I am caught in a spontaneous, joyful moment by the gaze of the camera.

3   I have looked at that picture a lot. It is the way I want to be seen in everyday, spontaneous moments, when soft studio lights are not at my rescue and I am vulnerable: I am pleased with the image. When I am asked for the photograph, my instinctive response is, "But it's the only copy I have," which I blurt out before I realize how narcissistic I sound. We are not to let on that we monitor ourselves so closely. We are to be head-tossing and laughing-eyed without being conscious of our beauty.

4   Why do I need pictures of myself? Because I like them. They are interesting to me. I like to see myself in relation to other people, to see myself how other people see me. I study photographs of myself intently, critically—always appraising, always analyzing, carefully assessing what I see there.

5   I take other opportunities to survey and assess. Most women do. I have mastered a swift glance over my right shoulder at mirrors and windows as I walk by, careful not to linger and let voyeurs behind the glass see my interest in my own image. The left profile is less reassuring, and with scarcely a conscious thought I place people to my right. This self-observation is not vanity. It is a play for approval, and a request to be treated well, with respect and admiration. It says, "I don't want to bore you during the entire journey."

6   The result of the demand for women to be beautiful, combined with a woman's need for approval, according to Berger, is that a woman's "own sense of being in herself is supplanted by a sense of being appreciated by another." Laura Riding's epigraph to the first chapter of Sandra M. Gilbert and Susan Gubar's *The Madwoman in the Attic* addresses this replacement of a woman's self-image with a male's-eye view:

> And the lady of the house was seen only as she appeared in each room, according to the nature of the lord of the room. None saw the whole of her, none but herself. For the light which she was was both her mirror and her body. None could tell the whole of her, none but herself.

7   The chapter, entitled "The Queen's Looking Glass," makes some important observations about "images of women," especially as portrayed in the Grimm brothers' fairy tale "Little Snow White." They note that "female bonding is extraordinarily difficult in patriarchy: women almost inevitably turn against women because the voice of the looking-glass sets them against each other." Thus we are set up as rivals for each other by the male voice of the looking glass, and Gilbert and Gubar see little hope for female solidarity. They share Anne Sexton's view that Snow White must inevitably become the wicked Queen. Having escaped from one display case (the glass coffin), she has traded it for another, the mirror. The Prince's home itself is a prison, the same one her mother encountered, where she appears "according to the nature of the lord of the room." To escape her new prison she must become the witch. She must become assertive and therefore monstrous and misogynistic to destroy the "angel woman" Galatea in herself.

8   That the perfect Snow White should become the evil Queen is horrifying to me, although Gilbert and Gubar endorse the witch's actions and sympathize with

her. It rings true, however, and it turns me to look at my relationship with my own mother. She despises the appearance-oriented environment in which women live, and she fears that I have bought into it. She has sometimes lamented that I was not born unattractive: she is afraid I will have everything given to me, that I'll never know what it is to really earn rewards. She too has bought into the system, however, and perhaps it is that which she laments. Five feet two, beautiful and blonde, a southern-Californian ex-Homecoming Queen, she has been handed a lot on the tarnished silver platter of prettiness. And while carefully maintaining that prettiness, she has despised it. She has always wanted to be tall, dark-haired and magnificent so people would take her seriously. My mother, trapped in her surfer-girl image and unable to transform her appearance, instead majored in microbiology, which she hated, in an attempt to earn the respect she craved.

9   She has since abandoned microbiology and her model-loveliness is beginning to abandon her. It makes me nervous. Old pictures of her from college and early marriage are breathtaking, with her tousled hair, her smooth tan skin, her perfect cheekbones, and her brilliant Homecoming Queen smile. (Holly Near, singing of her own Queen experience, has observed, "That's what Homecoming Queens do, is smile.") These images, however, are disconcerting. They are reminders for me of the death and disappearance of youth and of what is culturally defined as desirable. I wish I could look forward to such changes, to rejoice in the inner richness that replaces outward worth, but I shudder with the vanity of youth and dread the wrinkles and sagging flesh of age. I delight with Snow White that I am still "the fairest of them all."

10   Because of my dread of becoming what my mother is, and what other older women are, I expect intimidation and jealousy. And because I watch other women, measuring myself against them and judging myself accordingly, I experience intimidation and jealousy. The dynamics of this watching myself/watching you watching me phenomenon create what Margaret Atwood has dubbed "that pale-mauve hostility that you often find among women." It is a shared secret, that we watch ourselves so carefully while feigning nonchalance. We appraise other women as a man would, appraise ourselves as a man would, and weigh the results. It is strangely comforting to find the other wanting. I think most women hate this trap, and hate the pale-mauve hostility. But we learn it as we learn to walk and to wear our hair in pigtails the way daddy likes it. It is our way of surviving in the world we are born into: One in which, like it or not, we must continually impress men.

11   We are taught our meticulous self-observation; it is a learned activity. At the onset of puberty, among the other ridiculously sexist boy-catching hints we receive, girls are often instructed to "learn how to take a compliment." We are expected to accept another person's sense of us as they have expressed it, and to consider it a reward. By accepting it we add it to our expectations of ourself—our checklist as we glance into the mirrors of shop windows, listen to ourselves speak, or choose our clothes, opinions, and other accessories.

12   When a girl "takes a compliment," she accepts the reward and accepts, as well, the requirement that earned her the compliment. Both become internalized.

She now needs to be able to earn that other person's sense of her from herself. She practices her "disarming smile" in mirrors, concentrates on "poise," and makes sure she's being "a good listener." Not all compliments are "taken," of course, although they may be acknowledged with a polite "thank you." Some are discarded because they do not fit her image as the watcher in her sees it, and these rejects can be disconcerting as they suggest discrepancy between the internal surveyor and the external one, but true compliments, the ones that congratulate a girl's or woman's mutable, monitored perception of herself, are internalized and added to the checklist.

13   Sometimes the internal surveyor goes out of control. I have been haunted for several days by the image of one of the homeless people in the city. She sits huddled in a doorstep in a beige coat with a scarf tied around her head, and she clutches a large white plastic bag. The first time I saw her I found myself staring, wondering at her face, which was colored a deep pink. As I neared her, I could make out the cakey texture of makeup and I caught the sweet chemical smell of the pink powder that covered her entire face: forehead, wrinkled cheeks, lips, eyes, eyebrows, and ears, and that was smeared across the lapels of her coat and mixed with the pattern of her headwrap. I fixed my eyes back on the sidewalk, which was covered with white face-powder, and braced for the inevitable request for money. It didn't come. She didn't even notice me; her eyes were riveted to a spot in the corner of the doorstep. I glanced back at that spot as I passed, expecting to see a mirror into which she was staring so intently. There was nothing there. Only the concrete wall stared back at her.

14   Later in the day she was gone, and only a white outline of her seated form remained in the scattered face powder on the sidewalk, along with a sandwich in a baggie that someone must have given her, abandoned there with one bite taken. Disconcerted, I sought my own reflection in a shop window, to replace that of the trembling, staring, cariacature of female vanity I had seen that morning. Even as I caught my own eye, I saw the irony in my means of escape. This poor, ill woman, to whom her own made-up self is more important than food, exists at the outer edge of the obsession with appearance that women learn from childhood.

15   I do not want to be John Berger's pathetically trapped woman, to merely "appear," and to be a composite of other people's perceptions of me. I do not want to value appearance over action, but I cannot escape the habit of constantly having one eye on my own image. In mirrors and windows, in photographs, in other people's glances, and in my own mind I am haunted by images of myself. I am continually critiquing my appearance, my reactions, my gestures, and my speech. I am already caught in the queen's looking glass, already in conspiracy with the made-up old woman in the street.

16   A Stephen Sondheim character sings of his mistress. "Look at her looking, forever in that mirror. What does she see?" He need not ask, for she sees through his eyes. She sees herself as lover, as desirable object, and as rival before she sees herself as a woman. She sees herself in relation to him and in light of his expectations, and she sees her imperfections in that light. She sees Snow White fading and growing old and yet she clings to the façade. It is what she knows.

QUESTIONS

Experience

· Maile Meloy begins her essay with a discussion of her concern for how she looks. She describes a picture of herself that she likes, and she admits to looking in shopwindows to "survey and assess" her looks. To what extent does she appear overly self-conscious about her looks? Do you, like Meloy, check yourself out first when looking at photographs that include you as one among others? Why, or why not?

· As you read through Meloy's essay, were you able to follow her shifts of direction as she introduced other texts—the references to Snow White and the wicked Queen, the literary analysis and interpretation, the Stephen Sondheim song? Did you find yourself putting those fragments together, linking them to construct from your reading a sense of a coherent whole? Why, or why not?

Interpretation

· What is the central idea of this essay? To what extent is Meloy suggesting that men are responsible for women's obsession with their physical attractiveness? To what extent are women themselves victims of their own vanity and self-regard?

· Do you agree that women see themselves in relation to men, that they look at themselves as if men were looking them over?

· Do you agree that women size each other up physically—measuring and assessing themselves against one another, even taking conscious pleasure in seeing themselves as more attractive than their competition?

· How important is aging to Meloy's discussion? Why does she bring her mother into the essay?

Evaluation

· Who is responsible for establishing beauty as a cultural norm for women? Where do the standards for beauty come from?

· What attitudes toward youth and age, intelligence and social poise, are displayed in this essay? What do you think of Meloy's comments about how girls and women "take compliments"? About her admission that even with what she knows, she clings to the façade of beauty?

WRITING

Exploring

· Write your own essay on the subject of women's beauty (or men's). If you like, you can describe your own experience, as Meloy does. You are also encouraged to include in your essay the kinds of references to things you've seen and heard and read such as photographs, bits of songs, and quotations from books.

Interpreting

· Analyze the structure of Meloy's essay. Identify each of the elements she incorporates into it, where she places them, how she relates them to one another, and what their cumulative effect is.

Evaluating

· Take issue with something asserted in this essay. That is, find a statement you disagree with, and argue against it by bringing to bear evidence from your observation, experience, and reading.

JOHN UPDIKE
(b. 1932)

A & P

John Updike was born in Shillington, Pennsylvania. He attended Harvard University, where he was a cartoonist for the Lampoon, *the student humor magazine. After college, Updike spent a year in England—in London and Oxford—where he studied art. Upon his return he worked a few years for* The New Yorker, *where his work has appeared for more than twenty-five years. Updike has published short stories, novels, poetry, art and literary criticism, essays, and reviews in abundance. He has won a number of major literary awards, including the Pulitzer Prize* (Rabbit Is Rich, *1981), the National Book Award (*The Centaur, *1963), and the National Critics Circle Award for* Hugging the Shore *(1983).*

"A & P" reveals Updike's gift for language and for displaying the details of everyday life. The story offers an opportunity to consider the sex roles and sex-typed behavior of its principal characters. One of the story's most distinctive stylistic features is Updike's use of concrete, specific language, particularly in the narrator's description of the shoppers and of the store's products. Another aspect of its style worth noting is Updike's striking metaphors, as, for example, his comparison of a teenage girl's breasts with "the two smoothest scoops of vanilla," a stylistic feature that takes us directly to the issue of sex stereotyping.

1   In walks these three girls in nothing but bathing suits. I'm in the third check-out slot, with my back to the door, so I don't see them until they're over by the bread. The one that caught my eye first was the one in the plaid green two-piece. She was a chunky kid, with a good tan and a sweet broad soft-looking can with those two crescents of white just under it, where the sun never seems to hit, at the top of the backs of her legs. I stood there with my hand on a box of HiHo crackers trying to remember if I rang it up or not. I ring it up again and the customer starts giving me hell. She's one of these cash-register-watchers, a witch about fifty with rouge on her cheekbones and no eyebrows, and I know it made her day to trip me up. She'd been watching cash registers for fifty years and probably never seen a mistake before.

2   By the time I got her feathers smoothed and her goodies into a bag—she gives me a little snort in passing, if she'd been born at the right time they would have burned her over in Salem—by the time I get her on her way the girls had circled around the bread and were coming back, without a pushcart, back my way along the counters, in the aisle between the check-outs and the Special bins. They didn't even have shoes on. There was this chunky one, with the two-piece—it was bright green and the seams on the bra were still sharp and her belly was still pretty pale so I guessed she just got it (the suit)—there was this one, with one of those chubby berry-faces, the lips all bunched together under her nose, this one, and a

tall one, with black hair that hadn't quite frizzed right, and one of these sunburns right across under the eyes, and a chin that was too long—you know, the kind of girl other girls think is very "striking" and "attractive" but never quite makes it, as they very well know, which is why they like her so much—and then the third one, that wasn't quite so tall. She was the queen. She kind of led them, the other two peeking around and making their shoulders round. She didn't look around, not this queen, she just walked straight on slowly, on these long white prima donna legs. She came down a little hard on her heels, as if she didn't walk in her bare feet that much, putting down her heels and then letting the weight move along to her toes as if she was testing the floor with every step, putting a little deliberate extra action into it. You never know for sure how girls' minds work (do you really think it's a mind in there or just a little buzz like a bee in a glass jar?) but you got the idea she had talked the other two into coming in here with her, and now she was showing them how to do it, walk slow and hold yourself straight.

3   She had on a kind of dirty-pink—beige maybe, I don't know—bathing suit with a little nubble all over it and, what got me, the straps were down. They were off her shoulders looped loose around the cool tops of her arms, and I guess as a result the suit had slipped a little on her, so all around the top of the cloth there was this shining rim. If it hadn't been there you wouldn't have known there could have been anything whiter than those shoulders. With the straps pushed off, there was nothing between the top of the suit and the top of her head except just *her,* this clean bare plane of the top of her chest down from the shoulder bones like a dented sheet of metal tilted in the light. I mean, it was more than pretty.

4   She had sort of oaky hair that the sun and salt had bleached, done up in a bun that was unravelling, and a kind of prim face. Walking into the A & P with your straps down, I suppose it's the only kind of face you *can* have. She held her head so high her neck, coming up out of those white shoulders, looked kind of stretched, but I didn't mind. The longer her neck was, the more of her there was.

5   She must have felt in the corner of her eye me and over my shoulder Stokesie in the second slot watching, but she didn't tip. Not this queen. She kept her eyes moving across the racks, and stopped, and turned so slow it made my stomach rub the inside of my apron, and buzzed to the other two, who kind of huddled against her for relief, and they all three of them went up the cat-and-dog-food-breakfast-cereal-macaroni-rice-raisins-seasonings-spreads-spaghetti-soft-drinks-crackers-and-cookies aisle. From the third slot I look straight up this aisle to the meat counter, and I watched them all the way. The fat one with the tan sort of fumbled with the cookies, but on second thought she put the packages back. The sheep pushing their carts down the aisle—the girls were walking against the usual traffic (not that we have one-way signs or anything)—were pretty hilarious. You could see them, when Queenie's white shoulders dawned on them, kind of jerk, or hop, or hiccup, but their eyes snapped back to their own baskets and on they pushed. I bet you could set off dynamite in an A & P and the people would by and large keep reaching and checking oatmeal off their lists and muttering "Let me see, there was a third thing, began with A, asparagus, no, ah, yes, applesauce!" or whatever it is they do mutter. But there was no doubt, this jiggled them. A few houseslaves in pin curlers even looked around after pushing their carts past to make sure what they had seen was correct.

6   You know, it's one thing to have a girl in a bathing suit down on the beach, where what with the glare nobody can look at each other much anyway, and another thing in the cool of the A & P, under the fluorescent lights, against all those stacked packages, with her feet paddling along naked over our checkerboard green-and-cream rubber-tile floor.

7   "Oh Daddy," Stokesie said beside me. "I feel so faint."

8   "Darling," I said. "Hold me tight." Stokesie's married, with two babies chalked up on his fuselage already, but as far as I can tell that's the only difference. He's twenty-two, and I was nineteen this April.

9   "Is it done?" he asks, the responsible married man finding his voice. I forgot to say he thinks he's going to be manager some sunny day, maybe in 1990 when it's called the Great Alexandrov and Petrooshki Tea Company or something.

10   What he meant was, our town is five miles from a beach, with a big summer colony out on the Point, but we're right in the middle of town, and the women generally put on a shirt or shorts or something before they get out of the car into the street. And anyway these are usually women with six children and varicose veins mapping their legs and nobody, including them, could care less. As I say, we're right in the middle of town, and if you stand at our front doors you can see two banks and the Congregational church and the newspaper store and three real-estate offices and about twenty-seven old freeloaders tearing up Central Street because the sewer broke again. It's not as if we're on the Cape; we're north of Boston and there's people in this town haven't seen the ocean for twenty years.

11   The girls had reached the meat counter and were asking McMahon something. He pointed, they pointed, and they shuffled out of sight behind a pyramid of Diet Delight peaches. All that was left for us to see was old McMahon patting his mouth and looking after them sizing up their joints. Poor kids, I began to feel sorry for them, they couldn't help it.

12   Now here comes the sad part of the story, at least my family says it's sad but I don't think it's sad myself. The store's pretty empty, it being Thursday afternoon, so there was nothing much to do except lean on the register and wait for the girls to show up again. The whole store was like a pinball machine and I didn't know which tunnel they'd come out of. After a while they come around out of the far aisle, around the light bulbs, records at discount of the Caribbean Six or Tony Martin Sings or some such gunk you wonder they waste the wax on, sixpacks of candy bars, and plastic toys done up in cellophane that fall apart when a kid looks at them anyway. Around they come, Queenie still leading the way, and holding a little gray jar in her hand. Slots Three through Seven are unmanned and I could see her wondering between Stokes and me, but Stokesie with his usual luck draws an old party in baggy gray pants who stumbles up with four giant cans of pineapple juice (what do these bums *do* with all that pineapple juice? I've often asked myself) so the girls come to me. Queenie puts down the jar and I take it into my fingers icy cold. Kingfish Fancy Herring Snacks in Pure Sour Cream: 49¢. Now her hands are empty, not a ring or a bracelet, bare as God made them, and I wonder where the money's coming from. Still with that prim look she lifts a folded dollar bill out of the hollow at the center of her nubbled pink top. The jar went heavy in my hand. Really, I thought that was so cute.

13   Then everybody's luck begins to run out. Lengel comes in from haggling with

a truck full of cabbages on the lot and is about to scuttle into that door marked MANAGER behind which he hides all day when the girls touch his eye. Lengel's pretty dreary, teaches Sunday school and the rest, but he doesn't miss that much. He comes over and says, "Girls, this isn't the beach."

14   Queenie blushes, though maybe it's just a brush of sunburn I was noticing for the first time, now that she was so close. "My mother asked me to pick up a jar of herring snacks." Her voice kind of startled me, the way voices do when you see the people first, coming out so flat and dumb yet kind of tony, too, the way it ticked over "pick up" and "snacks." All of a sudden I slid right down her voice into her living room. Her father and the other men were standing around in ice-cream coats and bow ties and the women were in sandals picking up herring snacks on toothpicks off a big plate and they were all holding drinks the color of water with olives and sprigs of mint in them. When my parents have somebody over they get lemonade and if it's a real racy affair Schlitz in tall glasses with "They'll Do It Every Time" cartoons stencilled on.

15   "That's all right," Lengel said. "But this isn't the beach." His repeating this struck me as funny, as if it had just occurred to him, and he had been thinking all these years the A & P was a great big dune and he was the head lifeguard. He didn't like my smiling—as I say he doesn't miss much—but he concentrates on giving the girls that sad Sunday-school-superintendent stare.

16   Queenie's blush is no sunburn now, and the plump one in plaid, that I liked better from the back—a really sweet can—pipes up, "We weren't doing any shop-ping. We just came in for the one thing."

17   "That makes no difference," Lengel tells her, and I could see from the way his eyes went that he hadn't noticed she was wearing a two-piece before. "We want you decently dressed when you come in here."

18   "We *are* decent," Queenie says suddenly, her lower lip pushing, getting sore now that she remembers her place, a place from which the crowd that runs the A & P must look pretty crummy. Fancy Herring Snacks flashed in her very blue eyes.

19   "Girls, I don't want to argue with you. After this come in here with your shoul-ders covered. It's our policy." He turns his back. That's policy for you. Policy is what the kingpins want. What the others want is juvenile delinquency.

20   All this while, the customers had been showing up with their carts but, you know, sheep, seeing a scene, they had all bunched up on Stokesie, who shook open a paper bag as gently as peeling a peach, not wanting to miss a word. I could feel in the silence everybody getting nervous, most of all Lengel, who asks me, "Sammy, have you rung up this purchase?"

21   I thought and said "No" but it wasn't about that I was thinking. I go through the punches, 4, 9, GROC, TOT—it's more complicated than you think, and after you do it often enough, it begins to make a little song, that you hear words to, in my case "Hello (*bing*) there, you (*gung*) hap-py *pee*-pul (*splat*)!"—the *splat* being the drawer flying out. I uncrease the bill, tenderly as you may imagine, it just having come from between the two smoothest scoops of vanilla I had ever known were there, and pass a half and a penny into her narrow pink palm, and nestle the her-rings in a bag and twist its neck and hand it over, all the time thinking.

22   The girls, and who'd blame them, are in a hurry to get out, so I say "I quit" to Lengel quick enough for them to hear, hoping they'll stop and watch me, their

unsuspected hero. They keep right on going, into the electric eye; the door flies open and they flicker across the lot to their car, Queenie and Plaid and Big Tall Goony-Goony (not that as raw material she was so bad), leaving me with Lengel and a kink in his eyebrow.

23   "Did you say something, Sammy?"

24   "I said I quit."

25   "I thought you did."

26   "You didn't have to embarrass them."

27   "It was they who were embarrassing us."

28   I started to say something that came out "Fiddle-de-doo." It's a saying of my grandmother's, and I know she would have been pleased.

29   "I don't think you know what you're saying," Lengel said.

30   "I know you don't," I said. "But I do." I pull the bow at the back of my apron and start shrugging it off my shoulders. A couple customers that had been heading for my slot begin to knock against each other, like scared pigs in a chute.

31   Lengel sighs and begins to look very patient and old and gray. He's been a friend of my parents for years. "Sammy, you don't want to do this to your Mom and Dad," he tells me. It's true, I don't. But it seems to me that once you begin a gesture it's fatal not to go through with it. I fold the apron, "Sammy" stitched in red on the pocket, and put it on the counter, and drop the bow tie on top of it. The bow tie is theirs, if you've ever wondered. "You'll feel this for the rest of your life," Lengel says, and I know that's true, too, but remembering how he made that pretty girl blush makes me so scrunchy inside I punch the No Sale tab and the machine whirs "pee-pul" and the drawer splats out. One advantage to this scene taking place in summer, I can follow this up with a clean exit, there's no fumbling around getting your coat and galoshes, I just saunter into the electric eye in my white shirt that my mother ironed the night before, and the door heaves itself open, and outside the sunshine is skating around on the asphalt.

32   I look around for my girls, but they're gone, of course. There wasn't anybody but some young married screaming with her children about some candy they didn't get by the door of a powder-blue Falcon station wagon. Looking back in the big windows, over the bags of peat moss and aluminum lawn furniture stacked on the pavement, I could see Lengel in my place in the slot, checking the sheep through. His face was dark gray and his back stiff, as if he'd just had an injection of iron, and my stomach kind of fell as I felt how hard the world was going to be to me hereafter.

QUESTIONS

Experience

· As you read this story, were you surprised by the things that occurred? Were you annoyed at any point? Were you amused? Engaged? Why, or why not?

· To what extent did you find yourself relating to the characters—to Sammy, Lengel, the girls? Did your feelings and reactions about the characters develop or change as the story progressed? Why or why not?

Interpretation

· How do you read Sammy? What do you learn about him from the way he talks and thinks? What do his metaphors suggest about how he sees the store and the shoppers?

· Why does Sammy quit? How do you interpret Sammy's response to his act of quitting? What does he mean by saying that he "felt how hard the world was going to be" for him afterward?

Evaluation

· How do you respond to Sammy's (and Updike's) language in describing Queenie—beginning with her name and including her "white prima donna legs" and her "two scoops of vanilla"? What does language reveal about Sammy? About Updike?

· Whose values does the story seem to endorse? Whose values are questioned? How do your own values about sex roles, about work, and about principle affect your response to "A & P"?

WRITING

Exploring

· Write an essay in which you describe a decisive action you took when your sexual identity was at issue or when your motive for action involved your sexual identity.

Interpreting

· Write a paper in which you analyze Updike's story, providing an interpretation of it. You may choose to focus on a character or character relationship, on the story's language, on a series of incidents, or on a particular moment. Give your paper a title that reflects your focus.

Evaluating

· Write an essay in which you argue for or against the values the story displays. Decide what values pervade the story or what values it seems to endorse. Then argue either for or against their validity.

**EMILY DICKINSON
(1830–1886)**

"I'm 'wife'—I've finished that"

Emily Dickinson, along with Walt Whitman, is America's premier nineteenth-century poet, and indisputably one of the finest poets of the last two hundred years. She lived nearly her entire life in Amherst, Massachusetts, most of it in the house where she was born. She never married, though from the evidence of her poems and letters, she was in love more than once.

Her poems, unusual in idiom, rhythm, rhyme, and often in thought, usually require a good deal of patient attention. Her earliest readers had great difficulty with her poems, perceiving them as eccentric and even incompetent. They wondered why she didn't rhyme correctly, or why she used her own system of punctuation, heavy on dashes. They had trouble too with the abruptness of her poems and with their lack of smooth fluency.

Dickinson writes in a compressed, highly suggestive style, using language that demands careful analysis and sustained thought. Since there are so few words in a typical Dickinson poem, each word is invested with substantial meaning. No words are wasted. In her early poem "I'm 'wife'—I've finished that—," Dickinson presents a speaker who is recently married. This speaker describes her state of mind and heart by means of a series of comparisons and contrasts that, taken together, convey the speaker's attitude toward her marriage.

> I'm "wife"—I've finished that—
> That other state—
> I'm Czar—I'm "Woman" now—
> It's safer so—
>
> 5 How odd the Girl's life looks
> Behind this soft Eclipse—
> I think that Earth feels so
> To folks in Heaven—now—
>
> 10 This being comfort—then
> That other kind—was pain—
> But why compare?
> I'm "Wife"! Stop there!

QUESTIONS

Experience

· To what extent does the image of "wife" presented by the poem's speaker reflect your own ideas and attitudes about being a wife, either as you have experienced these feelings or as you might imagine them, regardless of your own gender.

Interpretation

· What is the speaker actually saying about her experience of being a "wife"? What is her attitude toward the experience? And how does the comparison in the second stanza help readers understand what she feels?

Evaluation

· What values does the speaker associate with the word and position of "wife"? What values are associated with the terms she uses to describe her state in the poem—"Czar," "Woman," and "Girl's life"?

WRITING

Exploring

· Write an essay in which you explore your ideas about what it means to be a "wife" in the 1990s. You may refer to Dickinson's poem if you wish.

Interpreting

· Write an interpretation of Dickinson's poem by analyzing its stanzas and lines, one at a time. You may wish to provide an opening paragraph that explains your basic understanding, and a conclusion that wraps up and extends the idea you develop in the middle of your essay. Be sure to explain the meaning of the poem by looking closely at its language and details, especially the contrasts it suggests.

Evaluating

· Discuss the view of women and marriage Dickinson's poem suggests. You may wish to affirm, reject, or modify that view in your essay. You may also wish to introduce into your discussion another poem about women and marriage, perhaps by Dickinson, perhaps by another poet.

GENDER—CONSIDERATIONS FOR THINKING AND WRITING

1. A number of the writers in this section discuss stereotypical images of men or women or both. Discuss how two or three of the following use cultural stereotypes in developing their arguments: Paul Theroux's "Being a Man," Annie Dillard's "The Deer at Providencia," Susan Brownmiller's "Femininity," Emily Dickinson's "I'm 'wife'—I've finished that—."

2. Some of the essayists compare characteristics of men and women, making assertions about women in their essays on men and vice versa. Discuss the images of the opposite sex presented by two of the following writers: Paul Theroux, Scott Russell Sanders, Deborah Tannen, and Susan Brownmiller.

3. Three writers make explicit references to the way men and/or women talk. Discuss the ideas about men's or women's speech advanced by two of the following: Deborah Tannen, Maxine Hong Kingston, Gretel Ehrlich (see the Introduction). You may wish to argue for or against one or another writer's point of view.

4. The relation of place to gender roles and stereotypes assumes importance in some of these essays. Compare what two of the following writers say about place and the attitudes toward gender associated with the places described: Pat C. Hoy II (the South), Maxine Hong Kingston (China), Annie Dillard (Ecuador), Gretel Ehrlich (the West—see the Introduction).

5. A few of the essayists argue that men or women have easier lives than members of the opposite sex. Compare the views of Paul Theroux (end of essay), Scott Russell Sanders (beginning), and Pat C. Hoy II (middle) about the privileges and burdens involved in being a man or a woman.

6. Two of the writers make beauty a central concern of their essays while a third refers to it less thoroughly but equally specifically. Compare the ideas about beauty explored in Kingston's "No Name Woman," Meloy's "The Voice of the Looking-Glass," and Brownmiller's "Femininity."

7. Discuss how ideas about gender in our society are changing. Consider the direction in which attitudes toward gender appear to be heading and why they are headed there. Refer to one or more essays in this section and, if you wish, to gender images as reflected in the media, especially in advertisements, television shows, or recent films.

8. Do some research on an aspect of or issue concerning gender. You might wish to consider research on the attitudes and behaviors of men, women, or both to one of the following: eating, talking, working, traveling. Or you might investigate how women functioned on the early American frontier, how they compare with men as managers and corporate executives, or how women or men see themselves in relation to others of their own sex.

FOUR

Race

JAMES BALDWIN
   Notes of a Native Son

ROGER WILKINS
   In Ivory Towers

JUNE JORDAN
   Where Is the Love?

CORNEL WEST
   Race Matters

N. SCOTT MOMADAY
   from *The Way to Rainy Mountain*

RICHARD RODRIGUEZ
   Complexion

SHELBY STEELE
   The New Sovereignty

SUYIN SO
   Grotesques

RALPH ELLISON
   Battle Royal

LANGSTON HUGHES
   Theme for English B

Race continues to be a major social problem in the United States. The social and economic distance between the lives of many white and black Americans, for example, continues to spread. The Civil Rights Movement, though successful in opening doors to some minority individuals, has not been successful in eradicating prejudice and racial antagonism. Complicating the racial tensions prevalent in America has been the increasing numbers of new immigrant minorities, including Asians and various Hispanic populations. Each of these racial minorities has begun to compete politically for a share in the American dream. Limited resources and an occasionally troubled economy, however, have increased competition and exacerbated tensions among various races and ethnic communities.

The writers in this chapter help us to better understand races and cultures different from our own. Some of these writers analyze the social consequences of political decisions based on race. A few note how problems associated with race are also bound up with aspects of class and culture.

In "Race Matters," Cornel West points to a set of hitherto intractable problems and urges us in his best pulpit style to begin solving them before they destroy us. James Baldwin, in his classic essay "Notes of a Native Son" describes the dangers of racial hatred and how that hatred can destroy both its object and the person who hates. June Jordan suggests that hatred be replaced by love and that the answer to her title question "Where Is the Love?" is that self-love anchored in self-respect be the starting point for a solution to racial animosity. Taking another tack, Shelby Steele, in "The New Sovereignty," argues against the means by which diversity is being pursued in various entitlement programs. An opposite view is expressed in Roger Wilkins's "In Ivory Towers," in which Wilkins suggests that there should be more affirmative action programs, not fewer.

N. Scott Momaday celebrates his Kiowa heritage in "The Way to Rainy Mountain," and Langston Hughes considers the differences and similarities between a black student and his white teacher in his poem "Theme for English B." Ralph Ellison's story "Battle Royal," a chapter from his 1953 novel, *Invisible Man,* vividly portrays the struggle for racial equality and the terrible costs of an ugly and rampant racism. Richard Rodriguez describes his struggle with identity while growing up between two cultures, Mexican and American. And Suyin So tells her story of experiencing prejudice firsthand while in elementary school.

You may find yourself disagreeing with some of these writers' views and perspectives. This should not surprise you, however, since some of them disagree with each other on issues such as affirmative action and racial quotas. Nonetheless, each of the writers in this chapter offers us something to think about, something to respond to, and perhaps something to act upon as well.

JAMES BALDWIN
(1924–1987)

Notes of a Native Son

James Baldwin was born in Harlem and became, at 14, a preacher. At 17 he abandoned the ministry and devoted himself to the craft of writing. Baldwin received institutional support in the form of fellowships to help sustain him while he wrote his first two novels, Go Tell It on the Mountain *(1953) and Giovanni's Room *(1956). Sandwiched between these two works was a collection of essays,* Notes of a Native Son *(1955), which many readers consider his finest work.*

In his essays Baldwin struggled to define himself as an American, as a writer, and as a black man, all of which, for Baldwin, were inextricably intertwined. In coming to terms with what was the most difficult thing in his life, his blackness, Baldwin revealed himself to be a passionate and eloquent writer, whose most frequent subject has been the relations between the races.

"Notes of a Native Son" is among the finest pieces Baldwin ever wrote. It describes, in language that rises from simple speech to heights of oratorical eloquence, what it was like for Baldwin to be a black man in a white world. Among the many notable features of this essay are its blending of two vocabularies: simple, common words of Anglo-Saxon derivation mixed with formal, polysyllabic words of Latin derivation. Noteworthy also are the stunning effects Baldwin achieves with repetition of words and phrases—with coherence, continuity, and emphasis. These are apparent throughout the essay, but they are most beautifully exemplified in the essay's final paragraph.

I

1 On the 29th of July, in 1943, my father died. On the same day, a few hours later, his last child was born. Over a month before this, while all our energies were concentrated in waiting for these events, there had been, in Detroit, one of the bloodiest race riots of the century. A few hours after my father's funeral, while he lay in state in the undertaker's chapel, a race riot broke out in Harlem. On the morning of the 3rd of August, we drove my father to the graveyard through a wilderness of smashed plate glass.

2 The day of my father's funeral had also been my nineteenth birthday. As we drove him to the graveyard, the spoils of injustice, anarchy, discontent, and hatred were all around us. It seemed to me that God himself had devised, to mark my father's end, the most sustained and brutally dissonant of codas. And it seemed to me, too, that the violence which rose all about us as my father left the world had been devised as a corrective for the pride of his eldest son. I had declined to believe in that apocalypse which had been central to my father's vision; very well, life seemed to be saying, here is something that will certainly pass for an apoca-

lypse until the real thing comes along. I had inclined to be contemptuous of my father for the conditions of his life, for the conditions of our lives. When his life had ended I began to wonder about that life and also, in a new way, to be apprehensive about my own.

3   I had not known my father very well. We had got on badly, partly because we shared, in our different fashions, the vice of stubborn pride. When he was dead I realized that I had hardly ever spoken to him. When he had been dead a long time I began to wish I had. It seems to be typical of life in America, where opportunities, real and fancied, are thicker than anywhere else on the globe, that the second generation has no time to talk to the first. No one, including my father, seems to have known exactly how old he was, but his mother had been born during slavery. He was of the first generation of free men. He, along with thousands of other Negroes, came North after 1919 and I was part of that generation which had never seen the landscape of what Negroes sometimes call the Old Country.

4   He had been born in New Orleans and had been a quite young man there during the time that Louis Armstrong, a boy, was running errands for the dives and honky-tonks of what was always presented to me as one of the most wicked of cities—to this day, whenever I think of New Orleans, I also helplessly think of Sodom and Gomorrah. My father never mentioned Louis Armstrong, except to forbid us to play his records; but there was a picture of him on our wall for a long time. One of my father's strong-willed female relatives had placed it there and forbade my father to take it down. He never did, but he eventually maneuvered her out of the house and when, some years later, she was in trouble and near death, he refused to do anything to help her.

5   He was, I think, very handsome. I gather this from photographs and from my own memories of him, dressed in his Sunday best and on his way to preach a sermon somewhere, when I was little. Handsome, proud, and ingrown, "like a toenail," somebody said. But he looked to me, as I grew older, like pictures I had seen of African tribal chieftains: he really should have been naked, with war-paint on and barbaric mementos, standing among spears. He could be chilling in the pulpit and indescribably cruel in his personal life and he was certainly the most bitter man I have ever met; yet it must be said that there was something else in him, buried in him, which lent him his tremendous power and, even, a rather crushing charm. It had something to do with his blackness, I think—he was very black—with his blackness and his beauty, and with the fact that he knew that he was black but did not know that he was beautiful. He claimed to be proud of his blackness but it had also been the cause of much humiliation and it had fixed bleak boundaries to his life. He was not a young man when we were growing up and he had already suffered many kinds of ruin; in his outrageously demanding and protective way he loved his children, who were black like him and menaced, like him; and all these things sometimes showed in his face when he tried, never to my knowledge with any success, to establish contact with any of us. When he took one of his children on his knee to play, the child always became fretful and began to cry; when he tried to help one of us with our homework the absolutely unabating tension which emanated from him caused our minds and our tongues to become paralyzed, so that he, scarcely knowing why, flew into a rage and the child, not knowing why, was punished. If it ever entered his head to bring a sur-

prise home for his children, it was, almost unfailingly, the wrong surprise and even the big watermelons he often brought home on his back in the summertime led to the most appalling scenes. I do not remember, in all those years, that one of his children was ever glad to see him come home. From what I was able to gather of his early life, it seemed that this inability to establish contact with other people had always marked him and had been one of the things which had driven him out of New Orleans. There was something in him, therefore, groping and tentative, which was never expressed and which was buried with him. One saw it most clearly when he was facing new people and hoping to impress them. But he never did, not for long. We went from church to smaller and more improbable church, he found himself in less and less demand as a minister, and by the time he died none of his friends had come to see him for a long time. He had lived and died in an intolerable bitterness of spirit and it frightened me, as we drove him to the graveyard through those unquiet, ruined streets, to see how powerful and overflowing this bitterness could be and to realize that this bitterness now was mine.

6   When he died I had been away from home for a little over a year. In that year I had had time to become aware of the meaning of all my father's bitter warnings, had discovered the secret of his proudly pursed lips and rigid carriage: I had discovered the weight of white people in the world. I saw that this had been for my ancestors and now would be for me an awful thing to live with and that the bitterness which had helped to kill my father could also kill me.

7   He had been ill a long time—in the mind, as we now realized, reliving instances of his fantastic intransigence in the new light of his affliction and endeavoring to feel a sorrow for him which never, quite, came true. We had not known that he was being eaten up by paranoia, and the discovery that his cruelty, to our bodies and our minds, had been one of the symptoms of his illness was not, then, enough to enable us to forgive him. The younger children felt, quite simply, relief that he would not be coming home anymore. My mother's observation that it was he, after all, who had kept them alive all these years meant nothing because the problems of keeping children alive are not real for children. The older children felt, with my father gone, that they could invite their friends to the house without fear that their friends would be insulted or, as had sometimes happened with me, being told that their friends were in league with the devil and intended to rob our family of everything we owned. (I didn't fail to wonder, and it made me hate him, what on earth we owned that anybody else would want.)

8   His illness was beyond all hope of healing before anyone realized that he was ill. He had always been so strange and had lived, like a prophet, in such unimaginably close communion with the Lord that his long silences which were punctuated by moans and hallelujahs and snatches of old songs while he sat at the living-room window never seemed odd to us. It was not until he refused to eat because, he said, his family was trying to poison him that my mother was forced to accept as a fact what had, until then, been only an unwilling suspicion. When he was committed, it was discovered that he had tuberculosis and, as it turned out, the disease of his mind allowed the disease of his body to destroy him. For the doctors could not force him to eat, either, and, though he was fed intravenously, it was clear from the beginning that there was no hope for him.

9   In my mind's eye I could see him, sitting at the window, locked up in his ter-

rors; hating and fearing every living soul including his children who had betrayed him, too, by reaching towards the world which had despised him. There were nine of us. I began to wonder what it could have felt like for such a man to have had nine children whom he could barely feed. He used to make little jokes about our poverty, which never, of course, seemed very funny to us; they could not have seemed very funny to him, either, or else our all too feeble response to them would never have caused such rages. He spent great energy and achieved, to our chagrin, no small amount of success in keeping us away from the people who surrounded us, people who had all-night rent parties to which we listened when we should have been sleeping, people who cursed and drank and flashed razor blades on Lenox Avenue. He could not understand why, if they had so much energy to spare, they could not use it to make their lives better. He treated almost everybody on our block with a most uncharitable asperity and neither they, nor, of course, their children were slow to reciprocate.

10   The only white people who came to our house were welfare workers and bill collectors. It was almost always my mother who dealt with them, for my father's temper, which was at the mercy of his pride, was never to be trusted. It was clear that he felt their very presence in his home to be a violation: this was conveyed by his carriage, almost ludicrously stiff, and by his voice, harsh and vindictively polite. When I was around nine or ten I wrote a play which was directed by a young, white schoolteacher, a woman, who then took an interest in me, and gave me books to read and, in order to corroborate my theatrical bent, decided to take me to see what she somewhat tactlessly referred to as "real" plays. Theatergoing was forbidden in our house, but, with the really cruel intuitiveness of a child, I suspected that the color of this woman's skin would carry the day for me. When, at school, she suggested taking me to the theater, I did not, as I might have done if she had been a Negro, find a way of discouraging her, but agreed that she should pick me up at my house one evening. I then, very cleverly, left all the rest to my mother, who suggested to my father, as I knew she would, that it would not be very nice to let such a kind woman make the trip for nothing. Also, since it was a schoolteacher, I imagine that my mother countered the idea of sin with the idea of "education," which word, even with my father, carried a kind of bitter weight.

11   Before the teacher came my father took me aside to ask *why* she was coming, what *interest* she could possibly have in our house, in a boy like me. I said I didn't know but I, too, suggested that it had something to do with education. And I understood that my father was waiting for me to say something—I didn't quite know what; perhaps that I wanted his protection against this teacher and her "education." I said none of these things and the teacher came and we went out. It was clear, during the brief interview in our living room, that my father was agreeing very much against his will and that he would have refused permission if he had dared. The fact that he did not dare caused me to despise him: I had no way of knowing that he was facing in that living room a wholly unprecedented and frightening situation.

12   Later, when my father had been laid off from his job, this woman became very important to us. She was really a very sweet and generous woman and went to a great deal of trouble to be of help to us, particularly during one awful winter. My mother called her by the highest name she knew. She said she was a "christian."

My father could scarcely disagree but during the four or five years of our relatively close association he never trusted her and was always trying to surprise in her open, Midwestern face the genuine, cunningly hidden, and hideous motivation. In later years, particularly when it began to be clear that this "education" of mine was going to lead me to perdition, he became more explicit and warned me that my white friends in high school were not really my friends and that I would see, when I was older, how white people would do anything to keep a Negro down. Some of them could be nice, he admitted, but none of them were to be trusted and most of them were not even nice. The best thing was to have as little to do with them as possible. I did not feel this way and I was certain, in my innocence, that I never would.

13   But the year which preceded my father's death had made a great change in my life. I had been living in New Jersey, working in defense plants, working and living among southerners, white and black. I knew about the south, of course, and about how southerners treated Negroes and how they expected them to behave, but it had never entered my mind that anyone would look at me and expect *me* to behave that way. I learned in New Jersey that to be a Negro meant, precisely, that one was never looked at but was simply at the mercy of the reflexes the color of one's skin caused in other people. I acted in New Jersey as I had always acted, that is as though I thought a great deal of myself—I had to *act* that way—with results that were, simply, unbelievable. I had scarcely arrived before I had earned the enmity, which was extraordinarily ingenious, of all my superiors and nearly all my coworkers. In the beginning, to make matters worse, I simply did not know what was happening. I did not know what I had done, and I shortly began to wonder what *anyone* could possibly do, to bring about such unanimous, active, and unbearably vocal hostility. I knew about jim-crow but I had never experienced it. I went to the same self-service restaurant three times and stood with all the Princeton boys before the counter, waiting for a hamburger and coffee; it was always an extraordinarily long time before anything was set before me; but it was not until the fourth visit that I learned that, in fact, nothing had ever been set before me: I had simply picked something up. Negroes were not served there, I was told, and they had been waiting for me to realize that I was always the only Negro present. Once I was told this, I determined to go there all the time. But now they were ready for me and, though some dreadful scenes were subsequently enacted in that restaurant, I never ate there again.

14   It was the same story all over New Jersey, in bars, bowling alleys, diners, places to live. I was always being forced to leave, silently, or with mutual imprecations. I very shortly became notorious and children giggled behind me when I passed and their elders whispered or shouted—they really believed that I was mad. And it did begin to work on my mind, of course; I began to be afraid to go anywhere and to compensate for this I went places to which I really should not have gone and where, God knows, I had no desire to be. My reputation in town naturally enhanced my reputation at work and my working day became one long series of acrobatics designed to keep me out of trouble. I cannot say that these acrobatics succeeded. It began to seem that the machinery of the organization I worked for was turning over, day and night, with but one aim: to eject me. I was fired once, and contrived, with the aid of a friend from New York, to get back on

the payroll; was fired again, and bounced back again. It took a while to fire me for the third time, but the third time took. There were no loopholes anywhere. There was not even any way of getting back inside the gates.

15   That year in New Jersey lives in my mind as though it were the year during which, having an unsuspected predilection for it, I first contracted some dread, chronic disease, the unfailing symptom of which is a kind of blind fever, a pounding in the skull and fire in the bowels. Once this disease is contracted, one can never be really carefree again, for the fever, without an instant's warning, can recur at any moment. It can wreck more important things than race relations. There is not a Negro alive who does not have this rage in his blood—one has the choice, merely, of living with it consciously or surrendering to it. As for me, this fever has recurred in me, and does, and will until the day I die.

16   My last night in New Jersey, a white friend from New York took me to the nearest big town, Trenton, to go to the movies and have a few drinks. As it turned out, he also saved me from, at the very least, a violent whipping. Almost every detail of that night stands out very clearly in my memory. I even remember the name of the movie we saw because its title impressed me as being so patly ironical. It was a movie about the German occupation of France, starring Maureen O'Hara and Charles Laughton and called *This Land Is Mine.* I remember the name of the diner we walked into when the movie ended: it was the "American Diner." When we walked in the counterman asked what we wanted and I remember answering with the casual sharpness which had become my habit: "We want a hamburger and a cup of coffee, what do you think we want?" I do not know why, after a year of such rebuffs, I so completely failed to anticipate his answer, which was, of course, "We don't serve Negroes here." This reply failed to discompose me, at least for the moment. I made some sardonic comment about the name of the diner and we walked out into the streets.

17   This was the time of what was called the "brown-out," when the lights in all American cities were very dim. When we reentered the streets something happened to me which had the force of an optical illusion, or a nightmare. The streets were very crowded and I was facing north. People were moving in every direction but it seemed to me, in that instant, that all of the people I could see, and many more than that, were moving toward me, against me, and that everyone was white. I remember how their faces gleamed. And I felt, like a physical sensation, a *click* at the nape of my neck as though some interior string connecting my head to my body had been cut. I began to walk. I heard my friend call after me, but I ignored him. Heaven only knows what was going on in his mind, but he had the good sense not to touch me—I don't know what would have happened if he had—and to keep me in sight. I don't know what was going on in my mind, either; I certainly had no conscious plan. I wanted to do something to crush these white faces, which were crushing me. I walked for perhaps a block or two until I came to an enormous, glittering, and fashionable restaurant in which I knew not even the intercession of the Virgin would cause me to be served. I pushed through the doors and took the first vacant seat I saw, at a table for two, and waited.

18   I do not know how long I waited and I rather wonder, until today, what I could possibly have looked like. Whatever I looked like, I frightened the waitress who shortly appeared, and the moment she appeared all of my fury flowed

towards her. I hated her for her white face, and for her great, astounded, frightened eyes. I felt that if she found a black man so frightening I would make her
fright worthwhile.

19   She did not ask me what I wanted, but repeated, as though she had learned it
somewhere, "We don't serve Negroes here." She did not say it with the blunt,
derisive hostility to which I had grown so accustomed, but, rather, with a note of
apology in her voice, and fear. This made me colder and more murderous than
ever. I felt I had to do something with my hands. I wanted her to come close
enough for me to get her neck between my hands.

20   So I pretended not to have understood her, hoping to draw her closer. And
she did step a very short step closer, with her pencil poised incongruously over
her pad, and repeated the formula: ". . . don't serve Negroes here."

21   Somehow, with the repetition of that phrase, which was already ringing in
my head like a thousand bells of a nightmare, I realized that she would never
come any closer and that I would have to strike from a distance. There was nothing on the table but an ordinary water-mug half full of water, and I picked this up
and hurled it with all my strength at her. She ducked and it missed her and shattered against the mirror behind the bar. And, with that sound, my frozen blood
abruptly thawed, I returned from wherever I had been, I *saw,* for the first time,
the restaurant, the people with their mouths open, already, as it seemed to me,
rising as one man, and I realized what I had done, and where I was, and I was
frightened. I rose and began running for the door. A round, potbellied man
grabbed me by the nape of the neck just as I reached the doors and began to beat
me about the face. I kicked him and got loose and ran into the streets. My friend
whispered, *"Run!"* and I ran.

22   My friend stayed outside the restaurant long enough to misdirect my pursuers
and the police, who arrived, he told me, at once. I do not know what I said to
him when he came to my room that night. I could not have said much. I felt, in
the oddest, most awful way, that I had somehow betrayed him. I lived it over and
over and over again, the way one relives an automobile accident after it has happened and one finds oneself alone and safe. I could not get over two facts, both
equally difficult for the imagination to grasp, and one was that I could have been
murdered. But the other was that I had been ready to commit murder. I saw nothing very clearly but I did see this: that my life, my *real* life, was in danger, and not
from anything other people might do but from the hatred I carried in my own
heart.

II

23 I had returned home around the second week in June—in great haste because it
seemed that my father's death and my mother's confinement were both but a
matter of hours. In the case of my mother, it soon became clear that she had simply made a miscalculation. This had always been her tendency and I don't believe
that a single one of us arrived in the world, or has since arrived anywhere else, on
time. But none of us dawdled so intolerably about the business of being born as
did my baby sister. We sometimes amused ourselves, during those endless, sti-

fling weeks, by picturing the baby sitting within in the safe, warm dark, bitterly regretting the necessity of becoming a part of our chaos and stubbornly putting it off as long as possible. I understood her perfectly and congratulated her on showing such good sense so soon. Death, however, sat as purposefully at my father's bedside as life stirred within my mother's womb and it was harder to understand why he so lingered in that long shadow. It seemed that he had bent, and for a long time, too, all of his energies towards dying. Now death was ready for him but my father held back.

24 All of Harlem, indeed, seemed to be infected by waiting. I had never before known it to be so violently still. Racial tensions throughout this country were exacerbated during the early years of the war, partly because the labor market brought together hundreds of thousands of ill-prepared people and partly because Negro soldiers, regardless of where they were born, received their military training in the south. What happened in defense plants and army camps had repercussions, naturally, in every Negro ghetto. The situation in Harlem had grown bad enough for clergymen, policemen, educators, politicians, and social workers to assert in one breath that there was no "crime wave" and to offer, in the very next breath, suggestions as to how to combat it. These suggestions always seemed to involve playgrounds, despite the fact that racial skirmishes were occurring in the playgrounds, too. Playground or not, crime wave or not, the Harlem police force had been augmented in March, and the unrest grew—perhaps, in fact, partly as a result of the ghetto's instinctive hatred of policemen. Perhaps the most revealing news item, out of the steady parade of reports of muggings, stabbings, shootings, assaults, gang wars, and accusations of police brutality is the item concerning six Negro girls who set upon a white girl in the subway because, as they all too accurately put it, she was stepping on their toes. Indeed she was, all over the nation.

25 I had never before been so aware of policemen, on foot, on horseback, on corners, everywhere, always two by two. Nor had I ever been so aware of small knots of people. They were on stoops and on corners and in doorways, and what was striking about them, I think, was that they did not seem to be talking. Never, when I passed these groups, did the usual sound of a curse or a laugh ring out and neither did there seem to be any hum of gossip. There was certainly, on the other hand, occurring between them communication extraordinarily intense. Another thing that was striking was the unexpected diversity of the people who made up these groups. Usually, for example, one would see a group of sharpies standing on the street corner, jiving the passing chicks; or a group of older men, usually, for some reason, in the vicinity of a barber shop, discussing baseball scores, or the numbers or making rather chilling observations about women they had known. Women, in a general way, tended to be seen less often together—unless they were church women, or very young girls, or prostitutes met together for an unprofessional instant. But that summer I saw the strangest combinations: large, respectable, churchly matrons standing on the stoops or the corners with their hair tied up, together with a girl in sleazy satin whose face bore the marks of gin and the razor, or heavy-set, abrupt, no-nonsense older men, in company with the most disreputable and fanatical "race" men, or these same "race" men with the sharpies, or these sharpies with the churchly women. Seventh Day Adventists and

Methodists and Spiritualists seemed to be hobnobbing with Holyrollers and they were all, alike, entangled with the most flagrant disbelievers; something heavy in their stance seemed to indicate that they had all, incredibly, seen a common vision, and on each face there seemed to be the same strange, bitter shadow.

26   The churchly women and the matter-of-fact, no-nonsense men had children in the Army. The sleazy girls they talked to had lovers there, the sharpies and the "race" men had friends and brothers there. It would have demanded an unquestioning patriotism, happily as uncommon in this country as it is undesirable, for these people not to have been disturbed by the bitter letters they received, by the newspaper stories they read, not to have been enraged by the posters, then to be found all over New York, which described the Japanese as "yellow-bellied Japs." It was only the "race" men, to be sure, who spoke ceaselessly of being revenged—how this vengeance was to be exacted was not clear—for the indignities and dangers suffered by Negro boys in uniform; but everybody felt a directionless, hopeless bitterness, as well as that panic which can scarcely be suppressed when one knows that a human being one loves is beyond one's reach, and in danger. This helplessness and this gnawing uneasiness does something, at length, to even the toughest mind. Perhaps the best way to sum all this up is to say that the people I knew felt, mainly, a peculiar kind of relief when they knew that their boys were being shipped out of the south, to do battle overseas. It was, perhaps, like feeling that the most dangerous part of a dangerous journey had been passed and that now, even if death should come, it would come with honor and without the complicity of their countrymen. Such a death would be, in short, a fact with which one could hope to live.

27   It was on the 28th of July, which I believe was a Wednesday, that I visited my father for the first time during his illness and for the last time in his life. The moment I saw him I knew why I had put off this visit so long. I had told my mother that I did not want to see him because I hated him. But this was not true. It was only that I *had* hated him and I wanted to hold on to this hatred. I did not want to look on him as a ruin: it was not a ruin I had hated. I imagine that one of the reasons people cling to their hates so stubbornly is because they sense, once hate is gone, that they will be forced to deal with pain.

28   We traveled out to him, his older sister and myself, to what seemed to be the very end of a very Long Island. It was hot and dusty and we wrangled, my aunt and I, all the way out, over the fact that I had recently begun to smoke and, as she said, to give myself airs. But I knew that she wrangled with me because she could not bear to face the fact of her brother's dying. Neither could I endure the reality of her despair, her unstated bafflement as to what had happened to her brother's life, and her own. So we wrangled and I smoked and from time to time she fell into a heavy reverie. Covertly, I watched her face, which was the face of an old woman; it had fallen in, the eyes were sunken and lightless; soon she would be dying, too.

29   In my childhood—it had not been so long ago—I had thought her beautiful. She had been quick-witted and quick-moving and very generous with all the children and each of her visits had been an event. At one time one of my brothers and myself had thought of running away to live with her. Now she could no longer produce out of her handbag some unexpected and yet familiar delight. She made

me feel pity and revulsion and fear. It was awful to realize that she no longer caused me to feel affection. The closer we came to the hospital the more querulous she became and at the same time, naturally, grew more dependent on me. Between pity and guilt and fear I began to feel that there was another me trapped in my skull like a jack-in-the-box who might escape my control at any moment and fill the air with screaming.

30   She began to cry the moment we entered the room and she saw him lying there, all shriveled and still, like a little black monkey. The great, gleaming apparatus which fed him and would have compelled him to be still even if he had been able to move brought to mind, not beneficence, but torture; the tubes entering his arm made me think of pictures I had seen when a child, of Gulliver, tied down by the pygmies on that island. My aunt wept and wept, there was a whistling sound in my father's throat; nothing was said; he could not speak. I wanted to take his hand, to say something. But I do not know what I could have said, even if he could have heard me. He was not really in that room with us, he had at last really embarked on his journey; and though my aunt told me that he said he was going to meet Jesus, I did not hear anything except that whistling in his throat. The doctor came back and we left, into that unbearable train again, and home. In the morning came the telegram saying that he was dead. Then the house was suddenly full of relatives, friends, hysteria, and confusion and I quickly left my mother and the children to the care of those impressive women, who, in Negro communities at least, automatically appear at times of bereavement armed with lotions, proverbs, and patience, and an ability to cook. I went downtown. By the time I returned, later the same day, my mother had been carried to the hospital and the baby had been born.

III

31 For my father's funeral I had nothing black to wear and this posed a nagging problem all day long. It was one of those problems, simple, or impossible of solution, to which the mind insanely clings in order to avoid the mind's real trouble. I spent most of that day at the downtown apartment of a girl I knew, celebrating my birthday with whiskey and wondering what to wear that night. When planning a birthday celebration one naturally does not expect that it will be up against competition from a funeral and this girl had anticipated taking me out that night, for a big dinner and a night club afterwards. Sometime during the course of that long day we decided that we would go out anyway, when my father's funeral service was over. I imagine *I* decided it, since, as the funeral hour approached, it became clearer and clearer to me that I would not know what to do with myself when it was over. The girl, stifling her very lively concern as to the possible effects of the whiskey on one of my father's chief mourners, concentrated on being conciliatory and practically helpful. She found a black shirt for me somewhere and ironed it and, dressed in the darkest pants and jacket I owned, and slightly drunk, I made my way to my father's funeral.

32   The chapel was full, but not packed, and very quiet. There were, mainly, my father's relatives, and his children, and here and there I saw faces I had not seen

since childhood, the faces of my father's one-time friends. They were very dark and solemn now, seeming somehow to suggest that they had known all along that something like this would happen. Chief among the mourners was my aunt, who had quarreled with my father all his life; by which I do not mean to suggest that her mourning was insincere or that she had not loved him. I suppose that she was one of the few people in the world who had, and their incessant quarreling proved precisely the strength of the tie that bound them. The only other person in the world, as far as I knew, whose relationship to my father rivaled my aunt's in depth was my mother, who was not there.

33   It seemed to me, of course, that it was a very long funeral. But it was, if anything, a rather shorter funeral than most, nor, since there were no overwhelming, uncontrollable expressions of grief, could it be called—if I dare to use the word—successful. The minister who preached my father's funeral sermon was one of the few my father had still been seeing as he neared his end. He presented to us in his sermon a man whom none of us had ever seen—a man thoughtful, patient, and forbearing, a Christian inspiration to all who knew him, and a model for his children. And no doubt the children, in their disturbed and guilty state, were almost ready to believe this; he had been remote enough to be anything and, anyway, the shock of the incontrovertible, that it was really our father lying up there in that casket, prepared the mind for anything. His sister moaned and this grief-stricken moaning was taken as corroboration. The other faces held a dark, non-committal thoughtfulness. This was not the man they had known, but they had scarcely expected to be confronted with *him;* this was, in a sense deeper than questions of fact, the man they had not known, and the man they had not known may have been the real one. The real man, whoever he had been, had suffered and now he was dead: this was all that was sure and all that mattered now. Every man in the chapel hoped that when his hour came he, too, would be eulogized, which is to say forgiven, and that all of his lapses, greeds, errors, and strayings from the truth would be invested with coherence and looked upon with charity. This was perhaps the last thing human beings could give each other and it was what they demanded, after all, of the Lord. Only the Lord saw the midnight tears, only He was present when one of His children, moaning and wringing hands, paced up and down the room. When one slapped one's child in anger the recoil in the heart reverberated through heaven and became part of the pain of the universe. And when the children were hungry and sullen and distrustful and one watched them, daily, growing wilder, and further away, and running headlong into danger, it was the Lord who knew what the charged heart endured as the strap was laid to the backside; the Lord alone who knew what one *would* have said if one had had, like the Lord, the gift of the living word. It was the Lord who knew of the impossibility every parent in that room faced: how to prepare the child for the day when the child would be despised and how to *create* in the child—by what means?—a stronger antidote to this poison than one had found for oneself. The avenues, side streets, bars, billiard halls, hospitals, police stations, and even the playgrounds of Harlem—not to mention the houses of correction, the jails, and the morgue—testified to the potency of the poison while remaining silent as to the efficacy of whatever antidote, irresistibly raising the question of whether or not such an antidote existed; raising, which was worse, the question of whether or not an antidote

was desirable; perhaps poison should be fought with poison. With these several schisms in the mind and with more terrors in the heart than could be named, it was better not to judge the man who had gone down under an impossible burden. It was better to remember: *Thou knowest this man's fall; but thou knowest not his wrassling.*

34   While the preacher talked and I watched the children—years of changing their diapers, scrubbing them, slapping them, taking them to school, and scolding them had had the perhaps inevitable result of making me love them, though I am not sure I knew this then—my mind was busily breaking out with a rash of disconnected impressions. Snatches of popular songs, indecent jokes, bits of books I had read, movie sequences, faces, voices, political issues—I thought I was going mad; all these impressions suspended, as it were, in the solution of the faint nausea produced in me by the heat and liquor. For a moment I had the impression that my alcoholic breath, inefficiently disguised with chewing gum, filled the entire chapel. Then someone began singing one of my father's favorite songs and, abruptly, I was with him, sitting on his knee, in the hot, enormous, crowded church which was the first church we attended. It was the Abyssinia Baptist Church on 138th Street. We had not gone there long. With this image, a host of others came. I had forgotten, in the rage of my growing up, how proud my father had been of me when I was little. Apparently, I had had a voice and my father had liked to show me off before the members of the church. I had forgotten what he had looked like when he was pleased but now I remembered that he had always been grinning with pleasure when my solos ended. I even remembered certain expressions on his face when he teased my mother—had he loved her? I would never know. And when had it all begun to change? For now it seemed that he had not always been cruel. I remembered being taken for a haircut and scraping my knee on the footrest of the barber's chair and I remembered my father's face as he soothed my crying and applied the stinging iodine. Then I remembered our fights, fights which had been of the worst possible kind because my technique had been silence.

35   I remembered the one time in all our life together when we had really spoken to each other.

36   It was on a Sunday and it must have been shortly before I left home. We were walking, just the two of us, in our usual silence, to or from church. I was in high school and had been doing a lot of writing and I was, at about this time, the editor of the high school magazine. But I had also been a Young Minister and had been preaching from the pulpit. Lately, I had been taking fewer engagements and preached as rarely as possible. It was said in the church, quite truthfully, that I was "cooling off."

37   My father asked me abruptly, "You'd rather write than preach, wouldn't you?"

38   I was astonished at his question—because it was a real question. I answered, "Yes."

39   That was all we said. It was awful to remember that that was all we had *ever* said.

40   The casket now was opened and mourners were being led up the aisle to look for the last time on the deceased. The assumption was that the family was too overcome with grief to be allowed to make this journey alone and I watched while

my aunt was led to the casket and, muffled in black, and shaking, led back to her seat. I disapproved of forcing the children to look on their dead father, considering that the shock of his death, or, more truthfully, the shock of death as a reality, was already a little more than a child could bear, but my judgment in this matter had been overruled and there they were, bewildered and frightened and very small, being led, one by one, to the casket. But there is also something very gallant about children at such moments. It has something to do with their silence and gravity and with the fact that one cannot help them. Their legs, somehow, seem *exposed,* so that it is at once incredible and terribly clear that their legs are all they have to hold them up.

41   I had not wanted to go to the casket myself and I certainly had not wished to be led there, but there was no way of avoiding either of these forms. One of the deacons led me up and I looked on my father's face. I cannot say that it looked like him at all. His blackness had been equivocated by powder and there was no suggestion in that casket of what his power had or could have been. He was simply an old man dead, and it was hard to believe that he had ever given anyone either joy or pain. Yet, his life filled that room. Further up the avenue his wife was holding his newborn child. Life and death so close together, and love and hatred, and right and wrong, said something to me which I did not want to hear concerning man, concerning the life of man.

42   After the funeral, while I was downtown desperately celebrating my birthday, a Negro soldier, in the lobby of the Hotel Braddock, got into a fight with a white policeman over a Negro girl. Negro girls, white policemen, in or out of uniform, and Negro males—in or out of uniform—were part of the furniture of the lobby of the Hotel Braddock and this was certainly not the first time such an incident had occurred. It was destined, however, to receive an unprecedented publicity, for the fight between the policeman and the soldier ended with the shooting of the soldier. Rumor, flowing immediately to the streets outside, stated that the soldier had been shot in the back, an instantaneous and revealing invention, and that the soldier had died protecting a Negro woman. The facts were somewhat different— for example, the soldier had not been shot in the back, and was not dead, and the girl seems to have been as dubious a symbol of womanhood as her white counterpart in Georgia usually is, but no one was interested in the facts. They preferred the invention because this invention expressed and corroborated their hates and fears so perfectly. It is just as well to remember that people are always doing this. Perhaps many of those legends, including Christianity, to which the world clings began their conquest of the world with just some such concerted surrender to distortion. The effect, in Harlem, of this particular legend was like the effect of a lit match in a tin of gasoline. The mob gathered before the doors of the Hotel Braddock simply began to swell and to spread in every direction, and Harlem exploded.

43   The mob did not cross the ghetto lines. It would have been easy, for example, to have gone over Morningside Park on the west side or to have crossed the Grand Central railroad tracks at 125th Street on the east side, to wreak havoc in white neighborhoods. The mob seems to have been mainly interested in something more potent and real than the white face, that is, in white power, and the principal damage done during the riot of the summer of 1943 was to white busi-

ness establishments in Harlem. It might have been a far bloodier story, of course, if, at the hour the riot began, these establishments had still been open. From the Hotel Braddock the mob fanned out, east and west along 125th Street, and for the entire length of Lenox, Seventh, and Eighth avenues. Along each of these avenues, and along each major side street—116th, 125th, 135th, and so on— bars, stores, pawnshops, restaurants, even little luncheonettes had been smashed open and entered and looted—looted, it might be added, with more haste than efficiency. The shelves really looked as though a bomb had struck them. Cans of beans and soup and dog food, along with toilet paper, corn flakes, sardines and milk tumbled every which way, and abandoned cash registers and cases of beer leaned crazily out of the splintered windows and were strewn along the avenues. Sheets, blankets, and clothing of every description formed a kind of path, as though people had dropped them while running. I truly had not realized that Harlem *had* so many stores until I saw them all smashed open; the first time the word *wealth* ever entered my mind in relation to Harlem was when I saw it scattered in the streets. But one's first, incongruous impression of plenty was countered immediately by an impression of waste. None of this was doing anybody any good. It would have been better to have left the plate glass as it had been and the goods lying in the stores.

44   It would have been better, but it would also have been intolerable, for Harlem had needed something to smash. To smash something is the ghetto's chronic need. Most of the time it is the members of the ghetto who smash each other, and themselves. But as long as the ghetto walls are standing there will always come a moment when these outlets do not work. That summer, for example, it was not enough to get into a fight on Lenox Avenue, or curse out one's cronies in the barber shops. If ever, indeed, the violence which fills Harlem's churches, pool halls, and bars erupts outward in a more direct fashion, Harlem and its citizens are likely to vanish in an apocalyptic flood. That this is not likely to happen is due to a great many reasons, most hidden and powerful among them the Negro's real relation to the white American. This relation prohibits, simply, anything as uncomplicated and satisfactory as pure hatred. In order really to hate white people, one has to blot so much out of the mind—and the heart—that this hatred itself becomes an exhausting and self-destructive pose. But this does not mean, on the other hand, that love comes easily: the white world is too powerful, too complacent, too ready with gratuitous humiliation, and, above all, too ignorant and too innocent for that. One is absolutely forced to make perpetual qualifications and one's own reactions are always canceling each other out. It is this, really, which has driven so many people mad, both white and black. One is always in the position of having to decide between amputation and gangrene. Amputation is swift but time may prove that the amputation was not necessary—or one may delay the amputation too long. Gangrene is slow, but it is impossible to be sure that one is reading one's symptoms right. The idea of going through life as a cripple is more than one can bear, and equally unbearable is the risk of swelling up slowly, in agony, with poison. And the trouble, finally, is that the risks are real even if the choices do not exist.

45   "But as for me and my house," my father had said, "we will serve the Lord." I wondered, as we drove him to his resting place, what this line had meant for him. I had heard him preach it many times. I had preached it once myself, proudly giv-

ing it an interpretation different from my father's. Now the whole thing came back to me, as though my father and I were on our way to Sunday school and I were memorizing the golden text: *And if it seem evil unto you to serve the Lord, choose you this day whom you will serve; whether the gods which your fathers served that were on the other side of the flood, or the gods of the Amorites, in whose land ye dwell: but as for me and my house, we will serve the Lord.* I suspected in these familiar lines a meaning which had never been there for me before. All of my father's texts and songs, which I had decided were meaningless, were arranged before me at his death like empty bottles, waiting to hold the meaning which life would give them for me. This was his legacy: nothing is ever escaped. That bleakly memorable morning I hated the unbelievable streets and the Negroes and whites who had, equally, made them that way. But I knew that it was folly, as my father would have said, this bitterness was folly. It was necessary to hold on to the things that mattered. The dead man mattered, the new life mattered; blackness and whiteness did not matter; to believe that they did was to acquiesce in one's own destruction. Hatred, which could destroy so much, never failed to destroy the man who hated and this was an immutable law.

46   It began to seem that one would have to hold in the mind forever two ideas which seemed to be in opposition. The first idea was acceptance, the acceptance, totally without rancor, of life as it is, and men as they are: in the light of this idea, it goes without saying that injustice is a commonplace. But this did not mean that one could be complacent, for the second idea was of equal power: that one must never, in one's own life, accept these injustices as commonplace but must fight them with all one's strength. This fight begins, however, in the heart and it now had been laid to my charge to keep my own heart free of hatred and despair. This intimation made my heart heavy and, now that my father was irrecoverable, I wished that he had been beside me so that I could have searched his face for the answers which only the future would give me now.

QUESTIONS

Experience

· Describe your experience of reading Baldwin's essay. Which parts drew you into Baldwin's world most powerfully? Why? How did you respond to the restaurant incident? Why?

Interpretation

· Is this essay primarily about race relations? About family relations? About the state of American society at a particular point in history? Something else? Explain.

Evaluation

· What values does Baldwin hold up as dangerous and destructive? What values does he counter them with? Where do you find Baldwin explaining his values most clearly?

WRITING

Exploring

· Write an account of a racial incident in which you were a direct participant or to which you were a witness—even if only through the media. Describe the incident carefully, and explain its significance for you personally, and then more generally.

· Or write your own "Notes of a Native Son or Daughter." Try to come to terms with your racial (or ethnic) heritage and with your place in relation to the society of which you are a part.

Interpreting

· Explain what you think Baldwin means by the following quotation from the end of Part I of his essay:

> I could not get over two facts, both equally difficult for the imagination to grasp, and one was that I could have been murdered. But the other was that I had been ready to commit murder. I saw nothing very clearly but I did see this: that my life, my *real* life, was in danger, and not from anything other people might do but from the hatred I carried in my own heart.

Evaluating

· Explain whether you think Baldwin's essay successfully conveys what it is like to live within a black skin. Cite specific words, phrases, and details to support your view. Rely on your personal experience if it is relevant.

ROGER WILKINS
(b. 1932)

In Ivory Towers

Roger Wilkins is perhaps best known as a civil rights activist and commentator on race relations. After receiving a B.A. and a law degree from the University of Michigan, Wilkins served as United States Assistant Attorney General and a program director for the Ford Foundation. He also served on the editorial boards of both the Washington Post *and the* New York Times *before becoming a professor of history at George Mason University.*

In his article "In Ivory Towers," originally published in Mother Jones *magazine in 1990, Wilkins argues in favor of affirmative action policies. His piece can be seen as a counterpoint to Shelby Steele's questioning of those policies, though Wilkins's article is not a direct response to Steele's, which was written later. Wilkins limits his discussion to the issue of black self-esteem. His rhetorical strategy consists of presenting the opposition view on this issue and then suggesting how affirmative action policies do not do what the opponents claim. His strategy in arguing is to question and cast doubt on the legitimacy and persuasiveness of the claims advanced by holders of opposing views.*

1   **B**lacks are among those expressing second thoughts about affirmative action in college and university life these days. The first concern is expressed by a brilliant young black friend, who laments that despite his formidable intellectual accomplishments, people still judge him not as a splendid scholar, but only as a smart black. The second is a concern expressed by some black educators that students admitted under affirmative action programs may come to doubt their own capacities as a result.

2   These complaints proceed from the same idea: that the main thing to think about when considering affirmative action is the damage it does to black self-esteem—either because whites will doubt blacks' capacities, or because the remedy itself makes blacks doubt their own capacities. I understand this burden, having carried part of it all my adult life, but the simple colloquial response I give to black faculty members and black students who express similar concerns to me is: "You're upset because you think *affirmative action* makes white folks look at you funny. Hell, white folks were looking at black folks funny long before affirmative action was invented. They been lookin' at black folks funny since 1619."

3   The founding tenet of racism is that blacks are inferior, particularly when it comes to intellectual capability. And an underpinning of racism has been an all-out cultural onslaught on the self-esteem of blacks, to transform them from assertive and self-sufficient human beings into dependents, mere extensions of the will of the whites who choose to use them.

4   Affirmative action, even weakly and spottily deployed, opens doors of opportunity that would otherwise be slammed tight. As a result, the country is better

and stronger. It surely is one of the most effective antidotes to the widespread habit of undervaluing the capacities of minorities and women. It also serves as a counterbalance to the tendency to overvalue, as a recruitment tool, the effectiveness and fairness of old-boy networks.

5   But affirmative action did not magically erase racism. It simply pushed back the boundaries of the struggle a little bit, giving some of us better opportunities to fulfill our capacities, and higher perches from which to conduct our battles. Anyone who thinks there are no more battles to be fought, even on the highest battlements of the ivoriest of the ivory towers, simply doesn't understand America.

6   Whatever confusion I've had about such things was knocked out of me a long time ago. Almost everything that has happened to me since I was twenty-one has resulted from one sort of affirmative action or another. Thirty-seven years as the object of affirmative action in such places as the Department of Justice, the Ford Foundation, the *Washington Post* and the *New York Times* have given me a rich understanding of the endurance of U.S. racism. I have done battle and emerged with enough self-confidence to assert that all of the places that hired me because of affirmative action were better for having done so.

7   Nevertheless, I am sympathetic to the desire of my young black friend for the excellence of his mind to wash the color off his accomplishments. Unfortunately, even in 1990, color is not irrelevant in the United States at any level—and perhaps that is fortunate, for it maintains some fragmentary bond between my friend and poor black people who need his concern and strength. I am reminded, in this regard, of the wisdom embedded in an old joke that comes from deep in African-American culture. In this story, two old white men are rocking on a porch in a Southern town. Says the first, "Zeke, what do you call a black man with a Ph.D. who has just won the Nobel Prize in physics?" Replies Zeke, after a long pause and much contemplative rocking, "I calls him nigger."

8   Not all white people are as deeply racist as Zeke, of course, but enough are to make it wise for young black people to follow what our mothers and fathers have taught us over the generations: that white people's judgments of us are to be viewed with great skepticism, and that accepting those judgments whole is apt to be hazardous to our mental health. Thus, mental toughness and an independent sense of our own worth are elements as essential to the black survival kit in 1990 as they ever were.

9   Not only do black professors need to know this, but black students entering predominantly white campuses have to be taught it, as well. Such campuses are products of white-American culture, and most black youngsters, particularly those from the inner cities, find them to be alien places. Moreover, they sometimes get mixed messages. Often recruited assiduously, they frequently find pockets of hostility and seas of indifference.

10   That is not a reason for less affirmative action, but for more—at the faculty, staff level. There should be many black adults on those campuses to make them feel less foreign to black students and more like places of opportunity, full of challenges that can be overcome with excellence and effort. If the number of knowledgeable and sympathetic adults is minuscule, the youngsters will see that the commitment to an atmosphere where everyone can learn is crimped and limited.

11   In this imperfect world, racism remains a major affliction that burdens all Americans—and it hits black Americans right in the self-esteem. But it must surely be easier to firm up your self-regard when you are employed with tenure than when working as an itinerant researcher. Similarly, the task is undoubtedly easier for a college graduate—even one who had to struggle with self-doubt during college years because of affirmative action—than for someone who has never gone to college.

12   It would be nice to think that in the academy we could escape cultural habits wrought during more than three centuries of legal racial oppression. But that won't happen in this century. So black people—even those who are privileged—just have to suck it in and keep on pushing, breaking their own paths and making a way for those still struggling behind.

QUESTIONS

Experience

- To what extent have you experienced favorable treatment—perhaps in being hired for a job, admitted to a school or program, or selected for an award—because of race or ethnicity?
- What is your response to situations in which such favorable treatment has been accorded, whether or not you have experienced it directly yourself? Why?

Interpretation

- What arguments does Wilkins advance in support of affirmative action? Why does he say there should be not less affirmative action, but more?
- To what extent do you agree with Wilkins that "racism remains a major affliction that burdens all Americans—and it hits black Americans right in the self-esteem"?

Evaluation

- How persuasive do you find Wilkins's arguments in support of affirmative action? How convincing do you find his claims about self-esteem?
- How effective do you find Wilkins's use of his "young black friend" as a way to present his own counterview? Consider especially what Wilkins says about his friend in paragraphs 7 and 11.

WRITING

Exploring

- Write an essay describing a situation in which you were the beneficiary or the loser due to a type of preferential treatment.
- Or write a series of questions you would ask Wilkins if you had an opportunity to interview him about his article.

Interpreting

· Analyze Wilkins's argument concerning affirmative action. Identify his claim—his major assertion or idea. Identify the evidence he brings to bear in its support.

· Discuss the image of American race relations conveyed in Wilkins's article. Explain whether you do or do not share his perspective.

Evaluating

· Evaluate the success of Wilkins's use of his experience as part of his evidence. Consider, as well, the effectiveness of the joke he includes.

· Or imagine yourself as Wilkins's brilliant young academic friend, and write a letter to Wilkins responding to his article.

JUNE JORDAN
(b. 1936)

Where Is the Love?

June Jordan was born and raised in New York City. She has taught at City College of the City University of New York, Sarah Lawrence College, and the State University of New York. She is currently professor of Afro-American Studies and Women's Studies at the University of California at Berkeley. Her stories, essays, and poems have appeared in numerous periodicals, includ-ing Black World, Esquire, Essence, *the* Nation, Partisan Review, *and the* Vil-lage Voice. *Her books of essays include* Civil Wars *(1981),* On Call *(1986),* Moving Toward Home *(1989), and* Technical Difficulties: African American Notes on the State of the Union *(1992).*

In "Where Is the Love?" Jordan presents a rousing call to begin answering the title question by loving and respecting herself as a black woman and as a feminist. Jordan's essay was first a speech, and its oral character is amply evident, especially in the way she uses repetition of word and phrase. In paragraph 4, for example, Jordan makes her point by insistently repeating three words: "powerless," "powerful," and "majority." And at many differ-ent places in her essay, she asks the title question: "Where Is the Love?"

1   As I think about anyone or any thing—whether history or literature or my father or political organizations or a poem or a film—as I seek to evaluate the potentiality, the life-supportive commitment/possibilities of anyone or any thing, the decisive question is, always, *Where is the love?* The energies that flow from hatred, from negative and hateful habits and attitudes and dogma do not promise something good, something I would choose to cherish, to honor with my own life. It is always the love, whether we look to the spirit of Fannie Lou Hamer, or to the spirit of Agostinho Neto, it is always the love that will carry action into positive new places, that will carry your own nights and days beyond demoralization and away from suicide.

2   I am a feminist, and what that means to me is much the same as the meaning of the fact that I am Black: it means that I must undertake to love myself and to respect myself as though my very life depends upon self-love and self-respect. It means that I must everlastingly seek to cleanse myself of the hatred and the con-tempt that surrounds and permeates my identity, as a woman, and as a Black human being, in this particular world of ours. It means that the achievement of self-love and self-respect will require inordinate, hourly vigilance, and that I am entering my soul into a struggle that will most certainly transform the experience of all the peoples of the earth, as no other movement can, in fact, hope to claim: because the movement into self-love, self-respect, and self-determination is the movement now galvanizing the true, the unarguable majority of human beings everywhere. This movement explicitly demands the testing of the viability of a moral idea: that the health, the legitimacy of any status quo, any governing force,

must be measured according to the experiences of those who are, comparatively, powerless. Virtue is not to be discovered in the conduct of the strong vis-à-vis the powerful, but rather it is to be found in our behavior and policies affecting those who are different, those who are weaker, or smaller than we. How do the strong, the powerful, treat children? How do we treat the aged among us? How do the strong and the powerful treat so-called minority members of the body politic? How do the powerful regard women? How do they treat us?

3   Easily you can see that, according to this criterion, the overwhelming reality of power and government and tradition is evil, is diseased, is illegitimate, and deserves nothing from us—no loyalty, no accommodation, no patience, no understanding—except a clear-minded resolve to utterly change this total situation and, thereby, to change our own destiny.

4   As a Black woman, as a Black feminist, I exist, simultaneously, as part of the powerless and as part of the majority peoples of the world in two ways: I am powerless as compared to any man because women, per se, are kept powerless by men/by the powerful; I am powerless as compared to anyone white because Black and Third World peoples are kept powerless by whites/by the powerful. I am the majority because women constitute the majority gender. I am the majority because Black and Third World peoples constitute the majority of life on this planet.

5   And it is here, in this extreme, inviolable coincidence of my status as a Black feminist, my status as someone twice stigmatized, my status as a Black woman who is twice kin to the despised majority of all the human life that there is, it is here, in that extremity, that I stand in a struggle against suicide. And it is here, in this extremity, that I ask, of myself, and of any one who would call me sister, *Where is the love?*

6   The love devolving from my quest for self-love and self-respect and self-determination must be, as I see it, something you can verify in the ways that I present myself to others, and in the ways that I approach people different from myself. How do I reach out to the people I would like to call my sisters and my brothers and my children and my lovers and my friends? If I am a Black feminist serious in the undertaking of self-love, then it seems to me that the legitimate, the morally defensible character of that self-love should be such that I gain and gain and gain in the socio-psychic strength needed so that I may, without fear, be able and willing to love and respect women, for example, who are not like me, women who are not feminists, women who are not professionals, women who are not as old or as young as I am, women who have neither job nor income, women who are not Black.

7   And it seems to me that the socio-psychic strength that should follow from a morally defensible Black feminism will mean that I become able and willing, without fear, to love and respect all men who are willing and able, without fear, to love and respect me. In short, if the acquirement of my self-determination is part of a worldwide, an inevitable, and a righteous movement, then I should become willing and able to embrace more and more of the whole world, without fear, and also without self-sacrifice.

8   This means that, as a Black feminist, I cannot be expected to respect what somebody else calls self-love if that concept of self-love requires my suicide to

any degree. And this will hold true whether that somebody else is male, female, Black, or white. My Black feminism means that you cannot expect me to respect what somebody else identifies as the Good of The People, if that so-called Good (often translated into *manhood* or *family* or *nationalism*) requires the deferral or the diminution of my self-fulfillment. We *are* the people. And, as Black women, we are most of the people, any people, you care to talk about. And, therefore, nothing that is Good for The People is good unless it is good for me, as I determine myself.

9   When I speak of Black feminism, then, I am speaking from an exacerbated consciousness of the truth that we, Black women, huddle together, miserably, on the very lowest levels of the economic pyramid. We, Black women, subsist among the most tenuous and least likely economic conditions for survival.

10   When I speak of Black feminism, then, I am not speaking of sexuality. I am not speaking of heterosexuality or lesbianism or homosexuality or bisexuality; whatever sexuality anyone elects for his or her pursuit is not my business, nor the business of the state. And, furthermore, I cannot be persuaded that one kind of sexuality, as against another, will necessarily provide for the greater happiness of the two people involved. I am not talking about sexuality. I am talking about love, about a steady-state deep caring and respect for every other human being, a love that can only derive from a secure and positive self-love.

11   As a Black woman/feminist, I must look about me, with trembling, and with shocked anger, at the endless waste, the endless suffocation of my sisters: the bitter sufferings of hundreds of thousands of women who are the sole parents, the mothers of hundreds of thousands of children, the desolation and the futility of women trapped by demeaning, lowest-paying occupations, the unemployed, the bullied, the beaten, the battered, the ridiculed, the slandered, the trivialized, the raped, and the sterilized, the lost millions and multimillions of beautiful, creative, and momentous lives turned to ashes on the pyre of gender identity. I must look about me and, as a Black feminist, I must ask myself: *Where is the love?* How is my own lifework serving to end these tyrannies, these corrosions of sacred possibility?

12   As a Black feminist poet and writer I must look behind me with trembling, and with shocked anger, at the fate of Black women writers until now. From the terrible graves of a traditional conspiracy against my sisters in art, I must exhume the works of women writers and poets such as Georgia Douglas Johnson (who?).

13   In the early flush of the Harlem Renaissance, Georgia Johnson accomplished an astonishing, illustrious life experience. Married to Henry Lincoln Johnson, U.S. Recorder of Deeds in Washington, D.C., the poet, in her own right, became no less than Commissioner of Conciliation for the U.S. Department of Labor *(who was that again? Who?).* And she, this poet, furthermore enjoyed the intense, promotional attention of Dean Kelley Miller, here at Howard, and W. E. B. Du Bois, and William Stanley Braithwaite, and Alain Locke. And she published three volumes of her own poetry and I found her work in Countee Cullen's anthology, *Caroling Dusk,* where, Countee Cullen reports, she, Georgia Douglas Johnson, thrived as a kind of Gwendolyn Brooks, holding regular Saturday night get-togethers with the young Black writers of the day.

14   And what did this poet of such acclaim, achievement, connection, and gen-

erosity, what did this poet have to say in her poetry, and who among us has ever heard of Georgia Douglas Johnson? And is there anybody in this room who can tell me the name of two or three other women poets from the Harlem Renaissance? And why did she die, and why does the work of all women die with no river carrying forward the record of such grace? How is it the case that whether we have written novels or poetry or whether we have raised our children or cleaned and cooked and washed and ironed, it is all dismissed as "women's work"; it is all, finally, despised as nothing important, and there is no trace, no echo of our days upon the earth?

15   Why is it not surprising that a Black woman as remarkably capable and gifted and proven as Georgia Douglas Johnson should be the poet of these pathetic, beggarly lines:

> I'm folding up my little dreams
> within my heart tonight
> And praying I may soon forget
> the torture of their sight
> *"My Little Dreams"*

How long, how long will we let the dreams of women serve merely to torture and not to ignite, to enflame, and to ennoble the promise of the years of every lifetime? And here is Georgia Douglas Johnson's poem "The Heart of a Woman":

> The heart of a woman goes forth with the dawn,
> As a lovebird, softwinging, so restlessly on,
> Afar o'er life's turrets and vales does it roam
> In the wake of those echoes the heart calls home.
>
> The heart of a woman falls back with the night
> And enters some alien cage in its plight,
> And tries to forget it has dreamed of the stars,
> While it breaks, breaks, breaks on the sheltering bars.

16   And it is against such sorrow, and it is against such suicide, and it is against such deliberated strangulation of the possible lives of women, of my sisters, and of powerless peoples—men and children—everywhere, that I work and live, now, as a feminist trusting that I will learn to love myself well enough to love you (whoever you are), well enough so that you will love me well enough so that we will know exactly where is the love: that it is here, between us, and growing stronger and growing stronger.

QUESTIONS

Experience

· What is it like to read this speech made into an essay? What do you imagine it would be like to hear June Jordan read it or speak it aloud? Why? How might the experience of hearing it delivered as a speech differ from reading the printed text?

Interpretation

· What is Jordan's central idea? How does she use her central idea or theme to communicate not merely her point but a feeling, as well?

· Why does she put her title in the form of a question? And what is the answer to that question?

Evaluation

· Jordan speaks as a black woman and as a feminist. To what extent do these dual aspects of her identity converge? To what extent do they diverge?

· Where does Jordan emphasize the values of race, and where does she stress aspects of women's lives?

WRITING

Exploring

· Write a letter to Jordan in which you react to what she says. You can ask questions, offer advice, reveal your agreement or disagreement with things she says, or say anything else that's on your mind.

Interpreting

· Analyze how Jordan uses repetition and questions to convey feeling, engage her audience, and express her central idea.

Evaluating

· Explain whether or not you think Jordan communicates with her audience effectively. You can choose to focus your discussion on her piece as writing or as speech. Provide reasons, and cite Jordan's text to support your view.

CORNEL WEST
(b. 1953)

Race Matters

Cornel West grew up in Tulsa, Oklahoma. He graduated from Harvard and Princeton Universities and taught at Union Theological Seminary and the Yale University Divinity School. He has also taught at Harvard and the University of Paris, and he is presently director of the Afro-American Studies Department at Princeton. His many books include Breaking Bread: Insurgent Black Intellectual Life *(1991) and* Race Matters *(1993), from which the following selection has been taken.*

West explores the roots of the race problem in the United States. One of his essay's distinctive features is the way West attempts less to argue a point than to bring disparate groups together to begin solving a hitherto intractable problem. He uses the rhetorical strategy of building common ground with his audience. Rather than insisting upon a particular solution to the problems he discusses, West urges his readers to share his concern and to join him in beginning the task of devising workable solutions.

> Since the beginning of the nation, white Americans have suffered from a deep inner uncertainty as to who they really are. One of the ways that has been used to simplify the answer has been to seize upon the presence of black Americans and use them as a marker, a symbol of limits, a metaphor for the "outsider." Many whites could look at the social position of blacks and feel that color formed an easy and reliable gauge for determining to what extent one was or was not American. Perhaps that is why one of the first epithets that many European immigrants learned when they got off the boat was the term "nigger"—it made them feel instantly American. But this is tricky magic. Despite his racial difference and social status, something indisputably American about Negroes not only raised doubts about the white man's value system but aroused the troubling suspicion that whatever else the true American is, he is also somehow black.
>
> —RALPH ELLISON, "What America Would Be Like without Blacks" (1970)

What happened in Los Angeles in April of 1992 was neither a race riot nor a class rebellion. Rather, this monumental upheaval was a multiracial, trans-class, and largely male display of justified social rage. For all its ugly, xenophobic resentment, its air of adolescent carnival, and its downright barbaric behavior, it signified the sense of powerlessness in American society. Glib attempts to reduce its meaning to the pathologies of the black underclass, the criminal actions of hoodlums, or the political revolt of the oppressed urban masses miss the mark. Of those arrested, only 36 percent were black, more than a third had full-time jobs, and most claimed to shun political affiliation. What we witnessed in Los Angeles was the consequence of a lethal linkage of economic decline, cultural decay, and political lethargy in American life. Race was the visible catalyst, not the underlying cause.

2   The meaning of the earthshaking events in Los Angeles is difficult to grasp because most of us remain trapped in the narrow framework of the dominant liberal and conservative views of race in America, which with its worn-out vocabulary leaves us intellectually debilitated, morally disempowered, and personally depressed. The astonishing disappearance of the event from public dialogue is testimony to just how painful and distressing a serious engagement with race is. Our truncated public discussions of race suppress the best of who and what we are as a people because they fail to confront the complexity of the issue in a candid and critical manner. The predictable pitting of liberals against conservatives, Great Society Democrats against self-help Republicans, reinforces intellectual parochialism and political paralysis.

3   The liberal notion that more government programs can solve racial problems is simplistic—precisely because it focuses *solely* on the economic dimension. And the conservative idea that what is needed is a change in the moral behavior of poor black urban dwellers (especially poor black men, who, they say, should stay married, support their children, and stop committing so much crime) highlights immoral actions while ignoring public responsibility for the immoral circumstances that haunt our fellow citizens.

4   The common denominator of these views of race is that each still sees black people as a "problem people," in the words of Dorothy I. Height, president of the National Council of Negro Women, rather than as fellow American citizens with problems. Her words echo the poignant "unasked question" of W. E. B. Du Bois, who, in *The Souls of Black Folk* (1903), wrote:

> They approach me in a half-hesitant sort of way, eye me curiously or compassionately, and then instead of saying directly, How does it feel to be a problem? they say, I know an excellent colored man in my town. . . . Do not these Southern outrages make your blood boil? At these I smile, or am interested, or reduce the boiling to a simmer, as the occasion may require. To the real question, How does it feel to be a problem? I answer seldom a word.

Nearly a century later, we confine discussions about race in America to the "problems" black people pose for whites rather than consider what this way of viewing black people reveals about us as a nation.

5   This paralyzing framework encourages liberals to relieve their guilty consciences by supporting public funds directed at "the problems"; but at the same time, reluctant to exercise principled criticism of black people, liberals deny them the freedom to err. Similarly, conservatives blame the "problems" on black people themselves—and thereby render black social misery invisible or unworthy of public attention.

6   Hence, for liberals, black people are to be "included" and "integrated" into "our" society and culture, while for conservatives they are to be "well behaved" and "worthy of acceptance" by "our" way of life. Both fail to see that the presence and predicaments of black people are neither additions to nor defections from American life, but rather *constitutive elements of that life.*

7   To engage in a serious discussion of race in America, we must begin not with the problems of black people but with the flaws of American society—flaws rooted

in historic inequalities and longstanding cultural stereotypes. How we set up the terms for discussing racial issues shapes our perception and response to these issues. As long as black people are viewed as a "them," the burden falls on blacks to do all the "cultural" and "moral" work necessary for healthy race relations. The implication is that only certain Americans can define what it means to be American—and the rest must simply "fit in."

8   The emergence of strong black-nationalist sentiments among blacks, especially among young people, is a revolt against this sense of having to "fit in." The variety of black-nationalist ideologies, from the moderate views of Supreme Court Justice Clarence Thomas in his youth to those of Louis Farrakhan today, rest upon a fundamental truth: White America has been historically weak-willed in ensuring racial justice and has continued to resist fully accepting the humanity of blacks. As long as double standards and differential treatment abound—as long as the rap performer Ice-T is harshly condemned while former Los Angeles Police Chief Daryl F. Gates's antiblack comments are received in polite silence, as long as Dr. Leonard Jeffries's anti-Semitic statements are met with vitriolic outrage while presidential candidate Patrick J. Buchanan's anti-Semitism receives a genteel response—black nationalisms will thrive.

9   Afrocentrism, a contemporary species of black nationalism, is a gallant yet misguided attempt to define an African identity in a white society perceived to be hostile. It is gallant because it puts black doings and sufferings, not white anxieties and fears, at the center of discussion. It is misguided because—out of fear of cultural hybridization and through silence on the issue of class, retrograde views on black women, gay men, and lesbians, and a reluctance to link race to the common good—it reinforces the narrow discussions about race.

10   To establish a new framework, we need to begin with a frank acknowledgment of the basic humanness and Americanness of each of us. And we must acknowledge that as a people—*E Pluribus Unum*—we are on a slippery slope toward economic strife, social turmoil, and cultural chaos. If we go down, we go down together. The Los Angeles upheaval forced us to see not only that we are not connected in ways we would like to be but also, in a more profound sense, that this failure to connect binds us even more tightly together. The paradox of race in America is that our common destiny is more pronounced and imperiled precisely when our divisions are deeper. The Civil War and its legacy speak loudly here. And our divisions are growing deeper. Today, eighty-six percent of white suburban Americans live in neighborhoods that are less than one percent black, meaning that the prospects for the country depend largely on how its cities fare in the hands of a suburban electorate. There is no escape from our interracial interdependence, yet enforced racial hierarchy dooms us as a nation to collective paranoia and hysteria—the unmaking of any democratic order.

11   The verdict in the Rodney King case which sparked the incidents in Los Angeles was perceived to be wrong by the vast majority of Americans. But whites have often failed to acknowledge the widespread mistreatment of black people, especially black men, by law enforcement agencies, which helped ignite the spark. The verdict was merely the occasion for deep-seated rage to come to the surface. This rage is fed by the "silent" depression ravaging the country—in which real weekly

wages of all American workers since 1973 have declined nearly twenty percent, while at the same time wealth has been upwardly distributed.

12   The exodus of stable industrial jobs from urban centers to cheaper labor markets here and abroad, housing policies that have created "chocolate cities and vanilla suburbs" (to use the popular musical artist George Clinton's memorable phrase), white fear of black crime, and the urban influx of poor Spanish-speaking and Asian immigrants—all have helped erode the tax base of American cities just as the federal government has cut its supports and programs. The result is unemployment, hunger, homelessness, and sickness for millions.

13   And a pervasive spiritual impoverishment grows. The collapse of meaning in life—the eclipse of hope and absence of love of self and others, the breakdown of family and neighborhood bonds—leads to the social deracination and cultural denudement of urban dwellers, especially children. We have created rootless, dangling people with little link to the supportive networks—family, friends, school—that sustain some sense of purpose in life. We have witnessed the collapse of the spiritual communities that in the past helped Americans face despair, disease, and death and that transmit through the generations dignity and decency, excellence and elegance.

14   The result is lives of what we might call "random nows," of fortuitous and fleeting moments preoccupied with "getting over"—with acquiring pleasure, property, and power by any means necessary. (This is not what Malcolm X meant by this famous phrase.) Post-modern culture is more and more a market culture dominated by gangster mentalities and self-destructive wantonness. This culture engulfs all of us—yet its impact on the disadvantaged is devastating, resulting in extreme violence in everyday life. Sexual violence against women and homicidal assaults by young black men on one another are only the most obvious signs of this empty quest for pleasure, property, and power.

15   Last, this rage is fueled by a political atmosphere in which images, not ideas, dominate, where politicians spend more time raising money than debating issues. The functions of parties have been displaced by public polls, and politicians behave less as thermostats that determine the climate of opinion than as thermometers registering the public mood. American politics has been rocked by an unleashing of greed among opportunistic public officials—who have followed the lead of their counterparts in the private sphere, where, as of 1989, one percent of the population owned thirty-seven percent of the wealth and ten percent of the population owned eighty-six percent of the wealth—leading to a profound cynicism and pessimism among the citizenry.

16   And given the way in which the Republican Party since 1968 has appealed to popular xenophobic images—playing the black, female, and homophobic cards to realign the electorate along race, sex, and sexual-orientation lines—it is no surprise that the notion that we are all part of one garment of destiny is discredited. Appeals to special interests rather than to public interests reinforce this polarization. The Los Angeles upheaval was an expression of utter fragmentation by a powerless citizenry that includes not just the poor but all of us.

17   What is to be done? How do we capture a new spirit and vision to meet the challenges of the post-industrial city, post-modern culture, and post-party politics?

18   First, we must admit that the most valuable sources for help, hope, and power consist of ourselves and our common history. As in the ages of Lincoln, Roosevelt, and King, we must look to new frameworks and languages to understand our multilayered crisis and overcome our deep malaise.

19   Second, we must focus our attention on the public square—the common good that undergirds our national and global destinies. The vitality of any public square ultimately depends on how much we *care* about the quality of our lives together. The neglect of our public infrastructure, for example—our water and sewage systems, bridges, tunnels, highways, subways, and streets—reflects not only our myopic economic policies, which impede productivity, but also the low priority we place on our common life.

20   The tragic plight of our children clearly reveals our deep disregard for public well-being. About one out of every five children in this country lives in poverty, including one out of every two black children and two out of every five Hispanic children. Most of our children—neglected by overburdened parents and bombarded by the market values of profit-hungry corporations—are ill-equipped to live lives of spiritual and cultural quality. Faced with these facts, how do we expect ever to constitute a vibrant society?

21   One essential step is some form of large-scale public intervention to ensure access to basic social goods—housing, food, health care, education, child care, and jobs. We must invigorate the common good with a mixture of government, business, and labor that does not follow any existing blueprint. After a period in which the private sphere has been sacralized and the public square gutted, the temptation is to make a fetish of the public square. We need to resist such dogmatic swings.

22   Last, the major challenge is to meet the need to generate new leadership. The paucity of courageous leaders—so apparent in the response to the events in Los Angeles—requires that we look beyond the same elites and voices that recycle the older frameworks. We need leaders—neither saints nor sparkling television personalities—who can situate themselves within a larger historical narrative of this country and our world, who can grasp the complex dynamics of our peoplehood and imagine a future grounded in the best of our past, yet who are attuned to the frightening obstacles that now perplex us. Our ideals of freedom, democracy, and equality must be invoked to invigorate all of us, especially the landless, propertyless, and luckless. Only a visionary leadership that can motivate "the better angels of our nature," as Lincoln said, and activate possibilities for a freer, more efficient, and stable America—only that leadership deserves cultivation and support.

23   This new leadership must be grounded in grass-roots organizing that highlights democratic accountability. Whoever *our* leaders will be as we approach the twenty-first century, their challenge will be to help Americans determine whether a genuine multiracial democracy can be created and sustained in an era of global economy and a moment of xenophobic frenzy.

24   Let us hope and pray that the vast intelligence, imagination, humor, and courage of Americans will not fail us. Either we learn a new language of empathy and compassion, or the fire this time will consume us all.

QUESTIONS

Experience

· West begins by referring to the Los Angeles riots of April 1992. How did you respond to seeing those riots in the media? How did others you know speak about them?

Interpretation

· What do you think is West's central point? How is that point related to his purpose? Does his argument help you understand what he calls the "paradox of race in America"? Why, or why not?

Evaluation

· What social and cultural values animate West's argument? What does he think is required for the issue of racial discord to be resolved? What do you think of the suggestions he makes for improving relations between the races?

WRITING

Exploring

· Write an essay in which you explore your own thoughts and feelings about race in America. You may choose to tell a story (or more than one story). You may prefer to spin your thoughts around references to events such as the Los Angeles riots, civil rights marches or demonstrations, or other public happenings.

Interpreting

· Analyze and interpret West's piece by dividing it into sections and explaining both what he argues and how he supports his claims in each of those sections. You may wish to begin by identifying the introduction, body, and conclusion of West's essay. Divide the body further into smaller sections, explaining the point and purpose of each of these subsections.

Evaluating

· Discuss the political or cultural values that lie behind the approaches of different groups to the race problem in America. Consider what West says about liberals and conservatives and why he finds their approaches inadequate.

N. SCOTT MOMADAY
(b. 1934)

from *The Way to Rainy Mountain*

N. Scott Momaday was born in Oklahoma in 1934 and educated at New Mexico University and at Stanford, where he earned a Ph.D. For the past decade and a half he has taught at the University of Arizona. Momaday won the 1969 Pulitzer Prize for his novel House Made of Dawn. *He is also the author of a children's book,* Owl in the Cedar Tree; *poetry; and an autobiographical memoir,* The Way to Rainy Mountain. *More recent work includes* The Ancient Child *(1989) and* In the Presence of the Sun: Stories and Poems *(1991).*

In the following passage from Rainy Mountain *Momaday provides a sense of what has been lost from his grandmother's Kiowa heritage. One of the most striking moments in the piece occurs during Momaday's paragraph-long description of his grandmother. His carefully selected details, especially those describing her singing, make for a memorable portrait. The sentences in that passage are long and loaded with specific details, as Momaday brings the vision of his grandmother's memory vividly before us.*

1   A single knoll rises out of the plain in Oklahoma, north and west of the Wichita range. For my people, the Kiowas, it is an old landmark, and they gave it the name Rainy Mountain. The hardest weather in the world is there. Winter brings blizzards, hot tornadic winds arise in the spring, and in summer the prairie is an anvil's edge. The grass turns brittle and brown, and it cracks beneath your feet. There are green belts along the rivers and creeks, linear groves of hickory and pecan, willow and witch hazel. At a distance in July or August the steaming foliage seems almost to writhe in fire. Great green and yellow grasshoppers are everywhere in the tall grass, popping up like corn to sting the flesh, and tortoises crawl about on the red earth, going nowhere in the plenty of time. Loneliness is an aspect of the land. All things in the plain are isolate; there is no confusion of objects in the eye, but *one* hill or *one* tree or *one* man. To look upon that landscape in the early morning, with the sun at your back, is to lose the sense of proportion. Your imagination comes to life, and this, you think, is where Creation was begun.

2   I returned to Rainy Mountain in July. My grandmother had died in the spring, and I wanted to be at her grave. She had lived to be very old and at last infirm. Her only living daughter was with her when she died, and I was told that in death her face was that of a child.

3   I like to think of her as a child. When she was born, the Kiowas were living the last great moment of their history. For more than a hundred years they had controlled the open range from the Smoky Hill River to the Red, from the headwaters

of the Canadian to the fork of the Arkansas and Cimarron. In alliance with the Comanches, they had ruled the whole of the Southern Plains. War was their sacred business, and they were the finest horsemen the world has ever known. But warfare for the Kiowas was preeminently a matter of disposition rather than of survival, and they never understood the grim, unrelenting advance of the U.S. Cavalry. When at last, divided and ill provisioned, they were driven onto the Staked Plains in the cold of autumn, they fell into panic. In Palo Duro Canyon they abandoned their crucial stores to pillage and had nothing then but their lives. In order to save themselves, they surrendered to the soldiers at Fort Sill and were imprisoned in the old stone corral that now stands as a military museum. My grandmother was spared the humiliation of those high gray walls by eight or ten years, but she must have known from birth the affliction of defeat, the dark brooding of old warriors.

4   Her name was Aho, and she belonged to the last culture to evolve in North America. Her forebears came down from the high country in western Montana nearly three centuries ago. They were a mountain people, a mysterious tribe of hunters whose language has never been classified in any major group. In the late seventeenth century they began a long migration to the south and east. It was a journey toward the dawn, and it led to a golden age. Along the way the Kiowas were befriended by the Crows, who gave them the culture and religion of the Plains. They acquired horses, and their ancient nomadic spirit was suddenly free of the ground. They acquired Tai-me, the sacred sun-dance doll, from that moment the object and symbol of their worship, and so shared in the divinity of the sun. Not least, they acquired the sense of destiny, therefore courage and pride. When they entered upon the Southern Plains they had been transformed. No longer were they slaves to the simple necessity of survival; they were a lordly and dangerous society of fighters and thieves, hunters and priests of the sun. According to their origin myth, they entered the world through a hollow log. From one point of view, their migration was the fruit of an old prophecy, for indeed they emerged from a sunless world.

5   Though my grandmother lived out her long life in the shadow of Rainy Mountain, the immense landscape of the continental interior lay like memory in her blood. She could tell of the Crows, whom she had never seen, and of the Black Hills, where she had never been. I wanted to see in reality what she had seen more perfectly in the mind's eye, and drove fifteen hundred miles to begin my pilgrimage.

6   A dark mist lay over the Black Hills, and the land was like iron. At the top of a ridge I caught sight of Devil's Tower upthrust against the gray sky as if in the birth of time the core of the earth had broken through its crust and the motion of the world was begun. There are things in nature that engender an awful quiet in the heart of man; Devil's Tower is one of them. Two centuries ago, because of their need to explain it, the Kiowas made a legend at the base of the rock. My grandmother said:

7   "Eight children were there at play, seven sisters and their brother. Suddenly the boy was struck dumb; he trembled and began to run upon his hands and feet. His fingers became claws, and his body was covered with fur. There was a bear

where the boy had been. The sisters were terrified; they ran, and the bear after them. They came to the stump of a great tree, and the tree spoke to them. It bade them climb upon it, and as they did so, it began to rise into the air. The bear came to kill them, but they were just beyond its reach. It reared against the tree and scored the bark all around with its claws. The seven sisters were borne into the sky, and they became the stars of the Big Dipper." From that moment, and so long as the legend lives, the Kiowas have kinsmen in the night sky. Whatever they were in the mountains, they could be no more. However tenuous their well-being, however much they had suffered and would suffer again, they had found a way out of the wilderness.

8   My grandmother had a reverence for the sun, a holy regard that now is all but gone out of mankind. There was a wariness in her, and an ancient awe. She was a Christian in her later years, but she had come a long way about, and she never forgot her birthright. As a child she had been to the sun dances; she had taken part in that annual rite, and by it she had learned the restoration of her people in the presence of Tai-me. She was about seven when the last Kiowa sun dance was held in 1887 on the Washita River above Rainy Mountain Creek. The buffalo were gone. In order to consummate the ancient sacrifice—to impale the head of a buffalo bull upon the Tai-me tree—a delegation of old men journeyed into Texas, there to beg and barter for an animal from the Goodnight herd. She was ten when the Kiowas came together for the last time as a living sun-dance culture. They could find no buffalo; they had to hang an old hide from the sacred tree. Before the dance could begin, a company of soldiers rode out from Fort Sill under orders to disperse the tribe. Forbidden without cause the essential act of their faith, having seen the wild herds slaughtered and left to rot upon the ground, the Kiowas backed away forever from the tree. That was July 20, 1890, at the great bend of the Washita. My grandmother was there. Without bitterness, and for as long as she lived, she bore a vision of deicide.

9   Now that I can have her only in memory, I see my grandmother in the several postures that were peculiar to her: standing at the wood stove on a winter morning and turning meat in a great iron skillet; sitting at the south window, bent above her beadwork, and afterwards when her vision failed, looking down for a long time into the fold of her hands; going out upon a cane, very slowly as she did when the weight of age came upon her; praying. I remember her most often at prayer. She made long, rambling prayers out of suffering and hope, having seen many things. I was never sure that I had the right to hear, so exclusive were they of all mere custom and company. The last time I saw her she prayed standing by the side of her bed at night, naked to the waist, the light of a kerosene lamp moving upon her dark skin. Her long black hair, always drawn and braided in the day, lay upon her shoulders and against her breasts like a shawl. I do not speak Kiowa, and I never understood her prayers, but there was something inherently sad in the sound, some merest hesitation upon the syllables of sorrow. She began in a high and descending pitch, exhausting her breath to silence; then again and again—and always the same intensity of effort, of something that is, and is not, like urgency in the human voice. Transported so in the dancing light among the shadows of her room, she seemed beyond the reach of time. But that was illusion; I think I knew then that I should not see her again.

10   Houses are like sentinels in the plain, old keepers of the weather watch. There, in a very little while, wood takes on the appearance of great age. All colors wear soon away in the wind and rain, and then the wood is burned gray and the grain appears and the nails turn red with rust. The window panes are black and opaque; you imagine there is nothing within, and indeed there are many ghosts, bones given up to the land. They stand here and there against the sky, and you approach them for a longer time than you expect. They belong in the distance; it is their domain.

11   Once there was a lot of sound in my grandmother's house, a lot of coming and going, feasting and talk. The summers there were full of excitement and reunion. The Kiowas are a summer people; they abide the cold and keep to them-selves, but when the season turns and the land becomes warm and vital they can-not hold still; an old love of going returns upon them. The aged visitors who came to my grandmother's house when I was a child were made of lean and leather, and they bore themselves upright. They wore great black hats and bright ample shirts that shook in the wind. They rubbed fat upon their hair and wound their braids with strips of colored cloth. Some of them painted their faces and carried the scars of old and cherished enmities. They were an old council of warlords, come to remind and be reminded of who they were. Their wives and daughters served them well. The women might indulge themselves; gossip was at once the mark and compensation of their servitude. They made loud and elaborate talk among themselves, full of jest and gesture, fright and false alarm. They went abroad in fringed and flowered shawls, bright beadwork and German silver. They were at home in the kitchen, and they prepared meals that were banquets.

12   There were frequent prayer meetings, and nocturnal feasts. When I was a child I played with my cousins outside, where the lamplight fell upon the ground and the singing of the old people rose up around us and carried away into the dark-ness. There were a lot of good things to eat, a lot of laughter and surprise. And afterwards, when the quiet returned, I lay down with my grandmother and could hear the frogs away by the river and feel the motion of the air.

13 Now there is a funereal silence in the rooms, the endless wake of some final word. The walls have closed in upon my grandmother's house. When I returned to it in mourning, I saw for the first time in my life how small it was. It was late at night, and there was a white moon, nearly full. I sat for a long time on the stone steps by the kitchen door. From there I could see out across the land; I could see the long row of trees by the creek, the low light upon the rolling plains, and the stars of the Big Dipper. Once I looked at the moon and caught sight of a strange thing. A cricket had perched upon the handrail, only a few inches away. My line of vision was such that the creature filled the moon like a fossil. It had gone there, I thought, to live and die, for there, of all places, was its small definition made whole and eternal. A warm wind rose up and purled like the longing within me.

14   The next morning, I awoke at dawn and went out on the dirt road to Rainy Mountain. It was already hot, and the grasshoppers began to fill the air. Still, it was early in the morning, and birds sang out of the shadows. The long yellow grass on the mountain shone in the bright light, and a scissortail hied above the land. There, where it ought to be, at the end of a long and legendary way, was my

grandmother's grave. She had at last succeeded to that holy ground. Here and there on the dark stones were ancestral names. Looking back once, I saw the mountain and came away.

QUESTIONS

Experience

· What feelings does Momaday induce in you as you read about his return to his ancestral home? As you read about the last, aborted Kiowa sun dance ceremony?

· What impression of his grandmother and of her people do you come away with when you finish reading Momaday's piece?

Interpretation

· How does Momaday convey his sense of the value of his heritage? Why does he mention the history of the Kiowas? Why does he describe the land so carefully?

Evaluation

· What especially does Momaday value about his grandmother and the vanishing culture she represents? What specific attitudes, beliefs, and behaviors does Momaday respectfully allude to?

WRITING

Exploring

· Write a short memoir about a place or person from your past. Try to describe the person or place (or both) in such a way as to convey the beliefs, attitudes, and values the person or place reflects or embodies.

Interpreting

· Choose one passage from Momaday's piece that you find especially effective. Examine its language carefully, and explain why the passage is important and what it conveys.

Evaluating

· Discuss the cluster of beliefs, attitudes, and practices that reflect the cultural values of the Kiowas as Momaday describes them here. You may wish to comment on those values by relating them to your own values or to those of contemporary urban, suburban, or country life.

RICHARD RODRIGUEZ
(b. 1944)

Complexion

Richard Rodriguez was born in San Francisco, the son of Mexican American immigrants. He was educated in a Catholic grammar school before earning a B.A. from Stanford University and an M.A. from Columbia University. He has been awarded a Fulbright fellowship and has attended the Warburg Institute in London. Rodriguez has contributed articles to many periodicals, including Harper's, the American Scholar, *the* New York Times, *and the* Los Angeles Times, *among others. His most recent book is* Days of Obligation: An Argument with My Mexican Father *(1992).*

The story of his assimilation into the American social and educational scene is described in an earlier work, Hunger of Memory *(1987), from which the following selection has been excerpted. Of particular interest to many readers is the way Rodriguez explores tensions resulting from the conflicting values of the two worlds he inhabits. Noteworthy about "Complexion" is Rodriguez's use of simile and metaphor and his inclusion of Spanish words. Especially striking is his use of short sentences and sentence fragments for emphasis, as exemplified in the beginning and ending of the piece.*

1 Complexion. My first conscious experience of sexual excitement concerns my complexion. One summer weekend, when I was around seven years old, I was at a public swimming pool with the whole family. I remember sitting on the damp pavement next to the pool and seeing my mother, in the spectators' bleachers, holding my younger sister on her lap. My mother, I noticed, was watching my father as he stood on a diving board, waving to her. I watched her wave back. Then saw her radiant, bashful, astonishing smile. In that second I sensed that my mother and father had a relationship I knew nothing about. A nervous excitement encircled my stomach as I saw my mother's eyes follow my father's figure curving into the water. A second or two later, he emerged. I heard him call out. Smiling, his voice sounded, buoyant, calling me to swim to him. But turning to see him, I caught my mother's eye. I heard her shout over to me. In Spanish she called through the crowd: 'Put a towel on over your shoulders.' In public, she didn't want to say why. I knew.

2 That incident anticipates the shame and sexual inferiority I was to feel in later years because of my dark complexion. I was to grow up an ugly child. Or one who thought himself ugly. *(Feo.)* One night when I was eleven or twelve years old, I locked myself in the bathroom and carefully regarded my reflection in the mirror over the sink. Without any pleasure I studied my skin. I turned on the faucet. (In my mind I heard the swirling voices of aunts, and even my mother's voice, whispering, whispering incessantly about lemon juice solutions and dark, *feo* children.) With a bar of soap, I fashioned a thick ball of lather. I began soaping my arms. I took my father's straight razor out of the medicine cabinet. Slowly,

with steady deliberateness, I put the blade against my flesh, pressed it as close as I could without cutting, and moved it up and down across my skin to see if I could get out, somehow lessen, the dark. All I succeeded in doing, however, was in shaving my arms bare of their hair. For as I noted with disappointment, the dark would not come out. It remained. Trapped. Deep in the cells of my skin.

3   Throughout adolescence, I felt myself mysteriously marked. Nothing else about my appearance would concern me so much as the fact that my complexion was dark. My mother would say how sorry she was that there was not money enough to get braces to straighten my teeth. But I never bothered about my teeth. In three-way mirrors at department stores, I'd see my profile dramatically defined by a long nose, but it was really only the color of my skin that caught my attention.

4   I wasn't afraid that I would become a menial laborer because of my skin. Nor did my complexion make me feel especially vulnerable to racial abuse. (I didn't really consider my dark skin to be a racial characteristic. I would have been only too happy to look as Mexican as my light-skinned older brother.) Simply, I judged myself ugly. And, since the women in my family had been the ones who discussed it in such worried tones, I felt my dark skin made me unattractive to women.

5   Thirteen years old. Fourteen. In a grammar school art class, when the assignment was to draw a self-portrait, I tried and tried but could not bring myself to shade in the face on the paper to anything like my actual tone. With disgust then I would come face to face with myself in mirrors. With disappointment I located myself in class photographs—my dark face undefined by the camera which had clearly described the white faces of classmates. Or I'd see my dark wrist against my long-sleeved white shirt.

6   I grew divorced from my body. Insecure, overweight, listless. On hot summer days when my rubber-soled shoes soaked up the heat from the sidewalk, I kept my head down. Or walked in the shade. My mother didn't need anymore to tell me to watch out for the sun. I denied myself a sensational life. The normal, extraordinary, animal excitement of feeling my body alive—riding shirtless on a bicycle in the warm wind created by furious self-propelled motion—the sensations that first had excited in me a sense of my maleness, I denied. I was too ashamed of my body. I wanted to forget that I had a body because I had a brown body. I was grateful that none of my classmates ever mentioned the fact.

7   I continued to see the *braceros,* those men I resembled in one way and, in another way, didn't resemble at all. On the watery horizon of a Valley afternoon, I'd see them. And though I feared looking like them, it was with silent envy that I regarded them still. I envied them their physical lives, their freedom to violate the taboo of the sun. Closer to home I would notice the shirtless construction workers, the roofers, the sweating men tarring the street in front of the house. And I'd see the Mexican gardeners. I was unwilling to admit the attraction of their lives. I tried to deny it by looking away. But what was denied became strongly desired.

8   In high school physical education classes, I withdrew, in the regular company of five or six classmates, to a distant corner of a football field where we smoked and talked. Our company was composed of bodies too short or too tall, all graceless and all—except mine—pale. Our conversation was usually witty. (In fact we

were intelligent.) If we referred to the athletic contests around us, it was with sarcasm. With savage scorn I'd refer to the 'animals' playing football or baseball. It would have been important for me to have joined them. Or for me to have taken off my shirt, to have let the sun burn dark on my skin, and to have run barefoot on the warm wet grass. It would have been very important. Too important. It would have been too telling a gesture—to admit the desire for sensation, the body, my body.

9   Fifteen, sixteen. I was a teenager shy in the presence of girls. Never dated. Barely could talk to a girl without stammering. In high school I went to several dances, but I never managed to ask a girl to dance. So I stopped going. I cannot remember high school years now with the parade of typical images: bright drive-ins or gliding blue shadows of a Junior Prom. At home most weekend nights, I would pass evenings reading. Like those hidden, precocious adolescents who have no real-life sexual experiences, I read a great deal of romantic fiction. 'You won't find it in your books,' my brother would playfully taunt me as he prepared to go to a party by freezing the crest of the wave in his hair with sticky pomade. Through my reading, however, I developed a fabulous and sophisticated sexual imagination. At seventeen, I may not have known how to engage a girl in small talk, but I had read *Lady Chatterley's Lover.*

10 It annoyed me to hear my father's teasing: that I would never know what 'real work' is; that my hands were so soft. I think I knew it was his way of admitting pleasure and pride in my academic success. But I didn't smile. My mother said she was glad her children were getting their educations and would not be pushed around like *los pobres.* I heard the remark ironically as a reminder of my separation from *los braceros.* At such times I suspected that education was making me effeminate. The odd thing, however, was that I did not judge my classmates so harshly. Nor did I consider my male teachers in high school effeminate. It was only myself I judged against some shadowy, mythical Mexican laborer—dark like me, yet very different.

11   Language was crucial. I knew that I had violated the ideal of the *macho* by becoming such a dedicated student of language and literature. *Machismo* was a word never exactly defined by the persons who used it. (It was best described in the 'proper' behavior of men.) Women at home, nevertheless, would repeat the old Mexican dictum that a man should be *feo, fuerte, y formal.* 'The three F's,' my mother called them, smiling slyly. *Feo* I took to mean not literally ugly so much as ruggedly handsome. (When my mother and her sisters spent a loud, laughing afternoon determining ideal male good looks, they finally settled on the actor Gilbert Roland, who was neither too pretty nor ugly but had looks 'like a man.') *Fuerte,* 'strong,' seemed to mean not physical strength as much as inner strength, character. A dependable man is *fuerte. Fuerte* for that reason was a characteristic subsumed by the last of the three qualities, and the one I most often considered— *formal.* To be *formal* is to be steady. A man of responsibility, a good provider. Someone *formal* is also constant. A person to be relied upon in adversity. A sober man, a man of high seriousness.

12   I learned a great deal about being *formal* just by listening to the way my father and other male relatives of his generation spoke. A man was not silent neces-

sarily. Nor was he limited in the tones he could sound. For example, he could tell a long, involved, humorous story and laugh at his own humor with high-pitched giggling. But a man was not talkative the way a woman could be. It was permitted a woman to be gossipy and chatty. (When one heard many voices in a room, it was usually women who were talking.) Men spoke much less rapidly. And often men spoke in monologues. (When one voice sounded in a crowded room, it was most often a man's voice one heard.) More important than any of this was the fact that a man never verbally revealed his emotions. Men did not speak about their unease in moments of crisis or danger. It was the woman who worried aloud when her husband got laid off from work. At times of illness or death in the family, a man was usually quiet, even silent. Women spoke up to voice prayers. In distress, women always sounded quick ejaculations to God or the Virgin; women prayed in clearly audible voices at a wake held in a funeral parlor. And on the subject of love, a woman was verbally expansive. She spoke of her yearning and delight. A married man, if he spoke publicly about love, usually did so with playful, mischievous irony. Younger, unmarried men more often were quiet. (The *macho* is a silent suitor. *Formal.*)

13   At home I was quiet, so perhaps I seemed *formal* to my relations and other Spanish-speaking visitors to the house. But outside the house—my God!—I talked. Particularly in class or alone with my teachers, I chattered. (Talking seemed to make teachers think I was bright.) I often was proud of my way with words. Though, on other occasions, for example, when I would hear my mother busily speaking to women, it would occur to me that my attachment to words made me like her. Her son. Not *formal* like my father. At such times I even suspected that my nostalgia for sounds—the noisy, intimate Spanish sounds of my past—was nothing more than effeminate yearning.

14   High school English teachers encouraged me to describe very personal feelings in words. Poems and short stories I wrote, expressing sorrow and loneliness, were awarded high grades. In my bedroom were books by poets and novelists—books that I loved—in which male writers published feelings the men in my family never revealed or acknowledged in words. And it seemed to me that there was something unmanly about my attachment to literature. Even today, when so much about the myth of the *macho* no longer concerns me, I cannot altogether evade such notions. Writing these pages, admitting my embarrassment or my guilt, admitting my sexual anxieties and my physical insecurity, I have not been able to forget that I am not being *formal.*

15   So be it.

QUESTIONS

Experience

· To what extent have you experienced the kinds of self-doubt, particularly doubts about your physical features, that Rodriguez describes about himself?

· How important is your "complexion" or some other of your physical features to you? Why?

Interpretation

· What does Rodriguez imply by his last sentence? What does he mean earlier when he writes that he suspected that education was making him "effeminate"? What standard was he comparing himself against?

· What does each of the Spanish words Rodriguez uses in this selection mean? What is the effect of his using Spanish words rather than English translations?

Evaluation

· What two sets of values came into conflict in Rodriguez's world as he grew up? How does he convey his sense of failure in not measuring up to (or in being different from) what were considered acceptable looks, interests, and behavior for a man of his world? What is your own view of the issue?

WRITING

Exploring

· Describe a time in your life when you felt out of synch with the cultural values of the world of your family or friends. Explain what caused your sense of difference, how you felt, and what you did to find your place in that world or to distance yourself from it.

Interpreting

· Select one paragraph you consider especially important in conveying either Rodriguez's feelings or an aspect of his main idea. Analyze the paragraph, explaining how Rodriguez uses facts, experience, example, and language to convey what he does.

Evaluating

· Discuss the conflicting cultural values Rodriguez identifies, especially as they impinge on his gender identity. Consider the extent to which Rodriguez is able to accommodate himself to his feeling of differentness and the extent to which he has moved beyond what concerned him so powerfully in his youth.

SHELBY STEELE
(b. 1946)

The New Sovereignty

Shelby Steele is a professor of English at San Jose State University. He is the author of The Content of Our Character, *which won the National Book Critics Circle Award for nonfiction in 1991. His essays have appeared in* Harper's, *the* American Scholar, *the* New Republic, *the* New York Times Magazine, *and many other publications.*

In "The New Sovereignty" he enters the debate about the validity and usefulness of group entitlements, or what has come to be better known as affirmative action. Steele's writing is characterized by a willingness to engage tough issues head on, by a clear and direct style, and by careful and logically developed argument. Especially noteworthy is his rhetorical stance, one that is both assertive and prepared for reasoned debate.

1   Toward the end of a talk I gave recently at a large midwestern university, I noticed a distinct tension in the audience. All respectful audiences are quiet, but I've come to understand that when there is disagreement with what's being said at the podium the silence can become pure enough to constitute a statement. Fidgeting and whispering cease, pencils stay still in notetakers' hands—you sense the quiet filling your pauses as a sign of disquiet, even resistance. A speaker can feel ganged-up on by such a silence.

2   I had gotten myself into this spot by challenging the orthodoxy of diversity that is now so common on university campuses—not the *notion* of diversity, which I wholly subscribe to, but the rigid means by which it is pursued. I had told the students and faculty members on hand that in the late 1960s, without much public debate but with many good intentions, America had embarked upon one of the most dramatic social experiments in its history. The federal government, radically and officially, began to alter and expand the concept of entitlement in America. Rights to justice and to government benefits were henceforth to be extended not simply to individuals but to racial, ethnic, and other groups. Moreover, the essential basis of all entitlement in America—the guarantees of the Constitution—had apparently been found wanting; there was to be redress and reparation of past grievances, and the Constitution had nothing to say about that.

3   I went on to explain that Martin Luther King and the early civil rights leaders had demanded only constitutional rights; they had been found wanting, too. By the late sixties, among a new set of black leaders, there had developed a presumption of collective entitlement (based on the redress of past grievances) that made blacks eligible for rights beyond those provided for in the Constitution, and thus beyond those afforded the nation's nonblack citizens. Thanks to the civil rights movement, a young black citizen as well as a young white citizen could not be turned away from a college because of the color of his or her skin; by the early seventies a young black citizen, poor or wealthy, now qualified for certain grants

and scholarships—might even be accepted for admission—simply *because* of the color of his or her skin. I made the point that this new and rather unexamined principle of collective entitlement had led America to pursue a democracy of groups as well as of individuals—that collective entitlement enfranchised groups just as the Constitution enfranchised individuals.

4   It was when I introduced a concept I call the New Sovereignty that my audience's silence became most audible. In America today, I said, sovereignty—that is, power to act autonomously—is bestowed upon any group that is able to construct itself around a perceived grievance. With the concept of collective entitlement now accepted not only at the federal level but casually at all levels of society, any aggrieved group—and, for that matter, any assemblage of citizens that might or might not have previously been thought of as such a group—could make its case, attract attention and funding, and build a constituency that, in turn, would increase attention and funding. Soon this organized group of aggrieved citizens would achieve sovereignty, functioning within our long-sovereign nation and negotiating with that nation for a separate, exclusive set of entitlements. And here I pointed to America's university campuses, where, in the name of their grievances, blacks, women, Hispanics, Asians, Native Americans, gays, and lesbians had hardened into sovereign constituencies that vied for the entitlements of sovereignty—separate "studies" departments for each group, "ethnic" theme dorms, preferential admissions and financial aid policies, a proportionate number of faculty of their own group, separate student lounges and campus centers, and so on. This push for equality among groups, I said, necessarily made for an inequality among individuals that prepared the ground for precisely the racial, gender, and ethnic divisiveness that, back in the sixties, we all said we wanted to move beyond.

5   At the reception that followed the talk I was approached by a tall, elegant woman who introduced herself as the chairperson of the women's studies department. Anger and the will to be polite were at war in her face so that her courteous smile at times became a leer. She wanted to "inform" me that she was proud of the fact that women's studies was a separate department at her university. I asked her what could be studied in this department that could not be studied in other departments. Take the case of, say, Virginia Woolf: in what way would a female academic teaching in a women's studies department have a different approach to Woolf's writing than a woman professor in the English department? Above her determined smile her eyes became fierce. "You must know as a black that they won't accept us"—meaning women, blacks, presumably others—"in the English department. It's an oppressive environment for women scholars. We're not taken seriously there." I asked her if that wasn't all the more reason to be there, to fight the good fight, and to work to have the contributions of women broaden the entire discipline of literary studies. She said I was naive. I said her strategy left the oppressiveness she talked about unchallenged. She said it was a waste of valuable energy to spend time fighting "old white males." I said that if women were oppressed, there was nothing to do *but* fight.

6   We each held tiny paper plates with celery sticks and little bricks of cheese, and I'm sure much body language was subdued by the tea party postures these plates imposed on us. But her last word was not actually a word. It was a look. She parodied an epiphany of disappointment in herself, as if she'd caught herself

in a bizarre foolishness. *Of course, this guy is the enemy. He is the very oppressiveness I'm talking about. How could I have missed it?* And so, suddenly comfortable in the understanding that I was hopeless, she let her smile become gracious. Grace was something she could afford now. An excuse was made, a hand extended, and then she was gone. Holding my little plate, I watched her disappear into the crowd.

7   Today there are more than five hundred separate women's studies departments or programs in American colleges and universities. There are nearly four hundred independent black studies departments or programs, and hundreds of Hispanic, Asian, and Native American programs. Given this degree of entrenchment, it is no wonder this woman found our little debate a waste of her time. She would have had urgent administrative tasks awaiting her attention—grant proposals to write, budget requests to work up, personnel matters to attend to. And suppose I had won the debate? Would she have rushed back to her office and begun to dismantle the women's studies department by doling out its courses and faculty to long-standing departments like English and history? Would she have given her secretary notice and relinquished her office equipment? I don't think so.

8   I do think I know how it all came to this—how what began as an attempt to address the very real grievances of women wound up creating newly sovereign fiefdoms like this women's studies department. First there was collective entitlement to redress the grievances, which in turn implied a sovereignty for the grievance group, since sovereignty is only the formalization of collective entitlement. Then, since sovereignty requires autonomy, there had to be a demand for separate and independent stature within the university (or some other institution of society). There would have to be a separate territory, with the trappings that certify sovereignty and are concrete recognition of the grievance identity—a building or suite of offices, a budget, faculty, staff, office supplies, letterhead, et cetera.

9   And so the justification for separate women's and ethnic studies programs has virtually nothing to do with strictly academic matters and everything to do with the kind of group-identity politics in which the principle of collective entitlement has resulted. My feeling is that there can be no full redress of the woeful neglect of women's intellectual contributions until those contributions are entirely integrated into the very departments that neglected them in the first place. The same is true for America's minorities. Only inclusion answers history's exclusion. But now the sovereignty of grievance-group identities has confused all this.

10   It was the sovereignty issue that squelched my talk with the women's studies chairperson. She came to see me as an enemy not because I denied that women writers had been neglected historically; I was the enemy because my questions challenged the territorial sovereignty of her department and of the larger grievance identity of women. It was not a matter of fairness—of justice—but of power. She would not put it that way, of course. For in order to rule over her sovereign fiefdom it remains important that she seem to represent the powerless, the aggrieved. It remains important, too, that my objection to the New Sovereignty can be interpreted by her as sexist. When I failed to concede sovereignty, I became an enemy of women.

11   In our age of the New Sovereignty the original grievances—those having to

do with fundamental questions such as basic rights—have in large measure been addressed, if not entirely redressed. But that is of little matter now. The sovereign fiefdoms are ends in themselves—providing career tracks and bases of power. This power tends to be used now mostly to defend and extend the fiefdom, often by exaggerating and exploiting secondary, amorphous, or largely symbolic complaints. In this way, America has increasingly become an uneasy federation of newly sovereign nations.

12   In *The True Believer,* Eric Hoffer wrote presciently of this phenomenon I have come to call the New Sovereignty: "When a mass movement begins to attract people who are interested in their individual careers, it is a sign that it has passed its vigorous stage; that it is no longer engaged in molding a new world but in possessing and preserving the present. It ceases then to be a movement and becomes an enterprise."

13   If it is true that great mass movements begin as spontaneous eruptions of long-smoldering discontent, it is also true that after significant reform is achieved they do not like to pass away or even modify their grievance posture. The redressing of the movement's grievances wins legitimacy for the movement. Reform, in this way, also means recognition for those who struggled for it. The movement's leaders are quoted in the papers, appear on TV, meet with elected officials, write books—they come to embody the movement. Over time, they and they alone speak for the aggrieved; and, of course, they continue to speak *of* the aggrieved, adding fresh grievances to the original complaint. It is their vocation now, and their means to status and power. The idealistic reformers thus become professional spokespersons for the seemingly permanently aggrieved. In the civil rights movement, suits and briefcases replaced the sharecropper's denim of the early years, and $500-a-plate fund-raisers for the National Association for the Advancement of Colored People replaced volunteers and picket signs. The raucous bra burning of late sixties feminism gave way to women's studies departments and direct-mail campaigns by the National Organization for Women.

14   This sort of evolution, however natural it may appear, is not without problems for the new grievance-group executive class. The winning of reform will have dissipated much of the explosive urgency that started the movement; yet the new institutionalized movement cannot justify its existence without this urgency. The problem becomes one of maintaining a reformist organization after considerable reforms have been won.

15   To keep alive the urgency needed to justify itself, the grievance organization will do three things. First, it will work to inspire a perpetual sense of grievance in its constituency so that grievance becomes the very centerpiece of the group itself. To be black, or a woman, or gay, is, in the eyes of the NAACP, NOW, or Act Up, to be essentially threatened, victimized, apart from the rest of America. Second, these organizations will up the ante on what constitutes a grievance by making support of sovereignty itself the new test of grievance. If the women's studies program has not been made autonomous, this constitutes a grievance. If the National Council of La Raza hasn't been consulted, Hispanics have been ignored. The third strategy of grievance organizations is to arrange their priorities in a way that will maximize their grievance profile. Often their agendas will be

established more for their grievance potential than for the actual betterment of the group. Those points at which there is resistance in the larger society to the group's entitlement demands will usually be made into top-priority issues, thereby emphasizing the status of victim and outsider necessary to sustain the sovereign organization.

16   Thus, at its 1989 convention, the NAACP put affirmative action at the very top of its agenda. Never mind the fact that studies conducted by both proponents and opponents of affirmative action indicate the practice has very little real impact on the employment and advancement of blacks. Never mind, too, that surveys show most black Americans do not consider racial preferences *their* priority. In its wisdom the NAACP thought (and continues to think) that the national mood against affirmative action programs is a bigger problem for black men and women than teen pregnancy, or the disintegrating black family, or black-on-black crime. Why? Because the very resistance affirmative action meets from the larger society makes it an issue of high grievance potential. Affirmative action can generate the urgency that justifies black sovereignty far more than issues like teen pregnancy or high dropout rates, which carry no load of collective entitlement and which the *entire* society sees as serious problems.

17   In the women's movement, too, the top-priority issues have been those with the highest grievance potential. I think so much effort and resources went into the now-failed Equal Rights Amendment because, in large part, it carried a tremendous load of collective entitlement (a constitutional amendment for a specific group rather than for all citizens) and because it faced great resistance from the larger society. It was a win-win venture for the women's movement. If it succeeded there would be a great bounty of collective entitlement; if it failed, as it did, the failure could be embraced as a grievance—an indication of America's continuing unwillingness to assure equality for women. *America does not want to allow us in!*—that is how the defeat of the ERA could be interpreted by NOW executives and by female English professors eager to run their own departments; the defeat of the ERA was a boon for the New Sovereignty.

18   I also believe this quest for sovereignty at least partially explains the leap of abortion rights to the very top of the feminist agenda on the heels of the ERA's failure. Abortion has always been an extremely divisive, complex, and emotionally charged issue. And for this reason it is also an issue of enormous grievance potential for the women's movement—assuming it can be framed solely in terms of female grievance. My own belief is that abortion is a valid and important issue for the women's movement to take up, and I completely support the pro-choice position the movement advocates. However, I think women's organizations like NOW have framed the issue in territorial terms in order to maximize its grievance potential. When they make women's control of their own bodies the very centerpiece of their argument for choice, they are making the fact of pregnancy the *exclusive* terrain of women, despite the obvious role of men in conception and despite the fact that the vast majority of married women deciding to have abortions reach their decisions with their husbands. Framed exclusively as a woman's right, abortion becomes not a societal issue or even a family issue but a grievance issue in the ongoing struggle of the women's movement. Can women's organizations continue to frame pro-choice as a grievance issue—a question of a right—and

expect to garner the votes in Congress or in the state legislatures, which is where the abortion question is headed?

19   I don't think this framing of the issue as a right is as much about abortion as it is about the sovereignty and permanency of women's organizations. The trick is exclusivity. If you can make the issue exclusively yours—within your territory of final authority—then all who do not capitulate are aggrieving you. And then, of course, you must rally and expand your organization to meet all this potential grievance.

20   But this is a pattern that ultimately puts grievance organizations out of touch with their presumed constituencies, who grow tired of the hyperbole. I think it partially explains why so many young women today resist the feminist label and why the membership rolls of the NAACP have fallen so sharply in recent years, particularly among the young. The high grievance profile is being seen for what it mostly is—a staying-in-business strategy.

21 How did America evolve its now rather formalized notion that groups of its citizens could be entitled collectively? I think it goes back to the most fundamental contradiction in American life. From the beginning America has been a pluralistic society, and one drawn to a radical form of democracy—emphasizing the freedom and equality of *individuals*—that could meld such diversity into a coherent nation. In this new nation no group would lord it over any other. But, of course, beneath this America of its ideals there was from the start a much meaner reality, one whose very existence mocked the notion of a nation made singular by the equality of its individuals. By limiting democracy to their own kind—white, male landowners—the Founding Fathers collectively entitled themselves and banished all others to the edges and underside of American life. There, individual entitlement was either curtailed or—in the case of slavery—extinguished.

22   The genius of the civil rights movement that changed the fabric of American life in the late 1950s and early 1960s was its profound understanding that the enemy of black Americans was not the ideal America but the unspoken principle of collective entitlement that had always put the lie to true democracy. This movement, which came to center stage from America's underside and margins, had as its single, overriding goal the eradication of white entitlement. And, correspondingly, it exhibited a belief in democratic principles at least as strong as that of the Founding Fathers, who themselves had emerged from the (less harsh) margins of English society. In this sense the civil rights movement reenacted the American Revolution, and its paramount leader, Martin Luther King, spoke as twentieth-century America's greatest democratic voice.

23   All of this was made clear to me for the umpteenth time by my father on a very cold Saturday afternoon in 1959. There was a national campaign under way to integrate the lunch counters at Woolworth stores, and my father, who was more a persuader than an intimidator, had made it a point of honor that I join him on the picket line, civil rights being nothing less than the religion of our household. By this time, age twelve or so, I was sick of it. I'd had enough of watching my parents heading off to still another meeting or march; I'd heard too many tedious discussions on everything from the philosophy of passive resistance to the symbolism of going to jail. Added to this, my own experience of picket lines

and peace marches had impressed upon me what so many people who've par-
taken of these activities know: that in themselves they can be crushingly boring—
around and around and around holding a sign, watching one's own feet fall, feeling the minutes like hours. All that Saturday morning I hid from my father and
tried to convince myself of what I longed for—that he would get so busy that if he
didn't forget the march he would at least forget me.

24   He forgot nothing. I did my time on the picket line, but not without building
up enough resentment to start a fight on the way home. What was so important
about integration? We had never even wanted to eat at Woolworth's. I told him
the truth, that he never took us to *any* restaurants anyway, claiming always that
they charged too much money for bad food. But he said calmly that he was proud
of me for marching and that he knew *I* knew food wasn't the point.

25   My father—forty years a truck driver, with the urges of an intellectual—went
on to use my little rebellion as the occasion for a discourse, in this case on the
concept of integration. Integration had little to do with merely rubbing shoulders
with white people, eating bad food beside them. It was about the right to go
absolutely anywhere white people could go being the test of freedom and equality. To be anywhere they could be and do anything they could do was the point.
Like it or not, white people defined the horizon of freedom in America, and if you
couldn't touch their shoulder you weren't free. For him integration was the *evidence* of freedom and equality.

26   My father was a product of America's margins, as were all the blacks in the
early civil rights movement, leaders and foot soldiers alike. For them integration
was a way of moving from the margins into the mainstream. Today there is considerable ambivalence about integration, but in that day it was nothing less than
democracy itself. Integration is also certainly about racial harmony, but it is more
fundamentally about the ultimate extension of democracy—beyond the racial entitlements that contradict it. The idea of racial integration is quite simply the most
democratic principle America has evolved, since all other such principles depend
on its reality and are diminished by its absence.

27   But the civil rights movement did not account for one thing: the tremendous
release of black anger that would follow its victories. The 1964 Civil Rights Act
and the 1965 Voting Rights Act were, on one level, admissions of guilt by American society that it had practiced white entitlement at the expense of all others.
When the oppressors admit their crimes, the oppressed can give full vent to their
long repressed rage because now there is a moral consensus between oppressor
and oppressed that a wrong was done. This consensus gave blacks the license to
release a rage that was three centuries deep, a rage that is still today everywhere
visible, a rage that—in the wake of the Rodney King verdict, a verdict a vast
majority of all Americans thought unfair—fueled the worst rioting in recent American history.

28   By the mid-sixties, the democratic goal of integration was no longer enough
to appease black anger. Suddenly for blacks there was a sense that far more was
owed, that a huge bill was due. And for many whites there was also the feeling
that some kind of repayment was truly in order. This was the moral logic that followed inevitably from the new consensus. But it led to an even simpler logic: if
blacks had been oppressed collectively, that oppression would now be redressed

by entitling them collectively. So here we were again, in the name of a thousand good intentions, falling away from the hard challenge of a democracy of individuals and embracing the principle of collective entitlement that had so corrupted the American ideal in the first place. Now this old sin would be applied in the name of uplift. And this made an easy sort of sense. If it was good enough for whites for three hundred years, why not let blacks have a little of it to get ahead? In the context of the sixties—black outrage and white guilt—a principle we had just decided was evil for whites was redefined as a social good for blacks. And once the formula was in place for blacks, it could be applied to other groups with similar grievances. By the 1970s more than 60 percent of the American population—not only blacks but Hispanics, women, Asians—would come under the collective entitlement of affirmative action.

29   In the early days of the civil rights movement, the concept of solidarity was essentially a moral one. That is, all people who believed in human freedom, fairness, and equality were asked to form a solid front against white entitlement. But after the collaboration of black rage and white guilt made collective entitlement a social remedy, the nature of solidarity changed. It was no longer the rallying of diverse peoples to breach an oppressive group entitlement. It was the very opposite: a rallying of people within a grievance group to pursue their own group entitlement. As early as the mid-sixties, whites were made unwelcome in the civil rights movement, just as, by the mid-seventies, men were no longer welcome in the women's movement. Eventually, collective entitlement *always* requires separatism. And the irony is obvious: those who once had been the victims of separatism, who had sacrificed so dearly to overcome their being at the margins, would later create an ethos of their own separatism. After the sixties, solidarity became essentially a separatist concept, an exclusionary principle. One no longer heard words like "integration" or "harmony"; one heard about "anger" and "power." Integration is anathema to grievance groups for precisely the same reason it was anathema to racist whites in the civil rights era: because it threatens their collective entitlement by insisting that no group be entitled over another. Power is where it's at today—power to set up the organization, attract the following, run the fiefdom.

30   But it must also be said that this could not have come to pass without the cooperation of the society at large and its institutions. Why did the government, the public and private institutions, the corporations and foundations, end up supporting principles that had the effect of turning causes into sovereign fiefdoms? I think the answer is that those in charge of America's institutions saw the institutionalization and bureaucratization of the protest movements as ultimately desirable, at least in the short term, and the funding of group entitlements as ultimately a less costly way to redress grievances. The leaders of the newly sovereign fiefdoms were backing off from earlier demands that America live up to its ideals. Gone was the moral indictment. Gone was the call for difficult, soulful transformation. The language of entitlements is essentially the old, comforting language of power politics, and in the halls of power it went down easily enough.

31   With regard to civil rights, the moral voice of Dr. King gave way to the demands and cajolings of poverty program moguls, class action lawyers, and

community organizers. The compromise that satisfied both political parties was to shift the focus from democracy, integration, and developmental uplift to collective entitlements. This satisfied the institutions because entitlements were cheaper in every way than real change. Better to set up black studies and women's studies departments than to have wrenching debates within existing departments. Better to fund these new institutions clamoring for money because who knows what kind of fuss they'll make if we turn down their proposals. Better to pass laws permitting Hispanic students to get preferred treatment in college admission—it costs less than improving kindergartens in East Los Angeles.

32   And this way to uplift satisfied the grievance-group "experts" because it laid the ground for their sovereignty and permanency: You negotiated with *us.* You funded *us.* You shared power, at least a bit of it, with *us.*

33   This negotiation was carried out in a kind of quasi-secrecy. Quotas, set-asides, and other entitlements were not debated in Congress or on the campaign trail. They were implemented by executive orders and Equal Employment Opportunity Commission guidelines without much public scrutiny. Also the courts played a quiet but persistent role in supporting these orders and guidelines and in further spelling out their application. Universities, corporations, and foundations implemented their own grievance entitlements, the workings of which are often kept from the public.

34   Now, it should surprise no one that all this entitlement has most helped those who least need it—white middle-class women and the black middle class. Poor blacks do not guide the black grievance groups. Working-class women do not set NOW's agenda. Poor Hispanics do not clamor for bilingualism. Perhaps there is nothing wrong with middle-class people being helped, but their demands for entitlements are most often in the name of those less well off than themselves. The negotiations that settled on entitlements as the primary form of redress after the sixties have generated a legalistic grievance industry that argues the interstices of entitlements and does very little to help those truly in need.

35 In a liberal democracy, collective entitlements based upon race, gender, ethnicity, or some other group grievance are always undemocratic expedients. Integration, on the other hand, is the most difficult and inexpedient expansion of the democratic ideal; for in opting for integration, a citizen denies his or her impulse to use our most arbitrary characteristics—race, ethnicity, gender, sexual preference—as the basis for identity, as a key to status, or for claims to entitlement. Integration is twentieth-century America's elaboration of democracy. It eliminates such things as race and gender as oppressive barriers to freedom, as democrats of an earlier epoch eliminated religion and property. Our mistake has been to think of integration only as a utopian vision of perfect racial harmony. I think it is better to see integration as the inclusion of all citizens into the same sphere of rights, the same range of opportunities and possibilities that our Founding Fathers themselves enjoyed. Integration is not social engineering or group entitlements; it is a fundamental *absence* of arbitrary barriers to freedom.

36   If we can understand integration as an absence of barriers that has the effect of integrating all citizens into the same sphere of rights, then it can serve as a principle of democratic conduct. Anything that pushes anybody out of this sphere is

undemocratic and must be checked, no matter the good intentions that seem to justify it. Understood in this light, collective entitlements are as undemocratic as racial and gender discrimination, and a group grievance is no more a justification for entitlement than the notion of white supremacy was at an earlier time. We are wrong to think of democracy as a gift of freedom; it is really a kind of discipline that avails freedom. Sometimes its enemy is racism and sexism; other times the enemy is our expedient attempts to correct these ills.

37   I think it is time for those who seek identity and power through grievance groups to fashion identities apart from grievance, to grant themselves the widest range of freedom, and to assume responsibility for that freedom. Victimhood lasts only as long as it is accepted, and to exploit it for an empty sovereignty is to accept it. The New Sovereignty is ultimately about vanity. It is the narcissism of victims, and it brings only a negligible power at the exorbitant price of continued victimhood. And all the while integration remains the real work.

QUESTIONS

Experience

· To what extent does what Steele describes as the "new sovereignty" appear in evidence on your campus or on others with which you are familiar? Are there separate studies departments for various racial and ethnic groups? Does your school have ethnic-theme dorms, lounges, and campus centers? Preferential admissions and financial policies? What do you think about each of these?

Interpretation

· Why does Steele believe that group entitlements are a bad idea? Why does he mention Martin Luther King, Jr., in the course of his argument? What place does the Constitution hold in his argument? Why?

Evaluation

· What conflicting values does Steele identify and use as the center of his argument? To what extent does his argument center on the conflict between individual and group values and individual and group entitlements?
· What political issues are at stake in the entitlement debate? Who stands to gain and lose if Steele's ideas are put into effect? Why?

WRITING

Exploring

· Compose a questionnaire asking students, faculty, and administrators what they think of Steele's objections to group entitlements—regardless of the degree to which they exist at your school. Then write up a few pages describing what you find out.

Interpretation

· Steele's essay can be divided into five parts (identified as such by the white space between them). For each part, write a paragraph in which you summarize Steele's argument. Then provide a concluding paragraph in which you pull together his individual points.

Evaluation

· Explain whether you essentially agree or disagree with Steele's argument. Cite passages in his argument to praise or criticize. You may, of course, agree with one part of his argument and disagree with another.

SUYIN SO
(b. 1973)

Grotesques

Suyin So wrote this essay while taking a summer writing course at Harvard University. At the time, she was still a high school student with her senior year ahead of her. Her initial assignment was to tell a story about herself and make it vivid for her readers. Subsequent assignments asked her to tell additional stories and to link them together to illustrate an idea.

Suyin So's essay describes in memorable detail the occasions in which she was the subject of prejudice. Among her essay's most notable aspects are the way she links her stories and the way she makes sense of them. She is also adept at presenting a scene vividly. Two examples stand out: the boy taunting her while bowing and saying "Ah-so" and the man with his face pressed up against a car window.

1   During childhood, all of us are equal. Innocent babes, we look upon each other with complete frankness and acceptance. For a brief time, it matters not whether your father drives a Mercedes, or that you have a different skin color than the others around you. What matters is how well your mom makes cherry Kool-Aid, how well you can play kickball. Eventually, though, this peaceful idyl is shattered. Prejudices are learned, barriers set, suspicions aroused. Innocence vanishes.

2   Flashback: A dingy cafeteria, inside a parochial elementary school, where mothers attempt to shelter their children from the unwholesome elements in public schools. A class of first graders furtively devours mashed potatoes and white bread, painfully aware of its lowly first-grade status. A class of older students traipses in: third grade? Fourth grade? It doesn't matter; to the first graders, big kids are big kids. As the older class lines up in front of the younger, one of them catches sight of the Asian-American girl sitting with her classmates. He begins to pick on her, bowing deeply at the waist with his hands clasped together as if in prayer. He is singsonging, "Ah-so, Ah-so." An expression of sheer pleasure illuminates his face, and a smile spreads across his mouth. He continues his revelry until he gets his food and sits down in a different area.

3   And what of the girl? What becomes of her?

4   She is digesting what she will later recognize as the first racial slur she has ever experienced. Presently she doesn't know this. She doesn't think, "Ah, here is an uncouth youngster assaulting my racial heritage and demeaning my cultural identity." There is no such startling realization. Instead, she is bewildered, hurt. Perhaps subconsciously, though, there is the knowledge that he is insulting some inherent quality, some intangible "thing" about her. Something she cannot erase or hide. She is also realizing that this quality instantly sets her apart and makes her different than the others around her.

5   The girl, of course, was me, and the boy someone named Allen, I think. Eleven years later, I can't remember much of my first grade year other than this

important moment. The experience remained in the front of my mind for quite some time, occasionally reminding me of itself when I was in danger of forgetting about it. Similar incidents, like when my classmates would screw up the corners of their eyes and scream with laughter, brought more attention to what I eventually wanted desperately to hide: the fact that I am Asian-American. I attempted to whitewash myself.

6   I pondered the malevolence of fate that had rendered me different from my friends, my name difficult for teachers to pronounce and impossible to find on personalized sets of stationery and keychains. Even though I never wrote letters nor carried keys, these mundane objects held a special attraction for me, perhaps because I knew I would not find a "Suyin" keychain nestled between "Sue" and "Suzanne." I longed for a different name, one that my teachers would not stumble over, one I could find on pink paper with red hearts scattered around it. A nice, bland, "normal" name.

7   Once I asked my father whether he thought, if we weren't what we were, we would be black or white. He looked at me in profound astonishment and with a hint of irritation. "Suyin," he told me, "we are Asian." Unsatisfied, I pressed him for a more specific answer. He repeated himself. "We are Asians. We cannot change what we are."

8   Yet I actually wanted, sometimes, to be able to change what I am. I wanted to believe that my family was like the families of my friends, with turkey and stuffing on Thanksgiving and grandparents just a block away. But we usually had chicken or duck—if we celebrated Thanksgiving at all—and my grandparents were half a world away.

9   This feeling passed, luckily, as other youthful follies probably do. I went to summer school in New Hampshire, realized that there were other teenagers with similar backgrounds, equally unusual names. I was overwhelmed at the sheer volume of Asian-Americans. It was a reassuring feeling. Suddenly, rather than being some oddity that people in my town stared and pointed at, I was simply another face in a sea of Asians, a homogeneous crowd. It seems strange that one should want to be lost in a crowd, identified immediately as a part of a whole. Yet it is not so surprising considering the former lack of sense of belonging.

10   This story does not end here, though. Pride replaces shame; acceptance, rejection. Something else is now present—a different sense of belonging.

11   Flashback II: Seven years old now, I am in Indonesia, that torturously hot country where my parents were born. We sit in a rickety old blue pickup truck, the pride of my uncle, traveling through the dusty, crowded streets of Surabaya, perhaps the second or third largest city of the country. I have no clue as to where we are traveling, and I cling to my mother, terrified by the strange images outside us: the calls of the street vendors, the people thronging in the roads, the wails of the babies. We stop abruptly. A man runs into the window, smashing his face against the dirty glass. His eyes are gruesomely red, the black pupils glazed over. He curses as he runs into the window, and hits the window a few times before another man appears to lead him away. Both men are filthy, dressed in once-white yellowish tee shirts, their pants splattered with mud. I watch them as they walk away, holding on to each other, swiveling my neck after we pass them.

12   "What's wrong with him?" I pester my mother, poking her. My uncle answers me.

13   "One of them is blind, the first man that came up to the truck. The man that led him away is deaf. They live together, rather than in an institution."

14   So there they are. A man without sight, but still able to hear; his companion without hearing, but still able to see. The two, helping each other down the sidewalk, functioning as a unit, a single entity.

15   Strangely enough, I feel a sense of kinship with them and others with similar afflictions. Not so much because I am physically disadvantaged, but more because I will always cheer on the underdog. Like the kid in class labeled the nerd, with four pocket protectors, five calculators and no friends, who would trade his intellect for a position on the football team. Or the girl thirty pounds overweight who eats lunch by herself in the corner of the cafeteria, who believes that if she were slimmer, trimmer, she would be perfect. Or, for that matter, the young black boy who thinks his only choices as a young black man are professional basketball or jail.

16   I share this weird bond with them because I know what it is to reject a part of your self and yearn to be something else. I have felt others' rejection, like the people at school who called me a chink, and the kind, grandfatherly old man who pleasantly told me he believed all non-Caucasian peoples to be inferior to the "superior Aryan race."

17   Yet that rejection of the self must pass, as it did with me. Acceptance comes eventually. Like the two men assisting each other in life, what was rejected before is confronted and dealt with. It becomes a source of pride and strength. I know a girl, her legs useless, who confided to me that one of the best things about being in a wheelchair was that she could pop a wheelie every so often.

18   Truly, I have no idea how it feels to be blind, to be deaf, or in a wheelchair. I am fortunate in that respect. Yet we are all the same in that we are victims of those twisted prejudices and barriers set up early in life. We are all the underdogs, defective and deformed, intimidated by the perfect, completely intact people who exist only in theory. We are, though, like Sherwood Anderson's grotesques, our ugly and twisted features shining with truth and beauty. We are happy in our defectiveness.

QUESTIONS

Experience

· How did you respond as you read Suyin So's essay? Did your response change at any point? Did it become stronger or more intense at any point? Where? Why?

Interpretation

· What is the writer's main point in this essay? Where does she make that point most directly? How do her stories illustrate, support, or otherwise clarify her idea?

Evaluation

· What social and cultural values does "Grotesques" touch on? What does Suyin So help us understand about the behavior of others that she describes? What does she help us understand about her?

WRITING

Exploring

· Write about a time when you were made to feel different by others. Tell the story of your experience, including salient details of description and dialogue that will clarify how you felt and what you may have learned from the experience.

Interpreting

· Analyze the structure of "Grotesques." Divide it into parts, and explain what each part contributes to the essay as a whole.

Evaluating

· Evaluate the effectiveness of "Grotesques" overall. Consider the writer's use of language; her inclusion of dialogue, questions, and short sentences and paragraphs; her references to the girl in a wheelchair and Sherwood Anderson; her title and her last sentence.

RALPH ELLISON
(1914–1994)

Battle Royal

Ralph Ellison won the 1954 National Book Award for Invisible Man, *an outstanding example of American postwar fiction. Born in Oklahoma, he moved to New York in 1938 and taught literature at a number of distinguished American universities, including Yale and the University of Chicago. Author of criticism and essays as well as fiction, Ellison published in* Partisan Review, American Review, *and* Iowa Review. *He was also a recipient of the Rockefeller Award and the Medal of Freedom. The nameless hero of Ellison's novel, excerpted below, bears the weight of black experience with a finality and symbolism reminiscent of Franz Kafka.*

Ellison's story can be neatly divided into six scenes, each of which contains a sharply etched descriptive focus. In the first and last of these scenes, the narrator invokes his grandfather, whose presence haunts him, and whom Ellison uses to anchor the story's ironies. Perhaps the story's most remarkable feature is its stunning descriptions—of the white woman dancer, the black boxers, and the strongly satirized pillars of the community.

1   It goes a long way back, some twenty years. All my life I had been looking for something, and everywhere I turned someone tried to tell me what it was. I accepted their answers too, though they were often in contradiction and even self-contradictory. I was naive. I was looking for myself and asking everyone except myself questions which I, and only I, could answer. It took me a long time and much painful boomeranging of my expectations to achieve a realization everyone else appears to have been born with: That I am nobody but myself. But first I had to discover that I am an invisible man!

2   And yet I am no freak of nature, nor of history. I was in the cards, other things having been equal (or unequal) eighty-five years ago. I am not ashamed of my grandparents for having been slaves. I am only ashamed of myself for having at one time been ashamed. About eighty-five years ago they were told that they were free, united with others of our country in everything pertaining to the common good, and, in everything social, separate like the fingers of the hand. And they believed it. They exulted in it. They stayed in their place, worked hard, and brought up my father to do the same. But my grandfather is the one. He was an odd old guy, my grandfather, and I am told I take after him. It was he who caused the trouble. On his deathbed he called my father to him and said, "Son, after I'm gone I want you to keep up the fight. I never told you, but our life is a war and I have been a traitor all my born days, a spy in the enemy's country ever since I give up my gun back in the Reconstruction. Live with your head in the lion's mouth. I want you to overcome 'em with yeses, undermine 'em with grins, agree 'em to death and destruction, let 'em swoller you till they vomit or bust wide open." They thought the old man had gone out of his mind. He had been the

meekest of men. The younger children were rushed from the room, the shades drawn and the flame of the lamp turned so low that it sputtered on the wick like the old man's breathing. "Learn it to the younguns," he whispered fiercely; then he died.

3　　　But my folks were more alarmed over his last words than over his dying. It was as though he had not died at all, his words caused so much anxiety. I was warned emphatically to forget what he had said and, indeed, this is the first time it has been mentioned outside the family circle. It had a tremendous effect upon me, however. I could never be sure of what he meant. Grandfather had been a quiet old man who never made any trouble, yet on his deathbed he had called himself a traitor and a spy, and he had spoken of his meekness as a dangerous activity. It became a constant puzzle which lay unanswered in the back of my mind. And whenever things went well for me I remembered my grandfather and felt guilty and uncomfortable. It was as though I was carrying out his advice in spite of myself. And to make it worse, everyone loved me for it. I was praised by the most lily-white men of the town. I was considered an example of desirable conduct—just as my grandfather had been. And what puzzled me was that the old man had defined it as *treachery*. When I was praised for my conduct I felt a guilt that in some way I was doing something that was really against the wishes of the white folks, that if they had understood they would have desired me to act just the opposite, that I should have been sulky and mean, and that that really would have been what they wanted, even though they were fooled and thought they wanted me to act as I did. It made me afraid that some day they would look upon me as a traitor and I would be lost. Still I was more afraid to act any other way because they didn't like that at all. The old man's words were like a curse. On my graduation day I delivered an oration in which I showed that humility was the secret, indeed, the very essence of progress. (Not that I believed this—how could I, remembering my grandfather?—I only believed that it worked.) It was a great success. Everyone praised me and I was invited to give the speech at a gathering of the town's leading white citizens. It was a triumph for our whole community.

4　　　It was in the main ballroom of the leading hotel. When I got there I discovered that it was on the occasion of a smoker, and I was told that since I was to be there anyway I might as well take part in the battle royal to be fought by some of my schoolmates as part of the entertainment. The battle royal came first.

5　　　All of the town's big shots were there in their tuxedos, wolfing down the buffet foods, drinking beer and whiskey and smoking black cigars. It was a large room with a high ceiling. Chairs were arranged in neat rows around three sides of a portable boxing ring. The fourth side was clear, revealing a gleaming space of polished floor. I had some misgivings over the battle royal, by the way. Not from a distaste for fighting, but because I didn't care too much for the other fellows who were to take part. They were tough guys who seemed to have no grandfather's curse worrying their minds. No one could mistake their toughness. And besides, I suspected that fighting a battle royal might detract from the dignity of my speech. In those pre-invisible days I visualized myself as a potential Booker T. Washington. But the other fellows didn't care too much for me either, and there were nine of them. I felt superior to them in my way, and I didn't like the manner in which we were all crowded together into the servants' elevator. Nor did they like my being there. In fact, as the warmly lighted floors flashed past the elevator we had words over the fact that I, by taking part in the fight, had knocked one of their friends out of a night's work.

6   We were led out of the elevator through a rococo hall into an anteroom and told to get into our fighting togs. Each of us was issued a pair of boxing gloves and ushered out into the big mirrored hall, which we entered looking cautiously about us and whispering, lest we might accidentally be heard above the noise of the room. It was foggy with cigar smoke. And already the whiskey was taking effect. I was shocked to see some of the most important men of the town quite tipsy. They were all there—bankers, lawyers, judges, doctors, fire chiefs, teachers, merchants. Even one of the more fashionable pastors. Something we could not see was going on up front. A clarinet was vibrating sensuously and the men were standing up and moving eagerly forward. We were a small tight group, clustered together, our bare upper bodies touching and shining with anticipatory sweat; while up front the big shots were becoming increasingly excited over something we still could not see. Suddenly I heard the school superintendent, who had told me to come, yell, "Bring up the shines, gentlemen! Bring up the little shines!"

7   We were rushed up to the front of the ballroom, where it smelled even more strongly of tobacco and whiskey. Then we were pushed into place. I almost wet my pants. A sea of faces, some hostile, some amused, ringed around us, and in the center, facing us, stood a magnificent blonde—stark naked. There was a dead silence. I felt a blast of cold air chill me. I tried to back away, but they were behind me and around me. Some of the boys stood with lowered heads, trembling. I felt a wave of irrational guilt and fear. My teeth chattered, my skin turned to goose flesh, my knees knocked. Yet I was strongly attracted and looked in spite of myself. Had the price of looking been blindness, I would have looked. The hair was yellow like that of a circus kewpie doll, the face heavily powdered and rouged, as though to form an abstract mask, the eyes hollow and smeared a cool blue, the color of a baboon's butt. I felt a desire to spit upon her as my eyes brushed slowly over her body. Her breasts were firm and round as the domes of East Indian temples, and I stood so close as to see the fine skin texture and beads of pearly perspiration glistening like dew around the pink and erected buds of her nipples. I wanted at one and the same time to run from the room, to sink through the floor, or go to her and cover her from my eyes and the eyes of the others with my body; to feel the soft thighs, to caress her and destroy her, to love her and murder her, to hide from her, and yet to stroke where below the small American flag tattooed upon her belly her thighs formed a capital V. I had a notion that of all in the room she saw only me with her impersonal eyes.

8   And then she began to dance, a slow sensuous movement; the smoke of a hundred cigars clinging to her like the thinnest of veils. She seemed like a fair bird-girl girdled in veils calling to me from the angry surface of some gray and threatening sea. I was transported. Then I became aware of the clarinet playing and the big shots yelling at us. Some threatened us if we looked and others if we did not. On my right I saw one boy faint. And now a man grabbed a silver pitcher from a table and stepped close as he dashed ice water upon him and stood him up and forced two of us to support him as his head hung and moans issued from

his thick bluish lips. Another boy began to plead to go home. He was the largest of the group, wearing dark red fighting trunks much too small to conceal the erection which projected from him as though in answer to the insinuating low-registered moaning of the clarinet. He tried to hide himself with his boxing gloves.

9   And all the while the blonde continued dancing, smiling faintly at the big shots who watched her with fascination, and faintly smiling at our fear. I noticed a certain merchant who followed her hungrily, his lips loose and drooling. He was a large man who wore diamond studs in a shirtfront which swelled with the ample paunch underneath, and each time the blonde swayed her undulating hips he ran his hand through the thin hair of his bald head and, with his arms upheld, his posture clumsy like that of an intoxicated panda, wound his belly in a slow and obscene grind. This creature was completely hypnotized. The music had quickened. As the dancer flung herself about with a detached expression on her face, the men began reaching out to touch her. I could see their beefy fingers sink into the soft flesh. Some of the others tried to stop them and she began to move around the floor in graceful circles, as they gave chase, slipping and sliding over the polished floor. It was mad. Chairs went crashing, drinks were spilt, as they ran laughing and howling after her. They caught her just as she reached a door, raised her from the floor, and tossed her as college boys are tossed at a hazing, and above her red, fixed-smiling lips I saw the terror and disgust in her eyes, almost like my own terror and that which I saw in some of the other boys. As I watched, they tossed her twice and her soft breasts seemed to flatten against the air and her legs flung wildly as she spun. Some of the more sober ones helped her to escape. And I started off the floor, heading for the anteroom with the rest of the boys.

10   Some were still crying and in hysteria. But as we tried to leave we were stopped and ordered to get into the ring. There was nothing to do but what we were told. All ten of us climbed under the ropes and allowed ourselves to be blindfolded with broad bands of white cloth. One of the men seemed to feel a bit sympathetic and tried to cheer us up as we stood with our backs against the ropes. Some of us tried to grin. "See that boy over there?" one of the men said. "I want you to run across at the bell and give it to him right in the belly. If you don't get him, I'm going to get you. I don't like his looks." Each of us was told the same. The blindfolds were put on. Yet even then I had been going over my speech. In my mind each word was as bright as flame. I felt the cloth pressed into place, and frowned so that it would be loosened when I relaxed.

11   But now I felt a sudden fit of blind terror. I was unused to darkness. It was as though I had suddenly found myself in a dark room filled with poisonous cottonmouths. I could hear the bleary voices yelling insistently for the battle royal to begin.

12   "Get going in there!"

13   "Let me at the big nigger!"

14   I strained to pick up the school superintendent's voice, as though to squeeze some security out of that slightly more familiar sound.

15   "Let me at those black sonsabitches!" someone yelled.

16   "No, Jackson, no!" another voice yelled. "Here, somebody, help me hold Jack."

17   "I want to get at that ginger-colored nigger. Tear him limb from limb," the first voice yelled.

18   I stood against the ropes trembling. For in those days I was what they called ginger-colored, and he sounded as though he might crunch me between his teeth like a crisp ginger cookie.

19   Quite a struggle was going on. Chairs were being kicked about and I could hear voices grunting as with a terrific effort. I wanted to see, to see more desperately than ever before. But the blindfold was as tight as a thick skin-puckering scab and when I raised my gloved hands to push the layers of white aside a voice yelled, "Oh, no you don't, black bastard! Leave that alone!"

20   "Ring the bell before Jackson kills him a coon!" someone boomed in the sudden silence. And I heard the bell clang and the sound of feet scuffling forward.

21   A glove smacked against my head. I pivoted, striking out stiffly as someone went past, and felt the jar ripple along the length of my arm to my shoulder. Then it seemed as though all nine of the boys had turned upon me at once. Blows pounded me from all sides while I struck out as best I could. So many blows landed upon me that I wondered if I were not the only blindfolded fighter in the ring, or if the man called Jackson hadn't succeeded in getting me after all.

22   Blindfolded, I could no longer control my motions. I had no dignity. I stumbled about like a baby or a drunken man. The smoke had become thicker and with each new blow it seemed to sear and further restrict my lungs. My saliva became like hot bitter glue. A glove connected with my head, filling my mouth with warm blood. It was everywhere. I could not tell if the moisture I felt upon my body was sweat or blood. A blow landed hard against the nape of my neck. I felt myself going over, my head hitting the floor. Streaks of blue light filled the black world behind the blindfold. I lay prone, pretending that I was knocked out, but felt myself seized by hands and yanked to my feet. "Get going, black boy! Mix it up!" My arms were like lead, my head smarting from blows. I managed to feel my way to the ropes and held on, trying to catch my breath. A glove landed in my midsection and I went over again, feeling as though the smoke had become a knife jabbed into my guts. Pushed this way and that by the legs milling around me, I finally pulled erect and discovered that I could see the black, sweat-washed forms weaving in the smoky-blue atmosphere like drunken dancers weaving to the rapid drumlike thuds of blows.

23   Everyone fought hysterically. It was complete anarchy. Everybody fought everybody else. No group fought together for long. Two, three, four, fought one, then turned to fight each other, were themselves attacked. Blows landed below the belt and in the kidney, with the gloves open as well as closed, and with my eye partly opened now there was not so much terror. I moved carefully, avoiding blows, although not too many to attract attention, fighting from group to group. The boys groped about like blind, cautious crabs crouching to protect their midsections, their heads pulled in short against their shoulders, their arms stretched nervously before them, with their fists testing the smoke-filled air like the knobbed feelers of hypersensitive snails. In the corner I glimpsed a boy violently punching the air and heard him scream in pain as he smashed his hand against a ring post. For a second I saw him bent over holding his hand, then going down as a blow

caught his unprotected head. I played one group against the other, slipping in and throwing a punch then stepped out of range while pushing the others into the melee to take the blows blindly aimed at me. The smoke was agonizing and there were no rounds, no bells at three minute intervals to relieve our exhaustion. The room spun around me, a swirl of lights, smoke, sweating bodies surrounded by tense white faces. I bled from both nose and mouth, the blood spattering upon my chest.

24 The men kept yelling, "Slug him, black boy! Knock his guts out!"

25 "Uppercut him! Kill him! Kill that big boy!"

26 Taking a fake fall, I saw a boy going down heavily beside me as though we were felled by a single blow, saw a sneaker-clad foot shoot into his groin as the two who had knocked him down stumbled upon him. I rolled out of range, feeling a twinge of nausea.

27 The harder we fought the more threatening the men became. And yet, I had begun to worry about my speech again. How would it go? Would they recognize my ability? What would they give me?

28 I was fighting automatically when suddenly I noticed that one after another of the boys was leaving the ring. I was surprised, filled with panic, as though I had been left alone with an unknown danger. Then I understood. The boys had arranged it among themselves. It was custom for the two men left in the ring to slug it out for the winner's prize. I discovered this too late. When the bell sounded two men in tuxedos leaped into the ring and removed the blindfold. I found myself facing Tatlock, the biggest of the gang. I felt sick at my stomach. Hardly had the bell stopped ringing in my ears than it clanged again and I saw him moving swiftly toward me. Thinking of nothing else to do I hit him smash on the nose. He kept coming, bringing the rank sharp violence of stale sweat. His face was a black blank of a face, only his eyes alive—with hate of me and aglow with a feverish terror from what had happened to us all. I became anxious. I wanted to deliver my speech and he came at me as though he meant to beat it out of me. I smashed him again and again, taking his blows as they came. Then on a sudden impulse I struck him lightly and as we clinched, I whispered, "Fake like I knocked you out, you can have the prize."

29 "I'll break your behind," he whispered hoarsely.

30 "For *them?*"

31 "For *me*, sonofabitch."

32 They were yelling for us to break it up and Tatlock spun me half around with a blow, and as a joggled camera sweeps in a reeling scene, I saw the howling red faces crouching tense beneath the cloud of blue-gray smoke. For a moment the world wavered, unraveled, flowed, then my head cleared and Tatlock bounced before me. The fluttering shadow before my eyes was his jabbing left hand. Then falling forward, my head against his damp shoulder, I whispered.

33 "I'll make it five dollars more."

34 "Go to hell!"

35 But his muscles relaxed a trifle beneath my pressure and I breathed. "Seven?"

36 "Give it to your ma," he said, ripping me beneath the heart.

37 And while I still held him I butted him and moved away. I felt myself bombarded with punches. I fought back with hopeless desperation. I wanted to deliver

my speech more than anything else in the world, because I felt only these men could judge truly my ability, and now this stupid clown was ruining my chances. I began fighting carefully now, moving in to punch him and out again with my greater speed. A lucky blow to his chin and I had him going too—until I heard a loud voice yell, "I got my money on the big boy."

38   Hearing this, I almost dropped my guard. I was confused: Should I try to win against the voice out there? Would not this go against my speech, and was not this a moment for humility, for nonresistance? A blow to my head as I danced about sent my right eye popping like a jack-in-the-box and settled my dilemma. The room went red as I fell. It was a dream fall, my body languid and fastidious as to where to land, until the floor became impatient and smashed up to meet me. A moment later I came to. An hypnotic voice said FIVE emphatically. And I lay there, hazily watching a dark red spot of my own blood shaping itself into a butterfly, glistening and soaking into the soiled gray world of the canvas.

39   When the voice drawled TEN I was lifted up and dragged to a chair. I sat dazed. My eye pained and swelled with each throb of my pounding heart and I wondered if now I would be allowed to speak. I was wringing wet, my mouth still bleeding. We were grouped along the wall now. The other boys ignored me as they congratulated Tatlock and speculated as to how much they would be paid. One boy whimpered over his smashed hand. Looking up front, I saw attendants in white jackets rolling the portable ring away and placing a small square rug in the vacant space surrounded by chairs. Perhaps, I thought, I will stand on the rug to deliver my speech.

40   Then the M.C. called to us, "Come on up here boys and get your money."

41   We ran forward to where the men laughed and talked in their chairs, waiting. Everyone seemed friendly now.

42   "There it is on the rug," the man said. I saw the rug covered with coins of all dimensions and a few crumpled bills. But what excited me, scattered here and there, were the gold pieces.

43   "Boys, it's all yours," the man said. "You get all you grab."

44   "That's right, Sambo," a blond man said, winking at me confidentially.

45   I trembled with excitement, forgetting my pain. I would get the gold and the bills, I thought. I would use both hands. I would throw my body against the boys nearest me to block them from the gold.

46   "Get down around the rug now," the man commanded, "and don't anyone touch it until I give the signal."

47   "This ought to be good," I heard.

48   As told, we got around the square rug on our knees. Slowly the man raised his freckled hand as we followed it upward with our eyes.

49   I heard, "These niggers look like they're about to pray!"

50   Then, "Ready," the man said. "Go!"

51   I lunged for a yellow coin lying on the blue design on the carpet, touching it and sending a surprised shriek to join those rising around me. I tried frantically to remove my hand but could not let go. A hot, violent force tore through my body, shaking me like a wet rat. The rug was electrified. The hair bristled up on my head as I shook myself free. My muscles jumped, my nerves jangled, writhed. But I saw that this was not stopping the other boys. Laughing in fear and embarrassment,

some were holding back and scooping up the coins knocked off by the painful contortions of the others. The men roared above us as we struggled.

52   "Pick it up, goddamnit, pick it up!" someone called like a bass-voiced parrot. "Go on, get it!"

53   I crawled rapidly around the floor, picking up the coins, trying to avoid the coppers and to get greenbacks and the gold. Ignoring the shock by laughing, as I brushed the coins off quickly, I discovered that I could contain the electricity—a contradiction, but it works. Then the men began to push us onto the rug. Laughing embarrassedly, we struggled out of their hands and kept after the coins. We were all wet and slippery and hard to hold. Suddenly I saw a boy lifted into the air, glistening with sweat like a circus seal, and dropped, his wet back landing flush upon the charged rug, heard him yell and saw him literally dance upon his back, his elbows beating a frenzied tattoo upon the floor, his muscles twitching like the flesh of a horse stung by many flies. When he finally rolled off, his face was gray and no one stopped him when he ran from the floor amid booming laughter.

54   "Get the money," the M.C. called. "That's good hard American cash!"

55   And we snatched and grabbed, snatched and grabbed. I was careful not to come too close to the rug now, and when I felt the hot whiskey breath descend upon me like a cloud of foul air I reached out and grabbed the leg of a chair. It was occupied and I held on desperately.

56   "Leggo nigger! Leggo!"

57   The huge face wavered down to mine as he tried to push me free. But my body was slippery and he was too drunk. It was Mr. Colcord, who owned a chain of movie houses and "entertainment palaces." Each time he grabbed me I slipped out of his hands. It became a real struggle. I feared the rug more than I did the drunk, so I held on, surprising myself for a moment by trying to topple *him* upon the rug. It was such an enormous idea that I found myself actually carrying it out. I tried not to be obvious, yet when I grabbed his leg, trying to tumble him out of the chair, he raised up roaring with laughter, and, looking at me with soberness dead in the eye, kicked me viciously in the chest. The chair leg flew out of my hand and I felt myself going and rolled. It was as though I had rolled through a bed of hot coals. It seemed a whole century would pass before I would roll free, a century in which I was seared through the deepest levels of my body to the fearful breath within me and the breath seared and heated to the point of explosion. It'll all be over in a flash, I thought as I rolled clear. It'll all be over in a flash.

58   But not yet, the men on the other side were waiting, red faces swollen as though from apoplexy as they bent forward in their chairs. Seeing their fingers coming toward me I rolled away as a fumbled football rolls off the receiver's fingertips, back into the coals. That time I luckily sent the rug sliding out of place and heard the coins ringing against the floor and the boys scuffling to pick them up and the M.C. calling, "All right, boys, that's all. Go get dressed and get your money."

59   I was limp as a dish rag. My back felt as though it had been beaten with wires.

60   When we had dressed the M.C. came in and gave us each five dollars, except Tatlock, who got ten for being last in the ring. Then he told us to leave. I was not to get a chance to deliver my speech, I thought. I was going out into the dim

Georgia O'Keeffe.
Black Iris III. 1926. Oil on
Canvas. 36" x 29 7/8".
The Metropolitan Museum
of Art, Alfred Stieglitz
Collection, 1969.

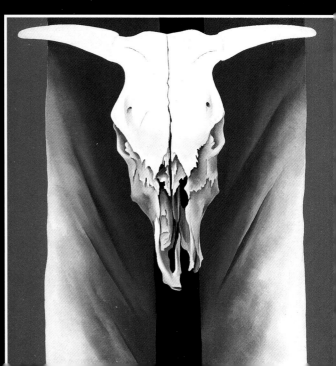

Georgia O'Keeffe.
*Cow's Skull: Red, White,
and Blue.* 1931. Oil on
canvas. 39 7/8" x 35 7/8".
The Metropolitan Museum
of Art, Alfred Stieglitz
Collection, 1952.
Photograph by
Malcolm Varon.

Edward Hopper. *House by the Railroad*. 1925. Oil on canvas. 24" x 29". The Museum of Modern Art, New York. Given Anonymously. Photograph © 1995 The Museum of Modern Art, New York.

Edward Hopper. *Rooms by the Sea*. 1951. Oil on canvas. 29" x 40 1/8". The Yale University Art Gallery. Bequest of

Jean Auguste Dominique Ingres. *La Grande Odalisque*. 1814. Oil on canvas. 35 1/4
Paris, France. Giraudon/Art Resource.

alley in despair when I was stopped and told to go back. I returned to the ball-room, where the men were pushing back their chairs and gathering in groups to talk.

61 The M.C. knocked on a table for quiet. "Gentlemen," he said, "we almost forgot an important part of the program. A most serious part, gentlemen. This boy was brought here to deliver a speech which he made at his graduation yes-terday . . ."

62 "Bravo!"

63 "I'm told that he is the smartest boy we've got out there in Greenwood. I'm told that he knows more big words than a pocket-sized dictionary."

64 Much applause and laughter.

65 "So now, gentlemen, I want you to give him your attention."

66 There was still laughter as I faced them, my mouth dry, my eye throbbing. I began slowly, but evidently my throat was tense, because they began shouting, "Louder! Louder!"

67 "We of the younger generation extol the wisdom of that great leader and educator," I shouted, "who first spoke these flaming words of wisdom. 'A ship lost at sea for many days suddenly sighted a friendly vessel. From the mast of the unfortunate vessel was seen a signal: "Water, water; we die of thirst!" The answer from the friendly vessel came back: "Cast down your bucket where you are." The captain of the distressed vessel, at last heeding the injunction, cast down his bucket, and it came up full of fresh sparkling water from the mouth of the Amazon River.' And like him I say, and in his words, 'To those of my race who depend upon bettering their condition in a foreign land, or who underestimate the impor-tance of cultivating friendly relations with the Southern white man, who is his next-door neighbor, I would say: "Cast down your bucket where you are"—cast it down in making friends in every manly way of the people of all races by whom we are surrounded. . . .' "

68 I spoke automatically and with such fervor that I did not realize that the men were still talking and laughing until my dry mouth, filling up with blood from the cut, almost strangled me. I coughed, wanting to stop and go to one of the tall brass, sand-filled spittoons to relieve myself, but a few of the men, especially the superintendent, were listening and I was afraid. So I gulped it down, blood, saliva, and all, and continued. (What powers of endurance I had during those days! What enthusiasm! What a belief in the rightness of things!) I spoke even louder in spite of the pain. But still they talked and still they laughed, as though deaf with cotton in dirty ears. So I spoke with greater emotional emphasis. I closed my ears and swallowed blood until I was nauseated. The speech seemed a hundred times as long as before, but I could not leave out a single word. All had to be said, each memorized nuance considered, rendered. Nor was that all. Whenever I uttered a word of three or more syllables a group of voices would yell for me to repeat it. I used the phrase "social responsibility" and they yelled:

69 "What's that word you say, boy?"

70 "Social responsibility," I said.

71 "What?"

72 "Social . . ."

73   "Louder."

74   ". . . responsibility."

75   "More!"

76   "Respon—"

77   "Repeat!"

78   "—sibility."

79   The room filled with the uproar of laughter until, no doubt, distracted by having to gulp down my blood, I made a mistake and yelled a phrase I had often seen denounced with newspaper editorials, heard debated in private.

80   "Social . . ."

81   "What?" they yelled.

82   ". . . equality—"

83   The laughter hung smokelike in the sudden stillness. I opened my eyes, puzzled. Sounds of displeasure filled the room. The M.C. rushed forward. They shouted hostile phrases at me. But I did not understand.

84   A small dry mustached man in the front row blared out, "Say that slowly, son!"

85   "What, sir?"

86   "What you just said!"

87   "Social responsibility, sir," I said.

88   "You weren't being smart, were you, boy?" he said, not unkindly.

89   "No, sir!"

90   "You sure that about 'equality' was a mistake?"

91   "Oh, yes, sir," I said. "I was swallowing blood."

92   "Well, you had better speak more slowly so we can understand. We mean to do right by you, but you've got to know your place at all times. All right, now, go on with your speech."

93   I was afraid. I wanted to leave but I wanted also to speak and I was afraid they'd snatch me down.

94   "Thank you, sir," I said, beginning where I had left off, and having them ignore me as before.

95   Yet when I finished there was a thunderous applause. I was surprised to see the superintendent come forth with a package wrapped in white tissue paper, and, gesturing for quiet, address the men.

96   "Gentlemen, you see that I did not overpraise this boy. He makes a good speech and some day he'll lead his people in the proper paths. And I don't have to tell you that that is important in these days and times. This is a good, smart boy, and so to encourage him in the right direction, in the name of the Board of Education I wish to present him a prize in the form of this . . ."

97   He paused, removing the tissue paper and revealing a gleaming calfskin briefcase.

98   ". . . in the form of this first-class article from Shad Whitmore's shop."

99   "Boy," he said, addressing me, "take this prize and keep it well. Consider it a badge of office. Prize it. Keep developing as you are and some day it will be filled with important papers that will help shape the destiny of your people."

100   I was so moved that I could hardly express my thanks. A rope of bloody saliva

forming a shape like an undiscovered continent drooled upon the leather and I wiped it quickly away. I felt an importance that I had never dreamed.

101 "Open it and see what's inside," I was told.

102 My fingers a-tremble, I complied, smelling the fresh leather and finding an official-looking document inside. It was a scholarship to the state college for Negroes. My eyes filled with tears and I ran awkwardly off the floor.

103 I was so overjoyed; I did not even mind when I discovered that the gold pieces I had scrambled for were brass pocket tokens advertising a certain make of automobile.

104 When I reached home everyone was excited. Next day the neighbors came to congratulate me. I even felt safe from grandfather, whose deathbed curse usually spoiled my triumphs. I stood beneath his photograph with my briefcase in hand and smiled triumphantly into his stolid black peasant's face. It was a face that fascinated me. The eyes seemed to follow everywhere I went.

105 That night I dreamed I was at a circus with him and that he refused to laugh at the clowns no matter what they did. Then later he told me to open my briefcase and read what was inside and I did, finding an official envelope stamped with the state seal; and inside the envelope I found another and another, endlessly, and I thought I would fall of weariness. "Them's years," he said. "Now open that one." And I did and in it I found an engraved document containing a short message in letters of gold. "Read it," my grandfather said. "Out loud."

106 "To Whom It May Concern," I intoned. "Keep This Nigger-Boy Running."

107 I awoke with the old man's laughter ringing in my ears.

108 (It was a dream I was to remember and dream again for many years after. But at that time I had no insight into its meaning. First I had to attend college.)

QUESTIONS

Experience

· What is it like for you to read this story? How did you respond to the boxing scene, to the scene of the woman dancing, and to the narrator's speech? Which of these scenes affected you most strongly? Why?

Interpretation

· Why does the author begin and end the story with scenes concerning the narrator's grandfather? What does the last sentence of the story mean? And what does the grandfather mean when he tells his grandson to "overcome 'em with yeses, undermine 'em with grins, agree 'em to death and destruction"?

· How many meanings of "battle royal" can you think of?

Evaluation

· What racist ideas does the story illustrate in its portrayal of the white men who attend the gathering? What is the effect of Ellison's making them pillars of the community? What is the narrator's attitude toward these men? Why?

WRITING

Exploring

· Describe an occasion when you were on public display. Explain what the circumstances were, and give an account of how you felt during the episode.
· Or explore a memory you have of a time when you either witnessed or participated in a humiliating event. Describe the emotions you experienced.

Interpreting

· Analyze one of the six scenes that make up "Battle Royal." Look carefully at Ellison's language and selection of detail. Explain what those choices contribute to the scene, and explain how the scene fits into the story overall.

Evaluating

· Evaluate one important idea that emerges from your reading of Ellison's story. Consider the way Ellison conveys this idea dramatically through description and dialogue. One possibility is the speaker's slip of the tongue while giving his speech. Another is the behavior of the men during the speech or during the battle royal.

LANGSTON HUGHES
(1902–1967)

Theme for English B

Langston Hughes was born in Joplin, Missouri. As a young man he worked as a merchant seaman and traveled widely, living for a time in Paris and Rome. He published his first volume of poems, The Weary Blues *(1926), three years before he graduated from Lincoln University, where he had won a scholarship. A major figure of the Harlem Renaissance, Hughes wrote prolifically, producing fiction and folklore, drama, song lyrics, essays, memoirs, and children's books, as well as many poems.*

In "Theme for English B," Hughes explores the differences in background and experience between a white Jewish college teacher and a black undergraduate. The poem takes the form of a personal statement that resembles, in part, a letter and, in part, an exploratory essay. Its words and sentences are informal, even conversational, and its tone is friendly.

The instructor said,

> *Go home and write*
> *a page tonight.*
> *And let that page come out of you—*
5 > *Then, it will be true.*

I wonder if it's that simple?

I am twenty-two, colored, born in Winston-Salem
I went to school there, then Durham, then here
to this college on the hill above Harlem.
10 I am the only colored student in my class.
The steps from the hill lead down into Harlem,
through a park, then I cross St. Nicholas,
Eighth Avenue, Seventh, and I come to the Y,
the Harlem Branch Y, where I take the elevator
15 up to my room, sit down, and write this page:

It's not easy to know what is true for you or me
at twenty-two, my age. But I guess I'm what
I feel and see and hear. Harlem, I hear you:
hear you, hear me—we two—you, me, talk on this page.
20 (I hear New York, too.) Me—who?

Well, I like to eat, sleep, drink, and be in love.
I like to work, read, learn, and understand life.
I like a pipe for a Christmas present,

25 or records—Bessie, bop, or Bach.
    I guess being colored doesn't make me *not* like
    the same things other folks like who are other races.

    So will my page be colored that I write?
    Being me, it will not be white.
    But it will be
30 a part of you, instructor.
    You are white—
    yet a part of me, as I am a part of you.
    That's American.
    Sometimes perhaps you don't want to be a part of me.
35 Nor do I often want to be a part of you.
    But we are, that's true!
    As I learn from you,
    I guess you learn from me—
    although you're older—and white—
40 and somewhat more free.

    This is my page for English B.

QUESTIONS

Experience

· To what extent does Hughes's poem touch on your own experience? Do you have to be of a different race than an instructor to understand the sameness and difference Hughes's speaker alludes to?

Interpretation

· What is the theme of "Theme for English B"? What idea about race and/or identity does the poem convey?

Evaluation

· What are the speaker's values? What are his goals? What is his background? How does Hughes suggest these aspects of his speaker's experience?

WRITING

Exploring

· Write your own page for English B. You can compose a loosely structured poem as Hughes does. Or you can simply write a page or so of prose in which you ask some of the kinds of questions and touch on some of the issues raised in Hughes's poem.

Interpreting

· Write an interpretation of the poem in which you explain each of its sections. Summarize the idea and the feeling that come through in each section. And explain the overall purpose and point of the poem.

Evaluating

· Provide an evaluation of "Theme for English B." Decide whether or not this is a convincing or engaging poem. Explain your view by citing words, phrases, and lines to substantiate it.

RACE—CONSIDERATIONS FOR THINKING AND WRITING

1. Discuss the depiction of being black in any two or more of the following: Baldwin's "Notes of a Native Son," Hurston's "How It Feels to Be Colored Me" (see p. 3 of the Introduction), Wilkins's "In Ivory Towers," Ellison's "Battle Royal," and Hughes's "Theme for English B." If you wish, you may bring into your discussion selections that touch on race from other chapters. Possibilities include "In Search of Our Mothers' Gardens" ("Communities") and "2 Live Crew, Decoded" ("Culture and Society").

2. Compare the way issues of race are treated in two of the following: Richard Rodriguez's "Complexion," N. Scott Momaday's "The Way to Rainy Mountain," Suyin So's "Grotesques," or James Baldwin's "Notes of a Native Son." Consider what each writer reveals about racial attitudes, preferences, or issues.

3. Create a dialogue between Roger Wilkins ("In Ivory Towers") and Shelby Steele ("The New Sovereignty"). Introduce, if you wish, additional remarks that Cornel West ("Race Matters") might make if invited to enter the conversation.

4. Discuss the connections between race and family or heritage described in two or more of the following: Baldwin's "Notes of a Native Son," Momaday's "The Way to Rainy Mountain," Rodriguez's "Complexion," Walker's "In Search of Our Mothers' Gardens" (in "Communities").

5. Select any writer in this chapter who also appears in another chapter and discuss connections you can make between two works by that author. Some possibilities include James Baldwin, Richard Rodriguez, Ralph Ellison, and Langston Hughes.

6. Compare the way two or more of the following writers discuss place or environment in relation to race: Baldwin, Hurston, Momaday, Rodriguez, or Ellison. Consider how the writers characterize the places they have lived and how issues of race color their experience of living in those places.

7. Write an imaginative or creative piece on the subject of race. You might write a poem, song, short story, or a scene for a short play or film. Or you might

create a dialogue on race between two or three of the writers from this chapter.

8. Do some research on an aspect of the race problem in America—on educational inequality, racial stereotyping, race and intelligence, for example. Write a research essay based on your findings. Try to focus on a specific question that you can answer in your essay.

FIVE

Language

MICHIKO KAKUTANI
  The Word Police

ROBIN LAKOFF
  Talking Like a Lady

BARBARA LAWRENCE
  Four-Letter Words Can Hurt You

NANCY MAIRS
  On Being a Cripple

NEIL POSTMAN
  "Now . . . This"

JAMES BALDWIN
  If Black English Isn't a Language, Then Tell Me, What Is?

GEORGE ORWELL
  Politics and the English Language

LISA BOGDONOFF
  Police! Police!

GISH JEN
  What Means Switch?

PABLO NERUDA
  The Word

Language is both within us and around us. We hear it spoken in our homes and classrooms, on television and the radio, in our cars and in our heads. We hear voices, watch facial expressions, and participate in the reciprocal process of understanding and being understood. In fact, language is such an enveloping presence that we may not pay much attention to it. It is simply there.

More and more, however, at work and play, in school and out, we need to attend carefully to language. We need to be alert for how language is used to influence our thoughts, feelings, and responses. And we need to learn to use language ourselves accurately, honestly, clearly, appropriately.

This chapter invites you to listen to a range of views about language and to listen to different voices express themselves, sometimes in more than one language. The writers of the works in this section take language seriously and encourage you to do the same. They show, among other things, how language is bound up with identity—how our speech and our writing reveal who we are and how we imagine ourselves.

Nancy Mairs, for example, sees herself as a "cripple" and refuses to accept any of the euphemisms, such as "disabled" or "handicapped," that others sometimes use to describe her. Robin Lakoff explains how certain linguistic choices are sex-marked as feminine and how particular feminine ways of talking are devalued. Barbara Lawrence explains how four-letter words, including the popular "fuck," convey powerfully oppressive and derogatory attitudes toward women. James Baldwin looks at a few systematic features of black English and argues that it deserves the status of a full-blown language with its own rules and linguistic principles.

In "Politics and the English Language" George Orwell argues that the decline of language is both cause and consequence of the decline of thought, and he identifies seven principles to avoid bad writing. Neil Postman criticizes the language used on television news broadcasts as being largely responsible for diminishing viewers' capacity for sustained thought and analysis. And Michiko Kakutani takes to task all those who would limit writers' ability to use the language they want because of political correctness and cultural sensitivity, both of which, she argues, have gotten out of hand. Gish Jen, on the other hand, explores the ability of people from different cultures and with different languages to communicate with one another.

And, finally, Lisa Bogdonoff explores the connotations and changing meanings of the various words used for law enforcement officials, while Pablo Neruda, in his poem "The Word," celebrates the living power of language inherent in words.

MICHIKO KAKUTANI
(b. 1955)

The Word Police

Michiko Kakutani is a book reviewer for The New York Times. *In addition to her regular reviewing, Ms. Kakutani writes articles on language and other timely subjects. Her book* The Poet at the Piano *collects the best of her reviews. The following selection appeared as an article in the "Styles" section of the Sunday edition of the* New York Times.

In "The Word Police," Kakutani argues that writers are at the mercy of political correctness, whose methods she laments because they diminish the permissible range of expression. An engaging element of Kakutani's essay is the richness and variety of her examples, which she culls from books, conferences, and popular culture. She develops her argument by citing what she considers the most ridiculous and outrageous suggestions of the "word police" and laughing at them. Her essay, however, makes larger claims, as she introduces an important question about the issue into her conclusion.

1   This month's inaugural festivities, with their celebration, in Maya Angelou's words, of "humankind"—"the Asian, the Hispanic, the Jew/ The African, the Native American, the Sioux,/ The Catholic, the Muslim, the French, the Greek/ The Irish, the Rabbi, the Priest, the Sheik,/ The Gay, the Straight, the Preacher,/ The privileged, the homeless, the Teacher"—constituted a kind of official embrace of multiculturalism and a new politics of inclusion.

2   The mood of political correctness, however, has already made firm inroads into popular culture. Washington boasts a store called Politically Correct that sells pro-whale, anti-meat, ban-the-bomb T-shirts, bumper stickers and buttons, as well as a local cable television show called "Politically Correct Cooking" that features interviews in the kitchen with representatives from groups like People for the Ethical Treatment of Animals.

3   The Coppertone suntan lotion people are planning to give their longtime cover girl, Little Miss (Ms?) Coppertone, a male equivalent, Little Mr. Coppertone. And even Superman (Superperson?) is rumored to be returning this spring, reincarnated as four ethnically diverse clones: an African-American, an Asian, a Caucasian and a Latino.

4   Nowhere is this P.C. mood more striking than in the increasingly noisy debate over language that has moved from university campuses to the country at large—a development that both underscores Americans' puritannical zeal for reform and their unwavering faith in the talismanic power of words.

5   Certainly no decent person can quarrel with the underlying impulse behind political correctness: a vision of a more just, inclusive society in which racism, sexism and prejudice of all sorts have been erased. But the methods and fervor of the self-appointed language police can lead to a rigid orthodoxy—and unintentional self-parody—opening the movement to the scorn of conservative opponents and the mockery of cartoonists and late-night television hosts.

6   It's hard to imagine women earning points for political correctness by saying "ovarimony" instead of "testimony"—as one participant at the recent Modern Language Association convention was overheard to suggest. It's equally hard to imagine people wanting to flaunt their lack of prejudice by giving up such words and phrases as "bull market," "kaiser roll," "Lazy Susan," and "charley horse."

7   Several books on bias-free language have already appeared, and the 1991 edition of the Random House Webster's College Dictionary boasts an appendix titled "Avoiding Sexist Language." The dictionary also includes such linguistic mutations as "womyn" (women, "used as an alternative spelling to avoid the suggestion of sexism perceived in the sequence m-e-n") and "waitron" (a gender-blind term for waiter or waitress).

8   Many of these dictionaries and guides not only warn the reader against offensive racial and sexual slurs, but also try to establish and enforce a whole new set of usage rules. Take, for instance, "The Bias-Free Word Finder, a Dictionary of Nondiscriminatory Language" by Rosalie Maggio (Beacon Press)—a volume often indistinguishable, in its meticulous solemnity, from the tongue-in-cheek "Official Politically Correct Dictionary and Handbook" put out last year by Henry Beard and Christopher Cerf (Villard Books). Ms. Maggio's book supplies the reader intent on using kinder, gentler language with writing guidelines as well as a detailed listing of more than 5,000 "biased words and phrases."

9   Whom are these guidelines for? Somehow one has a tough time picturing them replacing "Fowler's Modern English Usage" in the classroom, or being adopted by the average man (sorry, individual) in the street.

10   The "pseudogeneric 'he,' " we learn from Ms. Maggio, is to be avoided like the plague, as is the use of the word "man" to refer to humanity. "Fellow," "king," "lord" and "master" are bad because they're "male-oriented words," and "king," "lord" and "master" are especially bad because they're also "hierarchical, dominator society terms." The politically correct lion becomes the "monarch of the jungle," new-age children play "someone on the top of the heap," and the "Mona Lisa" goes down in history as Leonardo's "acme of perfection."

11   As for the word "black," Ms. Maggio says it should be excised from terms with a negative spin: she recommends substituting words like "mouse" for "black eye," "ostracize" for "blackball," "payola" for "blackmail" and "outcast" for "black sheep." Clearly, some of these substitutions work better than others: somehow the "sinister humor" of Kurt Vonnegut or "Saturday Night Live" doesn't quite make it; nor does the "denouncing" of the Hollywood 10.

12   For the dedicated user of politically correct language, all these rules can make for some messy moral dilemmas. Whereas "battered wife" is a gender-biased term, the gender-free term "battered spouse," Ms. Maggio notes, incorrectly implies "that men and women are equally battered."

13   On one hand, say Francine Wattman Frank and Paula A. Treichler in their book "Language, Gender, and Professional Writing" (Modern Language Association), "he or she" is an appropriate construction for talking about an individual (like a jockey, say) who belongs to a profession that's predominantly male—it's a way of emphasizing "that such occupations are not barred to women or that women's concerns need to be kept in mind." On the other hand, they add, using masculine pronouns rhetorically can underscore ongoing male dominance in those fields, implying the need for change.

14   And what about the speech codes adopted by some universities in recent years? Although they were designed to prohibit students from uttering sexist and racist slurs, they would extend, by logic, to blacks who want to use the word "nigger" to strip the term of its racist connotations, or homosexuals who want to use the word "queer" to reclaim it from bigots.

15   In her book, Ms. Maggio recommends applying bias-free usage retroactively: she suggests paraphrasing politically incorrect quotations, or replacing "the sexist words or phrases with ellipsis dots and/or bracketed substitutes," or using "sic" "to show that the sexist words come from the original quotation and to call attention to the fact that they are incorrect."

16   Which leads the skeptical reader of "The Bias-Free Word Finder" to wonder whether "All the King's Men" should be retitled "All the Ruler's People"; "Pet Semetary," "Animal Companion Graves"; "Birdman of Alcatraz," "Birdperson of Alcatraz," and "The Iceman Cometh," "The Ice Route Driver Cometh"?

17   Will making such changes remove the prejudice in people's minds? Should we really spend time trying to come up with nonmale-based alternatives to "Midas touch," "Achilles' heel," and "Montezuma's revenge"? Will tossing out Santa Claus—whom Ms. Maggio accuses of reinforcing "the cultural male-as-norm system"—in favor of Belfana, his Italian female alter ego, truly help banish sexism? Can the avoidance of "violent expressions and metaphors" like "kill two birds with one stone," "sock it to 'em" or "kick an idea around" actually promote a more harmonious world?

18   The point isn't that the excesses of the word police are comical. The point is that their intolerance (in the name of tolerance) has disturbing implications. In the first place, getting upset by phrases like "bullish on America" or "the City of Brotherly Love" tends to distract attention from the real problems of prejudice and injustice that exist in society at large, turning them into mere questions of semantics. Indeed, the emphasis currently put on politically correct usage has uncanny parallels with the academic movement of deconstruction—a method of textual analysis that focuses on language and linguistic pyrotechnics—which has become firmly established on university campuses.

19   In both cases, attention is focused on surfaces, on words and metaphors; in both cases, signs and symbols are accorded more importance than content. Hence, the attempt by some radical advocates to remove "The Adventures of Huckleberry Finn" from curriculums on the grounds that Twain's use of the word "nigger" makes the book a racist text—never mind the fact that this American classic (written in 1884) depicts the spiritual kinship achieved between a white boy and a runaway slave, never mind the fact that the "nigger" Jim emerges as the novel's most honorable, decent character.

20   Ironically enough, the P.C. movement's obsession with language is accompanied by a strange Orwellian willingness to warp the meaning of words by placing them under a high-powered ideological lens. For instance, the "Dictionary of Cautionary Words and Phrases"—a pamphlet issued by the University of Missouri's Multicultural Management Program to help turn "today's journalists into tomorrow's multicultural newsroom managers"—warns that using the word "articulate" to describe members of a minority group can suggest the opposite, "that 'those people' are not considered well educated, articulate and the like."

21   The pamphlet patronizes minority groups, by cautioning the reader against

using the words "lazy" and "burly" to describe any member of such groups; and it issues a similar warning against using words like "gorgeous" and "petite" to describe women.

22   As euphemism proliferates with the rise of political correctness, there is a spread of the sort of sloppy, abstract language that Orwell said is "designed to make lies sound truthful and murder respectable, and to give an appearance of solidity to pure wind." "Fat" becomes "big boned" or "differently sized"; "stupid" becomes "exceptional"; "stoned" becomes "chemically inconvenienced."

23   Wait a minute here! Aren't such phrases eerily reminiscent of the euphemisms coined by the Government during Vietnam and Watergate? Remember how the military used to speak of "pacification," or how President Richard M. Nixon's press secretary, Ronald L. Ziegler, tried to get away with calling a lie an "inoperative statement"?

24   Calling the homeless "the underhoused" doesn't give them a place to live; calling the poor "the economically marginalized" doesn't help them pay the bills. Rather, by playing down their plight, such language might even make it easier to shrug off the seriousness of their situation.

25   Instead of allowing free discussion and debate to occur, many gung-ho advocates of politically correct language seem to think that simple suppression of a word or concept will magically make the problem disappear. In the "Bias-Free Word Finder," Ms. Maggio entreats the reader not to perpetuate the negative stereotype of Eve. "Be extremely cautious in referring to the biblical Eve," she writes; "this story has profoundly contributed to negative attitudes toward women throughout history, largely because of misogynistic and patriarchal interpretations that labeled her evil, inferior, and seductive."

26   The story of Bluebeard, the rake (whoops!—the libertine) who killed his seven wives, she says, is also to be avoided, as is the biblical story of Jezebel. Of Jesus Christ, Ms. Maggio writes: "There have been few individuals in history as completely androgynous as Christ, and it does his message a disservice to overinsist on his maleness." She doesn't give the reader any hints on how this might be accomplished; presumably, one is supposed to avoid describing him as the Son of God.

27   Of course the P.C. police aren't the only ones who want to proscribe what people should say or give them guidelines for how they may use an idea; Jesse Helms and his supporters are up to exactly the same thing when they propose to patrol the boundaries of the permissible in art. In each case, the would-be censor aspires to suppress what he or she finds distasteful—all, of course, in the name of the public good.

28   In the case of the politically correct, the prohibition of certain words, phrases and ideas is advanced in the cause of building a brave new world free of racism and hate, but this vision of harmony clashes with the very ideals of diversity and inclusion that the multi-cultural movement holds dear, and it's purchased at the cost of freedom of expression and freedom of speech.

29   In fact, the utopian world envisioned by the language police would be bought at the expense of the ideals of individualism and democracy articulated in the "The Gettysburg Address": "Fourscore and seven years ago our fathers brought forth on this continent a new nation, conceived in liberty and dedicated to the proposition that all men are created equal."

30   Of course, the P.C. police have already found Lincoln's words hopelessly "phallocentric." No doubt they would rewrite the passage: "Fourscore and seven years ago our foremothers and forefathers brought forth on this continent a new nation, formulated with liberty, and dedicated to the proposition that all humankind is created equal."

QUESTIONS

Experience

· Comment on your experience with using or hearing different types of biased language. Discuss how forms of reference to women and minorities have changed in movies and on television.

Interpretation

· To what extent do you agree that biased language exists? To what extent do you think the problem may be exaggerated? Why?
· To what extent is Kakutani's idea simply that there is too much politically correct language being used now? What else does she express concern about? Why?

Evaluation

· Many of the examples cited in this piece concern gender bias. Do you think that there is more gender-biased language than other types? Why, or why not?

WRITING

Exploring

· Keep a record for a week or two of examples of biased language you hear on TV or read in newspapers and magazines. For each example you record, explain why the language is biased and against whom.

Interpreting

· Write a brief paper explaining the connection Kakutani makes between political correctness, euphemism, and abstract language. Explain why she alludes to Maya Angelou's inaugural poem "On the Pulse of Morning" and to George Orwell's essay "Politics and the English Language."

Evaluating

· Support, qualify, or refute Kakutani's argument by elaborating on her ideas or criticizing them. Cite evidence and examples from your experience, your observation, and your reading to develop your paper.

ROBIN LAKOFF
(b. 1942)

Talking Like a Lady

Robin Lakoff was born and raised in Brooklyn, New York. She is currently a professor of linguistics at the University of California, Berkeley. Among her books are Face Value: The Politics of Beauty *(1984) and* Language and a Woman's Place *(1985), from which the following selection has been excerpted. In "Talking Like a Lady" Lakoff explores ways women's language differs from men's.*

Among the essay's notable features are its multitude of examples from everyday language situations, including casual observation and conversation. Lakoff's examples clarify and illustrate her idea and provide convincing evidence for the part of her argument in which she claims different uses of language for men and women.

1 "Women's language" shows up in all levels of the grammar of English. We find differences in the choice and frequency of lexical items; in the situations in which certain syntactic rules are performed; in intonational and other superseg-mental patterns. As an example of lexical differences, imagine a man and a woman both looking at the same wall, painted a pinkish shade of purple. The woman may say:

1. The wall is mauve,

with no one consequently forming any special impression of her as a result of the words alone; but if the man should say (1), one might well conclude he was imitating a woman sarcastically or was a homosexual or an interior decorator. Women, then, make far more precise discriminations in naming colors than do men; words like *beige, ecru, aquamarine, lavender,* and so on are unremarkable in a woman's active vocabulary, but absent from that of most men. I have seen a man helpless with suppressed laughter at a discussion between two other people as to whether a book jacket was to be described as "lavender" or "mauve." Men find such discussion amusing because they consider such a question trivial, irrelevant to the real world.

2 We might ask why fine discrimination of color is relevant for women, but not for men. A clue is contained in the way many men in our society view other "unworldly" topics, such as high culture and the Church, as outside the world of men's work, relegated to women and men whose masculinity is not unquestionable. Men tend to relegate to women things that are not of concern to them, or do not involve their egos. Among these are problems of fine color discrimination. We might rephrase this point by saying that since women are not expected to make decisions on important matters, such as what kind of job to hold, they are relegated the noncrucial decisions as a sop. Deciding whether to name a color "lavender" or "mauve" is one such sop.

3   If it is agreed that this lexical disparity reflects a social inequity in the position of women, one may ask how to remedy it. Obviously, no one could seriously recommend legislating against the use of the terms "mauve" and "lavender" by women, or forcing men to learn to use them. All we can do is give women the opportunity to participate in the real decisions of life.

4   Aside from specific lexical items like color names, we find differences between the speech of women and that of men in the use of particles that grammarians often describe as "meaningless." There may be no referent for them, but they are far from meaningless: they define the social context of an utterance, indicate the relationship the speaker feels between himself and his addressee, between himself and what he is talking about.

5   As an experiment, one might present native speakers of standard American English with pairs of sentences, identical syntactically and in terms of referential lexical items, and differing merely in the choice of "meaningless" particles, and ask them which was spoken by a man, which a woman. Consider:

2. a. Oh dear, you've put the peanut butter in the refrigerator again.
    b. Shit, you've put the peanut butter in the refrigerator again.

6   It is safe to predict that people would classify the first sentence as part of "women's language," the second as "men's language." It is true that many self-respecting women are becoming able to use sentences like (2)(b) publicly without flinching, but this is a relatively recent development, and while perhaps the majority of Middle America might condone the use of (b) for men, they would still disapprove of its use by women. (It is of interest, by the way, to note that men's language is increasingly being used by women, but women's language is not being adopted by men, apart from those who reject the American masculine image [for example, homosexuals]. This is analogous to the fact that men's jobs are being sought by women, but few men are rushing to become housewives or secretaries. The language of the favored group, the group that holds the power, along with its nonlinguistic behavior, is generally adopted by the other group, not vice versa. In any event, it is a truism to state that the "stronger" expletives are reserved for men, and the "weaker" ones for women.)

7   Now we may ask what we mean by "stronger" and "weaker" expletives. (If these particles were indeed meaningless, none would be stronger than any other.) The difference between using "shit" (or "damn," or one of many others) as opposed to "oh dear," or "goodness," or "oh fudge" lies in how forcefully one says how one feels—perhaps, one might say, choice of particle is a function of how strongly one allows oneself to feel about something, so that the strength of an emotion conveyed in a sentence corresponds to the strength of the particle. Hence in a really serious situation, the use of "trivializing" (that is, "women's") particles constitutes a joke, or at any rate, is highly inappropriate. (In conformity with current linguistic practice, throughout this work an asterisk [*] will be used to mark a sentence that is inappropriate in some sense, either because it is syntactically deviant or used in the wrong social context.)

3. a. *Oh fudge, my hair is on fire.
    b. *Dear me, did he kidnap the baby?

8   As children, women are encouraged to be "little ladies." Little ladies don't scream as vociferously as little boys, and they are chastised more severely for throwing tantrums or showing temper: "high spirits" are expected and therefore tolerated in little boys; docility and resignation are the corresponding traits expected of little girls. Now, we tend to excuse a show of temper by a man where we would not excuse an identical tirade from a woman: women are allowed to fuss and complain, but only a man can bellow in rage. It is sometimes claimed that there is a biological basis for this behavior difference, though I don't believe conclusive evidence exists that the early differences in behavior that have been observed are not the results of very different treatment of babies of the two sexes from the beginning; but surely the use of different particles by men and women is a learned trait, merely mirroring nonlinguistic differences again, and again pointing out an inequity that exists between the treatment of men, and society's expectations of them, and the treatment of women. Allowing men stronger means of expression than are open to women further reinforces men's position of strength in the real world: for surely we listen with more attention the more strongly and forcefully someone expresses opinions, and a speaker unable—for whatever reason—to be forceful in stating his views is much less likely to be taken seriously. Ability to use strong particles like "shit" and "hell" is, of course, only incidental to the inequity that exists rather than its cause. But once again, apparently accidental linguistic usage suggests that women are denied equality partially for linguistic reasons, and that an examination of language points up precisely an area in which inequity exists. Further, if someone is allowed to show emotions, and consequently does, others may well be able to view him as a real individual in his own right, as they could not if he never showed emotion. Here again, then, the behavior a woman learns as "correct" prevents her from being taken seriously as an individual, and further is considered "correct" and necessary for a woman precisely because society does *not* consider her seriously as an individual.

9   Similar sorts of disparities exist elsewhere in the vocabulary. There is, for instance, a group of adjectives which have, besides their specific and literal meanings, another use, that of indicating the speaker's approbation or admiration for something. Some of these adjectives are neutral as to sex of speaker: either men or women may use them. But another set seems, in its figurative use, to be largely confined to women's speech. Representative lists of both types are below:

neutral	women only
great	adorable
terrific	charming
cool	sweet
neat	lovely
	divine

10   As with the color words and swear words already discussed, for a man to stray into the "women's" column is apt to be damaging to his reputation, though here a woman may freely use the neutral words. But it should not be inferred from this that a woman's use of the "women's" words is without its risks. Where a

woman has a choice between the neutral words and the women's words, as a man has not, she may be suggesting very different things about her own personality and her view of the subject matter by her choice of words of the first set or words of the second.

4. a. What a terrific idea!
   b. What a divine idea!

It seems to me that (a) might be used under any appropriate conditions by a female speaker. But (b) is more restricted. Probably it is used appropriately (even by the sort of speaker for whom it was normal) only in case the speaker feels the idea referred to be essentially frivolous, trivial, or unimportant to the world at large—only an amusement for the speaker herself. Consider, then, a woman advertising executive at an advertising conference. However feminine an advertising executive she is, she is much more likely to express her approval with (4)(a) than with (b), which might cause raised eyebrows, and the reaction: "That's what we get for putting a woman in charge of this company."

11   On the other hand, suppose a friend suggests to the same woman that she should dye her French poodles to match her cigarette lighter. In this case, the suggestion really concerns only her, and the impression she will make on people. In this case, she may use (b), from the "women's language." So the choice is not really free: words restricted to "women's language" suggest that concepts to which they are applied are not relevant to the real world of (male) influence and power.

12   One may ask whether there really are no analogous terms that are available to men—terms that denote approval of the trivial, the personal; that express approbation in terms of one's own personal emotional reaction, rather than by gauging the likely general reaction. There does in fact seem to be one such word: it is the hippie invention "groovy," which seems to have most of the connotations that separate "lovely" and "divine" from "great" and "terrific" excepting only that it does not mark the speaker as feminine or effeminate.

5. a. What a terrific steel mill!
   b. *What a lovely steel mill! (male speaking)
   c. What a groovy steel mill!

I think it is significant that this word was introduced by the hippies, and, when used seriously rather than sarcastically, used principally by people who have accepted the hippies' values. Principal among these is the denial of the Protestant work ethic: to a hippie, something can be worth thinking about even if it isn't influential in the power structure, or moneymaking. Hippies are separated from the activities of the real world just as women are—though in the former case it is due to a decision on their parts, while this is not uncontroversially true in the case of women. For both these groups, it is possible to express approval of things in a personal way—though one does so at the risk of losing one's credibility with members of the power structure. It is also true, according to some speakers, that upper-class British men may use the words listed in the "women's" column, as well as the specific color words and others we have categorized as specifically feminine, without raising doubts as to their masculinity among other speakers of the same dialect. (This is not true for lower-class Britons, however.) The reason may be that commitment to the work ethic need not necessarily be displayed: one may be or appear to be a gentleman of leisure, interested in various pursuits, but not involved in mundane (business or political) affairs, in such a culture, without incurring disgrace. This is rather analogous to the position of a woman in American middle-class society, so we should not be surprised if these special lexical items are usable by both groups. This fact points indeed to a more general conclusion. These words aren't, basically, "feminine"; rather, they signal "uninvolved," or "out of power." Any group in a society to which these labels are applicable may presumably use these words; they are often considered "feminine," "unmasculine," because women are the "uninvolved," "out-of-power" group par excellence.

13   Another group that has, ostensibly at least, taken itself out of the search for power and money is that of academic men. They are frequently viewed by other groups as analogous in some ways to women—they don't really work, they are supported in their frivolous pursuits by others, what they do doesn't really count in the real world, and so on. The suburban home finds its counterpart in the ivory tower: one is supposedly shielded from harsh realities in both. Therefore it is not too surprising that many academic men (especially those who emulate British norms) may violate many of these sacrosanct rules I have just laid down: they often use "women's language." Among themselves, this does not occasion ridicule. But to a truck driver, a professor saying, "What a lovely hat!" is undoubtedly laughable, all the more so as it reinforces his stereotype of professors as effete snobs.

14   When we leave the lexicon and venture into syntax, we find that syntactically too women's speech is peculiar. To my knowledge, there is no syntactic rule in English that only women may use. But there is at least one rule that a woman will use in more conversational situations than a man. (This fact indicates, of course, that the applicability of syntactic rules is governed partly by social context—the positions in society of the speaker and addressee, with respect to each other, and the impression one seeks to make on the other.) This is the rule of tag-question formation.[1]

---

[1] Within the lexicon itself, there seems to be a parallel phenomenon to tag-question usage, which I refrain from discussing in the body of the text because the facts are controversial and I do not understand them fully. The intensive *so*, used where purists would insist upon an absolute superlative, heavily stressed, seems more characteristic of women's language than of men's, though it is found in the latter, particularly in the speech of male academics. Consider, for instance, the following sentences:

(a) I feel *so* unhappy!
(b) That movie made me *so* sick!

Men seem to have the least difficulty using this construction when the sentence is unemotional, or nonsubjective—without reference to the speaker himself:

(c) That sunset is *so* beautiful!
(d) Fred is *so* dumb!

Substituting an equative like *so* for absolute superlatives (like *very, really, utterly*) seems to be a way of backing out of committing oneself strongly to an opinion, rather like tag questions (cf. discussion below, in the text). One might hedge in this way with perfect right in making aesthetic judgments, as in (c), or intellectual judgments, as in (d). But it is somewhat odd to hedge in describing one's own mental or emotional state: who, after all, is qualified to contradict one on this? To hedge in this situation is to seek to avoid making any strong statement: a characteristic, as we have noted already and shall note further, of women's speech.

15   A tag, in its usage as well as its syntactic shape (in English), is midway between an outright statement and a yes-no question: it is less assertive than the former, but more confident than the latter. Therefore it is usable under certain contextual situations: not those in which a statement would be appropriate, nor those in which a yes-no question is generally used, but in situations intermediate between these.

16   One makes a statement when one has confidence in his knowledge and is pretty certain that his statement will be believed; one asks a question when one lacks knowledge on some point and has reason to believe that this gap can and will be remedied by an answer by the addressee. A tag question, being intermediate between these, is used when the speaker is stating a claim, but lacks full confidence in the truth of that claim. So if I say:

> 6. Is John here?

I will probably not be surprised if my respondent answers "no"; but if I say

> 7. John is here, isn't he?

instead, chances are I am already biased in favor of a positive answer, wanting only confirmation by the addressee. I still want a response from him, as I do with a yes-no question; but I have enough knowledge (or think I have) to predict that response, much as with a declarative statement. A tag question, then, might be thought of as a declarative statement without the assumption that the statement is to be believed by the addressee: one has an out, as with a question. A tag gives the addressee leeway, not forcing him to go along with the views of the speaker.

17   There are situations in which a tag is legitimate, in fact the only legitimate sentence form. So, for example, if I have seen something only indistinctly, and have reason to believe my addressee had a better view, I can say:

> 8. I had my glasses off. He was out at third, wasn't he?

18   Sometimes we find a tag question used in cases in which the speaker knows as well as the addressee what the answer must be, and doesn't need confirmation. One such situation is when the speaker is making "small talk," trying to elicit conversation from the addressee:

> 9. Sure is hot here, isn't it?

19   In discussing personal feelings or opinions, only the speaker normally has any way of knowing the correct answer. Strictly speaking, questioning one's own opinions is futile. Sentences like (10) are usually ridiculous.

> 10. *I have a headache, don't I?

But similar cases do, apparently, exist, in which it is the speaker's opinions, rather than perceptions, for which corroboration is sought, as in (11):

> 11. The way prices are rising is horrendous, isn't it?

20   While there are of course other possible interpretations of a sentence like this, one possibility is that the speaker has a particular answer in mind—"yes" or

"no"—but is reluctant to state it baldly. It is my impression, though I do not have precise statistical evidence, that this sort of tag question is much more apt to be used by women than by men. If this is indeed true, why is it true?

21   These sentence types provide a means whereby a speaker can avoid committing himself, and thereby avoid coming into conflict with the addressee. The problem is that, by so doing, a speaker may also give the impression of not being really sure of himself, of looking to the addressee for confirmation, even of having no views of his own. This last criticism is, of course, one often leveled at women. One wonders how much of it reflects a use of language that has been imposed on women from their earliest years.

22   Related to this special use of a syntactic rule is a widespread difference perceptible in women's intonational patterns. There is a peculiar sentence intonation pattern, found in English as far as I know only among women, which has the form of a declarative answer to a question, and is used as such, but has the rising inflection typical of a yes-no question, as well as being especially hesitant. The effect is as though one were seeking confirmation, though at the same time the speaker may be the only one who has the requisite information.

12. a.   When will dinner be ready?
    b.   Oh . . . around six o'clock . . . ?

It is as though (b) were saying, "Six o'clock, if that's OK with you, if you agree." (a) is put in the position of having to provide confirmation, and (b) sounds unsure. Here we find unwillingness to assert an opinion carried to an extreme. One likely consequence is that these sorts of speech patterns are taken to reflect something real about character and play a part in not taking a woman seriously or trusting her with any real responsibilities, since "she can't make up her mind" and "isn't sure of herself." And here again we see that people form judgments about other people on the basis of superficial linguistic behavior that may have nothing to do with inner character, but has been imposed upon the speaker, on pain of worse punishment than not being taken seriously.

23   Such features are probably part of the general fact that women's speech sounds much more "polite" than men's. One aspect of politeness is as we have just described: leaving a decision open, not imposing your mind, or views, or claims on anyone else. Thus a tag question is a kind of polite statement, in that it does not force agreement or belief on the addressee. A request may be in the same sense a polite command, in that it does not overtly require obedience, but rather suggests something be done as a favor to the speaker. An overt order (as in an imperative) expresses the (often impolite) assumption of the speaker's superior position to the addressee, carrying with it the right to enforce compliance, whereas with a request the decision on the face of it is left up to the addressee. (The same is true of suggestions: here, the implication is not that the addressee is in danger if he does not comply—merely that he will be glad if he does. Once again, the decision is up to the addressee, and a suggestion therefore is politer than an order.) The more particles in a sentence that reinforce the notion that it is a request, rather than an order, the politer the result. The sentences of (13) illustrate these points: (a) is a direct order, (b) and (c) simple requests, and (d) and (e) compound requests.

13. a. Close the door.
     b. Please close the door.
     c. Will you close the door?
     d. Will you please close the door?
     e. Won't you close the door?

24   Let me first explain why (e) has been classified as a compound request. (A sentence like *Won't you please close the door* would then count as a doubly compound request.) A sentence like (13)(c) is close in sense to "Are you willing to close the door?" According to the normal rules of polite conversation, to agree that you are willing is to agree to do the thing asked of you. Hence this apparent inquiry functions as a request, leaving the decision up to the willingness of the addressee. Phrasing it as a positive question makes the (implicit) assumption that a "yes" answer will be forthcoming. Sentence (13)(d) is more polite than (b) or (c) because it combines them: *please* indicating that to accede will be to do something for the speaker, and *will you,* as noted, suggesting that the addressee has the final decision. If, now, the question is phrased with a negative, as in (13)(e), the speaker seems to suggest the stronger likelihood of a negative response from the addressee. Since the assumption is then that the addressee is that much freer to refuse, (13)(e) acts as a more polite request than (13)(c) or (d); (c) and (d) put the burden of refusal on the addressee, as (e) does not.

25   Given these facts, one can see the connection between tag questions and tag orders and other requests. In all these cases, the speaker is not committed as with a simple declarative or affirmative. And the more one compounds a request, the more characteristic it is of women's speech, the less of men's. A sentence that begins *Won't you please* (without special emphasis on *please*) seems to me at least to have a distinctly unmasculine sound. Little girls are indeed taught to talk like little ladies, in that their speech is in many ways more polite than that of boys or men, and the reason for this is that politeness involves an absence of a strong statement, and women's speech is devised to prevent the expression of strong statements.

QUESTIONS

Experience

· To what extent do you talk in ways Lakoff indicates that you do (as a man or as a woman)? To what extent and in what kinds of situations does your speech not fit her description? How does it differ, and why?

Interpretation

· Although Lakoff uses many examples of women's speech to distinguish it from men's, she is more interested in making a point about power and equity than in describing differences in language use. What does she suggest about why women use particular forms of speech, such as tag questions? What, according to Lakoff, is the reason women have a larger color vocabulary than men? And what is her purpose in introducing special groups such as hippies, homosexual men, and upper-class British males into her discussion?

Evaluation

· Assess the persuasiveness of Lakoff's argument. Consider ways she supports (or does not support) her assertions with evidence, example, or logic. Look, for example, at the opening sentence of paragraph 3, which seems to assume the reader's agreement about an important point—that lexical disparity reflects social disparity—without providing evidence or argumentative support for it. Cite other examples of Lakoff's assertions that assume the reader's agreement.

WRITING

Exploring

· Keep a record for a week of the ways men and women talk. You can make observations of television newscasters, characters in situation comedies, and films, as well as in your classes (both students and teachers). Write up your notes, and comment on what you find.

Interpreting

· Offer your own explanation for what you perceive as differences or growing similarities among the ways men and women use language.

· Or, if you prefer, make your analysis not of differences between men's and women's language, but of ways language is used by speakers from different social classes, speakers with different sexual orientations, or speakers talking in different contexts. You can use some of Lakoff's examples as well as your own observations.

Evaluating

· Write an essay in which you argue that society would be better off if men used language more the way women do, or if women used language more the way men do. Or argue that retaining the differences Lakoff describes has advantages over the alternatives.

BARBARA LAWRENCE

Four-Letter Words Can Hurt You

Barbara Lawrence is professor of language and literature at the State University of New York, Old Westbury. Her publications include articles and reviews on aspects of language—especially those related to feminist concerns. The following selection originally appeared in 1973 as an Op-Ed piece in the New York Times.

In "Four-Letter Words Can Hurt You," Lawrence considers various examples of sexist and racist language, arguing that such words "deform identity, deny individuality and humanness." Lawrence suggests, moreover, that obscene language trivializes the complexity of human experience by reducing it to simplistic and infantile functions. Her essay is replete with specific examples, some of which Lawrence investigates historically.

1   Why should any words be called obscene? Don't they all describe natural human functions? Am I trying to tell them, my students demand, that the "strong, earthy, gut-honest"—or, if they are fans of Norman Mailer, the "rich, liberating, existential"—language they use to describe sexual activity isn't preferable to "phony-sounding, middle-class words like 'intercourse' and 'copulate'?" "Cop You Late!" they say with fancy inflections and gagging grimaces. "Now, what is *that* supposed to mean?"

2   Well, what is it supposed to mean? And why indeed should one group of words describing human functions and human organs be acceptable in ordinary conversations and another, describing presumably the same organs and functions, be tabooed—so much so, in fact, that some of these words still cannot appear in print in many parts of the English-speaking world?

3   The argument that these taboos exist only because of "sexual hang-ups" (middle-class, middle-age, feminist), or even that they are a result of class oppression (the contempt of the Norman conquerors for the language of their Anglo-Saxon serfs), ignores a much more likely explanation, it seems to me, and that is the sources and functions of the words themselves.

4   The best known of the tabooed sexual verbs, for example, comes from the German *ficken,* meaning "to strike"; combined, according to Partridge's etymological dictionary *Origins,* with the Latin sexual verb *futuere;* associated in turn with the Latin *fustis,* "a staff or cudgel"; the Celtic *buc,* "a point, hence to pierce"; the Irish *bot,* "the male member"; the Latin *battuere,* "to beat"; the Gaelic *batair,* "a cudgeller"; the Early Irish *bualaim,* "I strike"; and so forth. It is one of what etymologists sometimes call "the sadistic group of words for the man's part in copulation."

5   The brutality of this word, then, and its equivalents ("screw," "bang," etc.), is not an illusion of the middle class or a crotchet of Women's Liberation. In their

origins and imagery these words carry undeniably painful, if not sadistic, implications, the object of which is almost always female. Consider, for example, what a "screw" actually does to the wood it penetrates; what a painful, even mutilating, activity this kind of analogy suggests. "Screw" is particularly interesting in this context, since the noun, according to Partridge, comes from words meaning "groove," "nut," "ditch," "breeding sow," "scrofula" and "swelling," while the verb, besides its explicit imagery, has antecedent associations to "write on," "scratch," "scarify," and so forth—a revealing fusion of a mechanical or painful action with an obviously denigrated object.

6   Not all obscene words, of course, are as implicitly sadistic or denigrating to women as these, but all that I know seem to serve a similar purpose: to reduce the human organism (especially the female organism) and human functions (especially sexual and procreative) to their least organic, most mechanical dimension; to substitute a trivializing or deforming resemblance for the complex human reality of what is being described.

7   Tabooed male descriptives, when they are not openly denigrating to women, often serve to divorce a male organ or function from any significant interaction with the female. Take the word "testes," for example, suggesting "witnesses" (from the Latin *testis*) to the sexual and procreative strengths of the male organ; and the obscene counterpart of this word, which suggests little more than a mechanical shape. Or compare almost any of the "rich," "liberating" sexual verbs, so fashionable today among male writers, with that much-derided Latin word "copulate" ("to bind or join together") or even that Anglo-Saxon phrase (which seems to have had no trouble surviving the Norman Conquest) "make love."

8   How arrogantly self-involved the tabooed words seem in comparison to either of the other terms, and how contemptuous of the female partner. Understandably so, of course, if she is only a "skirt," a "broad," a "chick," a "pussycat" or a "piece." If she is, in other words, no more than her skirt, or what her skirt conceals; no more than a breeder, or the broadest part of her; no more than a piece of a human being or a "piece of tail."

9   The most severely tabooed of all the female descriptives, incidentally, are those like a "piece of tail," which suggest (either explicitly or through antecedents) that there is no significant difference between the female channel through which we are all conceived and born and the anal outlet common to both sexes—a distinction that pornographers have always enjoyed obscuring.

10   This effort to deny women their biological identity, their individuality, their humanness, is such an important aspect of obscene language that one can only marvel at how seldom, in an era preoccupied with definitions of obscenity, this fact is brought to our attention. One problem, of course, is that many of the people in the best position to do this (critics, teachers, writers) are so reluctant today to admit that they are angered or shocked by obscenity. Bored, maybe, unimpressed, aesthetically displeased, but—no matter how brutal or denigrating the material—never angered, never shocked.

11   And yet how eloquently angered, how piously shocked many of these same people become if denigrating language is used about any minority group other than women; if the obscenities are racial or ethnic, that is, rather than sexual. Words like "coon," "kike," "spic," "wop," after all, deform identity, deny individ-

uality and humanness in almost exactly the same way that sexual vulgarisms and obscenities do.

12   No one that I know, least of all my students, would fail to question the values of a society whose literature and entertainment rested heavily on racial or ethnic pejoratives. Are the values of a society whose literature and entertainment rest as heavily as ours on sexual pejoratives any less questionable?

QUESTIONS

Experience

· What has been your experience in using, hearing, or being on the receiving end of various types of sexist, racist, or ethnically charged language? Have you ever referred to women with the terms Lawrence includes, for example? Or have you referred to ethnic or racial groups with the examples she gives? What about other terms?

Interpretation

· Why does Lawrence include the etymologies, or origins, of words such as "screw"? What does she mean by referring to the function of this and other words? Are you convinced that a word's source or dictionary meaning contributes to or increases its obscenity? Why, or why not?

Evaluation

· Do you think that using obscenities and taboo words is a liberating act? Why, or why not? Do you think many people are shocked by obscenity—older people, perhaps? Why, or why not? What is the purpose of using obscenities, anyway?

WRITING

Exploring

· Interview some of your friends, classmates, family members, perhaps even teachers. Ask whether they ever use obscenities and, if so, when, why, and which ones. Gauge their attitudes toward using obscenities.

· Attend two commercially successful or popular films, and keep a record of obscenities used. Categorize the types of obscenities, their occasions, and the characters who use them. Provide explanations for any obscenities you hear in the films.

Interpreting

· Lawrence's essay breaks into two parts, the first on sexist obscenities and the second on ethnic slurs. Summarize her argument in each part, and identify the kinds of evidence and examples she uses to support each half of her argument.

Evaluating

· Lawrence believes that the kinds of words men use about women convey men's attitudes toward women. And she also believes that the words men use for sexual intimacy convey their way of thinking about sex. Do you agree with her? Why, or why not? Identify some words women use in talking about men and about sex. What attitudes or perspectives do these words suggest? Why?

· Agree or disagree with Lawrence's suggestion that many people today are not shocked by the use of obscenity. Consider to what extent social factors, such as contemporary films and television shows, contribute to people's response to obscene language.

NANCY MAIRS
(b. 1943)

On Being a Cripple

Nancy Mairs is a teacher, essayist, and prize-winning poet who has also worked as a technical editor at the Smithsonian Astrophysical Observatory, the MIT Press, and the Harvard Law School. Her books include Plaintext, Carnal Acts, Remembering the Bone House *(autobiography), and* All the Rooms of the Yellow House *(poems).*

In "On Being a Cripple," Mairs describes her struggle with multiple sclerosis and raises important questions about how those with disabling diseases wish to call themselves and how they wish others to describe them. Perhaps the essay's most noteworthy features are its honesty and its toughness. Mairs refuses to feel sorry for herself, yet she does not diminish the difficulties she and her family contend with as a result of her disease. There is a sense, too, that this essay functions for Mairs as a form of therapy. It is less an argument than an excursion, one that Mairs makes for herself and invites us along on for the ride.

> To escape is nothing. Not to escape is nothing.
>
> —Louise Bogan

1   The other day I was thinking of writing an essay on being a cripple. I was thinking hard in one of the stalls of the women's room in my office building, as I was shoving my shirt into my jeans and tugging up my zipper. Preoccupied, I flushed, picked up my book bag, took my cane down from the hook, and unlatched the door. So many movements unbalanced me, and as I pulled the door open I fell over backward, landing fully clothed on the toilet seat with my legs splayed in front of me: the old beetle-on-its-back routine. Saturday afternoon, the building deserted, I was free to laugh aloud as I wriggled back to my feet, my voice bouncing off the yellowish tiles from all directions. Had anyone been there with me, I'd have been still and faint and hot with chagrin. I decided that it was high time to write the essay.

2   First, the matter of semantics. I am a cripple. I choose this word to name me. I choose from among several possibilities, the most common of which are "handicapped" and "disabled." I made the choice a number of years ago, without thinking, unaware of my motives for doing so. Even now, I'm not sure what those motives are, but I recognize that they are complex and not entirely flattering. People—crippled or not—wince at the word "cripple," as they do not at "handicapped" or "disabled." Perhaps I want them to wince. I want them to see me as a tough customer, one to whom the fates/gods/viruses have not been kind, but who can face the brutal truth of her existence squarely. As a cripple, I swagger.

3   But, to be fair to myself, a certain amount of honesty underlies my choice. "Cripple" seems to me a clean word, straightforward and precise. It has an honorable history, having made its first appearance in the Lindisfarne Gospel in the

tenth century. As a lover of words, I like the accuracy with which it describes my condition: I have lost the full use of my limbs. "Disabled," by contrast, suggests any incapacity, physical or mental. And I certainly don't like "handicapped," which implies that I have deliberately been put at a disadvantage, by whom I can't imagine (my God is not a Handicapper General), in order to equalize chances in the great race of life. These words seem to me to be moving away from my condition, to be widening the gap between word and reality. Most remote is the recently coined euphemism "differently abled," which partakes of the same semantic hopefulness that transformed countries from "undeveloped" to "underdeveloped," then to "less developed," and finally to "developing" nations. People have continued to starve in those countries during the shift. Some realities do not obey the dictates of language.

4   Mine is one of them. Whatever you call me, I remain crippled. But I don't care what you call me, so long as it isn't "differently abled," which strikes me as pure verbal garbage designed, by its ability to describe anyone, to describe no one. I subscribe to George Orwell's thesis that "the slovenliness of our language makes it easier for us to have foolish thoughts." And I refuse to participate in the degeneration of the language to the extent that I deny that I have lost anything in the course of this calamitous disease; I refuse to pretend that the only differences between you and me are the various ordinary ones that distinguish any one person from another. But call me "disabled" or "handicapped" if you like. I have long since grown accustomed to them; and if they are vague, at least they hint at the truth. Moreover, I use them myself. Society is no readier to accept crippledness than to accept death, war, sex, sweat, or wrinkles. I would never refer to another person as a cripple. It is the word I use to name only myself.

5   I haven't always been crippled, a fact for which I am soundly grateful. To be whole of limb is, I know from experience, infinitely more pleasant and useful than to be crippled; and if that knowledge leaves me open to bitterness at my loss, the physical soundness I once enjoyed (though I did not enjoy it half enough) is well worth the occasional stab of regret. Though never any good at sports, I was a normally active child and young adult. I climbed trees, played hopscotch, jumped rope, skated, swam, rode my bicycle, sailed. I despised team sports, spending some of the wretchedest afternoons of my life, sweaty and humiliated, behind a field-hockey stick and under a basketball hoop. I tramped alone for miles along the bridle paths that webbed the woods behind the house I grew up in. I swayed through countless dim hours in the arms of one man or another under the scattered shot of light from mirrored balls, and gyrated through countless more as Tab Hunter and Johnny Mathis gave way to the Rolling Stones, Creedence Clearwater Revival, Cream. I walked down the aisle. I pushed baby carriages, changed tires in the rain, marched for peace.

6   When I was twenty-eight I started to trip and drop things. What at first seemed my natural clumsiness soon became too pronounced to shrug off. I consulted a neurologist, who told me that I had a brain tumor. A battery of tests, increasingly disagreeable, revealed no tumor. About a year and a half later I developed a blurred spot in one eye. I had, at last, the episodes "disseminated in space and time" requisite for a diagnosis: multiple sclerosis. I have never been sorry for the doctor's initial misdiagnosis, however. For almost a week, until the negative

results of the tests were in, I thought that I was going to die right away. Every day for the past nearly ten years, then, has been a kind of gift. I accept all gifts.

7   Multiple sclerosis is a chronic degenerative disease of the central nervous system, in which the myelin that sheathes the nerves is somehow eaten away and scar tissue forms in its place, interrupting the nerves' signals. During its course, which is unpredictable and uncontrollable, one may lose vision, hearing, speech, the ability to walk, control of bladder and/or bowels, strength in any or all extremities, sensitivity to touch, vibration, and/or pain, potency, coordination of movements—the list of possibilities is lengthy and, yes, horrifying. One may also lose one's sense of humor. That's the easiest to lose and the hardest to survive without.

8   In the past ten years, I have sustained some of these losses. Characteristic of MS are sudden attacks, called exacerbations, followed by remissions, and these I have not had. Instead, my disease has been slowly progressive. My left leg is now so weak that I walk with the aid of a brace and a cane; and for distances I use an Amigo, a variation on the electric wheelchair that looks rather like an electrified kiddie car. I no longer have much use of my left hand. Now my right side is weakening as well. I still have the blurred spot in my right eye. Overall, though, I've been lucky so far. My world has, of necessity, been circumscribed by my losses, but the terrain left me has been ample enough for me to continue many of the activities that absorb me: writing, teaching, raising children and cats and plants and snakes, reading, speaking publicly about MS and depression, even playing bridge with people patient and honorable enough to let me scatter cards every which way without sneaking a peek.

9   Lest I begin to sound like Pollyanna, however, let me say that I don't like having MS. I hate it. My life holds realities—harsh ones, some of them—that no right-minded human being ought to accept without grumbling. One of them is fatigue. I know of no one with MS who does not complain of bone-weariness; in a disease that presents an astonishing variety of symptoms, fatigue seems to be a common factor. I wake up in the morning feeling the way most people do at the end of a bad day, and I take it from there. As a result, I spend a lot of time *in extremis* and, impatient with limitation, I tend to ignore my fatigue until my body breaks down in some way and forces rest. Then I miss picnics, dinner parties, poetry readings, the brief visits of old friends from out of town. The offspring of a puritanical tradition of exceptional venerability, I cannot view these lapses without shame. My life often seems a series of small failures to do as I ought.

10   I lead, on the whole, an ordinary life, probably rather like the one I would have led had I not had MS. I am lucky that my predilections were already solitary, sedentary, and bookish—unlike the world-famous French cellist I have read about, or the young woman I talked with one long afternoon who wanted only to be a jockey. I had just begun graduate school when I found out something was wrong with me, and I have remained, interminably, a graduate student. Perhaps I would not have if I'd thought I had the stamina to return to a full-time job as a technical editor; but I've enjoyed my studies.

11   In addition to studying, I teach writing courses. I also teach medical students how to give neurological examinations. I pick up freelance editing jobs here and there. I have raised a foster son and sent him into the world, where he has made me two grandbabies, and I am still escorting my daughter and son through ado-

lescence. I go to Mass every Saturday. I am a superb, if messy, cook. I am also an enthusiastic laundress, capable of sorting a hamper full of clothes into five subtly differentiated piles, but a terrible housekeeper. I can do italic writing and, in an emergency, bathe an oil-soaked cat. I play a fiendish game of Scrabble. When I have the time and the money, I like to sit on my front steps with my husband, drinking Amaretto and smoking a cigar, as we imagine our counterparts in Leningrad and make sure that the sun gets down once more behind the sharp childish scrawl of the Tucson Mountains.

12 This lively plenty has its bleak complement, of course, in all the things I can no longer do. I will never run again, except in dreams, and one day I may have to write that I will never walk again. I like to go camping, but I can't follow George and the children along the trails that wander out of a campsite through the desert or into the mountains. In fact, even on the level I've learned never to check the weather or try to hold a coherent conversation: I need all my attention for my wayward feet. Of late, I have begun to catch myself wondering how people can propel themselves without canes. With only one usable hand, I have to select my clothing with care not so much for style as for ease of ingress and egress, and even so, dressing can be laborious. I can no longer do fine stitchery, pick up babies, play the piano, braid my hair. I am immobilized by acute attacks of depression, which may or may not be physiologically related to MS but are certainly its logical concomitant.

13 These two elements, the plenty and the privation, are never pure, nor are the delight and wretchedness that accompany them. Almost every pickle that I get into as a result of my weakness and clumsiness—and I get into plenty—is funny as well as maddening and sometimes painful. I recall one May afternoon when a friend and I were going out for a drink after finishing up at school. As we were climbing into opposite sides of my car, chatting, I tripped and fell, flat and hard, onto the asphalt parking lot, my abrupt departure interrupting him in mid-sentence. "Where'd you go?" he called as he came around the back of the car to find me hauling myself up by the door frame. "Are you all right?" Yes, I told him, I was fine, just a bit rattly, and we drove off to find a shady patio and some beer. When I got home an hour or so later, my daughter greeted me with "What have you done to yourself?" I looked down. One elbow of my white turtleneck with the green froggies, one knee of my white trousers, one white kneesock were blood-soaked. We peeled off the clothes and inspected the damage, which was nasty enough but not alarming. That part wasn't funny: The abrasions took a long time to heal, and one got a little infected. Even so, when I think of my friend talking earnestly, suddenly, to the hot thin air while I dropped from his view as though through a trap door, I find the image as silly as something from a Marx Brothers movie.

14 I may find it easier than other cripples to amuse myself because I live propped by the acceptance and the assistance and, sometimes, the amusement of those around me. Grocery clerks tear my checks out of my checkbook for me, and sales clerks find chairs to put into dressing rooms when I want to try on clothes. The people I work with make sure I teach at times when I am least likely to be fatigued, in places I can get to, with the materials I need. My students, with one anonymous exception (in an end-of-the-semester evaluation), have been unper-

turbed by my disability. Some even like it. One was immensely cheered by the information that I paint my own fingernails; she decided, she told me, that if I could go to such trouble over fine details, she could keep on writing essays. I suppose I became some sort of bright-fingered muse. She wrote good essays, too.

15   The most important struts in the framework of my existence, of course, are my husband and children. Dismayingly few marriages survive the MS test, and why should they? Most twenty-two- and nineteen-year-olds, like George and me, can vow in clear conscience, after a childhood of chickenpox and summer colds, to keep one another in sickness and in health so long as they both shall live. Not many are equipped for catastrophe: the dismay, the depression, the extra work, the boredom that a degenerative disease can insinuate into a relationship. And our society, with its emphasis on fun and its association of fun with physical performance, offers little encouragement for a whole spouse to stay with a crippled partner. Children experience similar stresses when faced with a crippled parent, and they are more helpless, since parents and children can't usually get divorced. They hate, of course, to be different from their peers, and the child whose mother is tacking down the aisle of a school auditorium packed with proud parents like a Cape Cod dinghy in a stiff breeze jolly well stands out in a crowd. Deprived of legal divorce, the child can at least deny the mother's disability, even her existence, forgetting to tell her about recitals and PTA meetings, refusing to accompany her to stores or church or the movies, never inviting friends to the house. Many do.

16   But I've been limping along for ten years now, and so far George and the children are still at my left elbow, holding tight. Anne and Matthew vacuum floors and dust furniture and haul trash and rake up dog droppings and button my cuffs and bake lasagne and Toll House cookies with just enough grumbling so I know that they don't have brain fever. And far from hiding me, they're forever dragging me by racks of fancy clothes or through teeming school corridors, or welcoming gaggles of friends while I'm wandering through the house in Anne's filmy pink babydoll pajamas. George generally calls before he brings someone home, but he does just as many dumb thankless chores as the children. And they all yell at me, laugh at some of my jokes, write me funny letters when we're apart—in short, treat me as an ordinary human being for whom they have some use. I think they like me. Unless they're faking. . . .

17   Faking. There's the rub. Tugging at the fringes of my consciousness always is the terror that people are kind to me only because I'm a cripple. My mother almost shattered me once, with that instinct mothers have—blind, I think, in this case, but unerring nonetheless—for striking blows along the fault-lines of their children's hearts, by telling me, in an attack on my selfishness, "We all have to make allowances for you, of course, because of the way you are." From the distance of a couple of years, I have to admit that I haven't any idea just what she meant, and I'm not sure that she knew either. She was awfully angry. But at the time, as the words thudded home, I felt my worst fear, suddenly realized. I could bear being called selfish: I am. But I couldn't bear the corroboration that those around me were doing in fact what I'd always suspected them of doing, professing fondness while silently putting up with me because of the way I am. A cripple. I've been a little cracked ever since.

18　　　Along with this fear that people are secretly accepting shoddy goods comes a relentless pressure to please—to prove myself worth the burdens I impose, I guess, or to build a substantial account of goodwill against which I may write drafts in times of need. Part of the pressure arises from social expectations. In our society, anyone who deviates from the norm had better find some way to compensate. Like fat people, who are expected to be jolly, cripples must bear their lot meekly and cheerfully. A grumpy cripple isn't playing by the rules. And much of the pressure is self-generated. Early on I vowed that, if I had to have MS, by God I was going to do it well. This is a class act, ladies and gentlemen. No tears, no recriminations, no faint-heartedness.

19　　　One way and another, then, I wind up feeling like Tiny Tim, peering over the edge of the table at the Christmas goose, waving my crutch, piping down God's blessing on us all. Only sometimes I don't want to play Tiny Tim. I'd rather be Caliban, a most scurvy monster. Fortunately, at home no one much cares whether I'm a good cripple or a bad cripple as long as I make vichyssoise with fair regularity. One evening several years ago, Anne was reading at the dining-room table while I cooked dinner. As I opened a can of tomatoes, the can slipped in my left hand and juice spattered me and the counter with bloody spots. Fatigued and infuriated, I bellowed, "I'm so sick of being crippled!" Anne glanced at me over the top of her book. "There now," she said, "do you feel better?" "Yes," I said, "yes, I do." She went back to her reading. I felt better. That's about all the attention my scurviness ever gets.

20　　　Because I hate being crippled, I sometimes hate myself for being a cripple. Over the years I have come to expect—even accept—attacks of violent self-loathing. Luckily, in general our society no longer connects deformity and disease directly with evil (though a charismatic once told me that I have MS because a devil is in me) and so I'm allowed to move largely at will, even among small children. But I'm not sure that this revision of attitude has been particularly helpful. Physical imperfection, even freed of moral disapprobation, still defies and violates the ideal, especially for women, whose confinement in their bodies as objects of desire is far from over. Each age, of course, has its ideal, and I doubt that ours is any better or worse than any other. Today's ideal woman, who lives on the glossy pages of dozens of magazines, seems to be between the ages of eighteen and twenty-five; her hair has body, her teeth flash white, her breath smells minty, her underarms are dry; she has a career but is still a fabulous cook, especially of meals that take less than twenty minutes to prepare; she does not ordinarily appear to have a husband or children; she is trim and deeply tanned; she jogs, swims, plays tennis, rides a bicycle, sails, but does not bowl; she travels widely, even to out-of-the-way places like Finland and Samoa, always in the company of the ideal man, who possesses a nearly identical set of characteristics. There are a few exceptions. Though usually white and often blonde, she may be black, Hispanic, Asian, or Native American, so long as she is unusually sleek. She may be old, provided she is selling a laxative or is Lauren Bacall. If she is selling a detergent, she may be married and have a flock of strikingly messy children. But she is never a cripple.

21　　　Like many women I know, I have always had an uneasy relationship with my body. I was not a popular child, largely, I think now, because I was peculiar: intelligent, intense, moody, shy, given to unexpected actions and inexplicable notions and emotions. But as I entered adolescence, I believed myself unpopular because

I was homely: my breasts too flat, my mouth too wide, my hips too narrow, my clothing never quite right in fit or style. I was not, in fact, particularly ugly, old photographs inform me, though I was well off the ideal; but I carried this sense of self-alienation with me into adulthood, where it regenerated in response to the depredations of MS. Even with my brace I walk with a limp so pronounced that, seeing myself on the videotape of a television program on the disabled, I couldn't believe that anything but an inchworm could make progress humping along like that. My shoulders droop and my pelvis thrusts forward as I try to balance myself upright, throwing my frame into a bony S. As a result of contractures, one shoulder is higher than the other and I carry one arm bent in front of me, the fingers curled into a claw. My left arm and leg have wasted into pipe-stems, and I try always to keep them covered. When I think about how my body must look to others, especially to men, to whom I have been trained to display myself, I feel ludicrous, even loathsome.

22   At my age, however, I don't spend much time thinking about my appearance. The burning egocentricity of adolescence, which assures one that all the world is looking all the time, has passed, thank God, and I'm generally too caught up in what I'm doing to step back, as I used to, and watch myself as though upon a stage. I'm also too old to believe in the accuracy of self-image. I know that I'm not a hideous crone, that in fact, when I'm rested, well dressed, and well made up, I look fine. The self-loathing I feel is neither physically nor intellectually substantial. What I hate is not me but a disease.

23   I am not a disease.

24   And a disease is not—at least not singlehandedly—going to determine who I am, though at first it seemed to be going to. Adjusting to a chronic incurable illness, I have moved through a process similar to that outlined by Elisabeth Kübler-Ross in *On Death and Dying*. The major difference—and it is far more significant than most people recognize—is that I can't be sure of the outcome as the terminally ill cancer patient can. Research studies indicate that, with proper medical care, I may achieve a "normal" life span. And in our society, with its vision of death as the ultimate evil, worse even than decrepitude, the response to such news is, "Oh well, at least you're not going to *die*." Are there worse things than dying? I think that there may be.

25   I think of two women I know, both with MS, both enough older than I to have served me as models. One took to her bed several years ago and has been there ever since. Although she can sit in a high-backed wheelchair, because she is incontinent she refuses to go out at all, even though incontinence pants, which are readily available at any pharmacy, could protect her from embarrassment. Instead, she stays at home and insists that her husband, a small quiet man, a retired civil servant, stay there with her except for a quick weekly foray to the supermarket. The other woman, whose illness was diagnosed when she was eighteen, a nursing student engaged to a young doctor, finished her training, married her doctor, accompanied him to Germany when he was in the service, bore three sons and a daughter, now grown and gone. When she can, she travels with her husband; she plays bridge, embroiders, swims regularly; she works, like me, as a symptomatic-patient instructor of medical students in neurology. Guess which woman I hope to be.

26   At the beginning, I thought about having MS almost incessantly. And because of the unpredictable course of the disease, my thoughts were always terrified. Each

night I'd get into bed wondering whether I'd get out again the next morning, whether I'd be able to see, to speak, to hold a pen between my fingers. Knowing that the day might come when I'd be physically incapable of killing myself, I thought perhaps I ought to do so right away, while I still had the strength. Gradually I came to understand that the Nancy who might one day lie inert under a bedsheet, arms and legs paralyzed, unable to feed or bathe herself, unable to reach out for a gun, a bottle of pills, was not the Nancy I was at present, and that I could not presume to make decisions for that future Nancy, who might well not want in the least to die. Now the only provision I've made for the future Nancy is that when the time comes—and it is likely to come in the form of pneumonia, friend to the weak and the old—I am not to be treated with machines and medications. If she is unable to communicate by then, I hope she will be satisfied with these terms.

27   Thinking all the time about having MS grew tiresome and intrusive, especially in the large and tragic mode in which I was accustomed to considering my plight. Months and even years went by without catastrophe (at least without one related to MS), and really I was awfully busy, what with George and children and snakes and students and poems, and I hadn't the time, let alone the inclination, to devote myself to being a disease. Too, the richer my life became, the funnier it seemed, as though there were some connection between largesse and laughter, and so my tragic stance began to waver until, even with the aid of a brace and a cane, I couldn't hold it for very long at a time.

28   After several years I was satisfied with my adjustment. I had suffered my grief and fury and terror, I thought, but now I was at ease with my lot. Then one summer day I set out with George and the children across the desert for a vacation in California. Part way to Yuma I became aware that my right leg felt funny. "I think I've had an exacerbation," I told George. "What shall we do?" he asked. "I think we'd better get the hell to California," I said, "because I don't know whether I'll ever make it again." So we went on to San Diego and then to Orange, up the Pacific Coast Highway to Santa Cruz, across to Yosemite, down to Sequoia and Joshua Tree, and so back over the desert to home. It was a fine two-week trip, filled with friends and fair weather, and I wouldn't have missed it for the world, though I did in fact make it back to California two years later. Nor would there have been any point in missing it, since in MS, once the symptoms have appeared, the neurological damage has been done, and there's no way to predict or prevent that damage.

29   The incident spoiled my self-satisfaction, however. It renewed my grief and fury and terror, and I learned that one never finishes adjusting to MS. I don't know now why I thought one would. One does not, after all, finish adjusting to life, and MS is simply a fact of my life—not my favorite fact, of course—but as ordinary as my nose and my tropical fish and my yellow Mazda station wagon. It may at any time get worse, but no amount of worry or anticipation can prepare me for a new loss. My life is a lesson in losses. I learn one at a time.

30   And I had best be patient in the learning, since I'll have to do it like it or not. As any rock fan knows, you can't always get what you want. Particularly when you have MS. You can't, for example, get cured. In recent years researchers and the organizations that fund research have started to pay MS some attention even though it isn't fatal; perhaps they have begun to see that life is something other

than a quantitative phenomenon, that one may be very much alive for a very long time in a life that isn't worth living. The researchers have made some progress toward understanding the mechanism of the disease: It may well be an autoimmune reaction triggered by a slow-acting virus. But they are nowhere near its prevention, control, or cure. And most of us want to be cured. Some, unable to accept incurability, grasp at one treatment after another, no matter how bizarre: megavitamin therapy, gluten-free diet, injections of cobra venom, hypothermal suits, lymphocytopharesis, hyperbaric chambers. Many treatments are probably harmless enough, but none are curative.

31   The absence of a cure often makes MS patients bitter toward their doctors. Doctors are, after all, the priests of modern society, the new shamans, whose business is to heal, and many an MS patient roves from one to another, searching for the "good" doctor who will make him well. Doctors too think of themselves as healers, and for this reason many have trouble dealing with MS patients, whose disease in its intransigence defeats their aims and mocks their skills. Too few doctors, it is true, treat their patients as whole human beings, but the reverse is also true. I have always tried to be gentle with my doctors, who often have more at stake in terms of ego than I do. I may be frustrated, maddened, depressed by the incurability of my disease, but I am not diminished by it, and they are. When I push myself up from my seat in the waiting room and stumble toward them, I incarnate the limitation of their powers. The least I can do is refuse to press on their tenderest spots.

32   This gentleness is part of the reason that I'm not sorry to be a cripple. I didn't have it before. Perhaps I'd have developed it anyway—how could I know such a thing?—and I wish I had more of it, but I'm glad of what I have. It has opened and enriched my life enormously, this sense that my frailty and need must be mirrored in others, that in searching for and shaping a stable core in a life wrenched by change and loss, change and loss, I must recognize the same process, under individual conditions, in the lives around me. I do not deprecate such knowledge, however I've come by it.

33   All the same, if a cure were found, would I take it? In a minute. I may be a cripple, but I'm only occasionally a loony and never a saint. Anyway, in my brand of theology God doesn't give bonus points for a limp. I'd take a cure; I just don't need one. A friend who also has MS startled me once by asking, "Do you ever say to yourself, 'Why me, Lord?' " "No, Michael, I don't," I told him, "because whenever I try, the only response I can think of is 'Why not?' " If I could make a cosmic deal, who would I put in my place? What in my life would I give up in exchange for sound limbs and a thrilling rush of energy? No one. Nothing. I might as well do the job myself. Now that I'm getting the hang of it.

QUESTIONS

Experience

· Were you surprised that Mairs prefers to be described as a "cripple" rather than by other available terms such as "disabled," "handicapped," or "differently abled"? Why, or why not? What other terms have you heard "handi-capped" people express a preference for?

Interpretation

· Explain what Mairs means when she writes, "I am not a disease." What's the difference between "being" a disease and "having" a disease? To what extent does the disease of MS define who Mairs is? How has it affected her life physically and emotionally?

Evaluation

· To what extent does Mairs help you understand what a person with a disease like MS experiences? To what extent does the essay evoke an emotional response from you? Do you think Mairs's personal, even intimate, revelations about her body strengthen the essay or not? Why?

WRITING

Exploring

· Write an essay about a type of handicap or limitation you may possess. It need not be a physical handicap. Alternately, write an essay about encounters, experiences, or other dealings you may have had with those who suffer from some type of disability.

Interpreting

· Analyze the ways Mairs talks about herself—her body and her mind and spirit. Select key passages, and explain what Mairs conveys about herself by looking closely at her language. Try to identify her tone.

Evaluating

· Write an essay in which you identify the values Mairs has come to see as central in her life. Consider, as well, your own assessment of Mairs's view of what's important to her.

· Or write an assessment about society's approach to those with disabling diseases or physical conditions such as deafness and blindness. Consider your own views on the language used to describe people with these and other conditions, and consider your attitude toward ways the federal government has been providing for such people.

NEIL POSTMAN
(b. 1931)

"Now . . . This"

Neil Postman is a professor of media ecology at New York University. He is the author of many books, including Teaching as a Subversive Activity *and* Teaching as a Conserving Activity *(both coauthored with Charles Weingartner). The following selection is excerpted from his* Amusing Ourselves to Death, *a book about the television habits of Americans.*

In "Now . . . This" Postman examines the ways broadcast news has trivialized its subject—the news of the day. Postman identifies the need to make the news entertaining as the primary cause of this trivialization. He supports his claim with evidence in the form of examples taken not only from television news but from print media as well. Among the noteworthy features of Postman's essay are his analysis of the characteristic features of media news and his use of respected authorities such as Robert MacNeil of The MacNeil/Lehrer News Hour—*a news show that opposes the typical news-as-entertainment view, which, as MacNeil characterizes it, is "that bite-sized is best, that complexity must be avoided."*

1 The American humorist H. Allen Smith once suggested that of all the worrisome words in the English language, the scariest is "uh oh," as when a physician looks at your X rays and with knitted brow says, "Uh oh." I should like to suggest that the words which are the title of this chapter are as ominous as any, all the more so because they are spoken without knitted brow—indeed, with a kind of idiot's delight. The phrase, if that's what it may be called, adds to our grammar a new part of speech, a conjunction that does not connect anything to anything but does the opposite: separates everything from everything. As such, it serves as a compact metaphor for the discontinuities in so much that passes for public discourse in present-day America.

2 "Now . . . this" is commonly used on radio and television newscasts to indicate that what one has just heard or seen has no relevance to what one is about to hear or see, or possibly to anything one is ever likely to hear or see. The phrase is a means of acknowledging the fact that the world as mapped by the speeded-up electronic media has no order or meaning and is not to be taken seriously. There is no murder so brutal, no earthquake so devastating, no political blunder so costly—for that matter, no ball score so tantalizing or weather report so threatening—that it cannot be erased from our minds by a newscaster saying, "Now . . . this." The newscaster means that you have thought long enough on the previous matter (approximately forty-five seconds), that you must not be morbidly preoccupied with it (let us say, for ninety seconds), and that you must now give your attention to another fragment of news or a commercial.

3 Television did not invent the "Now . . . this" world view. . . . It is the offspring of the intercourse between telegraphy and photography. But it is through televi-

sion that it has been nurtured and brought to a perverse maturity. For on television, nearly every half hour is a discrete event, separated in content, context, and emotional texture from what precedes and follows it. In part because television sells its time in seconds and minutes, in part because television must use images rather than words, in part because its audience can move freely to and from the television set, programs are structured so that almost each eight-minute segment may stand as a complete event in itself. Viewers are rarely required to carry over any thought or feeling from one parcel of time to another.

4   Of course, in television's presentation of the "news of the day," we may see the "Now . . . this" mode of discourse in its boldest and most embarrassing form. For there, we are presented not only with fragmented news but news without context, without consequences, without value, and therefore without essential seriousness; that is to say, news as pure entertainment.

5   Consider, for example, how you would proceed if you were given the opportunity to produce a television news show for any station concerned to attract the largest possible audience. You would, first, choose a cast of players, each of whom has a face that is both "likable" and "credible." Those who apply would, in fact, submit to you their eight-by-ten glossies, from which you would eliminate those whose countenances are not suitable for nightly display. This means that you will exclude women who are not beautiful or who are over the age of fifty, men who are bald, all people who are overweight or whose noses are too long or whose eyes are too close together. You will try, in other words, to assemble a cast of talking hairdo's. At the very least, you will want those whose faces would not be unwelcome on a magazine cover.

6   Christine Craft has just such a face, and so she applied for a co-anchor position on KMBC-TV in Kansas City. According to a lawyer who represented her in a sexism suit she later brought against the station, the management of KMBC-TV "loved Christine's look." She was accordingly hired in January 1981. She was fired in August 1981 because research indicated that her appearance "hampered viewer acceptance." What exactly does "hampered viewer acceptance" mean? And what does it have to do with the news? Hampered viewer acceptance means the same thing for television news as it does for any television show: Viewers do not like looking at the performer. It also means that viewers do not believe the performer, that she lacks credibility. In the case of a theatrical performance, we have a sense of what that implies: The actor does not persuade the audience that he or she is the character being portrayed. But what does lack of credibility imply in the case of a news show? What character is a co-anchor playing? And how do we decide that the performance lacks verisimilitude? Does the audience believe that the newscaster is lying, that what is reported did not in fact happen, that something important is being concealed?

7   It is frightening to think that this may be so, that the perception of the truth of a report rests heavily on the acceptability of the newscaster. In the ancient world, there was a tradition of banishing or killing the bearer of bad tidings. Does the television news show restore, in a curious form, this tradition? Do we banish those who tell us the news when we do not care for the face of the teller? Does television countermand the warnings we once received about the fallacy of the ad hominem argument?

8   If the answer to any of these questions is even a qualified "Yes," then here is an issue worthy of the attention of epistemologists. Stated in its simplest form, it is that television provides a new (or, possibly, restores an old) definition of truth: The credibility of the teller is the ultimate test of the truth of a proposition. "Credibility" here does not refer to the past record of the teller for making statements that have survived the rigors of reality-testing. It refers only to the impression of sincerity, authenticity, vulnerability or attractiveness (choose one or more) conveyed by the actor/reporter.

9   This is a matter of considerable importance, for it goes beyond the question of how truth is perceived on television news shows. If on television, credibility replaces reality as the decisive test of truth-telling, political leaders need not trouble themselves very much with reality provided that their performances consistently generate a sense of verisimilitude. I suspect, for example, that the dishonor that now shrouds Richard Nixon results not from the fact that he lied but that on television he looks like a liar. Which, if true, should bring no comfort to anyone, not even veteran Nixon-haters. For the alternative possibilities are that one may look like a liar but be telling the truth; or even worse, look like a truth-teller but in fact be lying.

10   As a producer of a television news show, you would be well aware of these matters and would be careful to choose your cast on the basis of criteria used by David Merrick and other successful impresarios. Like them, you would then turn your attention to staging the show on principles that maximize entertainment value. You would, for example, select a musical theme for the show. All television news programs begin, end, and are somewhere in between punctuated with music. I have found very few Americans who regard this custom as peculiar, which fact I have taken as evidence for the dissolution of lines of demarcation between serious public discourse and entertainment. What has music to do with the news? Why is it there? It is there, I assume, for the same reason music is used in the theater and films—to create a mood and provide a leitmotif for the entertainment. If there were no music—as is the case when any television program is interrupted for a news flash—viewers would expect something truly alarming, possibly life-altering. But as long as the music is there as a frame for the program, the viewer is comforted to believe that there is nothing to be greatly alarmed about; that, in fact, the events that are reported have as much relation to reality as do scenes in a play.

11   This perception of a news show as a stylized dramatic performance whose content has been staged largely to entertain is reinforced by several other features, including the fact that the average length of any story is forty-five seconds. While brevity does not always suggest triviality, in this case it clearly does. It is simply not possible to convey a sense of seriousness about any event if its implications are exhausted in less than one minute's time. In fact, it is quite obvious that TV news has no intention of suggesting that any story *has* any implications, for that would require viewers to continue to think about it when it is done and therefore obstruct their attending to the next story that waits panting in the wings. In any case, viewers are not provided with much opportunity to be distracted from the next story since in all likelihood it will consist of some film footage. Pictures have little difficulty in overwhelming words and short-circuiting introspection. As

a television producer, you would be certain to give both prominence and precedence to any event for which there is some sort of visual documentation. A suspected killer being brought into a police station, the angry face of a cheated consumer, a barrel going over Niagara Falls (with a person alleged to be in it), the President disembarking from a helicopter on the White House lawn—these are always fascinating or amusing and easily satisfy the requirements of an entertaining show. It is, of course, not necessary that the visuals actually document the point of a story. Neither is it necessary to explain why such images are intruding themselves on public consciousness. Film footage justifies itself, as every television producer well knows.

12   It is also of considerable help in maintaining a high level of unreality that the newscasters do not pause to grimace or shiver when they speak their prefaces or epilogs to the film clips. Indeed, many newscasters do not appear to grasp the meaning of what they are saying, and some hold to a fixed and ingratiating enthusiasm as they report on earthquakes, mass killings and other disasters. Viewers would be quite disconcerted by any show of concern or terror on the part of newscasters. Viewers, after all, are partners with the newscasters in the "Now . . . this" culture, and they expect the newscaster to play out his or her role as a character who is marginally serious but who stays well clear of authentic understanding. The viewers, for their part, will not be caught contaminating their responses with a sense of reality, any more than an audience at a play would go scurrying to call home because a character on stage has said that a murderer is loose in the neighborhood.

13   The viewers also know that no matter how grave any fragment of news may appear (for example, on the day I write a Marine Corps general has declared that nuclear war between the United States and Russia is inevitable), it will shortly be followed by a series of commercials that will, in an instant, defuse the import of the news, in fact render it largely banal. This is a key element in the structure of a news program and all by itself refutes any claim that television news is designed as a serious form of public discourse. Imagine what you would think of me, and this book, if I were to pause here, tell you that I will return to my discussion in a moment, and then proceed to write a few words in behalf of United Airlines or the Chase Manhattan Bank. You would rightly think that I had no respect for you and, certainly, no respect for the subject. And if I did this not once but several times in each chapter, you would think the whole enterprise unworthy of your attention. Why, then, do we not think a news show similarly unworthy? The reason, I believe, is that whereas we expect books and even other media (such as film) to maintain a consistency of tone and a continuity of content, we have no such expectation of television, and especially television news. We have become so accustomed to its discontinuities that we are no longer struck dumb, as any sane person would be, by a newscaster who having just reported that a nuclear war is inevitable goes on to say that he will be right back after this word from Burger King; who says, in other words, "Now . . . this." One can hardly overestimate the damage that such juxtapositions do to our sense of the world as a serious place. The damage is especially massive to youthful viewers who depend so much on television for their clues as to how to respond to the world. In watching television news, they, more than any other segment of the audience, are drawn into an epis-

temology based on the assumption that all reports of cruelty and death are greatly exaggerated and, in any case, not to be taken seriously or responded to sanely.

14   I should go so far as to say that embedded in the surrealistic frame of a television news show is a theory of anticommunication, featuring a type of discourse that abandons logic, reason, sequence and rules of contradiction. In aesthetics, I believe the name given to this theory is Dadaism; in philosophy, nihilism; in psychiatry, schizophrenia. In the parlance of the theater, it is known as vaudeville.

15   For those who think I am here guilty of hyperbole, I offer the following description of television news by Robert MacNeil, executive editor and co-anchor of the "MacNeil-Lehrer Newshour." The idea, he writes, "is to keep everything brief, not to strain the attention of anyone but instead to provide constant stimulation through variety, novelty, action, and movement. You are required . . . to pay attention to no concept, no character, and no problem for more than a few seconds at a time." He goes on to say that the assumptions controlling a news show are "that bite-sized is best, that complexity must be avoided, that nuances are dispensable, that qualifications impede the simple message, that visual stimulation is a substitute for thought, and that verbal precision is an anachronism."

16   Robert MacNeil has more reason than most to give testimony about the television news show as vaudeville act. The "MacNeil-Lehrer Newshour" is an unusual and gracious attempt to bring to television some of the elements of typographic discourse. The program abjures visual stimulation, consists largely of extended explanations of events and in-depth interviews (which even there means only five to ten minutes), limits the number of stories covered, and emphasizes background and coherence. But television has exacted its price for MacNeil's rejection of a show business format. By television's standards, the audience is minuscule, the program is confined to public-television stations, and it is a good guess that the combined salary of MacNeil and Lehrer is one-fifth of Dan Rather's or Tom Brokaw's.

17   If you were a producer of a television news show for a commercial station, you would not have the option of defying television's requirements. It would be demanded of you that you strive for the largest possible audience, and, as a consequence and in spite of your best intentions, you would arrive at a production very nearly resembling MacNeil's description. Moreover, you would include some things MacNeil does not mention. You would try to make celebrities of your newscasters. You would advertise the show, both in the press and on television itself. You would do "news briefs," to serve as an inducement to viewers. You would have a weatherman as comic relief, and a sportscaster whose language is a touch uncouth (as a way of his relating to the beer-drinking common man). You would, in short, package the whole event as any producer might who is in the entertainment business.

18   The result of all this is that Americans are the best entertained and quite likely the least well-informed people in the Western world. I say this in the face of the popular conceit that television, as a window to the world, has made Americans exceedingly well informed. Much depends here, of course, on what is meant by being informed. I will pass over the now tiresome polls that tell us that, at any given moment, 70 percent of our citizens do not know who is the Secretary of State or the Chief Justice of the Supreme Court. Let us consider, instead, the case

of Iran during the drama that was called the "Iranian Hostage Crisis." I don't suppose there has been a story in years that received more continuous attention from television. We may assume, then, the Americans know most of what there is to know about this unhappy event. And now, I put these questions to you: Would it be an exaggeration to say that not one American in a hundred knows what language the Iranians speak? Or what the word "Ayatollah" means or implies? Or knows any details of the tenets of Iranian religious beliefs? Or the main outlines of their political history? Or knows who the Shah was, and where he came from?

19   Nonetheless, everyone had an opinion about this event, for in America everyone is entitled to an opinion, and it is certainly useful to have a few when a pollster shows up. But these are opinions of a quite different order from eighteenth- or nineteenth-century opinions. It is probably more accurate to call them emotions rather than opinions, which would account for the fact that they change from week to week, as the pollsters tell us. What is happening here is that television is altering the meaning of "being informed" by creating a species of information that might properly be called *disinformation.* I am using this word almost in the precise sense in which it is used by spies in the CIA or KGB. Disinformation does not mean false information. It means misleading information—misplaced, irrelevant, fragmented or superficial information—information that creates the illusion of knowing something but which in fact leads one away from knowing. In saying this, I do not mean to imply that television news deliberately aims to deprive Americans of a coherent, contextual understanding of their world. I mean to say that when news is packaged as entertainment, that is the inevitable result. And in saying that the television news show entertains but does not inform, I am saying something far more serious than that we are being deprived of authentic information. I am saying we are losing our sense of what it means to be well informed. Ignorance is always correctable. But what shall we do if we take ignorance to be knowledge?

20   Here is a startling example of how this process bedevils us. A *New York Times* article is headlined on February 15, 1983:

REAGAN MISSTATEMENTS GETTING LESS ATTENTION

The article begins in the following way:

> President Reagan's aides used to become visibly alarmed at suggestions that he had given mangled and perhaps misleading accounts of his policies or of current events in general. That doesn't seem to happen much anymore.
>
> Indeed, the President continues to make debatable assertions of fact but news accounts do not deal with them as extensively as they once did. In the view of White House officials, the declining news coverage mirrors a *decline in interest by the general public.* (my italics)

21   This report is not so much a news story as a story about the news, and our recent history suggests that it is not about Ronald Reagan's charm. It is about how news is defined, and I believe the story would be quite astonishing to both civil libertarians and tyrants of an earlier time. Walter Lippmann, for example, wrote in 1920: "There can be no liberty for a community which lacks the means by which to detect lies." For all of his pessimism about the possibilities of restoring an eigh-

teenth- and nineteenth-century level of public discourse, Lippmann assumed, as did Thomas Jefferson before him, that with a well-trained press functioning as a lie-detector, the public's interest in a President's mangling of the truth would be piqued, in both senses of that word. Given the means to detect lies, he believed, the public could not be indifferent to their consequences.

22   But this case refutes his assumption. The reporters who cover the White House are ready and able to expose lies, and thus create the grounds for informed and indignant opinion. But apparently the public declines to take an interest. To press reports of White House dissembling the public has replied with Queen Victoria's famous line, "We are not amused." However, here the words mean something the Queen did not have in mind. They mean that what is not amusing does not compel their attention. Perhaps if the President's lies could be demonstrated by pictures and accompanied by music the public would raise a curious eyebrow. If a movie, like *All the President's Men,* could be made from his misleading accounts of government policy, if there were a break-in of some sort or sinister characters laundering money, attention would quite likely be paid. We do well to remember that President Nixon did not begin to come undone until his lies were given a theatrical setting at the Watergate hearings. But we do not have anything like that here. Apparently, all President Reagan does is *say* things that are not entirely true. And there is nothing entertaining in that.

23   But there is a subtler point to be made here. Many of the President's "misstatements" fall in the category of contradictions—mutually exclusive assertions that cannot possibly both, in the same context, be true. "In the same context" is the key phrase here, for it is context that defines contradiction. There is no problem in someone's remarking that he prefers oranges to apples, and also remarking that he prefers apples to oranges—not if one statement is made in the context of choosing a wallpaper design and the other in the context of selecting fruit for dessert. In such a case, we have statements that are opposites, but not contradictory. But if the statements are made in a single, continuous, and coherent context, then they are contradictions, and cannot both be true. Contradiction, in short, requires that statements and events be perceived as interrelated aspects of a continuous and coherent context. Disappear the context, or fragment it, and contradiction disappears. This point is nowhere made more clear to me than in conferences with my younger students about their writing. "Look here," I say. "In this paragraph you have said one thing. And in that you have said the opposite. Which is it to be?" They are polite, and wish to please, but they are as baffled by the question as I am by the response. "I know," they will say, "but that is *there* and this is *here.*" The difference between us is that I assume "there" and "here," "now" and "then," one paragraph and the next to be connected, to be continuous, to be part of the same coherent world of thought. That is the way of typographic discourse, and typography is the universe I'm "coming from," as they say. But they are coming from a different universe of discourse altogether: the "Now . . . this" world of television. The fundamental assumption of that world is not coherence but discontinuity. And in a world of discontinuities, contradiction is useless as a test of truth or merit, because contradiction does not exist.

24   My point is that we are by now so thoroughly adjusted to the "Now . . . this" world of news—a world of fragments, where events stand alone, stripped of any

connection to the past, or to the future, or to other events—that all assumptions of coherence have vanished. And so, perforce, has contradiction. In the context of *no context,* so to speak, it simply disappears. And in its absence, what possible interest could there be in a list of what the President says *now* and what he said *then?* It is merely a rehash of old news, and there is nothing interesting or entertaining in that. The only thing to be amused about is the bafflement of reporters at the public's indifference. There is an irony in the fact that the very group that has taken the world apart should, on trying to piece it together again, be surprised that no one notices much, or cares.

25   For all his perspicacity, George Orwell would have been stymied by this situation; there is nothing "Orwellian" about it. The President does not have the press under his thumb. *The New York Times* and *The Washington Post* are not *Pravda;* the Associated Press is not Tass. And there is no Newspeak here. Lies have not been defined as truth nor truth as lies. All that has happened is that the public has adjusted to incoherence and been amused into indifference. Which is why Aldous Huxley would not in the least be surprised by the story. Indeed, he prophesied its coming. He believed that it is far more likely that the Western democracies will dance and dream themselves into oblivion than march into it, single file and manacled. Huxley grasped, as Orwell did not, that it is not necessary to conceal anything from a public insensible to contradiction and narcoticized by technological diversions. Although Huxley did not specify that television would be our main line to the drug, he would have no difficulty accepting Robert MacNeil's observation that "Television is the *soma* of Aldous Huxley's *Brave New World.*" Big Brother turns out to be Howdy Doody.

26   I do not mean that the trivialization of public information is all accomplished *on* television. I mean that television is the paradigm for our conception of public information. As the printing press did in an earlier time, television has achieved the power to define the form in which news must come, and it has also defined how we shall respond to it. In presenting news to us packaged as vaudeville, television induces other media to do the same, so that the total information environment begins to mirror television.

27   For example, America's newest and highly successful national newspaper, *USA Today,* is modeled precisely on the format of television. It is sold on the street in receptacles that look like television sets. Its stories are uncommonly short, its design leans heavily on pictures, charts and other graphics, some of them printed in various colors. Its weather maps are a visual delight; its sports section includes enough pointless statistics to distract a computer. As a consequence, *USA Today,* which began publication in September 1982, has become the third largest daily in the United States (as of July 1984, according to the Audit Bureau of Circulations), moving quickly to overtake the *Daily News* and the *Wall Street Journal.* Journalists of a more traditional bent have criticized it for its superficiality and theatrics, but the paper's editors remain steadfast in their disregard of typographic standards. The paper's Editor-in-Chief, John Quinn, has said: "We are not up to undertaking projects of the dimensions needed to win prizes. They don't give awards for the best investigative paragraph." Here is an astonishing tribute to the resonance of television's epistemology: In the age of television, the paragraph is

becoming the basic unit of news in print media. Moreover, Mr. Quinn need not fret too long about being deprived of awards. As other newspapers join in the transformation, the time cannot be far off when awards will be given for the best investigative sentence.

28   It needs also to be noted here that new and successful magazines such as *People* and *Us* are not only examples of television-oriented print media but have had an extraordinary "ricochet" effect on television itself. Whereas television taught the magazines that news is nothing but entertainment, the magazines have taught television that nothing but entertainment is news. Television programs, such as "Entertainment Tonight," turn information about entertainers and celebrities into "serious" cultural content, so that the circle begins to close: Both the form and content of news become entertainment.

29   Radio, of course, is the least likely medium to join in the descent into a Huxleyan world of technological narcotics. It is, after all, particularly well suited to the transmission of rational, complex language. Nonetheless, and even if we disregard radio's captivation by the music industry, we appear to be left with the chilling fact that such language as radio allows us to hear is increasingly primitive, fragmented, and largely aimed at invoking visceral response; which is to say, it is the linguistic analogue to the ubiquitous rock music that is radio's principal source of income. As I write, the trend in call-in shows is for the "host" to insult callers whose language does not, in itself, go much beyond humanoid grunting. Such programs have little content, as this word used to be defined, and are merely of archeological interest in that they give us a sense of what a dialogue among Neanderthals might have been like. More to the point, the language of radio newscasts has become, under the influence of television, increasingly decontextualized and discontinuous, so that the possibility of anyone's knowing about the world, as against merely knowing *of* it, is effectively blocked. In New York City, radio station WINS entreats its listeners to "Give us twenty-two minutes and we'll give you the world." This is said without irony, and its audience, we may assume, does not regard the slogan as the conception of a disordered mind.

30   And so, we move rapidly into an information environment which may rightly be called trivial pursuit. As the game of that name uses facts as a source of amusement, so do our sources of news. It has been demonstrated many times that a culture can survive misinformation and false opinion. It has not yet been demonstrated whether a culture can survive if it takes the measure of the world in twenty-two minutes. Or if the value of its news is determined by the number of laughs it provides.

QUESTIONS

Experience

· What has been your experience watching television news broadcasts? To what extent have you experienced the quick shifts of focus that Postman describes? Have you become accustomed to the pace of TV news or not? Why, or why not?

Interpretation

· The "Now . . . This" of the title refers, as Postman suggests, both to the shift into a commercial ("now this message") and to a new fragment of "news"—to a different story. What is the larger point Postman makes about the frequent and abrupt shifts from one "now . . . this" bit of news or commercial to another? What does Postman see as television's effect on "the total information environment"?

Evaluation

· What link does Postman draw between the style and pace of television news and the expectations and attention spans of American viewers? What is Postman's attitude toward what he calls "news without context" and "news as pure entertainment"? What is your attitude?

· What do you think of *People* magazine? Of the newspaper *USA Today*? What is Postman's view of them? Why?

WRITING

Exploring

· Keep a notepad handy while you watch television news broadcasts on two different nights. Record the number of stories and commercials and their subjects. You may also wish to time them. When you have completed your little survey, write a paragraph or two on your thoughts about what you have noticed.

Interpreting

· Write a summary of Postman's essay in which you identify and briefly explain each of his major criticisms of TV news broadcasts. Which do you think is the most important of his criticisms? Why?

Evaluating

· Write an assessment of Postman's piece in which you consider the quality of his observations and the effectiveness of his approach. In your paper, consider the following questions: How effective is Postman's invitation to readers to imagine themselves as producers of a television news show (paragraphs 10 and 17)? How effective is his quotation from Robert MacNeil (paragraph 15)? How effective is his invitation to imagine his essay written in the format of a television news show (paragraph 13)?

JAMES BALDWIN
(1924–1987)

If Black English Isn't a Language, Then Tell Me, What Is?

James Baldwin was born in Harlem and became, at 14, a preacher. At 17 he abandoned the ministry and devoted himself to the craft of writing. Baldwin received institutional support in the form of fellowships to help sustain him while he wrote his first two novels, Go Tell It on the Mountain *(1953) and* Giovanni's Room *(1956). Sandwiched between these two works was a collection of essays,* Notes of a Native Son *(1955), which many readers consider his finest work.*

In his essays Baldwin struggled to define himself as an American, as a writer, and as a black man, all of which, for Baldwin, were inextricably intertwined. In coming to terms with what was the most difficult thing in his life, his blackness, Baldwin revealed himself to be a passionate and eloquent writer whose most frequent subject has been the relations between the races. His essay on black English is one example of this continuing concern. In it Baldwin argues that black English expresses a distinctive view of experience that could not be expressed in any other language or dialect. Baldwin makes his argument in part by comparing different black and white Englishes with the different French languages spoken by inhabitants of Paris, Quebec, Guadeloupe, and Senegal.

1   St. Paul De Vence, France—The argument concerning the use, or the status, or the reality, of black English is rooted in American history and has absolutely nothing to do with the question the argument supposes itself to be posing. The argument has nothing to do with language itself but with the *role* of language. Language, incontestably, reveals the speaker. Language, also, far more dubiously, is meant to define the other—and, in this case, the other is refusing to be defined by a language that has never been able to recognize him.

2   People evolve a language in order to describe and thus control their circumstances, or in order not to be submerged by a reality that they cannot articulate. (And, if they cannot articulate it, they *are* submerged.) A Frenchman living in Paris speaks a subtly and crucially different language from that of the man living in Marseilles; neither sounds very much like a man living in Quebec; and they would all have great difficulty in apprehending what the man from Guadeloupe, or Martinique, is saying, to say nothing of the man from Senegal—although the "common" language of all these areas is French. But each has paid, and is paying, a different price for this "common" language, in which, as it turns out, they are not saying, and cannot be saying, the same things: They each have very different realities to articulate, or control.

3   What joins all languages, and all men, is the necessity to confront life, in order, not inconceivably, to outwit death: The price for this is the acceptance, and achievement, of one's temporal identity. So that, for example, though it is not taught in the schools (and this has the potential of becoming a political issue) the south of France still clings to its ancient and musical Provençal, which resists being described as a "dialect." And much of the tension in the Basque countries, and in Wales, is due to the Basque and Welsh determination not to allow their languages to be destroyed. This determination also feeds the flames in Ireland for among the many indignities the Irish have been forced to undergo at English hands is the English contempt for their language.

4   It goes without saying, then, that language is also a political instrument, means, and proof of power. It is the most vivid and crucial key to identity: It reveals the private identity, and connects one with, or divorces one from, the larger, public, or communal identity. There have been, and are, times, and places, when to speak a certain language could be dangerous, even fatal. Or, one may speak the same language, but in such a way that one's antecedents are revealed, or (one hopes) hidden. This is true in France, and is absolutely true in England: The range (and reign) of accents on that damp little island make England coherent for the English and totally incomprehensible for everyone else. To open your mouth in England is (if I may use black English) to "put your business in the street": You have confessed your parents, your youth, your school, your salary, your self-esteem, and, alas, your future.

5   Now, I do not know what white Americans would sound like if there had never been any black people in the United States, but they would not sound the say they sound. *Jazz,* for example, is a very specific sexual term, as in *jazz me, baby,* but white people purified it into the Jazz Age. *Sock it to me,* which means, roughly, the same thing, has been adopted by Nathaniel Hawthorne's descendants with no qualms or hesitations at all, along with *let it all hang out* and *right on! Beat to his socks,* which was once the black's most total and despairing image of poverty, was transformed into a thing called the Beat Generation, which phenomenon was, largely, composed of *uptight,* middle-class white people, imitating poverty, trying to *get down,* to get *with it,* doing their *thing,* doing their despairing best to be *funky,* which we, the blacks, never dreamed of doing—we *were* funky, baby, like *funk* was going out of style.

6   Now, no one can eat his cake, and have it, too, and it is late in the day to attempt to penalize black people for having created a language that permits the nation its only glimpse of reality, a language without which the nation would be even more *whipped* than it is.

7   I say that this present skirmish is rooted in American history, and it is. Black English is the creation of the black diaspora. Blacks came to the United States chained to each other, but from different tribes: Neither could speak the other's language. If two black people, at that bitter hour of the world's history, had been able to speak to each other, the institution of chattel slavery could never have lasted as long as it did. Subsequently, the slave was given, under the eye, and the gun, of his master, Congo Square, and the Bible—or, in other words, and under these conditions, the slave began the formation of the black church, and it is within this unprecedented tabernacle that black English began to be formed.

This was not, merely, as in the European example, the adoption of a foreign tongue, but an alchemy that transformed ancient elements into a new language: *A language comes into existence by means of brutal necessity, and the rules of the language are dictated by what the language must convey.*

8   There was a moment, in time, and in this place, when my brother, or my mother, or my father, or my sister, had to convey to me, for example, the danger in which I was standing from the white man standing just behind me, and to convey this with a speed, and in a language, that the white man could not possibly understand, and that, indeed, he cannot understand, until today. He cannot afford to understand it. This understanding would reveal to him too much about himself, and smash that mirror before which he has been frozen for so long.

9   Now, if this passion, this skill, this (to quote Toni Morrison) "sheer intelligence," this incredible music, the mighty achievement of having brought a people utterly unknown to, or despised by "history"—to have brought this people to their present, troubled, troubling, and unassailable and unanswerable place—if this absolutely unprecedented journey does not indicate that black English is a language, I am curious to know what definition of language is to be trusted.

10   A people at the center of the Western world, and in the midst of so hostile a population, has not endured and transcended by means of what is patronizingly called a "dialect." We, the blacks, are in trouble, certainly, but we are not doomed, and we are not inarticulate because we are not compelled to defend a morality that we know to be a lie.

11   The brutal truth is that the bulk of the white people in America never had any interest in educating black people, except as this could serve white purposes. It is not the black child's language that is in question, it is not his language that is despised: It is his experience. A child cannot be taught by anyone who despises him, and a child cannot afford to be fooled. A child cannot be taught by anyone whose demand, essentially, is that the child repudiate his experience, and all that gives him sustenance, and enter a limbo in which he will no longer be black, and in which he knows that he can never become white. Black people have lost too many black children that way.

12   And, after all, finally, in a country with standards so untrustworthy, a country that makes heroes of so many criminal mediocrities, a country unable to face why so many of the non-white are in prison, or on the needle, or standing, futureless, in the streets—it may very well be that both the child, and his elder, have concluded that they have nothing whatever to learn from the people of a country that has managed to learn so little.

QUESTIONS

Experience

· To what extent have you experienced the differentness of people who speak dialects or forms of English other than your own? Have you heard accents, inflections, idioms, expressions, and the like from speakers who come from other parts of the United States or from other countries in which English is spoken?

· If you have not had much experience hearing different dialects or versions of English, comment on your sense of whether such linguistic variety is a benefit or a drawback for the language.

Interpretation

· According to Baldwin, what are the attributes or characteristics of a language as opposed to a dialect? What, according to Baldwin, is the relation between language and reality?
· What does a language do for its speakers, in Baldwin's view?

Evaluation

· How well does Baldwin articulate his position? What evidence does he bring in its support? Do you find his argument and his distinctions between a dialect and a language convincing? Why, or why not? Do you agree that black English is a language? Why, or why not?

WRITING

Exploring

· Illustrate from your own experience and knowledge how language is, as Baldwin says, "a political instrument, means, and proof of power."

Interpreting

· Discuss Baldwin's idea that language is a key to identity—both personal identity and social identity.

Evaluating

· Agree or disagree with Baldwin's comment that to open your mouth and speak is to confess "your parents, your youth, your school, your salary, your self-esteem, and, alas, your future."

GEORGE ORWELL
(1903–1950)

Politics and the English Language

George Orwell is the pen name of Eric Blair, born in 1903 to English parents in Bengal, India. Orwell was educated in England—at Crossgates School and at Eton as King's Scholar. After university, he went to Burma, where he served as subdivisional officer in the Indian Imperial Police.

Best known for his fictional allegories, Animal Farm *and* 1984, *Orwell has also written remarkable nonfiction, including both books and essays.* Homage to Catalonia *(1938) provides an eyewitness account of the Spanish civil war, Orwell having served as a soldier on the Republican side.* The Road to Wigan Pier *(1937) provides an angry account of mining conditions in northern England.*

His essay "Politics and the English Language" is a classic statement of the need for clear, direct, and honest language. Orwell argues against opaque, sloppy writing, which he sees as both a symptom and a result of slovenly thinking. Orwell's rhetorical strategy involves making his claim clearly at the beginning of the essay and then illustrating the problems with language he excoriates by citing offending passages and analyzing their problems. In the final part of his essay, Orwell offers advice for avoiding the kinds of bad writing he illustrates and condemns.

1   Most people who bother with the matter at all would admit that the English language is in a bad way, but it is generally assumed that we cannot by conscious action do anything about it. Our civilization is decadent and our language—so the argument runs—must inevitably share in the general collapse. It follows that any struggle against the abuse of language is a sentimental archaism, like preferring candles to electric light or hansom cabs to aeroplanes. Underneath this lies the half-conscious belief that language is a natural growth and not an instrument which we shape for our own purposes.

2   Now, it is clear that the decline of a language must ultimately have political and economic causes: it is not due simply to the bad influence of this or that individual writer. But an effect can become a cause, reinforcing the original cause and producing the same effect in an intensified form, and so on indefinitely. A man may take to drink because he feels himself to be a failure, and then fail all the more completely because he drinks. It is rather the same thing that is happening to the English language. It becomes ugly and inaccurate because our thoughts are foolish, but the slovenliness of our language makes it easier for us to have foolish thoughts. The point is that the process is reversible. Modern English, especially written English, is full of bad habits which spread by imitation and which can be avoided if one is willing to take the necessary trouble. If one gets rid of these habits one can think more clearly, and to think clearly is a necessary first step

towards political regeneration: so that the fight against bad English is not frivo-lous and is not the exclusive concern of professional writers. I will come back to this presently, and I hope that by that time the meaning of what I have said here will have become clearer. Meanwhile here are five specimens of the English lan-guage as it is now habitually written.

These five passages have not been picked out because they are especially bad—I could have quoted far worse if I had chosen—but because they illustrate various of the mental vices from which we now suffer. They are a little below the average, but are fairly representative samples. I number them so that I can refer back to them when necessary:

(1) I am not, indeed, sure whether it is not true to say that the Milton who once seemed not unlike a seventeenth-century Shelley had not become, out of an experience ever more bitter in each year, more alien [*sic*] to the founder of that Jesuit sect which nothing could induce him to tolerate.

Professor Harold Laski (Essay in *Freedom of Expression*)

(2) Above all, we cannot play ducks and drakes with a native battery of idioms which prescribes such egregious collocations of vocables as the Basic *put up with* for *tolerate* or *put at a loss* for *bewilder*.

Professor Lancelot Hogben (*Interglossa*)

(3) On the one side we have the free personality: by definition it is not neu-rotic, for it has neither conflict nor dream. Its desires, such as they are, are trans-parent, for they are just what institutional approval keeps in the forefront of con-sciousness; another institutional pattern would alter their number and intensity; there is little in them that is natural, irreducible, or culturally dangerous. But *on the other side,* the social bond itself is nothing but the mutual reflection of these self-secure integrities. Recall the definition of love. Is not this the very picture of a small academic? Where is there a place in this hall of mirrors for either personality or fraternity?

Essay on psychology in *Politics* (New York)

(4) All the "best people" from the gentlemen's clubs, and all the frantic fascist captains, united in common hatred of Socialism and bestial horror of the rising tide of the mass revolutionary movement, have turned to acts of provocation, to foul incendiarism, to medieval legends of poisoned wells, to legalize their own destruction of proletarian organizations, and rouse the agitated petty-bourgeoisie to chauvinistic fervor on behalf of the fight against the revolutionary way out of the crisis.

Communist pamphlet

(5) If a new spirit *is* to be infused into this old country, there is one thorny and contentious reform which must be tackled, and that is the humanization and gal-vanization of the B.B.C. Timidity here will bespeak canker and atrophy of the soul. The heart of Britain may be sound and of strong beat, for instance, but the British lion's roar at present is like that of Bottom in Shakespeare's *Midsummer Night's Dream*—as gentle as any sucking dove. A virile new Britain cannot continue indef-initely to be traduced in the eyes or rather ears, of the world by the effete lan-

guors of Langham Place, brazenly masquerading as "standard English." When the voice of Britain is heard at nine o'clock, better far and infinitely less ludicrous to hear aitches honestly dropped than the present priggish, inflated, inhibited, school-ma'amish arch braying of blameless bashful mewing maidens!

Letter in Tribune

4 Each of these passages has faults of its own, but, quite apart from avoidable ugliness, two qualities are common to all of them. The first is staleness of imagery; the other is lack of precision. The writer either has a meaning and cannot express it, or he inadvertently says something else, or he is almost indifferent as to whether his words mean anything or not. This mixture of vagueness and sheer incompetence is the most marked characteristic of modern English prose, and especially of any kind of political writing. As soon as certain topics are raised, the concrete melts into the abstract and no one seems able to think of turns of speech that are not hackneyed: prose consists less and less of *words* chosen for the sake of their meaning, and more and more of *phrases* tacked together like the sections of a prefabricated henhouse. I list below, with notes and examples, various of the tricks by means of which the work of prose-construction is habitually dodged:

DYING METAPHORS

5 A newly invented metaphor assists thought by evoking a visual image, while on the other hand a metaphor which is technically "dead" (e.g., *iron resolution*) has in effect reverted to being an ordinary word and can generally be used without loss of vividness. But in between these two classes there is a huge dump of worn-out metaphors which have lost all evocative power and are merely used because they save people the trouble of inventing phrases for themselves. Examples are: *Ring the changes on, take up the cudgels for, toe the line, ride roughshod over, stand shoulder to shoulder with, play into the hands of, no axe to grind, grist to the mill, fishing in troubled waters, on the order of the day, Achilles' heel, swan song, hotbed.* Many of these are used without knowledge of their meaning (what is a "rift," for instance?), and incompatible metaphors are frequently mixed, a sure sign that the writer is not interested in what he is saying. Some metaphors now current have been twisted out of their original meaning without those who use them even being aware of the fact. For example, *toe the line* is sometimes written *tow the line.* Another example is the *hammer and the anvil,* now always used with the implication that the anvil gets the worst of it. In real life it is always the anvil that breaks the hammer, never the other way about: a writer who stopped to think what he was saying would be aware of this, and would avoid perverting the original phrase.

OPERATORS OR VERBAL FALSE LIMBS

6 These save the trouble of picking out appropriate verbs and nouns, and at the same time pad each sentence with extra syllables which give it an appearance of

symmetry. Characteristic phrases are *render inoperative, militate against, make contact with, be subjected to, give rise to, give grounds for, have the effect of, play a leading part (role) in, make itself felt, take effect, exhibit a tendency to, serve the purpose of,* etc., etc. The keynote is the elimination of simple verbs. Instead of being a single word, such as *break, stop, spoil, mend, kill,* a verb becomes a *phrase,* made up of a noun or adjective tacked on to some general-purposes verb such as *prove, serve, form, play, render.* In addition, the passive voice is wherever possible used in preference to the active, and noun constructions are used instead of gerunds *(by examination of* instead of *by examining).* The range of verbs is further cut down by means of the *-ize* and *de-* formations, and the banal statements are given an appearance of profundity by means of the *not un-* formation. Simple conjunctions and prepositions are replaced by such phrases as *with respect to, having regard to, the fact that, by dint of, in view of, in the interests of, on the hypothesis that;* and the ends of sentences are saved from anticlimax by such resounding common-places as *greatly to be desired, cannot be left out of account, a development to be expected in the near future, deserving of serious consideration, brought to a satisfactory conclusion,* and so on and so forth.

PRETENTIOUS DICTION

7 Words like *phenomenon, element, individual* (as noun), *objective, categorical, effective, virtual, basic, primary, promote, constitute, exhibit, exploit, utilize, eliminate, liquidate,* are used to dress up simple statements and give an air of scientific impartiality to biased judgments. Adjectives like *epoch-making, epic, historic, unforgettable, triumphant, age-old, inevitable, inexorable, veritable,* are used to dignify the sordid processes of international politics, while writing that aims at glorifying war usually takes on an archaic color, its characteristic words being: *realm, throne, chariot, mailed fist, trident, sword, shield, buckler, banner, jack-boot, clarion.* Foreign words and expressions such as *cul de sac, ancien régime, deus ex machina, mutatis mutandis, status quo, gleichschaltung, weltanschauung,* are used to give an air of culture and elegance. Except for the useful abbreviations *i.e., e.g.,* and *etc.,* there is no real need for any of the hundreds of foreign phrases now current in English. Bad writers, and especially scientific, political and sociological writers, are nearly always haunted by the notion that Latin or Greek words are grander than Saxon ones, and unnecessary words like *expedite, ameliorate, predict, extraneous, deracinated, clandestine, subaqueous* and hundreds of others constantly gain ground from their Anglo-Saxon opposite numbers.[1] The jargon peculiar to Marxist writing (*hyena, hangman, cannibal, petty bourgeois, these gen-*

---

[1] An interesting illustration of this is the way in which the English flower names which were in use till very recently are being ousted by Greek ones, *snapdragon* becoming *antirrhinum, forget-me-not* becoming *myosotis,* etc. It is hard to see any practical reason for this change of fashion: it is probably due to an instinctive turning-away from the more homely word and a vague feeling that the Greek word is scientific.

try, lacquey, flunkey, mad dog, White Guard, etc.) consists largely of words and phrases translated from Russian, German or French; but the normal way of coining a new word is to use a Latin or Greek root with the appropriate affix and, where necessary, the *-ize* formation. It is often easier to make up words of this kind (*deregionalize, impermissible, extramarital, non-fragmentary,* and so forth) than to think up the English words that will cover one's meaning. The result, in general, is an increase in slovenliness and vagueness.

MEANINGLESS WORDS

8 In certain kinds of writing, particularly in art criticism and literary criticism, it is normal to come across long passages which are almost completely lacking in meaning.[2] Words like *romantic, plastic, values, human, dead, sentimental, natural, vitality,* as used in art criticism, are strictly meaningless, in the sense that they not only do not point to any discoverable object, but are hardly ever expected to do so by the reader. When one critic writes, "The outstanding feature of Mr. X's work is its living quality," while another writes, "The immediately striking thing about Mr. X's work is its peculiar deadness," the reader accepts this as a simple difference of opinion. If words like *black* and *white* were involved, instead of the jargon words *dead* and *living,* he would see at once that language was being used in an improper way. Many political words are similarly abused. The word *Fascism* has now no meaning except in so far as it signifies "something not desirable." The words *democracy, freedom, patriotic, realistic, justice,* have each of them several different meanings which cannot be reconciled with one another. In the case of a word like *democracy,* not only is there no agreed definition, but the attempt to make one is resisted from all sides. It is almost universally felt that when we call a country democratic we are praising it: consequently the defenders of every kind of regime claim that it is a democracy, and fear that they might have to stop using the word if it were tied down to any one meaning. Words of this kind are often used in a consciously dishonest way. That is, the person who uses them has his own private definition, but allows his hearer to think he means something quite different. Statements like, *Marshal Pétain was a true patriot, The Soviet Press is the freest in the world, The Catholic Church is opposed to persecution,* are almost always made with intent to deceive. Other words used in variable meanings, in most cases more or less dishonestly, are: *class, totalitarian, science, progressive, reactionary, bourgeois, equality.*

9 Now that I have made this catalogue of swindles and perversions, let me give another example of the kind of writing that they lead to. This time it must of its nature be an imaginary one. I am going to translate a passage of good English

---

[2] Example: "Comfort's catholicity of perception and image, strangely Whitmanesque in range, almost the exact opposite in aesthetic compulsion, continues to evoke that trembling atmospheric accumulative hinting at a cruel, an inexorably serene timelessness. . . . Wrey Gardiner scores by aiming at simple bull's-eyes with precision. Only they are not so simple, and through this contented sadness runs more than the surface bittersweet of resignation." *(Poetry Quarterly)*

into modern English of the worst sort. Here is a well-known verse from *Ecclesiastes:*

> I returned and saw under the sun, that the race is not to the swift, nor the battle to the strong, neither yet bread to the wise, nor yet riches to men of understanding, nor yet favour to men of skill; but time and chance happeneth to them all.

10   Here it is in modern English:

> Objective consideration of contemporary phenomena compels the conclusion that success or failure in competitive activities exhibits no tendency to be commensurate with innate capacity, but that a considerable element of the unpredictable must invariably be taken into account.

11   This is a parody, but a very gross one. Exhibit (3), above, for instance, contains several patches of the same kind of English. It will be seen that I have not made a full translation. The beginning and ending of the sentence follow the original meaning fairly closely, but in the middle the concrete illustrations—race, battle, bread—dissolve into the vague phrase "success or failure in competitive activities." This had to be so, because no modern writer of the kind I am discussing—no one capable of using phrases like "objective consideration of contemporary phenomena"—would ever tabulate his thoughts in that precise and detailed way. The whole tendency of modern prose is away from concreteness. Now analyse these two sentences a little more closely. The first contains forty-nine words but only sixty syllables, and all its words are those of everyday life. The second contains thirty-eight words of ninety syllables: eighteen of its words are from Latin roots, and one from Greek. The first sentence contains six vivid images, and only one phrase ("time and chance") that could be called vague. The second contains not a single fresh, arresting phrase, and in spite of its ninety syllables it gives only a shortened version of the meaning contained in the first. Yet without a doubt it is the second kind of sentence that is gaining ground in modern English. I do not want to exaggerate. This kind of writing is not yet universal, and outcrops of simplicity will occur here and there in the worst-written page. Still, if you or I were told to write a few lines on the uncertainty of human fortunes, we should probably come much nearer to my imaginary sentence than to the one from *Ecclesiastes.*

12   As I have tried to show, modern writing at its worst does not consist in picking out words for the sake of their meaning and inventing images in order to make the meaning clearer. It consists in gumming together long strips of words which have already been set in order by someone else, and making the results presentable by sheer humbug. The attraction of this way of writing is that it is easy. It is easier—even quicker, once you have the habit—to say *In my opinion it is not an unjustifiable assumption that* than to say *I think.* If you use ready-made phrases, you not only don't have to hunt about for words; you also don't have to bother with the rhythms of your sentences, since these phrases are generally so arranged as to be more or less euphonious. When you are composing in a hurry—when you are dictating to a stenographer, for instance, or making a public speech—it is natural to fall into a pretentious, Latinized style. Tags like *a consideration which we should do well to bear in mind* or *a conclusion to which all of us would readily*

assent will save many a sentence from coming down with a bump. By using stale metaphors, similes and idioms, you save much mental effort, at the cost of leaving your meaning vague, not only for your reader but for yourself. This is the significance of mixed metaphors. The sole aim of a metaphor is to call up a visual image. When these images clash—as in *The Fascist octopus has sung its swan song, the jackboot is thrown into the melting pot*—it can be taken as certain that the writer is not seeing a mental image of the objects he is naming; in other words he is not really thinking. Look again at the examples I gave at the beginning of this essay. Professor Laski (1) uses five negatives in fifty-three words. One of these is superfluous, making nonsense of the whole passage, and in addition there is the slip *alien* for *akin,* making further nonsense, and several avoidable pieces of clumsiness which increase the general vagueness. Professor Hogben (2) plays ducks and drakes with a battery which is able to write prescriptions, and, while disapproving of the everyday phrase *put up with,* is unwilling to look *egregious* up in the dictionary and see what it means; (3), if one takes an uncharitable attitude towards it, is simply meaningless: probably one could work out its intended meaning by reading the whole of the article in which it occurs. In (4), the writer knows more or less what he wants to say, but an accumulation of stale phrases chokes him like tea leaves blocking a sink. In (5), words and meaning have almost parted company. People who write in this manner usually have a general emotional meaning—they dislike one thing and want to express solidarity with another—but they are not interested in the detail of what they are saying. A scrupulous writer, in every sentence that he writes, will ask himself at least four questions, thus: What am I trying to say? What words will express it? What image or idiom will make it clearer? Is this image fresh enough to have an effect? And he will probably ask himself two more: Could I put it more shortly? Have I said anything that is avoidably ugly? But you are not obliged to go to all this trouble. You can shirk it by simply throwing your mind open and letting the ready-made phrases come crowding in. They will construct your sentences for you—even think your thoughts for you, to a certain extent—and at need they will perform the important service of partially concealing your meaning even from yourself. It is at this point that the special connection between politics and the debasement of language becomes clear.

13   In our time it is broadly true that political writing is bad writing. Where it is not true, it will generally be found that the writer is some kind of rebel, expressing his private opinions and not a "party line." Orthodoxy, of whatever color, seems to demand a lifeless, imitative style. The political dialects to be found in pamphlets, leading articles, manifestos, White Papers and the speeches of under-secretaries do, of course, vary from party to party, but they are all alike in that one almost never finds in them a fresh, vivid, homemade turn of speech. When one watches some tired hack on the platform mechanically repeating the familiar phrases—*bestial atrocities, iron heel, bloodstained tyranny, free peoples of the world, stand shoulder to shoulder*—one often has a curious feeling that one is not watching a live human being but some kind of dummy: a feeling which suddenly becomes stronger at moments when the light catches the speaker's spectacles and turns them into blank discs which seem to have no eyes behind them. And this is not altogether fanciful. A speaker who uses that kind of phraseology has

gone some distance towards turning himself into a machine. The appropriate noises are coming out of his larynx, but his brain is not involved as it would be if he were choosing his words for himself. If the speech he is making is one that he is accustomed to make over and over again, he may be almost unconscious of what he is saying, as one is when one utters the responses in church. And this reduced state of consciousness, if not indispensable, is at any rate favorable to political conformity.

14   In our time, political speech and writing are largely the defence of the indefensible. Things like the continuance of British rule in India, the Russian purges and deportations, the dropping of the atom bombs on Japan, can indeed be defended, but only by arguments which are too brutal for most people to face, and which do not square with the professed aims of political parties. Thus political language has to consist largely of euphemism, question-begging and sheer cloudy vagueness. Defenceless villages are bombarded from the air, the inhabitants driven out into the countryside, the cattle machine-gunned, the huts set on fire with incendiary bullets: this is called *pacification*. Millions of peasants are robbed of their farms and sent trudging along the roads with no more than they can carry: this is called *transfer of population* or *rectification of frontiers*. People are imprisoned for years without trial, or shot in the back of the neck or sent to die of scurvy in Arctic lumber camps: this is called *elimination of unreliable elements*. Such phraseology is needed if one wants to name things without calling up mental pictures of them. Consider for instance some comfortable English professor defending Russian totalitarianism. He cannot say outright, "I believe in killing off your opponents when you can get good results by doing so." Probably, therefore, he will say something like this:

> While freely conceding that the Soviet régime exhibits certain features which the humanitarian may be inclined to deplore, we must, I think, agree that a certain curtailment of the right to political opposition is an unavoidable concomitant of transitional periods, and that the rigors which the Russian people have been called upon to undergo have been amply justified in the sphere of concrete achievement.

15   The inflated style is itself a kind of euphemism. A mass of Latin words falls upon the facts like soft snow, blurring the outlines and covering up all the details. The great enemy of clear language is insincerity. When there is a gap between one's real and one's declared aims, one turns as it were instinctively to long words and exhausted idioms, like a cuttlefish squirting out ink. In our age there is no such thing as "keeping out of politics." All issues are political issues, and politics itself is a mass of lies, evasions, folly, hatred and schizophrenia. When the general atmosphere is bad, language must suffer. I should expect to find—this is a guess which I have not sufficient knowledge to verify—that the German, Russian and Italian languages have all deteriorated in the last ten or fifteen years, as a result of dictatorship.

16   But if thought corrupts language, language can also corrupt thought. A bad usage can spread by tradition and imitation, even among people who should and do know better. The debased language that I have been discussing is in some ways very convenient. Phrases like *a not unjustifiable assumption, leaves much to*

be desired, would serve no good purpose, a consideration which we should do well to bear in mind, are a continuous temptation, a packet of aspirins always at one's elbow. Look back through this essay, and for certain you will find that I have again and again committed the very faults I am protesting against. By this morning's post I have received a pamphlet dealing with conditions in Germany. The author tells me that he "felt impelled" to write it. I open it at random, and here is almost the first sentence that I see: "[The Allies] have an opportunity not only of achieving a radical transformation of Germany's social and political structure in such a way as to avoid a nationalistic reaction in Germany itself, but at the same time of laying the foundations of a cooperative and unified Europe." You see, he "feels impelled" to write—feels, presumably, that he has something new to say— and yet his words, like cavalry horses answering the bugle, group themselves automatically into the familiar dreary pattern. The invasion of one's mind by ready-made phrases *(lay the foundations, achieve a radical transformation)* can only be prevented if one is constantly on guard against them, and every such phrase anaesthetizes a portion of one's brain.

17   I said earlier that the decadence of our language is probably curable. Those who deny this would argue, if they produced an argument at all, that language merely reflects existing social conditions, and that we cannot influence its development by any direct tinkering with words and constructions. So far as the general tone or spirit of a language goes, this may be true, but it is not true in detail. Silly words and expressions have often disappeared, not through any evolutionary process but owing to the conscious action of a minority. Two recent examples were *explore every avenue* and *leave no stone unturned,* which were killed by the jeers of a few journalists. There is a long list of fly-blown metaphors which could similarly be got rid of if enough people would interest themselves in the job; and it should also be possible to laugh the *not un-* formation out of existence,[3] to reduce the amount of Latin and Greek in the average sentence, to drive out foreign phrases and strayed scientific words, and, in general, to make pretentiousness unfashionable. But all these are minor points. The defence of the English language implies more than this, and perhaps it is best to start by saying what it does *not* imply.

18   To begin with, it has nothing to do with archaism, with the salvaging of obsolete words and turns of speech, or with the setting up of a "standard English" which must never be departed from. On the contrary, it is especially concerned with the scrapping of every word or idiom which has outworn its usefulness. It has nothing to do with correct grammar and syntax, which are of no importance so long as one makes one's meaning clear, or with the avoidance of Americanisms, or with having what is called a "good prose style." On the other hand it is not concerned with fake simplicity and the attempt to make written English colloquial. Nor does it even imply in every case preferring the Saxon word to the Latin one, though it does imply using the fewest and shortest words that will cover one's meaning. What is above all needed is to let the meaning choose the word, and not the other way about. In prose, the worst thing one can do with words is

---

[3] One can cure one's self of the *not un-* formation by memorizing this sentence: *A not unblack dog was chasing a not unsmall rabbit across a not ungreen field.*

to surrender to them. When you think of a concrete object, you think wordlessly, and then, if you want to describe the thing you have been visualizing you probably hunt about till you find the exact words that seem to fit it. When you think of something abstract you are more inclined to use words from the start, and unless you make a conscious effort to prevent it, the existing dialect will come rushing in and do the job for you, at the expense of blurring or even changing your meaning. Probably it is better to put off using words as long as possible and get one's meaning as clear as one can through pictures or sensations. Afterwards one can choose—not simply *accept*—the phrases that will best cover the meaning, and then switch round and decide what impression one's words are likely to make on another person. This last effort of the mind cuts out all stale or mixed images, all prefabricated phrases, needless repetitions, and humbug and vagueness generally. But one can often be in doubt about the effect of a word or a phrase, and one needs rules that one can rely on when instinct fails. I think the following rules will cover most cases:

1. Never use a metaphor, simile, or other figure of speech which you are used to seeing in print.
2. Never use a long word where a short one will do.
3. If it is possible to cut a word out, always cut it out.
4. Never use the passive where you can use the active.
5. Never use a foreign phrase, a scientific word or a jargon word if you can think of an everyday English equivalent.
6. Break any of these rules sooner than say anything outright barbarous.

These rules sound elementary, and so they are, but they demand a deep change of attitude in anyone who has grown used to writing in the style now fashionable. One could keep all of them and still write bad English, but one could not write the kind of stuff that I quoted in those five specimens at the beginning of this article.

19   I have not here been considering the literary use of language, but merely language as an instrument for expressing and not for concealing or preventing thought. Stuart Chase and others have come near to claiming that all abstract words are meaningless, and have used this as a pretext for advocating a kind of political quietism. Since you don't know what Fascism is, how can you struggle against Fascism? One need not swallow such absurdities as this, but one ought to recognize that the present political chaos is connected with the decay of language, and that one can probably bring about some improvement by starting at the verbal end. If you simplify your English, you are freed from the worst follies of orthodoxy. You cannot speak any of the necessary dialects, and when you make a stupid remark its stupidity will be obvious, even to yourself. Political language— and with variations this is true of all political parties, from Conservatives to Anarchists—is designed to make lies sound truthful and murder respectable, and to give an appearance of solidity to pure wind. One cannot change this all in a moment, but one can at least change one's own habits, and from time to time

one can even, if one jeers loudly enough, send some worn-out and useless phrase—some *jackboot, Achilles' heel, hotbed, melting pot, acid test, veritable inferno* or other lump of verbal refuse—into the dustbin where it belongs.

QUESTIONS

Experience

· To what extent have you experienced difficulty reading books and articles that are poorly written? In what subject areas have you encountered excessive jargon? Where have you encountered vague, careless, or confusing writing?

Interpretation

· Explain what Orwell means when he writes that "the decline of a language must ultimately have political and economic causes." Do you agree with his assertion that "the slovenliness of our language makes it easier for us to have foolish thoughts"? Why, or why not?

Evaluation

· To what extent does Orwell adhere to his own advice for good writing in "Politics and the English Language"? Can you find evidence where he violates his own advice?

WRITING

Exploring

· Find an example of writing that fits Orwell's description of bad writing. It can come from one of your textbooks, if you like. Then select one paragraph, and revise it by applying Orwell's advice for clear writing.

Interpreting

· For the next two weeks, keep a journal of violations of Orwell's standards for political language. You can collect your examples from newspaper and magazine reports and from news broadcasts. For each example you find, explain what the writer or speaker is saying, along with how he or she is violating standards for clear, direct, or honest use of language.

Evaluating

· Write an essay that supports, qualifies, or refutes Orwell's claim that "thought corrupts language, [and] language can also corrupt thought." Be sure to explain what both halves of this statement mean.

LISA BOGDONOFF
(b. 1960)

Police! Police!

Lisa Bogdonoff wrote "Police! Police!" for a college composition course she took as a sophomore at Queens College of the City University of New York. Lisa was asked to write about the connotations of a group of related words. In response to the assignment, she decided to do some research in the Oxford English Dictionary and the Dictionary of Afro-American Slang, where she found historical information about the word "police" and related forms such as "cop," "fuzz," and "pig"—among others. Her essay is notable for the way she presents this historical information efficiently and gracefully.

1 It is the middle of the night. You peer out of your second story window in an attempt to find out what is causing the scratching noise that woke you from sleep. Frozen with fear, you realize that two shadowed amorphous forms on the ground below are breaking into your home. Groping for the phone, you call the police. Just as the cops arrive, you hear a voice rasp, "Here comes the Fuzz," and you barely see two potential burglars escaping under the cover of darkness.

2   Very often we refer to the conservators of public peace as "police," "cops," "fuzz," even "pigs." Although each of these words refers to members of the peacekeeping force, the implications connoted by each are quite different. Describing the scene of an accident, a news reporter would employ the more respectable term "police," whereas the man on the street would be inclined to give equal time to the substantive "cops." "Fuzz," an appellation which became popular in the 1930's and 40's, is a deprecating term not often used by the upper classes. More a slang term than a colloquial expression, "fuzz" has not yet achieved social respectability. Possibly derived from "fuss," one who is overly particular and difficult to please, "fuzz" originally referred to a prison warden or detective. The demeaning "pig" emerged in the riotous 1960's and blatantly expressed a disgust with the nation's police force. "Pig," also a nickname for a prison guard, resulted from a transformation of the Middle English "pigge," slang for a wanton woman. Like the slang "fuzz," "pig" tends to predominate among the young as a disrespectful and rebellious term for what they take to be an oppressive authority.

3   Not surprisingly, members of the force would preferably be called policemen and policewomen, and on occasion may even refer to themselves as "cops." Coined in 1530, "police" has its roots in the Greek "polis" or city, and branches its way up to the Lower Latin "politia" or governmental administration and to the French "poli" *(Oxford English Dictionary)*. By 1829, "policemen" and "policewomen" were known as those of the police force paid to keep order. During the same year, Sir Robert Peel organized London's police force: from Sir Robert (Bobby) came the term for London's police—"bobbies" *(World Book Encyclopedia)*.

4   In America the copper star-shaped badges that adorned the law enforcers' uniforms may have led to the nickname "cop." Another theory is that "cop" stood for "Constables on Patrol." More likely is the *Oxford English Dictionary's* explanation that "cop" is a variation on cap or capture, derived from the Old French "capere." Certain dialects of Black English also define "cop" as a prison *(Dictionary of Afro-American Slang)*. Under most circumstances, the average American will interchange cop and police, with "police" the preferred usage.

5   Daily use and disuse of such words dictate their life spans. And thus, it is likely that "fuzz" and "pigs" will follow "Peelers" and "beaks" into oblivion. While "cop" and "police" still predominate, new words with different connotations such as the C.B. term "smokies" will emerge. Curiously, the fate of these appellations in the language is in the mouths of people.

QUESTIONS

Experience

· Lisa Bogdonoff wrote this essay in 1980. Which of the terms she uses to refer to police are still current today? What new terms have emerged since then? How do you refer to the police? Why?

Interpretation

· What does the writer mean by her final observation that "the fate of these appellations in the language is in the mouths of people"? To what extent does she suggest that we have the power to alter the English language?

Evaluation

· How clearly does Lisa Bogdonoff make her point? How appropriate and accurate are her examples? How convincing do you find her argument? Why?

WRITING

Exploring

· Write your own essay on a group of related words for something. Explain differences in the connotations of the words. Some possibilities are (a) bathroom, toilet, powder room, can, john, jakes, men's and ladies' rooms; (b) intelligent, smart, brainy, egghead, nerd; (c) drunk, intoxicated, stoned, bombed, smashed, inebriated. Like Lisa Bogdonoff, you will need to use one or more good dictionaries or other reference works for information.

Interpreting

· Analyze the way a writer of another essay in this section on language discusses the meanings of related words. Some possibilities: Kakutani's

"The Word Police," Lakoff's "Talking Like a Lady," and Mairs's "On Being a Cripple."

Evaluating

· Examine the social, cultural, or political values suggested by three of the following words: (a) feminist, (b) jock, (c) politician, (d) liberal, (e) conservative, (f) Democrat, (g) Republican, (h) Catholic, (i) Muslim.

GISH JEN
(b. 1956)

What Means Switch?

Gish Jen was raised in Scarsdale, New York, where she attended school before heading off to Harvard, Stanford, and the Iowa Writers' Workshop. She has received support from a number of agencies, including the National Endowment for the Arts. Her work has appeared in periodicals such as The New Yorker *and the* Atlantic Monthly *and has been reprinted in such volumes as* Best American Stories 1988. *Her novel,* Typical American, *published in 1991, garnered wide praise.*

"What Means Switch?," which originally appeared in the Atlantic Monthly, *describes a young Chinese American girl's efforts to communicate with a Japanese classmate who does not speak English. One of the story's most notable features is the way the author varies Mona's way of communicating with her mother, with her friends, and with Sherman, the boy she likes. Another is the way the author limits the story's perpective to the point of view of its young narrator.*

1   There we are, nice Chinese family—father, mother, two born-here girls. Where should we live next? My parents slide the question back and forth like a cup of ginseng neither one wants to drink. Until finally it comes to them, what they really want is a milkshake (chocolate) and to go with it a house in Scarsdale. What else? The broker tries to hint: the neighborhood, she says. Moneyed. Many delis. Meaning rich and Jewish. But someone has sent my parents a list of the top ten schools nation-wide (based on the opinion of selected educators and others) and so *many-deli* or not we nestle into a Dutch colonial on the Bronx River Parkway. The road's windy where we are, very charming; drivers miss their turns, plough up our flower beds, then want to use our telephone. "Of course," my mom tells them, like it's no big deal, we can replant. We're the type to adjust. You know—the lady drivers weep, my mom gets out the Kleenex for them. We're a bit down the hill from the private plane set, in other words. Only in our dreams do our jacket zippers jam, what with all the lift tickets we have stapled to them, Killington on top of Sugarbush on top of Stowe, and we don't even know where the Virgin Islands are— although certain of us do know that virgins are like priests and nuns, which there were a lot more of in Yonkers, where we just moved from, than there are here.

2   This is my first understanding of class. In our old neighborhood everybody knew everything about virgins and non-virgins, not to say the technicalities of staying in-between. Or almost everybody, I should say. In Yonkers I was the laugh-along type. Here I'm an expert.

3   "You mean the man . . . ?" Pig-tailed Barbara Gugelstein spits a mouthful of coke back into her can. "That is *so* gross!"

4   Pretty soon I'm getting popular for a new girl, the only problem is Danielle Meyers, who wears blue mascara and has gone steady with two boys. "How do

you know," she starts to ask, proceeding to edify us all with how she French-kissed one boyfriend and just regular kissed another. ("Because, you know, he had braces.") We hear about his rubber bands, how once one popped right into her mouth. I begin to realize I need to find somebody to kiss too. But how?

5   Luckily, I just about then happen to tell Barbara Gugelstein I know karate. I don't know why I tell her this. My sister Callie's the liar in the family; ask anybody. I'm the one who doesn't see why we should have to hold our heads up. But for some reason I tell Barbara Gugelstein I can make my hands like steel by thinking hard. "I'm not supposed to tell anyone," I say.

6   The way she backs away, blinking, I could be the burning bush.

7   "I can't do bricks," I say—a bit of expectation management. "But I can do your arm if you want." I set my hand in chop position.

8   "Uhh, it's okay," she says. "I know you can, I saw it on TV last night."

9   That's when I recall that I too saw it on TV last night—in fact, at her house. I rush on to tell her I know how to get pregnant with tea.

10   "With *tea?*"

11   "That's how they do it in China."

12   She agrees that China is an ancient and great civilization that ought to be known for more than spaghetti and gunpowder. I tell her I know Chinese. *"Be-yeh fa-foon,"* I say. *"Shee-veh. Ji nu."* Meaning, "Stop acting crazy. Rice gruel. Soy sauce." She's impressed. At lunch the next day, Danielle Meyers and Amy Weinstein and Barbara's crush, Andy Kaplan, are all impressed too. Scarsdale is a liberal town, not like Yonkers, where the Whitman Road Gang used to throw crabapple mash at my sister Callie and me and tell us it would make our eyes stick shut. Here we're like permanent exchange students. In another ten years, there'll be so many Orientals we'll turn into Asians; a Japanese grocery will buy out that one deli too many. But for now, the mid-sixties, what with civil rights on TV, we're not so much accepted as embraced. Especially by the Jewish part of town—which, it turns out, is not all of town at all. That's just an idea people have, Callie says, and lots of them could take us or leave us same as the Christians, who are nice too; I shouldn't generalize. So let me not generalize except to say that pretty soon I've been to so many bar and bas mitzvahs, I can almost say myself whether the kid chants like an angel or like a train conductor, maybe they could use him on the commuter line. At seder I know to forget the bricks, get a good pile of that mortar. Also I know what is schmaltz. I know that I am a goy. This is not why people like me, though. People like me because I do not need to use deodorant, as I demonstrate in the locker room before and after gym. Also, I can explain to them, for example, what is tofu (*der-voo,* we say at home). Their mothers invite me to taste-test their Chinese cooking.

13   "Very authentic." I try to be reassuring. After all, they're nice people, I like them. "De-lish." I have seconds. On the question of what we eat, though, I have to admit, "Well, no, it's different than that." I have thirds. "What my mom makes is home style, it's not in the cookbooks."

14   *Not in the cookbooks!* Everyone's jealous. Meanwhile, the big deal at home is when we have turkey pot pie. My sister Callie's the one introduced them—Mrs. Wilder's, they come in this green-and-brown box—and when we have them, we

both get suddenly interested in helping out in the kitchen. You know, we stand in front of the oven and help them bake. Twenty-five minutes. She and I have a deal, though, to keep it secret from school, as everybody else thinks they're gross. We think they're a big improvement over authentic Chinese home cooking. Ox-tail soup—now that's gross. Stir-fried beef with tomatoes. One day I say, "You know Ma, I have never seen a stir-fried tomato in any Chinese restaurant we have ever been in, ever."

15 "In China," she says, real lofty, "we consider tomatoes are a delicacy."

16 "Ma," I say. "Tomatoes are *Italian.*"

17 "No respect for elders." She wags her finger at me, but I can tell it's just to try and shame me into believing her. "I'm tell you, tomatoes *invented* in China."

18 "*Ma.*"

19 "Is true. Like noodles. Invented in China."

20 "That's not what they said in *school.*"

21 "In *China,*" my mother counters, "we also eat tomatoes uncooked, like apple. And in summertime we slice them, and put some sugar on top."

22 "Are you sure?"

23 My mom says of course she's sure, and in the end I give in, even though she once told me that China was such a long time ago, a lot of things she can hardly remember. She said sometimes she has trouble remembering her characters, that sometimes she'll be writing a letter, just writing along, and all of sudden she won't be sure if she should put four dots or three.

24 "So what do you do then?"

25 "Oh, I just make a little sloppy."

26 "You mean you *fudge*?"

27 She laughed then, but another time, when she was showing me how to write my name, and I said, just kidding, "Are you sure that's the right number of dots now?" she was hurt.

28 "I mean, of course you know," I said. "I mean, *oy.*"

29 Meanwhile, what *I* know is that in the eighth grade, what people want to hear does not include how Chinese people eat sliced tomatoes with sugar on top. For a gross fact, it just isn't gross enough. On the other hand, the fact that somewhere in China somebody eats or has eaten or once ate living monkey brains—now that's conversation.

30 "They have these special tables," I say, "kind of like a giant collar. With a hole in the middle, for the monkey's neck. They put the monkey in the collar, and then they cut off the top of its head."

31 "Whadda they use for cutting?"

32 I think. "Scalpels."

33 "*Scalpels*?" says Andy Kaplan.

34 "Kaplan, don't be dense," Barbara Gugelstein says. "The Chinese *invented* scalpels."

35 Once a friend said to me, You know, everybody is valued for something. She explained how some people resented being valued for their looks; others resented being valued for their money. Wasn't it still better to be beautiful and rich than ugly and poor, though? You should be just glad, she said, that you have some-

thing people value. It's like having a special talent, like being good at ice-skating, or opera-singing. She said, You could probably make a career out of it.

36   Here's the irony: I am.

37 Anyway. I am ad-libbing my way through eighth grade, as I've described. Until one bloomy spring day, I come in late to homeroom, and to my chagrin discover there's a new kid in class.

38   Chinese.

39   So what should I do, pretend to have to go to the girls' room, like Barbara Gugelstein the day Andy Kaplan took his ID back? I sit down; I am so cool I remind myself of Paul Newman. First thing I realize, though, is that no one looking at me is thinking of Paul Newman. The notes fly:

40   "*I* think he's cute."

41   "Who?" I write back. (I am still at an age, understand, when I believe a person can be saved by aplomb.)

42   "I don't think he talks English too good. Writes it either."

43   "Who?"

44   "They might have to put him behind a grade, so don't worry."

45   "He has a crush on you already, you could tell as soon as you walked in, he turned kind of orangish."

46   I hope I'm not turning orangish as I deal with my mail, I could use a secretary. The second round starts:

47   "What do you mean who? Don't be weird. Didn't you *see* him??? Straight back over your right shoulder!!!!"

48   I have to look; what else can I do? I think of certain tips I learned in Girl Scouts about poise. I cross my ankles. I hold a pen in my hand. I sit up as though I have a crown on my head. I swivel my head slowly, repeating to myself, *I* could be Miss America.

49   "Miss Mona Chang."

50   Horror raises its hoary head.

51   "Notes, please."

52   Mrs. Mandeville's policy is to read all notes aloud.

53   I try to consider what Miss America would do, and see myself, back straight, knees together, crying. Some inspiration. Cool Hand Luke, on the other hand, would, quick, eat the evidence. And why not? I should yawn as I stand up, and boom, the notes are gone. All that's left is to explain that it's an old Chinese reflex.

54   I shuffle up to the front of the room.

55   "One minute please," Mrs. Mandeville says.

56   I wait, noticing how large and plastic her mouth is.

57   She unfolds a piece of paper.

58   And I, Miss Mona Chang, who got almost straight A's her whole life except in math and conduct, am about to start crying in front of everyone.

59 I am delivered out of hot Egypt by the bell. General pandemonium. Mrs. Mandeville still has her hand clamped on my shoulder, though. And the next thing I know, I'm holding the new boy's schedule. He's standing next to me like a big blank piece of paper. "This is Sherman," Mrs. Mandeville says.

60 "Hello," I say.

61 "*Non how a,*" I say.

62 I'm glad Barbara Gugelstein isn't there to see my Chinese in action.

63 "*Ji nu,*" I say. "*Shee veh.*"

64 Later I find out that his mother asked if there were any other Orientals in our grade. She had him put in my class on purpose. For now, though, he looks at me as though I'm much stranger than anything else he's seen so far. Is this because he understands I'm saying "soy sauce rice gruel" to him or because he doesn't?

65 "Sher-man," he says finally.

66 I look at his schedule card. Sherman Matsumoto. What kind of name is that for a nice Chinese boy?

67 (Later on, people ask me how I can tell Chinese from Japanese. I shrug. You just kind of know, I say. *Oy!*)

68 Sherman's got the sort of looks I think of as pretty-boy. Monsignor-black hair (not monk brown like mine), bouncy. Crayola eyebrows, one with a round bald spot in the middle of it, like a golf hole. I don't know how anybody can think of him as orangish; his skin looks white to me, with pink triangles hanging down the front of his cheeks like flags. Kind of delicate-looking, but the only truly uncool thing about him is that his spiral notebook has a picture of a kitty cat on it. A big white fluffy one, with a blue ribbon above each perky little ear. I get much opportunity to view this, as all the poor kid understands about life in junior high school is that he should follow me everywhere. It's embarrassing. On the other hand, he's obviously even more miserable than I am, so I try not to say anything. Give him a chance to adjust. We communicate by sign language, and by drawing pictures, which he's better at than I am; he puts in every last detail, even if it takes forever. I try to be patient.

69 A week of this. Finally I enlighten him. "You should get a new notebook."

70 His cheeks turn a shade of pink you mostly only see in hyacinths.

71 "Notebook." I point to his. I show him mine, which is psychedelic, with big purple and yellow stick-on flowers. I try to explain he should have one like this, only without the flowers. He nods enigmatically, and the next day brings me a notebook just like his, except that this cat sports pink bows instead of blue.

72 "Pret-ty," he says. "You."

73 He speaks English! I'm dumbfounded. Has he spoken it all this time? I consider: Pretty. You. What does that mean? Plus actually, he's said *plit-ty,* much as my parents would; I'm assuming he means pretty, but maybe he means pity. Pity. You.

74 "Jeez," I say finally.

75 "You are wel-come," he says.

76 I decorate the back of the notebook with stick-on flowers, and hold it so that these show when I walk through the halls. In class I mostly keep my book open. After all, the kid's so new; I think I really ought to have a heart. And for a livelong day nobody notices.

77 Then Barbara Gugelstein sidles up. "Matching notebooks, huh?"

78   I'm speechless.

79   "First comes love, then comes marriage, and then come chappies in a baby carriage."

80   "Barbara!"

81   "Get it?" she says. "Chinese Japs."

82   "Bar-*bra*," I say to get even.

83   "Just make sure he doesn't give you any *tea*," she says.

84   Are Sherman and I in love? Three days later, I hazard that we are. My thinking proceeds this way: I think he's cute, and I think he thinks I'm cute. On the other hand, we don't kiss and we don't exactly have fantastic conversations. Our talks *are* getting better, though. We started out, "This is a book." "Book." "This is a chair." "Chair." Advancing to, "What is this?" "This is a book." Now, for fun, he tests me.

85   "What is this?" he says.

86   "This is a book," I say, as if I'm the one who has to learn how to talk.

87   He claps. "Good!"

88   Meanwhile, people ask me all about him, I could be his press agent.

89   "No, he doesn't eat raw fish."

90   "No, his father wasn't a kamikaze pilot."

91   "No, he can't do karate."

92   "Are you sure?" somebody asks.

93   Indeed he doesn't know karate, but judo he does. I am hurt I'm not the one to find this out; the guys know from gym class. They line up to be flipped, he flips them all onto the floor, and after that he doesn't eat lunch at the girls' table with me anymore. I'm more or less glad. Meaning, when he was there, I never knew what to say. Now that he's gone, though, I seem to be stuck at the "This is a chair" level of conversation. Ancient Chinese eating habits have lost their cachet; all I get are more and more questions about me and Sherman. "I dunno," I'm saying all the time. *Are* we going out? We do stuff, it's true. For example, I take him to the department stores, explain to him who shops in Alexander's, who shops in Saks. I tell him my family's the type that shops in Alexander's. He says he's sorry. In Saks he gets lost; either that, or else I'm the lost one. (It's true I find him calmly waiting at the front door, hands behind his back, like a guard.) I take him to the candy store. I take him to the bagel store. Sherman is crazy about bagels. I explain to him that Lender's is gross, he should get his bagels from the bagel store. He says thank you.

94   "Are you going steady?" people want to know.

95   How can we go steady when he doesn't have an ID bracelet? On the other hand, he brings me more presents than I think any girl's ever gotten before. Oranges. Flowers. A little bag of bagels. But what do they mean? Do they mean thank you, I enjoyed our trip; do they mean I like you; do they mean I decided I liked the Lender's better even if they are gross, you can have these? Sometimes I think he's acting on his mother's instructions. Also I know at least a couple of the presents were supposed to go to our teachers. He told me that once and turned red. I figured it still might mean something that he didn't throw them out.

96   More and more now, we joke. Like, instead of "I'm thinking," he always says,

"I'm sinking," which we both think is so funny, that all either one of us has to do is pretend to be drowning and the other one cracks up. And he tells me things—for example, that there are electric lights everywhere in Tokyo now.

97 "You mean you didn't have them before?"

98 "Everywhere now!" He's amazed too. "Since Olympics!"

99 "Olympics?"

100 "1960," he says proudly, and as proof, hums for me the Olympic theme song. "You know?"

101 "Sure," I say, and hum with him happily. We could be a picture on a UNICEF poster. The only problem is that I don't really understand what the Olympics have to do with the modernization of Japan, any more than I get this other story he tells me, about that hole in his left eyebrow, which is from some time his father accidentally hit him with a lit cigarette. When Sherman was a baby. His father was drunk, having been out carousing; his mother was very mad but didn't say anything, just cleaned the whole house. Then his father was so ashamed he bowed to ask her forgiveness.

102 "Your mother cleaned the house?"

103 Sherman nods solemnly.

104 "And your father *bowed*?" I find this more astounding than anything I ever thought to make up. "That is so weird," I tell him.

105 "Weird," he agrees. "This I no forget, forever. *Father* bow to *mother*!"

106 We shake our heads.

107 As for the things he asks me, they're not topics I ever discussed before. Do I like it here? Of course I like it here, I was born here, I say. Am I Jewish? Jewish! I laugh. *Oy!* Am I American? "Sure I'm American," I say. "Everybody who's born here is American, and also some people who convert from what they were before. You could become American." But he says no, he could never. "Sure you could," I say. "You only have to learn some rules and speeches."

108 "But I Japanese," he says.

109 "You could become American anyway," I say. "Like I *could* become Jewish, if I wanted to. I'd just have to switch, that's all."

110 "But you Catholic," he says.

111 I think maybe he doesn't get what means switch.

112 I introduce him to Mrs. Wilder's turkey pot pies. "Gross?" he asks. I say they are, but we like them anyway. "Don't tell anybody." He promises. We bake them, eat them. While we're eating, he's drawing me pictures.

113 "This American," he says, and he draws something that looks like John Wayne. "This Jewish," he says, and draws something that looks like the Wicked Witch of the West, only male.

114 "I don't think so," I say.

115 He's undeterred. "This Japanese," he says, and draws a fair rendition of himself. "This Chinese," he says, and draws what looks to be another fair rendition of himself.

116 "How can you tell them apart?"

117 "This way," he says, and he puts the picture of the Chinese so that it is looking at the pictures of the American and the Jew. The Japanese faces the wall. Then he draws another picture, of a Japanese flag, so that the Japanese has that to con-

template. "Chinese lost in department store," he says. "Japanese know how go." For fun, he then takes the Japanese flag and fastens it to the refrigerator door with magnets. "In school, in ceremony, we this way," he explains, and bows to the picture.

118   When my mother comes in, her face is so red that with the white wall behind her she looks a bit like the Japanese flag herself. Yet I get the feeling I better not say so. First she doesn't move. Then she snatches the flag off the refrigerator, so fast the magnets go flying. Two of them land on the stove. She crumples up the paper. She hisses at Sherman, *"This is the U.S. of A., do you hear me!"*

119   Sherman hears her.

120   "You call your mother right now, tell her come pick you up."

121   *He* understands perfectly. *I,* on the other hand, am stymied. How can two people who don't really speak English understand each other better than I can understand them? "But Ma," I say.

122   "Don't *Ma* me," she says.

123   Later on she explains that World War II was in China, too. "Hitler," I say. "Nazis. Volkswagens." I know the Japanese were on the wrong side, because they bombed Pearl Harbor. My mother explains about before that. The Napkin Massacre. "*Nan*-king," she corrects me.

124   "Are you sure?" I say. "In school, they said the war was about putting the Jews in ovens."

125   "Also about ovens."

126   "About both?"

127   "Both."

128   "That's not what they said in school."

129   "*Just forget about school.*"

130   Forget about school? "I thought we moved here for the schools."

131   "We moved here," she says, "for your education."

132   Sometimes I have no idea what she's talking about.

133   "I like Sherman," I say after a while.

134   "He's nice boy," she agrees.

135   Meaning what? I would ask, except that my dad's just come home, which means it's time to start talking about whether we should build a brick wall across the front of the lawn. Recently a car made it almost into our livingroom, which was so scary, the driver fainted and an ambulance had to come. "We should have discussion," my dad said after that. And so for about a week, every night we do.

136   "Are you just friends, or more than just friends?" Barbara Gugelstein is giving me the cross-ex.

137   "Maybe," I say.

138   "Come on," she says, "I told you *everything* about me and Andy."

139   I actually *am* trying to tell Barbara everything about Sherman, but everything turns out to be nothing. Meaning, I can't locate the conversation in what I have to say. Sherman and I go places, we talk, one time my mother threw him out of the house because of World War II.

140   "I think we're just friends," I say.

141   "You think or you're sure?"

142   Now that I do less of the talking at lunch, I notice more what other people talk about—cheerleading, who likes who, this place in White Plains to get earrings. On none of these topics am I an expert. Of course, I'm still friends with Barbara Gugelstein, but I notice Danielle Meyers has spun away to other groups.

143   Barbara's analysis goes this way: To be popular, you have to have big boobs, a note from your mother that lets you use her Lord & Taylor credit card, and a boyfriend. On the other hand, what's so wrong with being unpopular? "We'll get them in the end," she says. It's what her dad tells her. "Like they'll turn out too dumb to do their own investing, and then they'll get killed in fees and then they'll have to move to towns where the schools stink. And my dad should know," she winds up. "He's a broker."

144   "I guess," I say.

145   But the next thing I know, I have a true crush on Sherman Matsumoto. *Mis*ter Judo, the guys call him now, with real respect; and the more they call him that, the more I don't care that he carries a notebook with a cat on it.

146   I sigh. "Sherman."

147   "I thought you were just friends," says Barbara Gugelstein.

148   "We were," I say mysteriously. This, I've noticed, is how Danielle Meyers talks; everything's secret, she only lets out so much; it's like she didn't grow up with everybody telling her she had to share.

149   And here's the funny thing: The more I intimate that Sherman and I are more than just friends, the more it seems we actually are. It's the old imagination giving reality a nudge. When I start to blush, he starts to blush; we reach a point where we can hardly talk at all.

150   "Well, there's first base with tongue, and first base without," I tell Barbara Gugelstein.

151   In fact, Sherman and I have brushed shoulders, which was equivalent to first base I was sure, maybe even second. I felt as though I'd turned into one huge shoulder; that's all I was, one huge shoulder. We not only didn't talk, we didn't breathe. But how can I tell Barbara Gugelstein that? So instead I say, "Well there's second base and second base."

152   Danielle Meyers is my friend again. She says, "I know exactly what you mean," just to make Barbara Gugelstein feel bad.

153   "Like *what* do I mean?" I say.

154   Danielle Meyers can't answer.

155   "You know what I think?" I tell Barbara the next day. "I think Danielle's giving us a line."

156   Barbara pulls thoughtfully on one of her pigtails.

157   If Sherman Matsumoto is never going to give me an ID to wear, he should at least get up the nerve to hold my hand. I don't think he sees this. I think of the story he told me about his parents, and in a synaptic firestorm realize we don't see the same things at all.

158   So one day, when we happen to brush shoulders again, I don't move away. He doesn't move away either. There we are. Like a pair of bleachers, pushed together but not quite matched up. After a while, I have to breathe, I can't help it. I breathe in such a way that our elbows start to touch too. We are in a crowd,

waiting for a bus. I crane my neck to look at the sign that says where the bus is going; now our wrists are touching. Then it happens: He links his pinky around mine.

159   Is that holding hands? Later, in bed, I wonder all night. One finger, and not even the biggest one.

160   Sherman is leaving in a month. Already! I think, well, I suppose he will leave and we'll never even kiss. I guess that's all right. Just when I've resigned myself to it, though, we hold hands all five fingers. Once when we are at the bagel shop, then again in my parents' kitchen. Then, when we are at the playground, he kisses the back of my hand.

161   He does it again not too long after that, in White Plains.

162   I invest in a bottle of mouthwash.

163   Instead of moving on, though, he kisses the back of my hand again. And again. I try raising my hand, hoping he'll make the jump from my hand to my cheek. It's like trying to wheedle an inchworm out the window. You know, *This way, this way.*

164   *All over the world people have their own cultures.* That's what we learned in social studies.

165   If we never kiss, I'm not going to take it personally.

166   It is the end of the school year. We've had parties. We've turned in our text-books. Hooray! Outside the asphalt already steams if you spit on it. Sherman isn't leaving for another couple of days, though, and he comes to visit every morning, staying until the afternoon, when Callie comes home from her big-deal job as a bank teller. We drink Kool-Aid in the backyard and hold hands until they are sweaty and make smacking noises coming apart. He tells me how busy his par-ents are, getting ready for the move. His mother, particularly, is very tired. Mostly we are mournful.

167   The very last day we hold hands and do not let go. Our palms fill up with water like a blister. We do not care. We talk more than usual. How much is airmail to Japan, that kind of thing. Then suddenly he asks, will I marry him?

168   *I'm only thirteen.*

169   *But when old? Sixteen?*

170   *If you come back to get me.*

171   *I come. Or you can come to Japan, be Japanese.*

172   *How can I be Japanese?*

173   *Like you become American. Switch.*

174   He kisses me on the cheek, again and again and again.

175   His mother calls to say she's coming to get him. I cry. I tell him how I've saved every present he's ever given me—the ruler, the pencils, the bags from the bagels, all the flower petals. I even have the orange peels from the oranges.

176   *All?*

177   *I put them in a jar.*

178   I'd show him, except that we're not allowed to go upstairs to my room. Any-way, something about the orange peels seems to choke him up too. *Mis*ter Judo,

but I've gotten him in a soft spot. We are going together to the bathroom to get some toilet paper to wipe our eyes when poor tired Mrs. Matsumoto, driving a shiny new station wagon, skids up onto our lawn.

179 "Very sorry!"

180 We race outside.

181 "Very sorry!"

182 Mrs. Matsumoto is so short that about all we can see of her is a green cotton sun hat, with a big brim. It's tied on. The brim is trembling.

183 I hope my mom's not going to start yelling about World War II.

184 "Is all right, no trouble," she says, materializing on the step behind me and Sherman. She's propped the screen door wide open; when I turn I see she's waving. "No trouble, no trouble!"

185 "No trouble, no trouble!" I echo, twirling a few times with relief.

186 Mrs. Matsumoto keeps apologizing; my mom keeps insisting she shouldn't feel bad, it was only some grass and a small tree. Crossing the lawn, she insists Mrs. Matsumoto get out of the car, even though it means trampling some lilies-of-the-valley. She insists that Mrs. Matsumoto come in for a cup of tea. Then she will not talk about anything unless Mrs. Matsumoto sits down, and unless she lets my mom prepare her a small snack. The coming in and the tea and the sitting down are settled pretty quickly, but they negotiate ferociously over the small snack, which Mrs. Matsumoto will not eat unless she can call Mr. Matsumoto. She makes the mistake of linking Mr. Matsumoto with a reparation of some sort, which my mom will not hear of.

187 "Please!"

188 "No no no no."

189 Back and forth it goes. "No no no no." "No no no no." "No no no no." What kind of conversation is that? I look at Sherman, who shrugs. Finally Mr. Matsumoto calls on his own, wondering where his wife is. He comes over in a taxi. He's a heavy-browed businessman, friendly but brisk—not at all a type you could imagine bowing to a lady with a taste for tie-on sun hats. My mom invites him in as if it's an idea she just this moment thought of. And would he maybe have some tea and a small snack?

190 Sherman and I sneak back outside for another farewell, by the side of the house, behind the forsythia bushes. We hold hands. He kisses me on the cheek again, and then—just when I think he's finally going to kiss me on the lips—he kisses me on the neck.

191 Is this first base?

192 He does it more. Up and down, up and down. First it tickles, and then it doesn't. He has his eyes closed. I close my eyes too. He's hugging me. Up and down. Then down.

193 He's at my collarbone.

194 Still at my collarbone. Now his hand's on my ribs. So much for first base. More ribs. The idea of second base would probably make me nervous if he weren't on his way back to Japan and if I really thought we were going to get there. As it is, though, I'm not in much danger of wrecking my life on the shoals of passion; his unmoving hand feels more like a growth than a boyfriend. He has his whole face

pressed to my neck skin so I can't tell his mouth from his nose. I think he may be licking me.

195   From indoors, a burst of adult laughter. My eyelids flutter. I start to try and wiggle such that his hand will maybe budge upward.

196   Do I mean for my top blouse button to come accidentally undone?

197   He clenches his jaw, and when he opens his eyes, they're fixed on that button like it's a gnat that's been bothering him for far too long. He mutters in Japanese. If later in life he were to describe this as a pivotal moment in his youth, I would not be surprised. Holding the material as far from my body as possible, he buttons the button. Somehow we've landed up too close to the bushes.

198   What to tell Barbara Gugelstein? She says, "Tell me what were his last words. He must have said something last."

199   "I don't want to talk about it."

200   "Maybe he said, Good-bye?" she suggests. "Sayonara?" She means well.

201   "I don't want to talk about it."

202   "Aw, come on, I told you everything about . . ."

203   I say, "Because it's private, excuse me."

204   She stops, squints at me as though at a far-off face she's trying to make out. Then she nods and very lightly places her hand on my forearm.

205   The forsythia seemed to be stabbing us in the eyes. Sherman said, more or less, *You will need to study how to switch.*

206   And I said, *I think you should switch. The way you do everything is weird.*

207   And he said, *You just want to tell everything to your friends. You just want to have boyfriend to become popular.*

208   Then he flipped me. Two swift moves, and I went sprawling through the air, a flailing confusion of soft human parts such as had no idea where the ground was.

209   It is the fall, and I am in high school, and still he hasn't written, so finally I write him.

210   *I still have all your gifts,* I write. *I don't talk so much as I used to. Although I am not exactly a mouse either. I don't care about being popular anymore. I swear. Are you happy to be back in Japan? I know I ruined everything. I was just trying to be entertaining. I miss you with all my heart, and hope I didn't ruin everything.*

211   He writes back, *You will never be Japanese.*

212   I throw all the orange peels out that day. Some of them, it turns out, were moldy anyway. I tell my mother I want to move to Chinatown.

213   "Chinatown!" she says.

214   I don't know why I suggested it.

215   "What's the matter?" she says. "Still boy-crazy? That Sherman?"

216   "No."

217   "Too much homework?"

218   I don't answer.

219   "Forget about school."

220   Later she tells me if I don't like school, I don't have to go everyday. Some days I can stay home.

221   "Stay home?" In Yonkers, Callie and I used to stay home all the time, but that was because the schools there were *waste of time.*

222   "No good for a girl be too smart anyway."

223 For a long time I think about Sherman. But after a while I don't think about him so much as I just keep seeing myself flipped onto the ground, lying there shocked as the Matsumotos get ready to leave. My head has hit a rock; my brain aches as though it's been shoved to some new place in my skull. Otherwise I am okay. I see the forsythia, all those whippy branches, and can't believe how many leaves there are on a bush—every one green and perky and durably itself. And past them, real sky. I try to remember about why the sky's blue, even though this one's gone the kind of indescribable grey you associate with the insides of old shoes. I smell grass. Probably I have grass stains all over my back. I hear my mother calling through the back door, "Mon-a! Everyone leaving now," and "Not coming to say good-bye?" I hear Mr. and Mrs. Matsumoto bowing as they leave—or at least I hear the embarrassment in my mother's voice as they bow. I hear their car start. I hear Mrs. Matsumoto directing Mr. Matsumoto how to back off the lawn so as not to rip any more of it up. I feel the back of my head for blood—just a little. I hear their chug-chug grow fainter and fainter, until it has faded into the whuzz-whuzz of all the other cars. I hear my mom singing, "*Mon*-a! *Mon*-a!" until my dad comes home. Doors open and shut. I see myself standing up, brushing myself off so I'll have less explaining to do if she comes out to look for me. Grass stains—just like I thought. I see myself walking around the house, going over to have a look at our churned-up yard. It looks pretty sad, two big brown tracks, right through the irises and the lilies of the valley, and that was a new dogwood we'd just planted. Lying there like that. I hear myself thinking about my father, having to go dig it up all over again. Adjusting. I think how we probably ought to put up that brick wall. And sure enough, when I go inside, no one's thinking about me, or that little bit of blood at the back of my head, or the grass stains. That's what they're talking about—that wall. Again. My mom doesn't think it'll do any good, but my dad thinks we should give it a try. Should we or shouldn't we? How high? How thick? What will the neighbors say? I plop myself down on a hard chair. And all I can think is, we are the complete only family that has to worry about this. If I could, I'd switch everything to be different. But since I can't, I might as well sit here at the table for a while, discussing what I know how to discuss. I nod and listen to the rest.

QUESTIONS

Experience

· Comment on any experience you may have had communicating with someone who does not know English or your native language. To what extent were you able to communicate in those situations? With what results?

Interpretation

· Although this story involves efforts to communicate among its central characters, it is very much concerned with cultural differences and with the need to become part of a community. Identify a scene in which each of these issues is foregrounded, and comment on its effectiveness.

Evaluation

· How do cultural differences affect the communication between Mona and Sherman? What else contributes to the tension between them?

· To what extent is it possible for someone to "switch" cultures, as Mona at one point advises Sherman?

WRITING

Exploring

· Write about an experience you have had in communicating with someone from another culture. Explain to what extent your ability to understand one another turned on your understanding of one another's language and to what extent it was influenced by different cultural ideals, customs, or values.

Interpreting

· Examine the way Mona talks with her friends, with her mother, and with Sherman. Explain the significance of the way she talks with each. You may also wish to discuss other conversations, such as that between Sherman's and Mona's mothers or those involving Mona's or Sherman's father.

Evaluating

· Discuss the way different types of values clash in this story. You may wish to consider the values of one ethnic group compared with those of another, the values of an individual versus a larger group, or the values of younger and older people.

PABLO NERUDA
(1904–1973)

The Word

TRANSLATED BY ALASTAIR REID

A writer and a diplomat, Pablo Neruda was born in Parral, Chile. A prolific poet, Neruda introduced innovative techniques and wrote in a wide variety of styles. Collections of his poetry include The Early Poems *(1969) and* Five Decades: Poems 1925–1970, *among others. A lifelong political activist, Neruda was elected in 1944 to Chile's national senate. In the early 1970s he served Chilean President Salvador Allende as ambassador to France. In 1971 Neruda was awarded the Nobel Prize for literature.*

In his poem "The Word," Neruda celebrates the power of language. Among the poem's noteworthy features is its use of metaphor, especially its conception of the word as a living creature that is born and grows to maturity. Neruda makes the word stand for language quick with life, the equivalent and equal of life itself.

The word
was born in the blood,
grew in the dark body, beating,
and took flight through the lips and the mouth.

5 Farther away and nearer
still, still it came
from dead fathers and from wandering races,
from lands which had turned to stone,
lands weary of their poor tribes,
10 for when grief took to the roads
the people set out and arrived
and married new land and water
to grow their words again.
And so this is the inheritance;
15 this is the wavelength which connects us
with dead men and the dawning
of new beings not yet come to light.

Still the atmosphere quivers
with the first word uttered
20 dressed up
in terror and sighing.
It emerged
from the darkness
and until now there is no thunder

25 that ever rumbles with the iron voice
of that word,
the first
word uttered—
perhaps it was only a ripple, a single drop,
30 and yet its great cataract falls and falls.

Later on, the word fills with meaning.
Always with child, it filled up with lives.
Everything was births and sounds—
affirmation, clarity, strength,
35 negation, destruction, death—
the verb took over all the power
and blended existence with essence
in the electricity of its grace.
Human word, syllable, flank
40 of extending light and solid silverwork,
hereditary goblet which receives
the communications of the blood—
here is where silence came together with
the wholeness of the human word,
45 and, for human beings, not to speak is to die—
language extends even to the hair,
the mouth speaks without the lips moving,
all of a sudden, the eyes are words.

I take the word and pass it through my senses
50 as though it were no more than a human shape;
its arrangements awe me and I find my way
through each resonance of the spoken word—
I utter and I am and, speechless, I approach
across the edge of words silence itself.

55 I drink to the word, raising
a word or a shining cup;
in it I drink
the pure wine of language
or inexhaustible water,
60 maternal source of words,
and cup and water and wine
give rise to my song
because the verb is the source
and vivid life—it is blood,
65 blood which expresses its substance
and so ordains its own unwinding.
Words give glass quality to glass, blood to blood,
and life to life itself.

QUESTIONS

Experience

· Which sections of "The Word" did you find clearest and easiest to follow, and which the most difficult? Why? Which lines are the most meaningful for you? Why?

Interpretation

· Identify places where Neruda compares uttering the word to pregnancy and birth. Explain the significance of these comparisons.

· Explain the relationships between words and silence or between words and feeling that are suggested in the poem.

Evaluation

· To what extent does Neruda get you thinking about language in ways you had not considered before? To what extent does he make words "live" in his poem?

WRITING

Exploring

· Write an essay describing a situation or a time in which language was crucial. Identify which words were spoken and in what context. Explain the significance of the language used.

Interpreting

· Write an interpretation of the poem. You may wish to discuss each stanza in turn, or you may choose to focus on a particular aspect of the poem, such as its imagery, diction, or use of comparisons.

Evaluating

· Write an essay agreeing or disagreeing with Neruda's idea that "for human beings, not to speak is to die." Explain what he means by this statement.

LANGUAGE—CONSIDERATIONS FOR THINKING AND WRITING

1. A number of writers in this section discuss acceptable and unacceptable language. Consider the kinds of language two or three of the following find unacceptable and why: Barbara Lawrence, George Orwell, Nancy Mairs, or Michiko Kakutani.

2. Two writers consider characteristics of men and women, making assertions about the ways men and women use language. Compare aspects of gender as

reflected in the essays by Robin Lakoff and Barbara Lawrence. You may also wish to broaden your discussion by looking at Deborah Tannen's "Different Words, Different Worlds" (in "Gender"), Maxine Hong Kingston's "Silence" (in "Communities"), and Gloria Anzaldúa's "How to Tame a Wild Tongue" (in "Culture and Society").

3. After reading Nancy Mairs's "On Being a Cripple" and Michiko Kakutani's "The Word Police," write an essay explaining what Kakutani would think of Mairs's choice of words to describe herself. Consider, as well, how you think Kakutani would react to the other choices her disability to label—choices that Mairs rejects.

4. Compare what George Orwell and Pablo Neruda have to say about the power and influence of words. Or read Neil Postman's comments on television news broadcasts in light of George Orwell's "Politics and the English Language." Explain how Postman's view supports Orwell's, or explain how Orwell's ideas about verbal power differ from Neruda's.

5. Compare James Baldwin's ideas about language in "If Black English Isn't a Language, Then Tell Me What Is" with Gloria Anzaldúa's ideas in "How to Tame a Wild Tongue" (in "Culture and Society"). Consider what these writers identify as a language versus their definition of a dialect.

6. Discuss how ideas about language in our society are changing. You might wish to discuss whether societal strictures against obscene language are loosening or tightening, and why. You could look for examples of changing uses of language in popular magazines as well as in TV shows, films, and song lyrics.

7. Write an imaginative or creative piece that explores or illustrates an aspect of language of interest to you. You might write a poem, song, short story, or a scene for a play or a film. You may wish to write an imitation of one of the writer's works from the chapter (or a work from another section of the book). For example, you could use a section of Gloria Anzaldúa's essay as a model for an essay in which you employ two languages. Or you could write your own poem on words in the style of Neruda's "The Word."

8. Research an issue of language, and write a short, focused paper on the topic. You may wish to explore an issue raised by a writer from this chapter, such as Baldwin's thoughts about black English, Lakoff's about women's language, or Lawrence's about denigrating terms for women's body parts. Or you may wish to pursue some other question about language, such as differences between English and another language you know, or how a person's use of language is related to his or her social class or ethnicity.

S I X

The Arts

JOAN DIDION
  Georgia O'Keeffe

RALPH ELLISON
  Living with Music

MARY GORDON
  Mary Cassatt

MARK STRAND
  Crossing the Tracks to Hopper's World

WILLIAM ZINSSER
  Shanghai

JAMES AGEE
  The Comic Acting of Buster Keaton

JOHN BERGER
  Looking at a Photograph

ELIZABETH MACDONALD
  Odalisque

JAMES BALDWIN
  Sonny's Blues

LANGSTON HUGHES
  Trumpet Player

The arts are all around us. Hardly a day goes by that we don't hear music, see still and moving images, observe some kind of performance. The arts—of music, literature, dance, photography, cinema, and others—provide ways for us to express ourselves and to enjoy the ways others have expressed themselves. Among the pleasures the arts provide is the pleasure of creating something that didn't exist before. Another is the pleasure of acknowledging and appreciating the beauty or insight of artistic productions and performances.

A famous Latin phrase—*ars longa, vita brevis* (art is long, life is short)—suggests that artists must devote much of their lives to the creation of artworks they hope will endure beyond their own life spans. But one might also suggest that life, too, can be long, and that one way to make our lives more interesting and enjoyable is to develop an appreciation of many types of art. As you read the selections in this chapter, you will be encouraged to think about forms of artistic expression you may already know and to consider others you may be unfamiliar with. In both instances you can enhance the enjoyment you currently take from the arts. You may even be led to develop an interest in and appreciation of forms of artistic expression you have previously neglected.

Half of the essays in this section reveal a deep respect for the various artists discussed. Joan Didion describes her engagement with Georgia O'Keeffe as woman and artist, while Mary Gordon describes her appreciation of the life and work of the American impressionist painter Mary Cassatt. The contemporary American poet Mark Strand explains his fascination with the paintings of the modern American painter Edward Hopper. Elizabeth MacDonald uses two artists, Ingres and De Chirico, to help explain her obsession with being thin. And James Agee reviews the films of the comic actor Buster Keaton, explaining the nature of Keaton's genius for silent film comedy.

Four of the selections involve music: Baldwin's "Sonny's Blues," which describes the potential of music as a medium of communication; William Zinsser's "Shanghai," which reveals the extent to which music can cross cultural barriers; Langston Hughes's poem "Trumpet Player," which conveys not only the sense of the music being described but also its effects on the musician performing it; and Ralph Ellison's glorious essay "Living with Music," which portrays something of Ellison's early obsession with music as well as his profound respect for it.

Finally, in "Looking at a Photograph," John Berger, novelist and art critic, examines a photograph by André Kertész. In doing so, Berger teaches us how to read such an image, using its title as an index to the relevant historical circumstances that help elucidate its meaning. At the same time, he argues that the significance of the photograph for viewers transcends the particulars of historical actuality, as later viewers interpret Kertész's photograph in terms of familiar yet important aspects of human experience—in this case, love and parting.

JOAN DIDION
(b. 1934)

Georgia O'Keeffe

Joan Didion, essayist and novelist, was born in Sacramento, California. Didion earned her B.A. from the University of California at Berkeley and won Vogue *magazine's Prix de Paris the year she graduated. She has been an associate editor at* Vogue; *has taught creative writing; and has contributed stories, articles, and reviews to numerous periodicals. Her books include* River Run, Play It as It Lays, A Book of Common Prayer, *and* Democracy *(all novels) and* Slouching Toward Bethlehem, The White Album, Salvador, *and* After Henry *(essays and journal articles).*

In the following essay, Joan Didion describes the character of the modern American painter Georgia O'Keeffe. Didion's portrait of O'Keeffe conveys the writer's unmistakable admiration for the painter. It conveys also a sense of O'Keeffe's individuality and her uncompromising sense of painting what she wanted in the way she wanted to paint it. Didion's essay is notable for suggesting in a few brief pages a sense of the character of Georgia O'Keeffe. Didion achieves this intense character portrayal in part by letting her subject speak for herself and in part by identifying the salient qualities that define the painter, then illustrating those qualities with brief but telling anecdotes.

1 "Where I was born and where and how I have lived is unimportant," Georgia O'Keeffe told us in the book of paintings and words published in her ninetieth year on earth. She seemed to be advising us to forget the beautiful face in the Stieglitz photographs. She appeared to be dismissing the rather condescending romance that had attached to her by then, the romance of extreme good looks and advanced age and deliberate isolation. "It is what I have done with where I have been that should be of interest." I recall an August afternoon in Chicago in 1973 when I took my daughter, then seven, to see what Georgia O'Keeffe had done with where she had been. One of the vast O'Keeffe "Sky Above Clouds" canvases floated over the back stairs in the Chicago Art Institute that day, dominating what seemed to be several stories of empty light, and my daughter looked at it once, ran to the landing, and kept on looking. "Who drew it," she whispered after a while. I told her. "I need to talk to her," she said finally.

2 My daughter was making, that day in Chicago, an entirely unconscious but quite basic assumption about people and the work they do. She was assuming that the glory she saw in the work reflected a glory in its maker, that the painting was the painter as the poem is the poet, that every choice one made alone— every word chosen or rejected, every brush stroke laid or not laid down—betrayed one's character. *Style is character.* It seemed to me that afternoon that I had rarely seen so instinctive an application of this familiar principle, and I recall being pleased not only that my daughter responded to style as character but that it was

Georgia O'Keeffe's particular style to which she responded: this was a hard woman who had imposed her 192 square feet of clouds on Chicago.

3   "Hardness" has not been in our century a quality much admired in women, nor in the past twenty years has it even been in official favor for men. When hardness surfaces in the very old we tend to transform it into "crustiness" or eccentricity, some tonic pepperiness to be indulged at a distance. On the evidence of her work and what she has said about it, Georgia O'Keeffe is neither "crusty" nor eccentric. She is simply hard, a straight shooter, a woman clean of received wisdom and open to what she sees. This is a woman who could early on dismiss most of her contemporaries as "dreamy," and would later single out one she liked as "a very poor painter." (And then add, apparently by way of softening the judgment: "I guess he wasn't a painter at all. He had no courage and I believe that to create one's own world in any of the arts takes courage.") This is a woman who in 1939 could advise her admirers that they were missing her point, that their appreciation of her famous flowers was merely sentimental. "When I paint a red hill," she observed coolly in the catalogue for an exhibition that year, "you say it is too bad that I don't always paint flowers. A flower touches almost everyone's heart. A red hill doesn't touch everyone's heart." This is a woman who could describe the genesis of one of her most well-known paintings—the "Cow's Skull: Red, White and Blue" owned by the Metropolitan—as an act of quite deliberate and derisive orneriness. "I thought of the city men I had been seeing in the East," she wrote. "They talked so often of writing the Great American Novel—the Great American Play—the Great American Poetry. . . . So as I was painting my cow's head on blue I thought to myself, 'I'll make it an American painting. They will not think it great with the red stripes down the sides—Red, White and Blue—but they will notice it.' "

4   *The city men. The men. They.* The words crop up again and again as this astonishingly aggressive woman tells us what was on her mind when she was making her astonishingly aggressive paintings. It was those city men who stood accused of sentimentalizing her flowers: "I made you take time to look at what I saw and when you took time to really notice my flower you hung all your associations with flowers on my flower and you write about my flower as if I think and see what you think and see—and I don't." *And I don't.* Imagine those words spoken, and the sound you hear is *don't tread on me.* "The men" believed it impossible to paint New York, so Georgia O'Keeffe painted New York. "The men" didn't think much of her bright color, so she made it brighter. The men yearned toward Europe so she went to Texas, and then New Mexico. The men talked about Cézanne, "long involved remarks about the 'plastic quality' of his form and color," and took one another's long involved remarks, in the view of this angelic rattlesnake in their midst, altogether too seriously. "I can paint one of those dismal-colored paintings like the men," the woman who regarded herself always as an outsider remembers thinking one day in 1922, and she did: a painting of a shed "all low-toned and dreary with the tree beside the door." She called this act of rancor "The Shanty" and hung it in her next show. "The men seemed to approve of it," she reported fifty-four years later, her contempt undimmed. "They seemed to think that maybe I was beginning to paint. That was my only low-toned dismal-colored painting."

5   Some women fight and others do not. Like so many successful guerrillas in the war between the sexes, Georgia O'Keeffe seems to have been equipped early with an immutable sense of who she was and a fairly clear understanding that she would be required to prove it. On the surface her upbringing was conventional. She was a child on the Wisconsin prairie who played with china dolls and painted watercolors with cloudy skies because sunlight was too hard to paint and, with her brother and sisters, listened every night to her mother read stories of the Wild West, of Texas, of Kit Carson and Billy the Kid. She told adults that she wanted to be an artist and was embarrassed when they asked what kind of artist she wanted to be: she had no idea "what kind." She had no idea what artists did. She had never seen a picture that interested her, other than a pen-and-ink Maid of Athens in one of her mother's books, some Mother Goose illustrations printed on cloth, a tablet cover that showed a little girl with pink roses, and the painting of Arabs on horseback that hung in her grandmother's parlor. At thirteen, in a Dominican convent, she was mortified when the sister corrected her drawing. At Chatham Episcopal Institute in Virginia she painted lilacs and sneaked time alone to walk out to where she could see the line of the Blue Ridge Mountains on the horizon. At the Art Institute in Chicago she was shocked by the presence of live models and wanted to abandon anatomy lessons. At the Art Students League in New York one of her fellow students advised her that, since he would be a great painter and she would end up teaching painting in a girls' school, any work of hers was less important than modeling for him. Another painted over her work to show her how the Impressionists did trees. She had not before heard how the Impressionists did trees and she did not much care.

6   At twenty-four she left all those opinions behind and went for the first time to live in Texas, where there were no trees to paint and no one to tell her how not to paint them. In Texas there was only the horizon she craved. In Texas she had her sister Claudia with her for a while, and in the late afternoons they would walk away from town and toward the horizon and watch the evening star come out. "That evening star fascinated me," she wrote. "It was in some way very exciting to me. My sister had a gun, and as we walked she would throw bottles into the air and shoot as many as she could before they hit the ground. I had nothing but to walk into nowhere and the wide sunset space with the star. Ten watercolors were made from that star." In a way one's interest is compelled as much by the sister Claudia with the gun as by the painter Georgia with the star, but only the painter left us this shining record. Ten watercolors were made from that star.

QUESTIONS

Experience

· How does Didion help you to gain a sense of the character of her subject, Georgia O'Keeffe? Where do you feel O'Keeffe's presence most powerfully? What passage best helps you understand who and what she was?

Interpretation

· What is Didion's main point about Georgia O'Keeffe? Which of O'Keeffe's qualities of character does Didion single out for highest praise? Why?

Evaluation

· What personal values animate the work and life of Georgia O'Keeffe? What social and cultural values interfere with, or at least cross in the path of, O'Keeffe's values?

WRITING

Exploring

· Write an essay in which you celebrate the values and qualities of character of someone you admire. Try to identify just what it is you find impressive about your subject. You may wish to use a few direct quotations to help bring your subject to life on the page.

Interpreting

· Analyze one or more of O'Keeffe's paintings for what they reveal about her character or for what they illustrate about her art. You may wish to write about the painting reproduced on the color insert.

Evaluating

· Evaluate the effectiveness of Didion's portrait of Georgia O'Keeffe. Consider Didion's use of evidence, her use of quotations, her organization, and the inclusion of her daughter in the essay. Explain why Didion succeeds or fails in conveying a sense of the artist.

RALPH ELLISON
(1914–1994)

Living with Music

Ralph Ellison won the 1954 National Book Award for Invisible Man, *an outstanding example of American postwar fiction. Born in Oklahoma, he moved to New York in 1938 and taught literature at a number of distinguished American universities, including Yale and the University of Chicago. Author of criticism and essays as well as fiction, Ellison published in* Partisan Review, American Review, *and* Iowa Review. *He was also a recipient of the Rockefeller Award and the Medal of Freedom.*

In the following essay, Ellison describes his experience growing up with two kinds of music, jazz and classical music. The essay reveals not only Ellison's passionate love of music but also his grace and elegance as a writer who can make sentences sing. Notable features of the essay include Ellison's contrast between music and noise, his humorous description of the contest between a vocalist and a trumpeter, and his masterful alternation between a portrayal of two musical traditions. Most notable of all, however, is the sheer beauty of Ellison's language. His sentences warrant close analysis and careful imitation, and his diction is cause for envy.

1   In those days it was either live with music or die with noise, and we chose rather desperately to live. In the process our apartment—what with its booby-trappings of audio equipment, wires, discs and tapes—came to resemble the Collier mansion, but that was later. First there was the neighborhood, assorted drunks and a singer.

2   We were living at the time in a tiny ground-floor-rear apartment in which I was also trying to write. I say "trying" advisedly. To our right, separated by a thin wall, was a small restaurant with a juke box the size of the Roxy. To our left, a night-employed swing enthusiast who took his lullaby music so loud that every morning promptly at nine Basie's brasses started blasting my typewriter off its stand. Our living room looked out across a small back yard to a rough stone wall to an apartment building which, towering above, caught every passing thoroughfare sound and rifled it straight down to me. There were also howling cats and barking dogs, none capable of music worth living with, so we'll pass them by.

3   But the court behind the wall, which on the far side came knee-high to a short Iroquois, was a forum for various singing and/or preaching drunks who wandered back from the corner bar. From these you sometimes heard a fair barbershop style "Bill Bailey," free-wheeling versions of "The Bastard King of England," the saga of Uncle Bud, or a deeply felt rendition of Leroy Carr's "How Long Blues." The preaching drunks took on any topic that came to mind: current events, the fate of the long-sunk *Titanic* or the relative merits of the Giants and the Dodgers. Naturally there was great argument and occasional fighting—none of it fatal but all of it loud.

4   I shouldn't complain, however, for these were rather entertaining drunks, who like the birds appeared in the spring and left with the first fall cold. A more dedicated fellow was there all the time, day and night, come rain, come shine. Up on the corner lived a drunk of legend, a true phenomenon, who could surely have qualified as the king of all the world's winos—not excluding the French. He was neither poetic like the others nor ambitious like the singer (to whom we'll presently come) but his drinking bouts were truly awe-inspiring and he was not without his sensitivity. In the throes of his passion he would shout to the whole wide world one concise command, "Shut up!" Which was disconcerting enough to all who heard (except, perhaps, the singer), but such were the labyrinthine acoustics of courtyards and areaways that he seemed to direct his command at me. The writer's block which this produced is indescribable. On one heroic occasion he yelled his obsessive command without one interruption longer than necessary to take another drink (and with no appreciable loss of volume, penetration or authority) for three long summer days and nights, and shortly afterwards he died. Just how many lines of agitated prose he cost me I'll never know, but in all that chaos of sound I sympathized with his obsession, for I, too, hungered and thirsted for quiet. Nor did he inspire me to a painful identification, and for that I was thankful. Identification, after all, involves feelings of guilt and responsibility, and since I could hardly hear my own typewriter keys I felt in no way accountable for his condition. We were simply fellow victims of the madding crowd. May he rest in peace.

5   No, these more involved feelings were aroused by a more intimate source of noise, one that got beneath the skin and worked into the very structure of one's consciousness—like the "fate" motif in Beethoven's Fifth or the knocking-at-the-gates scene in *Macbeth*. For at the top of our pyramid of noise there was a singer who lived directly above us, you might say we had a singer on our ceiling.

6   Now, I had learned from the jazz musicians I had known as a boy in Oklahoma City something of the discipline and devotion to his art required of the artist. Hence I knew something of what the singer faced. These jazzmen, many of them now world-famous, lived for and with music intensely. Their driving motivation was neither money nor fame, but the will to achieve the most eloquent expression of idea-emotions through the technical mastery of their instruments (which, incidentally, some of them wore as a priest wears the cross) and the give and take, the subtle rhythmical shaping and blending of idea, tone and imagination demanded of group improvisation. The delicate balance struck between strong individual personality and the group during those early jam sessions was a marvel of social organization. I had learned too that the end of all this discipline and technical mastery was the desire to express an affirmative way of life through its musical tradition and that this tradition insisted that each artist achieve his creativity within its frame. He must learn the best of the past, and add to it his personal vision. Life could be harsh, loud and wrong if it wished, but they lived it fully, and when they expressed their attitude toward the world it was with a fluid style that reduced the chaos of living to form.

7   The objectives of these jazzmen were not at all those of the singer on our ceiling, but though a purist committed to the mastery of the *bel canto* style, German *lieder*, modern French art songs and a few American slave songs sung as if *bel*

canto, she was intensely devoted to her art. From morning to night she vocalized, regardless of the condition of her voice, the weather or my screaming nerves. There were times when her notes, sifting through her floor and my ceiling, bouncing down the walls and ricocheting off the building in the rear, whistled like tenpenny nails, buzzed like a saw, wheezed like the asthma of a Hercules, trumpeted like an enraged African elephant—and the squeaky pedal of her piano rested plumb center above my typing chair. After a year of non-co-operation from the neighbor on my left I became desperate enough to cool down the hot blast of his phonograph by calling the cops, but the singer presented a serious ethical problem: Could I, an aspiring artist, complain against the hard work and devotion to craft of another aspiring artist?

8   Then there was my sense of guilt. Each time I prepared to shatter the ceiling in protest I was restrained by the knowledge that I, too, during my boyhood, had tried to master a musical instrument and to the great distress of my neighbors—perhaps even greater than that which I now suffered. For while our singer was concerned basically with a single tradition and style, I had been caught actively between two: that of the Negro folk music, both sacred and profane, slave song and jazz, and that of Western classical music. It was most confusing; the folk tradition demanded that I play what I heard and felt around me, while those who were seeking to teach the classical tradition in the schools insisted that I play strictly according to the book and express that which I was *supposed* to feel. This sometimes led to heated clashes of wills. Once during a third-grade music appreciation class a friend of mine insisted that it was a large green snake he saw swimming down a quiet brook instead of the snowy bird the teacher felt that Saint-Saëns' *Carnival of the Animals* should evoke. The rest of us sat there and lied like little black, brown and yellow Trojans about that swan, but our stalwart classmate held firm to his snake. In the end he got himself spanked and reduced the teacher to tears, but truth, reality and our environment were redeemed. For we were all familiar with snakes, while a swan was simply something the Ugly Duckling of the story grew up to be. Fortunately some of us grew up with a genuine appreciation of classical music *despite* such teaching methods. But as an inspiring trumpeter I was to wallow in sin for years before being awakened to guilt by our singer.

9   Caught mid-range between my two traditions, where one attitude often clashed with the other and one technique of playing was by the other opposed, I caused whole blocks of people to suffer.

10   Indeed, I terrorized a good part of an entire city section. During summer vacation I blew sustained tones out of the window for hours, usually starting—especially on Sunday mornings—before breakfast. I sputtered whole days through M. Arban's (he's the great authority on the instrument) double- and triple-tonguing exercises—with an effect like that of a jackass hiccupping off a big meal of briars. During school-term mornings I practiced a truly exhibitionist "Reveille" before leaving for school, and in the evening I generously gave the ever-listening world a long, slow version of "Taps," ineptly played but throbbing with what I in my adolescent vagueness felt was a romantic sadness. For it was farewell to day and a love song to life and a peace-be-with-you to all the dead and dying.

11   On hot summer afternoons I tormented the ears of all not blessedly deaf with

imitations of the latest hot solos of Hot Lips Paige (then a local hero), the leaping right hand of Earl "Fatha" Hines, or the rowdy poetic flights of Louis Armstrong. Naturally I rehearsed also such school-band standbys as the *Light Cavalry* Overture, Sousa's "Stars and Stripes Forever," the *William Tell* Overture, and "Tiger Rag." (Not even an after-school job as office boy to a dentist could stop my efforts. Frequently, by way of encouraging my development in the proper cultural direction, the dentist asked me proudly to render Schubert's *Serenade* for some poor devil with his jaw propped open in the dental chair. When the drill got going, or the forceps bit deep, I blew real strong.)

12   Sometimes, inspired by the even then considerable virtuosity of the late Charlie Christian (who during our school days played marvelous riffs on a cigar box banjo), I'd give whole summer afternoons and the evening hours after heavy suppers of black-eyed peas and turnip greens, cracklin' bread and buttermilk, lemonade and sweet potato cobbler, to practicing hard-driving blues. Such food oversupplied me with bursting energy, and from listening to Ma Rainey, Ida Cox and Clara Smith, who made regular appearances in our town, I knew exactly how I wanted my horn to sound. But in the effort to make it do so (I was no embryo Joe Smith or Tricky Sam Nanton) I sustained the curses of both Christian and infidel— along with the encouragement of those more sympathetic citizens who understood the profound satisfaction to be found in expressing oneself in the blues.

13   Despite those who complained and cried to heaven for Gabriel to blow a chorus so heavenly sweet and so hellishly hot that I'd forever put down my horn, there were more tolerant ones who were willing to pay in present pain for future pride.

14   For who knew what skinny kid with his chops wrapped around a trumpet mouthpiece and a faraway look in his eyes might become the next Armstrong? Yes, and send you, at some big dance a few years hence, into an ecstasy of rhythm and memory and brassy affirmation of the goodness of being alive and part of the community? Someone had to; for it was part of the group tradition— though that was not how they said it.

15   "Let that boy blow," they'd say to the protesting ones. "He's got to talk baby talk on that thing before he can preach on it. Next thing you know he's liable to be up there with Duke Ellington. Sure, plenty Oklahoma boys are up there with the big bands. Son, let's hear you try those "Trouble in Mind Blues." Now try and make it sound like ole Ida Cox sings it."

16   And I'd draw in my breath and do Miss Cox great violence.

17 Thus the crimes and aspirations of my youth. It had been years since I had played the trumpet or irritated a single ear with other than the spoken or written word, but as far as my singing neighbor was concerned I had to hold my peace. I was forced to listen, and in listening I soon became involved to the point of identification. If she sang badly I'd hear my own futility in the windy sound; if well, I'd stare at my typewriter and despair that I should ever make my prose so sing. She left me neither night nor day, this singer on our ceiling, and as my writing languished I became more and more upset. Thus one desperate morning I decided that since I seemed doomed to live within a shrieking chaos I might as well contribute my share; perhaps if I fought noise with noise I'd attain some small peace. Then a mir-

acle: I turned on my radio (an old Philco AM set connected to a small Pilot FM tuner) and I heard the words

Art thou troubled?
Music will calm thee . . .

I stopped as though struck by the voice of an angel. It was Kathleen Ferrier, that loveliest of singers, giving voice to the aria from Handel's *Rodelinda*. The voice was so completely expressive of words and music that I accepted it without question—what lover of the vocal art could resist her?

18   Yet it was ironic, for after giving up my trumpet for the typewriter I had avoided too close a contact with the very art which she recommended as balm. For I had started music early and lived with it daily, and when I broke I tried to break clean. Now in this magical moment all the old love, the old fascination with music superbly rendered, flooded back. When she finished I realized that with such music in my own apartment, the chaotic sounds from without and above had sunk, if not into silence, then well below the level where they mattered. Here was a way out. If I was to live and write in that apartment, it would be only through the grace of music. I had tuned in a Ferrier recital, and when it ended I rushed out for several of her records, certain that now deliverance was mine.

19   But not yet. Between the hi-fi record and the ear, I learned, there was a new electronic world. In that realization our apartment was well on its way toward becoming an audio booby trap. It was 1949 and I rushed to the Audio Fair. I have, I confess, as much gadget-resistance as the next American of my age, weight and slight income; but little did I dream of the test to which it would be put. I had hardly entered the fair before I heard David Sarser's and Mel Sprinkle's Musician's Amplifier, took a look at its schematic and, recalling a boyhood acquaintance with such matters, decided that I could build one. I did, several times before it measured within specifications. And still our system was lacking. Fortunately my wife shared my passion for music, so we went on to buy, piece by piece, a fine speaker system, a first-rate AM-FM tuner, a transcription turntable and a speaker cabinet. I built half a dozen or more preamplifiers and record compensators before finding a commercial one that satisfied my ear, and, finally, we acquired an arm, a magnetic cartridge and—glory of the house—a tape recorder. All this plunge into electronics, mind you, had as its simple end the enjoyment of recorded music as it was intended to be heard. I was obsessed with the idea of reproducing sound with such fidelity that even when using music as a defense behind which I could write, it would reach the unconscious levels of the mind with the least distortion. And it didn't come easily. There were wires and pieces of equipment all over the tiny apartment (I became a compulsive experimenter) and it was worth your life to move about without first taking careful bearings. Once we were almost crushed in our sleep by the tape machine, for which there was space only on a shelf at the head of our bed. But it was worth it.

20   For now when we played a recording on our system even the drunks on the wall could recognize its quality. I'm ashamed to admit, however, that I did not always restrict its use to the demands of pleasure or defense. Indeed, with such marvels of science at my control I lost my humility. My ethical consideration for the singer up above shriveled like a plant in too much sunlight. For instead of

soothing, music seemed to release the beast in me. Now when jarred from my writer's reveries by some especially enthusiastic flourish of our singer, I'd rush to my music system with blood in my eyes and burst a few decibels in her direction. If she defied me with a few more pounds of pressure against her diaphragm, then a war of decibels was declared.

21   If, let us say, she were singing *"Depuis le Jour"* from *Louise,* I'd put on a tape of Bidu Sayão performing the same aria, and let the rafters ring. If it was some song by Mahler, I'd match her spitefully with Marian Anderson or Kathleen Ferrier; if she offended with something from *Der Rosenkavalier,* I'd attack her flank with Lotte Lehmann. If she brought me up from my desk with art songs by Ravel or Rachmaninoff, I'd defend myself with Maggie Teyte or Jennie Tourel. If she polished a spiritual to a meaningless artiness I'd play Bessie Smith to remind her of the earth out of which we came. Once in a while I'd forget completely that I was supposed to be a gentleman and blast her with Strauss' *Zarathustra,* Bartók's *Concerto for Orchestra,* Ellington's "Flaming Sword," the famous crescendo from *The Pines of Rome,* or Satchmo scatting, "I'll be Glad When You're Dead" (you rascal you!). Oh, I was living with music with a sweet vengeance.

22   One might think that all this would have made me her most hated enemy, but not at all. When I met her on the stoop a few weeks after my rebellion, expecting her fully to slap my face, she astonished me by complimenting our music system. She even questioned me concerning the artists I had used against her. After that, on days when the acoustics were right, she'd stop singing until the piece was finished and then applaud—not always, I guessed, without a justifiable touch of sarcasm. And although I was now getting on with my writing, the unfairness of this business bore in upon me. Aware that I could not have withstood a similar comparison with literary artists of like caliber, I grew remorseful. I also came to admire the singer's courage and control, for she was neither intimidated into silence nor goaded into undisciplined screaming; she persevered, she marked the phrasing of the great singers I sent her way, she improved her style.

23   Better still, she vocalized more softly, and I, in turn, used music less and less as a weapon and more for its magic with mood and memory. After a while a simple twirl of the volume control up a few decibels and down again would bring a live-and-let-live reduction of her volume. We have long since moved from that apartment and that most interesting neighborhood and now the floors and walls of our present apartment are adequately thick and there is even a closet large enough to house the audio system; the only wire visible is that leading from the closet to the corner speaker system. Still we are indebted to the singer and the old environment for forcing us to discover one of the most deeply satisfying aspects of our living. Perhaps the enjoyment of music is always suffused with past experience; for me, at least, this is true.

24   It seems a long way and a long time from the glorious days of Oklahoma jazz dances, the jam sessions at Halley Richardson's place on Deep Second, from the phonographs shouting the blues in the back alleys I knew as a delivery boy and from the days when watermelon men with voices like mellow bugles shouted their wares in time with the rhythm of their horses' hoofs and farther still from the washerwomen singing slave songs as they stirred sooty tubs in sunny yards, and

a long time, too, from those intense, conflicting days when the school music program of Oklahoma City was tuning our earthy young ears to classical accents—with music appreciation classes and free musical instruments and basic instruction for any child who cared to learn and uniforms for all who made the band. There was a mistaken notion on the part of some of the teachers that classical music had nothing to do with the rhythms, relaxed or hectic, of daily living, and that one should crook the little finger when listening to such refined strains. And the blues and the spirituals—jazz—? they would have destroyed them and scattered the pieces. Nevertheless, we learned some of it all, for in the United States when traditions are juxtaposed they tend, regardless of what we do to prevent it, irresistibly to merge. Thus musically at least each child in our town was an heir of all the ages. One learns by moving from the familiar to the unfamiliar, and while it might sound incongruous at first, the step from the spirituality of the spirituals to that of the Beethoven of the symphonies or the Bach of the chorales is not as vast as it seems. Nor is the romanticism of a Brahms or Chopin completely unrelated to that of Louis Armstrong. Those who know their native culture and love it unchauvinistically are never lost when encountering the unfamiliar.

25   Living with music today we find Mozart and Ellington, Kirsten Flagstad and Chippie Hill, William L. Dawson and Carl Orff all forming part of our regular fare. For all exalt life in rhythm and melody; all add to its significance. Perhaps in the swift change of American society in which the meanings of one's origin are so quickly lost, one of the chief values of living with music lies in its power to give us an orientation in time. In doing so, it gives significance to all those indefinable aspects of experience which nevertheless help to make us what we are. In the swift whirl of time music is a constant, reminding us of what we were and of that toward which we aspired. Art thou troubled? Music will not only calm, it will ennoble thee.

QUESTIONS

Experience

· To what extent does Ellison's essay call up your own experience with learning to play a musical instrument or with listening to music you find affecting and moving?

· What are your earliest memories of music?

Interpretation

· What does Ellison mean when he writes that "those who know their native culture and love it unchauvinistically are never lost when encountering the unfamiliar"? How is this idea related to the stories he tells in "Living with Music"?

Evaluation

· In the last paragraph of the essay, Ellison explains just what values he finds in music. Comment on the values music holds for Ellison. Add any other values music holds for you.

WRITING

Exploring

· Write about an experience you have had with music. You might wish to write about your experience in learning to play an instrument. You may prefer to focus on describing one or more teachers of music you may have had.

Interpreting

· Select a work of music you admire, and write an analysis and interpretation of it. It can be a popular song or a famous work from the classical, folk, rock, or jazz repertoire.

· Or analyze and interpret Ellison's essay by explaining his central idea. Account for the different elements Ellison includes in his essay, especially the people he mentions and the experiences he describes.

Evaluating

· Write an essay in which you reflect on the social and cultural values music embodies in our society. You can range across different musical styles, or you can focus on a particular type of music such as reggae, country and western, or hard rock.

· Or write an essay about the rise or decline of a particular type or style of music—and how its rise or decline reflects a particular set of social or cultural values.

MARY GORDON
(b. 1949)

Mary Cassatt

*Mary Gordon was born in Far Rockaway, New York. She graduated with a
B.A. from Barnard College, where she now teaches, and she has also earned
an M.A. from Syracuse University. Her books include the fictional works
Final Payments (1978), The Company of Women (1981), Men and Angels
(1986), Temporary Shelter (1988), and The Other Side (1990). The following
selection, "Mary Cassatt," is taken from her collection of essays, Good Boys
and Dead Girls and Other Essays (1991). In this piece Gordon raises questions about gender, creativity, and power. She also describes a few of Cassatt's paintings, one of which can be found following in the color insert.*

*In the following essay, Gordon writes about the American impressionist
painter Mary Cassatt. Gordon focuses on issues of gender, though she
invites us to look closely at paintings as well, while providing a sense of the
painter's artistic palette. Gordon's essay is notable for the defense it makes
of Cassatt as a painter of women's themes. It is also noteworthy for the way
it blends biographical information about the artist with critical observations
about her paintings.*

1   When Mary Cassatt's father was told of her decision to become a painter, he
said: "I would rather see you dead." When Edgar Degas saw a show of Cassatt's etchings, his response was: "I am not willing to admit that a woman can
draw that well." When she returned to Philadelphia after twenty-eight years
abroad, having achieved renown as an Impressionist painter and the esteem of
Degas, Huysmans, Pissarro, and Berthe Morisot, the *Philadelphia Ledger* reported:
"Mary Cassatt, sister of Mr. Cassatt, president of the Pennsylvania Railroad,
returned from Europe yesterday. She has been studying painting in France and
owns the smallest Pekingese dog in the world."

2   Mary Cassatt exemplified the paradoxes of the woman artist. Cut off from the
experiences that are considered the entitlement of her male counterpart, she has
access to a private world a man can only guess at. She has, therefore, a kind of
information he is necessarily deprived of. If she has almost impossible good fortune—means, self-confidence, heroic energy and dedication, the instinct to avoid
the seductions of ordinary domestic life, which so easily become a substitute for
creative work—she may pull off a miracle: she will combine the skill and surety
that she has stolen from the world of men with the vision she brings from the
world of women.

3   Mary Cassatt pulled off such a miracle. But if her story is particularly female, it
is also American. She typifies one kind of independent American spinster who
keeps reappearing in our history in forms as various as Margaret Fuller and
Katharine Hepburn. There is an astringency in such women, a fierce discipline, a
fearlessness, a love of work. But they are not inhuman. At home in the world, they

embrace it with a kind of aristocratic greed that knows nothing of excess. Balance, proportion, an instinct for the distant and the formal, an exuberance, a vividness, a clarity of line: the genius of Mary Cassatt includes all these elements. The details of the combination are best put down to grace; the outlines may have been her birthright.

4   She was one of those wealthy Americans whose parents took the children abroad for their education and medical care. The James family comes to mind and, given her father's attitude toward her career, it is remarkable that Cassatt didn't share the fate of Alice James. But she had a remarkable mother, intelligent, encouraging of her children. When her daughter wanted to study in Paris, and her husband disapproved, Mrs. Cassatt arranged to accompany Mary as her chaperone.

5   From her beginnings as an art student, Cassatt was determined to follow the highest standards of craftsmanship. She went first to Paris, then to Italy, where she studied in Parma with Raimondi and spent many hours climbing up scaffolding (to the surprise of the natives) to study the work of Correggio and Parmigianino. Next, she was curious to visit Spain to look at the Spanish masters and to make use of the picturesque landscape and models. Finally, she returned to Paris, where she was to make her home, and worked with Degas, her sometime friend and difficult mentor. There has always been speculation as to whether or not they were lovers; her burning their correspondence gave the rumor credence. But I believe that they were not; she was, I think, too protective of her talent to make herself so vulnerable to Degas as a lover would have to be. But I suppose I don't believe it because I cherish, instead, the notion that a man and a woman can be colleagues and friends without causing an excuse for raised eyebrows. Most important, I want to believe they were not lovers because if they were, the trustworthiness of his extreme praise grows dilute.

6   She lived her life until late middle age among her family. Her beloved sister, Lydia, one of her most cherished models, had always lived as a semi-invalid and died early, in Mary's flat, of Bright's disease. Mary was closely involved with her brothers and their children. Her bond with her mother was profound: when Mrs. Cassatt died, in 1895, Mary's work began to decline. At the severing of her last close familial tie, when her surviving brother died as a result of an illness he contracted when traveling with her to Egypt, she broke down entirely. "How we try for happiness, poor things, and how we don't find it. The best cure is hard work— if only one has the health for it," she said, and lived that way.

7   Not surprisingly, perhaps, Cassatt's reputation has suffered because of the prejudice against her subject matter. Mothers and children: what could be of lower prestige, more vulnerable to the charge of sentimentality. Yet if one looks at the work of Mary Cassatt, one sees how triumphantly she avoids the pitfalls of sentimentality because of the astringent rigor of her eye and craft. The Cassatt iconography dashes in an instant the notion of the comfortable, easily natural fit of the maternal embrace. Again and again in her work, the child's posture embodies the ambivalence of his or her dependence. In *The Family,* the mother and child exist in positions of unease; the strong diagonals created by their postures of opposition give the pictures their tense strength, a strength that renders sentimental sweetness impossible. In *Ellen Mary Cassatt in a White Coat* and *Girl in the Blue Arm Chair,* the children seem imprisoned and dwarfed by the trappings of respectable

life. The lines of Ellen's coat, which create such a powerful framing device, entrap the round and living child. The sulky little girl in the armchair seems about to be swallowed up by the massive cylinders of drawing room furniture and the strong curves of emptiness that are the floor. In *The Bath,* the little girl has all the unformed charming awkwardness of a young child: the straight limbs, the loose stomach. But these are not the stuff of Gerber babies—even of the children of Millais. In this picture, the center of interest is not the relationship between the mother and the child but the strong vertical and diagonal stripes of the mother's dress, whose opposition shape the picture with an insistence that is almost abstract.

8   Cassatt changed the iconography of the depiction of mothers and children. Hers do not look out into and meet the viewer's eye; neither supplicating nor seductive, they are absorbed in their own inner thoughts. Minds are at work here, a concentration unbroken by an awareness of themselves as objects to be gazed at by the world.

9   The brilliance of Cassatt's colors, the clarity and solidity of her forms, are the result of her love and knowledge of the masters of European painting. She had a second career as adviser to great collectors: she believed passionately that America must, for the sake of its artists, possess masterpieces, and she paid no attention to the outrage of her European friends, who felt their treasures were being sacked by barbarians. A young man visiting her in her old age noted her closed mind regarding the movement of the moderns. She thought American painters should stay home and not become "café loafers in Paris. Why should they come to Europe?" she demanded. "When I was young it was different . . . Our Museums had not great paintings for the students to study. Now that has been corrected and something must be done to save our young over here."

10   One can hear the voice of the old, irascible, still splendid aunt in that comment and see the gesture of her stick toward the Left Bank. Cassatt was blinded by cataracts; the last years of her life were spent in a fog. She became ardent on the subjects of suffragism, socialism, and spiritualism; the horror of the First World War made her passionate in her conviction that mankind itself must change. She died at her country estate near Grasse, honored by the French, recipient of the Légion d'honneur, but unappreciated in America, rescued only recently from misunderstanding, really, by feminist art critics. They allowed us to begin to see her for what she is: a master of line and color whose great achievement was to take the "feminine" themes of mothers, children, women with their thoughts alone, to endow them with grandeur without withholding from them the tenderness that fits so easily alongside the rigor of her art.

QUESTIONS

Experience

· Clearly, Mary Gordon is very much taken with Cassatt's art. Can you think of an artist—whether painter, sculptor, or architect—who has captivated you? If so, who—and why? If not, why not?

Interpretation

· What is the effect of the two quotations presented in the opening paragraph? What does Gordon mean by saying that Cassatt pulled off a miracle (paragraph 2)? What kind of miracle?

Evaluation

· To what extent did gender stereotypes interfere with Cassatt's career? To what extent are viewers of her paintings still hampered by gender stereotyping? To what extent is it possible to get past such stereotyping? How?

WRITING

Exploring

· Write about a work of art that engages you. Describe an occasion when you saw a work that caught you up. Try to account for what impressed you about the work, how you responded to it, and why you responded as you did.

Interpreting

· Analyze and interpret a work of art you have either some knowledge of or an interest in learning more about. You may wish to do some research after looking carefully at a reproduction of the work. You might wish to write about a work reproduced in this book or perhaps a work by an artist mentioned in Gordon's essay on Cassatt.

Evaluating

· Discuss the value of Cassatt as painter and as woman for Mary Gordon. Explain also how Cassatt's life and work can be valuable for others besides the writer—both women and men.

MARK STRAND
(b. 1934)

Crossing the Tracks to Hopper's World

Mark Strand was born to American parents on Prince Edward Island, Canada. He was educated at Antioch College, Yale University, and the University of Iowa. He has taught at various universities, including Princeton, Virginia, and Utah, where he directs the creative writing program. His published work includes fiction, translations, and children's books, as well as poetry and essays. His most recent book is Hopper *(1994). Before becoming a writer, however, Strand studied painting. The following selection about the American painter Edward Hopper reflects Strand's interest in the estrangement he finds represented in Hopper's art.*

Two things are worth noting about Strand's essay on Hopper—one structural, the other rhetorical. Structurally, this brief essay splits neatly in half, the first part providing a way of thinking about Hopper's greatest paintings, the second commenting on the Hopper exhibition that gave rise to Strand's ruminations about the painter. Rhetorically, Strand quotes Hopper twice, once in an epigraph and later in the essay proper. On both occasions Strand appropriates Hopper's words to his own use; in one case he actually disagrees with the painter's comments about his artistic aims.

The blank concrete walls and steel constructions of modern industry, midsummer streets with the acid green of close-cut lawns, the dusty Fords and gilded movies—all the sweltering, tawdry life of the American small town, and behind all, the sad desolation of our suburban landscape. He derives daily stimulus from these, that others flee from or pass with indifference.

1   **E**dward Hopper wrote the preceding words about Charles Burchfield, but he might just as well have been writing about himself. He is the painter of American life at its most hopeless and provincial. Yet he has rescued it from the workaday rhythms in which it is demeaned and has given it a preserving character. Buildings, people and natural objects take on, in his work, an emblematic or pictorial unity. The formal properties of offices, hotel rooms and bleak tenement interiors reinforce the isolation of his people who seem always in the act of entering a meaningless future—meaningless because it is anticipated in the sterility of the present.

2   The remarkable number of roads, highways, and railroad tracks in his paintings speak for Hopper's fascination with passage. Often, while looking at his work, we are made to feel like transients, momentary visitors to a scene that will endure without us and that suffers our presence with aggressive reticence. His famous painting at the Museum of Modern Art, *The House by the Railroad Tracks,** is a good example of what I mean.

---
*See color insert.

3   Separated from the house by tracks, we *feel* separated by change, by progress, by motion, and ultimately by the conditions our own mortality imposes. The house glares at us from what seems like an enormous distance. It appears so withdrawn, in fact, that it stands as an emblem of refusal, a monument to the idea of enclosure. And Hopper's famous statement of his aims—"What I wanted to do was paint sunlight on the side of a house"—seems misleading in its simplicity, for the sunlight in his paintings illuminates the secretive without penetrating it. Thus we feel separated from something essential and, as a consequence, our lives seem frivolous. When we look at his paintings we are made to feel, more than we care to, like time's creatures. Each of us would have to cross the tracks to inhabit that Victorian mansion with its coffin-like finality. And across the tracks is Hopper's forbidden land, where the present is lived eternally, where the moment is without moment, where it is always just after and just before—in this case, just after the train has passed, just before the train will arrive.

4   Hopper's use of light is almost always descriptive of time. In many of his paintings, duration is given a substantial and heroic geometry. In *Rooms by the Sea,* for example, an enormous trapezoid of light fills a room, denying the moment its temporality. Hopper's ability to use space convincingly as a metaphor for time is extraordinary. It demonstrates the ratio between stillness and emptiness, so that we are able to experience the emptiness of moments, hours, a whole lifetime.

5   His paintings frequently take place at dawn or in late afternoon in a twilight of few or no people. Again, the focus is the transitional. The times which combine elements of night and day paradoxically give the world greater solidity than it has when it is fully illuminated. Night and day in their more local manifestations as shadows and light are so arranged that they dramatize and give extra significance to buildings or parts of buildings we would otherwise take for granted. Such significance is heightened in those paintings where a house, say, stands next to trees or woods. Hopper's trees are strangely opaque; we never enter the woods in his work, nor does light. Their mystery is preserved, acting as an ominous reminder of how fragile our world of measured verticals and horizontals is.

6   The current show at the Whitney of selections from the Hopper Bequest is fascinating. There is not one painting in it that ranks with his masterpieces and only a few that manage to communicate that quality of loneliness and desolation we associate with many of his best known works. One of those that does is *Stairway* (no date given), a small, eerie painting which looks down a stairway leading to an open door and a dark massing of trees or hills directly outside. Not as rigorously defined spatially as his more mature paintings, it nevertheless mystifies in the same way. The open door becomes not merely a passage connecting inside and outside, but the disturbing link between nowhere and nowhere, or, again, the spatial and tangible restoration of a moment that exists between events, the events of leavetaking or arrival.

7   Even in the early paintings, there are a great number of roads and embankments, though they do not have the weight they will have later. *El Station* (1908) is typical Hopper subject matter, but quite insubstantial. The people, merely indicated in a few strokes, do not emerge as presences; the sunlight, convincing as itself, is without psychological depth or effect. Another painting which appears to

have much in common with other, better known Hoppers is *Cape Cod Sunset* (1934), but it lacks their solidity, their monumental reticence and, in fact, displays an uncharacteristic frailty. There are a few handsome paintings of Cobb's barns and house in Truro, but these, too, lack the forcefulness we usually associate with Hopper.

8   The most important aspect of the show is the watercolors, prints and drawings. Many of the watercolors move beyond being mere notation, hurried and perfunctory in gesture, and take on the strangeness, the involved quiet, of his oils. The prints also have qualities in common with the major oils. Though less austere and surely less compelling, such prints as *Evening Wind* and *American Landscape* already incorporate themes that will appear again in future Hoppers. Also exhibited are sketches and preparatory drawings for many of his well known paintings. These more than anything else in the show bring us close to his greatest work. Something of the same quality is transmitted—an oddness, a disturbing quiet, a sense of being in a room with a man who insists on being with us, but always with his back turned.

QUESTIONS

Experience

· How do you respond to the paintings of Edward Hopper? How would you characterize your feelings upon viewing the paintings displayed on the insert? To what extent does Hopper's work remind you of places you have been or of images you have seen? Explain your response.

Interpretation

· How helpful do you find Strand's interpretation of Hopper's art? Why? How helpful is the epigraph Strand cites from Hopper's comments on another artist?

· What, after all, is Strand's point about Hopper's paintings?

Evaluation

· Clearly, Strand admires Hopper's art. What, specifically, does he find valuable about it? To what extent do you think Strand's evaluation reflects his own perspective on experience? To what extent do you think Hopper's painting reflects peculiarly American experience?

WRITING

Exploring

· Write a careful description of one of Hopper's paintings. You can select a painting reproduced in this book, or you can choose another. Focus first on the overall painting and objects depicted, then, on closer inspection, on details. Consider, as part of your viewing, the use of light and shadow, along with Hopper's choice of colors.

Interpreting

· Write a couple of paragraphs explaining the significance of one of Hopper's paintings.

· Or compare two of Hopper's paintings, drawing out similarities to arrive at an interpretation of both paintings.

· Or compare one of Hopper's paintings with one by another artist. Be sure that the two works share one or more significant features.

Evaluating

· After doing some research on Hopper, quote the views of a commentator on his work whose ideas you strongly agree with or disagree with. Explain why.

WILLIAM ZINSSER
(b. 1922)

Shanghai

William Zinsser is a writer, editor, and teacher who was born in New York and educated at Princeton University. He worked for the New York Herald Tribune *from 1947 through 1959 as a features editor, drama editor, film critic, and editorialist. Now a freelance writer, Zinsser has contributed articles to numerous publications and has written many books, among them* On Writing Well *and* Writing with a Word Processor.

In the following piece, which originally appeared in The New Yorker, *Zinsser takes us inside the imaginations of two outstanding jazz musicians and teachers. The essay is remarkable for its sense of how the musicians work and the ways in which they think about and perform their music. One of the essay's most notable compositional strategies is Zinsser's integration of quotations from his subjects, Mitchell and Ruff, as he plays those quotations off direct quotes from Professor Tan, the Chinese host of these two black American jazz musicians.*

1   Jazz came to China for the first time on the afternoon of June 2nd, when the American bassist and French-horn player Willie Ruff introduced himself and his partner, the pianist Dwike Mitchell, to several hundred students and professors who were crowded into a large room at the Shanghai Conservatory of Music. The professors and the students were all expectant, without knowing quite what to expect. They knew only that they were about to hear the first American jazz concert ever presented to the Chinese. Probably they were not surprised to find that the two musicians were black, though black Americans are a rarity in the People's Republic. What they undoubtedly didn't expect was that Ruff would talk to them in Chinese, and when he began they murmured with delight.

2   Ruff is a lithe, dapper man of fifty who takes visible pleasure in sharing his enthusiasms, and it was obvious that there was no place he would rather have been than in China's oldest conservatory, bringing the music of his people to still another country deprived of that commodity. In 1959, he and Mitchell—who have played together as the Mitchell-Ruff Duo for twenty-six years—introduced jazz to the Soviet Union, and for that occasion Ruff taught himself Russian, his seventh language. In 1979, he hit on the idea of making a similar trip to China, and he began taking intensive courses in Chinese at Yale, where he is a professor of both music and Afro-American studies. By last winter, he felt he was fluent enough in Mandarin to make the trip.

3   Now Ruff stood at the front of the room, holding several sheets of paper on which he had written, in Chinese characters, what he wanted to tell his listeners about the origins of jazz. He looked somewhat like an Oriental sage himself. "In the last three hundred and fifty years, black people in America have created a music that is a rich contribution to Western culture," he began. "Of course, three

hundred and fifty years, compared to the long and distinguished history of Chinese music seems like only a moment. But please remember that the music of American black people is an amalgam whose roots are deep in African history, and that it has also taken many characteristics from the music of Europe." Ruff has an amiable voice, and as he spoke the men and women in the room were attentive but relaxed—not an audience straining to decipher a foreigner's accent. "In Africa, the drum is the most important musical instrument," Ruff went on. "But to me the fascinating thing is that the people also use their drums to talk. Please imagine that the drum method of speech is so exquisite that Africans can, without recourse to words, recite proverbs, record history, and send long messages. The drum is to West African society what the book is to literate society."

4   I wondered what the audience would make of that. Not only was China the oldest of literate societies; we were in the one Asian city that was encrusted with Western thought as transmitted in books, in journals, and in musical notation. Even the architecture of Shanghai was a patchwork of Western shapes—a residue of the days when the city had a huge foreign population and was divided into districts that were controlled by different European countries. At the conservatory, we were in the former French concession, and its main building was in a red brick French Provincial style, with a sloping red tile roof and a porte cochère. Another French-style building housed the conservatory's library of a hundred thousand books about music. Newer buildings served as classrooms and practice rooms, and the music that eddied out of the windows was the dreary fare of Western academic rigor: vocal scales endlessly rising, piano arpeggios repeated until they were mastered, chamber groups starting and stopping and starting again. We could have been in Vienna of the nineties or Paris of the twenties. In any case, we were a long way from Africa. And we were farther still from music created spontaneously.

5   "In the seventeenth century, when West Africans were captured and brought to America as slaves, they brought their drums with them," Ruff continued. "But the slave-owners were afraid of the drum because it was so potent; it could be used to incite the slaves to revolt. So they outlawed the black people's music. Our ancestors had to develop a variety of drum substitutes. One of them, for example, was tap dancing—I'm sure you've all heard of that. Now I'd like to show you another drum substitute that you probably don't know about—one that uses the hands and the body to make rhythm. It's called hambone." There was no translating "hambone" into Mandarin, but Ruff quickly had an intricate rhythm going to demonstrate, slapping himself with the palms of his hands and smacking his open mouth to create a series of resonating pops. Applause greeted this proof that the body could be its own drum.

6   "By the time jazz started to develop, all African instruments in America had disappeared," Ruff went on. "So jazz borrowed the instruments of Western music, like the ones that we're playing here today." He went over to his bass and showed how he used it as a percussion instrument by picking the strings with his fingers instead of playing them with a bow. "Only this morning," he said, "I gave a lesson to your distinguished professor of bass, and he is already *very good.*"

7   Moving on from rhythm to terrain more familiar to his listeners, Ruff pointed out that jazz took its structural elements from European harmony. "Mr. Mitchell

will now give you an example of the music that American slaves found in the Christian churches—Protestant hymns that had been brought from Europe," he said. "Slaves were encouraged to embrace Christianity and to use its music. Please listen." Mitchell played an old Protestant hymn. "The slaves adopted these harmonized melodies and transformed them into their own, very emotional spirituals," Ruff said when Mitchell had finished. "Mr. Mitchell and I will sing you a famous Negro spiritual from the days of slavery. It's called 'My Lord, What a Morning.' " With Mitchell playing a joyful accompaniment, the two men sang five or six choruses of the lovely old song, Mitchell carrying the melody in his deep voice, Ruff taking the higher, second part. The moment, musically beautiful, had an edge of faraway sadness. I couldn't help thinking of another alien culture onto which the Protestant hymns of Europe had once been strenuously grafted. It was just beyond the conservatory gates.

8   "Mr. Mitchell will now show you how the piano can be used as a substitute for the instruments of the orchestra," Ruff said. "Please notice that he uses his left hand to play the bass and also to make his rhythm section. Later, he will use his right hand to play the main melody and to fill in the harmony. This style is called ragtime." Mitchell struck up a jaunty rag. The students perked up at the playful pattern of notes. Ruff looked out at his class and beamed. The teacher in him was beginning to slip away; the musician in him was telling him to start the concert.

9   Mitchell and Ruff met in 1947, when they were servicemen at Lockbourne Air Force Base, outside Columbus, Ohio. Mitchell, then seventeen and a pianist in the unit band, needed an accompanist, and he gave the newly arrived Ruff, a sixteen-year-old French-horn player, a crash course in playing the bass. Thus the duo was unofficially born. When they were discharged, they followed separate paths and lost contact. Mitchell went to the Philadelphia Musical Academy. Ruff went to the Yale School of Music, where he studied with Paul Hindemith. Venturing out with his master's degree in 1954, he was told that no American symphony orchestra would hire a black musician, and he accepted an offer to join the Tel Aviv Symphony as first French horn. Shortly before he was to leave, he happened to turn his television set on to "The Ed Sullivan Show." Lionel Hampton's orchestra was playing, and as the camera panned over to the piano Ruff saw a familiar figure at the keyboard. Mitchell, it turned out, had been Hampton's pianist for the past two years. Ruff telephoned him backstage at the CBS studio. Mitchell hinted of imminent vacancies in the brass section. A few days later, Israel lost—and Hampton got—a superb French horn.

10   The Mitchell-Ruff Duo—"the oldest continuous group in jazz without personnel changes," Ruff says—was formed in 1955, when the two men left Hampton and struck out on their own. They were booked regularly by the major night clubs as the second act with the great bands of the day: Louis Armstrong, Duke Ellington, Dizzy Gillespie, Miles Davis. "They were our mentors," Ruff recalls. "They'd play a set and then we'd play a set and they'd hang around and tell us what we could be doing better. We learned everything from those men. Count Basie's band raised us. In 1956, they were the hottest band in the country—they were the most expensive band and we were the cheapest—and we sold out Birdland every night. One evening, Miles Davis brought Billie Holiday in to hear us, and we just about fell through the floor. We were still just kids."

11   Meanwhile, they caught the attention of another set of patrons—a group of older women in New York who had formed an organization called Young Audiences to introduce elementary- and high-school students to chamber music. For teachers, the women chose young professionals who could communicate with words as well as with music, and Mitchell and Ruff were the first people they selected to teach jazz. Ruff recalls, "It was done under the supervision of the founders—Mrs. Lionello Perera, a great patron of music, and Mrs. Edgar Leventritt, who started the Leventritt Competition—and Nina Collier and several other ladies who sat on the board. They taught us definite techniques, such as how to catch the attention of children, and they also gave us lessons in grooming and enunciation and conduct. They were very stern and really quite unpleasant, but instructive. Everything they told us turned out to be true."

12   Armed with these graces, Mitchell and Ruff hit the road for Young Audiences, often giving seven or eight performances a day, going from school to school, first in New York and later in Boston, Baltimore, and San Francisco. They did a tour of Indian schools in New Mexico. The duo alternated these forays with its stands in Manhattan clubs. Then, in 1959, it went to Russia. Ruff himself arranged the trip with Soviet officials after the State Department, which had been trying for two years to get Louis Armstrong into the Soviet Union, declined to help. In Russia, the two Americans found a thirst for jazz that surprised even them; when they left Moscow, nine hundred people came to the station to see them off. Mitchell, in turn, still remembers being moved by Russian songs that resembled spirituals he had heard in the black churches of his boyhood. Whether a scholar could find any such link doesn't matter to him; in music, he operates on an emotional level that has no need for evidence. "I felt a mysterious bond between their people and my people," he says. "I think I connected with their suffering."

13   Not long after that trip, the house of jazz began to crumble. Television was the new medium and rock the new musical message. "Night clubs started closing in the very early sixties," Ruff recalls. "The number of jazz performers who quit, died, or just disappeared was astounding. Many of them moved to Europe. Three of the greatest rhythm players—Oscar Pettiford, Bud Powell, and Kenny Clarke—had been living in Paris and playing for peanuts because they couldn't find any work in the United States. How devastating it was for us to play in Europe—as we did quite a bit then—and see so many of these great men so reduced!"

14   Mitchell and Ruff survived because of their teaching bent. They caught the attention of two venerable booking agencies, Pryor-Menz and Alkahest, that wanted a young act to give concerts for college audiences and also explain the music, and thereby found the format—sixty or seventy concerts a year, mainly at colleges—that has been their principal source of income to this day.

15   A new tool came their way in 1967, when CBS Television sent them to Brazil to make a one-hour film tracing the African roots of Brazilian music. Ruff recognized the value of film as a teaching device, went back to college to study film, and has since visited Bali, Senegal, and the pygmies of the Central African Republic to make films about the drum music and language of those societies. He always came back to Yale (where he and I lived in the same college) elated by new rhythmical affinities that he had found among diverse cultures and among seemingly unrelated forms of life. His seminars on rhythm began to make startling connec-

tions as he brought Yale professors into them from such disciplines as neurology, limnology, geology, art, English, astronomy, physiology, and physics. The professors, in fact, became almost as elated as Ruff.

16 We flew to Shanghai on a Chinese 747—Ruff walked up and down the aisles trying out his Chinese on the passengers—and the next day we called on Professor Tan Shu-chen, deputy director of the Shanghai Conservatory of Music, who was, so far, our only contact. Two years ago, Ruff had sought the sponsorship of the Center for United States–China Arts Exchange, the group that has been sending American musicians to China, but he got no response. Ruff felt that no matter how many great American artists went to China—Isaac Stern, the Boston Symphony Orchestra, Roberta Peters—the music that they played and sang would be European music. The indigenous music of America was jazz, and the Chinese had never heard it in a live performance. (When Ruff asked a Chinese man on the plane whether his people were familiar with jazz, he said, "Oh, yes, we know Stephen Foster very well.") Lacking official support, Ruff decided to go anyway. He booked himself and Mitchell on a two-week tour to Shanghai and Peking, the two cities that had major conservatories, and then went looking for money. He got a grant from Coca-Cola that would cover their expenses and the costs of filming their visit.

17 To have Professor Tan as our host was all that we could have asked. He had come to New York last winter in connection with the film "From Mao to Mozart—Isaac Stern in China," in which he describes his imprisonment during China's Cultural Revolution. Ruff invited him to visit the Yale School of Music, in the long-range hope of fostering some kind of collaboration that would help both institutions—an exchange of teachers or students or manuscripts between Yale and the Shanghai Conservatory, for instance. While Professor Tan was at Yale, he attended a class in which Ruff and Mitchell were playing, and he invited them, in turn, to give a concert at the conservatory. That was all that a born improviser needed to hear. Now we were at the conservatory, and Professor Tan was showing us around. He had arranged the jazz concert for the next afternoon.

18 The Shanghai Conservatory of Music, which was founded in 1927, and which prides itself on being part of the cultural conscience of China, has six hundred and fifty students—the youngest are eight years old—and three hundred teachers. Most of the students live on the campus. Quite a few are from Shanghai, but a large number are recruited from all over China by faculty members, who hold regional auditions.

19 The conservatory has five departments of instruction—piano; voice; strings and winds; composing and conducting; and traditional Chinese instruments—and two of musicology. One of these is a musical-research institute. The other, devoted to Chinese traditional and folk music, was recently formed to broaden the conservatory's involvement with the heritage of its own country. But the tilt is definitely Westward. Most of the conservatory's original teachers were Europeans, and many of its graduates have lived in the West and won recognition there. The curriculum, from what I could hear of it, was rooted in Europe: Bach, Scarlatti, Mozart, Beethoven, Brahms, Schubert, Chopin, Verdi. The biggest class that we saw consisted of a forty-piece student orchestra, led by a student conductor, playing Dvořák's Cello Concerto.

20 Professor Tan was a product of this tradition—and was one of its first casualties

when the Cultural Revolution struck. He was born in 1907, and as a boy he studied violin privately with Dutch and Italian teachers who were living in China. When he joined the Shanghai Municipal Orchestra, in 1927, he was its first Chinese member. He recalls the conductor, an Italian named Mario Paci, as a man of such fierce temper that he constantly broke his baton. Thus he learned at an early age that one of the liveliest currents running through Western music is high emotion among its practitioners.

21   Professor Tan turned to teaching in 1929—at one point, he was teaching violin at six different colleges in Shanghai—and rejoined the symphony in 1937. By that time, it had four Chinese members; obviously, Shanghai was still a creature of the West. But that era would soon come to an end. During the Second World War, the Japanese occupied Shanghai, foreigners were interned in concentration camps, and the colonizing grip of the West was finally broken.

22   It was no time or place for a musician to make a living—"One month's salary would buy one shoe," Professor Tan recalled—and, seeking a more practical trade, he went to architecture school and earned his degree. He returned to music after the war, however, joining the Shanghai Conservatory in 1947, and becoming its deputy director in 1949, when the Communists came to power in China. The school then began its biggest era of growth. The student body and the faculty were greatly expanded, and European music regained its hold. But the older students were also required to go away and work for three months every year on farms and in factories. "The peasants and workers disliked Western music because it belonged to the rich people," Professor Tan recalled. "And our students couldn't practice much, because they met so much criticism. At the conservatory, we never knew where we stood. Periods of criticism would alternate with periods of relaxation. It was an uneasy time. In fact, just before the Cultural Revolution I was thinking of retiring from teaching. I had a sense of a coming storm. We are like animals—we can feel that."

23   The storm broke on June 5, 1966. The first winds of the Cultural Revolution hit the conservatory from within. "On the first day, posters were put up and meetings were held denouncing the director, Professor Ho Lu-ting," Professor Tan said. "The next day, the attack was aimed at me. I was accused of poisoning the minds of the students. My crime was that I was teaching Mozart. I happen to be a blind admirer of European and American people and music and culture, so everything I had been teaching was poison. Bach and Beethoven were poison. And Brahms. And Paganini.

24   "At first, it was only posters and meetings. Then the conservatory was closed, and much of our music was destroyed. We were beaten every day by students and by young people who came in from outside. Boys of ten or eleven would throw stones at us. They really believed we were bad people—especially any professor who was over forty. The older you were, the worse you were. For a year, more than a hundred of us older teachers were beaten and forced to spend every day shut up together in a closed shed. Then there was a year when we had to do hard labor. Ten professors died from the strain; one of them had a heart attack when a young guard made him run after him for a mile. He just dropped dead at the end. Then came the solitary confinement. Our director was kept in prison, in chains, for five years. I was put in the worst room they could find here—a very

small room in the basement, hardly any bigger than my bed. It had no light and no windows, and it was smelly because it was next to a septic tank, and there was nothing to do to pass the time. I was kept there for fourteen months."

25   In 1971, Professor Tan was allowed to go home to live with his family pending the verdict on his "crimes," but he still had to do physical labor at the conservatory during the day. Needless to say, no Western music was played there. Finally, in 1976, the Gang of Four was overthrown, the professors were declared innocent, and the conservatory was reopened. Professor Tan told me that among the students he readmitted were some who had beaten and tormented him. I said that I could hardly imagine such forbearance. "I didn't think about that," he said. "The past is the past."

26   Professor Tan is a small, gentle man with white hair and a modest manner. He dresses in the informal work clothes that everybody wears in Shanghai; nobody would take him for one of the city's cultural eminences. He moves somewhat slowly and wears fairly strong glasses—marks, perhaps, of his long captivity. "The students have made astonishing progress since 1976, because now they can play wholeheartedly," he told me. "I love being able to teach the violin again. It's such an enjoyment to hear people who are truly talented. Yesterday, a girl played the 'Scottish Fantasy' of Max Bruch, and although I was supposed to be teaching her, I only sat and listened and never said a word. It was just right." He was equally pleased by the thought of bringing jazz to his students. "I've never seen any jazz musicians in China," he said. "Nobody here knows anything about jazz. When I heard Mr. Ruff and Mr. Mitchell play at Yale, I realized that it was very important music. I wanted my teachers and my students to hear it. I wanted them to know what real American jazz is like."

27   When Mitchell finished his ragtime tune, the audience clapped—apparently glad to hear some of the converging elements that Ruff had talked about earlier. "Now we're going to give you an example of blues," Ruff said. "Blues" was another word that didn't lend itself to Mandarin, and it sounded unusually strung out: "blooooooze." Ruff continued, "One of the fundamental principles of jazz is form, and blues are a perfect illustration. Blues almost always have a twelve-bar form. This twelve-bar form never changes. It wouldn't change even if we stayed here and played it all night." He paused to let this sink in. "But you don't have to worry—we aren't going to play it that long." It was his first joke in Chinese, and it went over well. Mitchell then played an easygoing blues—a classic sample of what came up the river from New Orleans, with a strong left hand ornamented by graceful runs in the right hand. Ruff joined in on bass, and they played several twelve-bar choruses.

28   After that number, Ruff brought up the matter of improvisation, which he called "the lifeblood of jazz." He said that when he was young he had worried because his people hadn't developed from their experience in America a written tradition of opera, like Chinese opera, that chronicled great or romantic events. "But later I stopped worrying, because I saw that the master performers of our musical story—Louis Armstrong, Ella Fitzgerald, and so many others—have enriched our culture with the beauty of what they created spontaneously. Now please listen one more time to the blues form, and count the measures along with me." He wanted his listeners to count, he said, because the rules of jazz require

the improviser, however wild his melodic journeys, to repeat the harmonic changes that went into the first statement of the theme. "After you count with me a few times through, Mr. Mitchell will begin one of his famous improvisations," Ruff said.

29   Mitchell played a simple blues theme, emphasizing the chord changes, and Ruff counted the twelve bars aloud in English. Mitchell then restated the theme, embroidering it slightly, and this time Ruff counted in Chinese: *"Yi, cr, san, si, wu, liu, qi, ba . . ."* This so delighted the students that they forgot to join him. "I can't hear you," Ruff said, teacher-fashion, but they kept quiet and enjoyed his climb up the numerical ladder. Afterward, Mitchell embarked on a series of dazzling improvisations, some constructed of runs like those played by Art Tatum, some built on strong chord progressions (he can move immense chord clusters up and down the keyboard with incredible speed); next, Ruff took a chorus on the bass; then they alternated their improvised flights, moving in twelve-bar segments to an ending that seemed inevitable—as if they had played it a hundred times before.

30   Changing the mood, Ruff announced that Mitchell would play "Yesterdays." Jerome Kern's plaintive melody is hardly the stuff of traditional jazz, nor was Mitchell's rendition of it—a treatment of classical intricacy, closer to Rachmaninoff (one of his heroes) than to any jazz pianist. The students applauded with fervor. Staying in a relatively classical vein, Ruff switched to the French horn, and the two men played Billy Strayhorn's "Lush Life" in a vein that was slow and lyrical, almost like a German lied, and that perhaps surprised the students with its lack of an obvious rhythm.

31   The next number was one that I didn't recognize. It moved at a bright tempo and had several engaging themes that were brought back by the piano or the French horn—the usual jazzmen's game of statement and response. Twice, Mitchell briefly introduced a contrapuntal motif that was a deliberate imitation of Bach, and each time it drew a ripple of amusement from the professors and the students. It was the first time they had heard a kind of music that they recognized from their own studies.

32   "That number is called 'Shanghai Blues,' " Ruff said at the end. "We just made it up." The audience buzzed with amazement and pleasure.

33   I had been watching the professors and the students closely during the concert. Their faces had the look of people watching the slow approach of some great natural force—a tornado or a tidal wave. They had been listening to music that their experience had not prepared them to understand. Two black men were playing long stretches of music without resorting to any printed notes. Yet they obviously hadn't memorized what they were playing; their music took unexpected turns, seemingly at the whim of the musicians, straying all over the keyboard and all over the landscape of Western tonality. Nevertheless, there was order. Themes that had been abandoned came back in different clothes. If the key changed, as it frequently did, the two men were always in the same key. Often there was a playfulness between the two instruments, and always there was rapport. But if the two players were exchanging any signals, the message was too quick for the untrained eye.

34   I could tell that the music was holding the Chinese listeners in a strong grip. Their minds seemed to be fully engaged. Their bodies, however, were not. Only

three pairs of feet in the whole room were tapping—Ruff's, Mitchell's, and mine. Perhaps this was a Chinese characteristic, this stillness of listening. Moreover, the music wasn't easy. It never again approached the overt syncopation of the ragtime that Mitchell had played early in the program; that was where the essential gaiety of jazz had been most accessible. Nor did it have the flat-out gusto that an earlier generation of black musicians might have brought to China—the thumping rhythms and simpler harmonies of a James P. Johnson or a Fats Waller. It was not that Mitchell and Ruff were playing jazz that was pedantic or sedate. On the contrary, I have seldom heard Mitchell play with more exuberant shifts of energy and mood. But the music was full of subtleties; even a Westerner accustomed to jazz would have been charmed by its intelligence and wit. I had to remind myself that the Chinese had heard no Western music of any kind from 1966 to 1976. A twenty-one-year-old student in the audience, for instance, would have begun to listen to composers like Mozart and Brahms only within the past five years. The jazz that he was hearing now was not so different as to be a whole new branch of music. Mitchell was clearly grounded in Bach and Chopin; Ruff's French horn had echoes of all the classical works—Debussy's "Rêverie," Ravel's "Pavane"—in which that instrument has such uncanny power to move us.

35   After "Shanghai Blues," Ruff asked for questions.

36   "Where do people go to study jazz in America?" a student wanted to know. "What kind of courses do they take?"

37   Ruff explained that jazz courses, where they existed at all, would be part of a broad college curriculum that included, say, languages and history and physics. "But, really, jazz isn't learned in universities or conservatories," he said. "It's music that is passed on by older musicians to those of us who are younger."

38   It was not a helpful answer. What kind of subject didn't have its own academy? A shyness settled over the room, though the students seemed full of curiosity. Professor Tan got up and stood next to Ruff. "I urge you to ask questions," he said. "I can assure you that jazz has many principles that apply to your studies here. In fact, I have many questions myself."

39   An old professor stood up and asked, "When you created the 'Shanghai Blues' just now, did you have a form for it, or a logical plan?"

40   "I just started tapping my foot," Ruff replied, tapping his foot to reconstruct the moment. "And then I started to play the first thought that came into my mind with the horn. And Mitchell heard it. And he answered. And after that we heard and answered, heard and answered, heard and answered."

41   The old professor said, "But how can you ever play it again?"

42   "We never can," Ruff replied.

43   "That is beyond our imagination," the professor said. "Our students here play a piece a hundred times, or two hundred times, to get it exactly right. You play something once—something very beautiful—and then you just throw it away."

44   Now the questions tumbled out. What was most on the students' minds quickly became clear: it was the mystery of improvisation. (The Chinese don't even have a word for improvisation of this kind; Ruff translated it as "something created during the process of delivery.") All the questions poked at this central riddle—"Could a Chinese person improvise?" and "Could two strangers improvise together?" and "How can you compose at such speed?"—and during this

period Ruff took one question and turned it into a moment that stood us all on our ear.

45 Was it really possible, a student wanted to know, to improvise on any tune at all—even one that the musicians had never heard before?

46 Ruff's reply was casual. "I would like to invite one of the pianists here to play a short traditional Chinese melody that I'm sure we would not know, and we will make a new piece based on that," he said.

47 The room erupted in oohs and cheers. I caught a look on Mitchell's face that said, "This time you've gone too far." The students began to call the name of the young man they wanted to have play. When they found him in the crowd, he was so diffident that he got down on the floor to keep from being dragged out. But his friends dragged him out anyway, and, regaining his aplomb, he walked to the piano and sat down with the formality of a concert artist. He was about twenty-two. Mitchell stood to one side, looking grave.

48 The young man played his melody beautifully and with great feeling. It seemed to be his own composition, unknown to the other people. It began with four chords of distinctively Chinese structure, moved down the scale in a stately progression, paused, turned itself around with a transitional figure of lighter weight, and then started back up, never repeating itself and finally resolving the theme with a suspended chord that was satisfying because it was so unexpected. It was a perfect small piece, about fourteen bars long. The student walked back to his seat, and Mitchell went back to the piano. The room grew quiet.

49 Mitchell's huge hands hovered briefly over the keys, and then the young man's melody came back to him. It was in the same key; it had the same chords, slightly embellished near the end; and, best of all, it had the same mood. Having stated the theme, Mitchell broadened it the second time, giving it a certain majesty, coloring the student's chords with dissonances that were entirely apt. He gave the Chinese chords a jazz texture but still preserved their mood. Then Ruff joined him on his bass, and they took the melody through a number of variations, Mitchell giving it a whole series of new lives but never losing its integrity. I listened to his feat with growing excitement. For me, it was the climax of years of marvelling at his ear and at his sensitivity to the material at hand. The students were equally elated and astonished. For them, it was the ultimate proof—because it touched their own heritage—that for a jazz improviser no point of departure is alien.

50 After that number, a few more questions were asked, and Mitchell and Ruff concluded with a Gershwin medley from "Porgy and Bess" and a genial rendition of "My Old Flame." Professor Tan thanked the two men and formally ended the concert. Then he went over to Mitchell and took his hands in his own. "You are an artist," he said.

51 Later, I told Mitchell that I thought Ruff had given him an unduly nervous moment when he invited the students to supply a melody.

52 "Well, naturally I was nervous, because I didn't have any idea what to expect," he said. "But, you know, that boy phrased his piece *perfectly*. The minute he started to play, I got his emotions. I understood exactly what he was feeling, and the rest was easy. The notes and the chords just fell into place."

QUESTIONS

Experience

· Identify two things you didn't know about music until you read Zinsser's piece. Point to places in the text that either amaze or baffle you. And find one passage, specifically describing music, in which you feel Zinsser conveys the spirit of that music.

Interpretation

· What is this selection about? Music? Jazz? Communication? Intercultural understanding? Something else? Select one passage you consider of central importance to one of the essay's most significant ideas, and comment on it.

Evaluation

· What values does Zinsser find in the music of Mitchell and Ruff? What powers does music possess that Zinsser either discusses or simply mentions in this piece?

· What differences exist in the training of Chinese and western musicians?

WRITING

Exploring

· Write about one aspect of musical experience Zinsser describes that either baffles or delights you. Explain what strikes you and why.

Interpreting

· Explain what you understand by the term "improvisation." Include in your explanation some consideration of how Mitchell invents a song based on an original composition by a Chinese student—a work he hears once and immediately begins improvising on.

Evaluating

· Evaluate the extent to which Zinsser is successful in conveying a sense of the improvisatory nature of jazz, or evaluate the extent to which Zinsser illustrates the transcultural meanings of music.

JAMES AGEE
(1909–1955)

The Comic Acting of Buster Keaton

Born and raised in Tennessee, James Agee graduated from Harvard in 1932 and published his first book, a volume of poems, Permit Me Voyage, *in 1934. His best-known works are his novel* A Death in the Family *(1957) and* Let Us Now Praise Famous Men *(1941), a study of Alabama sharecroppers, which was accompanied by photographs taken by Walker Evans. In addition, Agee wrote for a number of periodicals, including* Fortune, Nation, *and* Time *magazines. The following selection, an excerpt from one of his essays on film (he was an outstanding film critic), is taken from* Agee on Film *(1959). In it Agee explains the peculiar comic genius of the silent-film actor Buster Keaton.*

Agee is one of the finest critics who ever wrote about films. His ability to zero in on an actor's singular gifts has never been equaled. His essay on Buster Keaton is noteworthy for this common facility of Agee's and also for its engaging description of what happens in Keaton's films. The description of the action of Keaton's The Navigator *makes readers feel as if they are actually watching Keaton on the screen.*

1　　Buster Keaton started work at the age of three and one-half with his parents in one of the roughest acts in vaudeville ("The Three Keatons"); Harry Houdini gave the child the name Buster in admiration for a fall he took down a flight of stairs. In his first movies Keaton teamed with Fatty Arbuckle under Sennett. He went on to become one of Metro's biggest stars and earners; a Keaton feature cost about $200,000 to make and reliably grossed $2,000,000. Very early in his movie career friends asked him why he never smiled on the screen. He didn't realize he didn't. He had got the dead-pan habit in variety; on the screen he had merely been so hard at work it had never occurred to him there was anything to smile about. Now he tried it just once and never again. He was by his whole style and nature so much the most deeply "silent" of the silent comedians that even a smile was as deafeningly out of key as a yell. In a way his pictures are like a transcendent juggling act in which it seems that the whole universe is in exquisite flying motion and the one point of repose is the juggler's effortless, uninterested face.

2　　Keaton's face ranked almost with Lincoln's as an early American archetype; it was haunting, handsome, almost beautiful, yet it was irreducibly funny; he improved matters by topping it off with a deadly horizontal hat, as flat and thin as a phonograph record. One can never forget Keaton wearing it, standing erect at the prow as his little boat is being launched. The boat goes grandly down the skids and, just as grandly, straight on to the bottom. Keaton never budges.

The last you see of him, the water lifts the hat off the stoic head and it floats away.

3 No other comedian could do as much with the dead pan. He used this great, sad, motionless face to suggest various related things: a one-track mind near the track's end of pure insanity; mulish imperturbability under the wildest of circumstances; how dead a human being can get and still be alive; an awe-inspiring sort of patience and power to endure, proper to granite but uncanny in flesh and blood. Everything that he was and did bore out this rigid face and played laughs against it. When he moved his eyes, it was like seeing them move in a statue. His short-legged body was all sudden, machinelike angles, governed by a daft aplomb. When he swept a semaphorelike arm to point, you could almost hear the electrical impulse in the signal block. When he ran from a cop his transitions from accelerating walk to easy jogtrot to brisk canter to headlong gallop to flogged-piston sprint—always floating, above this frenzy, the untroubled, untouchable face—were as distinct and as soberly in order as an automatic gearshift.

4 Keaton was a wonderfully resourceful inventor of mechanistic gags (he still spends much of his time fooling with Erector sets); as he ran afoul of locomotives, steamships, prefabricated and over-electrified houses, he put himself through some of the hardest and cleverest punishment ever designed for laughs. In *Sherlock Jr.,* boiling along on the handlebars of a motorcycle quite unaware that he has lost his driver, Keaton whips through city traffic, breaks up a tug-of-war, gets a shovelful of dirt in the face from each of a long line of Rockette-timed ditch-diggers, approaches a log at high speed which is hinged open by dynamite precisely soon enough to let him through and, hitting an obstruction, leaves the handlebars like an arrow leaving a bow, whams through the window of a shack in which the heroine is about to be violated, and hits the heavy feet-first, knocking him through the opposite wall. The whole sequence is as clean in motion as the trajectory of a bullet.

5 Much of the charm and edge of Keaton's comedy, however, lay in the subtle leverages of expression he could work against his nominal dead pan. Trapped in the side-wheel of a ferryboat, saving himself from drowning only by walking, then desperately running, inside the accelerating wheel like a squirrel in a cage, his only real concern was, obviously, to keep his hat on. Confronted by Love, he was not as dead pan as he was cracked up to be, either; there was an odd, abrupt motion of his head which suggested a horse nipping after a sugar lump.

6 Keaton worked strictly for laughs, but his work came from so far inside a curious and original spirit that he achieved a great deal besides, especially in his feature-length comedies. (For plain hard laughter his nineteen short comedies—the negatives of which have been lost—were even better.) He was the only major comedian who kept sentiment almost entirely out of his work, and he brought pure physical comedy to its greatest heights. Beneath his lack of emotion he was also uninsistently sardonic; deep below that, giving a disturbing tension and grandeur to the foolishness, for those who sensed it, there was in his comedy a freezing whisper not of pathos but of melancholia. With the humor, the craftsmanship and the action there was often, besides, a fine, still and sometimes dreamlike beauty. Much of his Civil War picture *The General* is within hailing distance of Mathew

Brady. And there is a ghostly, unforgettable moment in *The Navigator* when, on a deserted, softly rolling ship, all the pale doors along a deck swing open as one behind Keaton and, as one, slam shut, in a hair-raising illusion of noise. . . .

7   Up to the middle thirties Buster Keaton made several feature-length pictures (with such players as Jimmy Durante, Wallace Beery and Robert Montgomery); he also made a couple of dozen talking shorts. Now and again he managed to get loose into motion, without having to talk, and for a moment or so the screen would start singing again. But his dark, dead voice, though it was in keeping with the visual character, tore his intensely silent style to bits and destroyed the illusion within which he worked. He gallantly and correctly refuses to regard himself as "retired." Besides occasional bits, spots and minor roles in Hollywood pictures, he has worked on summer stages, made talking comedies in France and Mexico and clowned in a French circus. This summer he has played the straw hats in *Three Men on a Horse.* He is planning a television program. He also has a working agreement with Metro. One of his jobs there is to construct comedy sequences for Red Skelton.

8   The only man who really survived the flood was Chaplin, the only one who was rich, proud and popular enough to afford to stay silent. He brought out two of his greatest nontalking comedies, *City Lights* and *Modern Times,* in the middle of an avalanche of talk, spoke gibberish and, in the closing moments, plain English in *The Great Dictator,* and at last made an all-talking picture, *Monsieur Verdoux,* creating for that purpose an entirely new character who might properly talk a blue streak. *Verdoux* is the greatest of talking comedies though so cold and savage that it had to find its public in grimly experienced Europe.

9   Good comedy, and some that was better than good, outlived silence, but there has been less and less of it. The talkies brought one great comedian, the late, majestically lethargic W. C. Fields, who could not possibly have worked as well in silence; he was the toughest and the most warmly human of all screen comedians, and *It's a Gift* and *The Bank Dick,* fiendishly funny and incisive white-collar comedies, rank high among the best comedies (and best movies) ever made. Laurel and Hardy, the only comedians who managed to preserve much of the large, low style of silence and who began to explore the comedy of sound, have made nothing since 1945. Walt Disney, at his best an inspired comic inventor and teller of fairy stories, lost his stride during the war and has since regained it only at moments. Preston Sturges has made brilliant, satirical comedies, but his pictures are smart, nervous comedy-dramas merely italicized with slapstick. The Marx Brothers were sidesplitters but they made their best comedies years ago. Jimmy Durante is mainly a nightclub genius; Abbott and Costello are semiskilled laborers, at best; Bob Hope is a good radio comedian with a pleasing presence, but not much more, on the screen.

10   There is no hope that screen comedy will get much better than it is without new, gifted young comedians who really belong in movies, and without freedom for their experiments. For everyone who may appear we have one last, invidious comparison to offer as a guidepost.

11   One of the most popular recent comedies is Bob Hope's *The Paleface.* We take no pleasure in blackening *The Paleface;* we single it out, rather, because it is as good as we've got. Anything that is said of it here could be said, with interest,

of other comedies of our time. Most of the laughs in *The Paleface* are verbal. Bob Hope is very adroit with his lines and now and then, when the words don't get in the way, he makes a good beginning as a visual comedian. But only the beginning, never the middle or the end. He is funny, for instance, reacting to a shot of violent whisky. But he does not know how to get still funnier (*i.e.,* how to build and milk) or how to be funniest last (*i.e.,* how to top or cap his gag). The camera has to fade out on the same old face he started with.

12   One sequence is promisingly set up for visual comedy. In it, Hope and a lethal local boy stalk each other all over a cow town through streets which have been emptied in fear of their duel. The gag here is that through accident and stupidity they keep just failing to find each other. Some of it is quite funny. But the fun slackens between laughs like a weak clothesline, and by all the logic of humor (which is ruthlessly logical) the biggest laugh should come at the moment, and through the way, they finally spot each other. The sequence is so weakly thought out that at that crucial moment the camera can't afford to watch them; it switches to Jane Russell.

13   Now we turn to a masterpiece. In *The Navigator* Buster Keaton works with practically the same gag as Hope's duel. Adrift on a ship which he believes is otherwise empty, he drops a lighted cigarette. A girl finds it. She calls out and he hears her; each then tries to find the other. First each walks purposefully down the long, vacant starboard deck, the girl, then Keaton, turning the corner just in time not to see each other. Next time around each of them is trotting briskly, very much in earnest; going at the same pace, they miss each other just the same. Next time around each of them is going like a bat out of hell. Again they miss. Then the camera withdraws to a point of vantage at the stern, leans its chin in its hand and just watches the whole intricate superstructure of the ship as the protagonists stroll, steal and scuttle from level to level, up, down and sidewise, always managing to miss each other by hair's-breadths, in an enchantingly neat and elaborate piece of timing. There are no subsidiary gags to get laughs in this sequence and there is little loud laughter; merely a quiet and steadily increasing kind of delight. When Keaton has got all he can out of this fine modification of the movie chase he invents a fine device to bring the two together: the girl, thoroughly winded, sits down for a breather, indoors, on a plank which workmen have left across sawhorses. Keaton pauses on an upper deck, equally winded and puzzled. What follows happens in a couple of seconds at most: air suction whips his silk topper backward down a ventilator; grabbing frantically for it, he backs against the lip of the ventilator, jacknifes and falls in backward. Instantly the camera cuts back to the girl. A topper falls through the ceiling and lands tidily, right side up, on the plank beside her. Before she can look more than startled, its owner follows, head between his knees, crushes the topper, breaks the plank with the point of his spine and proceeds to the floor. The breaking of the plank smacks Boy and Girl together.

14   It is only fair to remember that the silent comedians would have as hard a time playing a talking scene as Hope has playing his visual ones, and that writing and directing are as accountable for the failure as Hope himself. But not even the humblest journeymen of the silent years would have let themselves off so easily. Like the masters, they knew, and sweated to obey, the laws of their craft.

QUESTIONS

Experience

· What was your experience of reading Agee's descriptions of Keaton's acting? Were you able to see the actor and his antics in your mind's eye? Why, or why not?

Interpretation

· Aside from analyzing Keaton's talent for comic acting, what else does Agee convey in this selection? What other important points about Keaton, about comic actors, about silent film, does Agee make?

Evaluation

· What values animate Agee's comments? What standards of evaluation does he use in comparing Bob Hope and Buster Keaton as comic actors? How persuasive do you find Agee's comparative analysis?

WRITING

Exploring

· Write an exploratory essay in which you identify and explain the peculiar talents of one of your favorite actors. Try to give the reader a sense of what is special about this actor and what it is like to watch him or her on screen.

Interpreting

· Write an analysis and interpretation of a classic or modern film that you have found intriguing or thought-provoking. Explain the significance of the film's action and character relationships. Avoid simply providing a plot summary of the film.

Evaluating

· Write a comparative analysis of two films on the same subject, of two actors playing similar roles, of two actors playing roles with something in common. Evaluate the films, roles, or performances by identifying and analyzing their successful and unsuccessful features. Avoid simply expressing an opinion or preference without explaining why you find one film, actor, or performance superior. Provide evidence and example to support your view.

JOHN BERGER
(b. 1926)

Looking at a Photograph

John Berger is a novelist and an art critic. His novels include A Painter of
Our Time *(1958) and* G *(1972). His books of art criticism include* About
Looking *(1980);* Ways of Seeing *(1972), based on the British Broadcasting
Corporation's television programs of the same title; and* Another Way of
Telling *(1982), from which the following passage and photograph have been
excerpted.*

*The remarkable thing about Berger's little piece is the way he imagines
the implications of the photograph by André Kertész that he both describes
and explains. Berger imports into his reading of the photograph a set of
historical circumstances that he then uses to make sense of it. He provides justification for his use of history by citing the title the photographer
gave the picture. Yet Berger does not allow himself to be confined to a historical interpretation of the photograph. He sees in it a particular human
experience that, while rooted in a particular historical circumstance, transcends it.*

1   A mother with her child is staring intently at a soldier. Perhaps they are speaking. We cannot hear their words. Perhaps they are saying nothing and everything is being said by the way they are looking at each other. Certainly a drama is
being enacted between them.

2   The caption reads: "A Red Hussar leaving, June 1919, Budapest." The photograph is by André Kertész.

3   So, the woman has just walked out of their home and will shortly go back
alone with the child. The drama of the moment is expressed in the difference
between the clothes they are wearing. His for travelling, for sleeping out, for fighting; hers for staying at home.

4   The caption can also entail other thoughts. The Hapsburg monarchy had fallen
the previous autumn. The winter had been one of extreme shortages (especially of
fuel in Budapest) and economic disintegration. Two months before, in March, the
socialist Republic of Councils had been declared. The Western allies in Paris, fearful lest the Russian and now the Hungarian example of revolution should spread
throughout Eastern Europe and the Balkans, were planning to dismantle the new
republic. A blockade was already imposed. General Foch himself was planning
the military invasion being carried out by Rumanian and Czech troops. On June
8th Clemenceau telegraphed an ultimatum to Béla Kun demanding a Hungarian
military withdrawal which would have left the Rumanians occupying the eastern
third of their country. For another six weeks the Hungarian Red Army fought on,
but it was finally overwhelmed. By August, Budapest was occupied and very soon
after, the first European fascist regime under Horthy was established.

André Kertész. Photograph: A Red Hussard leaving, June 1919. Budapest. Photo A. Kertész © Ministére de la Culture - France. Association Française Pour la Diffusion du Patrimoine Photographique, Paris.

5　　If we are looking at an image from the past and we want to relate it to ourselves, we need to know something of the history of that past. And so the foregoing paragraph—and much more than that might be said—is relevant to the reading of Kertész's photograph. Which is presumably why he gave it the caption he did and not just the title "Parting." Yet the photograph—or rather, the way this photograph demands to be read—cannot be limited to the historical.

6　　Everything in it is historical: the uniforms, the rifles, the corner by the Budapest railway station, the identity and biographies of all the people who are (or were) recognizable—even the size of the trees on the other side of the fence. And yet it also concerns a resistance to history: an opposition.

7　　This opposition is not the consequence of the photographer having said Stop! It is not that the resultant static image is like a fixed post in a flowing river. We know that in a moment the soldier will turn his back and leave; we presume that he is the father of the child in the woman's arms. The significance of the instant photographed is already claiming minutes, weeks, years.

8　　The opposition exists in the parting look between the man and the woman. This look is not directed towards the viewer. We witness it as the older soldier with the moustache and the woman with the shawl (perhaps a sister) do. The exclusivity of this look is further emphasized by the boy in the mother's arms; he is watching his father, and yet he is excluded from their look.

9　　This look, which crosses before our eyes, is holding in place what *is,* not specifically what is there around them outside the station, but what *is* their life, what *are* their lives. The woman and the soldier are looking at each other so that the image of what *is* now shall remain for them. In this look their being *is* opposed to their history, even if we assume that this history is one they accept or have chosen.

QUESTIONS

Experience

· To what extent does Berger's description of Kertész's photograph help you to see it better? To what extent does his explanation or interpretation help you understand the photograph?

· Do you see anything else in the photograph that Berger has not mentioned?

Interpretation

· Provide a different explanation for the photograph, offering another interpretation. How does your alternative explanation differ from Berger's? Which do you find more plausible? Why?

Evaluation

· In his fourth and longest paragraph Berger places the photograph in historical context. How important is this information for understanding the picture? Do you agree with what Berger says later—that "the way this photograph demands to be read—cannot be limited to the historical"? Why, or why not?

WRITING

Exploring

· Select a photograph that is interesting or important to you, and tell the story behind it. It may be an old family photograph, a photograph of someone you love, or a picture that simply engages your imagination.

Interpreting

· Find a photograph you would like to analyze and interpret. Try to avoid using something from your family or personal life. Instead, look through images used in print advertisements, or look through a collection of photographs by one of the following: Ansel Adams, Diane Arbus, Mathew Brady, Eugene Atget, André Kertész, Dorothea Lange, or Eugene Smith.

· Analyze the photograph, and explain its significance.

Evaluating

· Select a photograph by one of the photographers mentioned in the preceding list, or choose a visual image from print advertising, and explain the social, political, or cultural values it embodies.

ELIZABETH MACDONALD
(b. 1970)

Odalisque

Elizabeth MacDonald is a graduate of Harvard University, where she studied French and fine arts. She wrote the following essay as a student in a freshman expository writing course.

Elizabeth MacDonald's essay is notable for its amalgamation of personal experience with observations about paintings, photographs, and reading inspired by her interest in the actress and painters she writes about. A noteworthy feature of MacDonald's essay is the way she uses one-sentence paragraphs for emphasis and the way she relates her real-life obsession with being thin to images from the worlds of art and film.

1   I am in eighth grade—perhaps two weeks, or even a week before all the trouble started—and walking one evening with a friend on the east side of Manhattan. I catch sight of my reflection in a plateglass window and, in these formative years, observe what I am becoming. My hair is short and less feminine at this time, my face rounder, my body plumper. I was happy with what I saw.

2   I am in ninth grade and my waist is the thickness of a bottleneck. Lying on my bed I hear my parents talking about me as they walk along the hall.

3   "This diet has gone on too long," my mother is saying, "she's gotten very weak."

4   "She is very thin," says my father.

5   I am in tenth grade and fatter than I have ever been. In a book written during the Twiggy-influenced sixties I read that every day that you fast you lose two pounds of fat. This seems easier than recovering the discipline that I had once in such abundance and have now lost. I begin a regimen in which I eat enormous amounts for a few days and fast on the others. I want very much to regain the beauty that was once mine, to re-discover the indestructible, perfect creature of angles and spare planes that lies hidden under this amorphous mass of lumps. I want more than anything to be thin again. This seems to be a way. For a desperate girl who has no assurance that she will ever be desirable almost no price is too high.

6   I do not remember the first time that I made myself throw up. It may have been in eleventh grade, but the circumstances have faded under the shame and horror. As I understand it many people try self-induced vomiting. Few are successful on the first attempt and most give up. Some of us persist: some of us even become quite talented.

7   In that talent I originally found salvation. Self-indulgence and beauty seemed, for the first time, compatible. I could give myself everything I wanted and retain the figure of the ascetic. I could have my cake, and I could eat it too. Nothing, however, is that easy. Maintaining the façade becomes indispensable. Every com-

pliment is a knife in the gut and an impulse to retain what I have, though I pay, and pay dearly. There is a line in Yeats' "Adam's Curse" that cries bitterness—

> To be born woman is to know—
> Although they do not talk of it at school—
> That we must labor to be beautiful

I have only just discovered that I have been misquoting these lines for years. In my mind the last line, though essentially the same, has always had a slightly different nuance.

> . . . We must suffer to be beautiful.

8   The most famous photograph of Rita Hayworth, as Gilda, immortalizes her as an extraordinary beauty. In black satin she stands, mysterious and gorgeous—a stunning beauty, with allure and come-hither confidence. Her skin glows alabaster against a black background and on her beautiful face, slightly turned to the side, is a look of encouragement and, conversely, knowing distance. She tilts her chin up in the arrogance of her beauty: she knows very well that she stops traffic and hearts. Her hair is long, her waist is small, and her strapless dress clings to her perfect figure. Her self-presentation is more than feminine; it is the essence of female. Rita Hayworth played a woman all men wanted and all women wanted to be. She sets the standard of what it is to be an ideal woman—a flesh Goddess.

9   I have heard that she could not reconcile her beauty and herself, that she felt herself to be an illusion created by lights and other people's vision of what she should be. You could never tell that from this photograph. This woman revels in nothing more than her sexuality and beauty. And for all that, all the power and joy in her physical presence that she presents to the world in this still, Rita Hayworth never believed in the image she presented. She felt that the façade was fraudulent and that she was two people inhabiting a beautiful shell whose two sides were irreconcilable. Her most famous quotation is a cry of pain. "Every man I ever knew went to bed with Gilda and woke up with me." They saw in her the realization of all their dreams and found that she was just a woman. Men looked in her for Gilda and a goddess. Inside she knew that she was as mortal as Mary Sixpack and she could not bear the split between her image and what she felt to be her real self. She suffered in her beauty.

10   In the margins of most of my notebooks is the sketch of a woman's head in a three quarter view. Her hair is long and her cheekbones are far more pronounced than mine will ever be, no matter how thin I get. Her jaw is very defined. I gave her a name once, a name that has much to do with ethereality and fragility and a name as imaginary as is Gilda. I only christen the sketches that turn out well with that name. I only want to draw a Gilda, and I only want to be a Gilda, even knowing what Gilda did to Rita Hayworth.

11   I would never presume to compare my looks with those of Rita Hayworth, but I am a woman, and I know about laboring. I too have learned that there is a price to be paid for beauty. I live the same deception as she did. I am not what I seem, and the deception battles my soul.

12   "Yes, I am attracted," I overheard him say once, "but I don't think she's my type." He did not know me at that point. I was a shell and a body, long hair and green

eyes and long legs and a small waist, nice curves for one so thin. I know that he wants the flesh envelope that I walk in. I and others have seen him looking at me, my hair, my face, my legs. He has twisted around in chairs to watch me as I go by, and I know that he is aware of me whenever I am around him. My physicality is a magnet. He wants and he wants, but he just wants a body. He does not want me. He himself is easy in his corporeality: he has the athlete's presence and the athlete's ability to live within his skin and take pleasure in the way his body works. I think I felt that if he—so easy in his skin—believed in my entirety then I too would believe. Only my body sold. Uninterested in the interior, he cannot divorce himself of his attraction for the façade, and I am caught. The façade always sells first, and therefore the façade must always be maintained, no matter what.

13   I met him for breakfast one morning this winter when the snow was falling softly. I walked alone in the quiet of early morning. I could feel the snow collecting on the gauze of my hair. Alone with him in a near-empty dining hall, I felt cold, and my food had no taste. I ate very little. After breakfast I disappeared.

14   Sometimes, when I have disappeared and I am unrecognizable, invisible, I run my hands over the planes of my face, telling myself that I am, I am, I am. I exist, I am alive, I tell myself, running my fingertips over the sockets of bone in which those green eyes lie, and I discover the line of my jaw beneath my skin. My eyelashes tickle my hands, and my hands worship my flesh and my bones. I am reassuring myself that somewhere under my rib cage my heart beats, that though invisible I am not gone.

15   I remember the first time I threw up blood.

16   The modern artist Giorgio di Chirico painted in a classical manner. His subjects seem to be informed by Italian Renaissance models but the classical vision has been tortured and twisted and made strange. His paintings recede into depth in skewed perspective, and nature has been warped into something that is both recognizable and alien. In his lonely, dark settings the shadows are like none ever seen in reality but are still frighteningly real. "There are more enigmas in the shadow of a man who walks in the sun," he said, "than in all the religions of past, present and future." In the medium he devoted his life to he could find no answers: mysteries were easier than a simple darkness, the shadow of a man in the sun. The lines of his paintings are invariably ruler straight, but there is no peace or ease to be found in his art. His paintings are disorienting: they are the representation of a human imbalance and uncertainty in the world.

17   I am uneasy in my shell.

18   The neoclassical artist Ingres painted figures of dubious anatomical construction but used the questions to glorify the beauty of the human shape rather than to disorient the viewer. It is the male body that is said to represent best the human form for its shape follows the lines of the core and is undisguised by curves and softness. Ingres painted women. In "The Turkish Bath" many women lie in splendor, impossibly twisted into sensuous shapes. He celebrates the disguising curves and softness, emphasizing them, asserting roundness as beautiful. In another celebration of Woman, "La Grande Odalisque," a beautiful woman reclines alone. I

first saw this painting in grisaille, a technique that simulates statuary, molding the human shape in shades of grey.

19   The body of this Turkish harem slave is everything that I wish I could permit mine to be. It is voluptuous and smooth; it is classically feminine. In the line of breast and hip, of round arm and thigh, globes and arcs connect and flow, defining grace and beauty. Hers is a celebration of existence, of the flesh and the senses. Nude she reclines, luxuriating in herself as a living being and a body. Her setting reflects and enhances the luxury of her being: royal blue, oriental cushions, self indulgence and self love. She cares for her own pleasure. Her skin is pale, and the feminine aspects of her figure have been emphasized to the point of distortion. Her shoulders are narrow; her waist is small, and her lower back is far too long. The elongation highlights the flesh at the hip and leads into her legs. They appear shorter than they would were she thin. Her feet and hands are fragile, her visible eye luminous, and the bones of her face have a delicate beauty. She is direct and beautiful. She is sensuous and sensual. She is enigmatic and she is feminine. Her glance over her round shoulder beckons and arrogantly asserts her power. Nude, she revels in herself as a sexual being. She does not hide.

20   In my dreams, though, I take on the attributes not of the Odalisque, but of my impossibly idealized sketch. The world celebrates my fragility and stunning physical presence. I define gorgeous. The earth congratulates itself that I pass time on its surface. I am delicate and so breathtakingly beautiful that I put Gilda to shame.

21   Ingres chose not to make his Odalisque's body anatomically correct. By the standards of reality it is warped and strangely twisted, wrong like di Chirico's perspective. Her arm and her lower back are far too long, her leg twists around her other leg. Her body is more than imperfect, it is impossible, but in its impossibility the necessities of bone and blood have been sacrificed to the beauty of line and form. Where di Chirico skews perspective to disorient, Ingres twists a body and liberates it. Without the bones that constrain the normal human figure, she is freer in her flesh. She is more conscious of her own power and presence. She inhabits her body in joy, accepting it, loving her curves and sensuality, hedonism inherent in the hookah and crumpled sheets. She flows feminine.

22   In Ingres' world—though not in mine—she need not suffer to be easy in her skin.

QUESTIONS

Experience

· Did you find the writer's description of her experience compelling, convincing, or something else? Why?
· How did you respond to her shifts of time, scene, and focus? Why?

Interpretation

· To what extent is MacDonald's essay about her bulimia? To what extent is it a commentary about the pressure placed upon women to be thin and beautiful? To what extent is it about her own body as a work of art?

· Why do you think the writer introduces Rita Hayworth into her essay? What about the paintings by Ingres and De Chirico?

Evaluation

· What cultural values emerge most powerfully from a reading of this essay? Where does the writer seem to address aspects of culture and value most directly?

WRITING

Exploring

· Write an essay about your own experience of coming to terms with your physical self. You might write about dieting, an exercise program, or some other dimension of your life in which your physical attributes assumed importance either to you or to others.

Interpreting

· Analyze Elizabeth MacDonald's essay. Explain how it is organized. Identify each of the texts she introduces into it, and account for their various functions and effects.

Evaluating

· Write an essay about one of the cultural concerns that emerge from your reading of MacDonald's essay: women's beauty, a woman's (or a man's) body as a work of art, or the relationship between beauty and suffering.

JAMES BALDWIN
(1924–1987)

Sonny's Blues

James Baldwin was born in Harlem and became, at 14, a preacher. At 17 he abandoned the ministry and devoted himself to the craft of writing. Baldwin received institutional support in the form of fellowships to help sustain him while he wrote his first two novels: Go Tell It on the Mountain *(1953)* and Giovanni's Room *(1956). Sandwiched between these two works was a collection of essays,* Notes of a Native Son *(1955), which many readers consider his finest work.*

In his essays Baldwin struggled to define himself as an American, as a writer, and as a black man, all of which, for Baldwin, were inextricably intertwined. In coming to terms with what was the most difficult thing in his life (his blackness), Baldwin revealed himself to be a passionate and eloquent writer whose most frequent subject has been the relations between the races.

The story that follows, however, illustrates another of Baldwin's perennial concerns—the importance of communication and understanding between people of different interests and social classes. The story uses music as a metaphor for communication on the deepest levels.

"Sonny's Blues" dramatizes the differences between two brothers whose lives have diverged but who are brought together again partly through the agency of music. Baldwin's story is remarkable not only for its depiction of class differences but for its evocation of the world of the musician who does not want to live a bourgeois life. Some of the most powerful writing occurs in the last few pages, in which Baldwin describes the musicians' community and their ability to communicate through music. Baldwin shows us that we, along with the middle-class brother, can also understand the power of music to serve as a bridge to understanding, appreciation, respect, and love.

1   I read about it in the paper, in the subway, on my way to work. I read it, and I couldn't believe it, and I read it again. Then perhaps I just stared at it, at the newsprint spelling out his name, spelling out the story. I stared at it in the swinging lights of the subway car, and in the faces and bodies of the people, and in my own face, trapped in the darkness which roared outside.

2   It was not to be believed and I kept telling myself that, as I walked from the subway station to the high school. And at the same time I couldn't doubt it. I was scared, scared for Sonny. He became real to me again. A great block of ice got settled in my belly and kept melting there slowly all day long, while I taught my classes algebra. It was a special kind of ice. It kept melting, sending trickles of ice water all up and down my veins, but it never got less. Sometimes it hardened and seemed to expand until I felt my guts were going to come spilling out or that I was going to choke or scream. This would always be at a moment when I was remembering some specific thing Sonny had once said or done.

3   When he was about as old as the boys in my classes his face had been bright and open, there was a lot of copper in it; and he'd had wonderfully direct brown eyes, and great gentleness and privacy. I wondered what he looked like now. He had been picked up, the evening before, in a raid on an apartment downtown, for peddling and using heroin.

4   I couldn't believe it: but what I mean by that is that I couldn't find any room for it anywhere inside me. I had kept it outside me for a long time. I hadn't wanted to know. I had had suspicions, but I didn't name them, I kept putting them away. I told myself that Sonny was wild, but he wasn't crazy. And he'd always been a good boy, he hadn't ever turned hard or evil or disrespectful, the way kids can, so quick, so quick, especially in Harlem. I didn't want to believe that I'd ever see my brother going down, coming to nothing, all that light in his face gone out, in the condition I'd already seen so many others. Yet it had happened and here I was, talking about algebra to a lot of boys who might, every one of them for all I knew, be popping off needles every time they went to the head. Maybe it did more for them than algebra could.

5   I was sure that the first time Sonny had ever had horse, he couldn't have been much older than these boys were now. These boys, now, were living as we'd been living then, they were growing up with a rush and their heads bumped abruptly against the low ceiling of their actual possibilities. They were filled with rage. All they really knew were two darknesses, the darkness of their lives, which was now closing in on them, and the darkness of the movies, which had blinded them to that other darkness, and in which they now, vindictively, dreamed, at once more together than they were at any other time, and more alone.

6   When the last bell rang, the last class ended, I let out my breath. It seemed I'd been holding it for all that time. My clothes were wet—I may have looked as though I'd been sitting in a steam bath, all dressed up, all afternoon. I sat alone in the classroom a long time. I listened to the boys outside, downstairs, shouting and cursing and laughing. Their laughter struck me for perhaps the first time. It was not the joyous laughter which—God knows why—one associates with children. It was mocking and insular, its intent was to denigrate. It was disenchanted, and in this, also, lay the authority of their curses. Perhaps I was listening to them because I was thinking about my brother and in them I heard my brother. And myself.

7   One boy was whistling a tune, at once very complicated and very simple, it seemed to be pouring out of him as though he were a bird, and it sounded very cool and moving through all that harsh, bright air, only just holding its own through all those other sounds.

8   I stood up and walked over to the window and looked down into the courtyard. It was the beginning of the spring and the sap was rising in the boys. A teacher passed through them every now and again, quickly, as though he or she couldn't wait to get out of that courtyard, to get those boys out of their sight and off their minds. I started collecting my stuff. I thought I'd better get home and talk to Isabel.

9   The courtyard was almost deserted by the time I got downstairs. I saw this boy standing in the shadow of a doorway, looking just like Sonny. I almost called his name. Then I saw that it wasn't Sonny, but somebody we used to know, a boy

from around our block. He'd been Sonny's friend. He'd never been mine, having been too young for me, and, anyway, I'd never liked him. And now, even though he was a grown-up man, he still hung around that block, still spent hours on the street corners, was always high and raggy. I used to run into him from time to time and he'd often work around to asking me for a quarter or fifty cents. He always had some real good excuse, too, and I always gave it to him, I don't know why.

10 But now, abruptly, I hated him. I couldn't stand the way he looked at me, partly like a dog, partly like a cunning child. I wanted to ask him what the hell he was doing in the school courtyard.

11 He sort of shuffled over to me, and he said, "I see you got the papers. So you already know about it."

12 "You mean about Sonny? Yes, I already know about it. How come they didn't get you?"

13 He grinned. It made him repulsive and it also brought to mind what he'd looked like as a kid. "I wasn't there. I stay away from them people."

14 "Good for you." I offered him a cigarette and I watched him through the smoke. "You come all the way down here just to tell me about Sonny?"

15 "That's right." He was sort of shaking his head and his eyes looked strange, as though they were about to cross. The bright sun deadened his damp dark brown skin and it made his eyes look yellow and showed up the dirt in his kinked hair. He smelled funky. I moved a little away from him and I said, "Well, thanks. But I already know about it and I got to get home."

16 "I'll walk you a little ways," he said. We started walking. There were a couple of kids still loitering in the courtyard and one of them said goodnight to me and looked strangely at the boy beside me.

17 "What're you going to do?" he asked me. "I mean, about Sonny?"

18 "Look. I haven't seen Sonny for over a year, I'm not sure I'm going to do any-thing. Anyway, what the hell *can* I do?"

19 "That's right," he said quickly, "ain't nothing you can do. Can't much help old Sonny no more, I guess."

20 It was what I was thinking and so it seemed to me he had no right to say it.

21 "I'm surprised at Sonny, though," he went on—he had a funny way of talking, he looked straight ahead as though he were talking to himself—"I thought Sonny was a smart boy, I thought he was too smart to get hung."

22 "I guess he thought so too," I said sharply, "and that's how he got hung. And how about you? You're pretty goddamn smart, I bet."

23 Then he looked directly at me, just for a minute. "I ain't smart," he said. "If I was smart, I'd have reached for a pistol a long time ago."

24 "Look. Don't tell *me* your sad story, if it was up to me, I'd give you one." Then I felt guilty—guilty, probably, for never having supposed that the poor bas-tard *had* a story of his own, much less a sad one, and I asked, quickly, "What's going to happen to him now?"

25 He didn't answer this. He was off by himself some place. "Funny thing," he said, and from his tone we might have been discussing the quickest way to get to Brooklyn, "when I saw the papers this morning, the first thing I asked myself was if I had anything to do with it. I felt sort of responsible."

26   I began to listen more carefully. The subway station was on the corner, just before us, and I stopped. He stopped, too. We were in front of a bar and he ducked slightly, peering in, but whoever he was looking for didn't seem to be there. The juke box was blasting away with something black and bouncy and I half watched the barmaid as she danced her way from the juke box to her place behind the bar. And I watched her face as she laughingly responded to something someone said to her, still keeping time to the music. When she smiled one saw the little girl, one sensed the doomed, still-struggling woman beneath the battered face of the semi-whore.

27   "I never *give* Sonny nothing," the boy said finally, "but a long time ago I come to school high and Sonny asked me how it felt." He paused, I couldn't bear to watch him, I watched the barmaid, and I listened to the music which seemed to be causing the pavement to shake. "I told him it felt great." The music stopped, the barmaid paused and watched the juke box until the music began again. "It did."

28   All this was carrying me some place I didn't want to go. I certainly didn't want to know how it felt. It filled everything, the people, the houses, the music, the dark, quicksilver barmaid, with menace; and this menace was their reality.

29   "What's going to happen to him now?" I asked again.

30   "They'll send him away some place and they'll try to cure him." He shook his head. "Maybe he'll even think he's kicked the habit. Then they'll let him loose"— he gestured, throwing his cigarette into the gutter. "That's all."

31   "What do you mean, that's *all?*"

32   But I knew what he meant.

33   "I *mean,* that's *all.*" He turned his head and looked at me, pulling down the corners of his mouth. "Don't you know what I mean?" he asked, softly.

34   "How the hell *would* I know what you mean?" I almost whispered it, I don't know why.

35   "That's right," he said to the air, "how would *he* know what I mean?" He turned toward me again, patient and calm, and yet I somehow felt him shaking, shaking as though he were going to fall apart. I felt that ice in my guts again, the dread I'd felt all afternoon; and again I watched the barmaid, moving about the bar, washing glasses, and singing. "Listen. They'll let him out and then it'll just start all over again. That's what I mean."

36   "You mean—they'll let him out. And then he'll just start working his way back in again. You mean he'll never kick the habit. Is that what you mean?"

37   "That's right," he said, cheerfully. *"You* see what I mean."

38   "Tell me," I said at last, "why does he want to die? He must want to die, he's killing himself, why does he want to die?"

39   He looked at me in surprise. He licked his lips. "He don't want to die. He wants to live. Don't nobody want to die, ever."

40   Then I wanted to ask him—too many things. He could not have answered, or if he had, I could not have borne the answers. I started walking. "Well, I guess it's none of my business."

41   "It's going to be rough on old Sonny," he said. We reached the subway station. "This is your station?" he asked. I nodded. I took one step down. "Damn!" he said, suddenly. I looked up at him. He grinned again. "Damn it if I didn't leave all

my money home. You ain't got a dollar on you, have you? Just for a couple of days, is all."

42   All at once something inside gave and threatened to come pouring out of me. I didn't hate him any more. I felt that in another moment I'd start crying like a child.

43   "Sure," I said. "Don't swear." I looked in my wallet and didn't have a dollar, I only had a five. "Here," I said. "That hold you?"

44   He didn't look at it—he didn't want to look at it. A terrible, closed look came over his face, as though he were keeping the number on the bill a secret from him and me. "Thanks," he said, and now he was dying to see me go. "Don't worry about Sonny. Maybe I'll write him or something."

45   "Sure," I said. "You do that. So long."

46   "Be seeing you," he said. I went down the steps.

47   And I didn't write Sonny or send him anything for a long time. When I finally did, it was just after my little girl died, he wrote me back a letter which made me feel like a bastard.

48   Here's what he said:

Dear Brother,

You don't know how much I needed to hear from you. I wanted to write you many a time but I dug how much I must have hurt you and so I didn't write. But now I feel like a man who's been trying to climb up out of some deep, real deep and funky hole and just saw the sun up there, outside. I got to get outside.

I can't tell you much about how I got here. I mean I don't know how to tell you. I guess I was afraid of something or I was trying to escape from something and you know I have never been very strong in the head (smile). I'm glad Mama and Daddy are dead and can't see what's happened to their son and I swear if I'd known what I was doing I would never have hurt you so, you and a lot of other fine people who were nice to me and who believed in me.

I don't want you to think it had anything to do with me being a musician. It's more than that. Or maybe less than that. I can't get anything straight in my head down here and I try not to think about what's going to happen to me when I get outside again. Sometime I think I'm going to flip and *never* get outside and some-time I think I'll come straight back. I tell you one thing, though, I'd rather blow my brains out than go through this again. But that's what they all say, so they tell me. If I tell you when I'm coming to New York and if you could meet me, I sure would appreciate it. Give my love to Isabel and the kids and I was sure sorry to hear about little Gracie. I wish I could be like Mama and say the Lord's will be done, but I don't know it seems to me that trouble is the one thing that never does get stopped and I don't know what good it does to blame it on the Lord. But maybe it does some good if you believe it.

Your brother,
Sonny

49   Then I kept in constant touch with him and I sent him whatever I could and I went to meet him when he came back to New York. When I saw him many things

I thought I had forgotten came flooding back to me. This was because I had begun, finally, to wonder about Sonny, about the life that Sonny lived inside. This life, whatever it was, had made him older and thinner and it had deepened the distant stillness in which he had always moved. He looked very unlike my baby brother. Yet, when he smiled, when we shook hands, the baby brother I'd never known looked out from the depths of his private life, like an animal waiting to be coaxed into the light.

50   "How you been keeping?" he asked me.

51   "All right. And you?"

52   "Just fine." He was smiling all over his face. "It's good to see you again."

53   "It's good to see you."

54   The seven years' difference in our ages lay between us like a chasm: I wondered if these years would ever operate between us as a bridge. I was remembering, and it made it hard to catch my breath, that I had been there when he was born; and I had heard the first words he had ever spoken. When he started to walk, he walked from our mother straight to me. I caught him just before he fell when he took the first steps he ever took in this world.

55   "How's Isabel?"

56   "Just fine. She's dying to see you."

57   "And the boys?"

58   "They're fine, too. They're anxious to see their uncle."

59   "Oh, come on. You know they don't remember me."

60   "Are you kidding? Of course they remember you."

61   He grinned again. We got into a taxi. We had a lot to say to each other, far too much to know how to begin.

62   As the taxi began to move, I asked, "You still want to go to India?"

63   He laughed. "You still remember that. Hell, no. This place is Indian enough for me."

64   "It used to belong to them," I said.

65   And he laughed again. "They damn sure knew what they were doing when they got rid of it."

66   Years ago, when he was around fourteen, he'd been all hipped on the idea of going to India. He read books about people sitting on rocks, naked, in all kinds of weather, but mostly bad, naturally, and walking barefoot through hot coals and arriving at wisdom. I used to say that it sounded to me as though they were getting away from wisdom as fast as they could. I think he sort of looked down on me for that.

67   "Do you mind," he asked, "if we have the driver drive alongside the park? On the west side—I haven't seen the city in so long."

68   "Of course not," I said. I was afraid that I might sound as though I were humoring him, but I hoped he wouldn't take it that way.

69   So we drove along, between the green of the park and the stony, lifeless elegance of hotels and apartment buildings, toward the vivid, killing streets of our childhood. These streets hadn't changed, though housing projects jutted up out of them now like rocks in the middle of a boiling sea. Most of the houses in which we had grown up had vanished, as had the stores from which we had stolen, the

basements in which we had first tried sex, the rooftops from which we had hurled tin cans and bricks. But houses exactly like the houses of our past yet dominated the landscape, boys exactly like the boys we once had been found themselves smothering in these houses, came down into the streets for light and air and found themselves encircled by disaster. Some escaped the trap, most didn't. Those who got out always left something of themselves behind, as some animals amputate a leg and leave it in the trap. It might be said, perhaps, that I had escaped, after all, I was a school teacher; or that Sonny had, he hadn't lived in Harlem for years. Yet, as the cab moved uptown through streets which seemed, with a rush, to darken with dark people, and as I covertly studied Sonny's face, it came to me that what we both were seeking through our separate cab windows was that part of ourselves which had been left behind. It's always at the hour of trouble and confrontation that the missing member aches.

70   We hit 110th Street and started rolling up Lenox Avenue. And I'd known this avenue all my life, but it seemed to me again, as it had seemed on the day I'd first heard about Sonny's trouble, filled with a hidden menace which was its very breath of life.

71   "We almost there," said Sonny.

72   "Almost." We were both too nervous to say anything more.

73   We lived in a housing project. It hasn't been up long. A few days after it was up it seemed uninhabitably new, now, of course, it's already rundown. It looks like a parody of the good, clean, faceless life—God knows the people who live in it do their best to make it a parody. The beat-looking grass lying around isn't enough to make their lives green, the hedges will never hold out the streets, and they know it. The big windows fool no one, they aren't big enough to make space out of no space. They don't bother with the windows, they watch the TV screen instead. The playground is most popular with the children who don't play at jacks, or skip rope, or roller skate, or swing, and they can be found in it after dark. We moved in partly because it's not too far from where I teach, and partly for the kids; but it's really just like the houses in which Sonny and I grew up. The same things happen, they'll have the same things to remember. The moment Sonny and I started into the house I had the feeling that I was simply bringing him back into the danger he had almost died trying to escape.

74   Sonny has never been talkative. So I don't know why I was sure he'd be dying to talk to me when supper was over the first night. Everything went fine, the oldest boy remembered him, and the youngest boy liked him, and Sonny had remembered to bring something for each of them; and Isabel, who is really much nicer than I am, more open and giving, had gone to a lot of trouble about dinner and was genuinely glad to see him. And she's always been able to tease Sonny in a way that I haven't. It was nice to see her face so vivid again and to hear her laugh and watch her make Sonny laugh. She wasn't, or, anyway, she didn't seem to be, at all uneasy or embarrassed. She chatted as though there were no subject which had to be avoided and she got Sonny past his first, faint stiffness. And thank God she was there, for I was filled with that icy dread again. Everything I did seemed awkward to me, and everything I said sounded freighted with hidden meaning. I was trying to remember everything I'd heard about dope addiction

and I couldn't help watching Sonny for signs. I wasn't doing it out of malice. I was trying to find out something about my brother. I was dying to hear him tell me he was safe.

75 "Safe!" my father grunted, whenever Mama suggested trying to move to a neighborhood which might be safer for children. "Safe, hell! Ain't no place safe for kids, nor nobody."

76 He always went on like this, but he wasn't, ever, really as bad as he sounded, not even on weekends, when he got drunk. As a matter of fact, he was always on the lookout for "something a little better," but he died before he found it. He died suddenly, during a drunken weekend in the middle of the war, when Sonny was fifteen. He and Sonny hadn't ever got on too well. And this was partly because Sonny was the apple of his father's eye. It was because he loved Sonny so much and was frightened for him, that he was always fighting with him. It doesn't do any good to fight with Sonny. Sonny just moves back, inside himself, where he can't be reached. But the principal reason that they never hit it off is that they were so much alike. Daddy was big and rough and loud-talking, just the opposite of Sonny, but they both had—that same privacy.

77 Mama tried to tell me something about this, just after Daddy died. I was home on leave from the army.

78 This was the last time I ever saw my mother alive. Just the same, this picture gets all mixed up in my mind with pictures I had of her when she was younger. The way I always see her is the way she used to be on a Sunday afternoon, say, when the old folks were talking after the big Sunday dinner. I always see her wearing pale blue. She'd be sitting on the sofa. And my father would be sitting in the easy chair, not far from her. And the living room would be full of church folks and relatives. There they sit, in chairs all around the living room, and the night is creeping up outside, but nobody knows it yet. You can see the darkness growing against the windowpanes and you hear the street noises every now and again, or maybe the jangling beat of a tambourine from one of the churches close by, but it's real quiet in the room. For a moment nobody's talking, but every face looks darkening, like the sky outside. And my mother rocks a little from the waist, and my father's eyes are closed. Everyone is looking at something a child can't see. For a minute they've forgotten the children. Maybe a kid is lying on the rug, half asleep. Maybe somebody's got a kid in his lap and is absent-mindedly stroking the kid's head. Maybe there's a kid, quiet and big-eyed, curled up in a big chair in the corner. The silence, the darkness coming, and the darkness in the faces frightens the child obscurely. He hopes that the hand which strokes his forehead will never stop—will never die. He hopes that there will never come a time when the old folks won't be sitting around the living room, talking about where they've come from, and what they've seen, and what's happened to them and their kinfolk.

79 But something deep and watchful in the child knows that this is bound to end, is already ending. In a moment someone will get up and turn on the light. Then the old folks will remember the children and they won't talk any more that day. And when light fills the room, the child is filled with darkness. He knows that every time this happens he's moved just a little closer to that darkness outside. The darkness outside is what the old folks have been talking about. It's what they've come from. It's what they endure. The child knows that they won't talk any more because if he knows too much about what's happened to *them,* he'll know too much too soon, about what's going to happen to *him.*

80 The last time I talked to my mother, I remember I was restless. I wanted to get out and see Isabel. We weren't married then and we had a lot to straighten out between us.

81 There Mama sat, in black, by the window. She was humming an old church song, *Lord, you brought me from a long ways off.* Sonny was out somewhere. Mama kept watching the streets.

82 "I don't know," she said, "if I'll ever see you again, after you go off from here. But I hope you'll remember the things I tried to teach you."

83 "Don't talk like that," I said, and smiled. "You'll be here a long time yet."

84 She smiled, too, but she said nothing. She was quiet for a long time. And I said, "Mama, don't you worry about nothing. I'll be writing all the time, and you be getting the checks. . . ."

85 "I want to talk to you about your brother," she said, suddenly. "If anything happens to me he ain't going to have nobody to look out for him."

86 "Mama," I said, "ain't nothing going to happen to you *or* Sonny. Sonny's all right. He's a good boy and he's got good sense."

87 "It ain't a question of his being a good boy," Mama said, "nor of his having good sense. It ain't only the bad ones, nor yet the dumb ones that gets sucked under." She stopped, looking at me. "Your Daddy once had a brother," she said, and she smiled in a way that made me feel she was in pain. "You didn't never know that, did you?"

88 "No," I said, "I never knew that," and I watched her face.

89 "Oh, yes," she said, "your Daddy had a brother." She looked out of the window again. "I know you never saw your Daddy cry. But *I* did—many a time, through all these years."

90 I asked her. "What happened to his brother? How come nobody's ever talked about him?"

91 This was the first time I ever saw my mother look old.

92 "His brother got killed," she said, "when he was just a little younger than you are now. I knew him. He was a fine boy. He was maybe a little full of the devil, but he didn't mean nobody no harm."

93 Then she stopped and the room was silent, exactly as it had sometimes been on those Sunday afternoons. Mama kept looking out into the streets.

94 "He used to have a job in the mill," she said, "and, like all young folks, he just liked to perform on Saturday nights. Saturday nights, him and your father would drift around to different places, go to dances and things like that, or just sit around with people they knew, and your father's brother would sing, he had a fine voice, and play along with himself on his guitar. Well, this particular Saturday night, him and your father was coming home from some place, and they were both a little drunk and there was a moon that night, it was bright like day. Your father's brother was feeling kind of good, and he was whistling to himself, and he had his guitar slung over his shoulder. They was coming down a hill and beneath them was a road that turned off from the highway. Well, your father's brother, being always kind of frisky, decided to run down this hill, and he did, with that

guitar banging and clanging behind him, and he ran across the road, and he was making water behind a tree. And your father was sort of amused at him and he was still coming down the hill, kind of slow. Then he heard a car motor and that same minute his brother stepped from behind the tree, into the road, in the moonlight. And he started to cross the road. And your father started to run down the hill, he says he don't know why. This car was full of white men. They was all drunk, and when they seen your father's brother they let out a great whoop and holler and they aimed the car straight at him. They was having fun, they just wanted to scare him, the way they do sometimes, you know. But they was drunk. And I guess the boy, being drunk, too, and scared, kind of lost his head. By the time he jumped it was too late. Your father says he heard his brother scream when the car rolled over him, and he heard the wood of that guitar when it give, and he heard them strings go flying, and he heard them white men shouting, and the car kept on a-going and it ain't stopped till this day. And, time your father got down the hill, his brother weren't nothing but blood and pulp."

95   Tears were gleaming on my mother's face. There wasn't anything I could say.

96   "He never mentioned it," she said, "because I never let him mention it before you children. Your Daddy was like a crazy man that night and for many a night thereafter. He says he never in his life seen anything as dark as that road after the lights of that car had gone away. Weren't nothing; weren't nobody on that road, just your Daddy and his brother and that busted guitar. Oh, yes. Your Daddy never did really get right again. Till the day he died he weren't sure but that every white man he saw was the man that killed his brother."

97   She stopped and took out her handkerchief and dried her eyes and looked at me.

98   "I ain't telling you all this," she said, "to make you scared or bitter or to make you hate nobody. I'm telling you this because you got a brother. And the world ain't changed."

99   I guess I didn't want to believe this. I guess she saw this in my face. She turned away from me, toward the window again, searching those streets.

100   "But I praise my Redeemer," she said at last, "that He called your Daddy home before me. I ain't saying it to throw no flowers at myself, but, I declare, it keeps me from feeling too cast down to know I helped your father get safely through this world. Your father always acted like he was the roughest, strongest man on earth. And everybody took him to be like that. But if he hadn't had *me* there—to see his tears!"

101   She was crying again. Still, I couldn't move. I said, "Lord, Lord, Mama, I didn't know it was like that."

102   "Oh, honey," she said, "There's a lot that you don't know. But you are going to find it out." She stood up from the window and came over to me. "You got to hold on to your brother," she said, "and don't let him fall, no matter what it looks like is happening to him and no matter how evil you gets with him. You going to be evil with him many a time. But don't you forget what I told you, you hear?"

103   "I won't forget," I said. "Don't you worry, I won't forget. I won't let nothing happen to Sonny."

104   My mother smiled as though she were amused at something she saw in my face. Then, "You may not be able to stop nothing from happening. But you got to let him know you's *there.*"

105 Two days later I was married, and then I was gone. And I had a lot of things on my mind and I pretty well forgot my promise to Mama until I got shipped home on a special furlough for her funeral.

106 And, after the funeral, with just Sonny and me alone in the empty kitchen, I tried to find out something about him.

107 "What do you want to do?" I asked him.

108 "I'm going to be a musician," he said.

109 For he had graduated, in the time I had been away, from dancing to the juke box to finding out who was playing what, and what they were doing with it, and he had bought himself a set of drums.

110 "You mean, you want to be a drummer?" I somehow had the feeling that being a drummer might be all right for other people but not for my brother Sonny.

111 "I don't think," he said, looking at me very gravely, "that I'll ever be a good drummer. But I think I can play a piano."

112 I frowned. I'd never played the role of the older brother quite so seriously before, had scarcely ever, in fact, *asked* Sonny a damn thing. I sensed myself in the presence of something I didn't really know how to handle, didn't understand. So I made my frown a little deeper as I asked: "What kind of musician do you want to be?"

113 He grinned. "How many kinds do you think there are?"

114 "Be *serious*," I said.

115 He laughed, throwing his head back, and then looked at me. "I *am* serious."

116 "Well, then, for Christ's sake, stop kidding around and answer a serious question. I mean, do you want to be a concert pianist, you want to play classical music and all that, or—or what?" Long before I finished he was laughing again. "For Christ's *sake*, Sonny!"

117 He sobered, but with difficulty. "I'm sorry. But you sound so—*scared!*" and he was off again.

118 "Well, you may think it's funny now, baby, but it's not going to be so funny when you have to make your living at it, let me tell you *that.*" I was furious because I knew he was laughing at me and I didn't know why.

119 "No," he said, very sober now, and afraid, perhaps, that he'd hurt me, "I don't want to be a classical pianist. That isn't what interests me. I mean"—he paused, looking hard at me, as though his eyes would help me to understand, and then gestured helplessly, as though perhaps his hand would help—"I mean, I'll have a lot of studying to do, and I'll have to study *everything,* but, I mean, I want to play *with*—jazz musicians." He stopped. "I want to play jazz," he said.

120 Well, the word had never before sounded as heavy, as real, as it sounded that afternoon in Sonny's mouth. I just looked at him and I was probably frowning a real frown by this time. I simply couldn't see why on earth he'd want to spend his time hanging around nightclubs, clowning around on bandstands, while people pushed each other around a dance floor. It seemed—beneath him, somehow. I had never thought about it before, had never been forced to, but I suppose I had always put jazz musicians in a class with what Daddy called "goodtime people."

121 "Are you *serious?*"

122 "Hell, *yes,* I'm serious."

123 He looked more helpless than ever, and annoyed, and deeply hurt.

124 I suggested, helpfully: "You mean—like Louis Armstrong?"

125   His face closed as though I'd struck him. "No. I'm not talking about none of that old-time, down home crap."

126   "Well, look, Sonny, I'm sorry, don't get mad. I just don't altogether get it, that's all. Name somebody—you know, a jazz musician you admire."

127   "Bird."

128   "Who?"

129   "Bird! Charlie Parker! Don't they teach you nothing in the goddamn army?"

130   I lit a cigarette. I was surprised and then a little amused to discover that I was trembling. "I've been out of touch," I said. "You'll have to be patient with me. Now. Who's this Parker character?"

131   "He's just one of the greatest jazz musicians alive," said Sonny, sullenly, his hands in his pockets, his back to me. "Maybe *the* greatest," he added, bitterly, "that's probably why *you* never heard of him."

132   "All right," I said, "I'm ignorant. I'm sorry. I'll go out and buy all the cat's records right away, all right?"

133   "It don't," said Sonny, with dignity, "make any difference to me. I don't care what you listen to. Don't do me no favors."

134   I was beginning to realize that I'd never seen him so upset before. With another part of my mind I was thinking that this would probably turn out to be one of those things kids go through and that I shouldn't make it seem important by pushing it too hard. Still, I didn't think it would do any harm to ask: "Doesn't all this take a lot of time? Can you make a living at it?"

135   He turned back to me and half leaned, half sat, on the kitchen table. "Everything takes time," he said, "and—well, yes, sure, I can make a living at it. But what I don't seem to be able to make you understand is that it's the only thing I want to do."

136   "Well, Sonny," I said, gently, "you know people can't always do exactly what they *want* to do—"

137   "*No,* I don't know that," said Sonny, surprising me. "I think people *ought* to do what they want to do, what else are they alive for?"

138   "You getting to be a big boy," I said desperately, "it's time you started thinking about your future."

139   "I'm thinking about my future," said Sonny, grimly. "I think about it all the time."

140   I gave up. I decided, if he didn't change his mind, that we could always talk about it later. "In the meantime," I said, "you got to finish school." We had already decided that he'd have to move in with Isabel and her folks. I knew this wasn't the ideal arrangement because Isabel's folks are inclined to be dicty and they hadn't especially wanted Isabel to marry me. But I didn't know what else to do. "And we have to get you fixed up at Isabel's."

141   There was a long silence. He moved from the kitchen table to the window. "That's a terrible idea. You know it yourself."

142   "Do you have a *better* idea?"

143   He just walked up and down the kitchen for a minute. He was as tall as I was. He had started to shave. I suddenly had the feeling that I didn't know him at all.

144   He stopped at the kitchen table and picked up my cigarettes. Looking at me with a kind of mocking, amused defiance, he put one between his lips. "You mind?"

145   "You smoking already?"

146   He lit the cigarette and nodded, watching me through the smoke. "I just wanted to see if I'd have the courage to smoke in front of you." He grinned and blew a great cloud of smoke to the ceiling. "It was easy." He looked at my face. "Come on, now. I bet you was smoking at my age, tell the truth."

147   I didn't say anything but the truth was on my face, and he laughed. But now there was something very strained in his laugh. "Sure. And I bet that ain't all you was doing."

148   He was frightening me a little. "Cut the crap," I said. "We already decided that you was going to go and live at Isabel's. Now what's got into you all of a sudden?"

149   "*You* decided it," he pointed out. "*I* didn't decide nothing." He stopped in front of me, leaning against the stove, arms loosely folded. "Look, brother. I don't want to stay in Harlem no more, I really don't." He was very earnest. He looked at me, then over toward the kitchen window. There was something in his eyes I'd never seen before, some thoughtfulness, some worry all his own. He rubbed the muscle of one arm. "It's time I was getting out of here."

150   "Where do you want to *go*, Sonny?"

151   "I want to join the army. Or the navy, I don't care. If I say I'm old enough, they'll believe me."

152   Then I got mad. It was because I was so scared. "You must be crazy. You goddamn fool, what the hell do you want to go and join the *army* for?"

153   "I just told you. To get out of Harlem."

154   "Sonny, you haven't even finished *school*. And if you really want to be a musician, how do you expect to study if you're in the *army?*"

155   He looked at me, trapped and in anguish. "There's ways. I might be able to work out some kind of deal. Anyway, I'll have the G.I. Bill when I come out."

156   "*If* you come out." We stared at each other. "Sonny, please. Be reasonable. I know the setup is far from perfect. But we got to do the best we can."

157   "I ain't learning nothing in school," he said. "Even when I go." He turned away from me and opened the window and threw his cigarette out into the narrow alley. I watched his back. "At least, I ain't learning nothing you'd want me to learn." He slammed the window so hard I thought the glass would fly out, and turned back to me. "And I'm sick of the stink of these garbage cans!"

158   "Sonny," I said, "I know how you feel. But if you don't finish school now, you're going to be sorry later that you didn't." I grabbed him by the shoulders. "And you only got another year. It ain't so bad. And I'll come back and I swear I'll help you do *whatever* you want to do. Just try to put up with it till I come back. Will you please do that? For me?"

159   He didn't answer and he wouldn't look at me.

160   "Sonny. You hear me?"

161   He pulled away. "I hear you. But you never hear anything *I* say."

162   I didn't know what to say to that. He looked out of the window and then back at me. "OK," he said, and sighed. "I'll try."

163   Then I said, trying to cheer him up a little, "They got a piano at Isabel's. You can practice on it."

164   And as a matter of fact, it did cheer him up for a minute. "That's right," he said to himself. "I forgot that." His face relaxed a little. But the worry, the thought-

fulness, played on it still, the way shadows play on a face which is staring into the fire.

165 But I thought I'd never hear the end of that piano. At first, Isabel would write me, saying how nice it was that Sonny was so serious about his music and how, as soon as he came in from school, or wherever he had been when he was supposed to be at school, he went straight to that piano and stayed there until suppertime. And, after supper, he went back to that piano and stayed there until everybody went to bed. He was at the piano all day Saturday and all day Sunday. Then he bought a record player and started playing records. He'd play one record over and over again, all day long sometimes, and he'd improvise along with it on the piano. Or he'd play one section of the record, one chord, one change, one progression, then he'd do it on the piano. Then back to the record. Then back to the piano.

166 Well, I really don't know how they stood it. Isabel finally confessed that it wasn't like living with a person at all, it was like living with sound. And the sound didn't make any sense to her, didn't make any sense to any of them—naturally. They began, in a way, to be afflicted by this presence that was living in their home. It was as though Sonny were some sort of god, or monster. He moved in an atmosphere which wasn't like theirs at all. They fed him and he ate, he washed himself, he walked in and out of their door; he certainly wasn't nasty or unpleasant or rude, Sonny isn't any of those things; but it was as though he were all wrapped up in some cloud, some fire, some vision all his own; and there wasn't any way to reach him.

167 At the same time, he wasn't really a man yet, he was still a child, and they had to watch out for him in all kinds of ways. They certainly couldn't throw him out. Neither did they dare to make a great scene about that piano because even they dimly sensed, as I sensed, from so many thousands of miles away, that Sonny was at that piano playing for his life.   ·

168 But he hadn't been going to school. One day a letter came from the school board and Isabel's mother got it—there had, apparently, been other letters but Sonny had torn them up. This day, when Sonny came in, Isabel's mother showed him the letter and asked where he'd been spending his time. And she finally got it out of him that he'd been down in Greenwich Village, with musicians and other characters, in a white girl's apartment. And this scared her and she started to scream at him and what came up, once she began—though she denies it to this day—was what sacrifices they were making to give Sonny a decent home and how little he appreciated it.

169 Sonny didn't play the piano that day. By evening, Isabel's mother had calmed down but then there was the old man to deal with, and Isabel herself. Isabel says she did her best to be calm but she broke down and started crying. She says she just watched Sonny's face. She could tell, by watching him, what was happening with him. And what was happening was that they penetrated his cloud, they had reached him. Even if their fingers had been a thousand times more gentle than human fingers ever are, he could hardly help feeling that they had stripped him naked and were spitting on that nakedness. For he also had to see that his presence, that music, which was life or death to him, had been torture for them and that they had endured it, not at all for his sake, but only for mine. And Sonny

couldn't take that. He can take it a little better today than he could then but he's still not very good at it and, frankly, I don't know anybody who is.

170 The silence of the next few days must have been louder than the sound of all the music ever played since time began. One morning, before she went to work, Isabel was in his room for something and she suddenly realized that all of his records were gone. And she knew for certain that he was gone. And he was. He went as far as the navy would carry him. He finally sent me a postcard from some place in Greece and that was the first I knew that Sonny was still alive. I didn't see him any more until we were both back in New York and the war had long been over.

171 He was a man by then, of course, but I wasn't willing to see it. He came by the house from time to time, but we fought almost every time we met. I didn't like the way he carried himself, loose and dreamlike all the time, and I didn't like his friends, and his music seemed to be merely an excuse for the life he led. It sounded just that weird and disordered.

172 Then we had a fight, a pretty awful fight, and I didn't see him for months. By and by I looked him up, where he was living, in a furnished room in the Village, and I tried to make it up. But there were lots of other people in the room and Sonny just lay on his bed, and he wouldn't come downstairs with me, and he treated these other people as though they were his family and I weren't. So I got mad and then he got mad, and then I told him that he might just as well be dead as live the way he was living. Then he stood up and he told me not to worry about him any more in life, that he *was* dead as far as I was concerned. Then he pushed me to the door and the other people looked on as though nothing were happening, and he slammed the door behind me. I stood in the hallway, staring at the door. I heard somebody laugh in the room and then the tears came to my eyes. I started down the steps, whistling to keep from crying. I kept whistling to myself, *You going to need me, baby, one of these cold, rainy days.*

173 I read about Sonny's trouble in the spring. Little Grace died in the fall. She was a beautiful little girl. But she only lived a little over two years. She died of polio and she suffered. She had a slight fever for a couple of days, but it didn't seem like anything and we just kept her in bed. And we would certainly have called the doctor, but the fever dropped, she seemed to be all right. So we thought it had just been a cold. Then, one day, she was up, playing, Isabel was in the kitchen fixing lunch for the two boys when they'd come in from school, and she heard Grace fall down in the living room. When you have a lot of children you don't always start running when one of them falls, unless they start screaming or something. And, this time, Grace was quiet. Yet, Isabel says that when she heard that *thump* and then that silence, something happened in her to make her afraid. And she ran to the living room and there was little Grace on the floor, all twisted up, and the reason she hadn't screamed was that she couldn't get her breath. And when she did scream, it was the worst sound, Isabel says, that she'd ever heard in all her life, and she still hears it sometimes in her dreams. Isabel will sometimes wake me up with a low, moaning, strangled sound and I have to be quick to awaken her and hold her to me and where Isabel is weeping against me seems a mortal wound.

174   I think I may have written Sonny the very day that little Grace was buried. I was sitting in the living room in the dark, by myself, and I suddenly thought of Sonny. My trouble made his real.

175   One Saturday afternoon, when Sonny had been living with us, or, anyway, been in our house, for nearly two weeks, I found myself wandering aimlessly about the living room, drinking from a can of beer, and trying to work up the courage to search Sonny's room. He was out, he was usually out whenever I was home, and Isabel had taken the children to see their grandparents. Suddenly I was standing still in front of the living room window, watching Seventh Avenue. The idea of searching Sonny's room made me still. I scarcely dared to admit to myself what I'd be searching for. I didn't know what I'd do if I found it. Or if I didn't.

176   On the sidewalk across from me, near the entrance to a barbecue joint, some people were holding an old-fashioned revival meeting. The barbecue cook, wearing a dirty white apron, his conked hair reddish and metallic in the pale sun, and a cigarette between his lips, stood in the doorway, watching them. Kids and older people paused in their errands and stood there, along with some older men and a couple of very tough-looking women who watched everything that happened on the avenue, as though they owned it, or were maybe owned by it. Well, they were watching this, too. The revival was being carried on by three sisters in black, and a brother. All they had were their voices and their Bibles and a tambourine. The brother was testifying and while he testified two of the sisters stood together, seeming to say, amen, and the third sister walked around with the tambourine outstretched and a couple of people dropped coins into it. Then the brother's testimony ended and the sister who had been taking up the collection dumped the coins into her palm and transferred them to the pocket of her long black robe. Then she raised both hands, striking the tambourine against the air, and then against one hand, and she started to sing. And the two other sisters and the brother joined in.

177   It was strange, suddenly, to watch, though I had been seeing these street meetings all my life. So, of course, had everybody else down there. Yet, they paused and watched and listened and I stood still at the window. " *'Tis the old ship of Zion,"* they sang, and the sister with the tambourine kept a steady, jangling beat, *"it has rescued many a thousand!"* Not a soul under the sound of their voices was hearing this song for the first time, not one of them had been rescued. Nor had they seen much in the way of rescue work being done around them. Neither did they especially believe in the holiness of the three sisters and the brother, they knew too much about them, knew where they lived, and how. The woman with the tambourine, whose voice dominated the air, whose face was bright with joy, was divided by very little from the woman who stood watching her, a cigarette between her heavy, chapped lips, her hair a cuckoo's nest, her face scarred and swollen from many beatings, and her black eyes glittering like coal. Perhaps they both knew this, which was why, when, as rarely, they addressed each other, they addressed each other as Sister. As the singing filled the air the watching, listening faces underwent a change, the eyes focusing on something within; the music seemed to soothe a poison out of them; and time seemed, nearly, to fall away from the sullen, belligerent, battered faces, as though they were fleeing back to their first condition, while dreaming of their last. The barbecue cook half shook his head and smiled, and dropped his cigarette and disappeared into his joint. A man fumbled in his pockets for change and stood holding it in his hand impatiently, as though he had just remembered a pressing appointment further up the avenue. He looked furious. Then I saw Sonny, standing on the edge of the crowd. He was carrying a wide, flat notebook with a green cover, and it made him look, from where I was standing, almost like a schoolboy. The coppery sun brought out the copper in his skin, he was very faintly smiling, standing very still. Then the singing stopped, the tambourine turned into a collection plate again. The furious man dropped in his coins and vanished, so did a couple of the women, and Sonny dropped some change in the plate, looking directly at the woman with a little smile. He started across the avenue, toward the house. He has a slow, loping walk, something like the way Harlem hipsters walk, only he's imposed on this his own half-beat. I had never really noticed it before.

178   I stayed at the window, both relieved and apprehensive. As Sonny disappeared from my sight, they began singing again. And they were still singing when his key turned in the lock.

179   "Hey," he said.

180   "Hey, yourself. You want some beer?"

181   "No. Well, maybe." But he came up to the window and stood beside me, looking out. "What a warm voice," he said.

182   They were singing *If I could only hear my mother pray again!*

183   "Yes," I said, "and she can sure beat that tambourine."

184   "But what a terrible song," he said, and laughed. He dropped his notebook on the sofa and disappeared into the kitchen. "Where's Isabel and the kids?"

185   "I think they went to see their grandparents. You hungry?"

186   "No." He came back into the living room with his can of beer. "You want to come some place with me tonight?"

187   I sensed, I don't know how, that I couldn't possibly say no. "Sure. Where?"

188   He sat down on the sofa and picked up his notebook and started leafing through it. "I'm going to sit in with some fellows in a joint in the Village."

189   "You mean, you're going to play, tonight?"

190   "That's right." He took a swallow of his beer and moved back to the window. He gave me a sidelong look. "If you can stand it."

191   "I'll try," I said.

192   He smiled to himself and we both watched as the meeting across the way broke up. The three sisters and the brother, heads bowed, were singing *God be with you till we meet again.* The faces around them were very quiet. Then the song ended. The small crowd dispersed. We watched the three women and the lone man walk slowly up the avenue.

193   "When she was singing before," said Sonny, abruptly, "her voice reminded me for a minute of what heroin feels like sometimes—when it's in your veins. It makes you feel sort of warm and cool at the same time. And distant. And—and sure." He sipped his beer, very deliberately not looking at me. I watched his face. "It makes you feel—in control. Sometimes you've got to have that feeling."

194   "Do you?" I sat down slowly in the easy chair.

195   "Sometimes." He went to the sofa and picked up his notebook again. "Some people do."

196   "In order," I asked, "to play?" And my voice was very ugly, full of contempt and anger.

197   "Well"—he looked at me with great, troubled eyes, as though, in fact, he hoped his eyes would tell me things he could never otherwise say—"they *think* so. And *if* they think so—!"

198   "And what do *you* think?" I asked.

199   He sat on the sofa and put his can of beer on the floor. "I don't know," he said, and I couldn't be sure if he were answering my question or pursuing his thoughts. His face didn't tell me. "It's not so much to *play*. It's to *stand* it, to be able to make it at all. On any level." He frowned and smiled: "In order to keep from shaking to pieces."

200   "But these friends of yours," I said, "they seem to shake themselves to pieces pretty goddamn fast."

201   "Maybe." He played with the notebook. And something told me that I should curb my tongue, that Sonny was doing his best to talk, that I should listen. "But of course you only know the ones that've gone to pieces. Some don't—or at least they haven't *yet* and that's just about all *any* of us can say." He paused. "And then there are some who just live, really, in hell, and they know it and they see what's happening and they go right on. I don't know." He sighed, dropped the notebook, folded his arms. "Some guys, you can tell from the way they play, they on something *all* the time. And you can see that, well, it makes something real for them. But of course," he picked up his beer from the floor and sipped it and put the can down again, "they *want* to, too, you've got to see that. Even some of them that say they don't—*some*, not all."

202   "And what about you?" I asked—I couldn't help it. "What about you? Do *you* want to?"

203   He stood up and walked to the window and remained silent for a long time. Then he sighed. "Me," he said. Then: "While I was downstairs before, on my way here, listening to that woman sing, it struck me all of a sudden how much suffering she must have had to go through—to sing like that. It's *repulsive* to think you have to suffer that much."

204   I said: "But there's no way not to suffer—is there, Sonny?"

205   "I believe not," he said and smiled, "but that's never stopped anyone from trying." He looked at me. "Has it?" I realized, with this mocking look, that there stood between us, forever, beyond the power of time or forgiveness, the fact that I had held silence—so long!—when he had needed human speech to help him. He turned back to the window. "No, there's no way not to suffer. But you try all kinds of ways to keep from drowning in it, to keep on top of it, and to make it seem—well, like *you*. Like you did something, all right, and now you're suffering for it. You know?" I said nothing. "Well you know," he said, impatiently, "Why *do* people suffer? Maybe it's better to do something to give it a reason, *any* reason."

206   "But we just agreed," I said, "that there's no way not to suffer. Isn't it better, then, just to—take it?"

207   "But nobody just takes it," Sonny cried, "that's what I'm telling you! *Everybody* tries not to. You're just hung up on the *way* some people try—it's not *your* way!"

208   The hair on my face began to itch, my face felt wet. "That's not true," I said, "that's not true. I don't give a damn what other people do, I don't even care how they suffer. I just care how *you* suffer." And he looked at me. "Please believe me," I said, "I don't want to see you—die—trying not to suffer."

209   "I won't," he said, flatly, "die trying not to suffer. At least, not any faster than anybody else."

210   "But there's no need," I said, trying to laugh, "is there? in killing yourself."

211   I wanted to say more, but I couldn't. I wanted to talk about will power and how life could be—well, beautiful. I wanted to say that it was all within; but was it? or, rather, wasn't that exactly the trouble? And I wanted to promise that I would never fail him again. But it would all have sounded—empty words and lies.

212   So I made the promise to myself and prayed that I would keep it.

213   "It's terrible sometimes, inside," he said, "that's what's the trouble. You walk these streets, black and funky and cold, and there's not really a living ass to talk to, and there's nothing shaking, and there's no way of getting it out—that storm inside. You can't talk it and you can't make love with it, and when you finally try to get with it and play it, you realize *nobody's* listening. So *you've* got to listen. You got to find a way to listen."

214   And then he walked away from the window and sat on the sofa again, as though all the wind had suddenly been knocked out of him. "Sometimes you'll do *anything* to play, even cut your mother's throat." He laughed and looked at me. "Or your brother's." Then he sobered. "Or your own." Then: "Don't worry. I'm all right now and I think I'll *be* all right. But I can't forget—where I've been. I don't mean just the physical place I've been, I mean where I've *been*. And *what* I've been."

215   "What have you been, Sonny?" I asked.

216   He smiled—but sat sideways on the sofa, his elbow resting on the back, his fingers playing with his mouth and chin, not looking at me. "I've been something I didn't recognize, didn't know I could be. Didn't know anybody could be." He stopped, looking inward, looking helplessly young, looking old. "I'm not talking about it now because I feel *guilty* or anything like that—maybe it would be better if I did, I don't know. Anyway, I can't really talk about it. Not to you, not to anybody," and now he turned and faced me. "Sometimes, you know, and it was actually when I was most *out* of the world, I felt that I was in it, that I was *with* it, really, and I could play or I didn't really have to *play*, it just came out of me, it was there. And I don't know how I played, thinking about it now, but I know I did awful things, those times, sometimes, to people. Or it wasn't that I *did* anything to them—it was that they weren't real." He picked up the beer can; it was empty; he rolled it between his palms: "And other times—well, I needed a fix, I needed to find a place to lean, I needed to clear a space to *listen*—and I couldn't find it, and I—went crazy, I did terrible things to *me*, I was terrible *for* me." He began pressing the beer can between his hands, I watched the metal begin to give. It glittered, as he played with it, like a knife, and I was afraid he would cut himself, but I said nothing. "Oh well. I can never tell you. I was all by myself at the bottom of something, stinking and sweating and crying and shaking, and I smelled it, you know? *my* stink, and I thought I'd die if I couldn't get away from it and yet, all the same, I knew that everything I was doing was just locking me in

with it. And I didn't know," he paused, still flattening the beer can, "I didn't know, I still *don't* know, something kept telling me that maybe it was good to smell your own stink, but I didn't think that *that* was what I'd been trying to do—and—who can stand it?" and he abruptly dropped the ruined beer can, looking at me with a small, still smile, and then rose, walking to the window as though it were the lodestone rock. I watched his face, he watched the avenue. "I couldn't tell you when Mama died—but the reason I wanted to leave Harlem so bad was to get away from drugs. And then, when I ran away, that's what I was running from— really. When I came back, nothing had changed, *I* hadn't changed, I was just— older." And he stopped, drumming with his fingers on the windowpane. The sun had vanished, soon darkness would fall. I watched his face. "It can come again," he said, almost as though speaking to himself. Then he turned to me. "It can come again," he repeated. "I just want you to know that."

217   "All right," I said, at last. "So it can come again. All right."

218   He smiled, but the smile was sorrowful. "I had to try to tell you," he said.

219   "Yes," I said. "I understand that."

220   "You're my brother," he said, looking straight at me, and not smiling at all.

221   "Yes," I repeated, "yes. I understand that."

222   He turned back to the window, looking out. "All that hatred down there," he said, "all that hatred and misery and love. It's a wonder it doesn't blow the avenue apart."

223   We went to the only nightclub on a short, dark street, downtown. We squeezed through the narrow, chattering, jam-packed bar to the entrance of the big room, where the bandstand was. And we stood there for a moment, for the lights were very dim in this room and we couldn't see. Then, "Hello, boy," said a voice and an enormous black man, much older than Sonny or myself, erupted out of all that atmospheric lighting and put an arm around Sonny's shoulder. "I been sitting right here," he said, "waiting for you."

224   He had a big voice, too, and heads in the darkness turned toward us.

225   Sonny grinned and pulled a little away, and said, "Creole, this is my brother. I told you about him."

226   Creole shook my hand. "I'm glad to meet you, son," he said, and it was clear that he was glad to meet me *there* for Sonny's sake. And he smiled, "You got a real musician in *your* family," and he took his arm from Sonny's shoulder and slapped him, lightly, affectionately, with the back of his hand.

227   "Well. Now I've heard it all," said a voice behind us. This was another musician, and a friend of Sonny's, a coal-black, cheerful-looking man, built close to the ground. He immediately began confiding to me, at the top of his lungs, the most terrible things about Sonny, his teeth gleaming like a lighthouse and his laugh coming up out of him like the beginning of an earthquake. And it turned out that everyone at the bar knew Sonny, or almost everyone; some were musicians, working there, or nearby, or not working, some were simply hangers-on, and some were there to hear Sonny play. I was introduced to all of them and they were all very polite to me. Yet, it was clear that, for them, I was only Sonny's brother. Here, I was in Sonny's world. Or, rather: his kingdom. Here, it was not even a question that his veins bore royal blood.

228   They were going to play soon and Creole installed me, by myself, at a table in a dark corner. Then I watched them, Creole, and the little black man, and Sonny, and the others, while they horsed around, standing just below the bandstand. The light from the bandstand spilled just a little short of them and, watching them laughing and gesturing and moving about, I had the feeling that they, nevertheless, were being most careful not to step into that circle of light too suddenly: that if they moved into the light too suddenly, without thinking, they would perish in flame. Then, while I watched, one of them, the small, black man, moved into the light and crossed the bandstand and started fooling around with his drums. Then—being funny and being, also, extremely ceremonious—Creole took Sonny by the arm and led him to the piano. A woman's voice called Sonny's name and a few hands started clapping. And Sonny, also being funny and being ceremonious, and so touched, I think, that he could have cried, but neither hiding it nor showing it, riding it like a man, grinned, and put both hands to his heart and bowed from the waist.

229   Creole then went to the bass fiddle and a lean, very bright-skinned brown man jumped up on the bandstand and picked up his horn. So there they were, and the atmosphere on the bandstand and in the room began to change and tighten. Someone stepped up to the microphone and announced them. Then there were all kinds of murmurs. Some people at the bar shushed others. The waitress ran around, frantically getting in the last orders, guys and chicks got closer to each other, and the lights on the bandstand, on the quartet, turned to a kind of indigo. Then they all looked different there. Creole looked about him for the last time, as though he were making certain that all his chickens were in the coop, and then he—jumped and struck the fiddle. And there they were.

230   All I know about music is that not many people ever really hear it. And even then, on the rare occasions when something opens within, and the music enters, what we mainly hear, or hear corroborated, are personal, private, vanishing evocations. But the man who creates the music is hearing something else, is dealing with the roar rising from the void and imposing order on it as it hits the air. What is evoked in him, then, is of another order, more terrible because it has no words, and triumphant, too, for that same reason. And his triumph, when he triumphs, is ours. I just watched Sonny's face. His face was troubled, he was working hard, but he wasn't with it. And I had the feeling that, in a way, everyone on the bandstand was waiting for him, both waiting for him and pushing him along. But as I began to watch Creole, I realized that it was Creole who held them all back. He had them on a short rein. Up there, keeping the beat with his whole body, wailing on the fiddle, with his eyes half closed, he was listening to everything, but he was listening to Sonny. He was having a dialogue with Sonny. He wanted Sonny to leave the shoreline and strike out for the deep water. He was Sonny's witness that deep water and drowning were not the same thing—he had been there, and he knew. And he wanted Sonny to know. He was waiting for Sonny to do the things on the keys which would let Creole know that Sonny was in the water.

231   And, while Creole listened, Sonny moved, deep within, exactly like someone in torment. I had never before thought of how awful the relationship must be between the musician and his instrument. He has to fill it, this instrument, with the breath of life, his own. He has to make it do what he wants it to do. And a piano

is just a piano. It's made out of so much wood and wires and little hammers and big ones, and ivory. While there's only so much you can do with it, the only way to find this out is to try; to try and make it do everything.

232   And Sonny hadn't been near a piano for over a year. And he wasn't on much better terms with his life, not the life that stretched before him now. He and the piano stammered, started one way, got scared, stopped; started another way, panicked, marked time, started again; then seemed to have found a direction, panicked again, got stuck. And the face I saw on Sonny I'd never seen before. Everything had been burned out of it, and, at the same time, things usually hidden were being burned in, by the fire and fury of the battle which was occurring in him up there.

233   Yet, watching Creole's face as they neared the end of the first set, I had the feeling that something had happened, something I hadn't heard. Then they finished, there was scattered applause, and then, without an instant's warning, Creole started into something else, it was almost sardonic, it was *Am I Blue*. And, as though he commanded, Sonny began to play. Something began to happen. And Creole let out the reins. The dry, low, black man said something awful on the drums, Creole answered, and the drums talked back. Then the horn insisted, sweet and high, slightly detached perhaps, and Creole listened, commenting now and then, dry, and driving, beautiful and calm and old. Then they all came together again, and Sonny was part of the family again. I could tell this from his face. He seemed to have found, right there beneath his fingers, a damn brand-new piano. It seemed that he couldn't get over it. Then, for a while, just being happy with Sonny, they seemed to be agreeing with him that brand-new pianos certainly were a gas.

234   Then Creole stepped forward to remind them that what they were playing was the blues. He hit something in all of them, he hit something in me, myself, and the music tightened and deepened, apprehension began to beat the air. Creole began to tell us what the blues were all about. They were not about anything very new. He and his boys up there were keeping it new, at the risk of ruin, destruction, madness, and death, in order to find new ways to make us listen. For, while the tale of how we suffer, and how we are delighted, and how we may triumph is never new, it always must be heard. There isn't any other tale to tell, it's the only light we've got in all this darkness.

235   And this tale, according to that face, that body, those strong hands on those strings, has another aspect in every country, and a new depth in every generation. Listen, Creole seemed to be saying, listen. Now these are Sonny's blues. He made the little black man on the drums know it, and the bright, brown man on the horn. Creole wasn't trying any longer to get Sonny in the water. He was wishing him Godspeed. Then he stepped back, very slowly, filling the air with the immense suggestion that Sonny speak for himself.

236   Then they all gathered around Sonny and Sonny played. Every now and again one of them seemed to say, amen. Sonny's fingers filled the air with life, his life. But that life contained so many others. And Sonny went all the way back, he really began with the spare, flat statement of the opening phrase of the song. Then he began to make it his. It was very beautiful because it wasn't hurried and it was no longer a lament. I seemed to hear with what burning he had made it his, with what burning we had yet to make it ours, how we could cease lamenting. Freedom lurked around us and I understood, at last, that he could help us to be free if we would listen, that he would never be free until we did. Yet, there was no battle in his face now. I heard what he had gone through, and would continue to go through until he came to rest in earth. He had made it his: that long line, of which we knew only Mama and Daddy. And he was giving it back, as everything must be given back, so that, passing through death, it can live forever. I saw my mother's face again, and felt, for the first time, how the stones of the road she had walked on must have bruised her feet. I saw the moonlit road where my father's brother died. And it brought something else back to me, and carried me past it, I saw my little girl again and felt Isabel's tears again, and I felt my own tears begin to rise. And I was yet aware that this was only a moment, that the world waited outside, as hungry as a tiger, and that trouble stretched above us, longer than the sky.

237   Then it was over. Creole and Sonny let out their breath, both soaking wet, and grinning. There was a lot of applause and some of it was real. In the dark, the girl came by and I asked her to take drinks to the bandstand. There was a long pause, while they talked up there in the indigo light and after awhile I saw the girl put a Scotch and milk on top of the piano for Sonny. He didn't seem to notice it, but just before they started playing again, he sipped from it and looked toward me, and nodded. Then he put it back on top of the piano. For me, then, as they began to play again, it glowed and shook above my brother's head like the very cup of trembling.

QUESTIONS

Experience

· Describe your experience of reading Baldwin's story. Which aspects of the story did you find confusing—at least at first? Where did the story come together for you? Where did you begin to feel you understood what Baldwin was saying or suggesting?

Interpretation

· What kind of relationship do the brothers have? Why? To what extent does the older brother feel responsible for the younger one? Why? Why does Baldwin include a return visit to their old neighborhood? What do we learn about the brothers' past from this visit? What more general point is implied?

Evaluation

· To what extent does Baldwin dramatize the contrasting values espoused by each of the brothers? What details embody or illustrate their contrasting perspectives?

WRITING

Exploring

· Write an essay in which you explore your own relationship with a brother or sister. Trace the development of your relationship over time, highlighting significant incidents that contributed to it. You may wish to employ dialogue and description along with explanation and analysis of your relationship.

Interpreting

· Use one or more of the following focuses to analyze Baldwin's story on the way to providing an interpretation of its meaning.

1. The imagery of darkness and entrapment
2. The story of the brothers' uncle
3. The meanings of Sonny's "blues"
4. The extended passage near the end describing the musical performance of Creole, Sonny, and the others.

Evaluating

· Consider what the story implies about one or more of the following:

1. work
2. music
3. religion
4. drugs.

· Explain whose cultural values the story seems to endorse and how and why it seems to support them.

LANGSTON HUGHES
(1902–1967)

Trumpet Player

Langston Hughes was born in Joplin, Missouri. As a young man he worked as a merchant seaman and traveled widely, living for a time in Paris and Rome. He published his first volume of poems, The Weary Blues *(1926), three years before he graduated from Lincoln University, where he had won a scholarship. A major figure of the Harlem Renaissance, Hughes wrote prolifically, producing fiction and folklore, drama, song lyrics, essays, memoirs, and children's books as well as many poems. His work in all the genres in which he wrote celebrates the lives of the urban poor. In addition, many of his poems display a love of music, particularly blues and jazz.*

In "Trumpet Player" Hughes depicts a musician in the act of performing. Through carefully chosen words he conveys a sense not only of the music being played—the blues—but of the effect the music has on the musician performing it. Hughes's poem portrays a musician lost in his art and experiencing its healing powers.

The Negro
With the trumpet at his lips
Has dark moons of weariness
Beneath his eyes
5 Where the smoldering memory
Of slave ships
Blazed to the crack of whips
About his thighs.

The Negro
10 With the trumpet at his lips
Has a head of vibrant hair
Tamed down,
Patent-leathered now
Until it gleams
15 Like jet—
Were jet a crown.

The music
From the trumpet at his lips
Is honey
20 Mixed with liquid fire.
The rhythm
From the trumpet at his lips

Is ecstasy
Distilled from old desire—

25   Desire
That is longing for the moon
Where the moonlight's but a spotlight
In his eyes,
Desire
30   That is longing for the sea
Where the sea's a bar-glass
Sucker size.

The Negro
With the trumpet at his lips
35   Whose jacket
Has a *fine* one-button roll,
Does not know
Upon what riff the music slips
Its hypodermic needle
40   To his soul—

But softly
As the tune comes from his throat
Trouble
Mellows to a golden note.

QUESTIONS

Experience

· To what extent have you had an experience either making music or listening to it when your troubles seemed to melt away? Do you think music has the power to help us forget our problems? Why, or why not?

Interpretation

· What do you think the poet expresses with the following phrases:

1. The music / . . . Is honey / Mixed with liquid fire.
2. The rhythm / . . . Is ecstasy / Distilled from old desire.
3. Its hypodermic needle / To his soul.

Evaluation

· To what extent do you find Hughes's poem successful in conveying the spirit of the music and the feelings of the trumpet player? Why?

WRITING

Exploring

· Write an essay about your experience playing music or listening to it when you were caught up so thoroughly in the experience that you lost a sense of where you were. If you have never had this experience, describe another musical experience that made a strong impression on you.

Interpreting

· Analyze "Trumpet Player," paying especially close attention to language that describes the performer. Discuss the poem's central idea and the image of the performer it presents.

Evaluating

· Consider whether the poem might or might not be overstating the power of music or overvaluing its effects on performer or listener.

THE ARTS—CONSIDERATIONS FOR THINKING AND WRITING

1. A number of selections in this chapter present a writer's view of an artist. Compare the way two of the following characterize the artists written about: Joan Didion on Georgia O'Keeffe, Mary Gordon on Mary Cassatt, Mark Strand on Edward Hopper.

2. Compare the images of musicians presented in Baldwin's "Sonny's Blues," Hughes's "Trumpet Player," Ellison's "Living with Music," and Zinsser's "Shanghai." Consider also the way each writer describes the powers and pleasures of music.

3. Compare the way John Berger and James Agee use language to help readers see their subjects—Kertész's photographs and Keaton's film acting, respectively. Refer to specific passages and to particular words and phrases that best help you visualize what each writer describes.

4. Discuss the uses to which Elizabeth MacDonald puts the artists Ingres and di Chirico in her essay. Then compare her use of those artists with the uses to which Hopper's paintings are put in Mark Strand's "Crossing the Tracks to Hopper's World" or Cassatt's paintings are put by Mary Gordon in her essay on the painter.

5. Discuss the cultural and social values embodied in any two works in this section. Likely candidates include the essays by Didion, Gordon, Zinsser, MacDonald, and Baldwin. Be sure to identify specific elements in the art or music discussed in the essay and to show how those elements of the art or music reflect particular social or cultural values.

6. Discuss how ideas about music or one of the other arts are changing. Consider what new kinds of music or art have become prominent or marginal in recent years and what that style of art or music suggests about contemporary social or cultural values.

7. Try your hand at a piece of creative writing—a short story, poem, song, or a scene for a play or a film. Use your creative work to express an attitude, idea, or perspective on something you feel strongly about.

8. Do some research on one of the artists mentioned in this chapter. Write a research essay focusing on a specific question about that artist's work. For example, you might consider the image of family in the paintings of Mary Cassatt or the image of nature presented in the paintings of Georgia O'Keeffe.

SEVEN

Nature

SHARMAN APT RUSSELL
  The Mimbres

EDWARD HOAGLAND
  The Courage of Turtles

LEWIS THOMAS
  The World's Biggest Membrane

ANNIE DILLARD
  Living Like Weasels

GEORGE ORWELL
  Some Thoughts on the Common Toad

LESLIE MARMON SILKO
  Landscape, History, and the Pueblo Imagination

LOREN EISELEY
  The Flow of the River

MAILE MELOY
  Horse-Love

TESS GALLAGHER
  The Lover of Horses

ELIZABETH BISHOP
  The Fish

All people need to find their place in the natural world. For some that has meant learning to cope with hurricanes, tornadoes, earthquakes, and other natural disasters. For others it has meant learning to appreciate the natural resources around them. For still others it has meant leaving the urban concrete village (at least on occasion) for the open spaces, where the air is clear, the starlight bright, and plant and animal life abundant. Learning to live within the natural world has also come more and more to mean learning not only how to appreciate that world but also how to preserve it.

The writers in this chapter touch on a number of these issues and others, as well. These writers help us see aspects of the natural world in ways we may not have seen them before. Annie Dillard's "Living Like Weasels" and Edward Hoagland's "The Courage of Turtles," along with Elizabeth Bishop's poem "The Fish," can give us a heightened regard for animals we may not have thought about very much before. Sharman Apt Russell's account of the Mimbres River shows those among us who do not live near a river just how powerful a river can be. Unlike Russell's writing about the Mimbres River, which emphasizes its strength and beauty, Loren Eiseley, in "The Flow of the River," writes about the magic and mystery of water, including the ability of water to transport us beyond ourselves into imaginative, even mystical realms.

Many of these writers encourage us, with their love and respect for nature, to develop more fully these qualities in our own relationship with the natural world. For example, Leslie Marmon Silko's essay "Landscape, History, and the Pueblo Imagination" conveys a reverential attitude toward the land, a religious perspective that considers land as an element of nature to commune with, understand, and appreciate for what it is in and of itself.

George Orwell's "Some Thoughts on the Common Toad" is less about toads than about the necessity of enjoying nature and being in tune with it. Orwell argues that all writing and all living need not have an agenda—social, political, or otherwise—and that writing about nature and living within it, irrespective of political considerations, is necessary for sanity and survival.

Two writers share their love of horses—Tess Gallagher in her short story "The Lover of Horses" and Maile Meloy in her essay "Horse-Love." Both pieces celebrate the beauty and temperament of these magnificent creatures, conveying each writer's enthusiasm along with her knowledge.

And in "The World's Biggest Membrane," Lewis Thomas invites us to think of the earth as a giant living cell with the atmosphere as its outer membrane. Thomas thinks of the world as a single unified living organism, a metaphor that is both surprising and illuminating, and one that shakes up conventional ways of thinking.

SHARMAN APT RUSSELL
(b. 1945)

The Mimbres

Sharman Apt Russell teaches writing at Western New Mexico University, making her home with her husband and children in Mimbres, New Mexico. She has published in such journals as The Missouri Review, The Threepenny Review, *and* Quarterly West. *A number of her essays are collected in her book* Songs of the Fluteplayer *(1991), from which the following essay has been taken.*

In "The Mimbres," Russell describes the experiences she and her husband shared in moving to land they bought on the Mimbres River in southwestern New Mexico. Her essay conveys clearly and simply what it's like to live through a river's raging floods. Sandwiched between her stories of living with her husband along the Mimbres, including their building an adobe house with their own hands, is a history of the region and an account of its culture. One of the most striking features of Russell's essay is the way she blends these two intentions easily and gracefully.

1   Three years before my husband and I bought land on the Mimbres River, an unusual amount of winter snow and spring rain prompted what locals authoritatively called a "hundred-year flood." That left us ninety-seven years. We were also reassured by the large dikes built by the Army Corps of Engineers between our agricultural field and the riverbed. These dense gray mounds of gravel, contained improbably with heavy mesh wire, were ten feet high, twenty-five feet at the base, and ugly. They efficiently blocked our view of the river which, at that time, was not much of a loss. Although things were to change quickly, when we came to southwestern New Mexico, the price of copper stood high, unemployment was low, and—through our land—the Mimbres River stretched bone-dry.

2   Like many country dwellers not born in the country, we find it hard to believe we were once so naive. We actually sought out river bottom land. We didn't think in terms of rusted wheel bearings, smashed foot bridges, soil erosion, or property damage. We didn't think of rivers at all in terms of property: rivers were above real estate. They were gifts in the desert. They were frail blue lines that disappeared on the map. In the arid Southwest, rivers—even intermittent rivers—were to be coveted.

3   In the coming years, we came to know the Mimbres River better. On my part, it was not an idyllic relationship. The only road to our house is a rough and rutted trail of packed dirt that goes over the stream bed. When the river does run, about seven months of the year, water seeps into our car bearings and the brakes freeze at night. When the river runs too high, we stall in midstream and must be hauled out by a neighbor's four-wheel drive. Those of us on the wrong side of the Mimbres, a collection of seven families, tried to deal with the conflict of road and river. We got together for workdays and animated discussions in which we all pre-

tended to be engineers. We built an elegant wood and rope "swinging bridge" for pedestrians and at the gravelly bottom of the stream installed cement culverts—only to have both swept away by spring run-off and heavy rains. On the occasion of such rains, the Mimbres became impassable by any vehicle. Whenever this seemed imminent, my husband and I parked our car on the side of the river that led to town: fifty miles to Deming, New Mexico for his teaching job and thirty miles to Silver City for mine. The next day, we would get up painfully early, walk a half mile to the crossing, and wade.

4   The cold water didn't bother my husband; the problems of this part-time river only intrigued him. In the early 1970s, New Mexico's Soil and Conservation Service had experimented with our section of the Mimbres by cutting down all the cottonwoods. At that time, they believed eliminating these great trees, some more than a hundred years old, would mean more grass for cattle. Today, it seems as inspired an act as putting cans on a cat's tail. Without the cottonwoods to hold the soil with their roots and break the impact of water, subsequent small floods swept over the denuded ground like efficient mowing machines. When the channel was dry again, the eroded result could only charitably be called a river. My husband's dream was to bring the old Mimbres back. To this end, he planted branch after branch of cottonwood in the hope they would miraculously grow. Miraculously, they did. He charted the re-vegetation of willows, chamisa, and walnut. He personally scattered the fluff of cattails. In a meditative silence, he walked the gray dikes built by the Army Corps of Engineers and saw a greener future.

5   On the morning of the second "hundred-year flood," we woke to a triumphant roar and strangely clear view. Below our house, what had last night been a field of winter rye was a mass of brown water lapping at the goat's pen. Something important seemed to be missing. It took us longer than seems reasonable to realize what that was. The ugly gravel dikes were gone. A strange, dark, churning river had taken their place, a river that also included part of our land, much of our topsoil, and our entire car.

6   We didn't learn the fate of the Volkswagen until later that morning. Excited and impressed, my husband dressed and went down to inspect the situation. I stayed in the house with our two-month-old daughter. Everyone in the neighborhood was out inspecting, and those who had gotten up early had the chance to see our car—parked on the "town" side of the river—slowly lifted up and carried along in the force of the flood. The little Bug was in good company, with giant cottonwoods torn from their roots and the debris of upstream bridges and irrigation pipe. When my husband returned to confirm the destruction of our single and uninsured vehicle, his face showed a kind of pleasure. Looking out over the changed, aquatic world, his eyes gleamed. He almost laughed. This was a big flood. This was bigger than the last one-hundred-year flood, six years ago. This was a river.

7   Our neighborhood was once a small ranch now divided into forty, ten, and five-acre parcels, with a restriction that no one can further subdivide. This restriction, as well as the property's irrigated land, was part of our reason for being here. We also liked the people who had come before us. As the limited number of house sites sold, a sense of community emerged which resulted in a name: El Otro Lado (The Other Side). For our private street sign, Jack and Roberta Greene,

among the first to buy, painted this in informal and cock-eyed calligraphy on a wooden board they posted at the highway. Divorced, in his early fifties, Jack had once posted a want ad for a companion in the *Mother Earth News* and thus met the also divorced, forty-eight-year-old Roberta. This slightly comic, slightly suspicious background proved misleading, for the Greenes became our role models, the sanest couple we knew. Neighbors in a rural community, we were all bound by mutual needs. We borrowed hand saws and drill bits from each other's tool box. We shared the maintenance of a Rototiller, and if a friend went out of town, we fed their horses, goats, chickens, dogs, and cats. Inevitably, we were all building passive-solar adobe homes and had much to say to each other about greenhouses and R values. Despite ages that ranged from thirty to sixty, we became close and comfortable and gathered almost every Sunday night—movie night!—around Jack and Roberta's new VCR.

8   Now, with the flood, we were not alarmed at being cut off and isolated together. Phone lines had been washed away, and the power pole rocked precariously in the middle of the rushing brown water. Huddled in sweaters, we converged as a group to note its sway. Our main fear was that without electricity we could not use the VCR to watch Roberta's copy of a Lina Wertmuller film. The pole held, and a potluck was arranged where, over four different salads, we discussed the river, the weather, and our fields—three words for the same thing.

9   That easily, the flood became another community event, another movie, another bond.

10   Upstream, a friend almost lost his life when he tried to cross the water in his new jeep. All night, his pregnant wife walked the crumbling bank and called his name. In the morning he was found clinging to a log, much chastened. His was not the only four-wheeler to go down the river. A small family-owned sawmill contributed some equipment; a rancher lost his prize tractor. The best news, according to everyone, was the loss of the dikes. As it turned out, they had channeled the Mimbres in such a way as to increase its force and power. One landowner threatened to shoot any engineer who tried to re-erect them. This did not prove necessary since the state labeled the entire area a floodplain, a belated nod to nature that prevented further interference.

11   On our property, the water scoured the river bed as the channel shifted to carve out chunks of irrigated field. When the flood subsided, a matter of days, it left a muddy battleground strewn with logs, misshapen debris, and two rubber tires ten feet in diameter and three feet thick. The small, laboriously planted cottonwoods did not survive. In fact, not a blade of grass remained. Elsewhere on the Mimbres, where the ground had been protected by trees, the torrent overflowed the banks and took down a few of the older cottonwoods. In less than a month, that part of the river was green again.

12 In southwestern New Mexico, the Mimbres River winds from the pine-covered Gila National Forest, down to the scrub oak and juniper of our land, south to the high plains of the Chihuahuan Desert. In its sixty-mile length, the river drops 4,500 feet and covers four life zones. Narrow, intimate, made lush with irrigation, this area has a long history. I found my first pottery while digging a squash bed in the garden. Since then I have found many bits of clay, their edges irregular, like pieces

of a jigsaw puzzle scattered in the dirt. As sometimes happens, the first one was the best: a palm-sized shard of black-on-white ware, its painted lines straight and elegantly thin. Such lines mean that the original pot was made between A.D. 1000 and 1100, the "Classic Period" of the Mimbreno Indians.

13   In their hundreds of years here, this branch of the Mogollon culture farmed, hunted, gathered, and painted pots that are world-famous today. The designs are often fantastical: southwestern versions of the griffon and the unicorn. Many are natural drawings of animals and insects. Some are quite bawdy—penises as long as your arm! Some resemble Escher paintings with their mirrored images and field reversals. In all, they present an extraordinarily talented culture. Over six thousand Mimbres pots are stored across the world in museums like the Smithsonian; you can also find Mimbres ware for sale, discreetly advertised in the back pages of such magazines as *The New Yorker*. Apparently, once the artistic fervor hit them, these Indians made a lot of pots. Most are found in the burial sites beneath the homes and villages that the Indians abandoned around the thirteenth century. Most have a "kill hole" at the bottom of the bowl, which may have allowed the spirit of the dead to escape. And some scientists theorize that the pots were made exclusively by women, with certain artists or prehistoric celebrities producing on a regular basis.

14   Modern Mimbrenos are proud of their heritage and exploit it ruthlessly. Designs crafted a thousand years ago can be seen on locally made earrings, T-shirts, stationery, calendars, aprons, towels, and coffee cups. An ancient picture of a bighorn sheep, now extinct in the valley, might pop up on an advertisement for farm equipment or a recruiting poster for the nearby university. While such theft is easily sanctioned, the commercial value of the actual pots is controversial. A Mimbres bowl can be worth as much as $25,000, and pot hunters regularly bulldoze sites that an archeologist might take years to uncover. Pot hunting, of course, is illegal on state or federal land, which most of the valley is not. Although archeologists wax indignant, they are considered by some natives to be just another breed of pot hunters, ones who take their loot to be stored in far-off museums.

15   In truth, we are all pot hunters here. How could it be otherwise, when the glamor of the past combines with profit? We perk up our ears when we hear that someone down the valley found seventy-two pots in her front yard. Seventy-two! Closer to home—a quarter mile from my doorstep—a doctor and his wife inadvertently destroyed a Mimbres bowl when dozing a building pad for their new house. On the hill above us, an ancient burial is found complete with human body and turquoise beads.

16   Such stories confirm that the qualities of a good home site have not changed much in a thousand years. In digging the foundations for our adobe, my husband uncovered a large grinding stone or *metate* buried three feet deep. After that, we watched each shovelful, but no pot emerged that would pay off our land mortgage. Mimbres pots may still be under the forsythia or kitchen floor, but it offends our aesthetics to run about with a backhoe digging arbitrary holes. We remain pleased with the *metate* and, conventionally, keep it outside our doorstep with an associated collection of *manos*: fist-sized, hand-held rocks worn smooth with grinding. Like most people who live in the valley, we count continuum as a return on our money.

17   Mimbres pottery is glamorous for its age and beauty. But it is only part of a small museum scattered over our twelve acres. A band of Apaches called the *Tci-he-nde* or Red Paint people left their arrowheads, as well as a four-inch spearpoint now on a shelf of knickknacks. Named for a stripe of paint across the warrior's face, this tribe probably entered the area long after the Mimbrenos' exit. They continued the tradition of farming. At least, they tended their crops between times on the warpath, first with the Spanish and later with the Mexicans and Americans. In the nineteenth century, chiefs like Mangas Coloradas and Victorio found it increasingly hard to hold off the growing horde of gold-hungry, silver-hungry, copper-hungry, even meershaum-hungry miners. Where miners went, forts and soldiers followed. And by the late 1860s, Mexican and Anglo farmers had also settled the Mimbres and would supply the boom town of Silver City with bumper crops of potatoes. Such early entrepreneurs dry-farmed pinto beans where my front yard yields grama grass. In 1869, they established the irrigation system that waters my garden. Over the years, these men and women dropped their own mementos of baling wire, lavender glass, and bone white china. Most recently, I found in our field a perfect 6 1/2 ounce Coke bottle. Its thick shape, patterned with raised letters, dated from the 1940s—seemingly an emblem of the modern world, until we compared the heavy diminutive bottle with an aluminum can red-flagged NutraSweet.

18   The Mimbrenos, the Apaches, the dry farmers are all gone—and not just because they died. The sudden disappearance of the Mimbrenos, along with Indian groups like the Anasazi to the north, is still a mystery. In their ruins is a sense of calm which seems to preclude war or pestilence. Their dead are properly buried, their kitchen utensils neatly stored. In contrast, the Apaches were clearly driven out. At one point, an Indian agent promised them a reservation on their homeland, but the citizens of Silver City objected, and nothing came of it. In 1886, the famed year that Geronimo surrendered, the entire Red Paint people were put on boxcars and shipped to Florida and permanent exile. For the dry farmers, the weather simply changed, and it began to rain less. The river itself was no longer that "rapid, dashing stream, about fifteen feet wide and three feet deep" described in 1846 by an American soldier.

19   Oddly, or perhaps not, such disappearances continue today. They are a part of the valley's heritage. In the ten years we have lived here, we have seen most of our friends and many of our acquaintances leave. Most obviously, a failing local economy is to blame. The Mimbres Valley is in Grant County, one of New Mexico's richest mineralized areas. Twelve miles to the east, the Santa Rita Mines began producing copper as early as 1804, and for most of the twentieth century that yellow metal—not quite so yellow as gold but more abundant—was excavated from a hole that eventually swallowed the entire town of Santa Rita, including its hospital and schoolhouse. Mining is an extractive industry. In the 1980s, the Kennicott Mining Company declared that only forty years' worth of low-grade ore existed at the strip mine they advertised as "the world's prettiest copper pit." Many smaller operations in nearby Hanover and Pinos Altos had already played out, and the other major company in the area, Phelps Dodge, also began to count the years. No one employed by the mines paid much attention. No one even

mentioned it to newcomers like us, and we didn't ask. As it turned out, forty was not the magic and seemingly far-off number. For it wasn't the amount of copper that caught Grant County by surprise, but the price per pound. By the time that price fell to under fifty-eight cents in 1982, the layoffs had already begun.

20   Still, that is only part of the story. Most of our friends did not leave the Mimbres Valley because they could not find a job here but because they could not find the job they expected of life. They and we came to this area for the small-town ambiance and rural lifestyle. Not surprisingly, neither the small town nor the surrounding rural area required many editors, landscape architects, graphic designers, psychologists, or political lobbyists. More surprisingly, some of us discovered that we needed to be these things. We had embraced a concept of happiness that required escape from the contaminated, stressful cities. For love of land—for love of beauty, for love of the valley—we could adjust to a lower standard of living. We could not adjust (at least not all of us) to being high school teachers or car mechanics.

21   Our closest neighbor is the car mechanic. His real interest is solar energy systems, and he wonders why his back hurts and why he spends his time under the hoods of cars as old as himself. Another friend would like to build houses but the economy here is too depressed and he lives, instead, on odd carpentry jobs. For five years, my husband was the high school teacher. Because of the long drive, he left for work at six in the morning and returned from work when it was too dark to see the land he was working to pay for. Increasingly, he became frustrated by conditions in his job which prevented him from doing it well. He was angered by the blatant cultural contempt for teachers, even as he recognized in himself echos of that contempt. As one close relative told him, public school teaching is a "deviant career choice." Even the school administrators seemed to agree. Finally, for a number of reasons, none of which had to do with low salary or discipline problems, my husband left Deming High.

22   It hardly needs to be said that he does not want to leave the Mimbres Valley. For now he pursues part-time work which includes free-lance photography and outfitting in the Gila Wilderness. Together with my salary, this income does not add up to what we have discovered—another surprise—we would like to have. Still, in the privacy of the valley, we can pick and choose our conveniences. We have an outhouse; we also have a word processor. Social identity, not economics, is perhaps the more real dilemma. What is a man with a patchwork of jobs as insecure as our river? Will my husband be happy at the age of fifty-five?

23   We don't know the answers to these questions, and in the willful charting of our lives, we wonder what turns we are taking and what roads we irrevocably pass. We wonder if we will ever regret our choice to step outside what we were taught to consider the mainstream. Perhaps we should wonder why we feel that it was a choice, as though how and why we came here was a conscious navigation, as though we are not, all of us, riding logs down a river.

24   In the theme of departure, there are variations. Jack and Roberta Greene retired here to build a home, garden, and become potters. Together, that first year, they made enough forty-pound adobe bricks for a small, liveable studio. They would need another two thousand for their one-bedroom house. Meanwhile they

planted an orchard of peaches, plums, apples, cherries, and walnuts. A master gardener, Roberta also grew lavish rows of strawberries, chilies, tomatoes, lettuce, peas, eggplant, cucumbers, onions, leeks, radishes, potatoes, and corn. Their raspberry crops were famous. It was far more food than they could eat, and in the summer they took the surplus to Silver City's Farmer's Market. In their second year, the two thousand adobe bricks lay neatly stacked in lines that spilled over into Jack's vinyard. Enthusiastically, they began to lay up the walls. Jack studied wiring, and they did most of the work themselves, including a compost toilet and solar hot-water system. By the time they had been in the valley five years, they had a beautiful Santa Fe-style home, an established orchard, a shed of useful tools, and the acceptable identity of a retired couple. As part of the grand plan, Jack began a kiln for their pottery work.

25   We profited greatly from the Greenes' knowledge, as well as from their tool shed. But by the time we began to lay up our own walls, Jack and Roberta were showing signs of restlessness. Before his "radicalization" and divorce, Jack had owned a chain of liquor stores in California. Twenty years later, with a beard and a wife from *Mother Earth News,* he was still the businessman, still a driver. The dream house was built. Now he couldn't quite see truck gardening for minimum wage or making pots for less than that. One day he and Roberta bought a video store in Silver City. At that time, it was the only video store in town and contained less than fifty movies. With Jack's retailing expertise and the labor Roberta once spent on her garden, the business grew quickly. For a while, the Greenes tried to straddle two worlds. But inevitably the "simple life" (burning and hauling trash, commuting to town, crossing the river, chasing cows from the garden, fixing a broken windmill, canning tomatoes) proved too burdensome. Some time after the second hundred-year flood, they bought a furnished house in town and put the Mimbres adobe up for sale.

26   In the nineteenth century, the French visitor Alexis de Tocqueville observed: "An American will build a house in which to pass his old age and sell it before the roof is on; he will plant a garden and rent it just as the trees are bearing; he will clear a field and leave others to reap the harvest; he will take up a profession and leave it, settle in one place and soon go off elsewhere with his changing desires."

27   My husband used to quote this in wonderment. Now we see how easily it could apply to us. When Jack and Roberta left, taking with them our Sunday night movies, the disintegration of our community began. The car mechanic opened up a bicycle shop in Silver City, and it is only a matter of time before he moves there too. The wife of one couple is in law school in Albuquerque. Another neighbor job hunts in Santa Fe. As we count the number of friends who have left the valley, as well as El Otro Lado, we are surprised at their number. Suddenly, we are no longer newcomers; we are the ones who are left.

28   On the river bank, my husband has planted more cottonwoods. With the dikes gone, he hopes this batch will survive the next flood. Many cottonwoods have already started up on their own, for this, after all, is the work of flooding—to tear down dying trees and carry seeds to new parts of the river. The chamisa is returning too and small patches of willow. Although it has only been a few years, the flood seems to have happened long ago, to much younger people. These

days, my husband broods over the increase of mobile homes in the valley: the tiny aluminum squares that mar his view of rolling hills and the fang of Cooke's Peak. Insistent against a backdrop of mesas, these trailers represent a different vision of the country, a vision we had not foreseen as overnight they pop up on the treeless tracts of land a son is carving from his father's pasture. The valley, like the river, cannot be predicted.

29   In the marital urge for balance, we switch sides often now. This week it is I who grow depressed at the thought of leaving the Mimbres Valley. It is not only the green fields that hold me, but the loss of my naivete. I am not sure I want to spend another ten years learning new lessons. Here, at least, we know our enemies. In this mood, I tell my husband that mobile homes are democratic. I tell him that new friends will come. I tell him that he will find the right job or find he doesn't need to. I tell him that the next flood will be a hundred years away and, in the meantime, his cottonwoods will grow tall. Let's stay, I say this week. Let's stay.

QUESTIONS

Experience

· What do you think of the response Russell and her husband make to the natural dangers and difficulties they regularly confront? Can you imagine yourself living under similar conditions and circumstances? Why, or why not?

Interpretation

· What point does Russell make about the loss of the dikes in the flood? Why did the state decide not to re-erect them?

· What does she mean by saying that "the flood became another community event"?

Evaluation

· What social and environmental values are reflected in the way of life described by Russell?

· What personal qualities exhibited by Russell and her husband impress you most? Why?

WRITING

Exploring

· Write an essay about some difficulty you encountered and had either to overcome or come to terms with. It need not necessarily be an element of nature. You may wish to write about an experience involving people banding together in a common cause.

Interpreting

· Identify and explain the central idea of Russell's essay. Include in your discussion her attitude toward the Mimbres and her attitude toward the kind of life she has chosen to live near the river.

Evaluating

· Discuss the conflicting values represented by the families that leave the Mimbres River valley and those that remain. Consider to what extent the author and her husband themselves share these conflicting values.

EDWARD HOAGLAND
(b. 1932)

The Courage of Turtles

Edward Hoagland splits his time between New York City, where he was born and raised, and New England country, where he attended college (Harvard) and gets in touch with nature. Though Hoagland is perhaps best known as a nature writer, he is also a novelist and travel writer. Among his books are Red Wolves and Black Bears, The Tugman's Passage, *and* The Edward Hoagland Reader, *which offers a sampling of his writings in different genres.*

In "The Courage of Turtles" Hoagland describes turtles as exhibiting some important human qualities of character. Part of the essay's charm derives from Hoagland's ability to interest us in the stories he tells and in the turtle "characters" he describes. In a sense, we might describe the essay as a series of interconnected animal fables, all of which involve turtles. In another sense, we might describe it as a naturalist's observations vividly presented. In fact, Hoagland's careful description of his turtle subjects not only distinguishes them from one another, but makes them vividly present. Another notable element of Hoagland's style in "Turtles" is his diction, which ranges from the vulgar "pee" and "burp" to the elegant foreign borrowing idée fixe.

1   Turtles are a kind of bird with the governor turned low. With the same attitude of removal, they cock a glance at what is going on as if they need only to fly away. Until recently they were also a case of virtue rewarded, at least in the town where I grew up, because, being humble creatures, there were plenty of them. Even when we still had a few bobcats in the woods the local snapping turtles, growing up to forty pounds, were the largest carnivores. You would see them through the amber water, as big as greeny wash basins at the bottom of the pond, until they faded into the inscrutable mud as if they hadn't existed at all.

2   When I was ten I went to Dr. Green's Pond, a two-acre pond across the road. When I was twelve I walked a mile or so to Taggart's Pond, which was lusher, had big water snakes and a waterfall; and shortly after that I was bicycling way up to the adventuresome vastness of Mud Pond, a lake-sized body of water in the reservoir system of a Connecticut city, possessed of cat-backed little islands and empty shacks and a forest of pines and hardwoods along the shore. Otters, foxes and mink left their prints on the bank; there were pike and perch. As I got older, the estates and forgotten back lots in town were parceled out and sold for nice prices, yet, though the woods had shrunk, it seemed that fewer people walked in the woods. The new residents didn't know how to find them. Eventually, exploring, they did find them, and it required some ingenuity and doubling around on my part to go for eight miles without meeting someone. I was grown by now, I lived in New York, and that's what I wanted on the occasional weekends when I came out.

3   Since Mud Pond contained drinking water I had felt confident nothing untoward would happen there. For a long while the developers stayed away, until the drought of the mid-1960s. This event, squeezing the edges in, convinced the local water company that the pond really wasn't a necessity as a catch basin, however; so they bulldozed a hole in the earthen dam, bulldozed the banks to fill in the bottom, and landscaped the flow of water that remained to wind like an English brook and provide a domestic view for the houses which were planned. Most of the painted turtles of Mud Pond, who had been inaccessible as they sunned on their rocks, wound up in boxes in boys' closets within a matter of days. Their footsteps in the dry leaves gave them away as they wandered forlornly. The snappers and the little musk turtles, neither of whom leave the water except once a year to lay their eggs, dug into the drying mud for another siege of hot weather, which they were accustomed to doing whenever the pond got low. But this time it was low for good; the mud baked over them and slowly entombed them. As for the ducks, I couldn't stroll in the woods and not feel guilty, because they were crouched beside every stagnant pothole, or were slinking between the bushes with their heads tucked into their shoulders so that I wouldn't see them. If they decided I had, they beat their way up through the screen of trees, striking their wings dangerously, and wheeled about with that headlong, magnificent velocity to locate another poor puddle.

4   I used to catch possums and black snakes as well as turtles, and I kept dogs and goats. Some summers I worked in a menagerie with the big personalities of the animal kingdom, like elephants and rhinoceroses. I was twenty before these enthusiasms began to wane, and it was then that I picked turtles as the particular animal I wanted to keep in touch with. I was allergic to fur, for one thing, and turtles need minimal care and not much in the way of quarters. They're personable beasts. They see the same colors we do and they seem to see just as well, as one discovers in trying to sneak up on them. In the laboratory they unravel the twists of a maze with the hot-blooded rapidity of a mammal. Though they can't run as fast as a rat, they improve on their errors just as quickly, pausing at each crossroads to look left and right. And they rock rhythmically in place, as we often do, although they are hatched from eggs, not the womb. (A common explanation psychologists give for our pleasure in rocking quietly is that it recapitulates our mother's heartbeat *in utero*.)

5   Snakes, by contrast, are dryly silent and priapic. They are smooth movers, legalistic, unblinking, and they afford the humor which the humorless do. But they make challenging captives; sometimes they don't eat for months on a point of order—if the light isn't right, for instance. Alligators are sticklers too. They're like war-horses, or German shepherds, and with their bar-shaped, vertical pupils adding emphasis, they have the *idée fixe* of eating, eating, even when they choose to refuse all food and stubbornly die. They delight in tossing a salamander up towards the sky and grabbing him in their long mouths as he comes down. They're so eager that they get the jitters, and they're too much of a proposition for a casual aquarium like mine. Frogs are depressingly defenseless: that moist, extensive back, with the bones almost sticking through. Hold a frog and you're holding its skeleton. Frogs' tasty legs are the staff of life to many animals—herons, rac-

coons, ribbon snakes—though they themselves are hard to feed. It's not an enviable role to be the staff of life, and after frogs you descend down the evolutionary ladder a big step to fish.

6   Turtles cough, burp, whistle, grunt and hiss, and produce social judgments. They put their heads together amicably enough, but then one drives the other back with the suddenness of two dogs who have been conversing in tones too low for an onlooker to hear. They pee in fear when they're first caught, but exercise both pluck and optimism in trying to escape, walking for hundreds of yards within the confines of their pen, carrying the weight of that cumbersome box on legs which are cruelly positioned for walking. They don't feel that the contest is unfair; they keep plugging, rolling like sailorly souls—a bobbing, infirm gait, a brave, sea-legged momentum—stopping occasionally to study the lay of the land. For me, anyway, they manage to contain the rest of the animal world. They can stretch out their necks like a giraffe, or loom underwater like an apocryphal hippo. They browse on lettuce thrown on the water like a cow moose which is partly submerged. They have a penguin's alertness, combined with a build like a Brontosaurus when they rise up on tiptoe. Then they hunch and ponderously lunge like a grizzly going forward.

7   Baby turtles in a turtle bowl are a puzzle in geometrics. They're as decorative as pansy petals, but they are also self-directed building blocks, propping themselves on one another in different arrangements, before upending the tower. The timid individuals turn fearless, or vice versa. If one gets a bit arrogant he will push the others off the rock and afterwards climb down into the water and cling to the back of one of those he has bullied, tickling him with his hind feet until he bucks like a bronco. On the other hand, when this same milder-mannered fellow isn't exerting himself, he will stare right into the face of the sun for hours. What could be more lionlike? And he's at home in or out of the water and does lots of metaphysical tilting. He sinks and rises, with an infinity of levels to choose from; or, elongating himself, he climbs out on the land again to perambulate, sits boxed in his box, and finally slides back in the water, submerging into dreams.

8   I have five of these babies in a kidney-shaped bowl. The hatchling, who is a painted turtle, is not as large as the top joint of my thumb. He eats chicken gladly. Other foods he will attempt to eat but not with sufficient perseverance to succeed because he's so little. The yellow-bellied terrapin is probably a yearling, and he eats salad voraciously, but no meat, fish or fowl. The Cumberland terrapin won't touch salad or chicken but eats fish and all of the meats except for bacon. The little snapper, with a black crenelated shell, feasts on any kind of meat, but rejects greens and fish. The fifth of the turtles is African. I acquired him only recently and don't know him well. A mottled brown, he unnerves the green turtles, dragging their food off to his lairs. He doesn't seem to want to be green—he bites the algae off his shell, hanging meanwhile at daring, steep, head-first angles.

9   The snapper was a Ferdinand until I provided him with deeper water. Now he snaps at my pencil with his downturned and fearsome mouth, his swollen face like a napalm victim's. The Cumberland has an elliptical red mark on the side of his green-and-yellow head. He is benign by nature and ought to be as elegant as his scientific name *(Pseudemys scripta elegans),* except he has contracted a disease of

the air bladder which has permanently inflated it; he floats high in the water at an undignified slant and can't go under. There may have been internal bleeding, too, because his carapace is stained along its ridge. Unfortunately, like flowers, baby turtles often die. Their mouths fill up with a white fungus and their lungs with pneumonia. Their organs clog up from the rust in the water, or diet troubles, and, like a dying man's, their eyes and heads become too prominent. Toward the end, the edge of the shell becomes flabby as felt and folds around them like a shroud.

10   While they live they're like puppies. Although they're vivacious, they would be a bore to be with all the time, so I also have an adult wood turtle about six inches long. Her shell is the equal of any seashell for sculpturing, even a Cellini shell; it's like an old, dusty, richly engraved medallion dug out of a hillside. Her legs are salmon-orange bordered with black and protected by canted, heroic scales. Her plastron—the bottom shell—is splotched like a margay cat's coat, with black ocelli on a yellow background. It is convex to make room for the female organs inside, whereas a male's would be concave to help him fit tightly on top of her. Altogether, she exhibits every camouflage color on her limbs and shells. She has a turtleneck neck, a tail like an elephant's, wise old pachydermous hind legs and the face of a turkey—except that when I carry her she gazes at the passing ground with a hawk's eyes and mouth. Her feet fit to the fingers of my hand, one to each one, and she rides looking down. She can walk on the floor in perfect silence, but usually she lets her shell knock portentously, like a footstep, so that she resembles some grand, concise, slow-moving id. But if an earthworm is presented, she jerks swiftly ahead, poises above it and strikes like a mongoose, consuming it with wild vigor. Yet she will climb on my lap to eat bread or boiled eggs.

11   If put into a creek, she swims like a cutter, nosing forward to intercept a strange turtle and smell him. She drifts with the current to go downstream, maneuvering behind a rock when she wants to take stock, or sinking to the nether levels, while bubbles float up. Getting out, choosing her path, she will proceed a distance and dig into a pile of humus, thrusting herself to the coolest layer at the bottom. The hole closes over her until it's as small as a mouse's hole. She's not as aquatic as a musk turtle, not quite as terrestrial as the box turtles in the same woods, but because of her versatility she's marvelous, she's everywhere. And though she breathes the way we breathe, with scarcely perceptible movements of her chest, sometimes instead she pumps her throat ruminatively, like a pipe smoker sucking and puffing. She waits and blinks, pumping her throat, turning her head, then sets off like a loping tiger in slow motion, hurdling the jungly lumber, the pea vine and twigs. She estimates angles so well that when she rides over the rocks, sliding down a drop-off with her rugged front legs extended, she has the grace of a rodeo mare.

12   But she's well off to be with me rather than at Mud Pond. The other turtles have fled—those that aren't baked into the bottom. Creeping up the brooks to sad, constricted marshes, burdened as they are with that box on their backs, they're walking into a setup where all their enemies move thirty times faster than they. It's like the nightmare most of us have whimpered through, where we are weighted down disastrously while trying to flee; fleeing our home ground, we try to run.

13   I've seen turtles in still worse straits. On Broadway, in New York, there is a penny arcade which used to sell baby terrapins that were scrawled with bon mots in enamel paint, such as KISS ME BABY. The manager turned out to be a wholesaler as well, and once I asked him whether he had any larger turtles to sell. He took me upstairs to a loft room devoted to the turtle business. There were desks for the paper work and a series of racks that held shallow tin bins atop one another, each with several hundred babies crawling around in it. He was a smudgy-complexioned, serious fellow and he did have a few adult terrapins, but I was going to school and wasn't actually planning to buy; I'd only wanted to see them. They were aquatic turtles, but here they went without water, presumably for weeks, lurching about in those dry bins like handicapped citizens, living on gumption. An easel where the artist worked stood in the middle of the floor. She had a palette and a clip attachment for fastening the babies in place. She wore a smock and a beret, and was homely, short and eccentric-looking, with funny black hair, like some of the ladies who show their paintings in Washington Square in May. She had a cold, she was smoking, and her hand wasn't very steady, although she worked quickly enough. The smile that she produced for me would have looked giddy if she had been happier, or drunk. Of course the turtles' doom was sealed when she painted them, because their bodies inside would continue to grow but their shells would not. Gradually, invisibly, they would be crushed. Around us their bellies—two thousand belly shells—rubbed on the bins with a mournful, momentous hiss.

14   Somehow there were so many of them I didn't rescue one. Years later, however, I was walking on First Avenue when I noticed a basket of living turtles in front of a fish store. They were as dry as a heap of old bones in the sun; nevertheless, they were creeping over one another gimpily, doing their best to escape. I looked and was touched to discover that they appeared to be wood turtles, my favorites, so I bought one. In my apartment I looked closer and realized that in fact this was a diamondback terrapin, which was bad news. Diamondbacks are tidewater turtles from brackish estuaries, and I had no sea water to keep him in. He spent his days thumping interminably against the baseboards, pushing for an opening through the wall. He drank thirstily but would not eat and had none of the hearty, accepting qualities of wood turtles. He was morose, paler in color, sleeker and more Oriental in the carved ridges and rings that formed his shell. Though I felt sorry for him, finally I found his unrelenting presence exasperating. I carried him, struggling in a paper bag, across town to the Morton Street Pier on the Hudson. It was August but gray and windy. He was very surprised when I tossed him in; for the first time in our association, I think, he was afraid. He looked afraid as he bobbed about on top of the water, looking up at me from ten feet below. Though we were both accustomed to his resistance and rigidity, seeing him still pitiful, I recognized that I must have done the wrong thing. At least the river was salty, but it was also bottomless; the waves were too rough for him, and the tide was coming in, bumping him against the pilings underneath the pier. Too late, I realized that he wouldn't be able to swim to a peaceful inlet in New Jersey, even if he could figure out which way to swim. But since, short of diving in after him, there was nothing I could do, I walked away.

QUESTIONS

Experience

· To what extent have you shared any of the experiences Hoagland describes—with turtles, snakes, frogs, or other creatures he mentions?

· Have you ever read anything before about turtles? If so, to what extent was it like Hoagland's essay?

· Were you surprised by some of the things Hoagland says about turtles? Why, or why not?

Interpretation

· What do you think Hoagland's purpose is in this essay? To celebrate turtles? To explain something about them? Something else?

· Does the essay have a central idea? If so, what is it?

Evaluation

· Did you enjoy reading this essay? Why, or why not?

· Why does Hoagland like turtles? What values does he ascribe to them?

· What human qualities does he associate with them?

· How convincing is his essay?

WRITING

Exploring

· Write an essay about an animal (or plant) that interests or intrigues you. You can base your essay on your reading, observation, and experience. You may wish to zero in on one or two special qualities of your subject and provide details, examples, and other forms of evidence to explain and illustrate your point.

Interpreting

· Explain what Hoagland accomplishes with his description of his pet female turtle. Explain the effect of his story about the painted turtles and the story of the turtle that ends the essay.

Evaluating

· Discuss the value of having a pet—turtle or otherwise—or argue that having a pet such as a turtle is not a good idea.

LEWIS THOMAS
(1913–1994)

The World's Biggest Membrane

Lewis Thomas belonged to the special fraternity of doctors who are also writers. Trained in medicine at Harvard Medical School, Thomas pursued a career as a researcher and medical school administrator at Yale and Tulane universities. He taught at Cornell University Medical School, and he served as president and chancellor of Memorial Sloan-Kettering Cancer Center in New York. For twenty years Thomas wrote a column for the New England Journal of Medicine; *his columns furnished materials he culled for his books, including* The Lives of a Cell *(1974),* The Medusa and the Snail *(1979), and* The Fragile Species *(1979), among others. His essays have had a wide and popular audience, well beyond the medical community for which they were originally written.*

In "The World's Biggest Membrane" Thomas imagines the earth as a giant organism. Taking off from that imaginative metaphor, Thomas follows up on its implications, especially with his notion of the atmosphere as the earth's membrane. The result is an excursion into thought, a brief ride on the winds of an idea that Thomas presents with a dash of wit and a touch of humor. Worth noting as well is the way he uses comparisons to make his scientific explanations easier to understand.

1   Viewed from the distance of the moon, the astonishing thing about the earth, catching the breath, is that it is alive. The photographs show the dry, pounded surface of the moon in the foreground, dead as an old bone. Aloft, floating free beneath the moist, gleaming membrane of bright blue sky, is the rising earth, the only exuberant thing in this part of the cosmos. If you could look long enough, you would see the swirling of the great drifts of white cloud, covering and uncovering the half-hidden masses of land. If you had been looking for a very long, geologic time, you could have seen the continents themselves in motion, drifting apart on their crustal plates held afloat by the fire beneath. It has the organized, self-contained look of a live creature, full of information, marvelously skilled in handling the sun.

2   It takes a membrane to make sense out of disorder in biology. You have to be able to catch energy and hold it, storing precisely the needed amount and releasing it in measured shares. A cell does this, and so do the organelles inside. Each assemblage is poised in the flow of solar energy, tapping off energy from metabolic surrogates of the sun. To stay alive, you have to be able to hold out against equilibrium, maintain imbalance, bank against entropy, and you can only transact this business with membranes in our kind of world.

3   When the earth came alive it began constructing its own membrane for the general purpose of editing the sun. Originally, in the time of prebiotic elaboration

of peptides and nucleotides from inorganic ingredients in the water on the earth, there was nothing to shield out ultraviolet radiation except the water itself. The first thin atmosphere came entirely from the degassing of the earth as it cooled, and there was only a vanishingly small trace of oxygen in it. Theoretically, there could have been some production of oxygen by photodissociation of water vapor in ultraviolet light, but not much. This process would have been self-limiting, as Urey showed, since the wave lengths needed for photolysis are the very ones screened out selectively by oxygen; the production of oxygen would have been cut off almost as soon as it occurred.

4   The formation of oxygen had to await the emergence of photosynthetic cells, and these were required to live in an environment with sufficient visible light for photosynthesis but shielded at the same time against lethal ultraviolet. Berkner and Marshall calculate that the green cells must therefore have been about ten meters below the surface of water, probably in pools and ponds shallow enough to lack strong convection currents (the ocean could not have been the starting place).

5   You could say that the breathing of oxygen into the atmosphere was the result of evolution, or you could turn it around and say that evolution was the result of oxygen. You can have it either way. Once the photosynthetic cells had appeared, very probably counterparts of today's blue-green algae, the future respiratory mechanism of the earth was set in place. Early on, when the level of oxygen had built up to around 1 per cent of today's atmospheric concentration, the anaerobic life of the earth was placed in jeopardy, and the inevitable next stage was the emergence of mutants with oxidative systems and ATP.[1] With this, we were off to an explosive developmental stage in which great varieties of respiring life, including the multicellular forms, became feasible.

6   Berkner has suggested that there were two such explosions of new life, like vast embryological transformations, both dependent on threshold levels of oxygen. The first, at 1 per cent of the present level, shielded out enough ultraviolet radiation to permit cells to move into the surface layers of lakes, rivers, and oceans. This happened around 600 million years ago, at the beginning of the Paleozoic era, and accounts for the sudden abundance of marine fossils of all kinds in the record of this period. The second burst occurred when oxygen rose to 10 per cent of the present level. At this time, around 400 million years ago, there was a sufficient canopy to allow life out of the water and onto the land. From here on it was clear going, with nothing to restrain the variety of life except the limits of biologic inventiveness.

7   It is another illustration of our fantastic luck that oxygen filters out the very bands of ultraviolet light that are most devastating for nucleic acids and proteins, while allowing full penetration of the visible light needed for photosynthesis. If it had not been for this semipermeability, we could never have come along.

8   The earth breathes, in a certain sense. Berkner suggests that there may have been cycles of oxygen production and carbon dioxide consumption, depending on relative abundances of plant and animal life, with the ice ages representing periods of apnea. An overwhelming richness of vegetation may have caused the level of oxygen to rise above today's concentration, with a corresponding deple-

---

[1] *ATP:* Adenosine triphosphate, a chemical in cells that produces energy for physiological responses.

tion of carbon dioxide. Such a drop in carbon dioxide may have impaired the "greenhouse" property of the atmosphere, which holds in the solar heat otherwise lost by radiation from the earth's surface. The fall in temperature would in turn have shut off much of living, and, in a long sigh, the level of oxygen may have dropped by 90 per cent. Berkner speculates that this is what happened to the great reptiles; their size may have been all right for a richly oxygenated atmosphere, but they had the bad luck to run out of air.

9   Now we are protected against lethal ultraviolet rays by a narrow rim of ozone, thirty miles out. We are safe, well ventilated, and incubated, provided we can avoid technologies that might fiddle with that ozone, or shift the levels of carbon dioxide. Oxygen is not a major worry for us, unless we let fly with enough nuclear explosives to kill off the green cells in the sea; if we do that, of course, we are in for strangling.

10   It is hard to feel affection for something as totally impersonal as the atmosphere, and yet there it is, as much a part and product of life as wine or bread. Taken all in all, the sky is a miraculous achievement. It works, and for what it is designed to accomplish it is as infallible as anything in nature. I doubt whether any of us could think of a way to improve on it, beyond maybe shifting a local cloud from here to there on occasion. The word "chance" does not serve to account well for structures of such magnificence. There may have been elements of luck in the emergence of chloroplasts, but once these things were on the scene, the evolution of the sky became absolutely ordained. Chance suggests alternatives, other possibilities, different solutions. This may be true for gills and swimbladders and forebrains, matters of detail, but not for the sky. There was simply no other way to go.

11   We should credit it for what it is: For sheer size and perfection of function, it is far and away the grandest product of collaboration in all of nature.

12   It breathes for us, and it does another thing for our pleasure. Each day, millions of meteorites fall against the outer limits of the membrane and are burned to nothing by the friction. Without this shelter, our surface would long since have become the pounded powder of the moon. Even though our receptors are not sensitive enough to hear it, there is comfort in knowing that the sound is there overhead, like the random noise of rain on the roof at night.

QUESTIONS

Experience

· Describe your experience of reading Thomas's essay. If you had trouble at any point, or if you had to concentrate harder, where did you have that trouble, or why did you have to read with more concentrated attention?
· Did you find the beginning and ending easier than the middle or not? Why?

Interpretation

· What does Thomas mean by saying "the earth breathes"?
· What does he mean by saying the earth is "the grandest product of collaboration in all of nature"?

Evaluation

· What implicit values are embedded in Thomas's essay? How might our behavior toward the earth as well as our thinking about it be affected by what Thomas writes here?

WRITING

Exploring

· Thomas uses a metaphor—the earth as a membrane—as the controlling image of his essay. Thomas uses this image to explain and explore his ideas about the earth. Develop your own short essay around a metaphor in which you explain and explore your topic by thinking about the implications of the metaphor. You can write about the earth using a different metaphor, or you may wish to select another topic altogether.

Interpreting

· Analyze Thomas's essay by writing a sentence or two about each of his paragraphs. In your sentences, identify the purpose of each paragraph, and explain what it contributes to the essay as a whole.

Evaluating

· Discuss one or more of the environmental values implicit in Thomas's essay. Explain why this value is important, and consider how Thomas's essay supports your view.

ANNIE DILLARD
(b. 1945)

Living Like Weasels

Annie Dillard has taught creative writing at Wesleyan University in Connecticut. She lived for a time in Roanoke, Virginia—an experience she used to wonderful effect in her first book, Pilgrim at Tinker Creek *(1974), which won a Pulitzer Prize. Since then she has lived on Puget Sound and in Connecticut, teaching at Wesleyan, in Middletown. Dillard has written a number of books, including* Living by Fiction, *a critical study;* Teaching a Stone to Talk, *a collection of essays; and* An American Childhood, *a portion of her autobiography. Dillard's essays can be demanding both intellectually and emotionally.*

Her essay "Living Like Weasels" is both surprising and intellectually provocative. In it Dillard raises questions about what it can mean to live by necessity rather than by choice—to live the way animals do in nature rather than as human beings in a complex social world riddled with intractable problems. Dillard's writing in this essay is frequently taut, strong, compact. Her sentences are often short, crisp, biting. Yet there are moments when the writing opens up and soars eloquently into poetry. Listen, for example, to the use of sound play in this sentence from the end of Dillard's second paragraph: "Or did the eagle eat what he could reach, gutting the living weasel with his talons before his breast, bending his beak, cleaning the beautiful airborne bones?"

I

1   A weasel is wild. Who knows what he thinks? He sleeps in his underground den, his tail draped over his nose. Sometimes he lives in his den for two days without leaving. Outside, he stalks rabbits, mice, muskrats, and birds, killing more bodies than he can eat warm, and often dragging the carcasses home. Obedient to instinct, he bites his prey at the neck, either splitting the jugular vein at the throat or crunching the brain at the base of the skull, and he does not let go. One naturalist refused to kill a weasel who was socketed into his hand deeply as a rattlesnake. The man could in no way pry the tiny weasel off, and he had to walk half a mile to water, the weasel dangling from his palm, and soak him off like a stubborn label.

2   And once, says Ernest Thompson Seton—once, a man shot an eagle out of the sky. He examined the eagle and found the dry skull of a weasel fixed by the jaws to his throat. The supposition is that the eagle had pounced on the weasel and the weasel swiveled and bit as instinct taught him, tooth to neck, and nearly won. I would like to have seen that eagle from the air a few weeks or months before he was shot: was the whole weasel still attached to his feathered throat, a fur pendant? Or did the eagle eat what he could reach, gutting the living weasel with his talons before his breast, bending his beak, cleaning the beautiful airborne bones?

II

3 I have been reading about weasels because I saw one last week. I startled a weasel who startled me, and we exchanged a long glance.

4 Twenty minutes from my house, through the woods by the quarry and across the highway, is Hollins Pond, a remarkable piece of shallowness, where I like to go at sunset and sit on a tree trunk. Hollins Pond is also called Murray's Pond; it covers two acres of bottomland near Tinker Creek with six inches of water and six thousand lily pads. In winter, brown-and-white steers stand in the middle of it, merely dampening their hooves; from the distant shore they look like miracle itself, complete with miracle's nonchalance. Now, in summer, the steers are gone. The water lilies have blossomed and spread to a green horizontal plane that is terra firma to plodding blackbirds, and tremulous ceiling to black leeches, crayfish, and carp.

5 This is, mind you, suburbia. It is a five-minute walk in three directions to rows of houses, though none is visible here. There's a 55 mph highway at one end of the pond, and a nesting pair of wood ducks at the other. Under every bush is a muskrat hole or a beer can. The far end is an alternating series of fields and woods, fields and woods, threaded everywhere with motorcycle tracks—in whose bare clay wild turtles lay eggs.

6 So. I had crossed the highway, stepped over two low barbed-wire fences, and traced the motorcycle path in all gratitude through the wild rose and poison ivy of the pond's shoreline up into high grassy fields. Then I cut down through the woods to the mossy fallen tree where I sit. This tree is excellent. It makes a dry, upholstered bench at the upper, marshy end of the pond, a plush jetty raised from the thorny shore between a shallow blue body of water and a deep blue body of sky.

7 The sun had just set. I was relaxed on the tree trunk, ensconced in the lap of lichen, watching the lily pads at my feet tremble and part dreamily over the thrusting path of a carp. A yellow bird appeared to my right and flew behind me. It caught my eye; I swiveled around—and the next instant, inexplicably, I was looking down at a weasel, who was looking up at me.

III

8 Weasel! I'd never seen one wild before. He was ten inches long, thin as a curve, a muscled ribbon, brown as fruitwood, soft-furred, alert. His face was fierce, small and pointed as a lizard's; he would have made a good arrowhead. There was just a dot of chin, maybe two brown hairs' worth, and then the pure white fur began that spread down his underside. He had two black eyes I didn't see, any more than you see a window.

9 The weasel was stunned into stillness as he was emerging from beneath an enormous shaggy wild rose bush four feet away. I was stunned into stillness twisted backward on the tree trunk. Our eyes locked, and someone threw away the key.

10 Our look was as if two lovers, or deadly enemies, met unexpectedly on an overgrown path when each had been thinking of something else: a clearing blow

to the gut. It was also a bright blow to the brain, or a sudden beating of brains with all the charge and intimate grate of rubbed balloons. It emptied our lungs. It felled the forest, moved the fields, and drained the pond; the world dismantled and tumbled into that black hole of eyes. If you and I looked at each other that way, our skulls would split and drop to our shoulders. But we don't. We keep our skulls. So.

11   He disappeared. This was only last week, and already I don't remember what shattered the enchantment. I think I blinked, I think I retrieved my brain from the weasel's brain, and tried to memorize what I was seeing, and the weasel felt the yank of separation, the careening splashdown into real life and the urgent current of instinct. He vanished under the wild rose. I waited motionless, my mind suddenly full of data and my spirit with pleadings, but he didn't return.

12   Please do not tell me about "approach-avoidance conflicts." I tell you I've been in that weasel's brain for sixty seconds, and he was in mine. Brains are private places, muttering through unique and secret tapes—but the weasel and I both plugged into another tape simultaneously, for a sweet and shocking time. Can I help it if it was a blank?

13   What goes on in his brain the rest of the time? What does a weasel think about? He won't say. His journal is tracks in clay, a spray of feathers, mouse blood and bone: uncollected, unconnected, loose-leaf, and blown.

IV

14 I would like to learn, or remember, how to live. I come to Hollins Pond not so much to learn how to live as, frankly, to forget about it. That is, I don't think I can learn from a wild animal how to live in particular—shall I suck warm blood, hold my tail high, walk with my footprints precisely over the prints of my hands?—but I might learn something of mindlessness, something of the purity of living in the physical senses and the dignity of living without bias or motive. The weasel lives in necessity and we live in choice, hating necessity and dying at the last ignobly in its talons. I would like to live as I should, as the weasel lives as he should. And I suspect that for me the way is like the weasel's: open to time and death painlessly, noticing everything, remembering nothing, choosing the given with a fierce and pointed will.

V

15 I missed my chance. I should have gone for the throat. I should have lunged for that streak of white under the weasel's chin and held on, held on through mud and into the wild rose, held on for a dearer life. We could live under the wild rose wild as weasels, mute and uncomprehending. I could very calmly go wild. I could live two days in the den, curled, leaning on mouse fur, sniffing bird bones, blinking, licking, breathing musk, my hair tangled in the roots of grasses. Down is a good place to go, where the mind is single. Down is out, out of your ever-loving mind and back to your careless senses. I remember muteness as a prolonged and

giddy fast, where every moment is a feast of utterance received. Time and events are merely poured, unremarked, and ingested directly, like blood pulsed into my gut through a jugular vein. Could two live that way? Could two live under the wild rose, and explore by the pond, so that the smooth mind of each is as every-where present to the other, and as received and as unchallenged, as falling snow?

16   We could, you know. We can live any way we want. People take vows of poverty, chastity, and obedience—even of silence—by choice. The thing is to stalk your calling in a certain skilled and supple way, to locate the most tender and live spot and plug into that pulse. This is yielding, not fighting. A weasel doesn't "attack" anything; a weasel lives as he's meant to, yielding at every moment to the perfect freedom of single necessity.

VI

17   I think it would be well, and proper, and obedient, and pure, to grasp your one necessity and not let it go, to dangle from it limp wherever it takes you. Then even death, where you're going no matter how you live, cannot you part. Seize it and let it seize you up aloft even, till your eyes burn out and drop; let your musky flesh fall off in shreds, and let your very bones unhinge and scatter, loosened over fields, over fields and woods, lightly, thoughtless, from any height at all, from as high as eagles.

QUESTIONS

Experience

· Have you ever had an experience in which you became momentarily taken out of yourself through an encounter in nature? Have you ever experienced a moment out of time—looking at the stars, watching a sunrise or sunset, gazing into the eyes of an animal, experiencing the grandeur of a waterfall or a canyon? What has the experience meant to you? Why?

Interpretation

· What does the weasel symbolize in this essay?
· What does Dillard mean by saying we can live like the weasel?
· Why does Dillard not remain connected with the weasel?
· To what extent can any of us remain connected to the natural world, in the way Dillard describes, for any length of time?

Evaluation

· What values does Dillard associate with the weasel? What does she mean when she says that the weasel is "wild"?
· What values of the weasel does Dillard think we can also share?
· What differences does she establish between herself and the weasel?

WRITING

Exploring

· Write an essay in which you explore one or more connections between yourself and the natural world. You can use your own experience, or you can refer to things you have seen or read. Try to arrive at an idea about how the human and natural worlds are related or how they differ.

Interpreting

· Analyze Dillard's essay. Discuss what she conveys in each of the essay's numbered parts. Explain her central idea.

Evaluating

· Discuss the values Dillard associates with the weasel and the extent to which we as human beings can share those values. Consider, as well, what Dillard suggests about differences between human beings and animals.

GEORGE ORWELL
(1903–1950)

Some Thoughts on the Common Toad

George Orwell is the pen name of Eric Blair, born in 1903 to English parents in Bengal, India. Orwell was educated in England, at Crossgates School and at Eton as King's Scholar. After university, he went to Burma, where he served as subdivisional officer in the Indian Imperial Police.

Best known for his fictional allegories, Animal Farm *and* 1984, *Orwell has also written remarkable nonfiction, including both books and essays.* Homage to Catalonia *(1938) provides an eyewitness account of the Spanish Civil War, Orwell having served as a soldier on the Republican side. The* Road to Wigan Pier *(1937) offers an angry account of mining conditions in northern England.*

Orwell's essays are nothing if not polemical. Even when writing about nature, Orwell has an argumentative edge. In "Some Thoughts on the Common Toad," Orwell presents a defense of the toad as a harbinger of spring and as an example of the need for human beings to enjoy its pleasures, whether or not they prefer flowers and birds to amphibians. As Orwell notes, "The pleasures of spring are available to everybody, and cost nothing." Just past the halfway point, however, Orwell shifts gears and asks a question: "Is it wicked to take a pleasure in spring, and other seasonal changes?" This question launches a brief discussion of the place of nature-love in a society replete with unsolved political and social problems. So the essay, which begins as a celebration of nature and a defense of one of its less beloved creatures, ends as a defense of time spent enjoying nature in, of, and for itself—as an outlet for feeling and a solace for the imperfectness of life.

1   Before the swallow, before the daffodil, and not much later than the snowdrop, the common toad salutes the coming of spring after his own fashion, which is to emerge from a hole in the ground, where he has lain buried since the previous autumn, and crawl as rapidly as possible towards the nearest suitable patch of water. Something—some kind of shudder in the earth, or perhaps merely a rise of a few degrees in the temperature—has told him that it is time to wake up: though a few toads appear to sleep the clock round and miss out a year from time to time—at any rate, I have more than once dug them up, alive and apparently well, in the middle of the summer.

2   At this period, after his long fast, the toad has a very spiritual look, like a strict Anglo-Catholic toward the end of Lent. His movements are languid but purposeful, his body is shrunken, and by contrast his eyes look abnormally large. This allows one to notice, what one might not at another time, that a toad has about the most beautiful eye of any living creature. It is like gold, or more exactly it is

like the golden-colored semi-precious stone which one sometimes sees in signet rings, and which I think is called a chrysoberyl.

3   For a few days after getting into the water the toad concentrates on building up his strength by eating small insects. Presently he has swollen to his normal size again, and then he goes through a phase of intense sexiness. All he knows, at least if he is a male toad, is that he wants to get his arms round something, and if you offer him a stick, or even your finger, he will cling to it with surprising strength and take a long time to discover that it is not a female toad. Frequently one comes upon shapeless masses of ten or twenty toads rolling over and over in the water, one clinging to another without distinction of sex. By degrees, however, they sort themselves out into couples, with the male duly sitting on the female's back. You can now distinguish males from females, because the male is smaller, darker and sits on top, with his arms tightly clasped round the female's neck. After a day or two the spawn is laid in long strings which wind themselves in and out of the reeds and soon become invisible. A few more weeks, and the water is alive with masses of tiny tadpoles which rapidly grow larger, sprout hind legs, then forelegs, then shed their tails: and finally, about the middle of the summer, the new generation of toads, smaller than one's thumbnail but perfect in every particular, crawl out of the water to begin the game anew.

4   I mention the spawning of the toads because it is one of the phenomena of spring which most deeply appeal to me, and because the toad, unlike the skylark and the primrose, has never had much of a boost from the poets. But I am aware that many people do not like reptiles or amphibians, and I am not suggesting that in order to enjoy the spring you have to take an interest in toads. There are also the crocus, the missel thrush, the cuckoo, the blackthorn, etc. The point is that the pleasures of spring are available to everybody, and cost nothing. Even in the most sordid street the coming of spring will register itself by some sign or other, if it is only a brighter blue between the chimney pots or the vivid green of an elder sprouting on a blitzed site. Indeed it is remarkable how Nature goes on existing unofficially, as it were, in the very heart of London. I have seen a kestrel flying over the Deptford gasworks, and I have heard a first-rate performance by a blackbird in the Euston Road. There must be some hundreds of thousands, if not millions, of birds living inside the four-mile radius, and it is rather a pleasing thought that none of them pays a halfpenny of rent.

5   As for spring, not even the narrow and gloomy streets round the Bank of England are quite able to exclude it. It comes seeping in everywhere, like one of those new poison gases which pass through all filters. The spring is commonly referred to as "a miracle," and during the past five or six years this worn-out figure of speech has taken on a new lease of life. After the sort of winters we have had to endure recently, the spring does seem miraculous, because it has become gradually harder and harder to believe that it is actually going to happen. Every February since 1940 I have found myself thinking that this time winter is going to be permanent. But Persephone, like the toads, always rises from the dead at about the same moment. Suddenly, toward the end of March, the miracle happens and the decaying slum in which I live is transfigured. Down in the square the sooty privets have turned bright green, the leaves are thickening on the chestnut trees, the daf-

fodils are out, the wallflowers are budding, the policeman's tunic looks positively a pleasant shade of blue, the fish-monger greets his customers with a smile, and even the sparrows are quite a different color, having felt the balminess of the air and nerved themselves to take a bath, their first since last September.

6 Is it wicked to take a pleasure in spring, and other seasonal changes? To put it more precisely, is it politically reprehensible, while we are all groaning, under the shackles of the capitalist system, to point out that life is frequently more worth living because of a blackbird's song, a yellow elm tree in October, or some other natural phenomenon which does not cost money and does not have what the editors of the left-wing newspapers call a class angle? There is no doubt that many people think so. I know by experience that a favorable reference to "Nature" in one of my articles is liable to bring me abusive letters, and though the keyword in these letters is usually "sentimental," two ideas seem to be mixed up in them. One is that any pleasure in the actual process of life encourages a sort of political quietism. People, so the thought runs, ought to be discontented, and it is our job to multiply our wants and not simply to increase our enjoyment of the things we have already. The other idea is that this is the age of machines and that to dislike the machine, or even to want to limit its domination, is backward-looking, reactionary, and slightly ridiculous. This is often backed up by the statement that a love of Nature is a foible of urbanized people who have no notion what Nature is really like. Those who really have to deal with the soil, so it is argued, do not love the soil, and do not take the faintest interest in birds or flowers, except from a strictly utilitarian point of view. To love the country one must live in the town, merely taking an occasional week-end ramble at the warmer times of year.

7 This last idea is demonstrably false. Medieval literature, for instance, including the popular ballads, is full of an almost Georgian enthusiasm for Nature, and the art of agricultural peoples such as the Chinese and Japanese centers always round trees, birds, flowers, rivers, mountains. The other idea seems to me to be wrong in a subtler way. Certainly we ought to be discontented, we ought not simply to find out ways of making the best of a bad job, and yet if we kill all pleasure in the actual process of life, what sort of future are we preparing for ourselves? If a man cannot enjoy the return of spring, why should he be happy in a labor-saving Utopia? What will he do with the leisure that the machine will give him? I have always suspected that if our economic and political problems are ever really solved, life will become simpler instead of more complex, and that the sort of pleasure one gets from finding the first primrose will loom larger than the sort of pleasure one gets from eating an ice to the tune of a Wurlitzer. I think that by retaining one's childhood love of such things as trees, fishes, butterflies, and—to return to my first instance—toads, one makes a peaceful and decent future a little more probable, and that by preaching the doctrine that nothing is to be admired except steel and concrete, one merely makes it a little surer that human beings will have no outlet for their surplus energy except in hatred and leader-worship.

8 At any rate, spring is here, even in London, N.1, and they can't stop you enjoying it. This is a satisfying reflection. How many a time have I stood watching the toads mating, or a pair of hares having a boxing match in the young corn, and thought of all the important persons who would stop me enjoying this if they

could. But luckily they can't. So long as you are not actually ill, hungry, frightened, or immured in a prison or a holiday camp, spring is still spring. The atom bombs are piling up in the factories, the police are prowling through the cities, the lies are streaming from the loudspeakers, but the earth is still going round the sun, and neither the dictators nor the bureaucrats, deeply as they disapprove of the process, are able to prevent it.

QUESTIONS

Experience

· What expectations did you bring to an essay about the "common toad"? Why? Were you surprised at Orwell's description of the toad's eye as "about the most beautiful eye of any living creature"? Why, or why not? Did anything else he says here surprise you? Why?

Interpretation

· What is Orwell's central point? Is his essay primarily about toads, nature, politics, or something else? Explain.

Evaluation

· What values does Orwell ascribe to political activity? What values does he ascribe to nature? How does he justify a loving attentiveness to nature when there is so much ugliness, unhappiness, and evil in the world?

WRITING

Exploring

· Write an essay in which you explore your thoughts and feelings about an aspect of nature. If you wish, you can come to the defense of a plant or animal that is often maligned—such as the toad.

Interpreting

· Analyze the structure of Orwell's essay. Use the white space to identify his three major sections, explaining the significance of each. Be sure also to note how each section develops through the use of details, examples, and evidence. Explain the overall point and purpose of the essay.

Evaluating

· Support, refute, or qualify Orwell's argument in "Some Thoughts on the Common Toad." Use your experience, your reading, and your observation to support your viewpoint.

LESLIE MARMON SILKO
(b. 1948)

Landscape, History, and the Pueblo Imagination

*Leslie Marmon Silko was born in Albuquerque, New Mexico, and raised on the Laguna Pueblo. Her mixed ancestry—she is part Pueblo Indian, part Mexican, part white—is reflected in much of her writing, which includes three books and essays, stories, and poems that have appeared in periodicals. In addition to her books—*Ceremony *(1978),* Storyteller *(1981), and* Almanac of the Dead *(1991)—Silko has written screenplays. She has taught at Vassar College and at her alma mater, the University of New Mexico.*

In "Landscape, History, and the Pueblo Imagination," Silko explains the relationship between landscape and life for the Pueblo Indians of New Mexico. She explains how the Pueblo conception of landscape encompasses land, sky, and everything within them, including people, and how survival depends upon a harmonious cooperation among all these elements. One of the most interesting features of Silko's essay is the way she uses oral narratives to illustrate the attitude toward nature her "landscape" celebrates.

FROM A HIGH ARID PLATEAU IN NEW MEXICO

1 You see that after a thing is dead, it dries up. It might take weeks or years, but eventually if you touch the thing, it crumbles under your fingers. It goes back to dust. The soul of the thing has long since departed. With the plants and wild game the soul may have already been borne back into bones and blood or thick green stalk and leaves. Nothing is wasted. What cannot be eaten by people or in some way used must then be left where other living creatures may benefit. What domestic animals or wild scavengers can't eat will be fed to the plants. The plants feed on the dust of these few remains.

2 The ancient Pueblo people buried the dead in vacant rooms or partially collapsed rooms adjacent to the main living quarters. Sand and clay used to construct the roof make layers many inches deep once the roof has collapsed. The layers of sand and clay make for easy gravedigging. The vacant room fills with cast-off objects and debris. When a vacant room has filled deep enough, a shallow but adequate grave can be scooped in a far corner. Archaeologists have remarked over formal burials complete with elaborate funerary objects excavated in trash middens of abandoned rooms. But the rocks and adobe mortar of collapsed walls were valued by the ancient people. Because each rock had been carefully selected for size and shape, then chiseled to an even face. Even the pink clay adobe melting with each rainstorm had to be prayed over, then dug and carried some distance. Corn cobs and husks, the rinds and stalks and animal bones were not regarded by the ancient people as filth or garbage. The remains were merely resting at a midpoint in their journey back to dust. Human remains are not so different. They should rest with the bones and rinds where they all may benefit living

creatures—small rodents and insects—until their return is completed. The remains of things—animals and plants, the clay and the stones—were treated with respect. Because for the ancient people all these things had spirit and being.

3   The antelope merely consents to return home with the hunter. All phases of the hunt are conducted with love. The love the hunter and the people have for the Antelope People. And the love of the antelope who agree to give up their meat and blood so that human beings will not starve. Waste of meat or even the thoughtless handling of bones cooked bare will offend the antelope spirits. Next year the hunters will vainly search the dry plains for antelope. Thus it is necessary to return carefully the bones and hair, and the stalks and leaves to the earth who first created them. The spirits remain close by. They do not leave us.

4   The dead become dust, and in this becoming they are once more joined with the Mother. The ancient Pueblo people called the earth the Mother Creator of all things in this world. Her sister, the Corn Mother, occasionally merges with her because all succulent green life rises out of the depths of the earth.

5   Rocks and clay are part of the Mother. They emerge in various forms, but at some time before, they were smaller particles or great boulders. At a later time they may again become what they once were. Dust.

6   A rock shares this fate with us and with animals and plants as well. A rock has being or spirit, although we may not understand it. The spirit may differ from the spirit we know in animals or plants or in ourselves. In the end we all originate from the depths of the earth. Perhaps this is how all beings share in the spirit of the Creator. We do not know.

FROM THE EMERGENCE PLACE

7   Pueblo potters, the creators of petroglyphs and oral narratives, never conceived of removing themselves from the earth and sky. So long as the human consciousness remains *within* the hills, canyons, cliffs, and the plants, clouds, and sky, the term *landscape,* as it has entered the English language, is misleading "A portion of territory the eye can comprehend in a single view" does not correctly describe the relationship between the human being and his or her surroundings. This assumes the viewer is somehow *outside* or *separate from* the territory he or she surveys. Viewers are as much a part of the landscape as the boulders they stand on. There is no high mesa edge or mountain peak where one can stand and not immediately be part of all that surrounds. Human identity is linked with all the elements of Creation through the clan: you might belong to the Sun Clan or the Lizard Clan or the Corn Clan or the Clay Clan. Standing deep within the natural world, the ancient Pueblo understood the thing as it was—the squash blossom, grasshopper, or rabbit itself could never be created by the human hand. Ancient Pueblos took the modest view that the thing itself (the landscape) could not be improved upon. The ancients did not presume to tamper with what had already been created. Thus *realism,* as we now recognize it in painting and sculpture, did not catch the imaginations of Pueblo people until recently.

8   The squash blossom itself is *one thing:* itself. So the ancient Pueblo potter abstracted what she saw to be the key elements of the squash blossom—the four

symmetrical petals, with four symmetrical stamens in the center. These key elements, while suggesting the squash flower, also link it with the four cardinal directions. By representing only its intrinsic form, the squash flower is released from a limited meaning or restricted identity. Even in the most sophisticated abstract form, a squash flower or a cloud or a lightning bolt became intricately connected with a complex system of relationships which the ancient Pueblo people maintained with each other, and with the populous natural world they lived within. A bolt of lightning is itself, but at the same time it may mean much more. It may be a messenger of good fortune when summer rains are needed. It may deliver death, perhaps the result of manipulations by the Gunnadeyahs, destructive necromancers. Lightning may strike down an evil-doer. Or lightning may strike a person of good will. If the person survives, lightning endows him or her with heightened power.

9   Pictographs and petroglyphs of constellations or elk or antelope draw their magic in part from the process wherein the focus of all prayer and concentration is upon the thing itself, which, in its turn, guides the hunter's hand. Connection with the spirit dimensions requires a figure or form which is all-inclusive. A "lifelike" rendering of an elk is too restrictive. Only the elk *is* itself. A *realistic* rendering of an elk would be only one particular elk anyway. The purpose of the hunt rituals and magic is to make contact with *all* the spirits of the Elk.

10   The land, the sky, and all that is within them—the landscape—includes human beings. Interrelationships in the Pueblo landscape are complex and fragile. The unpredictability of the weather, the aridity and harshness of much of the terrain in the high plateau country explain in large part the relentless attention the ancient Pueblo people gave the sky and the earth around them. Survival depended upon harmony and cooperation not only among human beings, but among all things— the animate and the less animate, since rocks and mountains were known to move, to travel occasionally.

11   The ancient Pueblos believed the Earth and the Sky were sisters (or sister and brother in the post-Christian version). As long as good family relations are maintained, then the Sky will continue to bless her sister, the Earth, with rain, and the Earth's children will continue to survive. But the old stories recall incidents in which troublesome spirits or beings threaten the earth. In one story, a malicious ka'tsina, called the Gambler, seizes the Shiwana, or Rainclouds, the Sun's beloved children. The Shiwana are snared in magical power late one afternoon on a high mountain top. The Gambler takes the Rainclouds to his mountain stronghold where he locks them in the north room of his house. What was his idea? The Shiwana were beyond value. They brought life to all things on earth. The Gambler wanted a big stake to wager in his games of chance. But such greed, even on the part of only one being, had the effect of threatening the survival of all life on earth. Sun Youth, aided by old Grandmother Spider, outsmarts the Gambler and the rigged game, and the Rainclouds are set free. The drought ends, and once more life thrives on earth.

THROUGH THE STORIES WE HEAR WHO WE ARE

12 All summer the people watch the west horizon, scanning the sky from south to north for rain clouds. Corn must have moisture at the time the tassels form. Oth-

erwise pollination will be incomplete, and the ears will be stunted and shriveled. An inadequate harvest may bring disaster. Stories told at Hopi, Zuni, and at Acoma and Laguna describe drought and starvation as recently as 1900. Precipitation in west-central New Mexico averages fourteen inches annually. The western pueblos are located at altitudes over 5,600 feet above sea level, where winter temperatures at night fall below freezing. Yet evidence of their presence in the high desert plateau country goes back ten thousand years. The ancient Pueblo people not only survived in this environment, but many years they thrived. In A.D. 1100 the people at Chaco Canyon had built cities with apartment buildings of stone five stories high. Their sophistication as sky-watchers was surpassed only by Mayan and Inca astronomers. Yet this vast complex of knowledge and belief, amassed for thousands of years, was never recorded in writing.

13　　　Instead, the ancient Pueblo people depended upon collective memory through successive generations to maintain and transmit an entire culture, a world view complete with proven strategies for survival. The oral narrative, or "story," became the medium in which the complex of Pueblo knowledge and belief was maintained. Whatever the event or the subject, the ancient people perceived the world and themselves within that world as part of an ancient continuous story composed of innumerable bundles of other stories.

14　　　The ancient Pueblo vision of the world was inclusive. The impulse was to leave nothing out. Pueblo oral tradition necessarily embraced all levels of human experience. Otherwise, the collective knowledge and beliefs comprising ancient Pueblo culture would have been incomplete. Thus stories about the Creation and Emergence of human beings and animals into this World continue to be retold each year for four days and four nights during the winter solstice. The "humma-hah" stories related events from the time long ago when human beings were still able to communicate with animals and other living things. But, beyond these two preceding categories, the Pueblo oral tradition knew no boundaries. Accounts of the appearance of the first Europeans in Pueblo country or of the tragic encounters between Pueblo people and Apache raiders were no more and no less important than stories about the biggest mule deer ever taken or adulterous couples surprised in cornfields and chicken coops. Whatever happened, the ancient people instinctively sorted events and details into a loose narrative structure. Everything became a story.

15　Traditionally everyone, from the youngest child to the oldest person, was expected to listen and to be able to recall or tell a portion, if only a small detail, from a narrative account or story. Thus the remembering and retelling were a communal process. Even if a key figure, an elder who knew much more than others, were to die unexpectedly, the system would remain intact. Through the efforts of a great many people, the community was able to piece together valuable accounts and crucial information that might otherwise have died with an individual.

16　　　Communal storytelling was a self-correcting process in which listeners were encouraged to speak up if they noted an important fact or detail omitted. The people were happy to listen to two or three different versions of the same event or the same humma-hah story. Even conflicting versions of an incident were welcomed for the entertainment they provided. Defenders of each version might joke and tease one another, but seldom were there any direct confrontations. Implicit in the Pueblo oral tradition was the awareness that loyalties, grudges, and kinship must always influence the narrator's choices as she emphasizes to listeners this is the way *she* has always heard the story told. The ancient Pueblo people sought a communal truth, not an absolute. For them this truth lived somewhere within the web of differing versions, disputes over minor points, outright contradictions tangling with old feuds and village rivalries.

17   A dinner-table conversation, recalling a deer hunt forty years ago when the largest mule deer ever was taken, inevitably stimulates similar memories in listeners. But hunting stories were not merely after-dinner entertainment. These accounts contained information of critical importance about behavior and migration patterns of mule deer. Hunting stories carefully described key landmarks and locations of fresh water. Thus a deer-hunt story might also serve as a "map." Lost travelers, and lost piñon-nut gatherers, have been saved by sighting a rock formation they recognize only because they once heard a hunting story describing this rock formation.

18   The importance of cliff formations and water holes does not end with hunting stories. As offspring of the Mother Earth, the ancient Pueblo people could not conceive of themselves within a specific landscape. Location, or "place," nearly always plays a central role in the Pueblo oral narratives. Indeed, stories are most frequently recalled as people are passing by a specific geographical feature or the exact place where a story takes place. The precise date of the incident often is less important than the place or location of the happening. "Long, long ago," "a long time ago," "not too long ago," and "recently" are usually how stories are classified in terms of time. But the places where the stories occur are precisely located, and prominent geographical details recalled, even if the landscape is well-known to listeners. Often because the turning point in the narrative involved a peculiarity or special quality of a rock or tree or plant found only at that place. Thus, in the case of many of the Pueblo narratives, it is impossible to determine which came first: the incident or the geographical feature which begs to be brought alive in a story that features some unusual aspect of this location.

19   There is a giant sandstone boulder about a mile north of Old Laguna, on the road to Paguate. It is ten feet tall and twenty feet in circumference. When I was a child, and we would pass this boulder driving to Paguate village, someone usually made reference to the story about Kochininako, Yellow Woman, and the Estrucuyo, a monstrous giant who nearly ate her. The Twin Hero Brothers saved Kochininako, who had been out hunting rabbits to take home to feed her mother and sisters. The Hero Brothers had heard her cries just in time. The Estrucuyo had cornered her in a cave too small to fit its monstrous head. Kochininako had already thrown to the Estrucuyo all her rabbits, as well as her moccasins and most of her clothing. Still the creature had not been satisfied. After killing the Estrucuyo with their bows and arrows, the Twin Hero Brothers slit open the Estrucuyo and cut out its heart. They threw the heart as far as they could. The monster's heart landed there, beside the old trail to Paguate village, where the sandstone boulder rests now.

20   It may be argued that the existence of the boulder precipitated the creation of

a story to explain it. But sandstone boulders and sandstone formations of strange shapes abound in the Laguna Pueblo area. Yet most of them do not have stories. Often the crucial element in a narrative is the terrain—some specific detail of the setting.

21   A high dark mesa rises dramatically from a grassy plain fifteen miles southeast of Laguna, in an area known as Swanee. On the grassy plain one hundred and forty years ago, my great-grandmother's uncle and his brother-in-law were grazing their herd of sheep. Because visibility on the plain extends for over twenty miles, it wasn't until the two sheepherders came near the high dark mesa that the Apaches were able to stalk them. Using the mesa to obscure their approach, the raiders swept around from both ends of the mesa. My great-grandmother's relatives were killed, and the herd lost. The high dark mesa played a critical role: the mesa had compromised the safety which the openness of the plains had seemed to assure. Pueblo and Apache alike relied upon the terrain, the very earth herself, to give them protection and aid. Human activities or needs were maneuvered to fit the existing surroundings and conditions. I imagine the last afternoon of my distant ancestors as warm and sunny for late September. They might have been traveling slowly, bringing the sheep closer to Laguna in preparation for the approach of colder weather. The grass was tall and only beginning to change from green to a yellow which matched the late-afternoon sun shining off it. There might have been comfort in the warmth and the sight of the sheep fattening on good pasture which lulled my ancestors into their fatal inattention. They might have had a rifle whereas the Apaches had only bows and arrows. But there would have been four or five Apache raiders, and the surprise attack would have canceled any advantage the rifles gave them.

22   Survival in any landscape comes down to making the best use of all available resources. On that particular September afternoon, the raiders made better use of the Swanee terrain than my poor ancestors did. Thus the high dark mesa and the story of the two lost Laguna herders became inextricably linked. The memory of them and their story resides in part with the high black mesa. For as long as the mesa stands, people within the family and clan will be reminded of the story of that afternoon long ago. Thus the continuity and accuracy of the oral narratives are reinforced by the landscape—and the Pueblo interpretation of that landscape is *maintained.*

QUESTIONS

Experience

· How do you respond to Silko's opening paragraphs about the burial habits of the Pueblo Indians? How do you respond to her description of the Indian hunters' relationship to their prey, the antelope?

Interpretation

· What point does Silko make about the Pueblos' relationship to nature? What details illustrate that point?

· What motivates the special relationship of the Pueblo people to nature?

Evaluation

· How do the arts and crafts of the Pueblo people reflect their attitude toward nature?

· What social and cultural values are especially important to them? Why?

WRITING

Exploring

· Describe the importance of storytelling in your life. You may wish to restrict your focus to the role of stories in the life of your family or to a particular type of story form or pattern you use to make sense of your own life.

Interpreting

· Summarize each part of Silko's essay. For each part zero in on a few key sentences. Quote those sentences in whole or in part in your summary of each section, and explain their significance.

Evaluating

· Discuss the Pueblo cultural values Silko describes. Explain how Pueblo ritual and attitudes reflect those values, and offer your own perspective on them. You may wish to use some of the ideas about stories Silko explores in her essay.

LOREN EISELEY
(1917–1977)

The Flow of the River

Loren Eiseley was a professor of anthropology at the University of Pennsylvania and a highly regarded naturalist and writer. His books include poetry, science writing, essays, and an autobiography. One of his best-known works, The Immense Journey (1955), describes the evolutionary development of life forms. The following essay has been taken from that book.

In "The Flow of the River" Eiseley recounts a number of his adventures with water. He sets his experiences amidst scientific and philosophical reflections on the significance of water, on its place in evolutionary history. What is distinctive about this piece is the way Eiseley blends descriptions of mundane matters, such as putting a mudfish in a tub of water, with a poetic prose that sings the praises of water's mysteries. One example occurs early in the essay, at the end of Eiseley's second paragraph, in which he describes "common water" like this: "Its substance reaches everywhere: it touches the past and prepares the future; it moves under the poles and wanders thinly in the heights of air. It can assume forms of exquisite perfection in a snowflake, or strip the living to a single shining bone cast up by the sea." This passage, typical of the writing throughout the essay, is notable for its balanced phrasing, for its perfectly controlled rhythm, and for its stunning concluding image.

1　If there is magic on this planet, it is contained in water. Its least stir even, as now in a rain pond on a flat roof opposite my office, is enough to bring me searching to the window. A wind ripple may be translating itself into life. I have a constant feeling that some time I may witness that momentous miracle on a city roof, see life veritably and suddenly boiling out of a heap of rusted pipes and old television aerials. I marvel at how suddenly a water beetle has come and is submarining there in a spatter of green algae. Thin vapors, rust, wet tar and sun are an alembic remarkably like the mind; they throw off odorous shadows that threaten to take real shape when no one is looking.

2　Once in a lifetime, perhaps, one escapes the actual confines of the flesh. Once in a lifetime, if one is lucky, one so merges with sunlight and air and running water that whole eons, the eons that mountains and deserts know, might pass in a single afternoon without discomfort. The mind has sunk away into its beginnings among old roots and the obscure tricklings and movings that stir inanimate things. Like the charmed fairy circle into which a man once stepped, and upon emergence learned that a whole century has passed in a single night, one can never quite define this secret; but it has something to do, I am sure, with common water. Its substance reaches everywhere: it touches the past and prepares the future; it moves under the poles and wanders thinly in the heights of air. It can assume forms of exquisite perfection in a snowflake, or strip the living to a single shining bone cast up by the sea.

3   Many years ago, in the course of some scientific investigations in a remote western county, I experienced, by chance, precisely this sort of curious absorption by water—the extension of shape by osmosis—at which I have been hinting. You have probably never experienced in yourself the meandering roots of a whole watershed or felt your outstretched fingers touching, by some kind of clairvoyant extension, the brooks of snow-line glaciers at the same time that you were flowing toward the Gulf over the eroded debris of worn-down mountains. A poet, MacKnight Black, has spoken of being "limbed . . . with waters gripping pole and pole." He had the idea, all right, and it is obvious that these sensations are not unique, but they are hard to come by; and the sort of extension of the senses that people will accept when they put their ear against a sea shell, they will smile at in the confessions of a bookish professor. What makes it worse is the fact that because of a traumatic experience in childhood, I am not a swimmer, and am inclined to be timid before any large body of water. Perhaps it was just this, in a way, that contributed to my experience.

4   As it leaves the Rockies and moves downward over the high plains towards the Missouri, the Platte River is a curious stream. In the spring floods, on occasion, it can be a mile-wide roaring torrent of destruction, gulping farms and bridges. Normally, however, it is a rambling, dispersed series of streamlets flowing erratically over great sand and gravel fans that are, in part, the remnants of a mightier Ice Age stream bed. Quicksands and shifting islands haunt its waters. Over it the prairie suns beat mercilessly throughout the summer. The Platte, "a mile wide and an inch deep," is a refuge for any heat-weary pilgrim along its shores. This is particularly true on the high plains before its long march by the cities begins.

5   The reason that I came upon it when I did, breaking through a willow thicket and stumbling out through ankle-deep water to a dune in the shade, is of no concern to this narrative. On various purposes of science I have ranged over a good bit of that country on foot, and I know the kinds of bones that come gurgling up through the gravel pumps, and the arrowheads of shining chalcedony that occasionally spill out of water-loosened sand. On that day, however, the sight of sky and willows and the weaving net of water murmuring a little in the shallows on its way to the Gulf stirred me, parched as I was with miles of walking, with a new idea: I was going to float. I was going to undergo a tremendous adventure.

6   The notion came to me, I suppose, by degrees. I had shed my clothes and was floundering pleasantly in a hole among some reeds when a great desire to stretch out and go with this gently insistent water began to pluck at me. Now to this bronzed, bold, modern generation, the struggle I waged with timidity while standing there in knee-deep water can only seem farcical; yet actually for me it was not so. A near-drowning accident in childhood had scarred my reactions; in addition to the fact that I was a nonswimmer, this "inch-deep river" was treacherous with holes and quicksands. Death was not precisely infrequent along its wandering and illusory channels. Like all broad wastes of this kind, where neither water nor land quite prevails, its thickets were lonely and untraversed. A man in trouble would cry out in vain.

7   I thought of all this, standing quietly in the water, feeling the sand shifting away under my toes. Then I lay back in the floating position that left my face to the

sky, and shoved off. The sky wheeled over me. For an instant, as I bobbed into the main channel, I had the sensation of sliding down the vast tilted face of the continent. It was then that I felt the cold needles of the alpine springs at my fingertips, and the warmth of the Gulf pulling me southward. Moving with me, leaving its taste upon my mouth and spouting under me in dancing springs of sand, was the immense body of the continent itself, flowing like the river was flowing, grain by grain, mountain by mountain, down to the sea. I was streaming over ancient sea beds thrust aloft where giant reptiles had once sported; I was wearing down the face of time and trundling cloud-wreathed ranges into oblivion. I touched my margins with the delicacy of a crayfish's antennae, and felt great fishes glide about their work.

8   I drifted by stranded timber cut by beaver in mountain fastnesses; I slid over shallows that had buried the broken axles of prairie schooners and the mired bones of mammoth. I was streaming alive through the hot and working ferment of the sun, or oozing secretively through shady thickets. I *was* water and the unspeakable alchemies that gestate and take shape in water, the slimy jellies that under the enormous magnification of the sun writhe and whip upward as great barbeled fish mouths, or sink indistinctly back into the murk out of which they arose. Turtle and fish and the pinpoint chirpings of individual frogs are all watery projections, concentrations—as man himself is a concentration—of that indescribable and liquid brew which is compounded in varying proportions of salt and sun and time. It has appearances, but at its heart lies water, and as I was finally edged gently against a sand bar and dropped like any log, I tottered as I rose. I knew once more the body's revolt against emergence into the harsh and unsupporting air, its reluctance to break contact with that mother element which still, at this late point in time, shelters and brings into being nine tenths of everything alive.

9   As for men, those myriad little detached ponds with their own swarming corpuscular life, what were they but a way that water has of going about beyond the reach of rivers? I, too, was a microcosm of pouring rivulets and floating driftwood gnawed by the mysterious animalcules of my own creation. I was three fourths water, rising and subsiding according to the hollow knocking in my veins: a minute pulse like the eternal pulse that lifts Himalayas and which, in the following systole, will carry them away.

10   Thoreau, peering at the emerald pickerel in Walden Pond, called them "animalized water" in one of his moments of strange insight. If he had been possessed of the geological knowledge so laboriously accumulated since his time, he might have gone further and amusedly detected in the planetary rumblings and eructations which so delighted him in the gross habits of certain frogs, signs of that dark interior stress which has reared sea bottoms up to mountainous heights. He might have developed an acute inner ear for the sound of the surf on Cretaceous beaches where now the wheat of Kansas rolls. In any case, he would have seen, as the long trail of life was unfolded by the fossil hunters, that his animalized water had changed its shapes eon by eon to the beating of the earth's dark millennial heart. In the swamps of the low continents, the amphibians had flourished and had their day; and as the long skyward swing—the isostatic response of the crust—had come about, the era of the cooling grasslands and mammalian life had come into being.

11   A few winters ago, clothed heavily against the weather, I wandered several miles along one of the tributaries of that same Platte I had floated down years before. The land was stark and ice-locked. The rivulets were frozen, and over the marshlands the willow thickets made such an array of vertical lines against the snow that tramping through them produced strange optical illusions and dizziness. On the edge of a frozen backwater, I stopped and rubbed my eyes. At my feet a raw prairie wind had swept the ice clean of snow. A peculiar green object caught my eye; there was no mistaking it.

12   Staring up at me with all his barbels spread pathetically, frozen solidly in the wind-ruffled ice, was a huge familiar face. It was one of those catfish of the twisting channels, those dwellers in the yellow murk, who had been about me and beneath me on the day of my great voyage. Whatever sunny dream had kept him paddling there while the mercury plummeted downward and that Cheshire smile froze slowly, it would be hard to say. Or perhaps he was trapped in a blocked channel and had simply kept swimming until the tide contracted around him. At any rate, there he would lie till the spring thaw.

13   At that moment I started to turn away, but something in the bleak, whiskered face reproached me, or perhaps it was the river calling to her children. I termed it science, however—a convenient rational phrase I reserve for such occasions—and decided that I would cut the fish out of the ice and take him home. I had no intention of eating him. I was merely struck by a sudden impulse to test the survival qualities of high-plains fishes, particularly fishes of this type who get themselves immured in oxygenless ponds or in cut-off oxbows buried in winter drifts. I blocked him out as gently as possible and dropped him, ice and all, into a collecting can in the car. Then we set out for home.

14   Unfortunately, the first stages of what was to prove a remarkable resurrection escaped me. Cold and tired after a long drive, I deposited the can with its melting water and ice in the basement. The accompanying corpse I anticipated I would either dispose of or dissect on the following day. A hurried glance had revealed no signs of life.

15   To my astonishment, however, upon descending into the basement several hours later, I heard stirrings in the receptacle and peered in. The ice had melted. A vast pouting mouth ringed with sensitive feelers confronted me, and the creature's gills labored slowly. A thin stream of silver bubbles rose to the surface and popped. A fishy eye gazed up at me protestingly.

16   "A tank," it said. This was no Walden pickerel. This was a yellow-green, mud-grubbing, evil-tempered inhabitant of floods and droughts and cyclones. It was the selective product of the high continent and the waters that pour across it. It had outlasted the prairie blizzards that left cattle standing frozen upright in the drifts.

17   "I'll get the tank," I said respectfully.

18   He lived with me all that winter, and his departure was totally in keeping with his sturdy, independent character. In the spring a migratory impulse or perhaps sheer boredom struck him. Maybe, in some little lost corner of his brain, he felt, far off, the pouring of the mountain waters through the sandy coverts of the Platte. Anyhow, something called to him, and he went. One night when no one was about, he simply jumped out of his tank. I found him dead on the floor next morn-

ing. He had made his gamble like a man—or, I should say, a fish. In the proper place it would not have been a fool's gamble. Fishes in the drying shallows of intermittent prairie streams who feel their confinement and have the impulse to leap while there is yet time may regain the main channel and survive. A million ancestral years had gone into that jump, I thought as I looked at him, a million years of climbing through prairie sunflowers and twining in and out through the pillared legs of drinking mammoth.

19   "Some of your close relatives have been experimenting with air breathing," I remarked, apropos of nothing, as I gathered him up. "Suppose we meet again up there in the cottonwoods in a million years or so."

20   I missed him a little as I said it. He had for me the kind of lost archaic glory that comes from the water brotherhood. We were both projections out of that timeless ferment and locked as well in some greater unity that lay incalculably beyond us. In many a fin and reptile foot I have seen myself passing by—some part of myself, that is, some part that lies unrealized in the momentary shape I inhabit. People have occasionally written me harsh letters and castigated me for a lack of faith in man when I have ventured to speak of this matter in print. They distrust, it would seem, all shapes and thoughts but their own. They would bring God into the compass of a shopkeeper's understanding and confine Him to those limits, lest He proceed to some unimaginable and shocking act—create perhaps, as a casual afterthought, a being more beautiful than man. As for me, I believe nature capable of this, and having been part of the flow of the river, I feel no envy—any more than the frog envies the reptile or an ancestral ape should envy man.

21   Every spring in the wet meadows and ditches I hear a little shrilling chorus which sounds for all the world like an endlessly reiterated "We're here, we're here." And so they are, as frogs, of course. Confident little fellows. I suspect that to some greater ear than ours, man's optimistic pronouncements about his role and destiny may make a similar little ringing sound that travels a small way out into the night. It is only its nearness that is offensive. From the heights of a mountain, or a marsh at evening, it blends, not too badly, with all the other sleepy voices that, in croaks or chirrups, are saying the same thing.

22   After a while the skilled listener can distinguish man's noise from the katydid's rhythmic assertion, allow for the offbeat of a rabbit's thumping, pick up the autumnal monotone of crickets, and find in all of them a grave pleasure without admitting any to a place of preeminence in his thoughts. It is when all these voices cease and the waters are still, when along the frozen river nothing cries, screams or howls that the enormous mindlessness of space settles down upon the soul. Somewhere out in that waste of crushed ice and reflected stars, the black waters may be running, but they appear to be running without life toward a destiny in which the whole of space may be locked in some silvery winter of dispersed radiation.

23   It is then, when the wind comes straitly across the barren marshes and the snow rises and beats in endless waves against the traveler, that I remember best, by some trick of the imagination, my summer voyage on the river. I remember my green extensions, my catfish nuzzlings and minnow wrigglings, my gelatinous materializations out of the mother ooze. And as I walk on through the white smother, it is the magic of water that leaves me a final sign.

24   Men talk much of matter and energy, of the struggle for existence that molds the shape of life. These things exist, it is true; but more delicate, elusive, quicker than the fins in water, is that mysterious principle known as "organization," which leaves all other mysteries concerned with life stale and insignificant by comparison. For that without organization life does not persist is obvious. Yet this organization itself is not strictly the product of life, nor of selection. Like some dark and passing shadow within matter, it cups out the eyes' small windows or spaces the notes of a meadow lark's song in the interior of a mottled egg. That principle—I am beginning to suspect—was there before the living in the deeps of water.

25   The temperature has risen. The little stinging needles have given way to huge flakes floating in like white leaves blown from some great tree in open space. In the car, switching on the lights, I examine one intricate crystal on my sleeve before it melts. No utilitarian philosophy explains a snow crystal, no doctrine of use or disuse. Water has merely leapt out of vapor and thin nothingness in the night sky to array itself in form. There is no logical reason for the existence of a snowflake any more than there is for evolution. It is an apparition from that mysterious shadow world beyond nature, that final world which contains—if anything contains—the explanation of men and catfish and green leaves.

QUESTIONS

Experience

· What were your impressions as you read through Eiseley's musings about water? To what extent did he carry you with him on his meandering journey?
· Have you ever experienced a desire like the one Eiseley describes that he had—to go with the flow of nature, in his case the flow of the river? Why, or why not?

Interpretation

· What do you think Eiseley means when he says that "once in a lifetime, perhaps, one escapes the actual confines of the flesh"? How can you escape the finite limits of your body?
· What does Eiseley experience and learn from his journey as he flows with the river?

Evaluation

· How would you characterize Eiseley's attitude toward the natural world? To what extent is his thinking and behavior scientific? To what extent is it mystical?

WRITING

Exploring

· Write an essay about a time when you gave yourself over to an element of the natural world—water, snow, light, a river, mountain, lake. Or imagine what this kind of experience would be like for you. Describe how you felt (or how you imagine that you would feel) in this environment and what, if anything, you may have learned.

Interpreting

· Analyze the images of water Eiseley includes in his essay. Look especially at places where he compares water with other things, or points at which he describes something in terms of water.

Evaluating

· Discuss Eiseley's vision of nature as exhibited through his valuing of water. How does he see nature? How does he attempt to connect himself with it?

MAILE MELOY
(b. 1972)

Horse-Love

Maile Meloy is a recent graduate of Harvard University, where she majored in English. She did a part of her college study abroad, at Oxford University, where she studied Renaissance literature. She is currently completing an M.F.A. at Columbia University. Her essay considers the ways women are pressured by society to be concerned with their appearance. Weaving her reading into her experience growing up female, Meloy reflects on aspects of femininity she both relishes and disparages.

Meloy wrote "Horse-Love" for a freshman class in expository writing. She began by writing brief exercises about animals and childhood classmates. The one about animals interested her more, so she developed it further. After writing a number of pages, she decided that her real subject would be horses, and in subsequent drafts, she expanded her essay by adding other experiences with a family horse, Chanco, as well as references to horses in films. The essay is noteworthy for its careful descriptive detail and for its characterization of the special relationship that exists between horse-lovers and the splendid animals they love.

1   Nothing is more unapologetically physical and natural than the birth of a horse. In a stable warm and dank with horse sweat and human bodies, acrid manure fumes mingle with the sweet smell of fresh hay piled onto remains of molding straw. The mare's restless shuffling in the hay kicks up dust which hangs in the air, catching light and tickling nostrils until it floats down to stick in a gray film on the horse's sweating flanks. Around this strange nativity are gathered the worried midwives: unshaven and rumpled horsemen in plaid flannel, women in rubber boots caked with manure, a vet with rolled-up sleeves. Each stands by, blinking from lost sleep and patient vigilance, but alert. Finally the sticky, blue-gray, leggy mass is brought into the world.

2   A thoroughbred foal is not only a financial investment. No true horseperson will be able to look you in the eye and tell you there's no emotional attachment, that the stillbirth of a colt has never provoked tears, or that the sudden death of a mare does not cast a pervasive gloom over an otherwise perfect Sunday.

3   My father called tonight, with news that his favorite mare, Chanco, is overdue with her foal by a week. My birthday was the projected due date, but she hasn't yet delivered and the wait has been prolonged. "She's just pretty miserable out there," he told me. "All full of colt like that." After only a week, I could hear concern in his voice. Cambridge seems very removed from southwest Montana, but even at this distance I felt the tug of concern. Chanco is a California horse, used to California tracks and California winters. She suffers more in any winter than northern horses do, and with a foal on the way. . . . Talking to him, I was struck by the realization of horse-love, and of my connection to a world of ranches, horses, and Western clichés.

4   My exposure to the world of horses began at the age of six, when I watched with fascination and horror a stallion being castrated. Thick, black rubber-bands stretched the skin tight across his balls, and as the vet quickly and expertly slit the stretched skin down the middle, it burst forth with white and blue-veined shiny insides like Red Riding-Hood's granny leaping from the inside of the Wolf's belly. Disgusted and as offended as I thought I should be, I drew back as he began the second, but the morbidity that draws people inexorably to accidents and ambulances kept me gaping at the revolting operation.

5   Not all of my experiences with horses are bloody or unpleasant. Horses can be so mild and devoted that their great, reflective eyes take on a human quality. Our first horse was an old Tennessee Walker named Lancer who could easily be trusted with children. When my friend Chanda and I were riding double in a pasture, however, we slid right off Lancer's bare back onto the ground. When he realized what had happened, he stopped, turned around, and had all but picked us up off the ground before our frantic parents could reach us.

6   I remember the races, as well. In the hot, dry summer in a halter top and shorts with a chocolate-covered ice cream bar dripping slowly over my fingers, I would go to watch Winking Doll race. She was my uncle's horse, and when my grandfather would watch her run, he would put money on her for me—to win, not to place, although placing was a safer bet. When my ticket had won, we would get to go to the Winner's Circle with Winkie and her jockey and the trainers. The trainers look the same to me now as they did then. They seem not to have changed. They are wrinkled and tanned and wear worn boots, their hands smell like horse medicine, and they are devoted to their horses. Every little cough is worrisome to the trainers, every race is an event, and any injury is devastating. The horses have changed throughout the years, the devotion has not; twelve years ago it was Winking Doll, now it is Chanco, and in two years it will be Chanco's waiting foal.

7   Even those who have not experienced this symbiosis have a conception of the horse as it has been glorified in our culture. While race-horse movies like *Black Beauty, The Black Stallion,* and *Pharlap* bestow on horses human character and desire, a truer portrayal of the nature of horses is the American Western. Kevin Costner's charming and comic difficulties with his horse in this year's Oscar-winning *Dances with Wolves* provide some of the most memorable moments of the film. The Lone Ranger had his Silver and Roy Rogers his Trigger and the mounts are as well and as fondly remembered as the riders. The horses who appear in Westerns, in fact, often have longer resumes than the actors who ride them. While production assistants "wrangle" extras and corral them in stuffy buildings, the horse-actors are pampered and carefully watched. And well they should be, for they usually deliver more honest performances than their human counterparts. The headstrong but fiercely loyal horse characters that appear in the most contrived of Spaghetti Westerns ring true and echo the tradition of horse-love.

8   When I speak of horse-love, I'm not talking about ten-year-old girls in love with horses, girls who paper their walls with photographs of Appaloosas and obsess, Catherine-the-Great-style, about a giant dappled stallion named Misty. I'm referring to the ties that develop when people live with horses, live for horses, gain their living through horses, and develop a mutually supportive relationship with the powerful beasts. Horses are a conquered species. They are our slaves and our sport. Yet certain people seem to find communion with the restless, spir-

ited creatures who have learned to love their domestication. People who work with horses acquire their silence and strength. They exhibit a degree of awkwardness with other people. You can detect a glazing of the eye in social situations suggesting they would rather be where polite conversation is unnecessary and appearances can be dropped. They have come to expect the same honesty in humans that they find in horses, and, finding humans consistently lacking, they tend to prefer equine company.

9   There are still places in which horses are people's lifeblood. Richard III's "My kingdom for a horse" dependence has not yet been swallowed up by dirty cities and asphalt, and it's strangely comforting. I may have romanticized here the obvious use, for our purposes, of an animal that once embodied absolute freedom. But anyone who has stumbled sleepily out of bed in the pre-dawn darkness and pulled on boots to trudge through a foot of snow to the stables where great, black forms stamp their hooves impatiently on the frozen ground and snort gratefully, glad you've finally come with hay that blows into your eyes and sticky grain—anyone who has put horses first in his or her life, even for a little while, knows that there's something wonderful about this quiet communion.

10   And so I wait, concerned about the little foal who was supposed to have my birthday, and concerned about his cold, unhappy mother. As I ride the subway or take an umbrella against the mist, my mind skips to cold, dry Montana where a colt will be born into a world of stamping, impatient horses and humans awaiting his arrival. He will continue the tradition, serve and be served, be driven and glorified and take his part in the legacy of this oddly beautiful cross-special tie.

QUESTIONS

Experience

· If you have ever ridden a horse or been close to horses, how well does Maile Meloy's essay mesh with your experience of them? If you have not, how well does Maile Meloy convey her appreciation of horses to you?

Interpretation

· Does this essay have a main idea? If so, what is it? If not, what is the essay's purpose?

Evaluation

· What do you think the writer means by her "connection to a world of ranches, horses, and Western clichés"? What kinds of western clichés do you think she is referring to?

WRITING

Exploring

· Write your own essay about your love (or hatred?) for some aspect of the natural world. You may wish to write about an animal, a group of animals or plants, or some other element of nature. Try to convey your feeling and your attitude through specific examples and incidents.

Interpreting

· Analyze the structure and content of "Horse-Love." In addition to specific horses the writer mentions, what else does she include in her essay? Chart its organization, and explain the function of each element included—from the scene describing the birth of a foal to the reference to horses in *Dancing with Wolves*.

Evaluating

· Discuss the specific virtues and values Maile Meloy associates with horses. Explain why you think she believes that people who work with horses may "tend to prefer equine company." Does this feeling make sense to you? Why, or why not?

TESS GALLAGHER
(b. 1932)

The Lover of Horses

Tess Gallagher was born in Port Angeles, Washington, and attended the University of Washington, where she received both bachelor's and master's degrees. She also holds a master's from the University of Iowa. She has taught at a number of universities, including Syracuse, Arizona, and Montana. A poet as well as a writer of fiction, she has published several volumes of poetry, including Instructions to the Double *(1976)*, Under Stars *(1978)*, Willingly *(1984), and* Amplitude: New and Selected Poems *(1987). She has written two screenplays, a volume of criticism, and a collection of short stories,* The Lover of Horses *(1986), from which the following story has been taken.*

In "The Lover of Horses" Gallagher takes us into a world where it is possible for some people to communicate with horses, to talk sense into them. She conveys a sense of the mysterious bond that exists between humans and animals, and she also establishes a strong bond between her young female narrator and her father—a bond that is explicitly and strikingly memorialized in the narrator's final comment at the story's conclusion.

1   They say my great-grandfather was a gypsy, but the most popular explanation for his behavior was that he was a drunk. How else could the women have kept up the scourge of his memory all these years, had they not had the usual malady of our family to blame? Probably he was both a gypsy and a drunk.

2   Still, I have reason to believe the gypsy in him had more to do with the turn his life took than his drinking. I used to argue with my mother about this, even though most of the information I have about my great-grandfather came from my mother, who got it from her mother. A drunk, I kept telling her, would have had no initiative. He would simply have gone down with his failures and had nothing to show for it. But my great-grandfather had eleven children, surely a sign of industry, and he was a lover of horses. He had so many horses he was what people called "horse poor."

3   I did not learn, until I traveled to where my family originated at Collenamore in the west of Ireland, that my great-grandfather had most likely been a "whisperer," a breed of men among the gypsies who were said to possess the power of talking sense into horses. These men had no fear of even the most malicious and dangerous horses. In fact, they would often take the wild animal into a closed stall in order to perform their skills.

4   Whether a certain intimacy was needed or whether the whisperers simply wanted to protect their secret conversations with horses is not known. One thing was certain—that such men gained power over horses by whispering. What they whispered no one knew. But the effectiveness of their methods was renowned, and anyone for counties around who had an unruly horse could send for a whis-

perer and be sure that the horse would take to heart whatever was said and reform his behavior from that day forth.

5   By all accounts, my great-grandfather was like a huge stallion himself, and when he went into a field where a herd of horses was grazing, the horses would suddenly lift their heads and call to him. Then his bearded mouth would move, and though he was making sounds that could have been words, which no horse would have had reason to understand, the horses would want to hear; and one by one they would move toward him across the open space of the field. He could turn his back and walk down the road, and they would follow him. He was probably drunk, my mother said, because he was swaying and mumbling all the while. Sometimes he would stop deadstill in the road and the horses would press up against him and raise and lower their heads as he moved his lips. But because these things were only seen from a distance, and because they have eroded in the telling, it is now impossible to know whether my great-grandfather said anything of importance to the horses. Or even if it was his whispering that had brought about their good behavior. Nor was it clear, when he left them in some barnyard as suddenly as he'd come to them, whether they had arrived at some new understanding of the difficult and complex relationship between men and horses.

6   Only the aberrations of my great-grandfather's relationship with horses have survived—as when he would bathe in the river with his favorite horse or when, as my grandmother told my mother, he insisted on conceiving his ninth child in the stall of a bay mare named Redwing. Not until I was grown and going through the family Bible did I discover that my grandmother had been this ninth child, and so must have known something about the matter.

7   These oddities in behavior lead me to believe that when my great-grandfather, at the age of fifty-two, abandoned his wife and family to join a circus that was passing through the area, it was not simply drunken bravado, nor even the understandable wish to escape family obligations. I believe the gypsy in him finally got the upper hand, and it led to such a remarkable happening that no one in the family has so far been willing to admit it: not the obvious transgression—that he had run away to join the circus—but that he was in all likelihood a man who had been stolen by a horse.

8   This is not an easy view to sustain in the society we live in. But I have not come to it frivolously, and have some basis for my belief. For although I have heard the story of my great-grandfather's defection time and again since childhood, the one image which prevails in all versions is that of a dappled gray stallion that had been trained to dance a variation of the mazurka. So impressive was this animal that he mesmerized crowds with his sliding step-and-hop to the side through the complicated figures of the dance, which he performed, not in the way of Lippizaners*—with other horses and their riders—but riderless and with the men of the circus company as his partners.

9   It is known that my great-grandfather became one of these dancers. After that he was reputed, in my mother's words, to have gone "completely to ruin." The fact that he walked from the house with only the clothes on his back, leaving

---

* *Lippizaners:* world-famous Austrian show horses trained at the Spanish Riding School of Vienna.

behind his own beloved horses (twenty-nine of them to be exact), further supports my idea that a powerful force must have held sway over him, something more profound than the miseries of drink or the harsh imaginings of his abandoned wife.

10   Not even the fact that seven years later he returned and knocked on his wife's door, asking to be taken back, could exonerate him from what he had done, even though his wife did take him in and looked after him until he died some years later. But the detail that no one takes note of in the account is that when my great-grandfather returned, he was carrying a saddle blanket and the black plumes from the headgear of one of the circus horses. This passes by even my mother as simply a sign of the ridiculousness of my great-grandfather's plight—for after all, he was homeless and heading for old age as a "good for nothing drunk" and a "fool for horses."

11   No one has bothered to conjecture what these curious emblems—saddle blanket and plumes—must have meant to my great-grandfather. But he hung them over the foot of his bed—"like a fool," my mother said. And sometimes when he got very drunk he would take up the blanket and, wrapping it like a shawl over his shoulders, he would grasp the plumes. Then he would dance the mazurka. He did not dance in the living room but took himself out into the field, where the horses stood at attention and watched as if suddenly experiencing the smell of the sea or a change of wind in the valley. "Drunks don't care what they do," my mother would say as she finished her story about my great-grandfather. "Talking to a drunk is like talking to a stump."

12   Ever since my great-grandfather's outbreaks of gypsy necessity, members of my family have been stolen by things—by mad ambitions, by musical instruments, by otherwise harmless pursuits from mushroom hunting to childbearing or, as was my father's case, by the more easily recognized and popular obsession with card playing. To some extent, I still think it was failure of imagination in this respect that brought about his diminished prospects in the life of our family.

13   But even my mother had been powerless against the attraction of a man so convincingly driven. When she met him at a birthday dance held at the country house of one of her young friends, she asked him what he did for a living. My father pointed to a deck of cards in his shirt pocket and said, "I play cards." But love is such as it is, and although my mother was otherwise a deadly practical woman, it seemed she could fall in love with no man but my father.

14   So it is possible that the propensity to be stolen is somewhat contagious when ordinary people come into contact with people such as my father. Though my mother loved him at the time of the marriage, she soon began to behave as if she had been stolen from a more fruitful and upright life which she was always imagining might have been hers.

15   My father's card playing was accompanied, to no one's surprise, by bouts of drinking. The only thing that may have saved our family from a life of poverty was the fact that my father seldom gambled with money. Such were his charm and powers of persuasion that he was able to convince other players to accept his notes on everything from the fish he intended to catch next season to the sale of his daughter's hair.

16   I know about this last wager because I remember the day he came to me with

a pair of scissors and said it was time to cut my hair. Two snips and it was done. I cannot forget the way he wept onto the backs of his hands and held the braids together like a broken noose from which a life had suddenly slipped. I was thirteen at the time and my hair had never been cut. It was his pride and joy that I had such hair. But for me it was only a burdensome difference between me and my classmates, so I was glad to be rid of it. What anyone else could have wanted with my long shiny braids is still a mystery to me.

17 When my father was seventy-three he fell ill and the doctors gave him only a few weeks to live. My father was convinced that his illness had come on him because he'd hit a particularly bad losing streak at cards. He had lost heavily the previous month, and items of value, mostly belonging to my mother, had disappeared from the house. He developed the strange idea that if he could win at cards he could cheat the prediction of the doctors and live at least into his eighties.

18 By this time I had moved away from home and made a life for myself in an attempt to follow the reasonable dictates of my mother, who had counseled her children severely against all manner of rash ambition and foolhardiness. Her entreaties were leveled especially in my direction since I had shown a suspect enthusiasm for a certain pony at around the age of five. And it is true I felt I had lost a dear friend when my mother saw to it that the neighbors who owned this pony moved it to pasture elsewhere.

19 But there were other signs that I might wander off into unpredictable pursuits. The most telling of these was that I refused to speak aloud to anyone until the age of eleven. I whispered everything, as if my mind were a repository of secrets which could only be divulged in this intimate manner. If anyone asked me a question, I was always polite about answering, but I had to do it by putting my mouth near the head of my inquisitor and using only my breath and lips to make my reply.

20 My teachers put my whispering down to shyness and made special accommodations for me. When it came time for recitations I would accompany the teacher into the cloakroom and there whisper to her the memorized verses or the speech I was to have prepared. God knows, I might have continued on like this into the present if my mother hadn't plotted with some neighborhood boys to put burrs into my long hair. She knew by other signs that I had a terrible temper, and she was counting on that to deliver me into the world where people shouted and railed at one another and talked in an audible fashion about things both common and sacred.

21 When the boys shut me into a shed, according to plan, there was nothing for me to do but to cry out for help and to curse them in a torrent of words I had only heard used by adults. When my mother heard this she rejoiced, thinking that at last she had broken the treacherous hold of the past over me, of my great-grandfather's gypsy blood and the fear that against all her efforts I might be stolen away, as she had been, and as my father had, by some as yet unforeseen predilection. Had I not already experienced the consequences of such a life in our household, I doubt she would have been successful, but the advantages of an ordinary existence among people of a less volatile nature had begun to appeal to me.

22 It was strange, then, that after all the care my mother had taken for me in this

regard, when my father's illness came on him, my mother brought her appeal to me. "Can you do something?" she wrote, in her cramped, left-handed scrawl. "He's been drinking and playing cards for three days and nights. I am at my wit's end. Come home at once."

23   Somehow I knew this was a message addressed to the very part of me that most baffled and frightened my mother—the part that belonged exclusively to my father and his family's inexplicable manias.

24   When I arrived home my father was not there.

25   "He's at the tavern. In the back room," my mother said. "He hasn't eaten for days. And if he's slept, he hasn't done it here."

26   I made up a strong broth, and as I poured the steaming liquid into a Thermos I heard myself utter syllables and other vestiges of language which I could not reproduce if I wanted to. "What do you mean by that?" my mother demanded, as if a demon had leapt out of me. "What did you say?" I didn't—I couldn't—answer her. But suddenly I felt that an unsuspected network of sympathies and distant connections had begun to reveal itself to me in my father's behalf.

27   There is a saying that when lovers have need of moonlight, it is there. So it seemed, as I made my way through the deserted town toward the tavern and card room, that all nature had been given notice of my father's predicament, and that the response I was waiting for would not be far off.

28   But when I arrived at the tavern and had talked my way past the barman and into the card room itself, I saw that my father had an enormous pile of blue chips at his elbow. Several players had fallen out to watch, heavy-lidded and smoking their cigarettes like weary gangsters. Others were slumped on folding chairs near the coffee urn with its empty "Pay Here" styrofoam cup.

29   My father's cap was pushed to the back of his head so that his forehead shone in the dim light, and he grinned over his cigarette at me with the serious preoccupation of a child who has no intention of obeying anyone. And why should he, I thought as I sat down just behind him and loosened the stopper on the Thermos. The five or six players still at the table casually appraised my presence to see if it had tipped the scales of their luck in an even more unfavorable direction. Then they tossed their cards aside, drew fresh cards, or folded.

30   In the center of the table were more blue chips, and poking out from my father's coat pocket I recognized the promissory slips he must have redeemed, for he leaned to me and in a low voice, without taking his eyes from his cards, said, "I'm having a hell of a good time. The time of my life."

31   He was winning. His face seemed ravaged by the effort, but he was clearly playing on a level that had carried the game far beyond the realm of mere card playing and everyone seemed to know it. The dealer cocked an eyebrow as I poured broth into the plastic Thermos cup and handed it to my father, who slurped from it noisily, then set it down.

32   "Tell the old kettle she's got to put up with me a few more years," he said, and lit up a fresh cigarette. His eyes as he looked at me, however, seemed overbrilliant, as if doubt, despite all his efforts, had gained a permanent seat at his table. I squeezed his shoulder and kissed him hurriedly on his forehead. The men kept their eyes down, and as I paused at the door, there was a shifting of chairs and a clearing of throats. Just outside the room I nearly collided with the barman,

who was carrying in a fresh round of beer. His heavy jowls waggled as he recovered himself and looked hard at me over the icy bottles. Then he disappeared into the card room with his provisions.

33   I took the long way home, finding pleasure in the fact that at this hour all the stoplights had switched onto a flashing-yellow caution cycle. Even the teenagers who usually cruised the town had gone home or to more secluded spots. *Doubt,* I kept thinking as I drove with my father's face before me, that's the real thief. And I knew my mother had brought me home because of it, because she knew that once again a member of our family was about to be stolen.

34   Two more days and nights I ministered to my father at the card room. I would never stay long because I had the fear myself that I might spoil his luck. But many unspoken tendernesses passed between us in those brief appearances as he accepted the nourishment I offered, or when he looked up and handed me his beer bottle to take a swig from—a ritual we'd shared since my childhood.

35   My father continued to win—to the amazement of the local barflies who poked their faces in and out of the card room and gave the dwindling three or four stalwarts who remained at the table a commiserating shake of their heads. There had never been a winning streak like it in the history of the tavern, and indeed, we heard later that the man who owned the card room and tavern had to sell out and open a fruit stand on the edge of town as a result of my father's extraordinary good luck.

36   Twice during this period my mother urged the doctor to order my father home. She was sure my father would, at some fateful moment, risk the entire winnings in some mad rush toward oblivion. But his doctor spoke of a new "gaming therapy" for the terminally ill, based on my father's surge of energies in the pursuit of his gambling. Little did he know that my father was, by that stage, oblivious to even his winning, he had gone so far into exhaustion.

37   Luckily for my father, the hour came when, for lack of players, the game folded. Two old friends drove him home and helped him down from the pickup. They paused in the driveway, one on either side of him, letting him steady himself. When the card playing had ended there had been nothing for my father to do but to get drunk.

38   My mother and I watched from the window as the men steered my father toward the hydrangea bush at the side of the house, where he relieved himself with perfect precision on one mammoth blossom. Then they hoisted him up the stairs and into the entryway. My mother and I took over from there.

39   "Give 'em hell, boys," my father shouted after the men, concluding some conversation he was having with himself.

40   "You betcha," the driver called back, laughing. Then he climbed with his companion into the cab of his truck and roared away.

41   Tied around my father's waist was a cloth sack full of bills and coins which flapped and jingled against his knees as we bore his weight between us up the next flight of stairs and into the living room. There we deposited him on the couch, where he took up residence, refusing to sleep in his bed—for fear, my mother claimed, that death would know where to find him. But I preferred to think he enjoyed the rhythms of the household; from where he lay at the center of the

house, he could overhear all conversations that took place and add his opinions when he felt like it.

42   My mother was so stricken by the signs of his further decline that she did everything he asked, instead of arguing with him or simply refusing. Instead of taking his winnings straight to the bank so as not to miss a day's interest, she washed an old goldfish bowl and dumped all the money into it, most of it in twenty-dollar bills. Then she placed it on the coffee table near his head so he could run his hand through it at will, or let his visitors do the same.

43   "Money feels good on your elbow," he would say to them. "I played them under the table for that. Yes sir, take a feel of that!" Then he would lean back on his pillows and tell my mother to bring his guests a shot of whiskey. "Make sure she fills my glass up," he'd say to me so that my mother was certain to overhear. And my mother, who'd never allowed a bottle of whiskey to be brought into her house before now, would look at me as if the two of us were more than any woman should have to bear.

44   "If you'd only brought him home from that card room," she said again and again. "Maybe it wouldn't have come to this."

45   *This* included the fact that my father had radically altered his diet. He lived only on greens. If it was green he would eat it. By my mother's reckoning, the reason for his change of diet was that if he stopped eating what he usually ate, death would think it wasn't him and go look for somebody else.

46   Another request my father made was asking my mother to sweep the doorway after anyone came in or went out.

47   "To make sure death wasn't on their heels; to make sure death didn't slip in as they left." This was my mother's reasoning. But my father didn't give any reasons. Nor did he tell us finally why he wanted all the furniture moved out of the room except for the couch where he lay. And the money, they could take that away too.

48   But soon his strength began to ebb, and more and more family and friends crowded into the vacant room to pass the time with him, to laugh about stories remembered from his childhood or from his nights as a young man at the country dances when he and his older brother would work all day in the cotton fields, hop a freight train to town and dance all night. Then they would have to walk home, getting there just at daybreak in time to go straight to work again in the cotton fields.

49   "We were like bulls then," my father would say in a burst of the old vigor, then close his eyes suddenly as if he hadn't said anything at all.

50   As long as he spoke to us, the inevitability of his condition seemed easier to bear. But when, at the last, he simply opened his mouth for food or stared silently toward the far wall, no one knew what to do with themselves.

51   My own part in that uncertain time came to me accidentally. I found myself in the yard sitting on a stone bench under a little cedar tree my father loved because he liked to sit there and stare at the ocean. The tree whispered, he said. He said it had a way of knowing what your troubles were. Suddenly a craving came over me. I wanted a cigarette, even though I don't smoke, hate smoking, in fact. I was sitting where my father had sat, and to smoke seemed a part of some rightness

that had begun to work its way within me. I went into the house and bummed a pack of cigarettes from my brother. For the rest of the morning I sat under the cedar tree and smoked. My thoughts drifted with its shifting and murmurings, and it struck me what a wonderful thing nature is because it knows the value of silence, the innuendos of silence and what they could mean for a wordbound creature such as I was.

52　　　I passed the rest of the day in a trance of silences, moving from place to place, revisiting the sites I knew my father loved—the "dragon tree," a hemlock which stood at the far end of the orchard, so named for how the wind tossed its triangular head; the rose arbor where he and my mother had courted; the little marina where I sat in his fishing boat and dutifully smoked the hated cigarettes, flinging them one by one into the brackish water.

53　　　I was waiting to know what to do for him, he who would soon be a piece of useless matter of no more consequence than the cigarette butts that floated and washed against the side of his boat. I could feel some action accumulating in me through the steadiness of water raising and lowering the boat, through the sad petal-fall of roses in the arbor and the tossing of the dragon tree.

54　　　That night when I walked from the house I was full of purpose. I headed toward the little cedar tree. Without stopping to question the necessity of what I was doing, I began to break off the boughs I could reach and to pile them on the ground.

55　　　"What are you doing?" my brother's children wanted to know, crowding around me as if I might be inventing some new game for them.

56　　　"What does it look like?" I said.

57　　　"Pulling limbs off the tree," the oldest said. Then they dashed away in a pack under the orchard trees, giggling and shrieking.

58　　　As I pulled the boughs from the trunk I felt a painful permission, as when two silences, tired of holding back, give over to each other some shared regret. I made my bed on the boughs and resolved to spend the night there in the yard, under the stars, with the hiss of the ocean in my ear, and the maimed cedar tree standing over me like a gift torn out of its wrappings.

59　　　My brothers, their wives and my sister had now begun their nightly vigil near my father, taking turns at staying awake. The windows were open for the breeze and I heard my mother trying to answer the question of why I was sleeping outside on the ground—"like a damned fool" I knew they wanted to add.

60　　　"She doesn't want to be here when death comes for him," my mother said, with an air of clairvoyance she had developed from a lifetime with my father. "They're too much alike," she said.

61　　　The ritual of night games played by the children went on and on past their bedtimes. Inside the house, the kerosene lantern, saved from my father's childhood home, had been lit—another of his strange requests during the time before his silence. He liked the shadows it made and the sweet smell of the kerosene. I watched the darkness as the shapes of my brothers and sister passed near it, gigantic and misshapen where they bent or raised themselves or crossed the room.

62　　　Out on the water the wind had come up. In the orchard the children were spinning around in a circle, faster and faster until they were giddy and reeling with speed and darkness. Then they would stop, rest a moment, taking quick ecstatic breaths before plunging again into the opposite direction, swirling round and round in the circle until the excitement could rise no higher, their laughter and cries brimming over, then scattering as they flung one another by the arms or chased each other toward the house as if their lives depended on it.

63   I lay awake for a long while after their footsteps had died away and the car doors had slammed over the goodbyes of the children being taken home to bed and the last of the others had been bedded down in the house while the adults went on waiting.

64   It was important to be out there alone and close to the ground. The pungent smell of the cedar boughs was around me, rising up in the crisp night air toward the tree, whose turnings and swayings had altered, as they had to, in order to accompany the changes about to overtake my father and me. I thought of my great-grandfather bathing with his horse in the river, and of my father who had just passed through the longest period in his life without the clean feel of cards falling through his hands as he shuffled or dealt them. He was too weak now even to hold a cigarette; there was a burn mark on the hardwood floor where his last cigarette had fallen. His winnings were safely in the bank and the luck that was to have saved him had gone back to that place luck goes to when it is finished with us.

65   So this is what it comes to, I thought, and listened to the wind as it mixed gradually with the memory of children's voices which still seemed to rise and fall in the orchard. There was a soft crooning of syllables that was satisfying to my ears, but ultimately useless and absurd. Then it came to me that I was the author of those unwieldy sounds, and that my lips had begun to work of themselves.

66   In a raw pulsing of language I could not account for, I lay awake through the long night and spoke to my father as one might speak to an ocean or the wind, letting him know by that threadbare accompaniment that the vastness he was about to enter had its rhythms in me also. And that he was not forsaken. And that I was letting him go. That so far I had denied the disreputable world of dancers and drunkards, gamblers and lovers of horses to which I most surely belonged. But from that night forward I vowed to be filled with the first unsavory desire that would have me. To plunge myself into the heart of my life and be ruthlessly lost forever.

QUESTIONS

Experience

· What is your reaction to this story? How do you respond to the narrator's father? To the narrator herself? To the mysterious bond between them?

Interpretation

· What mystery of nature or human behavior does Gallagher's story attempt to convey? How would you describe the connection between the human and natural worlds in this story?

Evaluation

· What values does the narrator's father live by? How are his values related to those of the rest of the family? What is the narrator's attitude toward these competing sets of values?

WRITING

Exploring

· Write an informal response to this story in which you discuss either the character of the narrator, the character of her father, or both.

Interpreting

· Analyze all the passages about horses or all the passages about nature. Try to explain what those passages have in common and why they are important to an understanding of the story.

Evaluating

· Evaluate the story for the quality of its attraction. Consider how the writer draws us into its world, and the extent to which the story's mystery and surprises are engaging enough to be provocative and memorable.

ELIZABETH BISHOP
(1911–1979)

The Fish

Elizabeth Bishop was born in Massachusetts and graduated from Vassar in 1934. She resided for many years in Brazil and translated Portuguese poetry in addition to writing her own poems. Her books include North & South—A Cold Spring *(1955), for which she was awarded a Pulitzer Prize, and* Complete Poems *(1969), for which she won a National Book Award. She wrote often and well about the natural world, as the following poem testifies.*

"The Fish" is notable for its precise description and its lack of sentimentality. Bishop's speaker is clearly engaged by the fish, so much so that she compares the barnacles attached to it to "rosettes" and its swim bladder to "a big peony." The end of the poem is especially effective, with its repetition of "rainbow, rainbow, rainbow," which suggests a moment of special significance for the speaker.

I caught a tremendous fish
and held him beside the boat
half out of water, with my hook
fast in a corner of his mouth.
He didn't fight.
He hadn't fought at all.
He hung a grunting weight,
battered and venerable
and homely. Here and there
his brown skin hung in strips
like ancient wallpaper,
and its pattern of darker brown
was like wallpaper:
shapes like full-blown roses
stained and lost through age.
He was speckled with barnacles,
fine rosettes of lime,
and infested
with tiny white sea-lice,
and underneath two or three
rags of green weed hung down.
While his gills were breathing in
the terrible oxygen
—the frightening gills,
fresh and crisp with blood,
that can cut so badly—

I thought of the coarse white flesh
packed in like feathers,
the big bones and the little bones,
30   the dramatic reds and blacks
of his shiny entrails,
and the pink swim-bladder
like a big peony.
I looked into his eyes
35   which were far larger than mine
but shallower, and yellowed,
the irises backed and packed
with tarnished tinfoil
seen through the lenses
40   of old scratched isinglass.
They shifted a little, but not
to return my stare.
—It was more like the tipping
of an object toward the light.
45   I admired his sullen face,
the mechanism of his jaw,
and then I saw
that from his lower lip
—if you could call it a lip—
50   grim, wet, and weaponlike,
hung five old pieces of fish-line,
or four and a wire leader
with the swivel still attached,
with all their five big hooks
55   grown firmly in his mouth.
A green line, frayed at the end
where he broke it, two heavier lines,
and a fine black thread
still crimped from the strain and snap
60   when it broke and he got away.
Like medals with their ribbons
frayed and wavering,
a five-haired beard of wisdom
trailing from his aching jaw.
65   I stared and stared
and victory filled up
the little rented boat,
from the pool of bilge
where oil had spread a rainbow
70   around the rusted engine
to the bailer rusted orange,
the sun-cracked thwarts,

the oarlocks on their strings,
the gunnels—until everything
75 was rainbow, rainbow, rainbow!
And I let the fish go.

QUESTIONS

Experience

· What feelings surfaced as you read Bishop's poem? Did you find your feelings changing at different places? Why, or why not?
· If you were not engaged by the poem, what about it failed to interest you?

Interpretation

· Why does the speaker of the poem let the fish go?
· Why doesn't the fish fight when caught?
· If this poem is about something more than catching a fish and letting it go, then what else is it about?

Evaluation

· What attitude toward the natural world is reflected in "The Fish"? Where do you find this attitude expressed or suggested?

WRITING

Exploring

· Describe an occasion when you had a close encounter with an animal— whether a fish, a bird, or some other creature. Try to convey what the encounter was like and why it may have been important for you. Explore its significance.

Interpreting

· Analyze the poem's language and detail in order to arrive at an interpretation. Explain your understanding of Bishop's poem. Support your interpretation by referring to specific words, phrases, and lines. Be sure to consider the speaker's attitude toward the fish in your analysis.

Evaluating

· Discuss whether this is or is not an effective and memorable poem. Consider, as part of your criteria for judgment, whether you learn anything from reading it and whether the poem helps you to see a fish in a way you had not seen one before. Introduce any other standards of evaluation you think appropriate.

NATURE—CONSIDERATIONS FOR THINKING AND WRITING

1. Compare the depiction of animals in two of the following: Hoagland's "The Courage of Turtles," Orwell's "Some Thoughts on the Common Toad," Dillard's "Living Like Weasels," and Bishop's "The Fish." Consider how the writers describe the animals in their essays and what insight the animals lead the writers to.

2. Compare the depiction of water in Russell's "The Mimbres" with its portrayal in Eiseley's "The Flow of the River." Consider not only the effects of water each writer describes, but also the associations with and images of water each writer presents.

3. Compare the attitudes toward and perspectives on horses in Meloy's "Horse-Love" with those in Gallagher's "The Lover of Horses." Explain how each writer characterizes horses and what each suggests about the animals' relationship with people.

4. Discuss the images of the land as they appear in two or more of the following: Russell's "The Mimbres," Silko's "Landscape, History, and the Pueblo Imagination," Orwell's "Some Thoughts on the Common Toad," and Momaday's "The Way to Rainy Mountain" (in "Race").

5. Discuss the ideas about the environment implied or explicitly stated in Thomas's "The World's Biggest Membrane" and Silko's "Landscape, History, and the Pueblo Imagination." Consider how these two writers view the earth and what influences or motivates them to move toward describing the earth as they do.

6. Consider whether and how ideas about the natural world might be changing. Identify alternative ways of thinking about nature and why they are important or influential. You might consider, for example, the issue of limited natural resources or the conflict between business and environmental interests in the Pacific Northwest.

7. Write an imaginative or creative work about nature—a poem, song, short story, or a scene for a play or a film. In your writing, try to convey a sense of the natural world that reveals either an idea about it or an attitude toward it—perhaps more than one idea or attitude.

8. Do some research on an issue involving the natural world—on the building of levees, for example, or on the competing claims of environmentalists and loggers or ranchers. Write a research essay that takes a position or develops an idea about the issue you choose.

PERMISSIONS
ACKNOWLEDGMENTS

Agee, James, "The Comic Acting of Buster Keaton" from *Agee on Film* by James Agee. Reprinted by permission of The James Agee Trust.

Angelou, Maya, "On the Pulse of Morning" from *On the Pulse of Morning* by Maya Angelou. Copyright © 1993 by Maya Angelou. Reprinted by permission of Random House, Inc.

Anzaldua, Gloria, "How To Tame a Wild Tongue" from *Borderlands/La Frontera: The New Mestiza* by Gloria Anzaldua. Copyright © 1987 by Gloria Anzaldua. Reprinted with permission from Aunt Lute Books.

Baldwin, James, "If Black English Isn't A Language, Then Tell Me What Is?" by James Baldwin from *New York Times,* 1979. Copyright © 1979 by The New York Times Company. Reprinted by permission.

Baldwin, James, "Notes of a Native Son" from *Notes of a Native Son* by James Baldwin. Copyright © 1955, renewed 1983 by James Baldwin. Reprinted by permission of Beacon Press.

Baldwin, James, "Sonny's Blues" is collected in *Going to Meet the Man,* © 1965 by James Baldwin. Copyright renewed. Published by Vintage Books. Reprinted with permission of the James Baldwin Estate.

Berger, John and **Jean Mohr,** "Looking at a Photograph" from *Another Way of Telling* by John Berger and Jean Mohr. Copyright © 1982 by John Berger and Jean Mohr. Reprinted by permission of Pantheon Books, a division of Random House, Inc.

Bishop, Elizabeth. "The Fish" from *The Complete Poems 1927–1979* by Elizabeth Bishop. Copyright © 1979, 1983 by Alice Helen Methfessel. Reprinted by permission of Farrar, Straus & Giroux, Inc.

Brownmiller, Susan, "Femininity" from *Femininity* by Susan Brownmiller. Copyright © 1984 by Susan Brownmiller. Reprinted by permission of Simon & Schuster, Inc.

Didion, Joan, "Georgia O'Keefe" from *The White Album* by Joan Didion. Copyright © 1979 by Joan Didion. Reprinted by permission of Farrar, Straus & Giroux, Inc.

Didion, Joan, "Marrying Absurd" from *Slouching Towards Bethlehem* by Joan

Hughes, Langston, "Trumpet Player" from *Selected Poems* by Langston Hughes. Copyright 1947 by Langston Hughes. Reprinted by permission of Alfred A. Knopf, Inc.

Hurston, Zora Neale, "How It Feels to Be Colored Me" from *The World Tomorrow,* May 11, 1928. Reprinted by permission of the Estate of Zora Neale Hurston.

Jen, Gish, "What Means Switch?" Copyright 1990 by Gish Jen. First published in *The Atlantic.* Reprinted by permission of the author.

Jordan, June, "Where is the Love?" from *Civil Wars* by June Jordan. Copyright © 1995 by June Jordan. Reprinted by permission.

Kakutani, Michiko, "The Word Police" by Michiko Kakutani from *New York Times,* June 20, 1993. Copyright © 1993 by The New York Times Company. Reprinted by permission.

King, Larry L., "Playing Cowboy" from *Of Outlaws, Conmen, Whores, Politicians & Other Artists* by Larry L. King. Copyright © 1980 by Larry L. King. Used by permission of Viking Penguin, a division of Penguin Books USA Inc.

Kingston, Maxine Hong, "No Name Woman" from *The Woman Warrior* by Maxine Hong Kingston. Copyright © 1975, 1976 by Maxine Hong Kingston. Reprinted by permission of Alfred A. Knopf, Inc.

Kingston, Maxine Hong, "Silence" from *The Woman Warrior* by Maxine Hong Kingston. Copyright © 1975, 1976 by Maxine Hong Kingston. Reprinted by permission of Alfred A. Knopf, Inc.

Lakoff, Robin, "Talking Like a Lady" from *Language and Society.* Copyright © 1973 by Robin Lakoff. Reprinted by permission of Robin Lakoff.

Lawrence, Barbara, "Four-Letter Words Can Hurt You" by Barbara Lawrence from *New York Times,* Oct. 27, 1973. Copyright © 1973 by The New York Times Company. Reprinted by permission.

Mairs, Nancy, "On Being a Cripple" from *Plaintext.* Reprinted by permission of The University of Arizona Press.

Momaday, N. Scott. Excerpt from "The Way to Rainy Mountain" from *The Way to Rainy Mountain* by N. Scott Momaday. First published in "The Reporter", Jan. 26, 1967. Reprinted from *The Way to Rainy Mountain,* © 1969 by The University of New Mexico Press. Reprinted by permission.

Neruda, Pablo, "The Word" from *Fully Empowered* by Pablo Neruda, translated by Alastair Reid. Translation copyright © 1975 by Alastair Reid. Reprinted by permission of Farrar, Straus & Giroux, Inc.

Excerpt from "Reagan Misstatements Getting Less Attention" from *New York Times,* February 15, 1983. Copyright © 1983 by The New York Times Company. Reprinted by permission.

Orwell, George, "Marrakech" from *Such, Such Were the Joys* by George Orwell, copyright 1953 by Sonia Brownell Orwell and renewed 1981 by Mrs. George K. Perutz, Mrs. Miriam Gross, Dr. Michael Dickson, Executors of the Estate of Sonia Brownell Orwell, reprinted by permission of Harcourt Brace &

INDEX

About Looking (Berger), 443
"About Men" (Ehrlich), excerpts from, 11-16, 19
"After Henry" (Didion), 116, 407
Against Our Will (Brownmiller), 181
Agee, James, 406, 438
Agee on Film (Agee), 438
All the Rooms of the Yellow House (Mairs), 349
Almanac of the Dead (Silko), 170, 509
American Childhood, An (Dillard), 211, 500
American Reader, The (Ravitch), 140
Amusing Ourselves to Death (Postman), 359
Ancient Child, The (Momaday), 288
. . . *And Other Dirty Stories* (King), 120
Angelou, Maya, 31, 102
Animal Farm (Orwell), 156, 373, 505
Annotating, 10-13
Another Way of Telling (Berger), 443
Anzuldua, Gloria, 110, 130
"A&P" (Updike), 246-250
Arts, aspects of, in writing, 406-478
"Avey" (Toomer), 80

Baldwin, James, 9, 256, 257, 330, 369, 406, 451
"Battle Royal" (Ellison), 256, 313-323
"Being a Man" (Theroux), 180, 235-237
Berger, John, 240, 406, 443
Best Little Whorehouse in Texas, The (King), 120
Bishop, Elizabeth, 480, 537
Black Literature and Literacy Theory (Gates), 162
Bogan, Louise, 349
Bogdonoff, Lisa, 330, 384
Bonfire of the Vanities (Wolfe), 64, 111
Book of Common Prayer, A (Didion), 116, 407

Breaking Bread: Insurgent Black Intellectual Life (West), 282
Brownmiller, Susan, 180, 181

Carnal Acts (Mairs), 349
Casanova, 240
Centaur, The (Updike), 246
Ceremony (Silko), 170, 509
China Men (Kingston), 75, 201
Civil Wars (Jordan), 277
Colored People (Gates), 162
"Comic Acting of Buster Keaton, The" (Agee), 438-441
Community, aspects of, in writing, 30-107
Company of Women, The (Gordon), 43, 419
Complete Poems (Bishop), 537
"Complexion" (Rodriguez), 293-296
Confessions of a White Racist (King), 120
Content of Our Character, The (Steele), 298
"Courage of Turtles, The" (Hoagland), 480, 490-494
Crossing Ocean Parkway (Torgovnick), 48
"Crossing the Tracks to Hopper's World" (Strand), 423-425
Culture, aspects of, in writing, 1, 9, 110-178

Days of Obligation: An Argument with My Mexican Father (Rodriguez), 293
Death in the Family, A (Agee), 438
"Deer of Providencia, The" (Dillard), 9, 180, 211-214
Democracy (Didion), 116, 407
Dickinson, Emily, 180, 252
Didion, Joan, 110, 116, 406, 407
"Different Words, Different Worlds" (Tannen), 222-233
Dillard, Annie, 9, 180, 211, 480, 500

Early Poems, The (Neruda), 401
Edward Hoagland Reader, The (Hoagland), 490
Ehrlich, Gretel, 10-20
Eiseley, Loren, 480, 516
Ellison, Ralph, 256, 282, 313, 406, 411
Essay form, 18-20
  example of, 20-27
Evaluation in reading, 8-9, 17
Evans, Walker, 438
Experience in reading, 3-5, 17

Face Value: The Politics of Beauty (Lakoff), 336
"Family Portrait" (Kim), 30, 89-92
Faulkner, William, 94-100
Femininity (Brownmiller), excerpt from, 181-184
Final Payments (Gordon), 43, 419
"Fish, The" (Bishop), 480, 537-539
Five Decades: Poems 1925-1970 (Neruda), 401
"Flow of the River, The" (Eisley), 480, 516-521
"Four-Letter Words Can Hurt You" (Lawrence), 345-347
Fragile Species, The (Thomas), 496
Freewriting, 13-14
  examples of, 14-15

G (Berger), 443
Gallagher, Tess, 480, 527
Gasset, Ortega Y, 175
Gates, Henry Louis, Jr., 110, 162-164
Gather Together in My Name (Angelou), 102
Gender, aspects of, in writing, 1, 9, 180-254
"Georgia O'Keeffe" (Didion), 407-409
Giovanni's Room (Baldwin), 257, 369, 451
Go Tell It on the Mountain (Baldwin), 257, 369, 451
Good Boys and Dead Girls and Other Essays (Gordon), 43, 419
Gordon, Mary, 30, 43, 406, 419
"Grotesques" (So), 309-311

Haciendo Caras: Making Face/Making Soul (Anzuldua), 130
Haunting of Hill House, The (Jackson), 94
"Health Craze, The" (Ribisi), 110, 165-168
"History of My Life" (Casanova), 240
Hoagland, Edward, 480, 490

Homage to Catalonia (Orwell), 156, 373, 505
Hopper (Strand), 423
"Horse-Love" (Meloy), 480, 523-525
House Made of Dawn (Momaday), 288
"How It Feels to Be Colored" (Hurston), 3-10
"How to Tame a Wild Tongue" (Anzuldua), 110, 130-138
Hoy, Pat C., II, 180, 186
Hugging the Shore (Updike), 246
Hughes, Langston, 256, 325, 406, 475
Hunger of Memory (Rodriguez), 293
Hurston, Zora Neale, 3-10, 19-21

I Know Why the Caged Bird Sings (Angelou), 102
"If Black English Isn't a Language, Then Tell Me, What Is?" (Baldwin), 369-371
"I'm 'wife'—I've finished that" (Dickinson), 180, 252
Immense Journey, The (Eisley), 516
"In Ivory Towers" (Wilkins), 256, 273-275
"In Search of Our Mothers' Gardens" (Walker), 80-87
In the Presence of the Sun: Stories and Poems (Momaday), 288
Instinct for Survival (Hoy), 186
Instructions to the Double (Gallagher), 527
Interpretation in reading, 5-8, 17
Invisible Man (Ellison), 313, 411

Jen, Gish, 330, 387
Jordan, June, 256, 277
Joy Luck Club, The (Tan), 58

Kakutani, Michiko, 330, 331
Kandy-Kolored Tangerine-Flake Streamline Baby, The (Wolfe), 64, 111
Kertész, Andre, 443
Kim, Eric, 30, 89
King, Larry L., 110, 120
Kingston, Maxine Hong, 9, 75, 180, 201
Kitchen God's Wife, The (Tan), 58

Laguna Woman (Silko), 170
Lakoff, Robin, 330, 336
"Landscape, History, and the Pueblo Imagination" (Silko), 480, 509-514
Language, aspects of, in writing, 1, 330-404
Language and a Woman's Place (Lakoff), 336

Lawrence, Barbara, 330, 345
Let Us Now Praise Famous Men (Agee), 438
Life Among the Savages (Jackson), 94
Lives of a Cell, The (Thomas), 496
Living by Fiction (Dillard), 211, 500
"Living Like Weasels" (Dillard), 480, 500-503
"Living with Music" (Ellison), 406, 411-417
"Looking at a Photograph" (Berger), 406, 443-445
Love Medicine (Tan), 58
"Lover of Horses, The" (Gallagher), 480, 527-535

MacDonald, Elizabeth, 406, 446
Mairs, Nancy, 330, 349
"Man to Send Rain Clouds, The" (Silko), 110, 170-173
"Marrakech" (Orwell), 110, 156-160
"Marrying Absurd" (Didion), 116-118
"Mary Cassatt" (Gordon), 406, 419-421
Mauve Gloves & Madmen, Clutter & Vine (Wolfe), 64, 111
Medusa and the Snail, The (Thomas), 496
Meloy, Maile, 180, 240, 480, 523
Men and Angels (Gordon), 43, 419
"Men We Carry in Our Minds, The" (Sanders), 180, 216-220
"Mimbres, The" (Russell), 481-488
Momaday, N. Scott, 256, 288
"More Than Just a Shrine: Paying Homage to the Ghosts of Ellis Island" (Gordon), 43-46
"Mosaics of Southern Masculinity" (Hoy), 180, 186-199
"Mother Tongue" (Tan), 30, 58-62
Moving Toward Home (Jordan), 277
"Multiculturalism" (Ravitch), 140-154

Nature, aspects of, in writing, 480-540
Neruda, Pablo, 330, 401
"New Sovereignty, The" (Steele), 256, 298-307
1984 (Orwell), 156, 373, 505
"No Name Woman" (Kingston), 9, 201-209
None But a Blockhead (King), 120
North & South—A Cold Spring (Bishop), 537
Notebook, double-column, 15-17
"Notes of a Native Son" (Baldwin), 256-271, 369, 451
"Now. . . This" (Postman), 359-367

"Odalisque" (MacDonald), 446-449
Of Outlaws, Con Men, Whores, Politicians, and Other Artists (King), 120
"On Being a Cripple" (Mairs), 349-357
"On Being White, Female, and Born in Bensonhurst" (Torgovnick), 48-56
On Call (Jordan), 277
"On the Pulse of Morning" (Angelou), 31, 102-105
On Writing Well (Zinsser), 427
One-Eyed Man, The (King), 120
"Only One Life" (Wolfe), 111-114, 165
Orwell, George, 110, 156, 330, 373, 480, 505
Other Side, The (Gordon), 43, 407
Owl in the Cedar Tree (Momaday), 288

Painter of Our Time, A (Berger), 443
Paradise of Bombs, The (Sanders), 32, 216
Permit Me Voyage (Agee), 438
Pilgrim at Tinker Creek (Dillard), 211, 500
Plaintext (Mairs), 349
Play It as It Lays (Didion), 116, 407
"Playing Cowboy" (King), 120-128
Poet at the Piano, The (Kakutani), 331
"Police! Police!" (Bogdonoff), 384-385
"Politics and the English Language" (Orwell), 330, 373-383
Postman, Neil, 330, 359
Price, Reynolds, 186
Primary sources, 2
Pump House Gang, The (Wolfe), 64, 111

Questioning in reading, 12-13, 16-17

Rabbit Is Rich (Updike), 246
Race, aspects of, in writing, 1, 9, 256-328
Race Matters (West), excerpts from, 282-286
Ravitch, Diane, 110, 140
Reading:
    annotating while, 10-13
    approach to, 3-9
    and evaluation, 8-9, 17
    and experience, 3-5, 17
    and interpretation, 5-8, 17
    questioning in, 12-13, 16-17
    reasons for, 1-3
Red Wolves and Black Bears (Hoagland), 490
Remembering the Bone House (Mairs), 349
Ribisi, Marie, 110, 165

Right Stuff, The (Wolfe), excerpts from, 30, 64–73, 111
River Run (Didion), 116, 407
Road to Wigan Pier, The (Orwell), 156, 373, 505
Rose for Emily, A (Faulkner), 94–100
Rodriguez, Richard, 256, 293
Russell, Sharman Apt, 480, 481

"Salvador" (Didion), 116, 407
Sanders, Scott Russell, 30, 32, 180, 216
Secondary sources, 2
Secrets of the Universe (Sanders), 32, 216
"Shanghai Blues" (Zinsser), 406, 427–436
Signifying Monkey, The (Gates), 162
"Silence" (Kingston), 75–78
Silko, Leslie Marmon, 110, 170, 480, 509
Simpson Louis, 110, 175
Singin' and Swingin' and Gettin' Merry Like Christmas (Angelou), 102
"Slouching Toward Bethlehem" (Didion), 116, 407
Smith, Ray Gwyn, 130
So, Suyin, 256, 309
"Some Thoughts on the Common Toad" (Orwell), 480, 505–508
Songs of the Fluteplayer (Russell), 481
"Sonny's Blues" (Baldwin), 406, 451–473
Staying Put (Sanders), 32, 216
Steele, Shelby, 256, 298
Storyteller (Silko), 170, 509
Strand, Mark, 406, 423

"Talking Like a Lady" (Lakoff), 336–343
Tan, Amy, 30, 58
Tannen, Deborah, 180, 222
Teaching a Stone to Talk (Dillard), 211, 500
Teaching as a Subversive Activity (Postman), 359
Technical Difficulties: African American Notes on the State of the Union (Jordan), 277
Temporary Shelter (Gordon), 43, 419
"Theme for English B" (Hughes), 256, 325–326
Theroux, Paul, 180, 235
Thesis, 18
This Bridge Called My Back: Writing by Radical Women of Color (Anzuldua), 130
Thomas, Lewis, 480, 496
Toomer, Jean, 80
Torgovnick, Marianna De Marco, 30, 48
Tripmaster Monkey, The (Kingston), 75, 201

Troubled Crusade: American Education, 1945–1980, The (Ravitch), 140
"Trumpet Player" (Hughes), 406, 475–476
Tugman's Passage, The (Hoagland), 490
"2 Live Crew, Decoded" (Gates), 110, 162–163
Typical American (Jen), 387

Under Stars (Gallagher), 527
Updike, John, 180, 246

"Voice of the Looking-Glass, The" (Meloy), 240, 243

Walker, Alice, 80
"Walt Whitman at Bear Mountain" (Simpson), 110, 175–176
Waverly Place (Brownmiller), 181
Way to Rainy Mountain, The (Momaday), excerpt from, 256, 288–292
"Wayland" (Sanders), 30, 32–41
Ways of Seeing (Berger), 240, 443
We Have Always Lived in the Castle (Jackson), 94
Weary Blues, The (Hughes), 325, 475
West, Cornel, 256, 282
"What America Would Be Like Without Blacks" (Ellison), 282
What Do Our Seventeen-Year-Olds Know? (Ravitch), 140
"What Means Switch?" (Jen), 387–399
Wheeling and Dealing (King), 120
"Where Is the Love?" (Jordan), 256, 277–280
"White Album, The" (Didion), 116, 407
Wilkins, Roger, 256, 273
Willingly (Gallagher), 527
Wolfe, Tom, 30, 64, 110, 111, 165
Woman Warrior, The (Kingston), 75, 201
"Word, The" (Neruda), 330, 401–402
"Word Police, The" (Kakutani), 331–335
"World's Biggest Membrane, The" (Thomas), 480, 496–498
Writing:
  preliminary strategies for, 10–16
  reasons for, 2–3
Writing with a Word Processor (Zinsser), 427

You Just Don't Understand (Tannen), 222

Zinsser, William, 406, 427